July 23–25, 2014
Oxford, UK

**acm** Association for
Computing Machinery

*Advancing Computing as a Science & Profession*

# WiSec'14

Proceedings of the 7th ACM Conference on
## Security and Privacy in Wireless & Mobile Networks

*Sponsored by:*
## ACM SIGSAC

**Association for
Computing Machinery**

*Advancing Computing as a Science & Profession*

**The Association for Computing Machinery**
**2 Penn Plaza, Suite 701**
**New York, New York 10121-0701**

**Notice to Past Authors of ACM-Published Articles**

**ISBN:** 978-1-4503-2972-9 (Digital)

**ISBN:** 978-1-4503-3180-7 (Print)

Additional copies may be ordered prepaid from:

**ACM Order Department**
PO Box 30777
New York, NY 10087-0777, USA

Phone: 1-800-342-6626 (USA and Canada)
+1-212-626-0500 (Global)
Fax: +1-212-944-1318
E-mail: acmhelp@acm.org
Hours of Operation: 8:30 am – 4:30 pm ET

Printed in the USA

# Foreword

It is with great pleasure to welcome you to the *2014 ACM Conference on Security and Privacy in Wireless and Mobile Networks (WiSec'14). WiSec'14* brings together experts from industry, government and academia with the goal of tackling the greatest security challenges facing mobile and wireless networks and devices. Now in its seventh year, *WiSec'14* continues to deliver on objective, as we are certain you will see in our mix of research papers, invited speakers and impromptu discussions.

This year, *WiSec* received 96 complete paper submissions. Our program committee, which was carefully composed of experts from diverse sectors of employment, geographic location and background, selected a total of 25 papers for publication, which yielded an acceptance rate of approximately 26%. These long and short papers cover the gamut of research in wireless and mobile security: topics including physical layer jamming and mobile applications to the use of GPS by critical infrastructure and weaknesses in implementations of cryptographic algorithms. It is this diversity of coverage and depth of expertise that will make the next few days well worth your travels.

As a special note this year, we are happy to partner with the organizers of *RFIDSec* and co-locate our two events. Our topics have deep and obvious overlap, and creating possibilities for both communities to interact seemed like too good an opportunity to neglect. We hope that you will use this opportunity to seek out researchers and practitioners outside of your normal circles, and use this event as the seed for strong collaboration in the future.

Putting together WiSec'14 was a team effort. We thank the authors for providing the content of the program. We are grateful to the program committee that worked very hard in reviewing papers and providing feedback for authors. In addition, Kasper Rasmussen and Mathieu Cunche (Publicity Chairs), Aurelian Francillon (Poster/Demo Chair), Justin King-Lacroix (Web Chair) have each done a great deal to make WiSec'14 a success. We are significantly indebted to the local organizers Elizabeth Walsh and Andrea Pilot from the Department of Computer Science, University of Oxford for their support and hard work. We thank St Anne's College for hosting the conference and for providing accommodation to attendees. We gratefully acknowledge financial support for student travel grants from ACM SIGSAC.

Finally, we thank WiSec Steering Committee, and in particular its chair Gene Tsudik, for its wise advises and strong support.

In summary, we hope that this year's WiSec will be a thought-provoking and exciting event where you will be able to expand your horizons and have many opportunities to share cutting-edge research ideas and results.

**Andrew Martin**
*WiSec'14 General Chair*
*University of Oxford, UK*

**Ivan Martinovic**
*WiSec'14 General Chair*
*University of Oxford, UK*

**Claude Castelluccia**
*WiSec'14 Program Chair*
*Inria, France*

**Patrick Traynor**
*WiSec'14 Program Chair*
*University of Florida, USA*

# Table of Contents

# WiSec 2014 Conference Organization

**General Chairs:** Andrew Martin *(Oxford University, UK)*
Ivan Martinovic *(Oxford University, UK)*

**Program Chair:** Claude Castelluccia *(Inria, France)*
Patrick Traynor *(University of Florida, USA)*

**Proceedings Chair:** Gergely Acs *(Inria, France)*

**Poster/Demo Chair:** Aurélien Francillon *(Eurecom, France)*

**Publicity Chairs:** Kasper Rasmussen *(Oxford University, UK)*
Mathieu Cunche *(Inria, France)*

**Web Chair:** Justin King-Lacroix *(University of Oxford, UK)*

**Steering Committee Chair:** Gene Tsudik *(University of California, Irvine, USA)*

**Steering Committee:** Gene Tsudik *(University of California, Irvine, USA)*
N. Asokan *(University of Helsinki, Finland)*
Srdjan Capkun *(ETH Zürich, Switzerland)*
Claude Castelluccia *(Inria, France)*
Douglas Maughan *(Department of Homeland Security, USA)*
Ahmad-Reza Sadeghi *(Technische Universität Darmstadt, Germany)*

**Program Committee:** Claude Castelluccia *(Inria, France)*
Patrick Traynor *(Georgia Institute of Technology, USA)*
David Barrera *(Carleton University, Canada)*
Erik-Oliver Blass *(Northeastern University, USA)*
Elie Bursztein *(Google, USA)*
Kevin Butler *(University of Oregon, USA)*
Srdjan Capkun *(ETH Zürich, Switzerland)*
Nicolas Christin *(Carnegie Mellon University, USA)*
Emiliano De Cristofaro *(University College London, UK)*
Adrienne Felt *(Google, USA)*
Aurélien Francillon *(Eurecom, France)*
Julien Freudiger *(PARC, USA)*
Thorsten Holz *(Ruhr-Universität Bochum, Germany)*
Murtuza Jadliwala *(Wichita State University, USA)*
Sanjay Jha *(University of New South Wales, Australia)*
Apu Kapadia *(Indiana University, USA)*
Frank Kargl *(University of Ulm, Germany)*
Yongdae Kim *(KAIST, Republic of Korea)*

# Baton: Certificate Agility for Android's Decentralized Signing Infrastructure

David Barrera[†]          Daniel McCarney[†]

Jeremy Clark[‡]          Paul C. van Oorschot[†]

[†]Carleton University, Ottawa, ON, Canada
[‡]Concordia University, Montreal, QC, Canada

## ABSTRACT

Android's trust-on-first-use application signing model associates developers with a fixed code signing certificate, but lacks a mechanism to enable transparent key updates or certificate renewals. The model allows application updates to be recognized as authorized by a party with access to the original signing key. However, changing keys or certificates requires that end users manually uninstall/reinstall apps, losing all non-backed up user data. In this paper, we show that with appropriate OS support, developers can securely and without user intervention transfer signing authority to a new signing key. Our proposal, Baton, modifies Android's app installation framework enabling key agility while preserving backwards compatibility with current apps and current Android releases. Baton is designed to work consistently with current UID sharing and signature permission requirements. We discuss technical details of the Android-specific implementation, as well as the applicability of the Baton protocol to other decentralized environments.

## Categories and Subject Descriptors

D.4.6 [**Operating Systems**]: Security and Protection—*Cryptographic controls*

## Keywords

Android; application signing; mobile operating systems

## 1. INTRODUCTION

Modern operating systems use digital signatures as a mechanism to verify the integrity of downloaded software and/or authenticate developers. Platforms such as iOS, Windows Phone, and Blackberry use code signatures to restrict installation of third-party applications to only registered developers. These platforms use a centralized authority, where developer certificates or the software itself is signed by the

vendor prior to being distributed to user devices. A centralized authority is restrictive for users (*e.g.*, users *must* obtain software and updates from sources formally sanctioned by the platform vendor) while allowing vendor control over certificate issuance.

Android, one of the most widely deployed mobile operating systems, does not use a centralized authority. Instead, developers are responsible for obtaining suitable signing certificates (typically self-signed, but they can be issued by a certificate authority). On Android, the OS allows installation of app updates only if they are sanctioned by the same developer. Such *update integrity* is enforced in the OS by comparing the set of signing certificates embedded in the already installed application against the set in the updated version. If the updated version's set of certificates matches the set in the previously installed app, the update is allowed. Otherwise, the update fails. Since Android uses a trust-on-first-use [25] approach, initial app installations are not subject to such *certificate continuity verification*.

When the certificate sets during an update don't match, the only method to install the updated app is for the user to manually uninstall the old app (which deletes the app's user data) and then install the updated version as a new install. This process in effect revokes trust in the previous signing certificate set, replacing it with a newly trusted set.

Aside from this uninstall-reinstall method, Android, in its operating system and developer tools, has no mechanism for developers to renew, change, or revoke signing certificate(s). In this paper, we motivate, design, and implement Baton, a set of software changes to Android's app installation framework and developer tools that allow code signing certificates to be updated (informally called *key agility* or *certificate agility*) without user involvement, user data loss, or changes to the decentralized code signing model.

When using Baton, app updates include a certificate chain that is cryptographically verified at update time. Upon validation of a chain linking the signing certificate embedded in the currently installed version of an app to the certificate embedded in the newly installed version, updates are allowed (preserving user data) without requiring the user to uninstall/reinstall the app. Baton is designed to be incrementally deployable and fully backwards compatible with currently deployed apps. The Baton component of Android's installation framework is only invoked when certificate updates are required, imposing no new overhead during regular application use or software updates not involving signing key changes.

## 1.1 Limitations of Existing Proposals

The concept of forward certificate chains, where an old key signs a new key (or alternatively, the new key is transmitted over a channel secured with the old key) is a long-known key-management technique, almost as old as public key certificates, with applications to encrypted email [29], TLS certificates [3], and Linux files [24].

| | Enables Key Agility | Allows Skipping Updates | Compatible with Jarsigner | Incrementally Deployable | Allows Revocation |
|---|---|---|---|---|---|
| Stock Android [4] | | • | • | • | |
| Baton (Sec 4) | • | • | • | • | |
| Self-Signed Executables [23] | | | • | • | |
| Key-locking [24] | • | | | • | |
| Baton Alternative (Sec 4.2) | • | • | | • | |
| Central Certificate Authority | • | • | • | | • |

Table 1: **A comparison of proposed update integrity mechanisms, including ones with key agility. A •denotes the availability of a feature in the corresponding proposal.**

An early proposal [23] for binary file update integrity through self-signing suggests signed executables that include an embedded set of public signing keys, sufficient for verifying signatures. This approach, while functionally similar to Android's app update mechanism, does not allow key agility. In subsequent work [24], the verification key set is allowed to evolve which enables key agility. However, it requires the user to diligently download and install all issued updates sequentially; skipping updates could lead to missing verification keys for future updates, precluding such updates from being installed. By contrast, Baton enables key agility while allowing users to skip intermediate updates. In addition, Baton is designed specifically for Android in a way that is compatible with `jarsigner`. None of the above proposals fully enable revocation, which is known to be difficult in the absence of a central authority. We address revocation in Section 6.3. Our comparison is summarized in Table 1.

**Contributions.** We first clearly highlight, through analysis of real-world examples, problems that have resulted from Android's current design wherein application package signing lacks what would naively be considered "ordinary best practices" related to certificate and public key updates (what we refer to as *certificate agility*). We then demonstrate that public key evolution, notoriously difficult to get right in practice (which we believe explains its current absence in Android), can be retrofitted without negative impact to the existing ecosystem. Thus, we motivate, design, and implement a mechanism supporting certificate agility on Android. We build upon existing academic proposals to create a practical solution that fits within existing constraints in the Android ecosystem, preserving compatibility with currently deployed applications, and without negatively impacting Android's secure app interaction policy. We ex-

| Key algorithm/size | Occurrences | % of total |
|---|---|---|
| RSA 1024 | 4593 | 74.57 |
| RSA 2048 | 1340 | 21.76 |
| DSA 1024 | 202 | 3.28 |
| Other (non-default) | 24 | 0.39 |

Table 2: **Signing key algorithm and key size over a dataset of 6159 certificates from the Android Observatory.**

plain the Baton protocol, including the specific technical details regarding modified components which provide Android support. While our main focus herein is Android, the Baton architecture is of general interest beyond Android as it provides a low overhead, algorithm-agnostic, cryptographically verifiable mechanism to update signing certificates without depending on a centralized infrastructure.

## 2. MOTIVATION FOR KEY AGILITY

This section presents arguments in favor of enabling key agility on Android backed by an empirical dataset obtained from the Android Observatory project [8].

### 2.1 Absence of Secure Defaults

The Android developer tools provide a point-and-click wizard for signing applications. The wizard requests (as input from the developer) a certificate validity period (Google requires a validity of 25 years or more for apps submitted to the Play Store [4]), and then invokes Java's `keytool` to generate a suitable signing key and certificate. Parameters such as key type, key size or signing algorithm cannot be specified using this wizard. However, it does pass a `-keyalg RSA` parameter to `keytool`, generating a default 1024 or 2048 bit RSA key (on Java 6 and 7, respectively). When invoked outside the wizard (*e.g.*, from the command line) without any parameters, `keytool` generates a 1024 bit (in a 160 bit subgroup) DSA public key.

On a dataset of 6159 signing certificates obtained from a snapshot of the Android Observatory from September 6, 2013, we observe that over 99% of certificates were likely generated using the Android signing wizard (see Table 2). In fact, only 24 certificates appear to have been generated by passing manual (non-default) options to `keytool`. According to recommendations by the National Institute of Standards and Technology (NIST), signature generation with key sizes less than 2048 bits for RSA and DSA was deprecated in 2011 and disallowed in 2013 [7, 6]. By this recommendation, over 75% of keys in our dataset do not follow best practices, yet developers have no mechanism to transparently issue an updated certificate with a stronger key. Enabling certificate agility allows developers to change key algorithms or key sizes as best practices evolve.

### 2.2 Ownership Transfer

Applications can be sold or otherwise transferred between developers. Under the current model and to avoid user interaction, *transferring private signing keys* is a likely component of the ownership transfer process. However, such sharing of private signing keys is problematic if a developer signs multiple apps with the same signing certificate; surrendering a private key for one app allows the new owner of

**Certificate Reuse CDF**

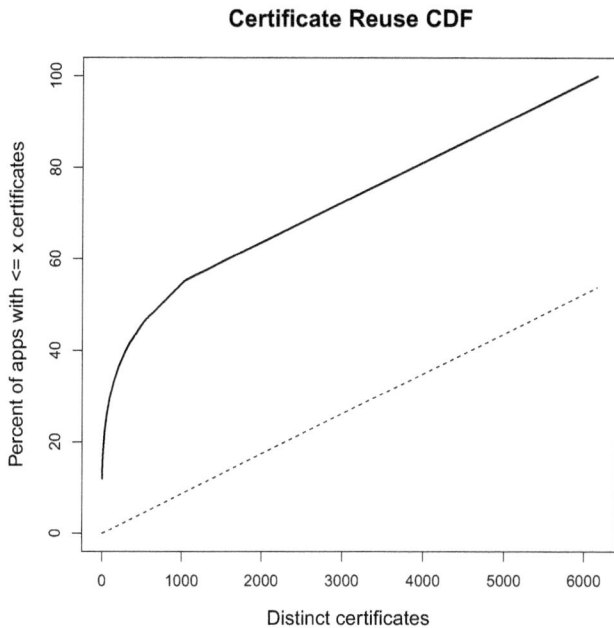

**Figure 1: CDF for certificate reuse in our dataset of 11452 apps and 6159 certificates. An $x = y$ line depicting a theoretical 1 distinct certificate per distinct app is plotted for reference.**

the key to issue updates to any other app signed with that key.

The September 6, 2013 snapshot of the Android Observatory consists of 11452 distinct[1] applications. On this dataset, we notice that key reuse (*i.e.*, using one key to sign more than one distinct app) happens frequently. Out of a total 6159 signing certificates, 1037 keys (16.83%) were used to sign 2 or more distinct apps. Figure 1 shows a cumulative distribution function of signing key reuse on our dataset. Some cases of reuse involve developers releasing a free (usually ad-supported) version of an app alongside a paid version signed with the same key. In other cases, software companies (*e.g.*, Rovio, Google, Yahoo, *etc.*) release a separate app for each service or game, but use a single signing key on all apps.

## 2.3 Logical Requirements

**Secure app interaction.** Developers (or development teams) can leverage Android's signature-level privileges for UID sharing or signature permissions (see Section 3) to securely integrate apps or app components. Without certificate agility, developers must decide ahead of time which apps should be granted the capability to interact securely. It may not always be possible to predict future functionality or required interaction of an application.

**External certificate management** Developers may wish to use certificates (perhaps previously acquired) issued by a certificate authority to assert a validated identity on their apps. However, many reputable CAs will not issue certifi-

cates with an essentially infinite lifespan (25 or more years). Some CAs (*e.g.*, Symantec[2]) will issue these long-lived certificates but will not release them to the developer; the developer must use a CA-provided signing service to sign applications, which is an additional cost and necessitates distinct certificates specifically for Android apps. Without certificate agility, developers cannot renew an expired certificate and still update user apps without user interaction.

## 2.4 Case Studies

This section describes two high-profile examples highlighting the potential benefits of certificate agility on Android.

*Google Authenticator.*

In March 2012, Google changed the signing certificate for their two-step authentication app Google Authenticator (package name `authenticator`[3]). Google released a new application (under package name `authenticator2`) signed with a new signing key and included a certificate used to sign other prominent Google properties (*e.g.*, Maps, Chrome, and the Play Store client). The certificate switch was ostensibly required to enable secure interaction (see Section 3) between Authenticator and this set of apps.

The upgrade path from one version of Authenticator to the other required that users take a series of steps, including a manual new install and uninstall. To assist users, Google created a help page[4] explaining the upgrade procedure. Below is an excerpt:

> *[...]Once you have confirmed as part of the previous step that you are able to successfully generate valid verification codes using the new Authenticator, it is safe to uninstall the old version of the app. Because both versions have the same icon, make sure to check the version number before uninstalling: you want to keep version 2.15.*

In Appendix A, we perform a usability analysis technique known as a cognitive walkthrough on this upgrade process. We find that the overall process is convoluted and should not involve the user. However, given the constraints, Google did mitigate many potential usability issues. With Baton, we aim to provide a mechanism by which, when developers update apps which include changed signing certificates, no additional interactions are triggered for end users when the updated apps install. Baton would have allowed Google to issue a standard update to `authenticator` which includes the new signing certificate.

*Mozilla Firefox for Android.*

Before releasing Firefox for Android in 2010, Mozilla's intention appeared to be to use their existing Microsoft Authenticode certificates or to purchase a 2 or 3 year certificate from Verisign to sign Firefox for Android.[5] Mozilla correctly

---

[1]We use the package name to differentiate between apps and to avoid counting app updates as key reuse.

[2]http://www.symantec.com/en/ca/verisign/code-signing/android

[3]The full package name is com.google.android.apps.authenticator2

[4]Upgrading to Google Authenticator v2.15 http://support.google.com/accounts/bin/answer.py?hl=en&topic=1099586&answer=2544996

[5]https://bugzilla.mozilla.org/show_bug.cgi?id=562843

3

concluded that there is no support in Android for certificate renewal, even if there is no change to the signing key pair. Mozilla filed a bug report[6] on Android asking for confirmation or motivation for why certificate renewal is not supported. The bug report was closed automatically getting marked as obsolete on June 23, 2013 despite the issue remaining unresolved and unacknowledged.

While the Android OS does not currently enforce certificate expiration (*i.e.,* apps with expired certificates can be installed as usual), the Android documentation [4] asserts that certificate validity is verified. This inconsistency leads us to believe that certificate expiration policies on Android may change in the future. Baton allows developers to use shorter lived (more typical lifespan) certificates, and update them as needed by issuing an application update. This may prove useful for companies, such as Mozilla, that already have (or wish to have) code signing certificates issued by certificate authorities.

## 3. BACKGROUND (ANDROID)

We quickly review, for convenience, background on the packaging and signing of Android apps and discuss the role of digital signatures on apps for application interaction.

Android applications are packaged and distributed as compressed (zip) archives, usually with an APK file extension. A typical app archive contains at least: digital signature data (in the `META-INF` directory); and application metadata such as version strings, unique package name, and permission declarations (*AndroidManifest.xml*).

Every installed Android app must have a unique, developer-chosen *package name* defined in *AndroidManifest.xml*, and should follow standard Java naming conventions to avoid collisions amongst applications. In general, developers reverse their domain name for uniqueness (possibly appending a name for an app if there is more than one app per domain, *e.g.,* `org.mozilla.firefox`). The package naming convention may be enforced by application markets such as Google Play, but developers are free to claim their package namespace, or re-use an existing namespace.

The *AndroidManifest.xml* file also contains a *version code*,[7] which is a developer-chosen monotonically increasing integer independent of the user-visible *version name* (*e.g.,* v1 or 2.5). During updates, the OS compares version codes and only allows installation if the version code is set to increase (*i.e.,* app downgrades are never allowed).

### Application signing and terminology.

All Android packages must be digitally signed to run on user devices or environment simulators [4]. During app development and testing, the standard development environment automatically creates self-signed debug certificates. For application release, Android allows developers to independently generate or obtain a key pair and a corresponding certificate that can be used for signing apps. The certificate may be self-signed, or issued by a certificate authority. While self-signed certificates are not required, they appear to be implicitly encouraged by Google, since the Play Store only allows apps with certificates expiring after 2033 to be

---
[6]`http://code.google.com/p/android/issues/detail?id=10020`
[7]`http://developer.android.com/tools/publishing/versioning.html`

published and many CAs won't issue certs with a 20 year lifespan.

Developers sign their code through the `jarsigner` tool, distributed as part of the standard Java development environment. During the signing process, `jarsigner` creates the `META-INF` directory inside the Android package, and adds three files:

1. `MANIFEST.MF` - A manifest file containing a list of every file name (except files in `META-INF`) in the archive at the time of signing, and a corresponding SHA1 hash for each entry.

2. `CERT.SF` - A file containing a SHA1 hash of each entry in `MANIFEST.MF` file, along with a corresponding file path.

3. `CERT.RSA` - The developer's X.509 certificate, usually self-signed using the RSA algorithm. This file also includes the signature of the entire `CERT.SF` file.

Apps can be signed with multiple keys, in which case the `META-INF` directory is populated with multiple certificates (one per signing key), manifests, and signature files. The signature(s) on an app can be stripped by deleting the `META-INF` directory.

### Initial install.

On initial installs (*i.e.,* where the package name of the application being installed is not already associated with an app on the device), Android only verifies the integrity of the app by performing a signature verification process on all files (except those in the `META-INF` directory). There is no external verification of the developer's certificate at install time, even if a certificate signed by a CA is used.

### Updates.

On application updates (*i.e.,* where there is already an app matching the package name of the app being installed), the signing certificate on the app being updated is compared with the certificate in the downloaded update. If the certificates are the same, the update is allowed following Android's certificate continuity verification. If the certificates are different, the update fails. We note that it is the certificates themselves that are compared, not the signatures. Thus, even if two certificates are signed with the same private key, updates are not allowed.

### Uninstalling apps.

Applications on Android cannot uninstall other applications without user interaction. Uninstalling an app typically requires the user to load the on-device application market or application manager. Uninstalling an app removes all locally stored user data, but applications may store data elsewhere, such as the cloud or the SD card. The method in which that data is handled after uninstallation is up to the developer.

### Secure application interaction.

Android uses signature information to allow apps sanctioned by the same developer(s) to communicate and share data securely. Two app interaction features rely on signatures:

1. *UID sharing.* Android apps are assigned unique UNIX UIDs at install-time to enforce application isolation

and sandboxing. When two or more apps are signed with the same key, developers can specify that they want these apps to be assigned the same UID, allowing mutual access to file storage or process space. UID sharing is common amongst modular applications such as plug-ins and extensions and eliminates the need to use excessive inter-process communication to transfer data between apps.

2. *Signature permissions.* Developers can define public interfaces available to other apps. Some interfaces may be sensitive, so they can be protected by developer-defined permissions. One type of developer-defined permissions is a signature permission, which can only be granted to applications signed with the same key as the application exposing the interface. Developers often use signature permissions to securely expose functionality and interact with other apps.

## 4. DESIGN AND IMPLEMENTATION OF BATON

Baton provides the ability for developers to delegate signing authority to a new private key. This is accomplished by creating a data structure (token) in which the old signing key is used to sign the new certificate and additional corresponding metadata. Each token is embedded in a certificate chain describing the history of delegations. The chain is cryptographically verifiable, and embedded inside the APK file of subsequently released Android apps after the first delegation occurs. The certificate chain and verifying code are implemented to meet the following design objectives:

1. *No user involvement.* Certificates and signatures are system-level components that need never be visible to the user. Baton provides a system-level mechanism to validate certificate changes and does not involve the user in any decisions or actions.

2. *Compatibility with Android's security model related to application signing.* Android uses certificates for software update continuity and for application interaction (see Section 3). Baton does not change the requirements for signature permissions and UID sharing.

3. *Minimal OS changes.* We add code to the Android application installation framework and developer tools, but make no other software modifications, and require no change of behavior by developers if certificates don't need to be changed.

4. *Backwards compatibility.* Baton supports incremental deployment with incremental benefit. Users with Baton-enabled Android will be able to upgrade applications that have changed their signing certificates (provided verification of the delegation succeeds). Users without a Baton-enabled Android build can still install and upgrade applications that include Baton certificate chains. These users, as with current Android, will be unable to transparently apply software updates if there is a certificate change; instead they must uninstall the current version and install the update as a first install.

Baton has two core components: (1) a set of patches to the Android installation framework, modifying packages responsible for parsing the *AndroidManifest.xml* file and verifying

application signatures; and (2) an Eclipse plug-in for assisting developers in generating key delegation metadata.

*Delegating Signing Authority.*

For a developer to successfully delegate (*i.e.*, endorse a new signing key) signing authority to a new signing key (shown as an example in Figure 2 as an update from $V2_{SigA}$ to $V3_{SigB}$), they must embed a valid delegation token in the update. In the example in Figure 2, a delegation token passing signing authority from $KeyA$ to $KeyB$ (*i.e.*, the private keys associated with certificates $A$ and $B$, respectively) must be present in the update. The delegation token generation is described as step one in the signing key endorsement protocol given in Protocol 1.

### 4.1 Threat Model and Goals

We consider the following security objectives to be necessary for any secure update mechanism, including Baton:

1. *No Unauthorized Updates.* Updates to installed apps must be authorized (either directly or transitively) by the signer(s) of the originally installed version of the app.

2. *No Replays.* Key delegation tokens should be bound to specific applications and versions. The tokens should not allow unintended delegations through embedding potentially modified tokens on unauthorized applications.

3. *Mitigating Social Engineering.* The update mechanism should only require user actions that are easily distinguishable from the actions a target victim user would take in a social engineering attack.

4. *No Unauthorized App Interaction.* Multiple apps may only interact through properly authorized privileged means (*e.g.*, sharing a UID or granting access to restricted APIs) with the mutual authorization of all the integrated apps.

We assume the attackers in the system to be computationally-bounded adversaries, who may hold their own signing keys, have their own apps released on application markets, and even have apps installed on a target user's phone. We assume adversaries are not capable of learning the private signing keys of other developers (we discuss key compromise in Section 6.2), nor are they able to modify or otherwise compromise the Android OS. We assume, however, that the adversary can tamper with any Android application package. A security analysis (see Section 5.3) is given after first describing the details of Baton.

### 4.2 Implementation

*Certificate Chain and Delegation Tokens.*

In Baton, a *certificate chain* is a sequence of one or more delegation tokens. Each delegation token in the certificate chain is a signed collection of metadata which contains the following information:

1. The application package name.
2. The application version code.
3. A set[8] of previously active certificates.

---

[8]Baton assumes developers may use multiple signing keys on the same application [10].

**Overview:** The holder of $KeyA$ wishes to delegate signing authority to a new key $KeyB$.

**Variables:**
$KeyA, KeyB$ - the private keys corresponding to the public keys in $CertA$ and $CertB$ respectively.
$CertA, CertB$ - the signature verification certificate used to verify signatures on current application release, and the certificate being delegated to, respectively. The certificates are self-signed.

**Pre-requisites:** The fingerprint of $CertB$ has been communicated to the holder of $KeyA$ over a channel with guaranteed integrity.

**Protocol:**

1. Holder of $KeyA$ generates $token=\text{Sig}_{KeyA}\{H(\text{pkg name, version code}, CertA, CertB \text{ fingerprint, previous token hash†})\}$.
2. $token$ is communicated to holder of $KeyB$.
3. Holder of $KeyB$ includes token in $AndroidManifest.xml$ when releasing updates signed with $KeyB$.

†: If there is no previous token to hash (*i.e.*, it is the first token to be included in a certificate chain) null may be substituted for the previous token hash value.

---

4. A set of currently active certificates.
5. A cryptographic hash of the previous delegation token in the certificate chain.

A Baton delegation token acts as a verifiable endorsement of a transition from one set of certificates to a new set of certificates whose corresponding private keys will be used to sign the new or current version of the application. The generation of the delegation token is described in Protocol 1.

Each delegation token, including a signed hash of the delegation token prior to itself in the chain, allows cryptographic verification of the entire certificate chain. This prevents an adversary from removing, adding, or rearranging delegation token elements in the chain. Inclusion of the package name scopes the delegation to only the specified application. For example, if a developer signs three applications with the same signing key and generates a Baton delegation token to update the certificate of only one of the three applications, the scope prevents this same token from being embedded in the other two applications, as the package name will not match.

*Baton XML.*
Baton applications embed into the $AndroidManifest.xml$ an XML representation of the certificate chain. To simplify the signing and verification procedure we detach[9] the delegation token signatures from the delegation token metadata to create two separate sets of nested elements, `certificate-chain` and `certificate-chain-signatures` (see Figure 3). The `delegation-token` elements in `certificate-chain` are matched to the corresponding `delegation-token-signature` elements in the `certificate-chain-signatures` by order within their parent element. The signing process is performed following the `xmldsig` [1] standard best practices[10] outlined by the W3C working group.

To allow signature validation in the case of missed intermediate updates, each delegation token includes a Base64 encoding of each certificate in the previous certificate set

as well as their fingerprints. We chose to embed the full certificate for each of the `previous-certs` as a convenience to handle updates from a very old version to a new version signed with certificates which would be valid only after processing several delegations. In this case, the certificates specified in intermediate tokens may not be present within the application and must be loaded from the encoded version in the token.

As a design alternative (listed as "Baton alternative" in Table 1), it is possible to avoid embedding a certificate chain at all by retaining all previous versions of $AndroidManifest.xml$ and the `META-INF` directory in future versions of the APK.[11] Thus, signing a new APK will bind the current $AndroidManifest.xml$ to the complete history of previously signed $AndroidManifest.xml$ files. In this alternative implementation, transitioning to a new set of signing certificates would require the $AndroidManifest.xml$ to specify the new certificate in an APK update signed by the currently valid certificate. This simpler implementation would require more involvement from developers to ensure that all prior versions of the `META-INF` directory are retained. `Jarsigner` would need to be invoked independently once the application archive is created. With Baton, certificate delegations only add a few lines to $AndroidManifest.xml$ instead of creating an archive of past files containing mostly no-longer valid data.

*AOSP Implementation.*
We modified The Android Open Source Project (AOSP) code to implement the Baton certificate verification functionality. The proposed set of patches totals under 500 lines of code which we plan to make available under an open source license compatible for inclusion in AOSP.

The `android.content.pm.PackageParser` core class was modified to correctly process of the new $AndroidManifest.xml$ entries. In the AOSP services sub-project, the `com.android.server.pm.PackageSignatures` class was modified to store a $SignatureChain$ reference, populated by the `PackageParser`. When the `com.android.server.pm.Settings` class loads or

---

[9]http://www.w3.org/TR/xmldsig-core/#def-SignatureDetached
[10]http://www.w3.org/TR/xmldsig-bestpractices/

[11]The hash tree structure of `MANIFEST.MF` allows the signature on a single file to be verified.

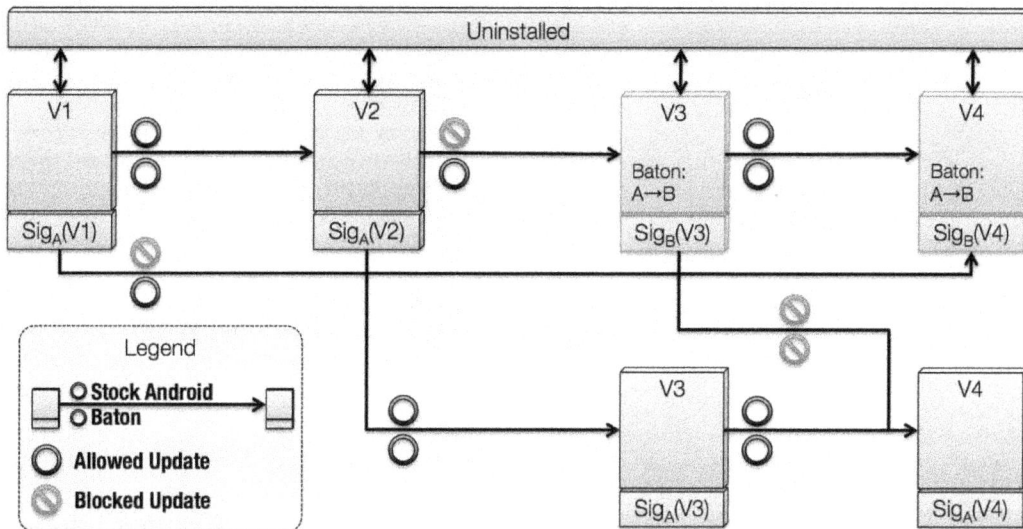

**Figure 2:** Version update diagram depicting updates that are allowed by stock Android (icons depicted over an arrow) and by Baton (icons depicted under the arrow). $\text{Sig}_A(Vn)$ and $\text{Sig}_B(Vn)$ are signatures on application version $n$ with signing keys $A$ and $B$, respectively. In all cases, updates are only allowed if signatures are successfully verified.

stores the on-disk *packages.xml* file, the *SignatureChain* is responsible for writing its own representation to the file, and restoring it when the operating system boots.

In addition to modifying existing classes, we created a new class (`com.android.server.pm.SignatureChain`). This class serves as an in-memory representation of the XML certificate chain from the *AndroidManifest.xml*. It contains the logic for reading the *SignatureChain* to and from XML, as well as verifying delegation token signatures.

Finally the `com.android.server.pm.PackageManagerService` class was modified to instrument the stock signature verification logic and package update procedure. When the modified `PackageManagerService` processes an update for an installed application, it will compare the installed application's set of signing certificates to the proposed update's set of signing certificates. If the sets match, the update proceeds following the existing Android certificate continuity policy. If the certificate sets do not match, then the `PackageManagerService` ensures that the proposed update must contain a delegation token for the correct version transition (*i.e.*, for the currently installed version to the update's version) endorsed by the installed application's certificate set. The version transition may be endorsed through one or more intermediate delegation tokens allowing the update to proceed in the event the user has missed interim updates.

The AOSP project does not include the `javax.xml.crypto.dsig` packages used to verify XML signatures. Therefore we additionally include the Apache Santuario[12] library, an independent implementation of the `xmldsig` [1] standard.

*Developer Tools.*

To facilitate adoption by developers, we augment the application signing life-cycle by integrating with the develop-

ment environment used to produce Android application releases. As of writing, the official Android Developer Tools (ADT) plugin for Eclipse[13] is closed source, impeding our ability to enable Baton support directly. In lieu of a patch to ADT, we have opted to provide a third party Eclipse plugin. After installing the Baton plugin in Eclipse, developers are able to export their Android projects as a Baton-enabled APK. In addition to the Eclipse plugin, our developer tools can operate as a stand-alone GUI, or a command line tool. The stand-alone versions of the plugin are better suited for integration with other IDEs that support external tools, or with more complex build management systems often used with large software projects.

To begin the process, the developer is prompted to select one or more signing certificates to endorse for future updates, or to enter a certificate fingerprint. For example, this may be a certificate generated by the new owner of the project if the developer is transferring control (*e.g.*, selling to another developer) of their application. The certificate may also be locally generated. The developer must also choose one or more signing certificates whose corresponding private keys will be used to sign the delegation token. In practice the developer will most often select the signing certificates presently used to sign production releases of their project. The version code and the package name values in the token are pre-filled from the values in the *AndroidManifest.xml* file. If necessary, the developer will be asked to enter a passphrase to unlock the private key. After unlocking the private keys (if required) the XML for the delegation token is generated, following Protocol 1. It is signed, and inserted into the certificate chain in the *AndroidManifest.xml* file. The token is also displayed on-screen to allow communication of the token to other parties if required.

---

[12]http://santuario.apache.org/

[13]http://developer.android.com/tools/index.html

```
<manifest ... >
 ...
  <certificate-chain>
    <delegation-token android:versionCode=
      "10">
      <previous-certs>
        <cert encoded="..." fingerprint=
"907EB3F2E8447054446A2A4B3ED8CA78DB04B188"
  />
      </previous-certs>
      <current-certs>
        <cert fingerprint=
"6E532E87A468052DA2EE8E9D6E56080181D3E2F9"
  />
      </current-certs>
      <previous-token hash="null" />
    </delegation-token>
  </certificate-chain>

  <ceritificate-chain-signatures>
    <delegation-token-signatures>
      <Signature>
        ....
      </Signature>
    </delegation-token-signatures>
  </certificate-chain-signatures>
  ...
</manifest>
```

**Figure 3: Example Baton certificate chain entry in *AndroidManifest.xml*. Base64 encoded certificate content and non-Baton related Android entries removed for brevity. Signature element defined in `xmldsig` [1] standard.**

## 5. EVALUATION

This Section discusses compatibility of Baton with other signature-based security mechanisms and previous versions of the OS. Additionally, we perform a security analysis of Baton.

### 5.1 Compatibility

*Compatibility with Related OS Functions.*

Android currently uses code signing certificates for security operations outside of application update integrity. Code signing certificates provide a form of access control, selectively allowing applications to join a shared UID group or to be granted a signature permission (see Section 3). At application install time, for the application to be allowed access to a signature protected resource (*e.g.*, UID group or permission), the certificates on the application must be identical to those associated with the protected resource. This requirement remains unchanged in Baton.

Using Baton, if one application in a shared UID group or an application providing a signature protected permission transitions to a new set of signing certificates, the certificates associated with the group or permission within the OS are updated to reflect the transition. As a consequence, future updates to other applications in the UID group, or requesting the signature permission must also transition to the new set of signing certificates.

We have designed Baton such that developers cannot issue a certificate transition to one application that "evicts" other applications from a UID group by changing the associated certificate set. This behavior is consistent with Android's current model, where applications cannot arbitrarily change UID groups during updates.[14] An eviction would, by definition, change the UID of the evicted application, leading to an inconsistent state. Our design instead honors the membership of already installed applications until they are updated. This prevents previously functional applications groups from losing functionality (by evicting a member) while introducing no detrimental security properties.

*Enabling Compatibility with Stock Android.*

Application releases that perform a certificate transition using Baton must package a modified *AndroidManifest.xml* containing a Baton certificate chain in the released APK. For this reason, we consider the compatibility of the modified application release with existing versions of Android (*i.e.,* those without Baton).

At application install-time, the Android OS parses the *AndroidManifest.xml* using the `android.content.pm.Package-Parser` class (located within the frameworks directory of AOSP). Once patched to enabled Baton support, the Android OS is aware of the new XML tags introduced for the certificate chain (see Figure 3), and can react accordingly. The default unmodified behavior of the `PackageParser` class, as of the time of writing, sets an internal `RigidParser` constant to **false**, causing unrecognized XML tags to be skipped without error. Based on the behavior of the code in AOSP, if an application carrying a delegation token is installed on an unpatched OS, the certificate chain will be ignored. The application will still install correctly pending successful (stock) certificate continuity validation.

If the Baton patches were merged into AOSP, we recommend developers who release applications containing a Baton certificate chain use the `android:minSdkVersion` parameter in *AndroidManifest.xml* to preclude install on systems lacking Baton support. It seems unavoidable that users without Baton support may only install application updates signed with a different set of signing certificates by first uninstalling the old application.

### 5.2 Implementation Evaluation

*Standard Update.*

We tested Baton by creating multiple releases (each with an incremental version code) of a test application, and side-loading each version on to an emulated Android environment in various orders (*e.g.,* V1→V2→V3, V1→V3, V2→V3→V1). All releases were signed with the same signing certificate and used the same package name. As per stock Android policy, updates succeeded but downgrades did not. The user experience was no different in the Baton environment and in the unmodified Android environment.

*Certificate Agility.*

We created a sample application with an embedded Baton certificate chain and tested delegating signing authority from one certificate to another (keeping the package name the same). After installing the application signed with one certificate, the app was transitioned to a new certificate by

---

[14]`https://android.googlesource.`
`com/platform/frameworks/base/+/`
`d0c5f515c05d05c9d24971695337daf9d6ce409c`

embedding a token generated by the Baton developer tools in an update. Baton successfully validated the delegation token, and user data related to the test app was preserved and accessible by the application with the new certificate. We also tested changing certificates but not including the Baton certificate chain, as well as changing certificates and including an invalid certificate chain. These updates failed with the "failed inconsistent certificate error" thrown by the Android OS as expected.

### *AOSP Unit Tests.*

We ran the bundled unit tests for the `PackageManagerService` class. These unit tests are included with the AOSP source code and are used for automated testing and to prevent any bugs from being introduced to previously functional code. We checked that the Baton system introduces no such regression errors by running the unit tests and verifying that a Baton patched system passes the tests without failure or warning.

### *AOSP Code Inspection.*

We searched the AOSP source code tree looking for references to signing certificates. Code found interacting with the `PackageManagerService` or with the `Signature` objects used internally to represent code signing certificates was manually inspected and examined for conflicts with Baton. No conflicts were discovered.

## 5.3 Security Analysis

Here, we analyze Baton under the security objectives and threat model presented in Section 4.1.

**No Unauthorized Updates.** Baton does not modify the requirements of Android's standard certificate continuity verification. Baton only introduces cryptographic verification of certificate chains. Thus, with Baton, an adversary must still compromise a developer's private signing key to issue an update or create a valid certificate chain to transition to a new signing certificate.

The certificate chain and delegation tokens in Baton are included in the *AndroidManifest.xml*. They are not secret; digital signatures provide integrity protection. Deleting the chain or delegation tokens inside the *AndroidManifest.xml* has the same effect as removing a signature from an Android package (deleting the `META-INF` directory, also known as signature stripping [8]). Apps without a Baton certificate chain or `META-INF` directory will fail to validate as legitimate updates and will not succeed in replacing an installed binary.

**No Replays.** Delegation tokens include a package name, version code, and are digitally signed. Replaying a delegation token on a different application (*i.e.*, copying the relevant section of the *AndroidManifest.xml* file into an application with a different package name) will prevent successful chain verification. Certificate transitions do not succeed unless all tokens in the chain reference the package name being updated, and corresponding signatures can be verified.

**Mitigating Social Engineering.** With Baton, users apply app updates as usual. However, unlike with stock Android, there is no legitimate reason to require the user to manually uninstall applications for the purpose of a key update. Training users that sometimes this action may be required

(which is the case, as of writing) can lead to social engineering attacks by malicious developers; Baton eliminates the need to do so, reducing this risk.

**No Unauthorized Interaction.** Baton does not modify UID sharing nor signature permission requirements. Applications must be signed with the same signing key(s) at install time to leverage signature privileges (see Section 5.1). It is not possible to leverage Baton to arbitrarily join a UID group for which a key is not held.

## 6. DISCUSSION

This Section discusses practical implications of enabling key agility on Android.

## 6.1 Certificate Expiration

The Android OS currently ignores the validity of signing certificates at install time, despite official documentation stating otherwise [4]. As of Android 4.2, we have verified that it is possible to install (without warning or user intervention) apps with a signing certificate that has expired. Additionally, the Google Play Store requires that all apps submitted carry a certificate valid for at least 25 years, making expiration verification redundant for marketplace installations. With Baton, certificate renewal becomes possible, which re-enables the possibility of enforcing certificate validity. Enforcing expiration may limit the impact of key compromises (see below) and allow the optional use of CA-issued signing certificates that have more generally acceptable validity periods (*e.g.*, 1–5 years).

Baton could be modified to limit the time during which an expired certificate can be used to authorize a key delegation. For example, limiting the ability for an expired certificate to authorize a key delegation one year after expiration. This mechanism can help reduce the exposure window where an adversary can gain access to an expired private key and roll it over to a new malicious key, while giving developers ample opportunity (*e.g.*, one year) to acquire and authorize new certificates after expiration.

## 6.2 Private Key Compromise

In the current Android security model, if a developer's private signing key is compromised by an attacker (*e.g.*, by physical keystore theft or by exploiting a crypto implementation bug [18]), the attacker may permanently release unauthorized updates. If the signing key is used on an app distributed on an application marketplace, the attacker would need to successfully gain access to the marketplace account to publish an update. Alternatively, the attacker could convince users to sideload the unauthorized version (*e.g.*, from a non-official site). Similarly with Baton, unauthorized updates will be possible if keys are compromised. This includes both standard updates as well as updates with a certificate chain. Developers using Baton must protect signing keys as usual. However, if key compromise or a crypto implementation bug is detected in a timely fashion, it may be possible for the legitimate developer to issue a Baton app update *before* the adversary, effectively "locking" users who upgraded into a new uncompromised replacement signing certificate.

## 6.3 Transferring Authority

Using Baton, developers can delegate signing authority to the holder of a different key, but the original certificate and corresponding key pair will remain authorized for issuing updates to versions of the app not containing the certificate chain. For example, when an app is being sold, the seller may continue to issue updates to the app under the original key (see $V2_{SigA} \rightarrow V3_{SigA}$ in Figure 2). Clients who do not update to the Baton version ($V3_{SigB}$) may be tricked into installing updates with the old signing certificate instead. While there is generally a trust relationship established when ownership of an app is being transferred (*e.g.,* the buyer is already exposed to potential backdoors in the app), best practices would encourage revoking the original certificate from updating the app. This must be a finer grained revocation than certificate revocation: a seller of an app may have other apps signed with the same certificate that are not being sold. We consider two conditions—with and without a marketplace—under which apps could require a proper transfer of signing authority.

**Assisted by a central marketplace.** When an app is installed through an application marketplace, there are effectively two authentication mechanisms in place to ensure source continuity: the signature enforced at the OS-level and the developer account with which the app is associated at the market-level. Application marketplaces such as Google Play allow developers to transfer apps to another account,[15] which effectively prevents an app seller from continuing to issue updates through the marketplace. For marketplace users, app updates will proceed as usual. Users who install apps from multiple markets or by sideloading may still be vulnerable to installing unauthorized updates that are signed with the original developer's key.

**Without a central marketplace.** When users install apps from only side-loaded sources, it seems difficult to communicate the revocation of a certificate's signing authority over a specific app. Certificate revocation remains an open problem in self-signed environments, where no single entity is authoritative except perhaps the OS itself.

**Detection instead of prevention.** It could prove advantageous to keep a public record of package names and associated certificate chains as a type of public notary to identify if different certificate chains emerge for the same app. This principle can be seen in other domains: *e.g.,* Convergence [25] and Certificate Transparency [2] which aim to detect fraudulent certificates in TLS. A similar system could be used in Android to confirm the uniqueness of a certificate chain at install-time. Baton could be augmented to submit certificate chains or query valid chains for a given application by leveraging an install-time server query mechanism like that of Barrera *et al.* [9]. The server-side component, which reports back on valid or invalid chains, would require manual curation by experts.

### 6.4 Applicability Beyond Android

The Baton protocol (see Protocol 1) is designed to be generically applicable in other decentralized signing environments. We only require that signed objects exist in a collision-free namespace. That is, the underlying OS prevents the existence of more than one signed object with the same name. In the case of Android, we use package names as

identifiers. However, Linux file system paths could also be used, resulting in an improvement over the key-locking proposal of van Oorschot and Wurster [24]. Baton also requires a way to keep track of versions to ensure correct validation of delegations. Object versioning can be implemented at the application level similar to Android's version code, or built in to the file system itself.

### 6.5 Limitations

One of Baton's main limitations is the need for developers to include the certificate chain (which includes corresponding full certificates) in potentially all[16] subsequent versions after a certificate transition. Failure to include the chain of certificates would prevent users who have not yet upgraded to the latest version from seamlessly upgrading, since there is otherwise no easy way to verify the chain. Android certificates are typically 600 bytes to 2 kilobytes in size, so overall application size is not expected to be adversely impacted by including several certificates. Since certificates and certificate chains are intended to be public, backup copies may without risk be stored in the cloud or on a shared drive.

Private key loss, even with Baton, remains a difficult problem. Losing a signing key means it is no longer possible to issue a Baton certificate update, unless a signature threshold system [22] is used. We believe solving this limitation would weaken Android's overall security model since a mechanism to issue an update without the original key could be abused by an adversary.

### 7. RELATED WORK

A comparison with proposals [23, 24] closely related to Baton was given in Section 1.1. In the broader literature on software updates, Cappos *et al.* [12] examine security issues in package managers which commonly distribute verifying keys as part of the installation media. Samuel *et al.* [20] describe a software update framework (TUF) that is resilient to a number of key compromise attacks. TUF is essentially an alternate PKI tailored to allow multiple roles (*e.g.,* release and timestamping) such that an adversary would have to compromise multiple keys to trick a user into installing a malicious update. Baton extends Android's trust-on-first-use model and focuses on the continuation and delegation of the initial trust without the need for a central PKI.

Specific to Android, Barrera *et al.* [8] examine Android's update integrity mechanisms, noting the lack of key agility and briefly discussing the Google Authenticator example. While the paper has several proposals, including improvements to UID sharing, none directly address key agility, the goal of Baton. Much of the existing body of Android security research has focused mainly on three areas: Android app analysis and malware [14, 16, 28]; permissions [15, 5]; and privilege escalation through IPC and covert channels [11, 21, 17]. Our work is focused on a less explored area of the Android security literature: the security of signing keys and certificate evolution.

### 8. CONCLUSION

The analysis of real-world examples and high-profile applications clearly illustrates the need for a mechanism to

---

[15]https://support.google.com/googleplay/android-developer/contact/publishing

[16]The certificate chain should be included in all subsequent versions from which the developer wishes to allow transparent upgrades, or as long as there is reason to believe not all users have performed the most recent certificate transition.

allow changing signing keys and certificates associated with Android apps. We have demonstrated its viability by providing a practical instantiation which has been tested and shown to be compatible with the current Android ecosystem. Baton demonstrates that what are typically considered as academic best practices for certificate update and package signing can be moved from theory to practice, to create a practical and lightweight mechanism that establishes cryptographically verifiable trust chains between certificates. With Baton, the responsibility of verifying integrity and authenticity of updates is placed on the developer and the OS, lightening the load on the user.

*Acknowledgements.*

This research is supported by the Natural Sciences and Engineering Research Council of Canada (NSERC)—the first author through a Canada Graduate Scholarship; the third through a Postdoctoral Fellowship; and the fourth through a Discovery Grant and as Canada Research Chair in Authentication and Computer Security. We also acknowledge support from NSERC ISSNet.

# 9. REFERENCES

[1] W3C Standard: XML signature syntax and processing. http://www.w3.org/TR/xmldsig-core/.

[2] Internet-Draft: Certificate transparency, 2012.

[3] Internet-Draft: Public key pinning extension for HTTP, 2012.

[4] Signing your applications. http://developer.android.com/tools/publishing/app-signing.html, Accessed Feb. 18, 2013.

[5] K. W. Y. Au, Y. F. Zhou, Z. Huang, and D. Lie. PScout: Analyzing the Android Permission Specification. In *ACM CCS*, 2012.

[6] E. Barker, W. Barker, W. Burr, W. Polk, and M. Smid. NIST Special Publication 800-57 Recommendation for Key Management. 2012.

[7] E. Barker and A. Roginsky. NIST Special Publication 800-131A Transitions: Recommendation for Transitioning the Use of Cryptographic Algorithms and Key Lengths, 2011.

[8] D. Barrera, J. Clark, D. McCarney, and P. C. van Oorschot. Understanding and Improving App Installation Security Mechanisms through Empirical Analysis of Android. In *ACM SPSM*, 2012.

[9] D. Barrera, W. Enck, and P. C. van Oorschot. Meteor: Seeding a Security-Enhancing Infrastructure for Multi-market Application Ecosystems. In *IEEE MoST*, 2012.

[10] D. Barrera, D. McCarney, J. Clark, and P. C. van Oorschot. Baton: Key Agility for Android without a Centralized Certificate Infrastructure. Technical Report TR-13-03, School of Computer Science, Carleton University, 2013.

[11] S. Bugiel, L. Davi, A. Dmitrienko, T. Fischer, A. Sadeghi, and B. Shastry. Towards taming privilege-escalation attacks on Android. In *NDSS*, 2012.

[12] J. Cappos, J. Samuel, S. Baker, and J. H. Hartman. A look in the mirror: Attacks on package managers. In *ACM CCS*, 2008.

[13] J. Clark, C. Adams, and P. C. van Oorschot. Usability of anonymous web browsing: An examination of Tor interfaces and deployability. In *SOUPS*, 2007.

[14] W. Enck, D. Octeau, P. McDaniel, and S. Chaudhuri. A study of Android application security. In *USENIX Security*, 2011.

[15] A. Felt, E. Chin, S. Hanna, D. Song, and D. Wagner. Android permissions demystified. In *ACM CCS*, 2011.

[16] A. Felt, M. Finifter, E. Chin, S. Hanna, and D. Wagner. A survey of mobile malware in the wild. *ACM SPSM*, 2011.

[17] A. P. Felt, H. J. Wang, A. Moshchuk, S. Hanna, and E. Chin. Permission re-delegation: Attacks and defenses. In *USENIX Security*, 2011.

[18] N. Heninger, Z. Durumeric, E. Wustrow, and J. A. Halderman. Mining your Ps and Qs: Detection of widespread weak keys in network devices. In *USENIX Security*, 2012.

[19] C. M. Karat, C. Brodie, and J. Karat. Usability Design and Evaluation for Privacy and Security Solutions. In L. Cranor and S. Garfinkel, editors, *Security and Usability*. O'Reilly, 2005.

[20] J. Samuel, N. Mathewson, J. Cappos, and R. Dingledine. Survivable key compromise in software update systems. In *ACM CCS*, 2010.

[21] R. Schlegel, K. Zhang, X. Zhou, M. Intwala, A. Kapadia, and X. Wang. Soundcomber: A Stealthy and Context-Aware Sound Trojan for Smartphones. In *NDSS*, 2011.

[22] V. Shoup. Practical Threshold Signatures. In *EuroCrypt*, 2000.

[23] P. C. van Oorschot and G. Wurster. Self-signed executables: Restricting replacement of program binaries by malware. In *USENIX HotSec*, 2007.

[24] P. C. van Oorschot and G. Wurster. Reducing Unauthorized Modification of Digital Objects. *IEEE Transactions on Software Engineering*, 38(1), 2012.

[25] D. Wendlandt, D. G. Andersen, and A. Perrig. Perspectives: Improving SSH-style host authentication with multi-path probing. In *USENIX ATC*, 2008.

[26] C. Wharton, J. Rieman, C. Lewis, and P. Polson. The cognitive walkthrough method: A practitioner's guide. In *Usability Inspection Methods*. Wiley & Sons, 1994.

[27] A. Whitten and J. Tygar. Why Johnny can't encrypt: a usability evaluation of PGP 5.0. In *USENIX Security*, 1999.

[28] Y. Zhou and X. Jiang. Dissecting android malware: Characterization and evolution. In *IEEE S&P*, 2012.

[29] P. Zimmermann and J. Callas. *The Evolution of PGP's Web of Trust*, chapter 7. O'Reilly, 2009.

# APPENDIX

# A. COGNITIVE WALKTHROUGH OF THE GOOGLE AUTHENTICATOR UPGRADE PROCESS

To illustrate the deficiencies in the process currently required to modify an application's signing certificate(s), *i.e.*, by requiring users to be involved in updating the application, we perform a cognitive walkthrough [26] of the update process as implemented by Google when switching signing keys for their Authenticator app (see Section 2). We refer to the versions of Authenticator with the initial signing key certificate[17] as Auth1 and the versions with the current certificate[18] as Auth2. Technically, these are considered by the OS to be distinct applications and thus must each have a unique package name[19]. However, users never see package names on Android. Apps are displayed to the user with an app name and icon, which are identical in both Auth1 and Auth2.

A cognitive walkthrough aims to shed light on the user experience of performing a specific task by relying on the interface for guidance. In a cognitive walkthrough, the evaluator (both a domain and usability expert) performs the core tasks required of the user and evaluates the experience against a set of guidelines or heuristics.

We consider a single core task: migrating from an installation of Auth1 to a fully functional installation of only Auth2. Since the core task is software installation, we looked to the literature for usability guidelines for installation, rather than regular software use, and borrow the installation-relevant guidelines from a cognitive walkthrough of the installation and use of Tor [13]. These guidelines, in turn curated from the literature, are:

**(G1)** Users should be aware of the steps they have to perform to complete a core task [27].

**(G2)** Users should be able to determine how to perform these steps [26, 27].

**(G3)** Users should know they have successfully completed each core task [26, 19].

**(G4)** Users should be able to recognize, diagnose, and recover from non-critical errors [26].

**(G5)** Users should not make dangerous errors from which they cannot recover [27].

**(G6)** Users should be comfortable with the terminology used in any interface dialogues or documentation [26, 19].

## A.1 Evaluation

Since Auth2 is technically a new installation instead of an update (we assume users can perform standard updates), it will not appear as an update in the Play Store. Thus, a user of Auth1 must first become aware of the existence of Auth2 through some other means (G1). Upon launching the latest (and last) version of Auth1 (v0.91), the user will encounter a prominent ribbon bar displayed at the top of the screen noting that the app will "no longer be supported." The phrase "Learn More" is offered as a link. The warning conforms to G6 but does not communicate the idea that a new version is available (G1), as opposed to the app simply being abandoned. Users may grasp that no more updates will be issued and then henceforth ignore the ribbon, never completing the core task of updating to Auth2.

If the user taps on "Learn More", they are then informed in plain language (G6) that a new version is available and are directed to the Play Store to download it. This information

[17]SHA: 38918A453D07199354F8B19AF05EC6562CED5788
[18]SHA: 24BB24C05E47E0AEFA68A58A766179D9B613A600
[19]Respectively: com.google.android.apps.authenticator and com.google.android.apps.authenticator2

in the app screen without requiring a user click-through to read it. The Play Store page for the application displays no information that distinguishes Auth2 from the already installed Auth1—it has the same app name and icon, and no language about the unusual update process for this particular app is present. A user may conclude they already have the app (contra G3). Diligent users, however, will notice the install button, which does not appear if an app is already installed (it is replaced with the option to open or uninstall).

If the user clicks to install Auth2, the app installs, automatically launches and transfers the user data from Auth1 to Auth2. (Technically, arranging for the app to open without a user click and securely transfer the data, which is private data used for authentication, requires sophisticated instrumentation of both apps by very good developers.) This automation prevents dangerous errors (G5). The user is then notified in plain language (G6) that the data has been transferred (G3) and is prompted to "uninstall the prior version of the app" (G1 and G2).

If the user clicks to uninstall the app, the OS displays a dialogue containing the app icon, app name (Authenticator), and question "do you want to uninstall this app" (G6)? In isolation, this screen does not adequately communicate to the user that the prior version is being uninstalled. Were the user instead to cancel the prompt to uninstall, perhaps believing that they do not want to uninstall what appears to be the exact app they just installed (based on the name and icon), they would have on their homescreen two identical icons with identical names and no indication of which is Auth1 and which is Auth2. If they manually uninstalled Auth2, they will lose their data (G5). However, if they opened Auth1, a warning would appear stating that the new version is already installed and offering to uninstall this version (G4). In addition, the user data is no longer available and the app is no longer functional (G4).

The user may successfully complete the core task by uninstalling Auth1 by following the instructions to do so when prompted during the installation of Auth2, or at any time later by following the prompts in either Auth1 or Auth2.

## A.2 Interpretation of Results

The intention of our cognitive walkthrough is not to criticize Google's handling of Authenticator's certificate migration. If anything, the process was relatively seamless, much of it automated, with care given to preventing dangerous errors and allowing recoverability. While there is room for improvement, this represents a nearly ideal execution of the certificate update process under the constraints of the OS. However in the hands of less skilled developers (*e.g.*, without clear instructions or the automation of the data transfer process upon install), the process could be much more difficult for users. Since Android currently leaves this migration process to app developers, we are apprehensive of how bad a less thoughtful execution could be, and note that a consequence of user error could be data loss.

By contrast, Baton removes all the uncertainty of developer execution and user behavior from the equation. With Baton, the same core task can be accomplished through a standard update indistinguishable from any other update, which we already assume a user can perform. Thus we can conclude, even without a cognitive walkthrough or user study, that any user able to update apps can use Baton to complete the core task.

is sufficient for G1 and G2, and should be displayed directly

# NativeWrap: Ad Hoc Smartphone Application Creation for End Users

Adwait Nadkarni
NC State University
Raleigh, North Carolina, USA
anadkarni@ncsu.edu

Vasant Tendulkar
NC State University
Raleigh, North Carolina, USA
tendulkar@ncsu.edu

William Enck
NC State University
Raleigh, North Carolina, USA
enck@cs.ncsu.edu

## ABSTRACT

Smartphones have become a primary form of computing. As a result, nearly every consumer, company, and organization provides an "app" for the popular smartphone platforms. Many of these apps are little more than a WebView widget that renders downloaded HTML and JavaScript content. In this paper, we argue that separating Web applications into separate OS principals has valuable security and privacy advantages. However, in the current smartphone application ecosystem, many such apps are fraught with privacy concerns. To this end, we propose *NativeWrap* as an alternative model for security and privacy conscious consumers to access Web content. NativeWrap "wraps" the domain for given URL into a native platform app, applying best practices for security configuration. We describe the design of a prototype of NativeWrap for the Android platform and test compatibility on the top 250 Alexa Websites. By using NativeWrap, third-party developers are removed from platform code, and users are placed in control of privacy sensitive operation.

## Categories and Subject Descriptors

D.4.6 [**Operating Systems**]: Security and Protection—*Access controls*

## Keywords

Web browsers; Mobile applications; Smartphone security

## 1. INTRODUCTION

Smartphones are now commonplace in much of the developed world, and their popularity continues to rise. A key feature of smartphones is the wide variety of available third-party applications, commonly known as "apps." Users can find apps to enhance nearly any daily activity and provide entertainment during idle periods. Indeed, the official application markets for Android and iOS both contain over 700,000 applications [55, 4].

Privacy is a significant problem for smartphone consumers. In the past several years, a number of research groups have identified

widespread privacy concerns with smartphone apps in both Android [18, 32, 19, 26, 25, 51] and iOS [15, 30]. Popular media investigators such as the Wall Street Journal have made similar independent findings [47]. Smartphone apps leak a range of privacy sensitive information, from seemingly innocent phone identifiers to geographic location to entire address books. Researchers often speculate that such data is collected and sold to data brokers that perform analytics for selling advertisements. Regardless of the actual use, it is clear that privacy sensitive data is being leaked by smartphone apps, often without user consent or information.

The current state of the smartphone application ecosystem leaves privacy conscious consumers with a dilemma: either use the app while being aware of the privacy risks, or do not install the app. Many privacy conscious consumers (including the authors) occasionally decide that an application's benefit outweighs its privacy risks. While recent research has proposed fine-grained privacy controls, none are likely to go mainstream. Solutions that modify the OS to allow finer-grained permission control [9, 43, 58], return fake values [6, 58, 32], or limit network connections with sensitive values [18, 32] require significant technical expertise to build and install the custom OS for a specific device. Furthermore, these research prototypes have not undergone rigorous testing, nor are they frequently updated to new OS versions that contain new features and security patches. More recently, an array of solutions have proposed adding inline reference monitors to applications [57, 37, 12, 31] rather than modifying the OS. Unfortunately, statically modifying an application package either results in a painful install process for the user, or requires an online trusted third-party to host modified apps (which to date does not exist). Finally, all of these solutions risk breaking applications in unknown ways, as developers frequently assume permissions are granted if the app is installed.

Privacy conscious consumers sometimes have third choice: use a mobile Website in the phone's Web browser. Many applications are simply a convenient way to access a popular Website from a mobile device. Increasingly, Website owners are developing and maintaining mobile versions of their websites, often with an "m." or "mobile." domain prefix. Frequently, the mobile Website functions very similar to the mobile app. However, there are security and privacy drawbacks to accessing the app through its corresponding mobile Website. First, authentication tokens are stored in the Web browser's cookie store, which has a larger attack surface than if they are stored in an app's private data storage. Second, the shared cookie store allows advertisers and social networking sites to track users [14].

In this paper, we propose *NativeWrap* as a new alternative model for privacy conscious consumers to use Web-based applications on smartphones. NativeWrap balances the security and privacy risks of using the smartphone application and the phone's Web browser.

When a user is visiting a Website in the phone's browser that she would like to run as a native app, she "shares" the URL with NativeWrap. NativeWrap then "wraps" the URL into a native platform app while configuring best-practice security options. In effect, NativeWrap removes the third-party developer from the platform code, placing the user in control.

Specifically, NativeWrap provides the following properties:

- *Isolated Cookie Store*: Web browsers have one cookie store and mediate access based on the same origin policy (SOP). Unfortunately, SOP is insufficient to prevent privacy loss when the same advertisement firm (e.g., DoubleClick) is used on many Websites. SOP also does not prevent large social networking sites (e.g., Facebook) from identifying user browser habits by simply encouraging Website owners to include social networking integration [14]. NativeWrap prevents such privacy loss by ensuring a separate cookie store for each wrapped Website. It also prevents a compromised browser from leaking authentication cookies for multiple Websites.

- *Phishing Prevention*: Phishing attacks are successful when the user clicks on a link and is fooled into entering sensitive information into a fake Website. On smartphones, phishing attacks are aided by Web browsers that remove the address bar to maximize the viewing area [22]. By using a native platform app, the user can be trained to always use the phone's application launcher to access security sensitive services (e.g., banking). NativeWrap provides the native platform app experience to any Website. It also pins the wrapped Website to a specific domain to ensure embedded elements (e.g., ads) do not redirect the user to a malicious site.

- *Correct SSL configuration*: Recent research has identified widespread misconfiguration of SSL in smartphone apps [20, 24]. NativeWrap not only ensures proper SSL verification, but it also can pin the Website to a certificate authority to remove dependence on a large root CA list. Furthermore, NativeWrap adapts HTTPS Everywhere [16] to optionally allow the user to force SSL within the wrapped Website [34].

- *Limited, User-controlled Permissions*: Developers of native mobile applications frequently include extra functionality that impinges on user privacy. NativeWrap defaults to Internet-only permission, with the ability for the user to add several common functional permissions when wrapping the Website.

**Our Contribution:** The primary contribution of this paper is the proposal of a new conceptual approach for privacy concerned consumers to access Web content from smartphones and mobile devices. We provide a prototype implementation for Android and note that the approach could be adopted by other platforms if it was integrated into the platform OS. We survey 12,500 applications from the Google Play Store to demonstrate the need for NativeWrap. Finally, we test the compatibility of NativeWrap with the Alexa top 250 websites.

The remainder of this paper proceeds as follows. Section 2 motivates NativeWrap. Section 3 describes the NativeWrap design. Section 4 details its implementation. Section 5 evaluates NativeWrap compatibility. Section 6 discusses deployment strategies. Section 7 describes related work. Section 8 concludes.

## 2. MOTIVATION

Before describing NativeWrap, we must first understand how and why many applications are developed. We begin with a short history of mobile application development while defining several key terms used throughout the paper. We then provide a survey of mobile apps from the Google Play Store to better characterize the significance of the problem.

### 2.1 Background

The first feature-enhanced mobile phones provided an Internet connection and a Web browser. Early users visited the same Websites as provided for personal computers; however, it quickly became clear that mobile versions of these Websites were required to cater to the small display sizes on mobile phones. These Websites, commonly known as *mobile WebApps* (or simply *WebApps*) are front ends developed specifically to suit the display and user interface aesthetics of mobile phones, and can be accessed by nearly any smartphone with a Web browser.

As mobile phone platforms with native application environments emerged, developers began porting WebApp functionality to the popular platforms. These native applications (or *native apps* for short) are platform-specific, and are hosted on application markets such as the Google Play Store or the Apple App Store, from which users discover, download, and install them to their devices.

Native apps possess the ability to closely interact with the user and use the phone's hardware features such as accelerometers and GPS receivers to provide a rich user experience. As the usefulness of native apps grew, so did their popularity, ultimately leading users to frequently choose a native app over visiting the corresponding WebApp in the phone's Web browser. In turn, more and more companies and organizations felt compelled to provide native app versions of their Websites to stay up-to-date and maintain company image.

Developing and maintaining native apps requires significant resources. First, the application must be developed for each popular platform. Android and iOS use vastly different programming languages and design abstractions. Second, native app updates must occur via the platform's application market, which can include timely review processes (e.g., iOS) or at minimum user annoyance when apps are updated frequently. As a consequence, hybrid applications began to emerge. These hybrid applications are essentially WebApps "wrapped" in a "WebView" class within a native app. Both Android and iOS provide WebView primitives, therefore only a very small amount of code needs to be written for each platform, and updates only need to occur at the Web server. Toolkits such as PhoneGap simplify this process even further by providing a common template. To simplify discussion, this paper terms these hybrid applications as *WebView apps*.

There are both security and privacy benefits and drawbacks to WebView apps verses using WebApps in the Web browser. On the positive side, WebView apps are treated as security principles within their native platforms. This separation provides extra protection of user credentials and other sensitive data. WebView apps can also deter phishing. Once a user downloads a native app (e.g., a banking app), she becomes implicitly trained to access the service through the phone's launcher, and potentially less likely to be fooled by a link in an Email. Finally, WebView apps have separate cookie storage, which limits cross-site privacy concerns. For example, if a user is logged into Facebook in the Web browser, whenever the users visits a Website with a Facebook "like button," Facebook is notified. In contrast, if the user accesses Facebook via a native or WebView app, the user's authenticated Facebook cookies are not present in the Web browser. Similar privacy concerns with Website advertisements are also mitigated.

WebView apps also have security and privacy drawbacks. WebView apps are generally relatively simple and their core function-

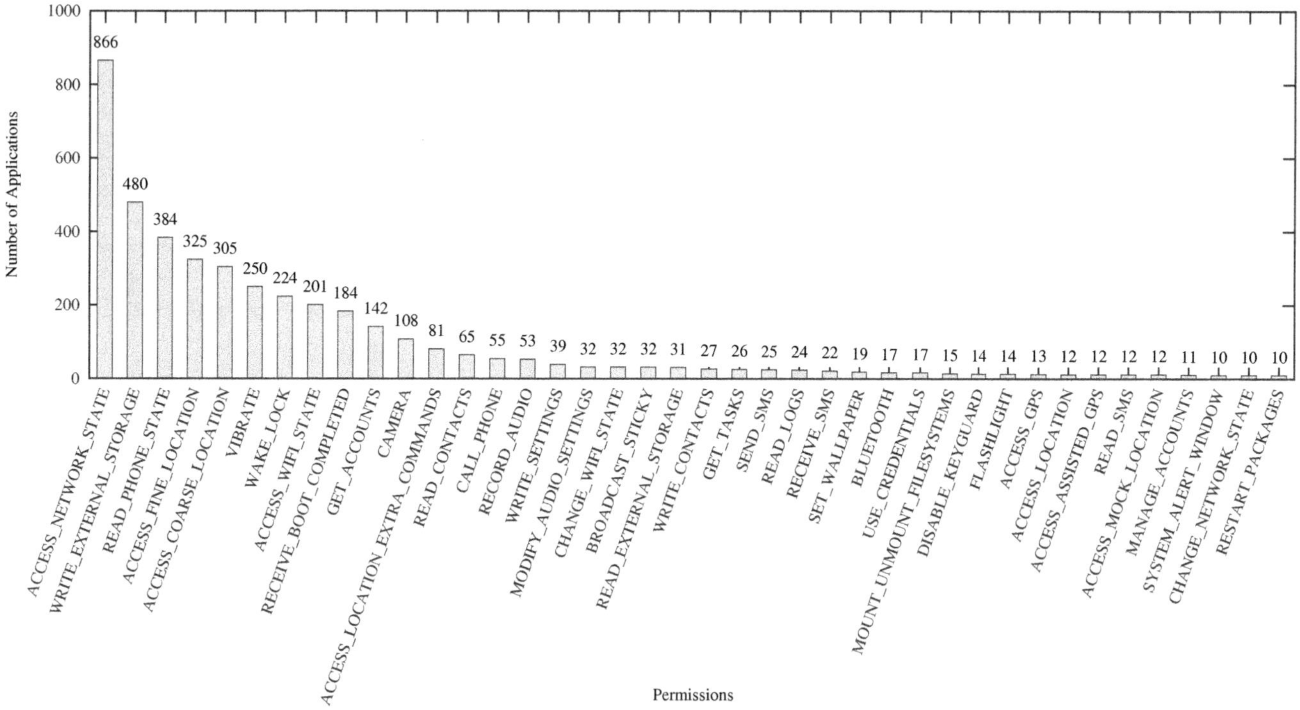

**Figure 1: Permissions frequently requested by WebView apps (only > 10 shown)**

**Table 1: Application Survey Results**

| Characteristic | # of Apps | Percentage |
|---|---|---|
| Total Apps | 12,500 | 100.00% |
| Apps that use WebViews | 10,165 | 81.32% |
| WebView Apps | 1,066 | 8.52% |
| Potentially over-privileged WebView Apps | 999 | 7.99% |

ality requires little more than permission to access the Internet. However, WebView apps often contain extra permissions. Many recent studies [18, 15, 32, 19] have identified privacy leaks of geographic location and phone identifiers, often by advertisement libraries [26]. Finally, WebView apps with extra permissions can potentially do more harm if exploited [21].

## 2.2 Application Survey

NativeWrap is an alternative to any mobile Website or native app that has a mobile Website. However, our primary target is to replace WebView applications, as they are little more than a WebView widget rendering the mobile version of a Website. To estimate a lower bound on the need for NativeWrap, we performed a survey of popular Android applications. Specifically, we sought to better understand *(1) what percentage of apps are WebView apps?* and *(2) what is the permission request profile of WebView apps?*

Our survey includes the top 500 free applications from each of the 25 application categories on the Google Play Store, as of January 2013. We excluded game and widget categories, as they are rarely full screen WebView apps. We disassembled the applications using baksmali [50] and extracted the `AndroidManifest.xml` file for each app using AXMLPrinter2 [2]. We then used lightweight static code analysis heuristics to classify the apps (described below). Our survey results are summarized in Table 1.

**Counting WebView apps:** We identified WebView apps in two steps. First, we used grep on the dissembled code to identify all applications that create or initialize WebView objects with URLs. We found that roughly 81% of applications used WebViews. However, upon closer inspection of randomly chosen applications, we found many apps use WebViews for extra functionality such as displaying company policies or advertisements. To estimate the lower bound of WebView apps, we identified the applications that use WebViews within the file that contains its main activity class. The main activity is specified in the application's `AndroidManifest.xml` and defines the first activity component started when the application is launched. If an app uses a WebView in its main activity class, it is highly likely that WebViews are core to the app's functionality. However, we stress that this is a lower bound, because developers may place WebView initializers in other classes called by the main activity class. This second search strategy identified 1,066 apps, or 8.52% of our sample set, which is significant enough a percentage of applications to be concerned about.

**Permission use by WebView apps:** Having identified a lower bound on the percentage of WebView apps, we turned to their security and privacy implications. Ideally a WebView app should only require the INTERNET permission. However, we found that nearly all of the identified WebView apps ($\approx$93%) required more permissions. These applications are called "potentially over-privileged WebView apps" in Table 1. Users installing these WebView apps have no way to deny specific undesired permissions.

The WebView apps requested a total of 436 unique extra permissions, of which 333 were custom permissions declared by the applications themselves. Figure 1 further breaks down the frequency of popularly requested permissions. The figure shows that most WebView apps request ACCESS_NETWORK_STATE, which is used to determine if the phone has a data connection, and can be used to differentiate cellular and WiFi connections. Addition-

15

ally, WRITE_EXTERNAL_STORAGE is reasonable for WebView apps storing caches on the SDcard. However, Figure 1 shows a wide variety of privacy and security relevant permissions. We note that the phone state and location permissions are the next highest requested permissions. These results clearly indicate WebView apps present privacy concerns.

**Stowaway [21]:** To characterize how many requested permissions are actually used by WebView app code, we analyzed 50 randomly selected applications with Stowaway [21]. We only analyzed 50 applications because Stowaway is not a stand-alone application and required us to manually upload the applications to a Website. The Stowaway results are useful as they help describe the potential for increased damage if the WebView app is compromised (e.g., due to a vulnerability in WebKit). We found that half of the 50 apps requested permissions that are never used. This result indicates that NativeWrap can also help increase application security.

## 2.3 Threat model

A fundamental premise behind our work is that both apps and mobile Websites have advantages and disadvantages with respect to security and privacy. Our NativeWrap solution is designed to leverage the advantages of each while removing the disadvantages.

Mobile applications are written by potentially untrusted third-party developers. Recent studies have clearly demonstrated that many legitimate (i.e., non-malware) apps leak privacy sensitive values such as phone identifiers, location, and address books [18, 32]. Often, these privacy leaks are a result of advertising and other non-required functionality. We seek to eliminate privacy loss due to non-required functionality.

Accessing mobile Websites through the device's Web browser also has security and privacy threats. We summarize these threats as follows.

**Cross-site Attacks:** WebApps contain Web elements from different origins. These elements can store cookies with the Web browser, and are frequently aware of the WebApp they are embedded within. By storing and retrieving cookies, the owners of these elements can track user's browsing habits. For example, consider a user logged into Facebook. Whenever the user visits a Website that embeds a Facebook "like button," Facebook is notified that the user visited the page, even if the user does not click the button [14]. Further investigations found that logging out of Facebook is not enough [11, 49]. To regain privacy, the user must clear the cookie store. Similar privacy concerns arise with Web advertisements that store cookies, i.e., a privacy concern DoubleClick is infamously known for. Browser state, including a range of browser cache methods, can be used to track the user [35]. By having per-WebApp cookie stores and state, NativeWrap significantly mitigates, if not removes, such privacy threats.

**Phishing:** Phishing attacks commonly trick users into clicking on URLs that direct them to a Website pretending to be the original (e.g., a bank Website). Web browsers on smartphones often make this easier, because the browser hides the address bar to maximize the page viewing area [22]. An example of such an attack is "Tab-nabbing" [46], wherein the attacker loads a fake page resembling some recently used website's login page into a browser tab that has been open, but inactive for a while. If the user is convinced the page is authentic, she may enter her credentials. NativeWrap seeks to mitigate such attacks by always clearly displaying the WebView app's name. NativeWrap further pins the WebView app to a domain to ensure phishing does not inadvertently originate from the domain, e.g., via advertisements that hijack the screen [1].

**Browser Compromise:** Upon compromising the Web browser, an attacker potentially gains access to all of the user's cookies, in-

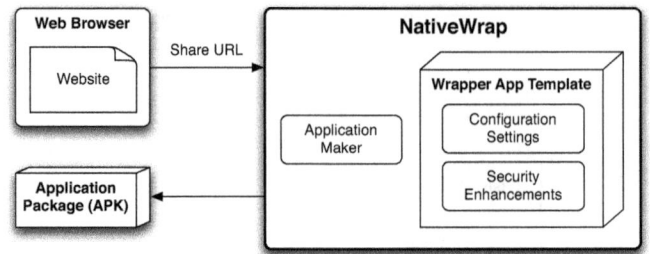

**Figure 2: The NativeWrap Architecture**

cluding those that are used for authentication. The compromise could also result in a Man-in-the-Browser attack [29], wherein the compromised browser logs all user activity and input. NativeWrap mitigates these threats by treating each WebApp as a different security principal in the host operating system. This includes separate cookie stores and separate runtime principals for each WebApp. We note that newer Web browser architectures such as Chrome for Android also provide defenses against such attacks. A more detailed comparison is provided in Section 7.

## 3. NATIVEWRAP DESIGN

NativeWrap provides an alternate model for accessing Web-based content by providing a balance between installing a third-party application and using the phone's Web browser. NativeWrap seamlessly allows end users to create safe and privacy friendly applications for any Website. To do this, the user must first visit the desired Website in the phone's Web browser. Once loaded, the user selects the "share" action that is often used to share a URL with messaging and social networking applications. When the user shares the URL, NativeWrap is available as a share target. Once NativeWrap receives a URL, it presents configuration screen to the user. NativeWrap uses the URL to specify best practices defaults (e.g., forcing SSL, CA pinning). Once the configuration is confirmed, NativeWrap parameterizes a pre-made WebView wrapper template and installs the newly created application package. This architecture is shown in Figure 2.

The remainder of this section describes the objectives and design of NativeWrap. We note that while many parts of the discussion are Android specific, NativeWrap is more general. We use Android where necessary to provide simplified and concrete discussion. Android also allows us to build and distribute a working NativeWrap prototype. We did not consider the other smartphone platforms for the prototype, because they cannot install applications without distributing them through the official application market. However, this need not necessarily be a limitation of NativeWrap. Other smartphone platforms (e.g., iOS) could easily include NativeWrap as part of the OS and provide it the ability to install the created applications.

## 3.1 Design Objectives

The primary objective of NativeWrap is to provide the user with a secure alternative to using WebView apps provided by third parties or accessing a WebApp via the browser. As such, NativeWrap seeks to achieve the following design objectives.

**1. Regulated permission set:** The WebView app should operate with the bare minimum privileges, i.e., network access. If additional privilege is required (e.g., to access external storage to upload photographs), the user should be provided the option to grant it. However, only network access should be enabled by default, and the WebView app should operate correctly with only network access (with the exception of the function requiring more privilege).

**2. Separate WebApp-specific resources:** In the browser, Web-Apps share a cookie store, bookmarks, and history. If the browser is compromised, the authentication cookies of all WebApps may be compromised. Furthermore, the same origin policy is insufficient to prevent privacy loss when a cookie provider is included as a page element on many Websites. Therefore, NativeWrap seeks to ensure separation of these resources. The resources should be specific to the WebApp; other WebApps should not be loaded into the original WebApp's container.

**3. Application-specific SSL configuration:** Web browsers must support the SSL needs of all Websites. In contrast, a NativeWrap app needs only to support the SSL needs of one Website. This feature must be leveraged to ensure the best possible SSL configuration for the app, including pinning the app to a CA certificate and forcing SSL if possible.

**4. Execution of trustworthy code:** The created WebView app should be free from known vulnerabilities and execute in a predictable manner. It should also prevent malicious arbitrary code from executing, and should be resistant to confused deputy attacks.

## 3.2 Design Elements

We fulfill these design objectives on Android in four parts: a secure configurable wrapper, domain pinning, SSL pinning, and forcing HTTPS where possible.

### 3.2.1 Secure Configurable Wrapper

In order to keep the resources of WebApps isolated, we wrap WebApps into native Android applications. Each Android application has a unique Linux UID making it a unique security principal. Therefore, native Android apps cannot access the private storages of other apps. By using this separation, we ensure protection for resources such as the cookie stores, saved passwords, etc.

Our native application template is actually an Android application built using a WebView as its primary layout view. The WebView is configured to display the WebApp associated with the URL supplied by the user. An alternate approach would have been modifying the default Android Open Source Project (AOSP) browser to support a single WebApp. After briefly considering this option, we determined that refactoring the browser app was a complex and error prone process that may leave unknown vulnerabilities. Therefore, we opted for a clean design.

We configure our wrapper template to request only the INTERNET permission. While studying WebApps, we recognized that some Websites allow users to upload files (e.g., photographs). WebViews can be programmed to relay file upload events to the Android OS. This feature will require the READ_EXTERNAL_STORAGE permission in future Android releases. Therefore, NativeWrap offers the user the option to add this permission while configuring the wrapper. Furthermore, the wrapper template is configured to only upload a file via the Android OS. Hence, the resulting app cannot directly access the external storage without the user's knowledge.

We note that NativeWrap could be too restrictive for some applications that genuinely require certain permissions (e.g., location) to execute their primary functionality. Our goal behind NativeWrap is to put the user in control, and such optional permissions can be added to NativeWrap's implementation if necessary.

### 3.2.2 Domain Pinning

The wrapper template is a native Android app that ensures that other native applications do not have access to the private resources of the WebApp wrapped in the template. To describe domain pin-

ning, we call this wrapped WebApp the "primary WebApp" and the corresponding URL the "primary URL." Domain pinning only affects the primary URL and not resources referenced by that page.

If the user navigates outside the primary WebApp, she may be exposed to phishing or cross-site attacks. These attacks often rely on the browser's ability to load multiple WebApps, which then share the same resources such as cookie stores, history and bookmarks. To prevent these attacks, we make the wrapper WebApp-specific by configuring the WebView to only work with the primary domain. Requests outside this domain are forwarded to the phone's default Web browser. To ensure the user is aware of this transition, we always display the name of the WebView App at the top of the screen. We also display a non-intrusive toast message when transitioning to the Web browser.

NativeWrap identifies the domain for the primary WebApp from the URL specified by the user. During our experimentation with initial versions of NativeWrap, we found that the full domain is not always appropriate. For example, `www.bestbuy.com` redirects to `www-ssl.bestbuy.com` for user login. Therefore, pinning the WebApp to `www.bestbuy.com` will not allow the user to log in, because the authentication cookies will be stored in the phone's browser. In this case, it is better to pin the WebView to `bestbuy.com` and allow all subdomains.

Pinning the WebApp to the second-level domain (e.g., `bestbuy.com`) is not always appropriate. For example, if the user is wrapping `foo.blogspot.com`, `blogspot.com` is too broad. However, we anecdotally observed that pinning the third-level domain is required significantly less frequently than the second-level domain. Therefore, we use the second-level domain as the default configuration, but also display the third-level domain as a clear option. We believe the cases when the third-level domain is needed will be obvious to most users.

Our experimentation with NativeWrap also uncovered redirection to other second-level domains. For example, `blogspot.com` redirects to `accounts.google.com` for authentication. Many Websites use third-parties such as Google and Facebook to authenticate. To address third-party authentication services, we suggest a whitelist solution. There are a relatively small number of authentication providers, which can be easily enumerated within the template. Furthermore, these domains generally are not the source of phishing attacks. Our current implementation only includes `accounts.google.com` and `facebook.com`, but additional entries can be easily added.

We note that including Facebook as trusted domain does not introduce privacy concerns unless the user actually logs into the WebApp via Facebook. In this case, Facebook may be notified of page visits within the primary WebApp if those pages contain Facebook like buttons.

### 3.2.3 SSL Pinning

Recent CA compromises have confirmed worst fears about the flaws of the CA model. An attack on Comodo in March 2011 resulted in it issuing 9 fake certificates for Websites including Google, Microsoft and Skype [40]. DigiNotar was compromised several months later [38], with the attacker(s) being able to issue over 500 fraudulent certificates, including a wildcard certificate for Google.

Fake SSL certificates are not limited to adversarial CA compromises. Nation states and other governing bodies can also force CAs to issue fake certificates. According to the Electronic Frontier Foundation's SSL Observatory, there are about 650-odd organizations that function as CAs [53]. An Android version ships 100s of such trusted CA certificates in its KeyStore, 140 for Android 4.2 [17]. If any one of these CAs is compromised, a fake SSL certificate for any Website can be created, allowing the holder of the fake certificate to perform DNS redirection or MITM attacks.

In the wake of the CA compromises and growing cyber-political tension, researchers have given increased attention to the CA model. Convergence [42] is a promising solution resulting from this discourse. Convergence is based on the idea of "trust agility," where the user chooses a set of notaries to validate certificates, and multiple notaries can be added or removed as needed. Notaries situated in different geographic areas can further reduce the possibility of an attacker fooling all notaries. One option is to include a Convergence module into NativeWrap. This would need to be coupled with defining an initial set of notaries, as well as allowing the user to configure the notary template used for all newly created applications. However, we currently use a simpler, and perhaps more appropriate mechanism: SSL CA pinning.

Creating WebApp-specific native applications makes NativeWrap suitable for using SSL CA pinning. Individual WebApps commonly only use one CA, therefore, it becomes possible to pin a root CA certificate to a particular wrapper application. SSL CA pinning significantly reduces the attack surface for many WebApps. For example, since Google uses Equifax as a CA, a compromise of Comodo would not affect the created WebView app. In fact, many third-party developers have begun using SSL pinning for their native apps. Unfortunately, doing so has proved to be error prone [20].

NativeWrap uses a first-use approach to acquire the CA certificate for the WebApp loaded in the native wrapper, i.e. we extract the CA certificate associated with the URL passed to NativeWrap. We then configure a TrustManager for the WebView class that only allows that root CA for SSL verification. We note that this approach is less flexible than Convergence, as the WebApp may wish to change its CA, which would require the WebView app to be recreated. This is not a problem for WebView apps created by third-parties, as they could simply distribute an updated version in the application market. The first-use approach is also subject to compromise during acquisition of the CA certificate used for the pinning. Finally, WebApps that use multiple CAs may nondeterministically fail. However, we did not experience any such problems during our compatibility study described in Section 5.1.

### 3.2.4 Force HTTPS

Many Websites provide both HTTP and HTTPS versions of their content. Unfortunately, URL references in content do not always use the HTTPS version of a URL when the user is visiting the HTTPS version of the site. ForceHTTPS [34] is a solution that allows Website owners to configure the site to inform the browser that HTTPS should be used for all connections. However, to take advantage of ForceHTTPS, the user must be aware that an HTTPS version of the site is available. For example, Google Search provides both HTTP and HTTPS versions, and until only recently, the user would need to type "`https://`" to visit the HTTPS version. To take advantage of the optional HTTPS versions of Websites, the Electronic Frontier Foundation (EFF) created the HTTPS Everywhere project [16]. This project provides an extension for Firefox and Chrome that consults a regular expression based rule set identifying Websites that have an HTTPS version. Users using the extension can ensure that they visit the HTTPS version of a Website whenever possible, without the need to type "`https://`".

We have incorporated the HTTPS Everywhere concept into NativeWrap. When the user shares a URL with NativeWrap, NativeWrap consults the HTTPS Everywhere rule set to determine if an HTTPS version of the Website is available. If so, the NativeWrap configuration template includes a "ForceHTTPS" checkbox, with the value selected by default.

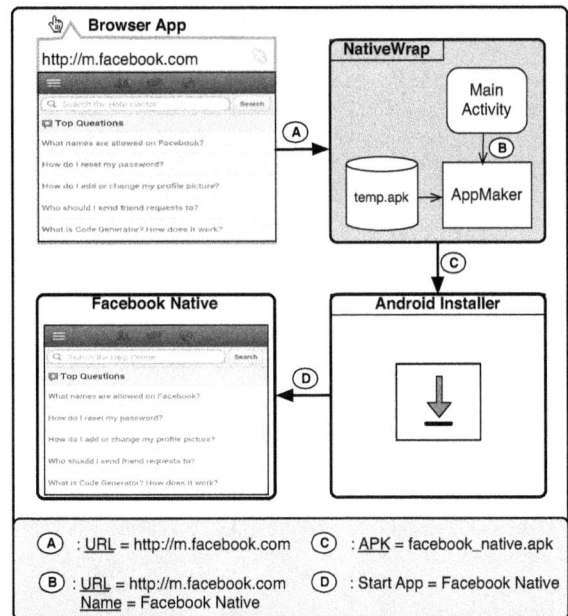

**Figure 3: NativeWrap Implementation: Wrapping the *Facebook* WebApp to create the *Facebook Native* application.**

If the user creates the app with the ForceHTTPS option enabled, the matched rule is included in the created WebView app. When the user uses the app, the rule is matched against every visited URL, substituting the HTTPS version whenever possible. Packaging a single rule works, since the wrapper is pinned to a single domain. This also works if the user selects the option to pin the wrapper to pin to the domain of the origin (e.g., `*.google.com` instead of `images.google.com`). In this case, the rule for `*.google.com` is applied, covering all its sub-domains.

We know that there are multiple ways to maintain the HTTPS Everywhere rule set. One option is to hard-code the rule set into the NativeWrap app, and update it by distributing a new version through the application market. However, this method is slow and potentially annoying for users. Therefore, NativeWrap currently retrieves the ruleset by making a secure connection to our remote server, where the rules are stored and regularly updated as soon as the EFF git repository is updated.

## 4. IMPLEMENTATION

In this section, we describe the implementation of NativeWrap for the Android OS. We describe the basic flow of events that takes place when a URL is native-wrapped. The core NativeWrap logic is implemented as an Android application that can be installed on any Android phone. The application includes a wrapper template that is in and of itself an Android APK package. An example execution using Facebook is shown in Figure 3. The source code for NativeWrap can be found at `http://research.csc.ncsu.edu/security/nativewrap/`.

**1. Sharing the URL:** The process begins with the user visiting the target URL in the phone's Web browser. Web browsers commonly have a "share" function that calls `startActivity` with an intent addressed to the ACTION_SEND action string and a data field containing the URL string of the current page. When Android resolves ACTION_SEND, multiple targets are available, therefore it opens a chooser dialog that allows the user to choose the target. NativeWrap defines an intent filter for ACTION_SEND on its main

18

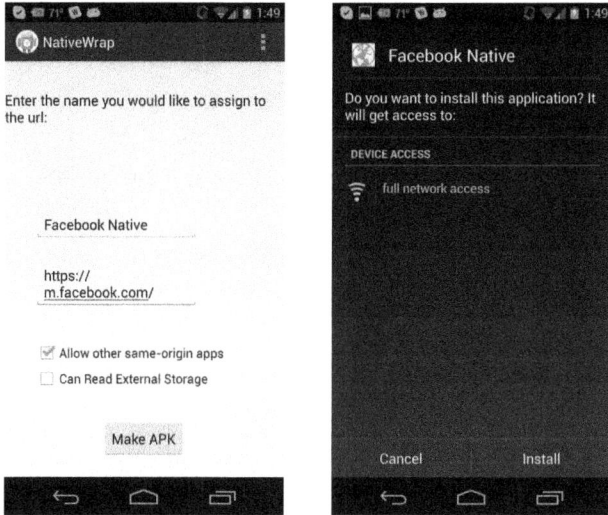

(a) NativeWrap Configuration Screen

(b) Android Installer

**Figure 4: Configuration and installation of a *Facebook Native* app.**

**Table 2: HTML5 Compatibility Score Comparison**

| Feature (Max points.) | Google Chrome | NativeWrap |
|---|---|---|
| Parsing rules (10) | 10 | 10 |
| Elements (30) | 25 | 25 |
| Forms (110) | 106 | 106 |
| Microdata (5) | 0 | 0 |
| Location and Orientation (20) | 20 | 20 |
| Output (10) | 5 | 5 |
| Input (20) | 13 | 3 |
| User Interaction (25) | 20 | 20 |
| Performance (25) | 25 | 20 |
| Security (40) | 28 | 28 |
| History and Navigation (10) | 10 | 10 |
| Communication (35) | 35 | 35 |
| Video (35) | 35 | 35 |
| Audio (30) | 25 | 20 |
| Peer To Peer (15) | 15 | 0 |
| 2D Graphics (25) | 19 | 19 |
| 3D Graphics (25) | 20 | 0 |
| Animation (5) | 5 | 5 |
| Web Applications (20) | 16 | 15 |
| Storage (30) | 28 | 28 |
| Files (10) | 10 | 10 |
| Other (20) | 14 | 14 |
| **Total (555)** | **484** | **428** |

activity. As such, NativeWrap is started automatically by Android, and there is no need for a persistent service.

**2. Customizing the Wrapper:** Once NativeWrap receives the intent, it extracts the URL and populates the configuration template with defaults, as described in Section 3. At this point, the user can modify the URL, the pinned domain, specify an application name, enable additional permissions, etc., as shown in Figure 4(a). The user then chooses to "Make the APK", which sends the customized parameters to the *AppMaker*, which is a private activity component.

**3. The AppMaker:** When AppMaker receives the customized parameters, it copies the default wrapper APK file to `temp.apk`. This APK is already configured to support SSL pinning, domain pinning, and some usability features to support a maximum number of web applications. It is also designed to retrieve the URL from an XML file in the `/assets` directory within the APK.

The *AppMaker* first extracts the `AndroidManifest.xml` from `temp.apk`. We parse and modify the manifest file using AXML [5], as it is in a binary XML format. We change the package name to "`com.nativewrap.wrapped<SERIAL>`", where "`<SERIAL>`" is a 32 bit integer serial number that is incremented to avoid repeating package names. NativeWrap does not use part of the URL as the package name to allow the user to make multiple WebView apps for the same domain, e.g., with different security settings.

AppMaker changes the package name only in the manifest file. It does not rebuild the application. To ensure that the application executes correctly, we use the full classname of activity components specified in the manifest. Using the default relative class names attempts to call a nonexistent class, since the package name in the manifest no longer matches the prefix on the Java classes.

Next, AppMaker modifies the `label` attribute of the main activity. This is the activity started by the phone's application launcher, and changing its `label` to the application name specified by user ensures the user can easily find the WebView app in the list of icons and in the settings menus. Additionally, if the user chooses external storage read access, AppMaker adds a `<uses-permission>` specification for READ_EXTERNAL_STORAGE.

Finally, AppMaker creates a new XML file for the Website URL, adds that file and the modified manifest file to `temp.apk`. The re-

sulting package is signed with a prespecified key and renamed to `<application-name>.apk`. In order to install the `.apk`, the installer must be able to read the file. The most obvious place to store the `.apk` is the SDcard, which is effectively readable by all applications. However, the SDcard is also effectively writable by all applications. If the `.apk` is writable, a malicious application may exploit a race condition by modifying the file before it is installed. To avoid this race condition, we place the `.apk` in the root of NativeWrap's `/data` directory and make the file world readable. Passing the full file path to the installer allows the package to be installed.

**4. Installing the APK:** Once the APK is created, AppMaker sends an intent message to the system with the full path to the APK to initiate its installation. As shown in Figure 4(b), this intent invokes the Android's installer, which presents the user with a screen to install the application. Once the user approves the permission list, the WebView app is available in the phone's application launcher.

## 5. EVALUATION

We begin the evaluation by comparing the HTML5 compatibility of NativeWrap with Google Chrome for Android, studying how NativeWrap affects the compatibility of WebApps. Then, we describe two case studies to demonstrate the functionality and security benefits of NativeWrap.

### 5.1 Compatibility

We test NativeWrap compatibility in two ways. First we test raw HTML5 compatibility using a standard benchmark. We then manually evaluate the top 250 Alexa Websites.

#### 5.1.1 HTML5 Compatibility Test

We performed a compatibility test for HTML5 support using `html5test.com`, on a Nexus 4 running Android 4.4.2. This test evaluates a Web browser on how well it supports the upcoming HTML5 standard, and generates a cumulative score chart for each aspect examined. We also compare the NativeWrap results with Chrome for Android (available for Android 4.0 and later).

Table 2 gives a comparison of Chrome for Android's and NativeWrap's wrapper's performance in the HTML5 compatibility test. We also note that NativeWrap performed exactly as well as the stock Android 4.4 browser, and much better than the reported values for the stock Android 4.0 browser (272 points as per `html5test.com`[1]), which confirms our choice to build the wrapper from scratch rather than refactoring the AOSP browser.

Our wrapper, and in turn the Android WebKit, only partially supports some HTML5 elements, while it does not support features like Microdata, 3D graphics, and peer to peer. However, we do support most other aspects of the standard, including form elements, essential parsing rules, audio, and video. NativeWrap's wrapper generally scores similar to Google Chrome for most of the features. Chrome scores better only in the input (access to webcam), audio (Web Audit API), peer to peer (WebRTC and Data Channel), 3D Graphics (WebGL 3D graphics), and Performance (Shared Workers), and Web applications (custom search providers) categories.

### 5.1.2  Alexa Top 250 study

To further verify our results, we manually tested NativeWrap for compatibility with the top 250 Websites in the world (filtering the duplicates, such as `google.in` and `google.cn`) from Alexa.com as of April 2013. Note that we skip websites in foreign languages that require login, therefore we actually consider the top testable 250 Websites. It is worth mentioning that as of September 2011, 34 of the top 100 websites had already converted to HTML5 [41]. Even by a conservative estimate, the number is likely to have gone higher since. We used a Samsung Galaxy Nexus phone running Android version 4.2.2 for this experiment and the case studies described in Section 5.2.

We made a native-wrapped application for each of these websites, and simultaneously tested the Website in Chrome for Android version 25. We tested the hypertext content as well as interactive multimedia content such as HTML5 audio and video tags, and also the intra-website navigation. None of the websites crash or exhibit broken functionality during our tests, with some minor exceptions[2], that exhibit similar behavior on the AOSP Browser as well due to HTML5 incompatibilities of the Webkit API. We infer the following from our results:

1) *Websites conservatively use HTML5 features*, using the ones commonly supported by most available browsers. For example, a developer would want to consider the Android 2.3 browser, which is still on about 46% of all Android devices as of February 2013 [27] and scores a modest 200 points on the compatibility test.

2) *Websites detect browser compatibility* and present only compatible features. Websites could also redirect the user to a HTML4 version, though we did not observe any redirection on our native-wrappers, possibly because it is compatible with most required HTML5 features that most websites currently use.

3) *Websites handle errors* and exceptions silently and transparently from the user, especially when they are related to HTML5, which is still not supported completely by most browsers.

4) *NativeWrap supports HTML4 content* well, and is completely compatible with websites that still work on HTML4.

## 5.2  Case Studies

### 5.2.1  Slick Deals

The Slick Deals WebApp keeps the user updated with the latest information on deals and offers on various products and services.

The Android app for Slick Deals is a WebView application, and does not use the native Android User Interface to a great extent. It is a fairly popular application installed in around 100,000 - 500,000 devices, with a four star ranking on the Google Play store. The app loads a WebView with the web address of the mobile WebApp, i.e., `http://m.slickdeals.net`.

Slick Deals was one of the over-privileged applications obtained from our application survey described in Section 2. An analysis with Stowaway detected that the app requests the Android location permissions (both coarse and fine location), but does not use any API that require these permissions. Even if it did call API that requested location, its purpose of displaying online deals would not justify the need for location information.

We created a new Slick Deals app using NativeWrap for this case study. The Slick Deals mobile website worked just as well on the new app as it did in the browser. At the same time, the original Slick Deals app did not offer any more functionality than the native wrapped app, apart from a different font and color combination, but was in fact vulnerable to activity hijacking attacks when scanned with ComDroid [8].

### 5.2.2  Facebook for Android

Facebook tops the Alexa rankings as the most visited website worldwide as of April 2013. The Facebook app is also the most popular free Android app based on the number of installs from the Google Play Store, somewhere between 100-500 million as of April 2013. Based on the sheer number of users whose privacy depends on Facebook, it is an ideal candidate for a case study.

We compared three methods of accessing Facebook from an Android device: 1) the Facebook WebApp accessed via the phone's Web browser shown in Figure 5(a), 2) the Facebook for Android native app (version 3.1) shown in Figure 5(b), and 3) the native-wrapped version of the Facebook app shown in Figure 5(c). We evaluate each approach on two main factors: *usability* which measures the convenience and features offered to the user, and *security* which is based on the vulnerabilities in the approach, possible attack surfaces and potential privacy violations.

**Accessing Facebook via the browser:** As described in Section 2.3, using the Facebook app in the Web browser exposes the user to various privacy and security problems, for e.g., the Facebook 'like' button privacy issue or phishing attacks like the 'tabnabbing'. The other two approaches do not face such problems as they are directly installed as independent native applications on the smartphone, and have their own separate resources.

The browser based approach also lacks the convenience of using a native app, as the user has to go through an additional step, i.e., the Web browser. The other two approaches provide dedicated apps for Facebook, and the native Facebook for Android app also utilizes some of the smartphone's resources and UI elements to provide a more immersive experience. Therefore, the Web browser-based approach clearly does not measure up to other two approaches, both in terms of usability and security. Hence, we now only focus on the remaining two approaches.

**Facebook for Android vs. Facebook-wrapped:** For this evaluation, we created a native-wrapped Facebook application with the URL `m.facebook.com`. We call it "Facebook-wrapped". We compare both the approaches on the basis of usability and security.

Facebook-wrapped and the Facebook for Android app are identical in terms of performing all of the core Facebook functionality, such as browsing pages and profiles, liking and sharing objects, uploading pictures, managing the user's account and privacy settings, etc. Facebook-wrapped lacks three primary features that Facebook for Android provides: 1) Android notifications, 2) contacts inte-

---

[1]Results accessed May 14, 2014.
[2]*Dailymotion* plays only the audio part of a video clip occasionally.

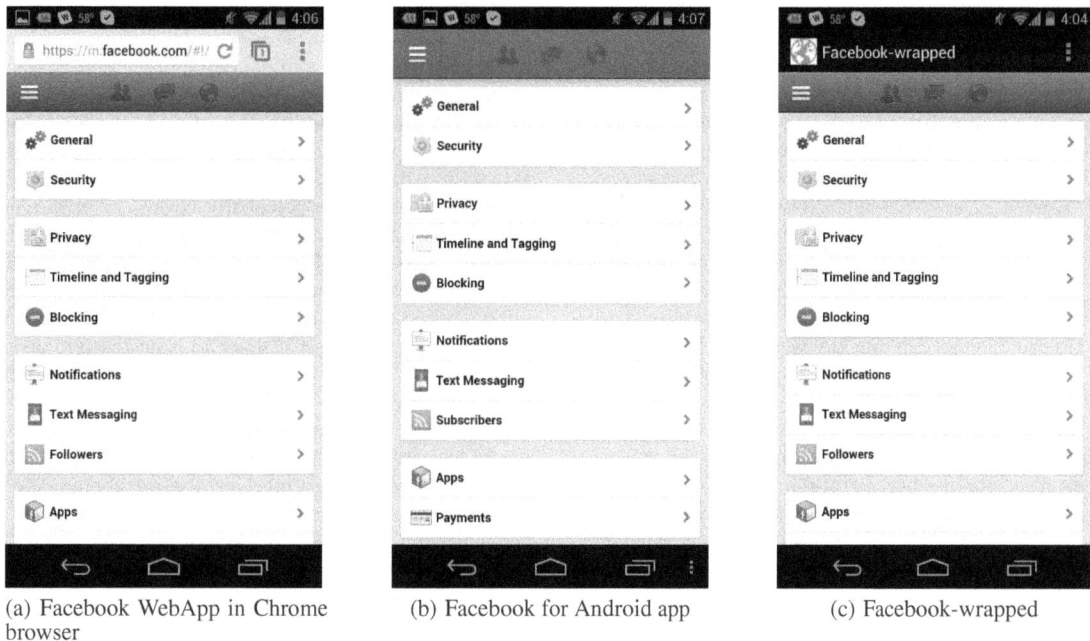

(a) Facebook WebApp in Chrome browser

(b) Facebook for Android app

(c) Facebook-wrapped

**Figure 5: Facebook Privacy Settings page.**

gration, and 3) geo-location checkin. However, users willing to sacrifice these features can benefit from privacy advantages.

Both the Facebook for Android and the Facebook-wrapped app are installed as native applications, and hence are not affected by the threats faced by the Web browser-based approach. The Facebook-wrapped app can perform all of the core Facebook functionality. Therefore, ideally, Facebook for Android should also not require more than the Internet permission. This is not the case, because Facebook for Android has many value-add features such as taking pictures and geo-location check-in. However, Facebook for Android also requests a number of non-obvious permissions. For example, it can access call logs, contacts, and recently added a permission allowing it to track what applications the user is currently running [45]. While there are likely reasonable justifications for all of Facebook for Android's permission requests based on various integration features, the functionality is not required by all users.

Facebook-wrapped on the other hand does not require any special privilege other than network access and the permission to read external storage (API 17 onwards, optional). The primary observed drawback was the inability to use geo-location check in. However, we view Facebook-wrapped as a privacy friendly alternative to Facebook for Android. Users interested in these privacy benefits are less likely to use the location feature.

## 6. DISCUSSION

When designing NativeWrap, we debated between bundling it with a custom Android and creating a stand-alone third party application that can be downloaded from Google Play. Clearly, a stand-alone third party application is more desirable and will reach a wider audience. Unfortunately, this deployment approach requires the user to modify the "Unknown Sources" application side-loading security setting. That is, the user has to choose to allow apps from unknown sources to install on the phone. Considering that most users are not security experts, allowing side-loading of apps from unknown sources may make the user vulnerable to attacks by

malicious applications. Expert users can reduce their vulnerability time frame by checking the option immediately before using NativeWrap, and unchecking it immediately afterwards. Testing showed that "Unknown Sources" was the only Android security option that needed to be disabled. NativeWrap was successfully tested with the "Verify Apps" feature activated.

The "Unknown Sources" limitation can be eliminated by making NativeWrap part of the Android OS. For example, NativeWrap could be deployed as a pre-installed system application and configured with the `ApplicationInfo.FLAG_PRIVILEGED` set in the package manager service. Doing so would inform the system package installer that NativeWrap install requests are not from an unknown source.

## 7. RELATED WORK

**Web browser hardening:** Web browsers are the central aspect of our Internet use. Anupam et al. analyzed JavaScript and VBScript based attacks on the Web application data in 1998 [3], and their work was one of the first to note how operating systems security primitives (e.g., 'ACL' [23], 'capabilities' [56, 39, 48]) apply to the multi-application environment in the browser. Since then, many approaches based on standard OS primitives have been proposed for enhancing the browser's security.

Tahoma [10] treats Web applications as first class objects, and uses virtual machines (VM) to isolate Web applications from each other and the browser from the underlying operating system. Each Web application instance starts in a new VM and has its own virtual disk space, screen, input devices, etc. A key difference with respect to NativeWrap is that Tahoma allows the Web application to specify the domains that will run in its VM instance in a manifest file. Delegating the browser configuration (domains to pin, security enhancements, etc.) to the Web application exposes the user to cross-site attacks and to some extent, phishing attacks described in Section 2.3. App Isolation [7] similarly allows web developers to configure domain pinning, and to optionally select isolated storage.

21

The OP Browser [28] splits the browser design into distinct function-specific components (e.g., webpage, storage, user interface) and makes the communication between these subsystems explicit, trusting the underlying operating system and the Java Virtual Machine (JVM) to maintain isolation between components. Such a model makes browser compromise difficult to achieve through exploits in individual subsystems, and provides strong isolation guarantees. Although OP Browser starts Web applications in new instances (processes), it still has a common cookie store for all Web application instances in the *storage* component. Although the reference monitor will follow the same origin policy, the common cookie store will lead to privacy issues such as the Facebook 'like' button problem. Instead of simply starting a new process, NativeWrap leverages the UID based separation provided by the underlying Android OS and ensures complete isolation between wrappers.

Google's Chrome for Android also leverages the UID based sandboxing provided by the Android OS. Every new browser 'tab' is started in a new principal instance, i.e., a process, and every such process has a different UID. This allows Chrome to regulate permissions allocated to each such principal, and provides isolation with respect to resources and data for each principal. A major limitation of the Chrome for Android browser is that is puts content from various origins in the same tab, i.e., in the same principal instance, meaning that the privileges allocated to a tab may still be accessible to the content from a different origin than the main content of the tab, leading to cross site attacks.

The Gazelle Web browser [54] recognizes the need for isolating Web application principals into separate instances. Content from different domains, even if accessed in the same tab or embedded in the same webpage, is put in separate principal instances. Therefore, Gazelle prevents embedded content of one principal executing code in another principal's context. In spite of such protections, principals in Chrome as well as Gazelle share common resources like cookie stores, which can result in privacy problems, some of which are described in this paper. The fundamental reason behind this difference is that NativeWrap's wrapper provides a single Web application environment, while Chrome for Android, Gazelle, OP browser and other similar approaches [52, 33, 36, 7] attempt to achieve complete app-specific isolation in a multi-app environment.

**Privacy violations by native apps:** Most Web browsers available today are vulnerable to many of the attacks described in our threat model (Section 2.3). Google's Chrome for Android is relatively resistant to browser compromise due to its UID based sandboxing, but is still vulnerable to phishing and cross-site attacks. Native WebView apps defined in Section 2.1 by default do not share browser state and cookie stores, and hence are not vulnerable to cross-site or browser phishing attacks. Nevertheless, native WebView apps that are over-privileged cause privacy concerns [18, 32, 19, 26, 25, 51].

There are different strategies for preventing privacy violations by such applications. Aurasium [57] repackages Android apps to make them policy compliant and to prevent privilege escalation attacks. A similar approach is taken by Dr. Android [37] and RetroSkeleton [12]. TISSA [58] allows the user to manage the private information granted to the app both during and after installation. It also has a provision to supply applications fake information. Apex [43] retrofits the Android package installer to install an application with custom policies. TaintDroid [18] uses taint tracking to alert the user when an application tries to export private data off the device. AppFence [32] and MockDroid [6] give the user a choice to provide fake information to apps that demand private data. In case the user needs to divulge information, AppFence prohibits the receiving app from exporting the data off the device.

Modifying an application package or its functionality may cause an application to break. Therefore, NativeWrap instead takes the control out of the hands of the developer, and packages a reliable template according to the security settings configured by the user.

**Other WebApp wrappers:** PhoneGap [44] allows developers to create native wrappers for HTML5 WebApps, and also provides JavaScript API to access the phone's resources. Thus, PhoneGap-based applications can potentially be just as privacy invasive as other native applications. PhoneGap is also only used by developers to wrap their HTML5 apps in native wrappers, and cannot be used by the user without the source code for the HTML5 app.

Finally, close in implementation, but drastically different in motivation, is the Fluid app [13]. Fluid is designed to create a native version of any Website for Mac OS X for user convenience. NativeWrap is designed specifically to address the security and privacy needs of smartphone users and is proposed as an alternate model for accessing Web content on smartphones. As such, Fluid does not provide the best practices security configuration provided by NativeWrap, nor does it provide the basic facility, i.e., a separate cookie store per wrapped WebApp in its free version.

## 8. CONCLUSION

Third-party native applications have become the *de facto* way for users to access Web content on smartphones. In this paper, we argued that native applications offer many security and privacy benefits over accessing the Web content using the phone's Web browser. Unfortunately, many of the native applications provided by third-parties contain privacy concerns in and of themselves. To resolve this tension, we proposed NativeWrap as an alternative approach for smartphone users to access Web content. NativeWrap "wraps" a given URL into a native application and applies security best practices configuration. In doing so, NativeWrap removes third-party developers from platform code and places users in control of privacy sensitive operation.

## Acknowledgements

This work was funded in part by the National Security Agency, and NSF grants CNS-1222680 and CNS-1253346. Any opinions, findings, and conclusions or recommendations expressed in this material are those of the authors and do not necessarily reflect the views of the funding agencies. We would also like to thank Tsung-Hsuan Ho, Ashwin Shashidharan, our shepherd Aurélien Francillon, and the anonymous reviewers for their valuable feedback during the writing of this paper.

## 9. REFERENCES

[1] C. Amrutkar, K. Singh, A. Verma, and P. Traynor. VulnerableMe: Measuring Systemic Weaknesses in Mobile Browser Security. In *Proceedings of the International Conference on Information Systems Security (ICISS)*, 2012.

[2] android4me - J2ME port of Google's Android. https://code.google.com/p/android4me/. Accessed August 2012.

[3] V. Anupam and A. Mayer. Security of web browser scripting languages: vulnerabilities, attacks, and remedies. In *Proceedings of the 7th USENIX Security Symposium*, pages 187–200, 1998.

[4] Apple. Apple Updates iOS to 6.1, Mar. 2013. http://www.apple.com/pr/library/2013/01/28Apple-Updates-iOS-to-6-1.html.

[5] axml - Read write android binary xml files.
`https://code.google.com/p/axml/`. Accessed
January 2013.

[6] A. R. Beresford, A. Rice, N. Skehin, and R. Sohan.
MockDroid: Trading Privacy for Application Functionality
on Smartphones. In *Proceedings of the 12th Workshop on
Mobile Computing Systems and Applications (HotMobile)*,
2011.

[7] E. Y. Chen, J. Bau, C. Reis, A. Barth, and C. Jackson. App
Isolation: Get the Security of Multiple Browsers with Just
One. In *Proceedings of the 18th ACM conference on
Computer and communications security. ACM*, 2011.

[8] E. Chin, A. P. Felt, K. Greenwood, and D. Wagner.
Analyzing Inter-Application Communication in Android. In
*Proceedings of the 9th Annual International Conference on
Mobile Systems, Applications, and Services (MobiSys)*, 2011.

[9] M. Conti, V. T. N. Nguyen, and B. Crispo. CRePE:
Context-Related Policy Enforcement for Android. In
*Proceedings of the 13th Information Security Conference
(ISC)*, Oct. 2010.

[10] R. S. Cox, J. G. Hanson, S. D. Gribble, and H. M. Levy. A
safety-oriented platform for web applications. In *2006 IEEE
Symposium on Security and Privacy*, pages 15–pp, 2006.

[11] N. Cubrilovic. Logging out of Facebook is not enough.
`http://www.nikcub.com/posts/`
`logging-out-of-facebook-is-not-enough`,
2011.

[12] B. Davis and H. Chen. RetroSkeleton: Retrofitting Android
Apps. In *Proceedings of the International Conference on
Mobile Systems, Applications, and Services (MobiSys)*, 2013.

[13] T. Ditchendorf. Turn Your Favorite Web Apps into Real Mac
Apps. http://fluidapp.com/about/, 2012. Accessed May 5,
2013.

[14] A. Efrati. 'Like' Button Follows Web Users.
`http://online.wsj.com/article/`
`SB10001424052748704281504576329441432995616.`
`html?mod=WSJ_Tech_LEADTop`, 2011.

[15] M. Egele, C. Kruegel, E. Kirda, and G. Vigna. PiOS:
Detecting Privacy Leaks in iOS Applications. In *Proceedings
of the ISOC Network and Distributed System Security
Symposium (NDSS)*, Feb. 2011.

[16] Electronic Frontier Foundation. HTTPS Everywhere.
`https://www.eff.org/https-everywhere`.
Accessed April 2013.

[17] N. Elenkov. Certificate pinning in Android 4.2.
`http://nelenkov.blogspot.com/2012/12/`
`certificate-pinning-in-android-42.html`,
2012.

[18] W. Enck, P. Gilbert, B.-G. Chun, L. P. Cox, J. Jung,
P. McDaniel, and A. N. Sheth. TaintDroid: An
Information-Flow Tracking System for Realtime Privacy
Monitoring on Smartphones. In *Proceedings of the 9th
USENIX Symposium on Operating Systems Design and
Implementation (OSDI)*, Oct. 2010.

[19] W. Enck, D. Octeau, P. McDaniel, and S. Chaudhuri. A
Study of Android Application Security. In *Proceedings of
the 20th USENIX Security Symposium*, August 2011.

[20] S. Fahl, M. Harbach, T. Muders, L. Baumgartner,
B. Freisleben, and M. Smith. Why eve and mallory love
android: an analysis of android SSL (in)security. In
*Proceedings of the 2012 ACM conference on Computer and
communications security(CCS)*, 2012.

[21] A. P. Felt, E. Chin, S. Hanna, D. Song, and D. Wagner.
Android Permissions Demystified. In *Proceedings of the
ACM Conference on Computer and Communications
Security (CCS)*, 2011.

[22] A. P. Felt and D. Wagner. Phishing on Mobile Devices. In
*Proceedings of the Workshop on Web 2.0 Security and
Privacy (W2SP)*, 2011.

[23] G. Fernandez and L. Allen. Extending the Unix Protection
Model with Access Control Lists. In *Proceedings of the
USENIX Summer Symposium*, pages 119–132, 1988.

[24] M. Georgiev, S. Iyengar, S. Jana, R. Anubhai, D. Boneh, and
V. Shmatikov. The most dangerous code in the world:
validating SSL certificates in non-browser software. In
*Proceedings of the ACM Conference on Computer and
Communications Security (CCS)*, pages 38–49, 2012.

[25] C. Gibler, J. Crussell, J. Erickson, and H. Chen.
AndroidLeaks: Automatically Detecting Potential Privacy
Leaks in Android Applications on a Large Scale. In *Trust
and Trustworthy Computing, Lecture Notes in Computer
Science Volume 7344*, 2012.

[26] M. Grace, W. Zhou, X. Jiang, and A.-R. Sadeghi. Unsafe
Exposure Analysis of Mobile In-App Advertisements. In
*Proceedings of the ACM Conference on Security and Privacy
in Wireless and Mobile Networks (WiSec)*, 2012.

[27] D. Graziano. Jelly Bean's market share is up but Gingerbread
just won't die.
`http://bgr.com/2013/02/08/android-`
`version-distribution-february-2013-316698/`,
2013. Accessed April 2013.

[28] C. Grier, S. Tang, and S. T. King. Secure web browsing with
the OP web browser. In *Proceedings of the 2008 IEEE
Symposium on Security and Privacy*, 2008.

[29] P. Guhring. Concepts against Man-in-the-Browser Attacks.
`http://www.cacert.at/svn/sourcerer/`
`CAcert/SecureClient.pdf`. Accessed December
2012.

[30] J. Han, Q. Yan, D. Gao, J. Zhou, and R. Deng. Comparing
Mobile Privacy Protection through Cross-Platform
Applications. In *Proceedings of the Annual Network and
Distributed System Security Symposium (NDSS)*, 2013.

[31] H. Hao, V. Singh, and W. Du. On the Effectiveness of
API-Level Access Control Using Bytecode Rewriting in
Android. In *Proceedings of the ACM SIGSAC Symposium on
Information Computer and Communications Security
(ASIACCS)*, 2013.

[32] P. Hornyack, S. Han, J. Jung, S. Schechter, and D. Wetherall.
These Aren't the Droids You're Looking For: Retrofitting
Android to Protect Data from Imperious Applications. In
*Proceedings of the ACM Conference on Computer and
Communications Security (CCS)*, 2011.

[33] L.-S. Huang, Z. Weinberg, C. Evans, and C. Jackson.
Protecting browsers from cross-origin CSS attacks. In
*Proceedings of the 17th ACM conference on Computer and
communications security*, pages 619–629, 2010.

[34] C. Jackson and A. Barth. ForceHTTPS: Protecting
High-Security Web Sites from Network Attacks. In
*Proceedings of the 17th International ACM Conference on
World Wide Web*, 2008.

[35] C. Jackson, A. Bortz, D. Boneh, and J. C. Mitchell.
Protecting browser state from web privacy attacks. In
*Proceedings of the 15th international conference on World
Wide Web*, pages 733–744. ACM, 2006.

[36] K. Jayaraman, W. Du, B. Rajagopalan, and S. J.Chapin. ESCUDO: A Fine-Grained Protection Model for Web Browsers. In *Proceedings of the 2010 IEEE 30th International Conference on Distributed Computing Systems (ICDCS)*, pages 231–240, 2010.

[37] J. Jeon, K. K. Micinski, J. A. Vaughan, A. Fogel, N. Reddy, J. S. Foster, and T. Millstein. Dr. Android and Mr. Hide: Fine-Grained Permissions in Android Applications. In *Proceedings of the ACM Workshop on Security and Privacy in Smartphones and Mobile Devices (SPSM)*, 2012.

[38] D. Kaplan. DigiNotar breach fallout widens as more details emerge. http://www.scmagazine.com/ diginotar-breach-fallout-widens-as-more- details-emerge/article/211349/, 2011.

[39] P. A. Karger and A. J. Herbert. An Augmented Capability Architecture to Support Lattice Security and Traceability of Access. In *Proceedings of the IEEE Symposium on Security and Privacy*, May 1984.

[40] W. Leonhard. Weaknesses in SSL certification exposed by Comodo security breach. https://www.infoworld .com/t/authentication/weaknesses-in-ssl- certification-exposed-comodo-security- breach-593, 2011.

[41] K. Maine. Percentage of Web sites Using HTML5. http://www.binvisions.com/articles/ how-many-percentage-web-sites-using-html5/, 2011. Accessed April 2013.

[42] Moxie Marlinspike. Convergence. http://convergence.io/. Accessed March 2013.

[43] M. Nauman, S. Khan, and X. Zhang. Apex: Extending Android Permission Model and Enforcement with User-defined Runtime Constraints. In *Proceedings of ASIACCS*, 2010.

[44] PhoneGap. http://phonegap.com/about/, 2012. Accessed May 5, 2013.

[45] E. Protalinski. Facebook's Android app can now retrieve data about what apps you use. http://thenextweb .com/facebook/2013/04/13/facebooks- android-app-can-now-retrieve-data- about-what-apps-you-use/, 2013.

[46] A. Raskin. Tabnabbing: A new type of phishing attack. http://www.azarask.in/blog/post/ a-new-type-of-phishing-attack/, 2010.

[47] Scott Thurm and Yukari Iwatani Kane. Your Apps Are Watching You. http://online.wsj.com/article/ SB10001424052748704694004576020083703574602. html.

[48] J. S. Shapiro. *EROS: A Capability System*. PhD thesis, University of Pennsylvania, 1999.

[49] B. Slawski. Facebook Patent Application Describes Receiving Data from Logged-Out Users to Target Ads. http://www.seobythesea.com/2011/09/ facebook-patent-application-target-ads/, 2011.

[50] smali - An Assembler/Disassembler for Android's dex Format. https://code.google.com/p/smali/. Accessed April 2013.

[51] R. Stevens, C. Gibler, J. Crussell, J. Erickson, and H. Chen. Investigating user privacy in android ad libraries. In *IEEE Mobile Security Technologies (MoST)*, 2012.

[52] S. Tang, H. Mai, and S. T. King. Trust and Protection in the Illinois Browser Operating System. In *Proceedings of the 9th USENIX conference on Operating systems design and implementation*, 2010.

[53] The Electronic Frontier Foundation. EFF SSL Observatory. https://www.eff.org/observatory. Accessed October 2012.

[54] H. J. Wang, C. Grier, A. Moshchuk, S. T. King, P. Choudhury, and H. Venter. The Multi-Principle OS Construction of the Gazelle Web Browser. In *Proceedings of the USENIX Security Symposium*, 2009.

[55] B. Womack. Google Says 700,000 Applications Available for Android. Bloomberg Businessweek, Oct. 2012. http: //www.businessweek.com/news/2012-10-29/ google-says-700-000-applications- available-for-android-devices.

[56] W. Wulf, E. Cohen, W. Corwin, A. Jones, R. Levin, C. Pierson, and F. Pollack. HYDRA: The Kernel of a Multiprocessor Operating Systems. *Communications of the ACM*, 17(6), June 1974.

[57] R. Xu, H. Saidi, and R. Anderson. Aurasium: Practical Policy Enforcement for Android Applications. In *Proceedings of the USENIX Security Symposium*, 2012.

[58] Y. Zhou, X. Zhang, X. Jiang, and V. W. Freeh. Taming Information-Stealing Smartphone Applications (on Android). In *Proceedings of the International Conference on Trust and Trustworthy Computing (TRUST)*, June 2011.

# ViewDroid: Towards Obfuscation-Resilient Mobile Application Repackaging Detection

Fangfang Zhang, Heqing Huang, Sencun Zhu, Dinghao Wu, and Peng Liu
The Pennsylvania State University
University Park, PA, USA
{fuz104, hhuang, szhu}@cse.psu.edu, {dwu, pliu}@ist.psu.edu

## ABSTRACT

In recent years, as mobile smart device sales grow quickly, the development of mobile applications (apps) keeps accelerating, so does mobile app repackaging. Attackers can easily repackage an app under their own names or embed advertisements to earn pecuniary profits. They can also modify a popular app by inserting malicious payloads into the original app and leverage its popularity to accelerate malware propagation. In this paper, we propose *ViewDroid*, a user interface based approach to mobile app repackaging detection. Android apps are user interaction intensive and event dominated, and the interactions between users and apps are performed through user interface, or views. This observation inspires the design of our new birthmark for Android apps, namely, *feature view graph*, which captures users' navigation behavior across app views. Our experimental results demonstrate that this birthmark can characterize Android apps from a higher level abstraction, making it resilient to code obfuscation. ViewDroid can detect repackaged apps at a large scale, both effectively and efficiently. Our experiments also show that the false positive and false negative rates of ViewDroid are both very low.

## Categories and Subject Descriptors

K.6.5 [**Management of Computing and Information Systems**]: [Security and Protection]; D.2.8 [**Software Engineering**]: Metrics

## Keywords

Mobile application; Repackaging; Obfuscation resilient; User interface

## 1. INTRODUCTION

In recent years, as the wide use and rapid development of mobile devices such as smartphones and tablets, mobile application (app) markets are growing rapidly. There were over $1,100,000$ apps available on the Google Play Android app market [5] on March 2014. Since popularity has become the core value among mobile platforms, many popular Android apps have been "copied," or repackaged, as reported by Gibler et al. [17]. One of the major reasons behind the emerging of Android app repackaging is that it is easy to reverse-engineer an Android app. When a user purchases and downloads an Android app, the installation package (i.e., the .apk file) is downloaded and stored on the user's mobile device. Given the openness of the Android platform, it is very easy to obtain the installation package from the device. After that, reverse engineering can be performed based on readily available tools such as apktool [1] and Baksmali/Smali [8], which can dissemble the compiled Dalvik EXecutable (dex) from the .apk file into a human readable Dalvik bytecode format (e.g., .smali files). At this point, the content of the app can be easily manipulated, modified, repackaged, and signed into a re-publishable APK file. Signing is not required to be bound with any official real ID of the developer and there is no certificate authority to sign apps. Moreover, due to the popularity of the Android platform, many unofficial app markets exist. Most of them do not enforce sanity checks on the apps listed on their web pages. As a result, the severity of app repackaging in the Android platform has been observed higher than in any other mobile platforms.

Generally speaking, there are two types of Android app repackaging. The purpose of the first type is to use other developers' apps to earn pecuniary profits. An attacker can easily repackage an app under his own name or embed different advertisements to gain ad benefits, and then republish it to an app market. Zhou et al. [34] found 5% to 13% of apps in the third-party app markets repackaged the apps from the official Android market. The second type is related to malware, where attackers modify a popular app by inserting some malicious payloads, e.g., sending out users' private information and purchasing apps without users' awareness, and leverage the popularity of the original app to accelerate the propagation of the malicious one. According to a recent study [35], 1083 (or 86.0%) of 1260 malware samples were repackaged from legitimate apps, indicating repackaging is a favorable vehicle for mobile malware propagation. Clearly, to maintain the health of an app market as well as for the security of mobile users, app repackaging detection is a critical issue to be addressed.

However, the problem of app repackaging detection is very challenging. On the one hand, due to the huge number of apps on an app market such as Google Play, efficiency and scalability of a detection scheme are highly demanded. On the other hand, the detection scheme must be resilient to code modification and existing automatic obfuscation techniques, because it is very easy to modify, obfuscate, and repackage Android apps without the source code of the original apps. Recently, several research works have been proposed for repackaging detection, based on Fuzzy Hashing [34], Program Dependence Graph (PDG) [15, 14], Feature Hashing [18], Module Decoupling [33], and Normal Compression Distance (NCD) [16]. These approaches can detect app repackaging efficiently based on certain "invariants" extracted from the app code. Such invariants are called *software birthmarks* as in the software engineering research [24, 25, 28, 30, 20]. A *software birthmark* is defined as a unique characteristic that a program or mobile app inherently possesses, and can be used to uniquely identify the program. All the above approaches use code-level birthmarks to characterize an app.

In this paper, we propose a novel repackaging detection system called *ViewDroid*, which leverages user interface based *birthmark* for detecting app repackaging on the Android platform. ViewDroid provides an alternative to the code-level detection approaches. It is motivated by two observations. First, smartphone apps are user behavior intensive and Android event-driven, and the interactions between users and apps are performed through user interfaces (i.e., app views). Some characteristics of views (e.g. the navigation between views) are unique for each independently developed app. Second, in both types of repackaging, because attackers want to leverage the popularity of a target app, they usually keep the repackaged apps' look-and-feel similar to the original one in the user interface level. Specifically, ViewDroid is built upon a robust birthmark called *view graph*. View graph is a graph constructed from all views through static analysis and catches the navigation relation among app views. In addition, we design features for both nodes and edges in view graph based on Android specific APIs. This can help pre-filter the non-relevant apps and improve the efficiency of the graph comparison algorithm.

ViewDroid is resilient to code obfuscation techniques for the following reasons. (1) View graph is a higher level representation of an app's behavior than the traditional code level birthmarks (e.g., opcode sequence, program dependence graph). In other words, ViewDroid does not need instruction-level details. Hence, it is resilient to code obfuscation such as noise instruction/data injection, instruction reordering, instruction splitting and aggregation and data dependence obfuscation, etc. (2) The generation of view graph relies on statically analyzing Android specific APIs (e.g., `startActivity` and `startActivityForResult`). These APIs are provided by the Android system and are hard to be replaced or modified. Therefore, view graph, as the birthmark, is more robust to obfuscation techniques such as API splitting, API renaming and API re-implementation. Our evaluation results demonstrate that ViewDroid is robust to many existing code obfuscation techniques.

Our paper makes the following contributions:

1. **View Graph**: We propose view graph, a user interface-based birthmark for Android apps. To the best of our knowledge, it is the first user interface level birthmark for software plagiarism or app repackaging detection.
2. **ViewDroid**: We propose ViewDroid, an Android app repackaging detection system based on view graph. ViewDroid is robust to many code obfuscation techniques, and both efficient and scalable. ViewDroid provides a complementary approach to current code-level repackaging detection methods.
3. **Obfuscation Resilience Evaluation**: We evaluated the obfuscation resilience of ViewDroid by 39 obfuscators from SandMarks [11] and KlassMaster [4], based on the evaluation framework proposed by Huang et al. [19]. The experimental results show that ViewDroid outperforms Androguard [16] in terms of obfuscation resilience.
4. **Large Scale Evaluation**: We tested ViewDroid on $10,311$ real-world apps ($573,872$ app pairs) from the Android market. It is detected that about $4.7\%$ apps are repackaging cases. We also evaluated the false negative of ViewDroid on a known repackaging app set. The false negative rate is $1.3\%$. The evaluation results demonstrate the efficiency and effectiveness of ViewDroid.

The remainder of the paper is structured as follows. Background of the Android platform and apps are given in Section 2. Section 3 generalizes the attack model and the design goals for repackaging detection. Section 4 describes the design of ViewDroid. Evaluation is presented in Section 5, followed by discussions in Section 6 and related work in Section 7. Finally we conclude the work with Section 8.

## 2. BACKGROUND

Android is a Linux-based platform for mobile devices. Users can download and install Android apps from various app markets. Android apps are published to the market in a compressed file format (i.e., .apk file). It contains a manifest file (i.e., AndroidManifest.xml), resource files (i.e., files in res directory), and compiled Dalvik Executable (i.e., classes.dex). The manifest file lists the package name, version number, critical components of the app, and the associate permissions to each component. The resource folder includes all the raw resource files, such as images and audio files, and the XML files which describe the layouts of user interfaces. The Dalvik executable contains all the classes that implement the functionality of all the primary components of an app. Some apps contain parts that are implemented by native languages. Since relatively few Android apps contain such components developed in the native languages C/C++ and they mostly serve as background services, our current ViewDroid design only takes into consideration the Dalvik executable, the relevant Android manifest file, and the layout files in the resource folder .

Components serve as the building blocks for Android apps. There are four types of components, namely, *Activity*, *Service*, *Broadcast Receivers*, and *Content Provider*. An *Activity* provides a screen for the user to interact with. An app requires one main activity to start but can have a number of other activities (roughly one per screen view). A stack is designed to organize activities. When a new activity starts, it goes to the top of the stack. A *Service* is a component that runs in the background, usually engaged in the performance of long-running tasks. In general, a service is used to perform any task that is asynchronous with respect to the main user interface. A *Broadcast Receiver* listens to special messages broadcasted by the system or individual apps and relays work to other services or activities. Finally, a *Content Provider* manages shared data and optionally exposes query and update capabilities for other components to invoke. A message-like *intent* is used to help the communications among components.

The execution sequence of an Android app usually starts from the main activity, specified in the manifest file. When the launching icon of an app is pressed by user, the main activity will be launched. It serves as the main entry point to the user interface. The app switches between activities by invoking platform APIs, `Context.startActivity()` or `Activity.startActivityForResult()` with `Intent` objects as parameter. An `Intent` object contains the information of the target activity. A user interface is loaded when an activity is initialized by the `onCreate()` method, which creates a new user view through APIs like `setContentView()`. The view is then put on the top of the view stack and becomes the running activity. Therefore, by analyzing the Android specific APIs within each `Activity` class, the user interface navigation relation information can be constructed to build our view graph. Note that, in our work, we only consider apps that have interactions with users (e.g., by key pressing, button clicking). Some other apps, which only have background services and do not interact with users, are out of our consideration.

## 3. PROBLEM STATEMENT

The most fundamental challenge of app repackaging detection is to find unique *birthmarks* to characterize apps. The proposed birthmark should be *accurate* and *unique* enough to identify an Android app. Moreover, as reported by Zhou et al. [34], the plagiarists and malware writers tend to use obfuscation on the repackaged apps to evade detection. Hence, to significantly raise the bar for stealthy repackaging, the designed detection scheme must be resilient against most code obfuscation techniques. Finally, since the Android app repackage problem is prevalent among most Android markets, it is very important to build a detection tool that can perform detection in large-scale scenarios.

**Scope of the paper.** In this paper, our purpose is to detect repackaging Android app pairs, but not to identify which is the original one and which is the repackaged one. We only focus on non-trivial Android apps that interact with users through user interface and are implemented as Dalvik executables. Apps that contains components implemented by native-code languages are out of the scope of our paper. Those only providing background services without user interactions are not under our consideration either.

### 3.1 Attack model

The general attack model in the Android app repackaging problem is: an attacker has access to the plaintiff Android app package (.apk file); he repackages the app by copying the code, making a few modifications (e.g., replacing the advertisement, attaching malicious payloads), and applying automatic code obfuscation techniques in order to evade detection; the repackaged app is then signed with a private key and republished to the app markets.

Based on the level of modification on the original APK files and the effort an attacker is willing to pay on the repackaging process, we further classify the repackaging attacks into the following three categories:

**Lazy attack:** A lazy attacker can make some simple changes over an app without changing its code. For in-

stance, repackaging an app with a different author name or with different advertisements is such rudimentary lazy attack. Non-developers can be easily trained to perform such tasks manually. More knowledgeable lazy attackers may apply current automatic code obfuscation tools to repackage an app without changing its functionality, following the procedure similar to what is shown in our evaluation section.

**Amateur attack:** An amateur attacker not only applies automatic code obfuscation but also changes/adds/deletes a small part of the functionalities. For example, an attacker can add some online social functionalities along with the online chat view to the original app. Attackers must pay more effort to understand and thus modify the code. For example, they have to read the Android manifest file to delete or append the components that they want to register for the app and to insert some interaction code into the original components to glue the newly added components.

**Malware:** A malware writer creates a malicious app that mimics a popular app by inserting some malicious payloads into the original program. In this way, the malicious app can leverage the popularity of the original app to increase its propagation speed. With this purpose, the attacker tries to make the functionalities and user interfaces of the repackaged app similar to the original one. Under this circumstance, an attacker actually has to perform most of tasks that an Amateur attacker has to do. In addition, the attacker needs to write the malicious payload either in Java or C/C++ and stealthily insert the payload into the app.

We further analyze how well ViewDroid can detect these attacks and other potential advanced attacks in Section 6.

### 3.2 Design Goals

In this paper, we design an app repackaging detection scheme named ViewDroid, with the following goals.

**Accurate Birthmark:** In order to measure the similarity between two Android apps, ViewDroid must select an accurate birthmark to characterize apps. This accurate birthmark should be able to reflect the primary semantics of Android apps and tell independently-developed apps apart. In other words, the designed birthmark should cause very few false positives.

**Obfuscation Resilience:** Code obfuscation is a technique to transform a sequence of code into a different sequence that preserves the semantics but is more difficult to understand or analyze. Obfuscation techniques can also be applied by attackers to evade repackaging detection. Hence, ViewDroid must be able to detect repackaging with the presence of various automated code obfuscation techniques. In other words, the designed birthmark should be robust against various obfuscators. Obfuscation resilient birthmarks will ensure low false negatives.

**Scalable Detection:** Because there are a huge number of apps on different Android app markets, ViewDroid must be efficient and scalable enough to detect repackaging in such a large-scale scenario.

## 4. DESIGN

### 4.1 Overview

It is critical while very challenging to identify an accurate and obfuscation resilient birthmark in the design of a repackaging detection tool. In the past, a good variety of birthmarks have been proposed and evaluated for different types of program languages (C, Java) and platforms (Linux, Windows). Some of these traditional birthmarks have been proposed to detect Android app repackaging [14, 18, 16, 34]. They are all code-level birthmarks. In this paper, instead of applying traditional software birthmarks, we propose a novel user interface-based one, namely *feature view graph*. It fully leverages a unique characteristic of smartphone apps – they are mostly UI intensive and event dominated [26]. Feature view graph represents a higher level abstraction of an Android app's semantics. Therefore, it has the potential to be more robust to code obfuscation. In order to meet the scalability requirement of Android repackaging detection, feature view graph is generated by static analysis of the dissembled installation file of an Android app (i.e., the APK file).

We define *view* in Definition 4.1 and *view graph* in Definition 4.2. View graph describes the user interface navigation relations of an Android app.

DEFINITION 4.1. *(View) A view is a user interface that is displayed to users for interaction with the mobile app. Each view has a corresponding activity class that defines the view's functionality. A view contains one or more visible components (e.g. buttons, trackball) on the screen. When touched, the components might trigger other activities or services.*

DEFINITION 4.2. *(View Graph) A view graph of a mobile app is a directed graph $G(V,E)$, where $V$ is a set of nodes, each of which represents a user interface view. $E$ is a set of edges $< a, b >$ such that $a \in V$, $b \in V$ and the smartphone display can switch from view $a$ to view $b$ by user interaction or other triggers.*

By adding features to each view and each edge, a view graph can represent an app more accurately and also improve the efficiency of app similarity measurement at the later stage. The features of a view could be the number, types or layout of the visible components (e.g., buttons, menus), or a set of Android platform specific APIs invoked in this view's activity. However, the former one (e.g., layout) is much easier for an attacker to manipulate because it does not represent the fundamental semantics of an app. The latter one (i.e., Android specific APIs) is much more stable and can reflect app's semantics; as a result, we only consider that as view features.

In a feature view graph, the feature of an edge is the event listener function (e.g., onClick(), onLongClick(), on-Touch(), etc.) that is directly triggered by user generated events. Generally, there are two types of events in Android platform, user-generated events and system-generated events. We only focus on user-generated events in our birthmark creation. This is because these events are highly associated with the functionality of an individual app and the corresponding user interaction with the app. For instance, the onClick() method of a registered listener is triggered when the corresponding button is pressed by a user, so we consider it as an edge feature. An example of system-generated events is when the system sends a short-message-received event, which triggers the onReceive() method registered for the SMS_RECEIVED intent in the manifest file. Clearly, this onReceive() method is not triggered by direct user interaction, so it is not considered as an edge feature. The *feature view graph* is defined in Definition 4.3.

DEFINITION 4.3. *(Feature View Graph) A feature view graph of a smartphone app is based on its view graph, $G(V, E)$, where certain features are selected and attached to $V$ and $E$.*

After creating the feature view graph of a plaintiff app and a suspicious app, ViewDroid measures the similarity between the two graphs by an applying subgraph isomorphism algorithm. Since it is an NP-complete problem, we need to improve the performance of graph matching. To this end, we apply a pre-filter to eliminate those more obvious non-matching pairs in advance.

## 4.2 System Architecture

Figure 1 shows the system architecture of ViewDroid, which has three primary components. Given two Android apps in *.apk* format, the *Code Extractor* will extract and parse the smali code (the dissembled version of Dalvik bytecode), human-readable Android Manifest file and layout XML files from each app's installation package. After that the *View Graph Constructor* performs some static analysis to generate a feature view graph for each app. A pre-filter is applied to remove app pairs that are not likely to be similar. Then the *Graph Similarity Checker* compares two feature view graphs and calculates a similarity score. Note that if two apps are signed by the same developer, we do not consider them as a repackaging case.

**Code Extractor.** The user interface layouts of an Android app are usually defined in XML files in the res/layout/ directory. The activity of a view is implemented in the *classes.dex*, which is compiled as Dalvik bytecode. Instead of focusing on the view layout that can be easily modified, we conduct the analysis on the activity class, which defines the functionality of a view and indicates the navigation between views. We choose to perform the static analysis directly on the smali code, which is an intermediate representation of Dalvik bytecode. This is because smali code is the direct dissembled version of Dalvik binary with rich annotation information. Our static analysis also uses some information from the Android manifest files and the layout component files. We leverage an existing tool apktool [1] to extract smali code and human-readable XML files from android app packages.

**View Graph Constructor.** As discussed in Section 2, the layout of an app view is usually defined in XML resource files and loaded by activity code during the execution to be presented to users. Most activities load a view by invoking the setContentView() function with an XML file name as the parameter, in its onCreate() function. A few special views are loaded by other functions, e.g., the Settings view is loaded by the addPreferencesFromResource() function. View navigation is implemented by activity switching. When an activity calls another activity, an instance of the callee activity is created, a new view associated with the callee will be loaded and put on the top of the system's view stack to be presented to users. An activity switches to another activity by invoking function startActivity() or startActivityForResult() with an Intent object as the parameter. As a result, we can construct the view graph by statically analyzing these function invocations.

The detailed steps of view graph construction are as follows:

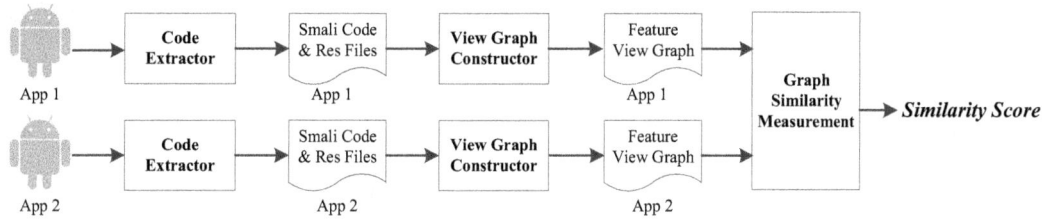

**Figure 1: The ViewDroid system architecture.**

1. **Generate view nodes**: We need to collect all the activities that are associated with potential UI views, each of which is usually a separate smali file loading a view layout in its `onCreate()` function. In each activity, we parse and grep the view loading function, such as `setContentView()` and `addPreferencesFromResource()` in the `onCreate()`function. The parameters of these view loading functions are the names of the XML resource files. After parsing all this relevant information, every view node and its relation to the corresponding activity class is generated.

2. **Extract view node features**: For the features of the view nodes, we only focus on the Android framework specific APIs. Since the Android platform use Java APIs that are built on a subset of the Apache Harmony Java implementation, we consider this set of APIs are more vulnerable to renaming attacks. Attackers can easily find semantic similar or equivalent APIs from other sources. However, the set of Android specific APIs, e.g., methods from the *android.security.KeyChain* or *android.nfc.NfcManager* classes, are very hard to be replaced. In order to interact with the Android platform, an app has to register certain permissions in the manifest files and use the relevant APIs to perform tasks. Based on this observation, we build the feature for each view node accordingly. We first analyze each activity class file associated with a view node to extract a set of invocations of the Android specific APIs. Then we can build an *invocation vector* for each view node. In such invocation vectors, instead of making a counter for each API, we only set a flag for the APIs that are invoked in the activities. This can protect ViewDroid from dummy code insertion attack and can also improve the efficiency on the invocations vector pattern matching.

3. **Generate edges**: Edges in the feature view graph represents the activity switch relationship among the set of views. The source view is associated with the caller activity of the `startActivity()` or `startActivityForResult()` functions. The target view is associated with the activity declared by the `Intent` object. There are six kinds of `Intent` constructors [3]:

(1) `Intent()`
(2) `Intent(Intent o)`
(3) `Intent(String action)`
(4) `Intent(String action, Uri uri)`
(5) `Intent(Context packageContext, Class<?> cls)`
(6) `Intent(String action, Uri uri, Context packageContext, Class<?> cls)`

As described in [32], constructors (5) and (6) specify the target activity in an explicit way with a particular class name. We can perform analysis to trace back to this hard-coded class name. Constructors (3) and (4) initialize an implicit Intent object by an action name, with or without a URI. The associated target activity, which could be within the same app or in another app, is selected by matching *intent filters* in the Android manifest files. The external target is undecidable without knowing other apps installed in a smartphone. In ViewDroid, we create a general destination node `external_activity` to represent all external targets and add an edge from the source activity to this node. Constructor (1) initializes an empty intent, which is surrounded by `setClass()`, `setComponent()` or `setAction()`. Hence, the identification of the target activity is the same as constructors (3)-(6). Constructor (2) copies another Intent object *o*. In this case, our analysis needs to trace back to the activity, which is specified by the constructor of the object *o*.

In order to figure out all the possible switching relationships among views, static analysis is performed. By analyzing all `startActivity()` and `startActivityForResult()` functions, we can stitch the caller activity and callee activity and therefore create an edge from the view of the caller activity to the view of the callee activity. Our view switching based invocation graph is more robust to code obfuscation than the traditional call graph, because it does not rely on the exact call sequence starting from one view node and ending at another view node. Whenever there is a view switching relationship, an edge is built to link the two views. It captures the user's real experience of view switching. Even though there might be several method invocations between an actual view switching, we ignore all the intermediary method calls, but just stitch the source and end view nodes for the corresponding activity classes. As long as attackers want to keep most functionality of the original app, the view switching relationship cannot be changed.

4. **Extract edge features**: In order to minimize false matches and improve the efficiency of similarity measurement in a latter stage, we add a feature to each edge. It is the user-generated event that triggers the view switch. During the static analysis, we can locate the `startActivity()` or `startActivityForResult()` functions and analyze which function call actually triggers the view switching. The trigger could be library provided event listener, such as `onClick()`, `onTouch()`, `OnItemSelected()` etc, or app developer self-defined functions. We consider these triggers to be the fea-

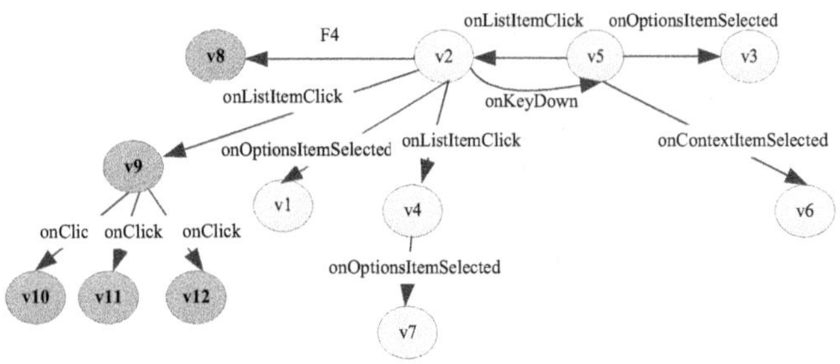

**Figure 3: The feature view graph of a repackaging app.**

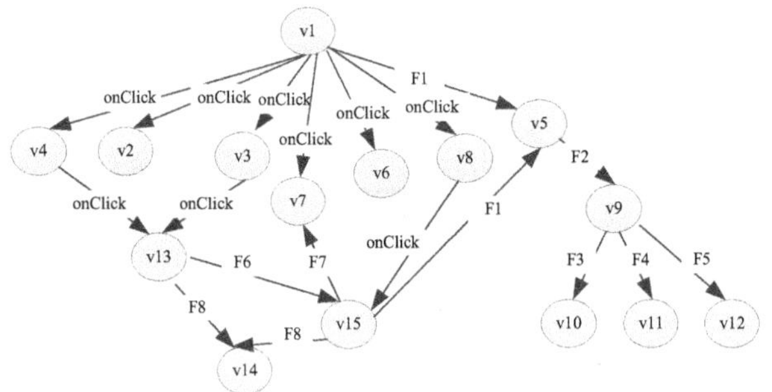

**Figure 4: The feature view graph of an independent app.**

tures of edges. Note that because the names of self-defined functions can be easily modified by an attacker, so we label all the developer self-defined trigger functions with the same name `self_defined_trigger` and consider them potentially matched with each other.

Figure 2 illustrates the steps of view graph construction for a simple Sudoku app. Figure 3 shows the feature view graph of an app that repackages the original app in Figure 2. The repackaged app copies the original app, adds an AdActivity (node $v8$) and additional social network functions (nodes $v9$, $v10$, $v11$, $v12$). Figure 4 shows the feature view graph of an independent app. Note that to make the graph clear in these figures, we omit the node features.

**Graph Similarity Checker.** We apply the VF2 [13] subgraph isomorphism algorithm to measure the similarity between two feature view graphs.

A pre-filter is leveraged to reduce the graph pairs that need to be compared. If one of the following three criteria meets, we will consider that they are not repackaging cases: (1) If the size of two view graphs differs a lot (specifically, the size of the bigger graph is at least 3 times of the smaller graph); (2) If the node features (i.e., those Android specific APIs considered in feature view graphs) in two view graphs have limited overlap (i.e., the number of overlapped features is below 1/3 of the size of the smaller graph). (3) If the sets of edge features in two view graphs have limited overlap (i.e., the number of overlapped edge features is below 1/3 of the edge number in the smaller graph).

When two graphs are compared by the subgraph isomorphism algorithm, only nodes and edges with similar features can be matched. We consider two view nodes are similar when their API invocation vectors have the Jaccard distance below 0.5. The Jaccard distance between two sets $A$ and $B$ is calculated with Formula 1. Edges with the same event listener are considered as a matched pair. Not only can this feature pre-comparison reduce false matches of nodes and edges, thus decreasing the false positives caused by simple view graphs, but it can also improve the efficiency of subgraph isomorphism computation.

$$J_d(A, B) = 1 - \frac{A \cap B}{A \cup B} \qquad (1)$$

If apps $A$ and $B$ have $m$ matched nodes, with $n_A$ and $n_B$ nodes in their feature view graphs, respectively, their similarity score is calculated as:

$$\text{similarity score} = \frac{m}{\min(n_A, n_B)} \qquad (2)$$

## 5. EVALUATION

ViewDroid is implemented in Python and Shell-script. The whole system consists of 2400 lines of Python code and 400 lines of Shell-scripts. Our experiments were conducted on a commodity machine with 1.6 GHz Intel Core i5 processor and 4 GB memory.

We have two sets of experiments. First, we conduct evaluation on a large set of real-world apps to measure the effectiveness and efficiency of ViewDroid. We also test the percentage of the repackaged malware cases. Second, we evaluate the obfuscation resilience of ViewDroid by applying different obfuscation techniques on existing apps and using ViewDroid to detect their similarities.

### 5.1 Real-world Large-scale Experiment

#### 5.1.1 False Positive and Efficiency

We crawl $10,311$ top Android apps from Google Play. These apps belong to 20 categories. We randomly choose 100 samples from each category and compare them with apps in the same category in a pairwise way. Totally $573,872$ app pairs are compared.

We set the similarity score threshold at 0.7. After applying ViewDroid to detect the repackaged apps, we manually check the detected pairs to measure false positives. The manual checking has two criteria: (1) We execute the app on a smartphone to check the similarity of their functionality; (2) We check the code, including smali files, layout files and the permissions. Only when both criteria are similar, we consider them as the real repackaging cases. We find 129 false matched pairs in total in 11 categories. Most of the false matches (112 out of 129) are caused by the invocations of ad libraries. When two apps share the same ad libraries and one app's graph size is relatively small, the matched nodes related to the common ad libraries will result in a high similarity score. These false matches can be eliminated by whitelisting known ad libraries. That is, we can simply ignore views that are generated by whitelisted libraries. The other 17 false matches are due to that one of the apps in each pair is very simple. For their view features, no special API is invoked and therefore nodes are not distinguishable. Moreover, their view graphs are small and easy to find matchable (sub)graphs. Our detection results, after adding a whitelist to rule out the known ad libraries, are shown in Table 1. The percentage column is the proportion

**Step 1: Generate Nodes**

| Node | Smali Code | XML File |
|------|-----------|----------|
| v1 | FileListActivity | file_list |
| v2 | FolderListActivity(Main Activity) | folder_list |
| v3 | SudokuEditActivity | sudoku_edit |
| v4 | SudokuExportActivity | sudoku_export |
| v5 | SudokuListActivity | sudoku_list |
| v6 | SudokuPlayActivity | sudoku_play |
| v7 | GameSettingsActivity | game_settings |

**Step 2: Extract Node Features**

| Node | Features |
|------|----------|
| v1 | (ListActivity ->onPrepareDialog, ...) |
| v2 | (Cursor->getColumnIndex,...) |
| v3 | (Activity->onWindowFocusChanged,...) |
| v4 | (ProgressDialog->setTitle,...) |
| v5 | (MenuItem->setshortcut,...) |
| v6 | (Window->setFlags,...) |
| v7 | (MenuItem->setIcon,...) |

**Step 3: Generate edges**

**Step 4: Extract edge features:**

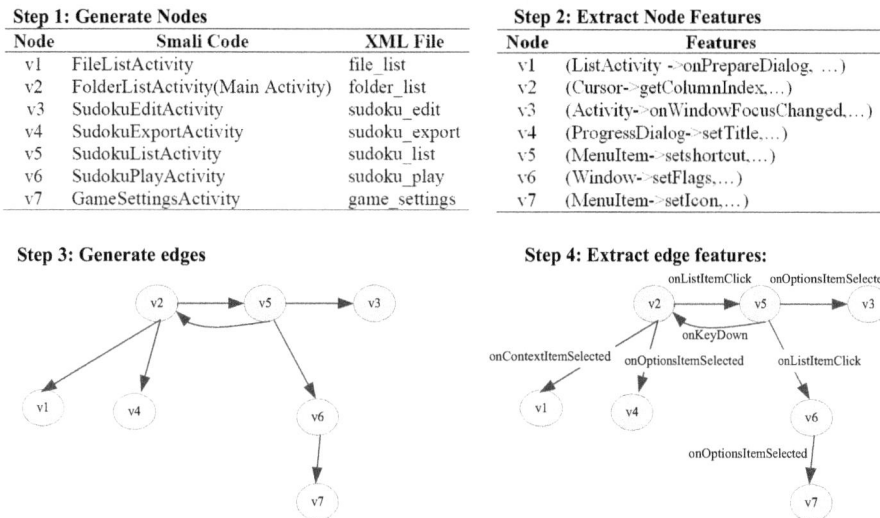

Figure 2: An example of view graph construction

of apps, which either repackage other apps or are repackaged by others, in all apps of each category. On average 4.7% among tested apps are found to be the real repackaging cases. The book and comic categories have more repackaging cases than other categories, because in both categories, there are existing products that can convert an ebook into an Android app. The apps generated by the same converting product are detected as repackaging pairs by ViewDroid. They are true positives since they share the same code base and the same views.

Among all 542 repackaging pairs, 262 of them belong to lazy attacks. The malware cases are analyzed in Section 5.1.3. The other pairs belong to the amateur attacks. Note that ViewDroid only measures the similarity between two apps. It does not identify which one is the original app and which one is the repackaged one.

The average execution time of ViewDroid for each testing is listed in Table 2. It is about 11$s$ per pair. In rare cases, the graph construction time and graph comparison time may take minutes. Only 0.6% apps take more than 1 minute to construct view graph and 0.2% pairs need more than 1 minute to conduct graph comparison. In addition, when applying ViewDroid to check a large number of apps, code extraction and view graph construction for each app is only performed once.

### 5.1.2 False Negative

In this section, we use a set of repackaged apps provided by a research group to measure the false negative rate of ViewDroid. These apps were collected from multiple Android markets. The app dataset includes totally 901 pairs of apps, whose view graphs have more than 3 view nodes. By setting the similarity score threshold at 0.7, as in Section 5.1.1, ViewDroid detects 868 pairs as repackaging cases. Among 659 of them, each pair of apps have the similarity score 1.0.

We then manually check the 33 pairs that are not detected by ViewDroid. They can be divided into three different categories. (1) For 11 pairs, two apps of each pair do not share or share very little common code. They do not have common functionalities or views either. As a result,

**Table 1: The repackaged apps detected by ViewDroid**

| Category | Pair# | App# | Repackaged Pair | Repackaged App | % |
|----------|-------|------|-----------------|----------------|---|
| Books | 34,550 | 495 | 81 | 55 | 11.1 |
| Business | 23,882 | 455 | 10 | 13 | 2.9 |
| Comics | 40,850 | 558 | 110 | 75 | 13.4 |
| Communication | 20,582 | 487 | 0 | 0 | 0.0 |
| Education | 40,950 | 559 | 7 | 11 | 2.0 |
| Entertainment | 25,758 | 512 | 10 | 16 | 3.1 |
| Finance | 37,650 | 526 | 9 | 13 | 2.5 |
| Game arcade | 30,496 | 543 | 64 | 37 | 6.8 |
| Game cards | 27,329 | 545 | 11 | 13 | 2.4 |
| Game casual | 20,662 | 509 | 12 | 18 | 3.5 |
| Health | 36,550 | 515 | 13 | 20 | 3.9 |
| Lifestyle | 20,538 | 509 | 10 | 13 | 2.6 |
| Media | 39,150 | 541 | 56 | 35 | 6.5 |
| Medical | 38,650 | 536 | 14 | 21 | 3.9 |
| Music | 19,655 | 496 | 21 | 20 | 4.0 |
| News | 10,466 | 495 | 21 | 24 | 4.8 |
| Personality | 37,050 | 520 | 31 | 25 | 4.8 |
| Photography | 23,914 | 518 | 17 | 22 | 4.2 |
| Shopping | 28,185 | 495 | 23 | 23 | 4.6 |
| Social | 17,005 | 497 | 22 | 26 | 5.2 |
| Total | 573,872 | 10,311 | 542 | 480 | 4.7 |

**Table 2: The execution time of ViewDroid (in seconds)**

|  | Code Extraction | Graph Construction | Graph Comparison |
|------|-----------------|--------------------|--------------------|
| Max | 15 | 146 | 590 |
| Avg | 4 | 6 | 1 |

not reporting them is the correct detection result for these 11 pairs. They were falsely included in the app dataset. (2) Another 10 pairs are not real repackaging cases either, although they do share some code between each other. The shared code is not related to the functionalities or the views of these apps, but is used as malicious payload to create ad shortcuts or to send out messages without users' awareness. That is, attackers use different apps to propagate the same malicious payload. Therefore, ViewDroid is correct again not reporting them. (3) The other 12 pairs are false negatives of ViewDroid at detection threshold 0.7. Here, each pair of apps have repackaged code related to their major functionalities, but have different code that implements

**Table 3: The malware attacks detected by View-Droid**

| Type | Number |
|---|---|
| Trojan.FakeApp/FakeFlash | 25 |
| Adware.Airpush | 14 |
| Adware.Plankton | 17 |
| Adware.LeadBolt | 26 |
| Other Adware | 10 |
| Virus | 1 |

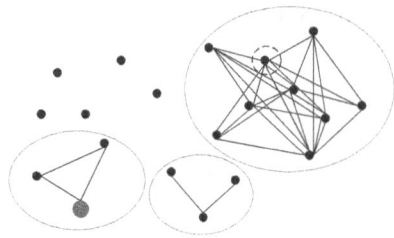

**Figure 5: The cluster of sudoku apps based on the similarity scores.**

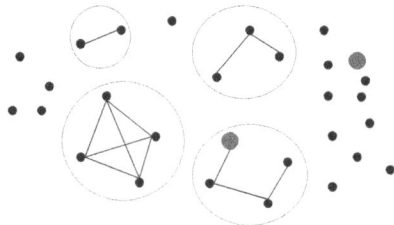

**Figure 6: The cluster of flashlight apps based on the similarity scores.**

"add-on" functions. These add-on components are relative large and complex compared to their carrier code. For example, two apps both implement a Ninja game. The matched view nodes detected by ViewDroid are the game itself, while the unmatched view nodes represent different social network functions. It is very likely that these two apps both repackaged another benign app by inserting their own customized social network library, which targets a specific market. The similarity scores of false negative cases are all between 0.5 and 0.7. It indicates that ViewDroid is able to find their common views. The false negative rate of ViewDroid at detection threshold 0.7 is 1.3%.

### 5.1.3 Malware

We use VirusTotal (`https://www.virustotal.com/en/`), an online malware detection service, to scan all the repackaged pairs detected in Section 5.1.1. Among the 480 apps identified as involved in repackaging cases (either the original ones or the repackaged ones) in our previous experiment, we detect 93 malware, which is 19.3% of repackaged apps. The malware types are listed in Table 3. They mainly belong to two different categories: Adware and Trojan horse. Adwares aggressively show advertisements to smartphone users. Trojan horses usually pretend to be legitimate apps, but steal sensitive information covertly. There is one virus detected. It is labeled as `Virus:BAT/Rbtg.gen`.

### 5.1.4 Category-based Evaluation

Next we illustrate a different kind of evaluation on real-world apps. We first search by some keywords in Google Play, and then download the returned apps and conduct pairwise measurement of their similarities. While our previous large-scale experiment randomly chooses pairs in the app market to evaluate the effectiveness and scalability of ViewDroid, this experiment is more interesting to individual app developers and app users to understand how repackaging may affect them.

We list two examples here. The first keyword is "sudoku" and we download 20 sudoku game apps. Based on the similarity scores, we cluster these apps as shown in Figure 5. An edge indicates two apps have a similarity score higher than 0.7. The largest cluster has 9 apps. The app with dashed circle is similar to all the other 8 apps in the cluster. The other two clusters both have 3 apps. Our manual checking verifies that the result has no false positives and false negatives. Further analysis indicates that there are 3 pairs belonging to lazy attack, where plagiarists only repackage the original apps without changing their functionality. The similarity scores of these pairs are 1.0. ViewDroid also discoveries one malware case, the red big node in Figure 5. VirusTotal identifies it as the Airpush Adware, which aggressively shows ads in the Android notification bar. This app inserts Airpush ads module into the original app and

slightly modifies the functionality by removing a strategy help view. The other repackaging pairs are all amateur attacks, where functionalities are added or removed, such as social network modules, help view, strategy hint views and advertisements.

In the second example, we search by the keyword "flashlight" and download 29 apps. We find 15 pairs with similarity scores higher than 0.7. Our manual checking indicates that 3 pairs are false positive cases. They are all caused by one app that has 4 views, only one Of which relates to its functionality whereas the other three are generated by an ad library. When compared to apps that share the same library with it, the three ad views are matched and the similarity scores are 0.75. Again, such false positives can be eliminated by whitelisting the ad libraries. The similarity cluster is shown in Figure 6. Four clusters have more than one app. Among all the 12 repackaged pairs, 2 belong to the lazy attacks, and 9 belong to the amateur attack where views are added or removed (e.g., the "about" view, "setting" view). One malware attack, shown as a big red node in Figure 6, is found. It is reported as a trojan horse by VirusTotal (there is indeed another malware in the 29 downloaded apps, but it is not the app repackaging case. It is identified as Plankton [7]).

## 5.2 Obfuscation Resilience

To test the obfuscation resilience of ViewDroid, we try to obfuscate the existing apps and malware with different obfuscators, and then check with ViewDroid the similarity score between each original app and its corresponding obfuscated one. Most existing popular obfuscation tools (e.g. ProGuard [6] and DexGuard [2]) work on Java source code level and their obfuscators are limited to method renaming, string encryption and class name encryption, etc. Therefore, we choose to use an obfuscation resilience evaluation tool developed by Huang et al. [19]. This evaluation framework can obfuscate and repackage apps by using one or multiple obfuscators from different Java bytecode obfuscation platforms (e.g., Sandmarks [11]). It directly targets the Dalvik bytecode. This actually mimics the real world scenarios where a plagiarist or repackager who only has access to the compiled Dalvik bytecode but not the Java source code and is eager to use various obfuscation techniques to evade detection. In our current obfuscation resilience test, we equip the framework to perform 39 obfuscators from both SandMarks [11] and KlassMaster [4]. To our knowledge, this is the broadest obfuscation resilience evaluation on Android repackaging detection.

First of all, we generate pairs of APK files from the obfuscation resilience evaluation tool. Then, we use ViewDroid to measure the similarity pairwisely between the obfuscated APK file and the original APK file. The higher similarity scores our ViewDroid returns for each specific obfuscator, the better resilience against that particular obfuscation.

We choose 50 apps from the Android app market based on different categories and 50 malwares from the malware Gnome project based on different families [35]. With this 100 Android app set, we perform *broadness* analysis and *depth* analysis to evaluate the obfuscation resilience aspect of ViewDroid provided by the evaluation framework. The broadness analysis result shows the general weakness and strength of ViewDroid against a broad range of obfuscation techniques. In this analysis, each obfuscator is applied individually. On the other hand, the depth analysis result evaluates the overall obfuscation resilience of ViewDroid against deep code manipulation by serializing a set of obfuscators. In this analysis, ViewDroid is evaluated against repackaged apps that have been obfuscated by multiple obfuscators. For example, an app may be obfuscated by variable renaming, followed by noise injection and/or control-flow flattening. With depth analysis, we can test the robustness of our detection scheme against more sophisticated obfuscation attacks.

### 5.2.1 Applying Single Obfuscation Algorithm

In our current evaluation setup, the *broadness* analysis is based on 39 obfuscation algorithms from *SandMarks* and *KlassMaster*. Table 4 shows the resilience comparison between ViewDroid and AndroGuard. The *Obfuscation Algorithm* columns indicate the names of the obfuscation algorithms applied in our framework. The *ViewDroid* columns list an average similar score for each obfuscation case. Specifically, in each obfuscation case, ViewDroid computes a similarity score for each original app (among totally 100 apps) and its obfuscated version and finally reports the average over 100 apps. The *AndroGuard* columns are the results reported by Huang et al. in [19], and we also compute three average similarity scores for AndroGuard based on three obfuscators from KlassMaster, which were not provided in the previous case study. All these three obfuscators have a *K*-tag at the beginning of the obfuscators' names in Table 4.

Based on the classification by Collberg et al. [12], all the single obfuscators can be categorized as *layout obfuscation*, *control based obfuscation* and *data based obfuscation*, which are tagged *L*, *C* and *D* after each obfuscator. The detailed explanation of the difference between these categories can be found in Huang et al. [19]. Overall, ViewDroid has better obfuscation resilience than AndroGuard. This is because in ViewDroid, repackaging detection is performed based on the similarity of the high level semantics of the app using the created feature view graph, while ignoring the detailed

control/data dependency or data structure. From the result, we can see that only 4 out of 39 obfuscators have an effect on ViewDroid, and the average similarity scores of all the other 35 obfuscators tested against ViewDroid are all 1.00.

The *Class Encrypter* obfuscator reduces the similarity score to 0, which is the only obfuscator that ViewDroid returns a lower score than AndroGuard. However, the score for AndroGuard is .03, which is very close to zero. This indicates that static analysis based detection schemes are not well-suited for encryption based obfuscation. By encrypting class files and decrypting them at runtime, Class Encrypter can completely hide the static structure of the program. However, certain heuristic can be built to preprocess these extreme encryption cases. For instance, whenever decryption or decoding is used in the program very intensively or is identified for a very large portion of the code, it can be flagged as suspicious. Usually, dynamic analysis based detection is needed in this situation, which is, however, lack of scalability. Overall, handling the heavy encryption and encoding based obfuscation is an interesting topic to explore in the future.

The other obfuscation algorithms that have some influence on ViewDroid are *Node Splitter*, *Method Madness* and *Class Splitter*. After further analysis of the feature view graph pairs computed from the 100 apps' obfuscated versions, we find that some graph nodes are split by obfuscators Node Spliter and Class Splitter, and the names of the methods that trigger view switching are replaced by some random names by Method Madness, which can potentially modify the feature of our view graph. However, from the overall similarity scores of these four obfuscators, we can see that these types of obfuscation cannot be performed frequently, as certain conditions have to be satisfied before these obfuscators make the actual manipulations. For instance, some class inheritance relationship has to be met in order to perform Node Splitter or Class Splitter, and also relevant specification in the Android manifest file should be changed accordingly. Furthermore, the obfuscation of method randomization in Method Madness cannot be performed directly on the Android framework APIs, tedious method rewriting work has to be performed before replacing the invocation of the Android APIs. For instance, simply changing the invocation *Landroid/app/Activity.dispatchTouchEvent ( Landroid/view/MotionEvent;)Z* into *Landroid/app/Activity. M103456d(Landroid/view/MotionEvent;)Z* does not work. As a result, we find that most APK files become non-executable after the Method Madness obfuscation.

### 5.2.2 Serializing Multiple Obfuscation Algorithms

Practically, especially when detection algorithms become more powerful, it is very possible that an attacker will try a combination of various obfuscation algorithms. Hence, besides the *broadness* analysis performed on ViewDroid, for *depth* analysis we also apply multiple obfuscators by serializing the top-three obfuscators reported from our broadness analysis, excluding the *Class Encrypter*. Due to the conflicts among various obfuscators, not all the obfuscated APK files are complete. We test various permutation cases with these three obfuscators and find two of all the permutations can be performed more successfully for the testing apps. One can output 99 out of 100 obfuscated APK files and the other outputs 96 out of 100 for all the tested ones. These two interesting permutations are shown as follows:

Table 4: **Average similarity score by ViewDroid compared with AndroGuard for each obfuscator used in broadness analysis**

| Obfuscation Algorithm | ViewDroid | AndroGuard | Obfuscation Algorithm | ViewDroid | AndroGuard |
|---|---|---|---|---|---|
| Const Pool Reorder (L) | 1.00 | 0.92 | Node Spliter (D) | 0.94 | 0.94 |
| Static Method Bodies (C) | 1.00 | 0.88 | Class Encrypter (D) | 0.00 | 0.03 |
| Method Merger (C) | 1.00 | 0.65 | Reorder Parameters (D) | 1.00 | 0.92 |
| Interleave Methods (C) | 1.00 | 0.56 | Promote Prim Register (D) | 1.00 | 0.92 |
| Opaque Pred Insert (C) | 1.00 | 0.92 | Promote Prim Types (D) | 1.00 | 0.93 |
| Branch Inverter (C) | 1.00 | 0.77 | Bludgeon Signatures (D) | 1.00 | 0.96 |
| Rand Dead Code (C) | 1.00 | 0.92 | Objectify (D) | 1.00 | 0.83 |
| Class Splitter (C) | 0.97 | 0.87 | Publicize Fields (D) | 1.00 | 0.91 |
| Method Madness (C) | 0.92 | 0.43 | Field Assignment (D) | 1.00 | 0.86 |
| Simple Opaque Pred (C) | 1.00 | 0.92 | Variable Reassign (D) | 1.00 | 0.85 |
| Reorder Instructions (C) | 1.00 | 0.89 | Parameter Alias (D) | 1.00 | 0.92 |
| Buggy Code (C) | 1.00 | 0.67 | Boolean Splitter (D) | 1.00 | 0.85 |
| Inliner (C) | 1.00 | 0.89 | String Encoder (D) | 1.00 | 0.87 |
| Branch Insert (C) | 1.00 | 0.87 | Overload Names (D) | 1.00 | 0.91 |
| Dynamic Inliner (C) | 1.00 | 0.84 | Duplicate Registers (D) | 1.00 | 0.89 |
| Irreducibility (C) | 1.00 | 0.86 | Rename Registers (D) | 1.00 | 0.96 |
| Opaque Branch Insert (C) | 1.00 | 0.85 | False Refactor (D) | 1.00 | 0.95 |
| Exception Branch (C) | 1.00 | 0.81 | Merge Local Int (D) | 1.00 | 0.94 |
| K-Flow Obfuscation (C) | 1.00 | 0.77 | K-Name Obfuscation (D) | 1.00 | 0.89 |
|  |  |  | K-String literals Encrypter (D) | 1.00 | 0.91 |

1. *[Node Spliter ⇒ Method Madness ⇒ Class Splitter]*
   Average Similarity Score of 99 apps : 0.915;
2. *[Class Splitter ⇒ Method Madness ⇒ Node Spliter]*
   Average Similarity Score of 96 apps : 0.906;

Both cases have the same three obfuscators but at a different serializing order. Although they can slightly reduce the average similarity scores by ViewDroid compared to the solely applying the obfuscator *Method Madness* case (with score 0.92), these scores are both above .90, sufficiently large for the obfuscated apps to be detected. *Case 1* reduces the average score from 0.92 to 0.915, which shows that applying serialized multiple obfuscators has only slightly higher influence on ViewDroid than applying a single obfuscator. For *Case 2*, the average similarity score is a little bit lower than *Case 1*. However, there are four apps that cannot finish the whole serialized obfuscations. This indicates that although serialized obfuscation is slightly more powerful, the attacker has to take the risk of ending up with incomplete obfuscation. We encountered more failures when performing other orders of serialization. Overall, our evaluation demonstrates that multiple obfuscations are hard to be serialized, and even if successfully performed, they have little impact on View-Droid's detection capability. Huang et al. [19] also reported that, in some scenarios, applying multiple obfuscations can lower the similarity scores reported by tools such as *Andro-Guard*. Our experiment shows that ViewDroid's high-level abstracted birthmark is not affected much by the low-level (multiple) code obfuscation.

# 6. DISCUSSION

## 6.1 Attack Analysis on ViewDroid

As discussed in Section 3, based on different repackaging purposes, ViewDroid might face various types of attacks.

- **Lazy attack:** In this attack, the attacker does not change the functionality of original apps but applies automatic code obfuscation tools to repackage an app. As a result, a lazy attack does not change the view navigation relations of an app. In addition, code obfuscation has little impact on the feature view graph generation, as demonstrated by evaluation in Section 5.2. Therefore, ViewDroid can effectively detect such attacks.

- **Amateur attack:** An attacker not only applies automatic code obfuscation but also makes small modifications on the functionalities. The feature view graph could be changed slightly. However, because we use the subgraph isomorphism algorithm to compare graphs, small changes of the view graph may reduce the similarity score a little but will not affect the overall detection result much. As a result, ViewDroid can tolerate small changes on app functionalities and views.

- **Malware:** An attacker inserts some malicious payload into the original program while trying to make the repackaged app look the same or similar to the original one in order to leverage the popularity of the original program for wide propagation. Clearly, their feature view graphs would also be very similar. Therefore, ViewDroid can effectively detect such repackaging.

**Other Potential Professional attacks:** An attacker, who knows ViewDroid, may attempt to change feature view graphs to evade detection. Attackers may (1) insert a dummy view into the path of two directly connected views; (2) split one view node into two view nodes; (3) self implement or obfuscate the invocation of `startActivity()` and `startActivityForResult()` functions. Since we use the subgraph isomorphism algorithm with a certain matching threshold (e.g., 0.7), in order to affect the detection result, attackers need to modify many views of the original apps. On one hand, it will significantly increase the workload of repackaging an app. On the other hand, the dummy nodes, edges and self-implemented functions will increase the code size and decrease the performance of apps. We have not seen such attacks in the real world yet.

ViewDroid helps defenders stay ahead of the current arms race with attackers.

## 6.2 Limitations and Future Work

ViewDroid can detect the repackaging of non-trivial apps effectively, but for the detection of apps with few views, more false positives may be reported. Even so, the API vector node features can significantly reduce such false positives, because only nodes with very similar API vectors can be matched.

ViewDroid can effectively detect the following three types of mobile app repackaging attacks: lazy attacks, amateur attacks and malware. However, some professional attacks can potentially change view graphs, regardless of the workload of attackers and the performance overhead of the repackaged apps. Dummy view insertion may be defeated by examining the trigger function of the view switches. If a switch is not triggered by user behavior, we can merge the target view with its predecessor/successor in the feature view graph. A similar strategy has been used by Chen et al. [10] to check for malicious behavior. In our future work, we are going to enhance ViewDroid to deal with such attacks.

As shown in our evaluation, ViewDroid has false negatives when the encrypter obfuscation is used. This is because encryption changes the code completely and hides all the static characteristics of an app. This is also a common problem of all static analysis based detection. To defeat against such attacks, dynamic analysis may be applied. However, dynamic analysis is not efficient enough to be used as a large-scale detection approach. This is the fundamental tradeoff between accuracy and performance. How to build a hybrid approach to leverage both dynamic and static analysis for encrypter obfuscation is also a very interesting and important topic.

## 7. RELATED WORK

**Smartphone App Similarity Measurement.** The smartphone app repackaging problem has drawn great attention from the research community. There are several relevant works on measuring the similarity between Android apps on code level. DroidMOSS [34] leverages fuzzy hash to detect app repackaging. A hash value is computed for each local unit of opcode sequence of the classes.dex, instead of computing a hash over the entire program opcode set. It can efficiently and effectively identify the opcode segments that were left untouched by the lazy repackager and works well when the bytecode is only manipulated at a few interesting points (e.g., the string names or hard-coded URLs). However, some obfuscation, such as noise injection, can evade the detection. DNADroid [14] proposed a program dependence graph (PDG) based detection approach, which considers the data dependency as the main characteristic of the apps for similarity comparison. The efficiency of the comparison is further improved in AnDarwin [15] by building semantic vectors from PDG for each method. In general, PDG is resilient against several control flow obfuscation techniques and noisy code insertion attacks that do not modify the data dependency. However, some specific data dependence obfuscations can be designed to evade this approach. For example, PDG can be changed by inserting intermediate variable assignment instructions into the code. Juxtapp [18] proposed a code-reuse evaluation framework which leverages k-grams of opcode sequences to build feature for the feature hashing approach. A sliding window will move within each basic block to map the features into bit vectors, which are further combined into a feature metric to help birthmark each app.

This detection scheme is able to effectively detect different code reuse situations, including piracy and code repackaging, malware existence, vulnerable code. Special designed code manipulation can potentially destruct the normal opcode pattern of Dalvik bytecode in a very dense fashion. Chen et al. [9] proposed a novel app birthmark, which is the geometry-characteristic-based encoding of control flow graph. This approach can effectively and efficiently detect cloned code which is syntactically similar with the original code. However, it cannot deal with app repackaging using code obfuscation techniques.

**Traditional software plagiarism detection** is another category of literatures that are relevant to smartphone app repackaging detection. MOSS [27] applies local fingerprinting to detect source code plagiarism. Liu et al. [22] proposed a program dependence graph (PDG) based approach. Lim et al. [21] used stack pattern based birthmark. These static analysis methods require the source code and are vulnerable to some code obfuscations. Myles et al. [25] statically analyzed executables and used K-gram techniques to measure the similarity. This approach is vulnerable to instruction reordering and junk instruction insertion. The dynamic software birthmarks include core values based birthmark [20, 31], dynamic opcode n-gram birthmark [23], whole program path (WPP) birthmark [24], dynamic API birthmark [29] and system call based birthmark [30]. The dynamic methods are not efficient enough to be performed on a large scale plagiarism detection scenario, like Android app markets.

**Smartphone App Security.** There are several publications in this category related to ViewDroid. They leverage the user interface feature of the Android platform, but use it for different purposes. SmartDroid [32] leverages user interfaces to find user interactions that will trigger sensitive APIs. It combines the static analysis and dynamic analysis. Chen et al. [10] developed a Permission Event Graph (PEG) to detect, or prove the absence of malicious behavior that is not authorized by users. Zhou et al. [33] proposed a module decoupling method to partition an app's code into primary and non-primary modules and thus to identify the malicious payloads reside in the benign apps. They also develop an approach to extracting feature vectors from those piggy backed apps to help improve the efficiency of the piggyback relationship detection. Our approach pays more attention to the repackaging detection from the primary functionalities of the Android apps and takes into account obfuscation resilience. We also identify certain features for the nodes and edges during the view graph construction to improve the efficiency of our detection.

## 8. CONCLUSION

In this paper, we proposed a user interface based Android app repackaging detection method, ViewDroid. The evaluation results show that ViewDroid can effectively detect Android app repackaging with the presence of various obfuscation techniques. ViewDroid is also efficient enough for performing large-scale experiments.

## 9. ACKNOWLEDGMENTS

This research was supported in part by the NSF Grant CCF-1320605, NSF Grant CNS-1223710, ARO W911NF-09-1-0525 (MURI), and ARO W911NF-13-1-0421 (MURI).

# 10. REFERENCES

[1] Android-Apktool: A tool for reverse engineering Android apk files. http://code.google.com/p/android-apktool/.

[2] Dexguard. http://www.saikoa.com/dexguard.

[3] Intent android developers. developer.android.com/reference/android/content/Intent.html.

[4] KlassMaster. http://www.zelix.com/klassmaster/docs/index.html.

[5] Number of avaliable Android applications. http://www.appbrain.com/stats/number-of-android-apps.

[6] Proguard. http://developer.android.com/tools/help/proguard.html/.

[7] Security alert: New stealthy android spyware - plankton - found in official android market. http://www.csc.ncsu.edu/faculty/jiang/Plankton/.

[8] Smali: An assembler/disassembler for Android's dex format. http://code.google.com/p/smali/.

[9] K. Chen, P. Liu, and Y. Zhang. Achieving accuracy and scalability simultaneously in detecting application clones on android markets. In *36th International Conference on Software Engineering (ICSE)*, 2014.

[10] K. Z. Chen, N. Johnson, V. D'Silva, S. Dai, K. MacNamara, T. Magrino, E. X. Wu, M. Rinard, and D. Song. Contextual policy enforcement in Android applications with permission event graphs. In *NDSS'13*, 2013.

[11] C. Collberg, G. Myles, and A. Huntwork. Sandmarks - a tool for software protection research. In *IEEE Security and Privacy, vol. 1, no. 4*, 2003.

[12] C. Collberg, C. Thomborson, and D. Low. A taxonomy of obfuscating transformations. Technical report, 1997.

[13] L. P. Cordella, P. Foggia, C. Sansone, and M. Vento. A (sub) graph isomorphism algorithm for matching large graphs. *Pattern Analysis and Machine Intelligence, IEEE Transactions on*, 26(10), 2004.

[14] J. Crussell, C. Gibler, and H. Chen. Attack of the clones: Detecting cloned applications on android markets. In *ESORICS*, pages 37–54, 2012.

[15] J. Crussell, C. Gibler, and H. Chen. Scalable semantics-based detection of similar android applications. In *ESORICS*, 2013.

[16] A. Desnos and G. Gueguen. Android: From reversing to decompilation. In *Black hat 2011, Abu Dhabi*.

[17] C. Gibler, R. Stevens, J. Crussell, H. Chen, H. Zang, and H. Choi. Adrob: Examining the landscape and impact of Android application plagiarism. In *Proceedings of 11th International Conference on Mobile Systems, Applications and Services*, 2013.

[18] S. Hanna, L. Huang, E. Wu, S. Li, C. Chen, and D. Song. Juxtapp: A scalable system for detecting code reuse among android applications. In *Proceedings of the 9th Conference on Detection of Intrusions and Malware & Vulnerability Assessment*, 2012.

[19] H. Huang, S. Zhu, P. Liu, and D. Wu. A framework for evaluating mobile app repackaging detection algorithms. In *Proceedings of the 6th International Conference on Trust & Trustworthy Computing*, 2013.

[20] Y.-C. Jhi, X. Wang, X. Jia, S. Zhu, P. Liu, and D. Wu. Value-based program characterization and its application to software plagiarism detection. In *Proceedings of the 33rd International Conference on Software Engineering*, pages 756–765. ACM, 2011.

[21] H. Lim, H. Park, S. Choi, and T. Han. Detecting theft of Java applications via a static birthmark based on weighted stack patterns. *IEICE - Trans. Inf. Syst.*, E91-D(9), 2008.

[22] C. Liu, C. Chen, J. Han, and P. S. Yu. GPLAG: detection of software plagiarism by program dependence graph analysis. In *KDD '06: Proceedings of the 12th ACM SIGKDD international conference on Knowledge discovery and data mining*, 2006.

[23] B. Lu, F. Liu, X. Ge, B. Liu, and X. Luo. A software birthmark based on dynamic opcode n-gram. *International Conference on Semantic Computing*, 2007.

[24] G. Myles and C. Collberg. Detecting software theft via whole program path birthmarks. *Information Security*, 3225/2004, 2004.

[25] G. Myles and C. Collberg. K-gram based software birthmarks. In *SAC '05: Proceedings of the 2005 ACM symposium on Applied computing*, 2005.

[26] J. Ostrander. *Android UI Fundamentals: Develop and Design*. Peachpit Press, 2012.

[27] S. Schleimer, D. S. Wilkerson, and A. Aiken. Winnowing: local algorithms for document fingerprinting. In *Proc. of ACM SIGMOD Int. Conf. on Management of Data*, 2003.

[28] D. Schuler, V. Dallmeier, and C. Lindig. A dynamic birthmark for Java. In *Proceedings of the twenty-second IEEE/ACM international conference on Automated software engineering*, 2007.

[29] H. Tamada, K. Okamoto, M. Nakamura, A. Monden, and K. ichi Matsumoto. Dynamic software birthmarks to detect the theft of windows applications. In *Int. Symp. on Future Software Technology*, 2004.

[30] X. Wang, Y.-C. Jhi, S. Zhu, and P. Liu. Detecting software theft via system call based birthmarks. In *Computer Security Applications Conference, 2009. ACSAC'09. Annual*, pages 149–158. IEEE, 2009.

[31] F. Zhang, Y. Jhi, D. Wu, P. Liu, and S. Zhu. A first step towards algorithm plagiarism detection. In *Proceedings of the 2012 International Symposium on Software Testing and Analysis*. ACM, 2012.

[32] C. Zheng, S. Zhu, S. Dai, G. Gu, X. Gong, X. Han, and W. Zou. SmartDroid: an automatic system for revealing UI-based trigger conditions in Android applications. In *Proceedings of the second ACM workshop on Security and privacy in smartphones and mobile devices*, pages 93–104. ACM, 2012.

[33] W. Zhou, Y. Zhou, M. Grace, X. Jiang, and S. Zou. Fast, scalable detection of piggybacked mobile applications. In *Proceedings of the third ACM conference on Data and application security and privacy*, pages 185–196. ACM, 2013.

[34] W. Zhou, Y. Zhou, X. Jiang, and P. Ning. Detecting repackaged smartphone applications in third-party Android marketplaces. In *Proceedings of the second ACM conference on Data and Application Security and Privacy*, 2012.

[35] Y. Zhou and X. Jiang. Dissecting Android malware: Characterization and evolution. *Security and Privacy, IEEE Symposium on*, 2012.

# On Mobile Malware Infections

## Abstract

### N. Asokan
Aalto University and University of Helsinki
Finland
asokan@acm.org

## Keywords

mobile malware; infection rate; Android; malware detection

## Categories and Subject Descriptors

D.4.6 [**Security and Protection**]: Invasive software

Concerns about mobile malware are not new. There is a steady stream of news stories about the exponential growth of malware targeted at specific smartphone operating systems. Given the extent of smartphone usage, a malware epidemic affecting smartphones could potentially have devastating consequences. Yet, anecdotal evidence seems to suggest that malware infection of smartphones in the wild is not at the same scale as malware infection of personal computers. Estimates of the rates of malware infection on mobile devices are surprisingly rare. Even the few available public estimates differ greatly (ranging between 0.0009% to about 5%). We found only one previous independent and rigorous estimate [1] which used an indirect method to estimate infection rate of mobile devices using a dataset of DNS queries made by users in the United States.

In this backdrop, we set out to estimate infection rates on Android devices directly by collecting data from a large number of devices (reported in [2]). In this talk, I will describe our experience and some lessons we learned.

Infection rates in our dataset, according the two malware datasets we used, were small (about 0.26%) but significantly higher than the previous independent estimate [1]. Different anti-malware vendors use different criteria for deciding if a given software package is malicious. We were surprised to find that none of the malware instances found in our dataset was flagged as malware by a majority of vendors.

Some application stores have a greater density of malicious applications than others. Advertising within applications and cross-promotional deals could potentially act as infection vectors whereby installing one application would lead to installing additional applications. Based on these observations we conjectured that the set of "clean" applications on a device can serve as an indicator for infection of that device. By analyzing our dataset, we found that while the set of applications alone is not an accurate indicator of infection a classifier trained using the application co-occurrence data performs up to five times better in identifying a vulnerable device than the baseline of random selection. Since the cost of this indicator is virtually nothing, we believe that it can serve as a useful technique for identifying the pool of devices on which more expensive monitoring and analysis mechanisms should be deployed. This is useful, for example, in the search for new or previously undetected malware: an anti-malware vendor could monitor devices flagged by the classifier as vulnerable and focus their analyses on applications found on those devices. It is therefore a technique that can complement standard malware scanning. With improved accuracy, the classifier may also help end users and enterprise IT administrators by providing early warning of impending infection of a device.

## 1. REFERENCES

[1] C. Lever, M. Antonakakis, B. Reeves, P. Traynor, and W. Lee. The core of the matter: Analyzing malicious traffic in cellular carriers. In *Proc. the 2013 Network and Distributed Systems Security Conference (NDSS 2013)*. Internet Society, 2013.

[2] H. T. T. Truong, E. Lagerspetz, P. Nurmi, A. J. Oliner, S. Tarkoma, N. Asokan, and S. Bhattacharya. The company you keep: Mobile malware infection rates and inexpensive risk indicators. In *Proceedings of the 23rd International Conference on World Wide Web*, WWW '14, pages 39–50. International World Wide Web Conferences Steering Committee, 2014.

*WiSec'14*, July 23–25, 2014, Oxford, UK.
ACM 978-1-4503-2972-9/14/07.
http://dx.doi.org/10.1145/2627393.2627420 .

# SPPEAR: Security & Privacy-Preserving Architecture for Participatory-Sensing Applications

Stylianos Gisdakis, Thanassis Giannetsos, Panos Papadimitratos
Networked Systems Security Group
KTH Royal Institute of Technology
Stockholm, Sweden
{gisdakis, athgia, papadim@kth.se}

## ABSTRACT

Recent advances in sensing, computing, and networking have paved the way for the emerging paradigm of participatory sensing (PS). The openness of such systems and the richness of user data they entail raise significant concerns for their security, privacy and resilience. Prior works addressed different aspects of the problem. But in order to reap the benefits of this new sensing paradigm, we need a comprehensive solution. That is, a secure and accountable PS system that preserves user privacy, and enables the provision of incentives to the participants. At the same time, we are after a PS system that is resilient to abusive users and guarantees privacy protection even against multiple misbehaving PS entities (servers). We address these seemingly contradicting requirements with our SPPEAR architecture. Our full blown implementation and experimental evaluation demonstrate that SPPEAR is efficient, practical, and scalable. Last but not least, we formally assess the achieved security and privacy properties. Overall, our system is a comprehensive solution that significantly extends the state-of-the-art and can catalyze the deployment of PS applications.

## Categories and Subject Descriptors

D.4.6 [**Operating Systems**]: Security and Protection; E.3 [**Data Encryption**]: Public Key Cryptosystems

## General Terms

Experimentation, Performance, Security

## Keywords

Participatory Sensing; Security; Privacy; Anonymity

## 1. INTRODUCTION

Mobile platforms with a broadening gamut of sensing capabilities are now available in increasing numbers. Unlike wireless sensor networks, which are deployed in a given area, smartphones (for example) are anyway carried around by numerous users. Leveraging their wide scale proliferation and sensing capabilities, one could collect valuable data of unprecedented quality and quantity, practically from everywhere. This new paradigm of *participatory* or *mobile crowd* sensing [1, 2] is brought forth by numerous research projects, ranging from environmental monitoring [3, 4] and urban sensing [5, 6] to intelligent transportation systems [7, 8], assistive health-care [9, 10] and public safety [11].

Participatory Sensing (PS) has the potential to offer a new understanding of our environment and lead to innovative applications that create added value for the contributing users. However, for this to materialize, users must embrace the initiatives *"from the people, for the people"* systems and participate in great numbers. The ubiquity of mobile devices renders mass participation feasible but, at the same time, users are increasingly concerned with the *security* and the *privacy* of their sensitive information; recent revelations of mass surveillance [12] aggravate such anxieties.

The more the users engage and are called upon by the PS system, the richer the data they contribute (or consume) and, thus, the more susceptible they are to privacy threats. Sensitive information, including daily routines, location and social relations, is given away [13]. The fine-grained nature of such personal data can lead to extensive user-profiling, unsolicited targeted advertisement or, even, personal attacks and stalking [14]. This is intensified when users belong to small groups that share similar characteristics (e.g., work/residence area, entertainment preferences [15]). However, as recent experience shows, assuming that users can simply trust the PS system they contribute sensitive data to, is no longer a viable option [16, 17]. Therefore, it is imperative to address privacy concerns because users perceive them to be significant; as a result, they may refuse to use or even oppose a service.

Even though protecting privacy is a necessary condition for user participation, it is not (by itself) a sufficient one. Indeed, the research community has identified the importance of *incentivizing* users so that they provide a continuous influx of contributions. The type of incentives and the way they materialize (i.e., reputation systems [18], service quotas [19], or monetary rewards [20]) largely depend on the stake-holder(s) that initiate the sensing tasks. However, it is necessary to provide such incentives in a privacy preserving manner. For example, users must be able to receive quotas for their contributions without associating themselves with the data or the task they participated in.

On the other hand, the desired openness of participatory sensing, i.e., anyone that *can* get involved *should* contribute

*WiSec'14,* July 23–25, 2014, Oxford, UK.
Copyright 2014 ACM 978-1-4503-2972-9/14/07 ...$15.00.
http://dx.doi.org/10.1145/2627393.2627402.

data, introduces a series of threats to the *trustworthiness* of the system as it does not preempt adversarial behavior and malicious (or erroneous) contributions. Attackers can interfere with the sensing process and, therefore, manipulate the results of the PS tasks. To this end, we need protocols that can hold offending users *accountable*, but without necessarily disclosing their identity.

To reap the benefits of this new community sensing paradigm, it is imperative to address all these issues while complying with the seemingly contradicting demands for privacy and accountability. This sets the challenge ahead: *How to build secure and accountable PS architectures that can safeguard user privacy while supporting various user incentive mechanisms?* Despite the plethora of research efforts, what remains is to consider the aforementioned problem as a whole. Existing works are concerned with parts of the problem at hand; they either ensure privacy and security without considering accountability [14, 21, 22, 23, 24]; or they differentiate between users that either contribute or consume information [25, 26]. At the same time, a separate body of research investigates incentive mechanisms for PS without considering user privacy [18, 19, 20].

*Contributions:* Our work meets this challenge, proposing SPPEAR; a comprehensive secure and privacy-preserving architecture for PS systems, which systematically addresses all key PS aspects, i.e., privacy, security, accountability and incentives provision. More specifically, SPPEAR (*i*) is scalable, dependable and applicable to any type of PS application, (*ii*) guarantees user non-identifiability and offers strong *privacy protection*, (*iii*) limits participation to legitimate users in a fully *accountable* manner, (*iv*) efficiently shuns out offending users without, necessarily, revealing their identity, (*v*) is resilient to compromised and colluding PS entities, and (*vi*) can support various incentive mechanisms in a privacy-preserving manner. We provide a full-blown implementation of our system, on real mobile devices, and extensively assess its efficiency and practicality. Furthermore, we present a formal analysis of the achieved security and privacy properties.

The paper is organized as follows: first, we survey the state-of-the-art research efforts in the area (Section 2). We then describe the system and adversarial models (Section 3) and discuss the PS security and privacy requirements (Section 4). In Section 5, we provide an overview of SPPEAR and the services it offers followed by a detailed presentation of all implemented components and protocols (Section 6). We present a formal assessment of the achieved properties (Section 7) and a detailed performance evaluation (Section 8). Finally, in Section 9 we conclude this work.

## 2. RELATED WORK

Participatory sensing has attracted the attention of the research community, especially in the context of security and privacy [27, 28]. [29] introduces the concept of participatory privacy regulations which allow participants to control the information they disclose. [14, 24, 30, 31, 32] preserve location privacy through *obfuscation* (i.e., by generalizing or peturbing spatiotemporal information associated to participants) and *anonymization* (i.e., by removing user identities).

The integrity and the authenticity of user-generated content is guaranteed by leveraging Trusted Platform Modules in [33] and [34]. However, these schemes do not consider other security aspects of the PS environment; i.e., system abuse by malicious (or erroneous) contributions or accountability for misbehaving users. This renders them vulnerable to information distortion and data pollution: malicious users can attack the data collection process by submitting faulty samples, without being held culpable for their actions.

AnonySense [21] is a general-purpose framework for secure and privacy preserving tasking and reporting. Reports are submitted through wireless access points, while leveraging Mix Networks [35] to de-associate the submitted data from their origin. However, the way it employs the short group signatures scheme defined in [36], for the cryptographic protection of submitted reports, renders it vulnerable to sybil attacks (Section 7). Although AnonySense can evict malicious users, filtering out their past and faulty contributions requires the *de-anonymization* of benign reports[1]; besides being a costly operation, this process violates the anonymity of legitimate participants. Misbehavior detection is a lengthy process that may occur even at the end of the sensing task when all contributions are available (e.g., by detecting outliers). SPPEAR shuns out offending users and filters out their malicious input through an efficient revocation mechanism (Section 6.6) that does not erode the privacy of benign users.

Other group signature schemes can prevent anonymity abuse by limiting the rate of user authentications (and, thus, of the samples they submit), to a predefined threshold ($k$) for a given time interval [37]. Exceeding this is considered misbehavior and results in user de-anonymization and revocation. Nonetheless, this technique cannot capture other types of misbehavior, i.e., when malicious users/devices pollute the data collection process by submitting ($k - 1$) faulty samples within a time interval. In contrast, SPPEAR is *misbehavior-agnostic* and *prevents* such anonymity abuse by leveraging authorization tokens and pseudonyms with non-overlapping validity periods (Section 7).

PEPSI [22] prevents unauthorized entities from querying the results of sensing tasks with provable security. It is based on a centralized solution that focuses on the privacy of data queriers; i.e., entities interested in sensing information. Unlike our work, PEPSI does not consider accountability and privacy-preserving incentive mechanisms and it does not ensure privacy against cellular Internet Service Providers (ISPs).

PEPPeR [26] protects the privacy of the parties querying mobile nodes (and not of the information contributing nodes), by decoupling the process of node discovery from the access control mechanisms used to query these nodes. PRISM [23] focuses on the secure deployment of sensing applications and does not consider privacy. It follows the *push model* for distributing tasks to nodes: service providers disseminate applications to mobile devices (according to criteria such as their location). This approach enables timely and scalable application deployment, but harms user privacy since service providers have knowledge of the device locations. On the contrary, our work provides comprehensive security and privacy protetion, in the presence of stronger adversaries, for all users irrespectively of their role (i.e., contributing or querying).

Complementary studies focus on the provision of *incentives* to stimulate user participation [18, 19, 20, 38, 39] by leveraging various incentive mechanisms such as auctions, dynamic pricing, monetary coupons, service quotas and reputation systems. However, as these mechanisms do not consider pri-

---

[1]Submitted by users that belong to the same group as the revoked ones.

vacy, they can reveal sensitive information by linking users to the data they contribute to the system.

## 3. SYSTEM AND ADVERSARY MODEL

**System Model**: We consider a generic Participatory Sensing (PS) system that consists of [40]:

- **Task Service Providers**: they initiate data collection campaigns, defining the scope and the domain of the sensing tasks (e.g., estimation of traffic congestion from 8 to 10 AM).

- **Users**: they carry mobile devices (e.g., smart phones, tablets, smart vehicles) equipped with embedded sensors (e.g., cameras, microphones, light sensors, gyroscopes) and navigation modules (e.g., GPS). Mobile devices collect sensory data and report them to the PS infrastructure[2]. Additionally, involved participants can also query the results of a sensing task.

- **Back-end infrastructure**: it is responsible for supporting the life cycle of a sensing task; it registers and authenticates users, collects and aggregates user-contributed reports and, finally, disseminates the results (of the sensing task) to all interested stake-holders and to the task service provider that initiated the task.

**Adversary Model**: The openness of PS systems renders them vulnerable to abuse by both *external* and *internal* adversaries.

External adversaries are entities without an association to the PS system, and thus, they have limited disruptive capabilities. They can eavesdrop communications (to gather information on task participation and user activities). They might manipulate the data collection process by submitting unauthorized samples or replaying the ones of benign users. They can also target the availability of the system by launching jamming and D(D)oS attacks. The latter attacks are beyond our scope and, therefore, we rely on the network operators (e.g., ISPs) for their mitigation.

Internal adversaries can be users or PS system entities that exhibit malicious behavior. Users, or their compromised devices, might contribute faulty measurements or attempt to impersonate other entities and pose with multiple identities (i.e., acting as a Sybil entity). Moreover, adversarial users could try to exploit the incentive mechanisms in an attempt to increase their utility (e.g., coupons, rewards, quotas, receipts) either without offering the required contributions (i.e., not *complying* with the requirements of the task [41]) or by *double-spending* already redeemed quotas.

At the same time, internal attacks can target user privacy, i.e., seek to identify, trace and profile users, notably through PS-specific actions[3]. This is especially so in the case of misbehaving infrastructure components. More specifically, we consider: (*i*) *fully compromised* entities that exhibit arbitrary malicious behavior, (*ii*) "*honest-but-curious*" entities executing correctly the protocols but curious to learn private user data, and (*iii*) *colluding* entities, collectively trying to harm user privacy.

---

[2]Devices leverage any type of telecommunication networks (e.g., 3/4G, WiFi, WiMax).
[3]For instance, user de-anonymization by examining the content of the reports they submit [21]

## 4. SECURITY & PRIVACY REQUIREMENTS

Recent revelations of mass surveillance [12] make people increasingly concerned about the security and privacy of their personal information. PS systems will not succeed if they require users to perform a leap of faith and contribute their sensitive data. Users demand strong security and privacy guarantees. However, security and privacy protection alone cannot ensure that users will embrace PS applications. To reap the benefits of this emerging paradigm, we need a synthesis of the above with *incentive* mechanisms.

SPPEAR, our security and privacy-preserving architecture for PS systems, offers a broadened security and privacy protection under weakened trust assumptions. In particular, we address:

**R1. Communication integrity, confidentiality and authentication**: The communication among the PS entities should be authenticated and protected from any alteration and/or disclosure to unauthorized entities.

**R2. Authorization and Access Control**: The participating user device should act according to the policies specified by the sensing task, defined by the corresponding initiator. To enforce such policies, the PS architecture should provide *access control* and *authorization* services.

**R3. Non-Repudiation and Accountability of Actions**: Actions should be non-repudiable and all system entities (i.e., users and infrastructure components) should be held accountable for their actions.

**R4. Anonymity**: Users (their devices and their actions) should not be identifiable. Observers should not be able to infer private information and whether a user performed or will perform a specific action. Moreover, no observer should be able to link an action to the user or infer if two (or more) actions were performed by the same user (device). Anonymity is *conditional* in the sense that it can be revoked when users deliberately disrupt the operation of the system or contaminate the data collection process (i.e., by submitting faulty reports)[4].

**R5. Fairness**: Misbehaving users should not be able to exploit the incentive mechanisms (e.g., receipts) to increase their utility without making the requested contributions [28].

## 5. SPPEAR ARCHITECTURE

In this section we provide an overview of SPPEAR, its entities and protocols.

### 5.1 System Entities

**Users (Information Prosumers)**: Users act both as *information producers* (i.e., submit data) and *information consumers* (i.e., request information from the system). User devices with sensing capabilities (e.g., mobile phones, vehicles), participate in tasks by submitting authenticated samples, or by querying for (collected) data.

**Task Service (TS)**: This entity initiates sensing tasks and campaigns. It also, defines and provides the rewards participants shall receive for their contributions [40].

**Group Manager (GM)**: It is responsible for the registration of user devices, issuing anonymous credentials to them. Furthermore, the Group Manager authorizes the par-

---

[4]The faulty behavior detection depends on the tasks, and it is orthogonal to this investigation.

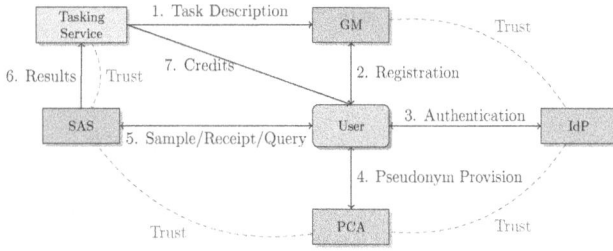

**Figure 1: SPPEAR Overview**

ticipation of devices in various tasks in an *oblivious manner*, using *authorization tokens*.

**Identity Provider (IdP):** It offers identity and credential management services (e.g., user authentication and access control, among others) to the PS system.

**Pseudonym Certification Authority (PCA):** It provides anonymized ephemeral credentials, termed *pseudonyms*, to the devices; they are used to cryptographically protect (i.e., ensure the integrity and the authenticity) the submitted samples, or to authenticate devices querying the results of the sensing task. To achieve *unlinkability*, devices obtain multiple pseudonyms from the PCA.

**Sample Aggregation Service (SAS):** User devices submit samples to this entity which is responsible for storing and processing the collected data. This is orthogonal to our work and it depends on the task/application. Although some privacy preserving data processing [42, 43, 44]) could be employed, we neither assume nor require such mechanisms. For each authentic submitted sample, the SAS issues a *receipt* to the device, which later submits it to claim credits for the sensing task. The SAS exposes interfaces that enable any *authenticated* and *authorized* user to query for the results of sensing tasks/campaigns.

**Resolution Authority (RA):** The entity responsible for the revocation of the anonymity of offending devices (e.g., devices that disrupt the system or pollute the data collection process).

SPPEAR separates processes and functions across entities, according to the *separation-of-duties* principle [45]: each entity is given the minimum information required to execute the desired task. This way, SPPEAR achieves its goals under weakened assumptions on the trustworthiness of the PS system. In particular, we ensure user privacy even in the case of "*honest-but-curious*" infrastructure and prevent a single PS entity from answering the user-information sensitive question: "*Which user (Who) submitted What sample, for which task (Where) and When*".

## 5.2 Trust Establishment

The aforementioned system entities need to establish trust relations. SPPEAR leverages Security Assertion Markup Language (SAML) assertions [46] that represent authentication and authorization claims, produced by one entity for another. To establish trust between the IdP and the PCA, a Web Service (WS)-Metadata exchange takes place. Metadata are XML-based entity descriptors that contain information such as authentication requirements, entity URIs, protocol bindings and digital certificates. The metadata published by the IdP contain the *X.509* certificates the PCA uses to verify the signatures of the assertions produced by the IdP. Similarly,

the PCA publishes metadata that contain its digital identifier and certificates.

To verify the authorization token, the IdP possesses the digital certificate of the GM. The pseudonyms issued to the user devices are signed with the PCA's private key. The SAS possesses the digital certificate of the PCA. An overview of our design and the trust relations of its components are illustrated in Figure 1.

The confidentiality and the integrity of the communication is guaranteed by end-to-end authenticated Transport Layer Security (TLS) channels established between the devices and the PS entities (i.e., IdP, PCA, SAS). Furthermore, to prevent de-anonymyzation on the basis of network identifiers, we leverage the TOR anonymization network [47].

## 6. SPPEAR PROTOCOLS

In a nutshell, the Task Service (TS) generates sensing tasks and campaigns. Each task is associated with the number of credits, $C$, that users shall receive from the TS for their participation, as long as they submit at least $n$ reports to the Sample Aggregation Service (SAS). The $(C, n)$ parameters are included in the task description. Once ready, the TS informs the Group Manager (GM) about the newly generated task. Then, the GM initializes a *group signature* scheme which allows each participant ($P_i$) to anonymously authenticate herself with a private key ($gsk_i$). The GM pushes the group public key to the Identity Provider (IdP) responsible for authenticating users (Section 6.1).

The GM publishes a list of active tasks that users regularly retrieve in order to select the ones they want to contribute to. The task description can be done with the use of task-specific languages similar to *AnonyTL* [21]. If a user is willing to participate in a task, she authorizes her device to obtain the group credentials (i.e., $gsk_i$) and an *authorization token* from the GM (Section 6.2). Then, the device initiates the authentication protocol with the IdP and it obtains pseudonyms from the Pseudonym Certification Authority (PCA) (Section 6.3). With these pseudonyms the device can (anonymously) authenticate the samples it submits to the SAS (and receive a credit receipt for each of them) or get authenticated to query the task results (Section 6.4). Finally, the device presents $n$ receipts to the TS to receive the task credits (Section 6.5).

## 6.1 Task Initialization

The life cycle of a sensing task starts when the TS registers it to the GM which, in turn, examines its requirements and generates a task descriptor, in XML format. Then, the GM instantiates a group signature scheme by computing a group public key, *gpk*.

Group signatures fall into two categories, in terms of *group dynamicity*: static and dynamic. The former requires a fixed number of group members, whereas the latter allows dynamic addition of members to the group. The selection of the appropriate scheme is coupled to the context of the sensing task. To exemplify this, assume a sensing campaign that requires the participation of only "premium" users. In this case, the number of eligible users is known and thus static group signature schemes are applicable. Otherwise, dynamic group signatures are necessary. SPPEAR supports, but is not limited to, two group signature schemes; *Short Group Signatures* [36] (static) and the *Camenisch-Groth* scheme [48] (dynamic).

**Algorithm 1:** *Authorization Token* Acquisition

**Result:** Device obtains *authorization token* $X_{i,j}$

| **Initialization Phase**(GM) | **Transfer Phase**(GM & DV) |
|---|---|
| **Data:** $N$ generated authentication tokens | **Data:** Computed token commitments $Y_{i,j}$ |
| **Begin** | **Begin** |
| **1.** GM $\twoheadrightarrow S : [\sqrt{N}, \sqrt{N}]$ | **1.** GM $\twoheadrightarrow \{r_R, r_C\}$ |
| **2.** GM $\twoheadrightarrow 2\sqrt{N}$ random keys $(R_1, ..., R_{\sqrt{N}}), (C_1, ..., C_{\sqrt{N}}),$ for each Row & Column | **2.** Randomize row & column keys: $(R_1 \cdot r_R, ...., R_{\sqrt{N}} \cdot r_R)$ $(C_1 \cdot r_C, ..., C_{\sqrt{N}} \cdot r_C)$ |
| **3. for** *every* $X_{i,j}$ *in S* **do** | **3. If** device wishes $X_{i,j}$ |
| GM $\twoheadrightarrow \{K_{i,j}, Y_{i,j}\}$, where $K_{i,j} = g^{R_i C_j}$, where $\{G_g, g\} \xrightarrow{DDH} \{Grp, Genr\}$ $Y_{i,j} = commit_{K_{i,j}}(X_{i,j})$ | **then** $OT_1^{\sqrt{N}}[GM, DV] \xrightarrow{Pick} R_i \cdot r_R$ $OT_1^{\sqrt{N}}[GM, DV] \xrightarrow{Pick} C_j \cdot r_C$ |
| **end** | **end** |
| **3.** GM sends to the device $Y_{1,1}, ..., Y{\sqrt{N}, \sqrt{N}}$ | **4.** GM sends $g^{\frac{1}{r_R r_C}}$ |
| | **5.** Device reconstructs $K_{i,j} = g^{(\frac{1}{r_R r_C} R_i) \cdot r_R C_j \cdot r_C}$ |
| | **6.** Obtain $X_{i,j}$ by opening $Y_{i,j}$ with $K_{i,j}$ |
| **End** | **End** |

## 6.2 Device Registration and Authorization Token Acquisition

To participate in a sensing task, a user must register her device to the Group Manager (GM) and obtain the private key $gsk_i$. Towards this end, the device initiates an interactive *JOIN* protocol with the GM.[5] This protocol guarantees *exculpability*: no entity can forge signatures besides the intended holder of the key [49].

The GM generates an *authorization token dispenser*, $D_{auth}$. Each token in it binds the identity of the registered user to the identifiers of the active tasks and the type of relevant access rights (submit samples or access the results of the sensing task). The binding is done with the use of secure and salted cryptographic hashes. Tokens are also signed by the GM to ensure their authenticity. More specifically, the dispenser is a vector of tokens, $D_{auth} = [t_1, t_2, ..., t_N]$, where each token $t_i$ is:

$$\{t_{id}, h(user_{id} \| task_i \| n), task_i, submit/query\}_{\sigma_{GM}}$$

$N$ denotes the number of currently active sensing tasks, $n$ is a nonce and $t_{id}$ is the token identifier. In order to participate in a task, the device must pick the corresponding token the dispenser.

Nevertheless, merely requesting a token would compromise users' privacy; besides being aware of the real identity of the user, the GM would learn the task she wishes to contribute to and this could lead to a breach of her privacy. For example, participating in a task that measures noise pollution during night hours within an area "A" can help the GM deduce sensitive user information such as home location and personal activities (among others) [50, 51].

To prevent this, SPPEAR employs *Private Information Retrieval (PIR)* techniques. Currently, we support the *"Oblivious Transfer with Adaptive Queries"* protocol [52]. The scheme has two phases (see Alg. 1): the initialization phase, performed by the GM, and the token acquisition phase involving both the device and the GM. For the former, the GM generates and arranges the $N$ authorization tokens in a two-dimensional

---

[5]Due to space limitations, we refer the reader to [36, 48]

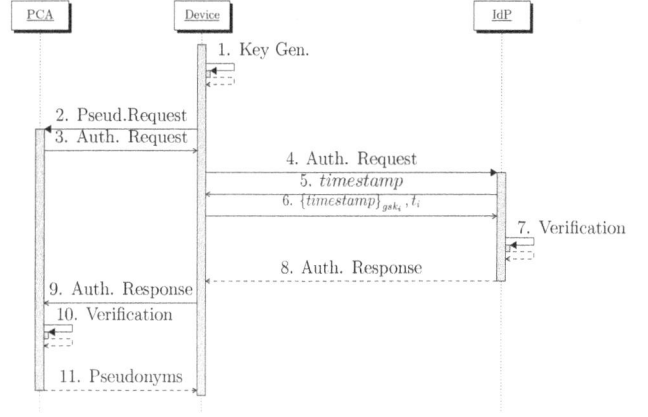

**Figure 2: Authentication Protocol**

array, $S$, with $\sqrt{N}$ rows and $\sqrt{N}$ columns. Then, it computes $2\sqrt{N}$ random keys, $(R_1, R_2, ..., R_{\sqrt{N}})$, $(C_1, C_2, ..., C_{\sqrt{N}})$, and a commitment, $Y_{i,j}$, for each element of the array. These commitments are sent to the device.

During the token acquisition phase, the GM randomizes the $2\sqrt{N}$ keys with two elements $r_R$ and $r_C$. Then, the device initiates two Oblivious Transfer sessions to obtain the desired token, $X_{i,j}$; one for the row key, $R_i \cdot r_R$, and another for the column key, $C_j \cdot r_C$. After receiving $g^{\frac{1}{r_R r_C}}$, from the GM, and with the acquired keys, the device can now obtain $X_{i,j}$ by opening the already received commitment, $Y_{i,j}$.

The security of this scheme relies on the Decisional Diffie-Helman (DDH) assumption [52]. As the token acquisition protocol leverages oblivious transfer, the GM does not know which token was obtained by the device and, thus, cannot deduce the task the user wishes to contribute to. In Sec. 8 we present the scheme complexity along with a quantitative analysis of its performance (Sec. 8.3).

## 6.3 Device Authentication

Having the signing key, $gsk_i$, and the authorization token, the device can now authenticate itself to the IdP and receive pseudonyms from PCA. A pseudonym is an X.509 certificate [53] that binds an anonymous identity with a public key. Figure 2 presents the authentication protocol, based on Web-Services, which is as follows:

**Phase 1:** The device generates the desired amount of key-pairs and creates the same number of Certificate Signing Requests (CSRs) (Step 1).

**Phase 2:** The device requests pseudonyms from the PCA with the generated CSRs (Step 2). Since the device is not yet authenticated, the PCA issues a SAML authentication request [46] (Step 3) to the IdP, signed with its private key and encrypted with the public key of the IdP. According to SAML specifications, the request contains a random *transient identifier* ($tr_{id}$) for identifying and managing the session during further execution of the protocol. The request is then relayed by the device to the IdP (Step 4), according to the protocol bindings agreed between the PCA and the IdP during the metadata exchange phase (Sec. 5.2).

**Phase 3:** The IdP decodes and decrypts the authentication request, verifies the XML signature of the PCA and initiates the authentication process with the device. Our authentication is based on group signatures. More specifically, the IdP sends a challenge (in the form of a timestamp/nonce) to the device (Step 5). The device, then, produces a group signature on the challenge with its signing key $gsk_i$. It also submits the token for the desired sensing task (Step 6). The IdP verifies the challenge with the use of the $gpk$ (obtained from the GM). Upon successful authentication (Step 7), the IdP generates a SAML authentication response signed with its private key and encrypted with the public key of the PCA. The response contains the $tr_{id}$ and an authentication statement (i.e., assertion): this asserts that the device was successfully authenticated anonymously through a group signature and it includes the authorization token and the access rights of the device. Finally, the SAML response is encoded and sent back to the device (Step 8).

**Phase 4:** The device delivers the SAML assertion to the PCA (Step 9), which decrypts it and verifies its signature and its fields (Step 10). Once the transaction is completed, the device is authenticated and it receives valid pseudonyms. The access rights of the device are included as attributes in these pseudonyms (Step 11).

Each pseudonym has a time validity that specifies the period (i.e., the pseudonym life time) for which the pseudonym can be used. If the obtained pseudonyms had overlapping life times, malicious users could expose multiple identities simultaneously, i.e., launch *sybil attacks*. To prevent this, we require that the PCA issue pseudonyms with non-overlapping life times (i.e., two pseudonyms are never valid during the same time interval).

## 6.4 Sample Submission and Incentives Support

With the acquired pseudonyms, the device can now participate in the sensing task by signing the samples and attaching the corresponding pseudonym. More specifically, each submitted sample, $s_i$, is of the form:

$$s_i = \{v \,||\, t \,||\, loc \,||\, \sigma_{PrvKey} \,||\, C_i\}$$

$v$ is the value of the sensed phenomenon, $t$ is a time-stamp, $loc$ are the coordinates of the device; $\sigma_{PrvKey}$ is the digital signature over all the sample fields, generated with the private key whose public key is included in the pseudonym $C_i$. The SAS verifies the signature and time-stamp, against the time validity of the pseudonym. If the sample is deemed authentic, the SAS prepares a receipt, $r_i$, for the device:

$$r_i = \{receipt_{id} \,||\, task_{id} \,||\, time \,||\, \sigma_{SAS}\}$$

$\sigma_{SAS}$ denotes the digital signature of the SAS. The device stores each received receipt until the end of the task.

To query the results of the task, the device can authenticate itself to the SAS with a pseudonym (using two-way authentication over TLS). The use of different pseudonyms for interacting with the SAS provides unlinkability. To ensure device anonymity, communications are done over TOR.

## 6.5 Task Finalization

As they submit reports to the SAS, devices accumulate a number of receipts. To receive the credits assigned to a sensing task, a device has to collect at least $n$ receipts (where $n$ is specified by the tasking service). When a device has the required amount of receipts, it submits them to the Task Service (TS). The TS verifies their signatures and then invalidates them (i.e., stores them in a database and marks them as used), so that they cannot be re-used by any other device. If the number of submitted receipts satisfies the task requirements (i.e., $n$ receipts), the $C$ credits are given to

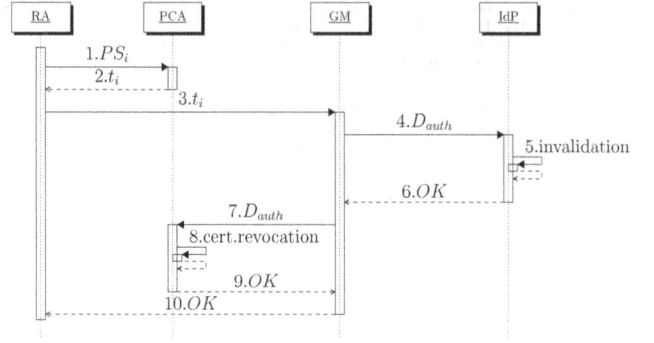

**Figure 3: Pseudonym Revocation**

the user; either in the form of reputation or in the form of a voucher. Again, to ensure the anonymity of the device, communications are done over TOR.

## 6.6 Pseudonym Revocation

If required, SPPEAR provides efficient means for shunning out offending users. Assume one device whose (anonymously) submitted samples significantly deviate from the rest. This could serve as an indication of misbehavior (e.g., an effort to *pollute* the results of the sensing task). In that case, the device should be prohibited from further participating in the task. If not deliberately misbehaving, one of the device sensors malfunctions. In that case, it might be required that the device is revoked from the affected tasks (e.g., the ones that rely on the specific malfunctioning sensor). To address the above scenarios, we design fine-grained revocation protocols, suitable for different levels of escalating misbehavior:

**Total Revocation:** The RA coordinates this protocol based on a (set of) pseudonym(s) $PS_i$ (see Figure 3). Upon completion, the device for which the pseudonym was issued is evicted from the system:

**Phase 1:** The RA provides the PCA with the $PS_i$ (Step 1). The PCA responds with the authorization token, $t_i$, included in the SAML assertion that authorized the generation of pseudonym $PS_i$ (Step 2). This token is passed by the RA to the GM (Step 3).

**Phase 2:** Based on $t_i$, the GM retrieves the whole token dispenser, $D_{auth}$, that included $t_i$. This dispenser is sent to the IdP (Step 4) that blacklists all its tokens and sends back a confirmation to the GM (Steps 5, 6). From this point on, the device can no longer get authenticated because all its tokens were invalidated.

**Phase 3:** To revoke the already issued pseudonyms, the GM sends the dispenser, $D_{auth}$, to the PCA. The PCA determines the tokens in the dispenser it has issued pseudonyms for. Then, it updates its Certificate Revocation List (CRL) with all the not yet expired pseudonyms of the device (Steps 7, 8). At this point, the device can no longer submit samples to the SAS because its pseudonyms have been revoked; clearly, SAS has access to the PCA's CRL.

**Partial Revocation:** This protocol evicts a device from a specific sensing task. The RA sends the pseudonym, $PS_i$, that needs to be revoked to the PCA, which retrieves the token, $t_i$, from the SAML assertion that authorized the issuance of $PS_i$. Consequently, the PCA revokes all the pseudonyms that were issued for $t_i$. As a device can be issued only one token per task, and this is now revoked, the device can no longer participate in the task. The partial revocation protocol does not involve the GM and thus, it does not remove the device anonymity; this is important for preserving the anonymity of malfunctioning (but not malicious) devices.

# 7. SECURITY AND PRIVACY ANALYSIS

In this section, we first discuss SPPEAR with respect to the requirements defined in Section 3. We then provide a formal analysis of the achieved security and privacy properties.

Communications take place over secure channels (TLS). This ensures communication *confidentiality* and *integrity*. Furthermore, each system entity has a digital certificate for authentication (thus we get $R_1$).

In SPPEAR, the GM is the *Policy Decision Point*, which issues authorization decisions with respect to the eligibility of a device for a specific sensing task. The IdP is the *Policy Enforcement Point* which authorizes the participation of a device on the basis of authorization tokens (thus we get $R_2$).

Malicious devices can leverage anonymity and inject faulty reports to "pollute" the collection process. As an example, let us consider a traffic monitoring task in which real-time traffic maps (of road networks) are built based on user submitted location and velocity reports. By abusing their pseudo- or anonymity or, if possible, by launching a sybil-attack, misbehaving users can provoke a false perception over the congestion levels of a road network and thus, disrupt traffic. State-of-the-art schemes (e.g., [21]) that rely on group signatures to authenticate submitted reports are vulnerable to abuse. More specifically, it is impossible to detect if two reports were generated by the same device without opening the signatures of all reports, irrespectively of the device that generated them. Besides being a costly operation,[6] this approach would violate the privacy of legitimate users.

We overcome this challenge with the use of authorization tokens: they indicate that the device was authenticated, for a given task, and that it received pseudonyms with non-overlapping time validities. This way, the PCA can corroborate the time validity of the previously issued pseudonyms and if requested by the device, provide it with new pseudonyms that do not overlap the previously issued ones. This prevents malicious devices from using multiple pseudonyms, simultaneously, and renders SPPEAR secure against Sybil attacks. Nevertheless, re-using the same pseudonym to cryptographically protect more than one reports trades off privacy (linkability) for overhead (Section 8.5 contains an extensive analysis on this).

The employed Private Information Retrieval scheme prevents a curious GM from deducing which task a user wishes to participate in. Moreover, devices get authenticated to the IdP without revealing their identity thanks to group-signatures. Finally, pseudonyms allow devices to anonymously, and without being linked, prove the authenticity of the samples they submit. By using multiple pseudonyms (ideally one per report) and by interacting with the SAS via TOR, devices can achieve enhanced sample/report unlinkability. Furthermore, TOR prevents the IdP, the PCA, and the cellular ISPs from de-anonymizing devices based on network identifiers, such as MAC and IP addresses ($R_4$). SPPEAR "hides" (by leveraging end-to-end encryption and TOR) from the cellular ISP all fine-grained and sensitive information exchanged in the PS

---

[6]Due to space limitations we refer the reader to [36].

| Datum | Entity | Secrecy | Strong Secrecy/ Unlinakbility |
|---|---|---|---|
| Dev. id (*id*) | GM | ✓ | ✓ |
| Auth. Token (*t*) | IdP, PCA | ✓ | ✓ |
| Subm. sample. (*s*) | SAS | ✓ | ✓ |
| Device pseud. (*PS*) | SAS, PCA | ✓ | ✓ |
| Receipt (*r*) | SAS | ✓ | ✓ |

**Table 1: Secrecy Analysis for Dolev-Yao Adversaries**

context. Essentially, the cellular ISPs gain no additional information from the participation of the device in the sensing task.

The first three columns of Table 1 present the information each SPPEAR entity possesses. Our approach (i.e., the separation of duties design principle) prevents a single infrastructure entity from accessing all user-sensitive pieces of information (we elaborate on colluding infrastructure entities in Section 7.1.2).

The cryptographic primitives employed by SPPEAR guarantee that no (offending) user can deny her actions. More specifically, due to the interactive protocols executed during the registration phase (Section 6.2), $gsk_i$ is known only to the user device and as a result, *exculpability* is ensured [36]. Furthermore, digital signatures are generated with keys known only to the device and thus, non-repudiation is achieved.

SPPEAR can shun out offending devices (see Section 6.6) without, necessarily, disclosing their identity ($R_3, R_4$). To achieve permanent eviction of misbehaving devices the registration phase can be enhanced with authentication methods that entail network operators (e.g., GBA [54]). However, we leave this as a future direction.

We consider operation in semi-trusted environments. More specifically, a PCA can be compromised and issue certificates for devices not authenticated by the IdP. If so, the PCA does not possess any SAML assertion for the issued pseudonyms, and thus, it can be held accountable for misbehavior. Moreover, the IdP cannot falsely authenticate non-registered devices: it cannot forge the authorization tokens included in the SAML assertions (see Section 6.3). As a result, the PCA will refuse issuing pseudonyms and, thus, the IdP will be held accountable. Moreover, SAML authentication responses (Section 6.3) are digitally signed by the IdP and thus cannot be forged or tampered by malicious devices. Overall, in SPPEAR, one entity can serve as a witness of the actions performed by another; this way we establish a strong *chain-of-custody* ($R_3$).

A special case of misbehavior is a malicious SAS that exploits the total revocation protocol (Section 6.6) to de-anonymize users. To mitigate such behavior, we require that strong indications of misbehavior be presented to the RA before the resolution and revocation protocols are executed. Nevertheless, such aspects are beyond the scope of this work.

Malicious users cannot generate receipts because they cannot forge the signature of the SAS. Furthermore, each receipt is bound to a task and, thus, cannot be used to earn credits from another task. Colluding malicious users can exchange sample receipts among them. Nevertheless, receipts are invalidated upon submission and cannot be "double-spent" (thus we get requirement $R_5$).

Receipts are generated by the SAS and validated by the Tasking Service (Section 6.4), neither of which knows the long-term identity of the user. As a result, the presented incentive mechanism preserves user anonymity ($R_4$).

| Honest-but-curious (colluding) entities | Information Leaked | Privacy Implications |
|---|---|---|
| GM | - | No sensitive information can be inferred. |
| IdP | $t$ | The IdP can simply infer that an anonymous user wishes to participate in a task. |
| PCA | $PS, t$ | The PCA will infer that an anonymous user wishes to receive pseudonyms for a given task. |
| SAS | $s, PS, r$ | The SAS knows that a given report was submitted for a specific sensing task. |
| GM, IdP | $t, id$ | The GM and the IdP can infer that a user with a known identity wishes to participate to a specific task. |
| GM, PCA | $t, id, PS$ | The GM and the PCA can infer that a user with a user with a known identity wishes to participate to a specific task and has received pseudonyms. |
| GM, SAS | $s, PS, r$ | When the GM and the SAS collude they can infer that a report was submitted by a pseudonymous user. |
| IdP, PCA | $t, PS$ | These authorities can infer that an anonymous user received pseudonyms for a specific task. |
| PCA, SAS | $t, PS, s, r$ | The PCA and the SAS can infer that an anonymous user received pseudonyms for a specific task and has submitted a report. |
| GM, PCA, SAS | all | Full de-anonymization of the user, the task she participates in and the reports she has submitted. |

Table 2: Honest-but-curious entities with ProVerif.

## 7.1 Formal Analysis

For the correctness of the employed cryptographic primitives (i.e., the group signature and the PIR schemes) we refer to [36, 48] and [52]. Here we formalize SPPEAR security and privacy properties with respect to the introduced entities and functionalities.

We use ProVerif, an automated protocol verifier [55], to model SPPEAR in $\pi$-Calculus [55]. In ProVerif, entities (infrastructure components and users) are described as processes. Protocols (i.e., authentication, Section 6.3, sample submission, Section 6.4, and revocation, Section 6.6) are modeled as a parallel composition of multiple copies of these processes. ProVerif assumes sets of *names* and *variables* along with a finite *signature*, $\Sigma$, comprising all the function symbols accompanied by their *arity*. The basic cryptographic primitives are modeled as symbolic operations over bit-strings representing messages encoded with the use of *constructors* and *destructors*. Constructors generate messages whereas destructors retrieve parts of the messages they operate on.

Adversaries in ProVerif follow the Dolev-Yao model [56]: they can eavesdrop, modify and forge messages according to the cryptographic keys they possess. To protect communications, every emulated PS entity in the analysis maintains its own private keys/credentials. This adversarial model captures any type of misbehavior besides curious and colluding system entities (considered in Section 7.1.2), as it assumes that the adversary does not have any knowledge on their corresponding cryptographic keys.

### 7.1.1 Secrecy, Strong Secrecy and Unlinkability

In ProVerif, the attacker's knowledge on a piece of information $i$, is queried with the use of the predicate $attacker(i)$. This initiates a resolution algorithm whose input is a set of Horn clauses that describe the protocol. If $i$ can be obtained by the attacker, the algorithm outputs *true* (along with a counter-example) or *false* otherwise. ProVerif can verify *strong-secrecy* properties implying the adversary cannot infer changes over secret values. To examine strong-secrecy for datum $i$, the predicate *noninterf* is used. We evaluate the properties of SPPEAR-specific data. Table 1 summarizes our findings: SPPEAR ensures not only secrecy but also strong-secrecy for all the critical pieces of information. Thus, it guarantees system security and user privacy.

As adversaries cannot infer changes over the aforementioned data, unlinkability [57] (with respect to Dolev-Yao adversaries) is achieved [58]. More specifically, given two tokens, $t_1$ and $t_2$, belonging to the same user, it is impossible for the adversary to relate them. The same holds for the rest of SPPEAR-specific data (i.e., samples, pseudonyms, receipts).

### 7.1.2 Honest-but-curious System Entities

We additionally consider the case of honest-but-curious system entities that collude to breach user privacy. We model such behavior in ProVerif by using a *spy channel* that is accessible by the adversary, and where a curious authority publishes its state, keys and variables. Accordingly, to emulate colluding infrastructure entities, we assume multiple spy channels for each of them. Consequently, the Dolev-Yao adversary (by monitoring these channels) will have access to all the information handled by these entities. Table 2 presents the pieces of information that leak (along with their semantics) for various combinations of honest-but-curious colluding entities.

Single system entities cannot fully de-anonymize users as they have limited access to user information (Table 1). Furthermore, SPPEAR also prevents de-anonymization even when two authorities collude. In order to completely de-anonymize users and their actions, it is required that the GM, the PCA and the SAS collaborate. In case these components are deployed within different administrative domains, their collusion is rather improbable. Nevertheless, if they are within the same administrative domain, the separation-of-duties requirement (according to which SPPEAR is designed) may no longer hold; thus, user privacy would not be guaranteed.[7].

## 8. PERFORMANCE EVALUATION

In this section, we discuss the complexity of the employed cryptographic primitives and provide a thorough assessment of SPPEAR's efficiency and dependability (with respect to both the devices and the infrastructure). Furthermore, through realistic simulations, we evaluate the (privacy) effectiveness of the pseudonym usage against a location/sample linking attack.

## 8.1 Complexity Analysis

Table 3 provides an overview of the complexity of the cryptographic primitives employed by SPPEAR. For group signatures, we focus on the number of *modular exponentiations* ($ME$) and *pairing evaluations* ($PE$). For sample submission and verification, we employ the Elliptic Curve Digital Signature Algorithm (ECDSA) with keys computed over 224

---

[7]Please note that any distributed architecture would fail to preserve privacy in this scenario.

| Function | Complexity | Entities |
|----------|-----------|----------|
| Authentication (BBS) | $12ME + 5PE$ [59] | IdP, User Device |
| Authentication (CG) | $10ME$ [59] | IdP, User Device |
| Sample Submission | $(6n+2)MM + MI + 5nSQ$ [60] | User Device |
| Sample Verification | $(12n+2)MM + MI + 10nSQ$ [60] | SAS |
| Receipt Generation | $(6n+2)MM + MI + 5nSQ$ [60] | SAS |

**Table 3: Complexity Analysis**

**Figure 4: Authentication Protocol**

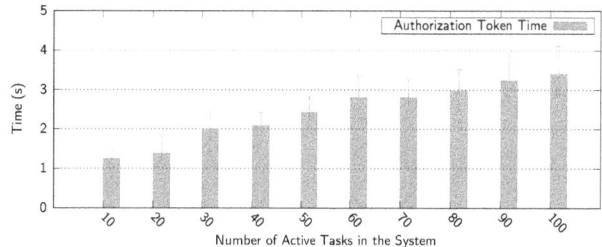

**Figure 5: Token Acquisition Time**

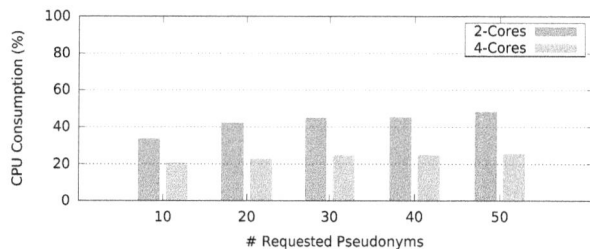

**Figure 6: CPU Consumption**

bit prime fields (*secp224k1* curve), thus, achieving a 112 bit security level [61]. We present the complexity of ECDSA with respect to *modular multiplications* ($MM$), *squaring* ($SQ$) and *modular inversions* ($MI$) for $n$-bit multiplication operands.

Recall from Section 6.2 that the PIR scheme requires $N$ exponentiations (the number of active tasks). Moreover, each of the two $OT$ transactions requires $O(\sqrt{N})$ steps.

## 8.2 System Setup

The IdP, GM, PCA, and RA are deployed, for testing purposes, on separate Virtual Machines (VMs) with dual-core 2.0 GHz CPUs. We distribute the services provided by PCA over two VMs for our dependability evaluation (the same can be applied to the other entities, but we omit the discussion due to space limitations). We use the OpenSSL [62] library for the cryptographic operations, i.e., the ECDSA and TLS and the JPBC [63] library for the group signature schemes. We have deployed our sensing application on Android smartphones with different specifications: 4-Cores/1 GB RAM and 2-Cores/1 GB RAM.

To emulate the real-world networks, we introduce an artificial network delay at the data link layer: the employed queuing discipline increases randomly the network latency following a normal distribution with a mean of $10\,ms$ and variance of $2.5\,s$.

For the infrastructure evaluation (see Section 8.4) we use Jmeter$^{\text{TM}}$ to emulate multiple devices that access the infrastructure concurrently. Additionally, we implement a *mobility tracker*, similar to the one presented in [64] based on Kalman Filters, to perform the privacy evaluation in Section 8.5.

## 8.3 User-Side Evaluation

Figure 4 illustrates the performance of the authentication and pseudonym acquisition protocol on the two Android devices. We assume a device requests an authorization token within a set of 10 tokens (i.e., 10 active tasks). We present the time needed to execute the different steps of the algorithm (i.e., pseudonym generation, acquisition time and authentication at the IdP), averaged over 50 observations. For the dual-core phone, the time needed to get authenticated and obtain 10 pseudonyms is around $8\,s$. This increases linearly as the device requests more pseudonyms: for 50 pseudonyms, the authentication protocol (Section 6.3) is executed in $22\,s$. On the IdP site, authentication (based on group signatures) requires $4\,s$. For the quad-core device, the protocol requires significantly less time (around $11\,s$ for 50 pseudonyms). When executing the protocol over TOR, overhead is introduced in the form of network latency. Due to space limitations, we present here the results only for the quad-core device. A latency of $10\,s$ is introduced, thus raising the authentication time to $23\,s$ for 50 pseudonyms. Even for demanding

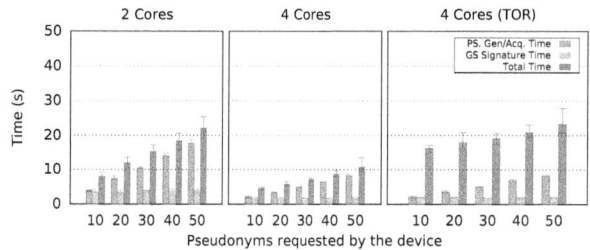

PS tasks, such a number of pseudonyms provides adequate privacy (Section 8.5).

We assess the efficiency of EC-based digital signatures compared to group-signature schemes on the quad-core device. We find that ECDSA with SHA512 is approximately 10 times faster compared to group signature schemes (BBS scheme [36] for the same security level). This is an important aspect of our design, also compared to AnonySense [21] that relies on group signatures: as devices are expected to submit a considerable amount of digitally signed samples, it is critical, from the energy consumption point of view, that the process is as efficient as possible.

For the implemented PIR scheme, Figure 5 shows the time needed to obtain an authorization token for one task on the quad-core device: it increases mildly with the number of active tasks in the system. Even for a set of 100 active tasks, the time needed to obtain one authorization token is approximately $3.5\,s$.

We assess *CPU* utilization for the two mobile devices (Figure 6). For the dual-core device, the amount of CPU required ranges from 36%, for 10 pseudonyms, to approximately 50% for 50 pseudonyms. For the quad-core phone the CPU consumption significantly drops, ranging from 20%, for 10 pseudonyms, to 23% for 50 pseudonyms. For comparison purposes, we measured the CPU consumption of the Facebook$^{\text{TM}}$ application on the quad-core device. On average the Facebook client consumes 18% of the CPU, that is close to the CPU consumption of our client on the same device (for 50 pseudonyms).

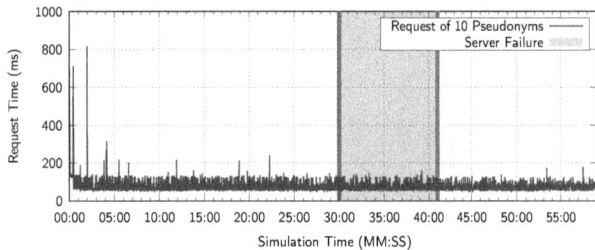

Figure 7: System Reliability in Real-World Scenario

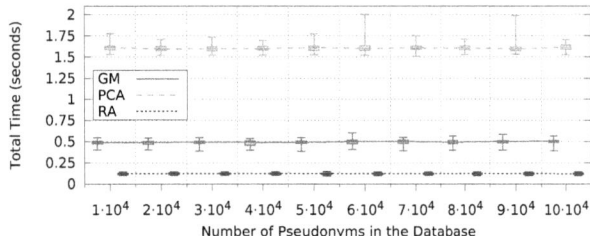

Figure 8: Device Revocation

## 8.4 Infrastructure-Side Evaluation

To assess the performance of the system under stressful, yet realistic, scenarios we assumed a privacy-demanding use case that includes *mobility*. The devices of car drivers or passengers get authenticated to our system and receive pseudonyms to submit data on encountered traffic conditions in a privacy-preserving manner. This scenario is a demanding case of participatory sensing, because it entails strict location privacy protection requirements.

To model such conditions, we use the "TAPAS" data set [65] that contains synthetic traffic traces from the city of Cologne (Germany) during a whole day. We assume a request policy of 10 pseudonyms every 10 minutes, i.e. pseudonym lifetime of 1 minute each [66]. By combining this policy with 5 000 randomly chosen vehicular traces from the data set, we create threads for Jmeter. Each thread is scheduled according to the TAPAS mobility traces, with journeys specified by start and end timestamps. Figure 7 shows that our system performs really well in this high-stress scenario: it serves each request, approximately, in less than $200\,ms$. Furthermore, during the 1 *hour* execution of this test, we simulate an outage of one of the two PCAs, disconnecting completely the VM from the network for 11 minutes. As shown in the grade area of Figure 7, the request latency does not increase and the system recovers transparently from the outage.

Figure 8 shows the time required for a single device revocation, as a function of the number of pseudonyms in the database. The RA queries the PCA for the token $t_i$ that the device used to request the pseudonym $PS$. After retrieving $t_i$, the RA asks the GM to translate $t_i$ to the device long term identifier ($lt_{id}$). Then, the GM invalidates all device tokens for which the $t_i$ was issued and informs the IdP (Section 6.6). Accordingly, the PCA revokes all device pseudonyms. These two processing delays are accounted for as the time spent on PCA ($t_{PCA}$) and GM ($t_{GM}$), respectively. The total time spent on RA is $t_{TOT} = t_{RA} + t_{PCA} + t_{GM}$, where $t_{TOT}$ is the total execution time of the pseudonym resolution protocol.

The pseudonym set is generated by assuming the same request policy for all devices. This approach maximizes the

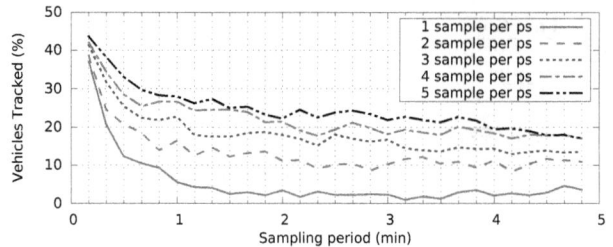

Figure 9: Privacy Evaluation for Mobility

entropy of the database set. Each assumed device obtained 10 tokens for requesting a set of 10 pseudonyms, thus giving the overall ratio 1 device : 10 tokens : 100 pseudonyms. The box-plots in Figure 8 depict the results averaged over 100 runs, with the pseudonym set increasing from 10 000 to 100 000 items linearly (i.e., we assume more devices). The performance of the system is not affected by the size of the set. On average, revocation of a device requires $2.3\,s$.

## 8.5 Pseudonyms and Protection

To evaluate privacy, notably, the unlinkability achieved by pseudonyms, we consider the following sensing task: drivers, with the use of their smartphones, report their current location and velocity to the SAS. We assume here that the SAS is not trusted: it performs no aggregation or obfuscation of the submitted data but rather tries to create detailed location profiles for each vehicle, by linking successive location samples submitted under the same or different pseudonyms. Various techniques that leverage location information and mobility can be employed to track vehicles. In this context, we emulate such adversarial behavior with a mobility tracker (Section 8.2). We consider 250 vehicles and a geographic area of 105 urban road links in the city of Stockholm. We generate mobility traces with the SUMO [67] microscopic road traffic simulator. Our objective is to understand the privacy implications of varying pseudonym utilization policies. In Figure 9, we present our findings: we plot the fraction of vehicles our tracker tracked for more than 50% of their trip, as a function of the report submission frequency (from $10\,s$ to $5\,min$) for different pseudonym reusage policies, i.e., the number of reports signed under the same pseudonym.

The tracker successfully tracks 37% of the vehicles[8] for a reporting frequency of $10\,s$ and a use of 1 pseudonym per report (maximum unlinkability). The tracking success significantly decreases as we move towards more realistic reporting frequencies: the Kalman Filter-based tracker receives less corrections and thus produces worse predictions. On the other hand, using the same pseudonym for multiple samples, trades-off privacy for overhead, but not significantly. For a sampling frequency of 1 *report*/*min*, we observe that approximately only 5% of the vehicles are tracked for more than 50% of their trips. By reusing the same pseudonym for 5 reports, this fraction goes to 27%. One interesting observation is that the effect of pseudonym reuse weakens as the sampling frequency decreases to frequencies more relevant to the context of PS, i.e., 1 *report*/*30s* [7].

As discussed in Section 8.3, the quad-core device needs approximately $10\,s$ to acquire 50 pseudonyms (Figure 4); which, based on the results of this section, can provide enhanced location privacy for mobility based participatory sensing tasks. Even when pseudonyms are reused, SPPEAR still

---

[8]Moreover, please note that the regularity of vehicular movement works in favor of the tracker.

offers strong location privacy. Nonetheless, the pseudonym usage policy can be tuned to the level of privacy users require.

## 9. CONCLUSIONS

Technological advances in sensing, microelectronics and their integration in everyday consumer devices laid the groundwork for the rise of people-centric sensing. However, its success requires effective protocols that guarantee security and privacy for PS systems and their users. To meet this challenge, we presented SPPEAR; a novel secure and accountable PS architecture that can safeguard user privacy while supporting user incentive mechanisms. SPPEAR achieves security, privacy and resilience in the presence of strong adversaries. Moreover, it enables the provision of incentives in a privacy-preserving manner; a catalyst for user participation. We formally evaluated the achieved security and privacy properties and provided a full-blown implementation of our system on actual devices.

## References

[1] J. Burke et al. "Participatory sensing". In: *Workshop on World-Sensor-Web: Mobile Device Centric Sensor Networks and Applications*. Boulder, USA, 2006.

[2] R. K. Ganti, F. Ye, and H. Lei. "Mobile crowdsensing: current state and future challenges." In: *IEEE Communications Magazine* 49.11 (2011), pp. 32–39.

[3] M. V. Kaenel, P. Sommer, and R. Wattenhofer. "Ikarus: Large-scale Participatory Sensing at High Altitudes". In: *Proceedings of the 12th Workshop on Mobile Computing Systems and Applications*. Phoenix, USA, 2011.

[4] D. Mendez et al. "P-Sense: A Participatory Sensing system for air pollution monitoring & control". In: *IEEE International Conference on Pervasive Computing and Communications (PerCom)*. Seattle, 2011.

[5] L. Deng and L. P. Cox. "LiveCompare: Grocery Bargain Hunting Through Participatory Sensing". In: *ACM 10th Workshop on Mobile Computing Systems and Applications (HotMobile)*. Santa Cruz, California, 2009.

[6] E. Miluzzo et al. "Tapping into the Vibe of the City Using VibN, a Continuous Sensing Application for Smartphones". In: *ACM 1st International Symposium From Digital Footprints to Social and Community Intelligence SCI*. Beijing, China, 2011.

[7] B. Hull et al. "CarTel: a distributed mobile sensor computing system". In: *Proceedings of the 4th International Conference on Embedded networked Sensor Systems*. Boulder, USA, 2006.

[8] A. Thiagarajan et al. "VTrack: Accurate, Energy-aware Road Traffic Delay Estimation Using Mobile Phones". In: *Proceedings of the 7th ACM Conference on Embedded Networked Sensor Systems*. Berkeley, USA, 2009.

[9] T. Giannetsos, T. Dimitriou, and N. R. Prasad. "People-centric sensing in assistive healthcare: Privacy challenges and directions". In: *Security and Communications Network* 4.11 (Nov. 2011), pp. 1295–1307.

[10] N. Lane et al. "BeWell: A Smartphone Application to Monitor, Model and Promote Wellbeing". In: *5th International ICST Conference on Pervasive Computing Technologies for Healthcare*. Dublin, Apr. 2012.

[11] J. Ballesteros et al. "Safe cities. A participatory sensing approach". In: *IEEE 37th Conference on Local Computer Networks*. 2012.

[12] G. Greenwald. *"NSA Prism Program Taps in to User Data of Apple, Google and Others"*. June 2013. URL: http://www.theguardian.com/world/2013/jun/06/us-tech-giants-nsa-data.

[13] S. Cleveland. "In search of user privacy protection in ubiquitous computing." In: *IEEE 13th Conference on Information Reuse and Integration (IRI)*. 2012, pp. 694–699.

[14] I. Boutsis and V. Kalogeraki. "Privacy Preservation for Participatory Sensing Data". In: *IEEE Conference on Pervasive Computing and Communications (PerCom)*. 2013.

[15] A. Singla and A. Krause. "Incentives for Privacy Tradeoff in Community Sensing". In: *Proceedings of the 1st AAAI Conference on Human Computation and Crowdsourcing (HCOMP)*. Palm Springs, 2013.

[16] E. Mills. *"Google sued over Android data location collection"*. 2011. URL: http://news.cnet.com/8301-27080_3-20058493-245.html.

[17] J. Lowensohn. *"Apple sued over location tracking in iOS"*. 2011. URL: http://news.cnet.com/8301-27076_3-20057245-248.html.

[18] E. Androulaki et al. "Reputation systems for anonymous networks". In: *Privacy Enhancing Technologies*. 2008.

[19] T. Luo and C. K. Tham. "Fairness and social welfare in incentivizing participatory sensing." In: *IEEE 9th Conference on Sensor, Mesh and Ad Hoc Communications and Networks (SECON)*. Seoul, 2012.

[20] I. Krontiris and A. Albers. "Monetary incentives in participatory sensing using multi-attributive auctions". In: *International Journal on Parallel Emerging Distributed Systems* 27.4 (2012), pp. 317–336.

[21] M. Shin et al. "AnonySense: A system for anonymous opportunistic sensing." In: *Pervasive and Mobile Computing* 7.1 (2011), pp. 16–30.

[22] E. De Cristofaro and C. Soriente. "Extended Capabilities for a Privacy-Enhanced Participatory Sensing Infrastructure (PEPSI)". In: *IEEE Transactions on Information Forensics and Security* 8.12 (2013), pp. 2021–2033.

[23] T. Das et al. "PRISM: platform for remote sensing using smartphones". In: *Proceedings of the 8th International Conference on Mobile Systems, Applications, and Services*. San Francisco, USA, 2010.

[24] L. Kazemi and C. Shahabi. "TAPAS: Trustworthy privacy-aware participatory sensing". In: *Knowledge and Information Systems* 37.1 (2013), pp. 105–128.

[25] L. Kazemi and C. Shahabi. "Towards preserving privacy in participatory sensing". In: *IEEE Workshop on Pervasive Computing and Communications (PerCom)*. Seattle, 2011.

[26] T. Dimitriou, I. Krontiris, and A. Sabouri. "PEPPeR: A querier's Privacy Enhancing Protocol for PaRticipatory sensing". In: *Security and Privacy in Mobile Information and Communication Systems*. Springer, 2012, pp. 93–106.

[27] D. Christin et al. "A Survey on Privacy in Mobile Participatory Sensing Applications". In: *J. Syst. Softw.* 84.11 (2011), pp. 1928–1946.

[28] A. Kapadia, D. Kotz, and N. Triandopoulos. "Opportunistic Sensing: Security Challenges for the New Paradigm". In: *Proceedings of the International Conference on COMmunication Systems And NETworks*. Bangalore, India, 2009.

[29] K. Shilton et al. "Participatory privacy in Urban Sensing." In: *International Workshop on Mobile Device and Urban Sensing (MODUS)*. St. Louis, USA, 2008.

[30] K. L. Huang, S. S. Kanhere, and W. Hu. "Towards privacy-sensitive participatory sensing". In: *IEEE Conference on Pervasive Computing and Communications*. Galveston, USA, Mar. 2009.

[31] C.Y. Chow, M. Mokbel, and X. Liu. "Spatial cloaking for anonymous location-based services in mobile P2P environments." In: *GeoInformatica* 15.2 (2011), pp. 351–380.

[32] S. Gao et al. "TrPF: A Trajectory Privacy-Preserving Framework for Participatory Sensing". In: *IEEE Transactions on Information Forensics & Security* 8.6 (2013), pp. 874–887.

[33] A. Dua et al. "Towards Trustworthy Participatory Sensing". In: *Proceedings of the 4th USENIX Conference on Hot Topics in Security.* Montreal, Canada, 2009.

[34] P. Gilbert et al. "Toward Trustworthy Mobile Sensing". In: *Proceedings of the 11th Workshop on Mobile Computing Systems & Applications.* Annapolis, USA, 2010.

[35] D. L. Chaum. "Untraceable Electronic Mail, Return Addresses, and Digital Pseudonyms". In: *ACM Communications* 24.2 (Feb. 1981), pp. 84–90.

[36] D. Boneh, X. Boyen, and H. Shacham. "Short group signatures". In: *Int. Cryptology Conference (CRYPTO).* 2004.

[37] J. Camenisch et al. "How to win the clonewars: efficient periodic n-times anonymous authentication". In: *ACM 13th conference on Computer and Communications Security.* New York, USA, 2006.

[38] J. S. Lee and B. Hoh. "Dynamic pricing incentive for participatory sensing." In: *Journal of Pervasive and Mobile Computing* 6.6 (2010), pp. 693–708.

[39] S. Reddy et al. "Examining Micro-payments for Participatory Sensing Data Collections". In: *ACM 12th International Conference on Ubiquitous Computing.* Copenhagen, Denmark, 2010.

[40] T. Giannetsos, S. Gisdakis, and P. Papadimitratos. "Trustworthy People-Centric Sensing: Privacy, Security and User Incentives Road-map". In: *IEEE 13th Mediterranean Ad Hoc Networking Workshop (Med-hoc-Net).* Piran, Slovenia, 2014.

[41] J. Rula et al. "No "one-size fits all": Towards a principled approach for incentives in mobile crowdsourcing". In: *Proceedings of the 15th Workshop on Mobile Computing Systems and Applications (HotMobile).* Santa Barbara, CA, 2014.

[42] L. Sweeney. "k-anonymity: A Model for Protecting Privacy". In: *International Journal of Uncertainty, Fuzziness and Knowledge Based Systems.* 10.5 (Oct. 2002), pp. 557–570.

[43] N. Li and T. Li. "t-Closeness: Privacy Beyond k-Anonymity and l-Diversity". In: *IEEE 23rd International Conference on Data Engineering (ICDE).* Istanbul, 2007.

[44] A. Machanavajjhala et al. "L-diversity: Privacy beyond k-anonymity". In: *ACM Transactions on Knowledge Discovery Data* 1 (2007), pp. 1–47.

[45] J. H. Saltzer and M. D. Schroeder. "The protection of information in computer systems". In: *Proceedings of the IEEE* 63.9 (1975), pp. 1278–1308.

[46] S. Cantor et al. *Assertions and Protocols for the OASIS Security Assertion Markup Language (SAML) V2.0.* Tech. rep. OASIS Standard, Mar. 2005.

[47] R. Dingledine, N. Mathewson, and P. Syverson. "Tor: the second-generation onion router". In: *Proceedings of the 13th Conference on USENIX Security Symposium.* San Diego, USA, 2004.

[48] J. Camenisch and J. Groth. "Group signatures: Better efficiency and new theoretical aspects". In: *Security in Communication Networks.* Springer, 2005, pp. 120–133.

[49] G. Ateniese et al. "A practical and provably secure coalition-resistant group signature scheme". In: *Advances in Cryptology.* 2000.

[50] L. Pournajaf et al. *A Survey on Privacy in Mobile Crowd Sensing Task Management.* Tech. rep. TR-2014-00. Department of Mathematics and Computer Science, Emory University, 2014.

[51] A. Santos et al. "Context Inference for Mobile Applications in the UPCASE Project". In: *MobileWireless Middleware, Operating Systems, and Applications.* Vol. 7. Springer Berlin Heidelberg, 2009, pp. 352–365.

[52] M. Naor and B. Pinkas. "Oblivious Transfer with Adaptive Queries". In: *Proceedings of the 19th Conference on Advances in Cryptology (CRYPTO).* London, 1999.

[53] S. Santesson et al. *"Internet X.509 Public Key Infrastructure Qualified Certificates Profile".* RFC 3039 (Proposed Standard). Internet Engineering Task Force, Jan. 2001.

[54] 3rd Generation Partnership Project. *Technical Specification Group Services and System Aspects; Generic Authentication Architecture (GAA); Generic Bootstrapping Architecture (GBA).* 2011.

[55] B. Blanchet. "Automatic proof of strong secrecy for security protocols". In: *IEEE Symposium on Security & Privacy.* 2004.

[56] D. Dolev and A. C. Yao. *On the security of public key protocols.* Tech. rep. Stanford University, 1981.

[57] A. Pfitzmann and M. Koehntopp. "Anonymity, Unobservability, and Pseudonymity - A Proposal for Terminology". In: *Designing Privacy Enhancing Technologies.* Lecture Notes in Computer Science. Springer, 2001, pp. 1–9.

[58] M. Christofi and A. Gouget. "Formal Verification of the mERA-Based eServices with Trusted Third Party Protocol". In: *Information Security and Privacy Research.* Vol. 376. IFIP Advances in Information and Communication Technology. Springer Berlin Heidelberg, 2012, pp. 299–314.

[59] M. Manulis et al. *Group Signatures: Authentication with Privacy.* Tech. rep. Bundesamt fur Sicherheit in der Informationstechnik, 2012.

[60] J. Petit. "Analysis of ECDSA Authentication Processing in VANETs". In: *3rd International Conference on New Technologies, Mobility and Security.* Cairo, 2009.

[61] D. R. L. Brown. *Recommended Elliptic Curve Domain Parameters.* Tech. rep. Certicom Research, Jan. 2010.

[62] *"OpenSSL Project".* URL: http://www.openssl.org/.

[63] A. De Caro and V. Iovino. "jPBC: Java pairing based cryptography". In: *Proceedings of the 16th IEEE Symposium on Computers and Communications, ISCC 2011.* Kerkyra, Corfu, Greece, June 28 - July 1, 2011, pp. 850–855.

[64] B. Wiedersheim et al. "Privacy in Inter-Vehicular Networks: Why Simple Pseudonym Change Is Not Eenough". In: *International Conference on Wireless On-Demand Network Systems and Services.* Kranjska Gora, Slovenia, Feb. 2010.

[65] S. Uppoor and M. Fiore. "Large-scale urban vehicular mobility for networking research". In: *Proceedings of the 3rd IEEE Vehicular Networking Conference (VNC).* Amsterdam, Nov. 2011.

[66] G. Calandriello et al. "On the Performance of Secure Vehicular Communication Systems". In: *Dependable and Secure Computing, IEEE Transactions on* 8.6 (2011), pp. 898–912.

[67] D. Krajzewicz et al. "Recent Development and Applications of SUMO - Simulation of Urban MObility". In: *International Journal On Advances in Systems and Measurements* 5.4 (Dec. 2012), pp. 128–138.

# Short Paper: MVSec: Secure and Easy-to-Use Pairing of Mobile Devices with Vehicles

Jun Han[†‡], Yue-Hsun Lin[†], Adrian Perrig[‡], Fan Bai[§]
[†]Carnegie Mellon University  [‡]ETH Zurich  [§]General Motor Research
{junhan, tenma}@cmu.edu  adrian.perrig@inf.ethz.ch  fan.bai@gm.com

## ABSTRACT

With the increasing popularity of mobile devices, drivers and passengers will naturally want to connect their devices to their cars. Malicious entities can and likely will try to attack such systems in order to compromise other vehicular components or eavesdrop on privacy-sensitive information. It is imperative, therefore, to address security concerns from the onset of these technologies. While guaranteeing secure wireless vehicle-to-mobile communication is crucial to the successful integration of mobile devices in vehicular environments, usability is of equally critical importance. With *MVSec*, we propose novel approaches to secure vehicle-to-mobile communication tailored specifically for vehicular environments. We present novel security protocols and provide complete implementation and user study results.

## Categories and Subject Descriptors

C.2.0 [**General**]: Security and Protection; C.2.1 [**Network Architecture and Design**]: Wireless Communication

## Keywords

Secure key agreement; smartphone security; vehicle security

## 1. INTRODUCTION

With the proliferation of wireless devices using Wi-Fi and Bluetooth technologies, security of their communication is a vital concern as numerous real-world attacks have been reported [14]. Insecure wireless communication may allow attackers to eavesdrop or launch Man-in-the-Middle (MitM) attacks, impersonating legitimate communicating devices.

Efforts to eradicate such attacks have inspired many research proposals as well as industrial solutions, namely to provide secure pairing between the devices by "bonding" them to establish a secure channel. However, it is still significantly difficult for human users to easily determine which devices are being paired because of the invisible nature of wireless communication. Hence, researchers propose demonstrative identification, which affirms to the human user which

devices are actually communicating leveraging out-of-band channels. [3].

However, many naive solutions attempting to establish such secure pairing for any two devices introduces a tradeoff. In many cases, increasing security leads to decreased usability, which becomes a significant hindrance for wide adoption of the technology by the general public. On the other hand, decreased usability may cause a security breach in these protocols. This is exemplified by the use case scenario when a user tries to pair her phone with a friend's phone using Bluetooth. The state-of-the-art solutions require the user to either copy a passkey displayed on one device to the other, compare two passkeys displayed on both devices, or to enter a hard-to-guess passkey on both devices. However, the security of such protocols often rely on the passkey not being repeated or easy-to-guess, requiring the users to input hard-to-guess passkeys to guarantee the protocol security [10]. These designs, however, lead to multiple problems in practice. Many devices actually display a repeated and/or easy-to-guess passkeys (e.g., 000000, 123456, etc.) [17]. Also, many users tend to make fatal mistake of inputting easy-to-guess passkeys [15].

In this paper, we delve into a specific problem of vehicular environments. The proliferation of smartphones coupled with emerging smarter vehicles allows constant exchange of sensitive information over wireless communication. For example, different automotive manufacturers and smartphone companies established Car Connectivity Consortium (CCC) and have formed *Mirror Link*, a standard for integrating smartphones and the vehicles to enable access to the phones using car's control, display, and speakers [6]. In addition to pairing with personal cars, we expect more frequent pairing use cases for widely deployed rental car services – both traditional and short-term rental cars (e.g., Zipcar).

Unfortunately, coupling of smartphones and vehicles introduces a new avenue of potential attacks if the wireless channel is not secured. Although launching such attacks may not seem plausible at a first glance, they are certainly within the realm of possibility especially for high-value targets (e.g., celebrities, politicians, etc.) that provide more incentives for the attackers. Furthermore, such targets are more likely to drive luxury vehicles that embrace next-generation vehicle-to-mobile convergence systems. Are current cars effectively protected from remote attackers attempting to compromise vehicular components? Can we be convinced that the sensitive information in our vehicles is not being maliciously transmitted to attackers in other nearby cars on the road, or in parking lots connected via Bluetooth or Wi-Fi?

To address these problems, we present *MVSec*, the first secure key agreement scheme tailored specifically for vehicular environments, providing strong security guarantees and easy usability. MVSec leverages out-of-band channels such as sound or light as its communication medium because commodity hardware such as LED, ambient light sensor, speaker, and microphone are readily available in cars and/or smartphones. MVSec allows a user, typically the driver, to simply press a button on each device (the car and the phone) to initiate the protocols. For the protocols that leverage sound, all the user needs to do is to simply verify that both the car and the intended mobile device emit a short beep. Similarly, for protocols that leverage light emission, the user simply needs to place the mobile device in the glove compartment for a short amount of time. We present detailed explanation of more protocols and their security analysis in §4.

This paper makes the following **contributions**. We provide (1) a description of MVSec vehicle-to-mobile pairing protocols which leverages different cryptographic schemes based on various out-of-band channels readily available in commercial vehicles and mobile devices; (2) an implementation of the MVSec protocols on Android smartphones; and (3) experimental results to demonstrate the usability of MVSec, as it requires minimal user involvement.

## 2. PROBLEM DEFINITION

This section presents the goals we plan to achieve given the constraints, lists the assumptions we hold, and discusses the attacker model.

**Goals.** The main goal of MVSec is to present a complete system that provides a secure and usable communication between the car and the smartphone. If an attacker is present and launches an attack, it will be clear to the user that an error has occurred, so that the user can immediately abort the pairing process. The main properties MVSec tries to achieve are the following. MVSec achieves **secrecy** by allowing the driver's phone and the car to hide information from unintended devices. It also achieves **authenticity** and **integrity** by allowing the driver's phone and the car to validate that unaltered data arrived from the claimed sender. MVSec also achieves **demonstrative identification** by enabling the user to explicitly be aware of which devices are actually communicating via the wireless communication.

**Constraints.** We also categorize some of the constraints that pose challenges in achieving the aforementioned goals. The phone and the car initially do not share any prior secret, nor depend on any Trusted Third Party (TTP) for exchanging the secret. In addition, MVSec incurs minimal hardware cost by leveraging available hardware commonly installed in today's cars and smartphones to communicate via out-of-band (OOB) channels (discussed further in §4).

**Assumptions.** We make the following assumptions to achieve the aforementioned goals. We assume that the OOB channel *does not require user diligence*. This is a necessary assumption to ensure high usability. We also assume that there is *no malware* on the vehicle or mobile device. If there is malicious code on the mobile device, a pairing protocol will no longer securely establish a shared secret.

**Attacker Model.** We now present the attacker model by describing the attacker goals and capabilities.

*Attacker Goals.* The goals of the attacker is to break the aforementioned security properties, namely to break secrecy and authenticity of vehicle-to-mobile communication.

*Attacker Capabilities.* We assume that the attacker can perform both passive and active attacks. A passive attacker can perform attacks without actively participating in the protocol, such as eavesdropping. An active attacker follows a Dolev-Yao attacker model who are able to perform various types of attacks in addition to eavesdropping – data injection attacks, denial-of-service, man-in-the-middle (MitM), etc. In this paper, we concentrate on defending against the MitM attack.

## 3. RELATED WORK

Many researchers have investigated the problem of securely pairing two devices that do not share prior secret key. One of the main challenges in secure pairing, however, is to provide usability while guaranteeing security.

Wireless solutions such as Bluetooth or Wi-Fi have standards that attempt to provide a secure exchange of credentials (e.g., Bluetooth Secure Simple Pairing (SSP) [8] and Wi-Fi Protected Setup [1]). We illustrate as an example the details of one of the SSP protocols called *numeric comparison*. This protocol consists of two phases in performing a secure pairing. In the first phase, a pair of devices exchange public keys (e.g., Diffie Hellman). In the second phase, both devices perform verification on the received public keys by requiring the user to verify if the displayed numbers on both devices are identical. Once the user performs a successful verification, the devices then establish a secure connection. However, Kuo et al. [10] highlight that large attack surfaces for these specifications exist, and provide recommendations to improve usability. For example, the security of the *numeric comparison* method depends on the displayed number to be hard to guess and unrepeated. However, in many products, manufacturers are not careful in their implementations, and cause potential security vulnerabilities.

Different research proposals are suggested to achieve secure pairing while preserving usability. One approach is to leverage a visual channel. McCune et al. propose Seeing-is-Believing (SiB) [12], a solution that allows two smartphones to securely exchange each other's public keys using QR codes and phone cameras. SiB, however, is not well suited for a vehicular setting because it requires extra hardware such as cameras, which is not present in vehicles. SiB also requires user diligence as the users need to actively take pictures of the QR code.

## 4. MVSec PROTOCOLS

This section presents the overview of the MVSec protocols, discusses the OOB channel selection, and then delves into the protocol details. The main goal of MVSec is to allow a user to securely pair his/her smartphone with a vehicle such that an attacker will not successfully launch MitM attacks.

To achieve this goal, we first need to overcome the challenge of providing *demonstrative identification*, to ensure that the vehicle and the intended smartphone are in fact communicating with each other. We leverage out-of-band (OOB) communication channels as a solution. Different from the in-band channels used by the devices, e.g., Wi-Fi or Bluetooth, an OOB channel is a separate communication medium between the communicating devices (e.g, humans, light, sound, vibrations, etc.).

### 4.1 Out-of-band Channel Selection

MVSec leverages two types of OOB channels for the protocols described in detail in §4.2. They are categorized into *strong* and *weak* OOB channels.

**Strong OOB Channel.** A strong OOB channel guarantees both *secrecy* and *authenticity*. We select **light** in a vehicle's closed glove compartment as the strong OOB channel because it provides both of these security properties. We assume that the glove compartment does not leak any light signal, thus provides secrecy. This channel also provides authenticity because only the vehicle will emit light signals. This is because no other device is inside the compartment as the driver first verifies that other devices are not placed inside the compartment during protocol execution.

In addition to considering the security properties, we choose light to conform to the assumptions made in §2. The OOB channel needs to (1) be readily available in vehicles and smartphones today in order to be easily deployable, and (2) provide high usability, i.e., the OOB channel needs to have a relatively fast data rate and should not require user diligence nor annoy the users. We define relatively fast data rate to be faster than the OOB channel used as baseline case, which is manual human input (explained further in §5). This OOB channel allows such usability because the only task that the user performs is to press a button on both the vehicle and the smartphone, and place the smartphone inside the glove compartment. After waiting for a few seconds, during which the vehicle transmits signals via blinking lights to the smartphone, the pairing process successfully completes.

**Weak OOB Channel.** A weak OOB channel provides only *authenticity*. We select **sound** signals as the weak OOB channel. This channel provides authenticity because a user can easily identify that the sound beeps are originating only from the intended devices (e.g., vehicle and driver's smartphone). If an unintended device beeps, the user simply aborts the protocol. We assume that the beeps are sufficiently long and loud enough for the user to easily identify the origin of the beeps. We assert that this is a realistic assumption, because smartphone users generally distinguish who's phone is ringing when (s)he hears a phone ring. We also use sound signals because of the ubiquitous deployments of microphones and speakers in vehicles and smartphones.

## 4.2 MVSec Protocol Details

This section describes the MVSec protocols that leverage light and sound signals as strong and weak OOB channels, respectively. We present the underlying cryptographic primitives of these protocols.

---

**MVSec-I: Protocol using EKE**

1. $User$ : Presses start buttons on A and B. Places B in the glove compartment.
2. $A \xrightarrow{Light} B$ : $K_s$ where $K_s \xleftarrow{R} \{0,1\}^\ell$
3. $A \xrightarrow{BT} B$ : $\{g^a\}_{K_s}$; B decrypts $\{g^a\}_{K_s}$ with $K_s$;
   $B$ : Computes shared key $K' = (g^a)^b$.
4. $B \xrightarrow{BT} A$ : $\{g^b\}_{K_s} || M_{K'}(n_A)$ where $n_A = H(\{g^a\}_{K_s})$
   $A$ : Decrypts $\{g^b\}_{K_s}$; Computes shared key $K = (g^b)^a$;
   $M_{K'}(n_A) \overset{?}{=} M_K(H(\{g^a\}_{K_s}))$;
   Aborts if verification failed.
5. $A \xrightarrow{BT} B$ : $M_{K'}(n_B)$ where $n_B = H(\{g^b\}_{K_s})$
   $B$ : $M_{K'}(n_B) \overset{?}{=} M_K(H(\{g^b\}_{K_s}))$;
   Aborts if verification failed.

---

**Figure 1: MVSec-I using light as the strong OOB channel with $\ell = 20$.**

**MVSec-I: Protocol leveraging a strong OOB channel.** The first key agreement protocol leverages light as a strong OOB channel. This protocol makes use of the Encrypted Key Exchange (EKE) [4] and is depicted in Fig-

ure 1. A conventional EKE scheme allows two participating entities to use a shared low-entropy password to derive a temporary shared key that can be used to authenticate the key exchange messages. We use a variant of the EKE scheme by treating a short shared secret $K_s$ (20 bits) as a low entropy password. $K_s$ is first transmitted via the light signal in Step 2. In Steps 3 and 4, both the vehicle and the smartphone transmit their DH public keys encrypted with $K_s$. Then the vehicle and the mobile device also performs key confirmation in Steps 4 and 5.

---

**MVSec-II: Protocol using SAS with Hash**

1. $User$ : Presses start buttons on A and B. Aborts if devices other than A or B beep during execution.
2. $A \xrightarrow{BT} B$ : $C_A = H(g^a)$.
3. $B \xrightarrow{BT} A$ : $C_B = H(g^b)$.
4. $A \xrightarrow{BT} B$ : $g^a$
5. $B$ : $C_A \overset{?}{=} H(g^a)$ verifies $g^a$ and abort if verification fails. Computes shared key $K = (g^a)^b$.
   $B \xrightarrow{BT} A$ : $g^b$
6. $A$ : $C_B \overset{?}{=} H(g^b)$ verifies $g^b$ and abort if verification fails. Computes shared key $K' = (g^b)^a$.
7. $A \xRightarrow{Sound} B$ : $SAS_A = [H(K')]_\ell$.
   $B$ : $SAS_B = [H(K)]_\ell$;
   $SAS_A \overset{?}{=} SAS_B$; aborts if verification fails.
8. $B \xRightarrow{Sound} A$ : $SAS_B$.
   $A$ : $SAS_B \overset{?}{=} SAS_A$; aborts if verification fails.

*Key confirmation (check $K' \overset{?}{=} K$)*

9. $A$ : $n'_A \xleftarrow{R} \{0,1\}^\eta$.
   $A \xrightarrow{BT} B$ : $n'_A || M_{K'}(n'_A)$
10. $B$ : $n'_B \xleftarrow{R} \{0,1\}^\eta$.
    $B \xrightarrow{BT} A$ : $n'_B || M_K(n'_A || n'_B)$
11. $A$ : $M_K(n'_A || n'_B) \overset{?}{=} M_{K'}(n'_A || n'_B)$; abort if confirmation fails.
    $A \xrightarrow{BT} B$ : $M_{K'}(n'_B)$
12. $B$ : $M_{K'}(n'_B) \overset{?}{=} M_K(n'_B)$; abort if confirmation fails.

---

**Figure 2: MVSec-II using sound as the weak OOB channel with $\ell = 20$ and $\eta = 256$ (HMAC-SHA3).**

**MVSec-II: Protocol leveraging a weak OOB channel.** MVSec-II uses sound as the weak OOB channel in Figure 2. This protocol leverages *Short Authenticated Strings (SAS)* [16, 13, 11] which uses commitment/decommitment schemes prior to transmitting the short hash comparisons for verification. This approach is preferred over a naive approach of sending short hash values over the weak OOB channel for verification. The reason is that attackers may be able to launch attacks to find hash collisions. The vehicle and the smartphone transmit their commitment messages in Steps 2 and 3. These commitments are hash of their DH public keys. They reveal the public keys to each other in Steps 4 and 5. After verifying the public keys by comparing the hashes, both parties generate negotiated DH key $K$ and $K'$ in Steps 5 and 6. To confirm the correctness of negotiated DH key, two parties exchange the SAS messages in Steps 7 and 8 via the weak OOB channel. The SAS messages here are truncated to only 20 bits. Then, both parties verify whether the received SAS and the transmitted SAS matches. If successful, the two parties perform key confirmation as depicted in Steps 9 to 12.

## 4.3 Discussion of MVSec protocols.

In MVSec-I, the vehicle and the smartphone only share a short secret key $K_s$, because the low data rate of the OOB channel renders transmission of a longer key (e.g., 128-bit AES key) impractical. We do not use this key directly for data encryption or authentication, but rather as a short term shared secret. Otherwise, an attacker may perform brute-force attacks to derive this key.

The light in a glove compartment is a unidirectional OOB channel. In order to perform mutual authentication, we provide secrecy in addition to authenticity, hence a strong OOB channel. However, the sound channel is bidirectional, and therefore, does not require the additional secrecy property.

We analyze the security of the proposed protocols and how they successfully defend against MitM attacks. We also verify the protocols using AVISPA [2], a state-of-the-art automated security protocol validation tool. [1]

## 5. IMPLEMENTATION

We demonstrate working MVSec protocols using the Android platform. We use two Motorola Droid 1 phones running Android 2.2.3 (Froyo) - one to simulate the car and the other to represent the driver's smartphone respectively.

### 5.1 MVSec Pairing Walk-Through

We now provide a walk-through of the MVSec pairing protocols by describing our implementation prototypes leveraging both the weak and strong OOB channels.

**Weak OOB Channel.** First, both devices prompt the user with instructions and a "Pair Now" button on the car. Once the user initiates the pairing process, the device simulating the vehicle (car for short) will start transmitting light pulses by varying the light intensity levels of the screen. §5.3 also provides implementation detail. The phone will capture the varying light intensity levels in this step. Then the car and the phone will exchange messages over the in-band channel (i.e., Bluetooth) to complete MVSec-I protocol.

**Strong OOB Channel.** Once the user presses the "Pair Now" button, the two devices will initiate pairing messages over the in-band channel. Then the two devices transmit each other's SAS messages over the OOB channel (sound). As soon as the car finishes emitting the beep, the phone starts beeping, and the car listens. In §5.2, we present a detailed description of the encoding and decoding of the sound pulses. After the SAS messages have been exchanged, the two devices complete MVSec-II protocol by exchanging the key confirmation messages over the in-band channel.

### 5.2 Audio Channel

MVSec leverages sound as a weak OOB channel for the following reasons. First, the SAS messages only need to be authenticated, but not require to be secret. The audio channel provides authenticity because the driver can easily determine the source device of the sound beeps inside the car - i.e., whether the beep is originating from the car speakers and his intended mobile device, as opposed to other unintended devices (e.g., passenger smartphone). Second, the necessary hardware are already available in the car and the phone, which satisfies the constraints mentioned in §2. This is because all cars and phones have speakers and microphones.

In order to transmit 20 bits of the SAS message, we first encode the data into eight different frequencies, allowing 20 bits to be encoded to 8 pulses. It takes roughly 800 ms to transmit a pulse (including the pause), so it takes roughly 5.6 seconds to transmit all 20 bits of data. For example,

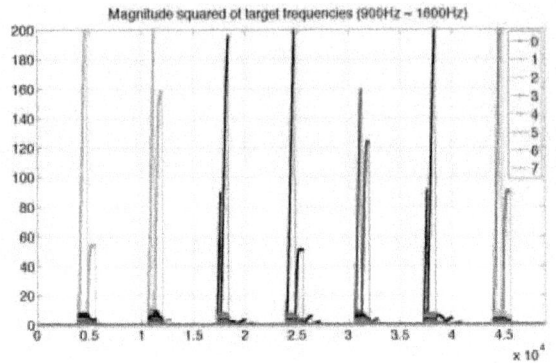

Figure 3: Magnitude squared of target frequencies 900Hz - 1600Hz. The decoding algorithm will process this to '2233531' (== 0x93759).

when the transmitter transmits 0x93759 as the SAS message, it is first encoded the message to '2233531' in base 8. On the receiver's side, we leverage Android's AudioRecord class to record the sound signal. Once the signal is recorded, we filter the signal by applying Goertzel algorithm [7, 5] for the eight target frequencies. We use eight frequencies evenly distributed from 900Hz to 1600Hz. The aggregate of the filtered frequencies represented by their magnitude squared ($mag^2$), is depicted in Figure 3. Each spike represents the pulse that correlates to a base 8 number. To finalize the decoding phase, we process the pulses by applying a sliding window technique to the $mag^2$ values. The sliding window algorithm is triggered when the $mag^2$ value exceeds a certain threshold, $th$. Upon triggering the sliding window algorithm, we check to see if the $mag^2$ value exceeds $th$ within a certain window size, $wnd$. If the value exceeds $th$, we increment a counter until it exceeds the detection threshold, $dth$. We then classify this window as a legitimate sound pulse. Using empirical analysis, we set $wnd$=4000, $th = 40$, and $dth$=200. The described processing increases the detection accuracy, and reduce false positives, and successfully decodes the pulses to the correct '2233531'(0x93759).

### 5.3 Visual Channel

MVSec leverages a strong OOB channel to transmit a short, temporary secret key to defend against the MitM attack. This OOB channel leverages the light bulb in a closed glove compartment to transmit messages, which will be detected by an ambient light sensor on the driver's phone. An Android phone is equipped with the sensor to measure the light intensity experienced by the phone. This sensor is generally used to detect light intensity for automatic brightness control and screen locking. We leverage Android's SensorManager class to implement the prototype. In our implementation, we fully implement the driver's smartphone, and simulate the car's glove box light source, by using another Android device, by varying the light intensity of the screen.

When the driver presses the start button on each device to initiate the protocol, the car will emit a sequence of light signals to the driver's smartphone. The signal is an encoding of a short temporary key (20 bits) as described in the protocol details in §4. Accounting for the low resolution of the ambient light sensor on the smartphones, the current prototype leverages four intensity levels to encode the corresponding bits: low, medium, high, and pause. Each level corresponds to the following lux values received by the receiver's ambient light sensor – 10 lx, 40 lx, 90 lx, and 160 lx.

---

[1]Due to the space limitation, we provide the details of the security analysis and AVISPA results in a technical report [9].

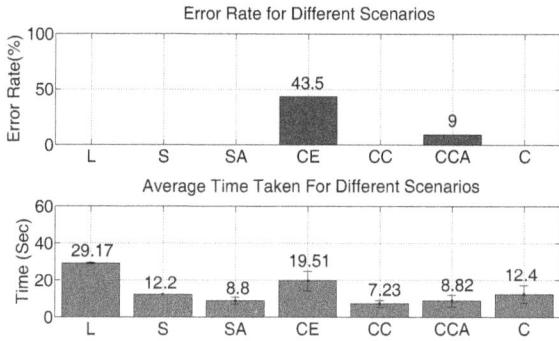

**Figure 4: Error rate and time measurements of different study types. Attack scenarios are also included.**

Due to the low sampling rate of the ambient sensor in the driver's phone, the car transmits one intensity level for every two seconds (one second for intensity value and another second for the pause bit), and takes a total of 26 seconds to transmit (20 bits encodes to 13 pulses). However, we envision that more responsive ambient sensors installed in newer phones will increase the speed.

MVSec uses the ambient light sensor as a proof-of-concept. However, we envision that using other sensors to read the light signal (e.g., camera) would increase the overall detection time and improve the performance.

## 6. EVALUATION

This section provides the evaluation of the usability, as well as the OOB channel detection accuracy. We present the results of the user study conducted by describing the participant profile, study process, and analysis of the results. We also evaluate how accurate the OOB channel is in terms of the detection accuracy. [2]

### 6.1 Usability Analysis

The main goal of this user study is to determine the usability of the MVSec. Specifically, we design our study to verify (1) whether MVSec reduces user errors as well as pairing timing, and (2) the user's perception of MVSec being more secure and simple to use compared to other solutions.

**Demographics.** We recruited 23 participants from different sources such as Craigslist and a university mailing lists (Varied participant pool in gender, age, and education background).

The participants' age range was 20–59; 13 are in twenties, 6 are in thirties, and 4 are in more than forties. These participants include 12 male and 11 female. Among 23 participants, 10 have undergraduate degree (e.g., master or doctorate degrees), 13 have college degree, and one participant has only high school diploma.

**User Study Process.** Participants are invited to the driver's seat in a car to perform user study. We present to them with two phones – one to simulate the car's control unit ($P_{car}$) and the other to be used as the driver's smartphone ($P_{driver}$). $P_{car}$ is attached to the car's dashboard to simulate the vehicle's infotainment system. We designed both the *light (L)* and *sound (S)* MVSec scenarios to be tested for the user study. Although we fully implemented the working

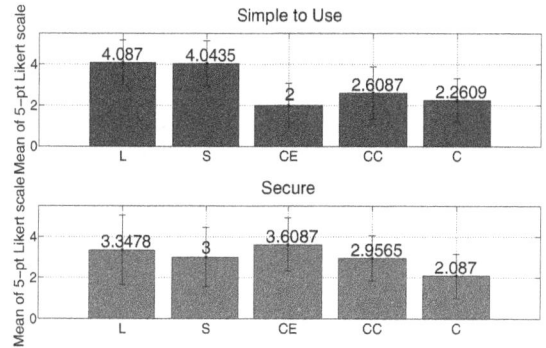

**Figure 5: Post-test questionnaire results that rate user's perceptions for simplicity/security.**

prototype for $L$ scenario as mentioned in §5, we simulated $L$ for the user study by asking the user to place $P_{driver}$ into the glove compartment and explained to them that the light in the compartment will be emitting secret light signal to $P_{driver}$.

For comparison, we implemented three baseline cases that are currently used as Bluetooth pairing schemes in vehicles. The three cases are *choose-and-enter (CE)*, *compare-and-confirm (CC)*, and *copy (C)*. *CE* allows the user to choose a hard-to-guess number and enter it on both of the devices. *CC* allows the user to compare the numbers displayed on each of the devices. *C* allows the user to copy a displayed number on the car, and input it into his phone.

In addition to these five scenarios, we also added two attack scenarios – one for MVSec and the other for the baseline case. First, we present *sound attack (SA)*, an attack on *sound* by having an unintended device beep, when the participant is performing sound pairing scenario, and test if the participant is able to detect the beep from the unintended device and aborts the pairing process. Second, we present *compare-and-confirm attack (CCA)*, an attack on *CC* by presenting two numbers that are different by a digit, and test if the participant can determine the difference. To reduce bias between the subjects, we present the seven scenarios in random order for different participants.

**Study Results.** During the execution of the scenarios, we measure the following two outputs for comparison – *error rate* and *time*. For non-attack scenarios (i.e., $L$, $S$, $CE$, $CC$, and $C$), we claim that an error occurs when the participant performs tasks in an incorrect manner resulting in an unsuccessful pairing. For attack scenarios, (i.e., $SA$ and $CCA$), an error occurs if the participant does not detect a problem, and continues the pairing procedure without aborting. Figure 4 depicts the comparison of the six scenarios with respect to error rate and timing.

The first graph in Figure 4 illustrates that the error rate is around 45% for $CE$, which is a significant percentage. This is because many participants chose easy-to-guess six digit number, when asked to come up with a six digit passkey. Because the security of this approach depends on the passkey to be unpredictable, this demonstrates a clear security problem. We also observe that for the attack scenario of *compare-and-confirm* (Scenario $SA$), about 10% of the participants mistakenly accepted different values displayed on the devices to be the same. However, we did not find any error caused by the participants when pairing via the $L$ and $S$. More interestingly, during the attack scenario of $S$, all participants distinguished the beeps from the intended devices as opposed to the unintended device, and pressed abort button as instructed.

The lower graph in Figure 4 depicts the average time taken for different scenarios. On average, $L$ took around 29 seconds, which is the longest to complete, due to the low resolution of the ambient light sensor. $CE$ followed $L$ with around 20 seconds of average completion time. This is because the participants had to come up with a six digit passkey, and enter the number twice, once on each device. $C$ and $S$ took about the same time of around 12 seconds. The fastest average completion time was $CC$, because this scenario did not require the user to enter any numbers on the devices.

Upon completion of all seven scenarios, we asked the participants to rate the scenarios (excluding the attack scenarios) with a five point Likert scale for *simplicity* and *security* (scale from 1 to 5: 1 being the least simple/secure and 5 being the simplest/most secure). Figure 5 depicts the average of the Likert scale. It is interesting to note that both $L$ and $S$ have significantly higher average (both above average value 4) than the baseline cases for simplicity, despite the fact that $L$ took the longest time to complete. It is also interesting to note that the user perception for security are relatively well distributed among different scenarios, fortifying the fact that the participants well represent average users without security expertise.

With the aforementioned results, we claim that MVSec provides a clear usability advantage over the baseline cases, which are used as industry standards in many of the vehicle-to-mobile pairing schemes. We find that MVSec simplifies user experience, while significantly reducing error rate.

## 7. DISCUSSION

We now discuss some of the relevant points that were not addressed in the above sections.

**Alternative Pairing Methods.** There are alternative pairing solutions that may seem to be valid at a first glance for performing a secure key agreement. However, we provide reasons for why they may not be adequate solutions. First, many cars are already equipped with built-in iPod jacks. While it is possible to perform secure key agreement using such cables, we find that not all existing cars today have such cables. We design MVSec to be deployed in all cars, including existing cars without such cables. Second, NFC may be used as an OOB channel to perform authentication. However, NFC suffers the same issue – not all cars are equipped with NFC chips today. To exacerbate this problem, many mobile devices today do not have NFC chips. In particular, iOS devices which have significant market share, ship without NFC chips. Hence, we find that NFC cannot meet our goal of deploying MVSec to all existing cars, while incurring minimal hardware cost.

**Visual Channel.** Recall that our solution leveraging visual channel was established by varying the light intensity in the glove compartment to emit signals to the phone inside the compartment. While current cars today only have a simple mechanical controller that turns on the light when the compartment door opens, we envision that the light source can be controlled by either installing a new ECU (Electronic Control Unit) or being controlled by existing ECU in the future. To support MVSec in existing cars, dealers can easily service existing cars to install such controllers.

**Access Control Policy.** MVSec employs an access control policy where the right to drive the vehicle equates to the right to pair a phone. In addition, the driver may delegate such rights to the passengers. However, there may be situations that such policy may not be sufficient. This is best exemplified when the driver leaves his car with valet parking or repair service center. If the glove compartment is unlocked, the valet or service personnel may pair their phones with the car. To resolve this issue, we envision MVSec to employ the following mechanism. MVSec may enforce the car to prompt the driver's phone for any additional pairing requests, so that the car would only proceed with the pairing process after the driver's authorization. (We assume that first phone to be paired does not require such authorization.)

## 8. CONCLUSION

Wireless device pairing is often vulnerable to MitM attacks. Thus, secure pairing between a vehicle and a phone is important for a successful industry deployment. The proposed protocols in this paper address solutions to protect against these attacks, while providing demonstrative identification to the human user. MVSec leverages readily available hardware to allow a car and a phone to perform secure key agreement without any pre-shared secret, and independent of a trusted third party, while still preserving usability.

## 9. REFERENCES

[1] W.F. Alliance. Wi-fi protected access: Strong, standards-based, interoperable security for today's wi-fi networks. *Retrieved March*, 1:2004, 2003.

[2] A. Armando, D. Basin, Y. Boichut, Y. Chevalier, L. Compagna, J. Cuéllar, P. Drielsma, P. Heám, O. Kouchnarenko, J. Mantovani, et al. The avispa tool for the automated validation of internet security protocols and applications. In *Computer Aided Verification*, pages 135–165. Springer, 2005.

[3] Dirk Balfanz, Diana K. Smetters, Paul Stewart, and H. Chi Wong. Talking to strangers: Authentication in ad-hoc wireless networks. In *NDSS*, 2002.

[4] S. M. Bellovin and M. Merritt. Encrypted key exchange: Password-based protocols secure against dictionary attacks. In *Proceedings of the IEEE Symposium on Security and Privacy*, 1992.

[5] Eric Cheng and Paul Hudak. Audio Processing and Sound Synthesis in Haskell. January 2009.

[6] Car Connectivity Consortium. Mirror Link. http://www.mirrorlink.com/.

[7] G. Goertzel. An algorithm for the evaluation of finite trigonometric series. *American Mathematical Monthly*, 65:34 – 35, 1958.

[8] Bluetooth Core Specification Working Group. Bluetooth simple pairing Whitepaper. Bluetooth SIG Whitepaper '06.

[9] Jun Han, Yue-Hsun Lin, Adrian Perrig, and Fan Bai. Mvsec: Secure and easy-to-use pairing of mobile devices with vehicles. In *CyLab Technical Report, May 2014, CMU-CyLab-14-006*.

[10] Cynthia Kuo, Jesse Walker, and Adrian Perrig. Low-cost manufacturing, usability, and security: An analysis of bluetooth simple pairing and wi-fi protected setup. In *USEC*, 2007.

[11] Sven Laur, N. Asokan, and Kaisa Nyberg. Efficient mutual data authentication using manuallyauthenticated strings. In *Cryptography and Network Security*, pages 90–107, 2006.

[12] Jonathan McCune, Adrian Perrig, and Michael Reiter. Seeing-is-believing: Using camera phones for human-verifiable authentication. In *Proceedings of the IEEE Symposium on Security and Privacy*, 2005.

[13] S. Pasini and S. Vaudenay. Sas-based authenticated key agreement. In *Theory and Practice of Public-Key Cryptography (PKC)*, 2006.

[14] Karen Scarfone and John Padgette. Guide to bluetooth security. *NIST Special Publication*, 800:121, 2008.

[15] Ersin Uzun, Kristiina Karvonen, and N. Asokan. Usability analysis of secure pairing methods. In *USEC*, 2007.

[16] Serge Vaudenay. Secure communications over insecure channels based on short authenticated strings. In *International Cryptology Conference (CRYPTO)*, 2005.

[17] Stefan Viehbock. Brute forcing Wi-Fi Protected Setup. When poor design meets poor implementation. http://sviehb.files.wordpress.com/2011/12/viehboeck_wps.pdf.

# Short Paper:
# A Dangerous 'Pyrotechnic Composition':
# Fireworks, Embedded Wireless and Insecurity-by-Design

Andrei Costin
EURECOM
Sophia Antipolis
France
andrei.costin@eurecom.fr

Aurélien Francillon
EURECOM
Sophia Antipolis
France
aurelien.francillon@eurecom.fr

## ABSTRACT

Fireworks are used around the world to salute popular events such as festivals, weddings, and public or private celebrations. Besides their entertaining effects fireworks are essentially colored explosives which are sometimes directly used as weapons. Modern fireworks systems heavily rely on *wireless pyrotechnic firing systems*. Those *embedded cyber-physical systems (ECPS)* are able to remotely control pyrotechnic composition ignition. The failure to properly secure these computer sub-systems may have disastrous, if not deadly, consequences.

We describe our experience in discovering and exploiting a wireless firing system in a short amount of time without any prior knowledge of such systems. In summary, we demonstrate our methodology starting from analysis of firmware, the discovery of vulnerabilities and finally by demonstrating a real world attack. The most recent version of the firmware of this device is not vulnerable anymore to those security issues. Unfortunately, there are more than 20 vendors of similar devices that may remain vulnerable to similar attacks, in particular some of them do not have a firmware update mechanism. This suggests more that a more strict certification, with requirements for wireless security, as a realistic long term solution to the problem.

## Categories and Subject Descriptors

C.3 [**SPECIAL - PURPOSE AND APPLICATION - BASED SYSTEMS**]: Real-time and embedded systems; C.2.1 [**Network Architecture and Design**]: Wireless communication; D.4.6 [**Security and Protection**]: Invasive software

## Keywords

Embedded; Wireless; Firing Systems; Security; Vulnerabilities; Exploitation

## 1. INTRODUCTION

Fireworks are essentially explosives used for entertainment purposes. A *fireworks event*, also called a *pyrotechnic show* or *fireworks show*, is a display of the effects produced by *fireworks devices*. Fireworks devices are designed to produce effects such as noise, light, smoke, floating materials (e.g., confetti). The fireworks event and fireworks devices are controlled by *fireworks firing systems*. Firing systems, besides fireworks, often serve other primary industries as well. This includes special effects and military training or simulation.

Despite the fact that fireworks are intended for celebrations, their usage is often associated with high risks of destruction, injuries, and even death. Many recent news and research studies show the dangers of fireworks [3, 24]. Sometimes fireworks are even used as real weapons in street clashes [12]. Fireworks accidents are often caused by equipment mishandling, not following safety rules or low quality of the fireworks devices. Another aggravating factor is that fireworks are generally intended to be displayed in densely crowded and public areas. All these accidents still happen despite the strict control of the distribution of fireworks and the need for a professional license to handle such devices.

Classically *fireworks firing systems* consist of mechanical or electrical switches and electric wiring (often called shooting wire). This type of setup is simple, efficient and relatively safe [5]. However, it dramatically limits the effects, complexity and capabilities of the fireworks systems and events. Advances in software, embedded and wireless technologies allows fireworks systems to take full benefit of them. A modern (wireless) firing system is at the same time a complete *embedded cyber-physical system (ECPS)* and an instance of *wireless sensor/actuator network (WSAN)*. Since fireworks firing systems are increasingly relying on wireless, embedded and software technologies, they are exposed to the very same risks as any other ECPS, WSAN or computer system.

Based on recent research, both critical and embedded systems of all types acquired a bad security reputation. For example, airplanes can be spoofed on new radar systems [15], a car control can be taken over [14, 22] and can be compromised to failure [21], an implanted insulin pump can be completely compromised [25] or an array of PLCs in a nuclear facility can be rendered nonfunctional [18, 23].

In this paper we approach the study of firing system risks from the perspective of computer, embedded and wireless security. We describe our experience in discovering and exploiting a wireless firing system in a short amount of time

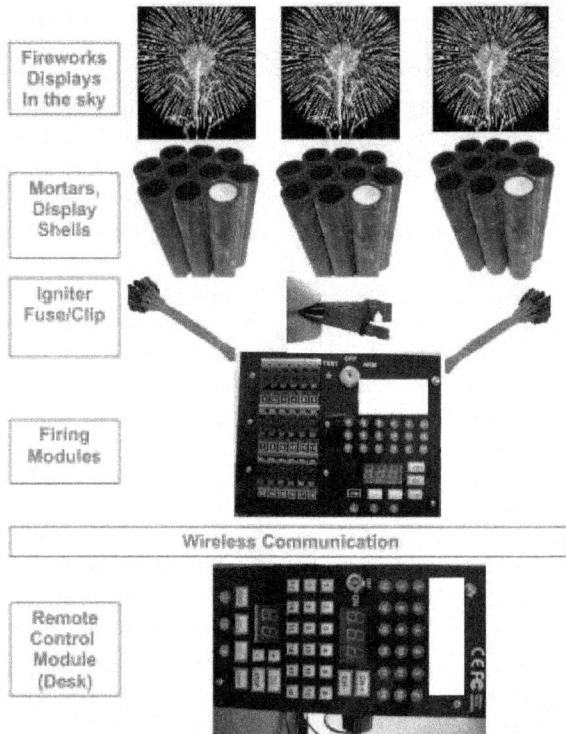

**Figure 1:** Generic diagram and components of a wireless firing system.

without any prior knowledge of such systems. In summary, we demonstrate our methodology starting from analysis of firmware to the discovery of vulnerabilities. Our static analysis helped our decision to acquire such a system which we analyzed in-depth. This allowed us to confirm the presence of exploitable vulnerabilities on the actual hardware. Finally, we stress on the need of hardware and software security and safety compliance enforcement for pyrotechnic firing systems.

## 2. OVERVIEW OF FIREWORKS SYSTEMS

Figure 1 presents a generic diagram of a fireworks firing system. A fireworks firing systems is composed of:

- *Remote control modules* (also sometimes known as *main control*) control the entire show, which includes sequencing cues and sending *fire* commands. They connect to firing modules by wired or wireless connections. In simple scenarios a single remote control module is paired with all firing modules, while in more complex shows there are several remote control modules, each one paired with a show-specific subset of firing modules. All remote control modules act independent of each other. Those devices rely on a microcontroller embedding its own firmware.

- *Firing modules* receive *fire* commands from remote control modules and activate minimum ignition current for the igniter clips. Firing modules are based on micro-controllers and have their own firmware.

- *Wired connections* are described here for completeness, however, these do not apply to our case study where remote control and firing modules are all wireless. Classic *fireworks firing systems* consist of electric wiring between remote control and firing modules [5]. Simple connection cables having End-Of-Line (EOL) resistors are used to securely terminate wire loops. EOL resistors allow the remote control to monitor the field wiring for open or short circuit conditions, hence detecting wiring problems and tampering.

- *Wireless transceivers* are enabling the wireless connections between the remote control modules and the firing modules. Those connections are often performed using 433.92 MHz modules (often capable of using *rolling codes* [2]), or 2.4GHz ZigBee compatible (IEEE 802.15.4) modules which support AES by standard. Those modules rely on microcontrollers that have their own firmware. The devices we study in section 3 are only communicating with *wireless* transceivers between the remote control modules and the firing modules, those actually support AES and several modes of operation, but do not use it.

- *Igniter clips* connect firing modules to the pyrotechnic devices housed inside mortars and ignite the fire once firing module activate the minimum necessary current.

- *Mortars* house the pyrotechnic devices; they also ensure safe launch and firing of the pyrotechnic device into the sky.

- *Pyrotechnic devices* are the actual pyrotechnic compositions which produce visual and sound effects in the sky once *fire* command is activated.

### 2.1 Regulation, Compliance and Certification

Many critical systems, including wireless firing systems, advertise as *"Simple, Reliable, Wireless"* or *"Proven, Secure, Reliable"*. However, such systems must first address regulation, compliance and certifications in order to be able and operate in certain geographical regions or conditions.

On the one hand, devices with fire-hazard risk, such as pyrotechnics and explosives, must conform to fire protection regulations of the country of manufacturing and/or operation. For USA, it is the National Fire Protection Association (NFPA). Specifically, NFPA-79 *"provides safeguards for industrial machinery to protect operators, equipment, facilities, and work-in-progress from fire and electrical hazards"* [9]. This standard applies to *"the electrical/electronic equipment, apparatus, or systems of industrial machines operating from a nominal voltage of 600 volts or less"*. The safety feature provided by this standard is the requirement of a key-switched operation before any potentially dangerous action can start.

This certification however does not apply to the hardware designs or the firmware implementations which control NFPA-certified *industrial machinery*.

On the other hand, all wireless or radio-frequency (RF) modules must comply with national radio-frequency licensing and allocation plans. This includes Federal Communications Commission (FCC), CE Marking (*Conformité Européenne*) and Industry Canada (IC) certification. The system we analyze contains a California Eastern Labs (CEL) IEEE 802.15.4 2.4GHz RF transceiver, which is CE and FCC certified. However, those certifications do not apply to the security of the communication channels or network protocols or of the firmware, but only to the transceiver.

We argue that, given the risk of the devices controlled by such equipment, a certification, based on a security evaluation of the architecture, firmware and communications should be mandatory. We show in this paper that this is not the case.

As a counter-example we consider the avionics field. Avionics encompass virtually the entire spectrum of hardware and software involved in the aviation field where safety and high-risk are considered. All avionics devices must pass strict compliance testing for both hardware (DO-254) and software (DO-178B) [20]. Despite those certifications there are recent examples of wireless avionics protocols shown to be deployed without security [15].

# 3. EXPERIMENTS AND RESULTS

## 3.1 Summary

In [16] we performed a large-scale firmware analysis by crawling the Internet for firmware images, reaching 172K firmware candidates. After unpacking firmware images, we run simple static analysis, correlation and reporting tools on each firmware image, which lead us to discover 38 previously unknown vulnerabilities. In this process, by pure chance, we discovered the firmware images of a wireless firing system. We deliberately omit the name of the vendor and the system for safety and ethical reasons.

Analysis of firmware images for that system has shown us components (strings, binary code, configurations) which appeared insecure [1]. The findings were convincing enough that we acquired the devices for a detailed analysis. Another factor to motivate the acquisition is that according to the vendor, this system is used by *"over 1000 customers in over 60 countries"*. Hence, these systems appear to be particularly popular among fireworks display companies and can be exploited on large geographical areas and can impact a wide range of public events.

## 3.2 Firmware Acquisition and Static Analysis

Among many others, our crawlers collected from the Internet several firmware images, in *Intel Hexadecimal Object Files (iHex)* format, dedicated to the the wireless firing system. After unpacking, we use several heuristics, including *keyword matching*. *keyword matching* searches for special keywords such as `backdoor, telnet, UART, shell` which often allows to find multiple vulnerabilities. The firmware images were matching the string `Shell>`. Based on this we isolated those firmware images and proceeded to analyze them further with automated and manual approaches.

We identified several security issues with the firmware images we analyzed. First, plain iHex format doesn't provide any encryption or authentication hence the functionality is openly accessible for study by the attacker and likely open to malicious firmware modifications. In addition to this, iHex format provides mechanisms that can be use by attackers to insert code or data into memory regions that might have not been designed to be accessible.

---

[1] This analysis was performed on the stable firmware as of Nov 2013, meanwhile a new firmware addressing most of the security issues we discovered was made stable, and is now deployed.

## 3.3 Hardware Acquisition and Analysis

The static analysis findings were convincing enough that we acquired the actual wireless firing system to analyze it further. Indeed, static analysis is known to be faster and to scale better than dynamic analysis as it does not require access to the physical devices. However, one important research challenge remains to confirm the results of static analysis. The analyzed firmware images were designed to run on specific embedded devices, without the actual hardware, it is very hard to confirm the discovered vulnerabilities. Indeed, findings of the static analysis study may be not exploitable in a live system, e.g., because the vulnerable code is not executed, or is activated by a configuration option. Even though this could be discovered by emulation, it is a tedious process in itself as it can be error prone and a generic emulator would need to be customized to emulate this particular platform.

These systems usually come bundled with firing modules and remote control modules. The exact number and placement of each module depends on the setup and choreography of each fireworks show. Both of these modules contain *CEL MeshConnect* 2.4GHz ZigBee (IEEE 802.15.4) transceivers [10]. Both modules are equipped with key-operated switches, as required by NFPA-79 chapter 9.2.

Both modules provide a servicing serial port (UART) which provides access to a built-in menu which displays the `Shell>` prompt we discovered earlier. This allows to testing, repair and debug the remote control module. This UART port is only accessible by physically removing the plastic chassis of the modules and as such, it can be abused only with physical attacks. When properly secured, this port could be used for example to restore or update the AES-128 encryption keys of the wireless ZigBee transceivers. In addition to the above, the USB *SNAP Stick SS200* [13] provides reprogramming and sniffing functions over 2.4GHz ZigBee (IEEE 802.15.4), and is tailored in particular for SNAP chipsets and software.

### Remote Control Module

A detailed view of main components of the remote control module can be seen on Figure 2. After remote control module's disassembly, we confirmed that it uses a *ColdFire MCF52254* processor from Freescale [8]. This is consistent with the result of *Motorola m68k family* provided by our architecture detection tool in Section 3.2. It also uses a *SST25VF032B* flash chip by Microchip [7].

The remote control module exposes a USB port. This port has two main functions. One function is to upload a fireworks show orchestration script. This orchestrator script is a CSV file which instructs the main processor of the remote control module to which firing module and when to send firing cue signals in order to achieve the planned visual, sound or smoke effects. Another function is to upgrade the firmware of the main (not wireless) micro-controller unit (MCU) of the device. This is done via an `.ihex` file, as described in Section 3.2.

## 3.4 Wireless Analysis

This systems, as many others from other vendors, contains a 2.4GHz ZigBee (IEEE 802.15.4) CEL MeshConnect transceiver. The discovery, configuration query and setup, pairing and firmware upgrade of these units is done through

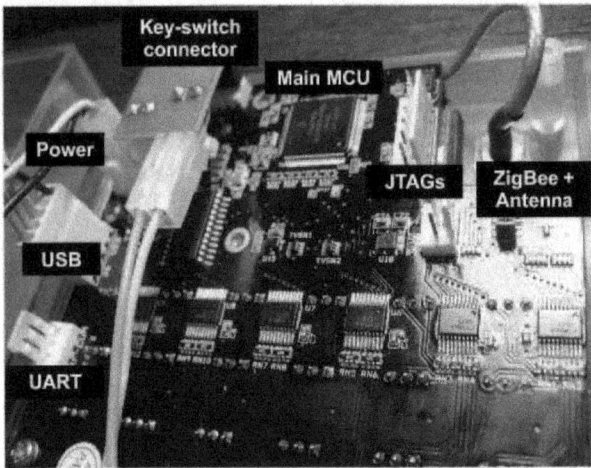

**Figure 2:** Remote control module's hardware.

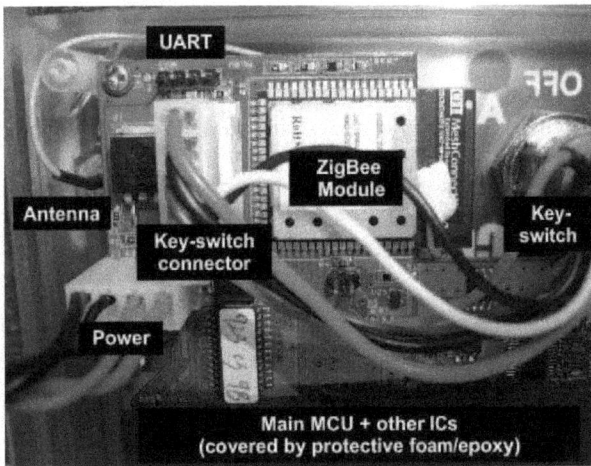

**Figure 3:** Firing module's hardware.

*Synapse Portal* [2] software. We installed *Synapse Portal* and then ran the discovery and configuration query. The wireless chipsets on remote control, firing and firmware reprogramming modules have AES-128 capable firmware installed. However, the encryption is not enabled, no encryption key is present and AES-128 seems to be unused. In addition to this, the system's documentation didn't seem to support AES-128 secured configuration steps. Surprisingly, even though those devices are standard compliant and as such have AES-128 capabilities, neither authentication nor encryption of the messages are used. This is most likely due to the difficulty to properly setup key management and distribution, and that could be perceived more as a risk of operational failure during a fireworks show, rather than a securing mechanism.

Further analysis revealed that it is possible to upload Python application scripts to remote wireless chipsets. These scripts are executed in a Python interpreter within the wireless chipset's MCU [10]. The provided interpreter framework is a subset of Python. Before being uploaded to target nodes, *Synapse Portal* compiles these Python scripts into binary form and stores them as SNAPpy files (with extension .spy) files [11]. The binary form is targeted for the specific

[2]http://www.synapse-wireless.com/
snap-components-free-developers-IDE-tools/portal

MCU which drives each wireless chipsets. These scripts expose entry-points (functions) that can be remotely called (via RPC) by other wireless nodes. These scripts can interact with the MCU of the wireless chipsets or with GPIO-ports of the wireless chipsets. Usually those GPIO-ports are connected to the main MCU of the remote control or of the firing module. This allows interaction with the main MCUs as well as with IO peripherals such as buttons, displays and igniter clips.

The typical use of script entry-points is as follows. The remote control modules process the CSV orchestration scripts. When it decides a *fire* command is required, it sends a Zig-Bee packet containing a higher-level message to call a specific entry-point on a specific remote module.

The usual procedure of *normal firing* is as follows. The firing modules are paired with a particular remote control module. Subsequently, firing modules will accept the *arm*, *disarm* and *fire* commands only from the paired remote control module. The pairing is enforced by checking remote control's 802.15.4 *short address* (similar to a MAC address filtering). The physical key on all firing modules are turned into *arm* position. The staff departs to the safe regulatory distance to fire the cues. The key on all remote control modules are turned to *on*. The staff confirms everything is safe and ready, and then presses the *arm* button on the remote control, which in turn wirelessly sends a *digital arm* command to firing modules. The firing modules enter a *confirmed arm*, ready for subsequent *fire* command. The staff starts the show by sending, either manually or scripted, *fire* commands to corresponding firing module's cues.

### 3.4.1 Wireless Attacks

The lack of encryption and mutual unit authentication, opens the system to multiple attacks, in particular sniffing, spoofing and replaying.

We describe a simple attack, yet which we consider as the most dangerous for the fireworks show staff members. The attacker would perform the following sequence of operations in a continuous manner. Eavesdrop the packets (broadcasts, multicasts, node-to-node), from those learn the 802.15.4 addresses of each remote control and firing modules, and learn their corresponding pairing. For each learned pair, the attacker spoofs the remote control's 802.15.4 addresses, spoofs the *digital arm* command to the pair's firing module, and immediately send *fire* command for all cues once *digital arm* confirmation comes from the firing module. The consequence of this attack is that as soon as the show operator will turn the physical key of a given firing module to *arm* position, it will immediately receive the sequence of *digital arm* and *fire* for all cues. This will fire all the pyrotechnic loads and in the worst case will not allow enough time for the staff to depart to the safe distance. Thus it will defeat the physical key safety and function separation. We *successfully implemented* this attack using components described in Section 3.4.2 and *tested* this attack in practice on the systems we acquired.

Alternatively, an attacker could easily replace default Python functions responsible for firing cues, with arbitrary malicious Python functions. For example, each malicious firing cue function could fire all cues at once instead of firing only it's own cue, thus potentially producing a massive chain explosion. Or it could not fire cues at all or fire them at random, rendering the fireworks show below expectations. Last but not least, an attacker can remotely set random encryption keys on remote nodes. This would result in a denial-of-service for the legitimate user, since her legitimate devices would not be able to communicate with exploited devices anymore. This can definitely ruin a holiday celebration or produce disadvantages to competitors in professional fireworks competitions.

### 3.4.2 Wireless Attack Implementation

*SNAP Stick SS200 [13].* It is mainly a firmware programmer for the remote control and firing modules and is based on well-known ATmega128RFA1 chipset from Atmel. Conveniently, using *SNAP Portal*'s utilities, and a special proprietary firmware for it, made available by Synapse as *ATmega128RFA1_Sniffer*, it can be turned into a SNAP-specific 802.15.4 sniffer, where it sniffs and decodes 802.15.4 packets based on Synapse's higher level protocol semantics (e.g., multicasts, broadcasts, peer or multicast RPC calls). We used it to sniff and record the packets between remote control and firing modules during their normal operations. Finally, we also used it to validate our packet injection and replay attacks. If this sniffer received them, then the remote control and firing modules would see our rogue packets. Otherwise we had to fix our injector (regardless the fact that our lower level raw packet sniffer could see them), and then test again sniffed packets and actual devices' behavior.

*Goodfet [1].* It is an embedded bus adapter for various microcontrollers and radios, additionally proving great open-source support for advanced attacks. It conveniently provides firmware for TelosB devices to allow sniffing among other functionalities. We tested our attack with this Goodfet firmware running on TelosB.

*KillerBee [6].* It is a framework and tools for exploiting ZigBee and 802.15.4 networks. It conveniently provides a pre-compiled Goodfet firmware for extra attack functionality. We tested our attack with this Goodfet firmware running on TelosB.

*Crossbow's TelosB.* The sniffer based on SS200 is useful for SNAP protocols and visualization, but it filters out and strips down the packets, hence is largely limiting. We required a lower level raw packet sniffer. We also required an inexpensive and open-source supported approach. TelosB hardware and Goodfet firmware was a perfect fit, so we used them as an additional, much more verbose and raw, sniffer. After learning the SS200 higher level packets for critical commands we correlated them with raw packets recorded by TelosB-Goodfet. Alternatively, a Zigduino [3] could have been used for this task.

*Econotag [4].* Econotag is a inexpensive and convenient open-source platform for 802.15.4 networks. We assembled sequences of packets instructing to arm and fire sent from the remote control module to the firing module. Finally, we coded an infinite loop of these sequences in a custom firmware. Once plugged, the Econotag successfully performs the attack on a firing module once it's key is turned to *physical arm* position. A Zigduino could have been used for this task as well.

---

[3] http://www.logos-electro.com/zigduino/

*Implementation notes.* We implemented a simple attack, however it is obvious and trivial to extend the implementation to automatically and continuously sniff new firing modules, and subsequently spoof remote control sequences.

## 3.5 Solutions

Below we summarize a set of recommendations that can dramatically increase the security of the hardware, firmware and wireless communication of the analyzed wireless firing system. With increased security, a safer operation of the entire system can be achieved:

- Provide "factory reset button" to a "factory safe" image and state – this can help reset the wireless chipsets to no encryption state when wireless crypto key (e.g., AES-128) is forgotten.

- In "basic mode" – a clear-text and insecure mode, allow only testing functionality (e.g., identification, communication, continuity).

- In "secure mode" – a mutual authenticated and encrypted mode, allow additional functionality such as *fire* command to igniter clips and firmware upgrade of the both main and wireless MCUs.

- Implement "secure scan" techniques [19] – to allow debugging, testing and restoring of the main MCU and board.

- Remote-code attestation – ensuring, via static or dynamic root of trust, that safety critical code is not tampered with; this could be achieved via minor hardware and firmware modifications, for example as presented in SMART [17].

- Formal verification – this can dramatically increase security and safety of firmware, hardware and communication protocols.

- Compliance standards and testing – strict compliance testing for both hardware and software, similar to DO-254 and DO-178B respectively.

## 4. FUTURE WORK

On the one hand, we aim at implementing an attack of wireless remote firmware upgrade of the main MCU via the 2.4GHz ZigBee (IEEE 802.15.4) chipsets. This is opposite to the current procedure, where the firmware upgrade is initiated from a USB stick connected locally to the device under attack. Since we have the actual devices under our full control, we also aim at using a dynamic analysis platform for firmware security testing, such as Avatar [26]. In Avatar, instructions are executed in an emulator, while the IO accesses to the embedded system's peripherals are forwarded to the real device. An additional aim is to find vulnerabilities in the CSV parser of the remote control to achieve a USB plug-and-exploit proof of concept.

On the other hand, we aim at finding solutions to help this particular category of devices. Solutions not specific to wireless firing systems, include secure firmware upgrades, encrypted and authorized wireless communication channels, secure restore and debug chains. Finally, wireless firing systems specific solutions include secure latency control and secure positioning.

## 5. CONCLUSIONS

We presented vulnerability discovery and exploitation of wireless firing systems in a short amount of time without prior knowledge of such systems. We started with an automated large-scale framework for firmware crawling and analysis [16], and employed simple heuristics (e.g., keyword matching) and very simple static analysis. We were able to quickly and automatically isolate firmwares of critically important remote firing systems and identify several potential vulnerabilities through both automatic and manual static analysis. These vulnerabilities include unauthenticated firmware upgrade, unauthenticated wireless communications, sniffing and spoofing wireless communications, arbitrary code injection and functionality trigger, temporary denial-of-service. We successfully implemented and tested an unsophisticated attack with potentially devastating consequences.

We conclude that, given the risk presented by their usage, the security of wireless firing systems should be taken very seriously. We also conclude that such systems must be more rigorously certified and regulated. We stress on the necessity and urgency to introduce software and hardware compliance verification similar to DO-178B and DO-254 respectively. We strongly believe these small improvement steps, along with solutions in Section 3.5, can definitely help increase the security and safety of such wireless embedded systems.

Last but not least, we discussed the issues with the vendor. A firmware update that is now deployed is addressing most of the security issues. Unfortunately, there are more than 20 vendors of wireless firing systems that may remain vulnerable to similar attacks, in particular some of them do not have a firmware update mechanism.

## Acknowledgments

We thank the anonymous reviewers, as well as Scott Smith, for their comments and suggestions for improving this paper. In particular we thank our shepherd, Jens Schmitt, for his valuable time and inputs guiding this paper for publication.

The research leading to these results was partially funded by the European Union Seventh Framework Programme (contract Nr 257007).

## Disclaimer

We remind that performing such attacks outside of a lab is an illegal activity prohibited by law. Eurecom cannot be held responsible in case of an abuse of such techniques.

## 6. REFERENCES

[1] https://github.com/travisgoodspeed/goodfet.
[2] Atmel AppNote AVR411: Secure Rolling Code Algorithm for Wireless Link.
[3] California Fireworks Display Goes Horribly Wrong: Dozens injured by catastrophic misfire during Simi Valley Fourth of July. ABCNews, 5th July 2013.
[4] Econotag. http://redwire.myshopify.com/.
[5] Fireworks Electric (Wired) Firing Systems. http://www.skylighter.com/fireworks/how-to/setup-electric-firing-systems.asp.
[6] KillerBee; Framework and tools for exploiting ZigBee and IEEE 802.15.4 networks. http://code.google.com/p/killerbee/.
[7] Microchip SST25VF032B Flash Chip Datasheet.
[8] Motorola ColdFire MCF52254 Processor Datasheet.
[9] NFPA 79: Electrical Standard for Industrial Machinery. http://www.nfpa.org/79.
[10] Synapse Module Comparison Chart. http://content.solarbotics.com/products/documentation/synapse_comparison_table.pdf.
[11] Synapse SNAP Network Operating System – Reference Manual, v2.4, 2012.
[12] Ukraine protests: Kiev fireworks 'rain on police'. http://www.bbc.com/news/world-europe-25820899.
[13] USB Snap Stick SS200. https://www.synapse-wireless.com/snap-components/usb-mesh-snap-stick.
[14] S. Checkoway, D. McCoy, D. Anderson, B. Kantor, S. Savage, K. Koscher, A. Czeskis, F. Roesner, and T. Kohno. Comprehensive Experimental Analysis of Autmototive Attack Surfaces. In *Proceedings of the USENIX Security Symposium*, San Francisco, CA, August 2011.
[15] A. Costin and A. Francillon. Ghost in the Air (Traffic): On insecurity of ADS-B protocol and practical attacks on ADS-B devices. *Black Hat USA*, July 2012.
[16] A. Costin, J. Zaddach, A. Francillon, and D. Balzarotti. A Large Scale Analysis of the Security of Embedded Firmwares. In *To appear at USENIX Security Symposium*, August 2014.
[17] K. El Defrawy, A. Francillon, D. Perito, and G. Tsudik. Smart: Secure and minimal architecture for (establishing a dynamic) root of trust. In *Proceedings of the Network & Distributed System Security Symposium, San Diego, CA*, 2012.
[18] N. Falliere, L. O. Murchu, and E. Chien. W32.Stuxnet Dossier. *White paper, Symantec Corp., Security Response*, 2011.
[19] D. Hely, F. Bancel, M.-L. Flottes, and B. Rouzeyre. Secure scan techniques: a comparison. In *On-Line Testing Symposium, 2006. IOLTS 2006. 12th IEEE International*, pages 6–pp. IEEE, 2006.
[20] V. Hilderman and T. Baghi. *Avionics certification: a complete guide to DO-178 (software), DO-254 (hardware)*. 2007.
[21] J. Hirsch and K. Bensinger. Toyota settles acceleration lawsuit after $3-million verdict. Los Angeles Times, October 25, 2013.
[22] K. Koscher, A. Czeskis, F. Roesner, S. Patel, T. Kohno, S. Checkoway, D. McCoy, B. Kantor, D. Anderson, H. Shacham, and S. Savage. Experimental security analysis of a modern automobile. *2010 IEEE Symposium on Security and Privacy*.
[23] R. Langner. Stuxnet: Dissecting a cyberwarfare weapon. *Security & Privacy, IEEE*, 9(3):49–51, 2011.
[24] V. Puri, S. Mahendru, R. Rana, and M. Deshpande. Firework injuries: a ten-year study. *Journal of Plastic, Reconstructive & Aesthetic Surgery*, 62(9), 2009.
[25] J. Radcliffe. Hacking Medical Devices for Fun and Insulin: Breaking the Human SCADA System, 2011.
[26] J. Zaddach, L. Bruno, A. Francillon, and D. Balzarotti. Avatar: A Framework to Support Dynamic Security Analysis of Embedded Systems' Firmwares. In *Network and Distributed System Security Symposium*, NDSS 14, February 2014.

# Short Paper: Speaking the Local Dialect: Exploiting differences between IEEE 802.15.4 Receivers with Commodity Radios for fingerprinting, targeted attacks, and WIDS evasion

Ira Ray Jenkins
jenkins@cs.dartmouth.edu
Dept. of Computer Science
Dartmouth College
Hanover, New Hampshire
USA

Rebecca Shapiro
bx@cs.dartmouth.edu
Dept. of Computer Science
Dartmouth College
Hanover, New Hampshire
USA

Sergey Bratus
sergey@cs.dartmouth.edu
Dept. of Computer Science
Dartmouth College
Hanover, New Hampshire
USA

Travis Goodspeed
travis@radiantmachines.com
Straw Hat

Ryan Speers
ryan@riverloopsecurity.com
River Loop Security, LLC

David Dowd
david@riverloopsecurity.com
River Loop Security, LLC

## ABSTRACT

Producing IEEE 802.15.4 PHY-frames reliably accepted by some digital radio receivers, but rejected by others—depending on the receiver chip's make and model—has strong implications for wireless security. Attackers could target specific receivers by crafting "shaped charges," attack frames that appear valid to the intended target and are ignored by all other recipients. By transmitting in the unique, slightly non-compliant "dialect" of the intended receivers, attackers would be able to create entire communication streams invisible to others, including wireless intrusion detection and prevention systems (WIDS/WIPS).

These scenarios are no longer theoretic. We present methods of producing such IEEE 802.15.4 frames with *commodity digital radio chips* widely used in building inexpensive 802.15.4-conformant devices. Typically, PHY-layer fingerprinting requires software-defined radios that cost orders of magnitude more than the chips they fingerprint; however, our methods do not require a software-defined radio and use the same inexpensive chips.

Knowledge of such differences, and the ability to fingerprint them is crucial for defenders. We investigate new methods of fingerprinting IEEE 802.15.4 devices by exploring techniques to differentiate between multiple 802.15.4-conformant radio-hardware manufacturers and firmware distributions. Further, we point out the implications of these results for WIDS, both with respect to WIDS evasion techniques and countering such evasion.

*WiSec'14,* July 23–25, 2014, Oxford, United Kingdom
Copyright 2014 ACM 978-1-4503-2972-9/14/07 ...$15.00.
http://dx.doi.org/10.1145/2627393.2627408.

## Categories and Subject Descriptors

C.2.1 [**Computer-Communication Networks**]: Network Architecture and Design—*Wireless communication*

## Keywords

IEEE 802.15.4; ZigBee; wireless sensor networks; security

## 1. INTRODUCTION

Wireless sensor networks (WSN) represent a massive and rapidly growing technology sector. Market research estimates 1 billion radio frequency integrated circuit (RFIC) devices will be deployed by 2017 [17], the majority of which will be IEEE 802.15.4 [2] and ZigBee [29] standards compliant.

Due to the increasing dependence on these digital radios it is important to understand their stacks from the ground up. In particular, manipulations of PHY- and LNK-frames achievable with commodity means—and other commodity stacks' reactions to them—are of special interest. Overlooked capabilities of commodity hardware leads to nasty surprises for the defenders of a deployed base previously considered reasonably secure. For example, discovery of methods to inject arbitrary crafted 802.11 LNK-frames with commodity 802.11 hardware around 2005 led to the embarrassing "Month of Kernel Bugs" (MoKB) in 2006 that exposed multiple vulnerabilities in Wi-Fi drivers across all operating systems and in many embedded implementations.

We demonstrate that commodity 802.15.4 digital radios are capable of producing PHY-frames that differ in appearance between various 802.15.4 receivers; while being accepted as valid by some receivers, these frames may be rejected by others—depending on the radio chip's make (and, occasionally, firmware). Using this physical-frame-level technique the attacker can craft and broadcast "shaped charges" to covertly communicate with target nodes by constructing a "dialect" of IEEE 802.15.4 PHY-frames intelligible to only

| Symbols: 8 | 2 | 2 | | variable |
|---|---|---|---|---|
| Preamble | SFD | Frame length (7 bits) | Reserved | PSDU |
| SHR | | PHR | | PHY payload |

**Figure 1: An IEEE 802.15.4 standard physical frame.**

these nodes. This allows attackers to bypass WIDS/WIPS systems that utilize different digital radio receivers, as a monitor(s), than that of the network nodes they protect.

The purpose of this work is to expand the state-of-the-art in IEEE 802.15.4 physical-layer manipulation achievable with commodity 802.15.4/ZigBee devices, enabling device identification, targeted attacks, and WIDS/WIPS bypasses. We have built an experimental framework, code-named Isotope, around commodity hardware and open-source software. We have also developed several techniques effective in differentiating between multiple devices' hardware.

The remainder of this paper is organized as follows: Section 2 discusses previous work and provides context for our contributions; Section 3 provides a brief primer on the IEEE 802.15.4 standard and introduces the frame crafting techniques we have developed; Section 4 describes our experimental setup; Section 5 reveals our results; and Section 6 offers concluding remarks and a nod toward future work.

## 2. PREVIOUS WORK

Our work extends previous work on *active fingerprinting* from our lab [6, 10, 12, 26]. It also harkens back to the classic work on evading intrusion detection and prevention systems (IDS/IPS) [16, 23] that exploited differences in network streams reassembly by the attack targets and the IDS/IPS protecting them—which have since been generalized as *parser differential* attacks [19, 25].

Our work is similar to independently created results by Ramsey, Mullins, and Kulesza [20, 24]. They showed shortening the preambles made the packets non-receivable to some sniffers. We present such a result, in addition to other observations at the 802.15.4 PHY-layer, but using only commodity hardware and open-source software.

### 2.1 Digital Radio Fingerprinting

Fingerprinting endeavors to exploit unique characteristics in the digital circuitry or firmware implementation of a device. Slight imperfections in the radio circuitry, introduced during the manufacturing process, might be detectable during radio transmissions. In addition, bugs or deviations from the standard in the firmware implementation may also be observable during radio operation and can act as a fingerprint. For a more detailed understanding, Danev, Zanetti, and Capkun provide a thorough survey of the state-of-the-art in wireless fingerprinting [11].

In passive fingerprinting methods, a third party attempts to unobtrusively sniff the communications channel [13, 14, 18]. Unique signals or transmission timing may be considered a fingerprint. Naturally, this approach is often lossy or error prone due to the potential lack of traffic over the wire or interference from the multiple layers of the radio stack [23]. Alternatively, active techniques attempt to interact with a device, often by sending specially crafted requests, in hopes of eliciting a response [6, 10]. Both the data contained in the response and the response itself can be considered a fingerprint.

*Applications of Fingerprinting.* Attackers have used fingerprinting techniques to find systems known to be vulnerable, see through defensive deceptions such as false bannering or redirecting honeypots [5], and to impersonate trusted nodes on a network. Not surprisingly, as soon as fingerprinting techniques became a part of standard TCP/IP network

reconnaissance an arms race ensued with tools offering functionality to deceive fingerprinting techniques by imitating known signatures. Meanwhile, defenders use fingerprinting techniques to identify nodes on their network, both benign and malignant, and to find vulnerable software, firmware, and hardware combinations. The IEEE 802.15.4 and ZigBee standards offer no exception to this rule. By design, these are commodity technologies (in particular, much more so at their origins than 802.11/Wi-Fi).

## 3. METHODS

In this section, we look at the IEEE 802.15.4 standard and describe the receiver fingerprinting and targeting techniques we have developed.

### 3.1 IEEE 802.15.4 Standard

The IEEE created the 802.15 workgroup for Wireless Personal Area Networks (WPAN) in the early 2000s to establish standards for Layers 1 and 2 (physical and link, respectively). The IEEE 802.15 workgroup defined standards that include 802.15.1, a derivative of Bluetooth intended for general WPANs, and 802.15.4, designed for low-rate WPANs (LR-WPANs). LR-WPANs are attractive for low-power, low-range, low-bandwidth, and low-cost applications of wireless networking, particularly for industrial control and embedded systems.

ZigBee is a Layer 3 (network layer) specification which layers on top of 802.15.4 and is more well-known. While ZigBee is ripe for investigation in many different forms of fingerprinting; this paper focuses on the layer beneath ZigBee—the IEEE 802.15.4 standard.

In the IEEE 802.15.4 standard, the smallest amount of information that can be sent over the air is four bits, or a symbol. The standard defines four types of physical frames: beacon, data, acknowledgement, and command. The standard physical frame layout, for all frames, is shown in Figure 1. A standard frame consists of a synchronization header (SHR), a physical layer (PHY) header (PHR), and a payload within the physical service data unit (PSDU). The physical frames differ in their payload, but all contain a standard SHR and PHR. The SHR comprises an 8-symbol preamble of zeros (0x0) and the start-of-frame delimiter (SFD), which must be 0xA7. This header, as its name implies, serves to synchronize the receiving radio with the transmitting radio so that symbols are correctly pulled out of the signal. The frame length, a 7-bit number representing the number of octets in the physical payload, and a single reserved bit compose the PHR. The payload follows the length and contains all the data for Layer 2 and higher. Each type of physical frame requires a different payload structure.

### 3.2 Crafting Physical Frame Headers

Before introducing the designed methods, it should be noted that many commodity radios cannot craft arbitrary physical frame headers, SHR and PHR. By design, the ra-

| Variable Preamble | SFD | Length | Payload |

(a) Variable preamble length

| 0x0s | 0xFs | SFD | Length | Payload |

(b) Franconian Notch

| Preamble | 0xFs | SFD | Length | Payload |

(c) Franconian Bridge

| Preamble | SFD (bad) | 0xFs | Preamble | SFD | Length | Payload |

(d) Cumberland Gap

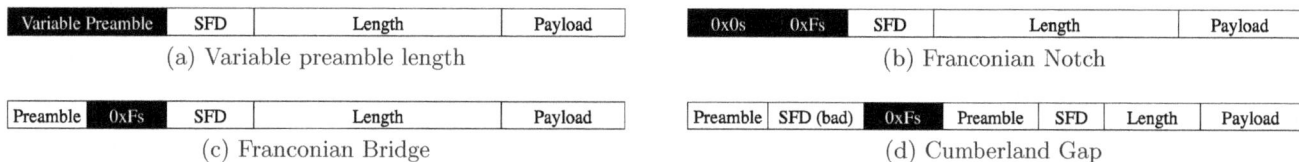

Figure 2: New fingerprinting frames.

dio hardware manages the frame headers to assure proper functionality. In order to fully control a physical frame's contents, we make use of our good neighbor Travis Goodspeed, et al's packets-in-packets (PIP) frame-injection technique [15].

The 802.15.4 standard requires the SFD to be 0xA7. If an 802.15.4-compliant radio receives an SFD of any other value, the receiving radio resets itself into a fresh receiving state, listening again for a new SHR; however, some radios permit us to specify the SFD value via a register, which allows us to transmit frames with non-compliant SFDs. Any receivers expecting the standard SFD will reset themselves after seeing the unexpected symbols. The transmitting radio, however, will continue to send the remainder of the frame. If the remainder of the frame contains a standard SHR the receiver will think it is receiving a fresh packet. In this way, we are able to transmit a non-standard physical frame that contains a fully-standard physical frame, or a packet in a packet.

## 3.3 Fingerprinting Techniques

Here we will describe four new techniques for fingerprinting IEEE 802.15.4 stacks, with a focus on the physical layer. Each technique is active—a stimulus frame with a non-standard physical-layer header is transmitted and the target's response or lack thereof is recorded. Our hypothesis is that we can distinguish different radio chipsets by which type of stimulus packets they are willing to receive. To determine whether a given chipset has indeed received a packet, we send a frame whose payload triggers a response by a higher layer—such as beacon request. If we receive the correct response to our stimulus, we assume that our crafted frame was received.

*A Variable Preamble Length.* While the IEEE 802.15.4 standard defines the preamble length to be eight zero (0x0) symbols some radios might accept frames with fewer than the stated number, while others do not. Figure 2a shows the general layout of a frame generated to test a target's response to non-standard preambles. The aim of this technique is to measure the number of zero symbols, before the SFD, a chipset requires in order to accept a frame.

*A Franconian Notch.* According to the IEEE 802.15.4 specification, a preamble field should contain eight zero (0x0) symbols. However, some chipsets may accept non-standard preambles. For example, the CC2420 [28] can be programmed to ignore some of the least significant symbols in the synchronization header to help it be more resilient to noise. Figure 2b shows the physical frame crafted for the Franconian Notch[1] method. Here we modulate each subsequent

symbol of the standard preamble from 0x0 to 0xF , going from all zeros (0x0s) to six 0xF symbols (thus introducing a "notch"). The aim of this technique is to measure the number of invalid preamble symbols a radio is willing to accept.

*A Franconian Bridge.* Inspired by the previous approaches, the Franconian Bridge method "spans the gap" between the variable preamble length and Franconian Notch techniques. As shown in Figure 2c, the Franconian Bridge investigates how a target responds to having a varying number of 0xF symbols placed between the fully-standard preamble and the SFD. Technically, this will evaluate a radio's behavior in the presence of a seemingly non-standard SFD.

*A Cumberland Gap.* The Cumberland Gap[2] technique, as seen in Figure 2d, measures how a target behaves with respect to receiving a standard frame immediately after receiving a valid preamble and an invalid SFD, thus introducing a "gap" between a bad frame and a good frame.

It is important to remember that when radios are listening for data, they read whatever they find into a symbol. Therefore, it is quite common for a radio to be prepared to accept a frame when it is merely listening to interference and reading garbage as symbols. There are a few discrete states that a radio state machine has to go through when finding an SFD. In this method, we intentionally make the SFD very close to the standard to nudge the receiver as close as possible to the state in which it receives a full frame without outright telling it to take the remainder of the frame. When the incorrect SFD arrives, the chip goes back to listening for a preamble—we seek to measure the timing of this behavior. The fewer symbols that we can inject and still get a response may imply a faster turn-over time, and might also signify a fingerprint.

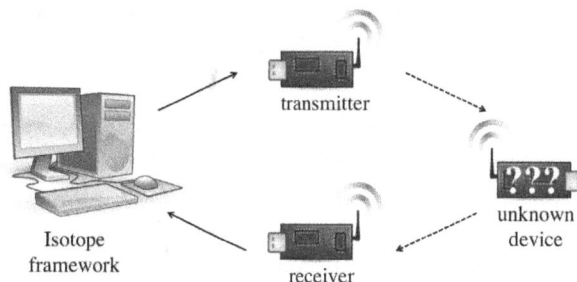

Figure 3: The fingerprinting testbed.

---

[1] The Franconian Notch is a mountain pass through the White Mountains of New Hampshire.

[2] The Cumberland Gap is a mountain pass through the Appalachian Mountains between Tennessee, Kentucky, and Virginia.

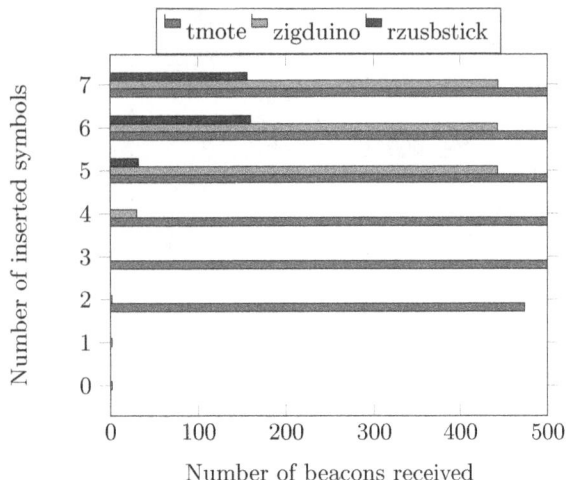

**Figure 4: Variable preamble results.**

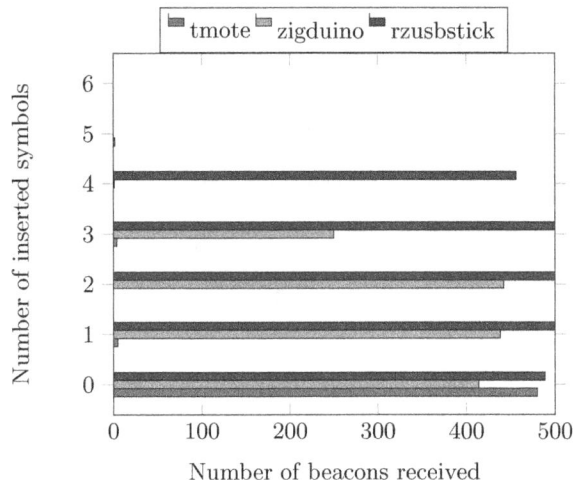

**Figure 5: Franconian Notch results.**

## 4. EXPERIMENTAL SETUP

To test the functionality of our proposed fingerprinting methods, we built a testbed to examine how different IEEE 802.15.4 stacks respond to the types of non-standard physical headers previously described.

### 4.1 Testbed Layout

Our testbed consists of only commodity hardware and open-source software. As shown in Figure 3, two IEEE 802.15.4-conformant radios are connected (via serial over USB) to a single workstation running Isotope, our fingerprinting software. Isotope is a Python framework that utilizes the open source libraries Scapy [4], to build 802.15.4 physical frames, and KillerBee [3], to configure the radios, monitor communications traffic, and inject arbitrary frames. One radio is used solely to transmit crafted frames and the other radio is used to sniff all traffic on a particular channel. The third, unknown, device is setup to listen on a specific channel and respond to beacon requests.

### 4.2 Hardware and Software

We experimented with several different radio devices, namely Zigduinos [21], RZUSBsticks [9], and the popular (but now discontinued) Tmote Sky [22]. Each of these devices contain different on-board radio chips, namely an Atmel AT-mega128RFA1 [8], an Atmel AT86RF230 [7], and a Chipcon CC2420 [28], respectively. Each device was tested with the GoodFET [1] open-source firmware.

## 5. RESULTS

*A variable preamble length.* Figure 4 shows the results of varying the number of preamble symbols. Clearly, the Tmote device responds to the fewest number of preamble symbols. It is possible that this is by design. Remember, the Tmote contains a CC2420 radio chip which allows a programmable number of preamble bits to be accepted. Assuming normal function, it seems obvious that the Tmote is distinguishable from the Zigduino and RZUSBstick.

*A Franconian Notch.* Figure 5 showcases the results of transforming the preamble from 8 zero (0x0) symbols to 6

0xF symbols. Zero (0) on the Y-axis represents a fully standard physical frame, with zero 0xF symbols present. It appears as though the Tmote, previously loose with the standard, is now fully compliant. Since the Tmote previously accepted fewer preamble symbols, this could be an artifact of the radio interpreting the additional 0xF symbols as an invalid SFD, or it could have to do with the RF demodulator's sync circuit being thrown out of state by the additional bit transitions. At the other end of the spectrum, we find the RZUSBstick also stands out by accepting as many as 4 0xF symbols within the preamble. Both the Tmote and RZUSBstick look to be distinguishable from each other and the Zigduino.

*A Franconian Bridge.* The results for the Franconian Bridge method are shown in Figure 6. Recall that this technique inserts garbage between a valid preamble and a valid SFD. Ideally, a radio would interpret the garbage as an invalid SFD. As in the previous method's results, the Tmote strictly adheres to the standard; while, the RZUSBstick accepts up to 5 garbage symbols interposed between the preamble and SFD. We also find the Zigduino occasionally responding to as many as 6 symbols.

*A Cumberland Gap.* The results for the Cumberland Gap method, seen in Figure 7, do not seem encouraging. It appears as though the Tmote has the fastest turnaround time, responding to any number of garbage symbols spliced between a bad SFD and a good packet. Meanwhile, the RZUSBstick maintains the slowest. This may be attributed to fact that the RZ uses an on-board antenna versus the Tmote and Zigduino's external antennas.

## 6. CONCLUSIONS

With the number of wireless sensor networks exploding, a large portion being IEEE 802.15.4 and ZigBee devices, it is essential that we be able to secure and protect these devices and networks for mission-critical systems. Fingerprinting these radio devices is a first step along the path to achieving that security. Device identification, both passive and active, has been used on many other wireless network protocols.

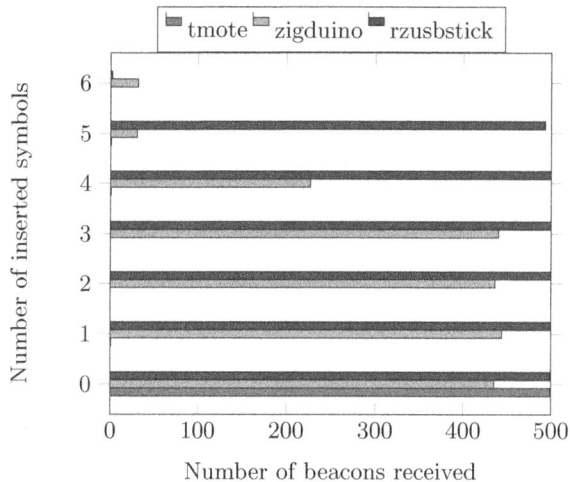

**Figure 6: Franconian Bridge results.**

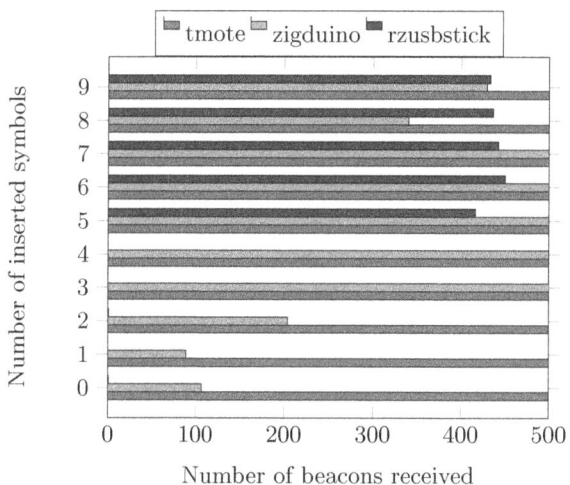

**Figure 7: Cumberland Gap results.**

Our work seeks to apply it to IEEE 802.15.4-conformant radio devices. By accurately identifying different devices, we have another tool, on-top of PKI authentication schemes, for verifying trusted nodes in a network. Similarly, by analyzing how frames and packets make their way through the firmware and radio circuitry, it is possible that we may uncover hidden vulnerabilities and attack vectors.

With preliminary results, it appears that the Tmote devices, with the Chipcon CC2420 radio chipset, and the RZ-USBsticks, with the Atmel AT86RF230 radio chipset, are differentiable (at least between themselves and a Zigduino receiver). The Tmotes clearly respond to very non-standard preamble lengths, whether by design or flaw; however, the same devices seem to be very strict on preamble and SFD content. It appears that the RZUSBsticks accept very non-standard preamble and SFD content. Currently, the CC2420 chips look like the top contender so far to avoid WIDS detection.

## 6.1 Future Work

We feel this work is ripe for research. There are many more possible firmware and hardware combinations to test—

we have really only just begun. Moving forward, it is critical to obtain and test additional devices (both firmware and radio chips). The Tmote devices, our main contender for WIDS evasion, are no longer in production. We have recently begun producing a new device, the ApiMote, based on the CC2420. We suspect the two devices will react similarly; however, those results are forthcoming. It will also be necessary to conduct additional tests in high noise environments and within an isolated RF chamber. Of course, our software framework, Isotope, will also require some additional refinements to make it more robust. Typically, in device identification, a database of fingerprints is used in combination with some sort of machine learning method to analyze and evaluate fingerprint matches. Our current work constitutes only the first stage of identifying possible fingerprints. We anticipate potential vulnerabilites lie within these device-specific dialects, such as possible length overflows. Lastly, we would like to explore the potential for WIDS evasion by these commodity radios [27].

## 7. ACKNOWLEDGEMENTS

This research was supported in part by the National Science Foundation, under Grant Award Number 1016782, and the Department of Energy, under Grant Award Number DE-OE0000097. This report was prepared as an account of work sponsored by an agency of the United States Government. Neither the United States Government nor any agency thereof, nor any of their employees, makes any warranty, express or implied, or assumes any legal liability or responsibility for the accuracy, completeness, or usefulness of any information, apparatus, product, or process disclosed, or represents that its use would not infringe privately owned rights. Reference herein to any specific commercial product, process, or service by trade name, trademark, manufacturer, or otherwise does not necessarily constitute or imply its endorsement, recommendation, or favoring by the United States Government or any agency thereof. The views and opinions of authors expressed herein do not necessarily state or reflect those of the United States Government or any agency thereof.

## 8. REFERENCES

[1] GoodFET. http://goodfet.sourceforge.net.
[2] IEEE Computer Society. http://www.ieee.org.
[3] KillerBee. http://code.google.com/p/killerbee/.
[4] Scapy. http://www.secdev.org/projects/scapy/.
[5] Tiny Honeypot. http://freecode.com/projects/thp.
[6] C. Arackaparambil, S. Bratus, A. Shubina, and D. Kotz. On the reliability of wireless fingerprinting using clock skews. In *Proceedings of the 3rd ACM conference on Wireless network security*, pages 169–174. ACM, 2010.
[7] Atmel Corporation. AT86RF230 datasheet. http://www.atmel.com/Images/doc5131.pdf.
[8] Atmel Corporation. ATmega128RFA1 datasheet. http://www.atmel.com/Images/doc8266.pdf.
[9] Atmel Corporation. RZUSBstick. http://www.atmel.com/tools/RZUSBSTICK.aspx.
[10] S. Bratus, C. Cornelius, D. Kotz, and D. Peebles. Active behavioral fingerprinting of wireless devices. In *Proceedings of the first ACM conference on Wireless network security*, pages 56–61. ACM, 2008.

[11] B. Danev, D. Zanetti, and S. Capkun. On physical-layer identification of wireless devices. *ACM Computing Surveys (CSUR)*, 45(1):6, 2012.

[12] D. D. Dowd. *Isotope: Active Behavioral Fingerprinting of IEEE 802.15.4 Devices.* Senior honors thesis, Dartmouth College, Computer Science, August 2012.

[13] J. P. Ellch. Fingerprinting 802.11 devices. Master's thesis, Naval Postgraduate School, 2006.

[14] J. Franklin, D. McCoy, P. Tabriz, V. Neagoe, J. V. Randwyk, and D. Sicker. Passive data link layer 802.11 wireless device driver fingerprinting. In *Proceedings of the 15th USENIX Security Symposium*, pages 167–178, 2006.

[15] T. Goodspeed, S. Bratus, R. Melgares, R. Shapiro, and R. Speers. Packets in Packets: Orson Welles' In-Band Signaling Attacks for Modern Radios. In *5th USENIX Workshop on Offensive Technologies (WOOT)*, pages 54–61, August 2011.

[16] M. Handley, V. Paxson, and C. Kreibich. Network Intrusion Detection: Evasion, Traffic Normalization, and End-to-End Protocol Semantics. In *Proceedings of the USENIX Security Conference*, 2001.

[17] M. Hatler, D. Gurganious, and C. Chi. 802.15.4 & ZigBee: Expanding markets, growing threats. Technical report, A Market Dynamics report (9th edition), 2012.

[18] S. Jana and S. K. Kasera. On fast and accurate detection of unauthorized wireless access points using clock skews. *Mobile Computing, IEEE Transactions on*, 9(3):449–462, 2010.

[19] D. Kaminsky, L. Sassaman, and M. Patterson. PKI Layer Cake: New Collision Attacks Against The Global X.509 CA Infrastructure. Black Hat USA, August 2009.

[20] N. Kulesza, B. W. P. Ramsey, and B. E. Mullins. Wireless intrusion detection through preamble manipulation. In *Proceedings of the 9th Int'l Conf on Cyber Warfare and Security*, pages 132–139, 2014.

[21] Logos Electromechanical LLC. Zigduino. http://logos-electro.com/zigduino/.

[22] Moteiv Corporation. Tmote Sky datasheet. http://www.snm.ethz.ch/snmwiki/pub/uploads/Projects/tmote_sky_datasheet.pdf.

[23] T. H. Ptacek and T. N. Newsham. Insertion, evasion, and denial of service: Eluding network intrusion detection. Technical report, Secure Networks Inc, 1998.

[24] B. W. P. Ramsey and B. E. Mullins. In J. Butts and S. Shenoi, editors, *Critical Infrastructure Protection*, IFIP Advances in Information and Communication Technology, pages 63–79. Springer.

[25] L. Sassaman, M. L. Patterson, S. Bratus, and M. E. Locasto. Security Applications of Formal Language Theory. *IEEE Systems Journal*, 7(3), September 2013.

[26] R. Speers. IEEE 802.15.4 Wireless Security: Self-Assessment Frameworks. Technical Report TR2011-687, Dartmouth College, Computer Science, Hanover, NH, June 2011.

[27] R. Speers, J. Vazquez, and S. Bratus. Making (and Breaking) an IEEE 802.15.4 WIDS. In *Troopers*, 2014.

[28] Texas Instruments. CC2420 datasheet. http://www.ti.com/lit/ds/symlink/cc2420.pdf.

[29] Zigbee Alliance. ZigBee. http://www.zigbee.org.

# Violating Privacy Through Walls by Passive Monitoring of Radio Windows

Arijit Banerjee
University of Utah
Salt Lake City, UT, USA
arijit@cs.utah.edu

Dustin Maas
Xandem Technology
Salt Lake City, UT, USA
dustin@xandem.com

Maurizio Bocca
Politecnico di Milano
Milano, Italy
maurizio.bocca@polimi.it

Neal Patwari
University of Utah & Xandem
Technology
Salt Lake City, UT, USA
npatwari@ece.utah.edu

Sneha Kasera
University of Utah
Salt Lake City, UT, USA
kasera@cs.utah.edu

## ABSTRACT

We investigate the ability of an attacker to passively use an otherwise secure wireless network to detect moving people through walls. We call this attack on privacy of people a "monitoring radio windows" (MRW) attack. We design and implement the MRW attack methodology to reliably detect when a person crosses the link lines between the legitimate transmitters and the attack receivers, by using physical layer measurements. We also develop a method to estimate the direction of movement of a person from the sequence of link lines crossed during a short time interval. Additionally, we describe how an attacker may estimate any artificial changes in transmit power (used as a countermeasure), compensate for these power changes using measurements from sufficient number of links, and still detect line crossings. We implement our methodology on WiFi and ZigBee nodes and experimentally evaluate the MRW attack by passively monitoring human movements through external walls in two real-world settings. We find that achieve close to 100% accuracy in detecting line crossings and determining direction of motion, even through reinforced concrete walls.

## Categories and Subject Descriptors

C.2 [**Computer-Communication Networks**]: Miscellaneous

## Keywords

Radio Window; WiFi; Signal strength; Line Crossing

## 1. INTRODUCTION

We investigate an attack to the privacy of the people moving in an area covered by a wireless network. People moving

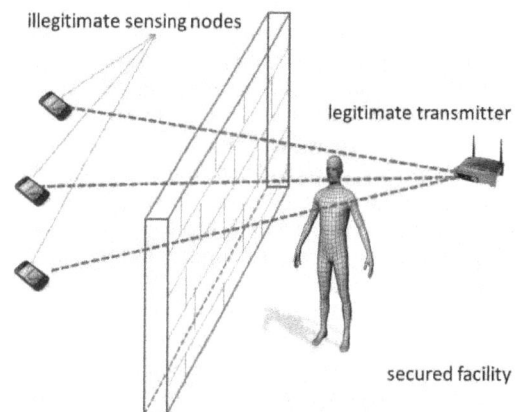

Figure 1: Monitoring Radio Windows (MRW) attack example.

in an area covered by one or more wireless networks affect the way radio signals propagate. We demonstrate that the presence, location and direction of movement of people not carrying any wireless device can be "eavesdropped" by using the channel information of wireless links artificially created by an attacker by deploying sensing devices or *receivers* that can passively "hear" *transmitters* such as WiFi access points (APs), composing the legitimate wireless network. Radio signals from transmitters passing through non-metal external walls are analogous to light from light bulbs passing through glass windows in that either can be used to "see" where building occupants are moving from outside of the building. Hence, we call this attack on privacy of people an "monitoring radio windows" (MRW) attack.

Consider a building where security is important (e.g., an embassy) with a concrete exterior wall. One or more wireless networks may have been set up in this building to transfer different types of data, including voice and video. We can expect these networks to implement advanced data security protocols to prevent eavesdropping of data. However, an attacker can still deploy receivers outside the wall of the building to passively measure different parameters of the received radio signals. By measuring the channel state information (CSI) or received signal strength (RSS), for example, of the links from the transmitters inside the building to the receivers deployed, the attacker can monitor the movements of people and objects inside the building in the area behind the wall in Figure 1. The information about people's movements can be put to malicious use including planning a physical attack on the personnel inside the building.

In this paper, we design and implement the MRW attack methodology for through wall people localization. Our methodology relies on reliably detecting when people cross the link lines between the legitimate transmitters and the attack receivers. We first develop a majority-vote based detection algorithm that reliably detects line of sight (LOS) crossing between the legitimate transmitter and the attack receivers by comparing short-term variances in link channel information with their long-term counterparts. We also develop a method to estimate the direction of movement of a person from the sequence of link lines crossed during a short time interval. Next, we implement our methodology on WiFi and ZigBee nodes and experimentally evaluate the MRW attack by monitoring people's movements through walls in two real-world settings – a hallway of a university building separated from the outside by a one-foot thick concrete wall, and a residential house. When we use two WiFi 802.11n nodes with normal antenna separation, or two groups of ZigBee nodes as attack receivers, we find that our methods achieve close to 100% accuracy in detecting line crossings and the direction of movement. We also find that our methods achieve 90 – 100% accuracy when we use a single 802.11n attack receiver. We note that our goal in this paper is not to precisely estimate the location of a moving person but rather, only detect line crossings and determine the direction of movement through walls. This coarse-granular location information violates the person's privacy and can be used by an attacker.

To protect the privacy of the location information from the MRW attack, the owner of the legitimate network may choose to implement a countermeasure in which the transmitters vary their transmit power during successive transmissions. The artificial transmit power changes can be either random or follow a pre-defined profile replicating the typical channel variations introduced when a person crosses a link line. This countermeasure is expected to introduce additional variability in the received signal measured by the attack receivers, which can be wrongly interpreted by the attacker as caused by moving people or objects crossing the link lines. In this paper, we demonstrate that an attacker who can measure a sufficient number of links can accurately estimate the artificial transmit power change, compensate for it, and ultimately locate people and monitor their movements. We base our compensation strategy on the following intuition: an artificial transmit power change at a transmitter will impact the measurements at all attack receivers with approximately the same magnitude of change, whereas genuine power changes due to human movement are likely to impact receivers each with a different magnitude. This intuition also suggests that protecting against radio window attacks is a very hard problem because any change at the source of transmission can be possibly compensated for by correlating measurements across multiple attack receivers.

The idea of using radio signals through walls for obtaining location information is not new and has been used in existing efforts including Radio Tomographic Imaging (RTI) [25],

WiVi [2], and WiTrack [1], among others. However, the existing literature does not demonstrate that an attacker can obtain location information 1) without transmitting (and thus not subject to jamming or source localization); and 2) through thick external walls (such as reinforced concrete) and in large buildings. Wilson et al. developed RTI [25] to track human movement through walls by deploying dozens of transceivers throughout or on many sides of a room in a residential home. However, RTI requires active transmission from all the deployed nodes, and, hence it can be detected by source localization and/or countered by jamming. Note that for solid external walls, penetration loss can be very high, e.g., about 20 dB/ft through concrete at 2.4 GHz [21]. Since the signal must penetrate external walls twice, once to enter and once to exit the building, transmit power must be very high in order to achieve useful range.

Adib et al. [2] developed WiVi to track moving humans through walls inside a closed room using WiFi signals. In a follow up work, Adib et al. [1] developed a 3-D through-wall motion tracking system, WiTrack, that can be used to track the 3D location of a moving person inside a room, and to detect falls and simple gestures. Though efficient, these methods also depend on active probing requiring custom hardware to send WiFi signals through a barrier (e.g., a wall) and measure the way it reflects back from objects on the other side. Like RTI, these methods are vulnerable to detection and jamming, and must penetrate an external wall twice. Note that WiTrack was demonstrated through drywall [1], which has a 0.5 dB penetration loss at 2.4 GHz [26]. Our work is stealthier in that purely *passive* receivers are deployed by an attacker to measure signals from the transmitters already deployed in existing infrastructure. The attack receivers do not transmit any signal or interfere with the existing transmissions in any way - hence they can not be detected using source localization and are immune to jamming. Furthermore, the active signal transmission from outside the wall, forces WiVi and WiTrack to perform a costly "nulling" procedure to counteract the flash effect - the strong reflection from the wall that overshadows signals reflected back from inside the room. We rely only on the transmitted signal from the existing infrastructure inside the facility to detect a person's movement, hence the flash effect does not apply. We can perform our location detection with simpler algorithms and off the shelf hardware. Unlike WiVi and WiTrack, our method enables the attacker to see through dense wall material, including 12 inch thick reinforced concrete walls. In a related work that is not directly concerned with location privacy [18], Pu et al. showed that Doppler shifts resulting from multipath distortions, due to reflections of wireless signals from a human body, can be used to identify human gestures. However, their work relies on classification of gestures based on extensive learning. One must actively perform a startup sequence of gestures in the direction of the wireless receiver(s) to get into the control system before sending the real gesture commands. Our research does not consider human gestures and hence does not require an extensive learning phase.

The remainder of the paper is organized as follows. Section 2 describes the adversary model, while in Section 3 we introduce the methods developed. Experimental setup and results are presented in Sections 4 and 5, respectively. Additional existing research in the area of location privacy attacks is discussed in Section 6. Conclusions are given in Section 7.

## 2. ADVERSARY MODEL

We make the following assumptions about the attacker (In this paper, we use the term attacker for anyone, whether malicious or genuine, who is trying to detect human movement):

- The attacker is able to deploy multiple wireless sensing devices within the transmission range of the legitimate transmitter(s) outside the area being monitored. The attacker is able to measure the physical layer information (RSS and/or CSI) of the links between the transmitter(s) and the attack receivers.

- The attacker does not have access to the content of the packets transmitted by the legitimate network nodes.

- The attacker does not deploy any transmitters, nor does it have any control over the legitimate transmitters. However, it requires the legitimate transmitters to transmit packets frequently to allow it perform the line crossing detections.

- The attacker does not make any assumption regarding the transmit power profile of the transmitters.

- The attacker nodes do not associate or interfere in any manner with the transmissions of the legitimate transmitter(s).

- The attacker may not know the precise location of the transmitters, however, we do assume that the transmitter is located well inside the perimeters of buildings for network coverage.

- The attacker may deploy the MRW attack when it is dark to minimize the chance of getting detected.

## 3. METHODOLOGY

In this section, we first develop a methodology to detect line crossings of a single person based on a majority vote for WiFi 802.11n receivers. We also develop a method that uses a sequence of line crossings to determine the direction of the movement. Next, we present our approaches for estimating transmit power change and its compensation, when the transmit power is artificially changed by the owner of the wireless transmitters, inside a secure building, with the hope of preserving location privacy. Last, we show how we adapt our methodology for IEEE 802.15.4 ZigBee attack receivers.

### 3.1 Line Crossing Detection

Many modern WiFi networks use the 802.11n standard, in which transceivers are equipped with multiple antennas in order to leverage the spatial diversity of the wireless channel. While these multiple-input multiple-output (MIMO) systems provide high data rates, they also provide a rich source of channel information to an adversary interested in localizing people inside a building.

The 802.11n wireless standard uses the well-known orthogonal frequency-division multiplexing (OFDM) modulation scheme, which encodes and transmits data across multiple subcarriers for each transmitter-receiver antenna pair.

When an 802.11n receiver receives a packet, it estimates the effect of the wireless channel on each MIMO OFDM subcarrier for the purpose of channel equalization. Since this channel state information (CSI), represented as a complex gain for each subcarrier, is measured during the unencrypted preamble of each WiFi packet, an adversary without legitimate access to data on the network can still measure the CSI for every packet.

We apply a windowed variance method for detecting abrupt changes in the CSI for a WiFi link. Let $H_{j,k}(n)$ be the magnitude of the signal strength for the $j$th transmitter-receiver antenna pair and the $k$th OFDM subcarrier for the $n$th packet. We define the windowed variance measurement at packet $n$ as follows. Let

$$v_{j,k}^w(n) = \frac{1}{w-1} \sum_{i=n-w+1}^{n} (H_{j,k}(i) - \bar{H}_{j,k}^w)^2, \qquad (1)$$

where, $w$ is the number of previous CSI samples in the window and $\bar{H}_{j,k}^w(n)$ is the average signal strength for the $j$th transmitter-receiver antenna pair computed over $w$.

We define the subcarrier-average variance and standard deviation for packet $n$ for a given antenna pair $j$ as

$$V_j^w(n) = \frac{1}{N} \sum_k v_{j,k}^w(n), S_j^w(n) = \frac{1}{N} \sum_k \sqrt{v_{j,k}^w(n)}. \qquad (2)$$

where $N$ is the number of subcarriers. We track both $V_j^w(n)$ and $S_j^w(n)$ over a short-term time window $w_s$, and a long-term time window $w_l$, and detect a line crossing when

$$\sum_{n \in D} V_j^{w_s}(n) - V_j^{w_l}(n) > \gamma(n), \qquad (3)$$

where $D$ is the most recent contiguous set of packets for which $V_j^{w_s}(n) - V_j^{w_l}(n) > 0$ and the threshold $\gamma(n)$ is defined as

$$\gamma(n) = V_j^{w_l}(n) + CS_j^{w_l}(n). \qquad (4)$$

$\gamma(n)$ determines the sensitivity of the detection system, smaller values of $\gamma(n)$ will ensure low missed detection rate but will increase the probability of false alarms. On the other hand, larger values of $\gamma(n)$ will lower false alarm rates at the expense of higher missed detection rates. The constant $C$ is included to allow the user to adjust the trade-off between false alarms and missed detections.

To improve robustness, in the case where there are more than two antenna pairs, we take the majority vote between antenna pairs over the short-term window to decide if a line crossing has occurred. More specifically, when a receiver antenna detects a line crossing, we count the line crossing detections for all the receiver antennas over the short-term window, $w_s$. For a $3 \times 3$ MIMO transmitter and receiver, this would mean computing a majority vote over nine measurements. When the majority of the receiver antennas detect a line crossing within $w_s$, we infer that a person has crossed the link line between the transmitter and the receiver. We will show that this majority vote method improves the performance of our detector by decreasing false alarms and missed detections.

We note that our window-based variance method differs from the method presented in [19, 28]. In [19, 28], Youssef et al. compare recent window-based variance measurements of RSSI at multiple WiFi links to measurements made during a static calibration period when nobody is moving in the area of interest. If a certain number of WiFi links within the area of interest detect motion within a certain time interval, a motion event is detected in the area of interest. Our attacker does not know if and/or when people are moving inside of the building, and therefore cannot create calibration measurements based on a static environment. Instead, we compare a short-term window variance to a long-term windowed variance. The long-term window allows us to capture the behavior of the wireless links when the majority of measurements are likely made while there is nobody crossing the link line. Additionally, in the case of 802.11n, we exploit the effect that line crossings have on each OFDM subcarrier and MIMO antenna pair.

## 3.2 Determining Direction of Motion

If the adversary measures the CSI at multiple receivers, or if a single receiver includes multiple antennas as is the case with 802.11n, it is also possible to infer the direction that a person is walking when line crossings are detected. The direction of motion is inferred from the time differences between the line crossing detections at each receiver, in the case of multiple receivers, or at each transmitter-receiver antenna pair, when the receivers include multiple antennas.

Consider the scenario where the attacker arranges the MIMO antenna array of an 802.11n receiver such that the antennas are roughly parallel to a hallway as shown in Figure 2(a). The spatial order of the antennas with reference to the hallway is known, and each transmitter-receiver antenna is given an index according to its spatial order. Based on the adversary model assumption that a transmitter is located well inside the perimeter, the attacker, even without knowing the precise location of the transmitter or the arrangement of its antennas, may treat the antennas of the wireless transmitter as if they are co-located and still achieve reliable results.

In the single WiFi receiver case, if a link crossing is detected by majority vote for a given short-term window, we find the line that best fits the set of points $\{(d_j, n_j) : j \in P\}$, where $d_j$ is the spatial index of antenna pair $j$ representing it's location relative to the other links, $n_j$ is the packet index indicating when a detection occurred at antenna pair $j$ according to (3), and $P$ is the set of antenna pairs ending at the WiFi receiver which detected a line crossing during the short-term window. The sign of the slope of this line indicates the direction of motion. Figure 2 shows an example which uses CSI measurements from three antennas at the WiFi transmitter and three antennas at WiFi RX1 (9 antenna pairs). In the case of two single-input single-output (SISO) WiFi receivers, a similar method may be applied, but the two spatial and packet indexes directly determine the line and its slope.

## 3.3 Compensation of Transmit Power Change

In this subsection, we propose a methodology to detect artificial transmit power changes (if any) and compensate for the same. The signal strength for the $j$th transmitter-receiver antenna pair and the $k$th OFDM subcarrier for packet $n$ is given by

$$H_{j,k}(n) = T_x(n) + G_t + G_r - L_{j,k}(n) + \Psi_{j,k}(n), \quad (5)$$

where $T_x(n)$ is the transmit power of the transmitter for packet $n$, $G_t$ and $G_r$ are the transmitter and receiver an-

tenna gains, respectively, $L_{j,k}(n)$ is the path loss, and $\Psi_{j,k}(i)$ is a noise term.

The attacker does not know the transmit power or antenna gains, so she relies on the difference between the signal strength for the packet $n$ and the reference packet ($n = 0$) as follows.

$$h_{j,k}(n) \triangleq H_{j,k}(n) - H_{j,k}(0). \quad (6)$$

From (5), we see that

$$h_{j,k}(n) = t_x(n) - l_{j,k}(n) + \psi_{j,k}(n), \quad (7)$$

where $t_x(n) = T_x(n) - T_x(0)$, $l_{j,k}(n) = L_{j,k}(n) - L_{j,k}(0)$, and $\psi_{j,k}(n) = \Psi_{j,k}(n) - \Psi_{j,k}(0)$.

In absense of any transmit power changes, $h_{j,k}(n)$ is dominated by path loss changes caused when a person crosses the link and abrupt variation in $h_{j,k}(n)$ can be used to detect line crossings. However, any transmit power change (introduced artificially) at the transmitter dominates the $h_{j,k}(n)$ term and masks the effect of channel variation caused by human movement. A transmitter could thus presumably preserve location privacy by changing its transmit power frequently to introduce artifical signal strength variations.

We now propose a method that a smart attacker can use to estimate and remove the artificial power changes and accurately detect line crossings. In our method, the attacker estimates the artificial transmit power change amplitude by correlating measurements across all antenna pairs and all subcarriers, and removes the effect of transmit power changes from the received signal strength measurements. We propose to use the median of $h_{k,j}(n)$ for all available transmitter-receiver antenna pairs and corresponding subcarriers, as an estimator of the artificial transmit power change, as shown in the equation below:

$$\hat{t}_x(n) = \text{median} \{h_{j,k}(n) \forall j, k\}. \quad (8)$$

Our choice of this estimator is based on the following observations. First, we observe that $t_x(n)$ appears in the equation for $h_{k,j}(n)$ for all $j$ and $k$. This is because, any change in transmit power affects measurements across all transmitter-receiver antenna pairs and corresponding subcarriers simultaneously. We also know that the change in the path loss $l_{j,k}$ is just as likely to be positive as negative. Furthermore, any change due to human movement will not affect all the links simultaneously.

In the absence of an artificial transmit power change, $\hat{t}_x(n)$ is likely to be close to zero, i.e., our estimator does not require us to detect whether or not there is an artificial transmit power change for packet $n$.

The compensated signal strength for packet $n$, which we denote $\hat{H}_{j,k}(n)$, is given by

$$\hat{H}_{j,k}(n) = H_{j,k}(n) - \hat{t}_x(n). \quad (9)$$

Although the reference packet was sent with unknown transmit power $T_x(0)$, for $n > 0$, we consider $T_x(n)$ to be the relative dB shift in transmit power compared to $T_x(0)$. $\hat{H}_{j,k}(n)$ essentially, is an estimate of the subcarrier signal strength if there were no transmit power changes between the reference packet and packet $n$.

It is clear that, any error in the estimation of the transmit power changes amplitude will introduce additional noise in the measurements. However, the dynamics of the signal are still preserved and an attacker can use any variation in the

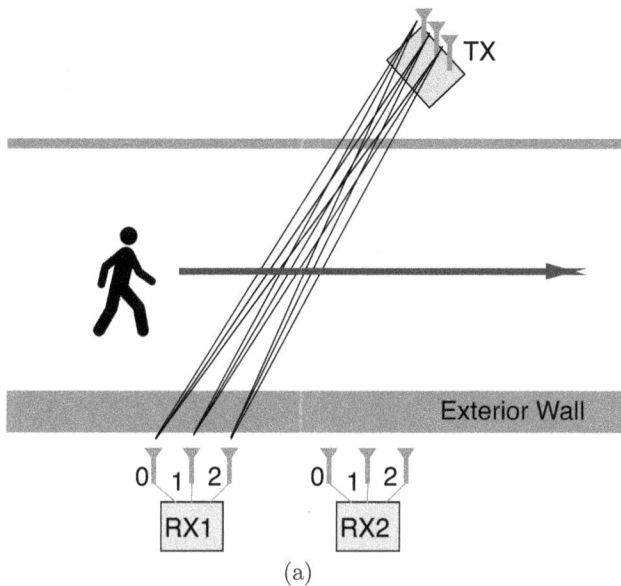

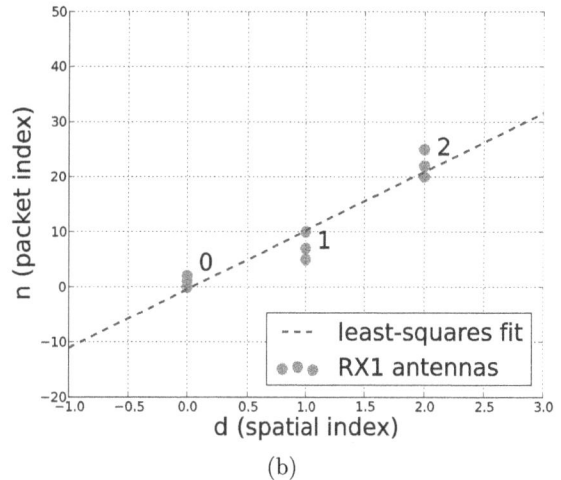

Figure 2: (a) The MIMO antenna array used for line crossing detection.(b) Direction of motion is determined by slope of the line fitted to the points created by the spatial indexes of the antennas and the packet indexes.

signal over a short time period in order to notice motion of a person near the link line.

### 3.4 ZigBee Networks

The methodologies described above are also applicable for IEEE 802.15.4 ZigBee nodes. However, the ZigBee nodes are generally equipped with a single antenna, so the MIMO setup is not available. Moreover, ZigBee nodes do not use OFDM for communication, so we use channel information from a single frequency channel (instead of averaging across all subcarriers as in the case of OFDM) to evaluate our methodologies. Furthermore, there is no tool to get the complete CSI at the receiver. Instead, we rely on the RSS value obtained from the receiver hardware. Thus, in the case of ZigBee we set $H_{j,k}(n)$ to the RSS value measured in decibel units for the $j$th transmitter-receiver antenna pair for packet $n$, also $k = 1, \forall j$ as we have measurements from a single channel only.

In order to create spatial diversity we use three closely located ZigBee receivers together to form a group as described in Section 4. We detect line crossings by applying our majority vote approach on the three links formed between the transmitter and the three receivers in the group. We detect direction of motion using two groups of receivers and observing sequence of groups crossed over a short time window. We estimate and compensate for artificial transmit power changes (if any) by applying the methods described in Section 3.3, and utilizing the fact that any change in transmit power affects all receivers simultaneously across all groups.

### 4. EXPERIMENTS

In this section, we describe the experimental setup. Section 4.1 describes the tools we use to measure the wireless channel, Section 4.2 describes the transmit power changes we apply, and Section 4.3 describes two real-world experimental deployments.

### 4.1 Tool Description

We use the following tools to measure the wireless channel and detect line crossings.

*WiFi:* We use laptops with Intel 5300 NICs that have three-antenna MIMO 802.11n radios. We use the CSI Tool [9], that has been built for these radios, to get channel state information from the WiFi transmitter. The CSI tool extracts 802.11n channel state information for 30 subcarrier at each antenna pair. Since we use three antennas at each node for communication, for each transmitter-receiver pair, we have $3 \times 3 = 9$ links each with 30 subcarrier groups. We use two kinds of antenna separations - in the normal case (WiFi_NORM), we place the antennas 6 cm apart, in the other case (WiFi_SEP), we use a larger antenna separation of 30 cm. The increased separation is accomplished by connecting the antennas to the Intel 5300 NIC with standard RF cables that are long enough to provide up to 30 cm separation. We program the transmitter to transmit packets at a rate of 10 Hz which is similar to beacon frame rates of a standard wireless access point. The attack receivers use the CSI Tool to obtain channel state information from the received packets which in turn is used to detect line crossings as described in Section 3.1.

*ZigBee:* For the ZigBee experiments, we use Texas Instrument CC2531 USB dongles [22], which are equipped with low-power, IEEE 802.15.4-compliant radios operating in the 2.4 GHz ISM band. The transmission frequency in this case is 12 Hz. A laptop is used to process the measured data at the attack receivers. There is no tool to obtain the CSI information in the case of ZigBee nodes. Therefore, we use the RSS value (in dBm) measured by the receiver hardware for our analysis, as described in Section 3.4.

### 4.2 Transmit Power Variations

We consider three different settings of transmit power variations for our experiments:

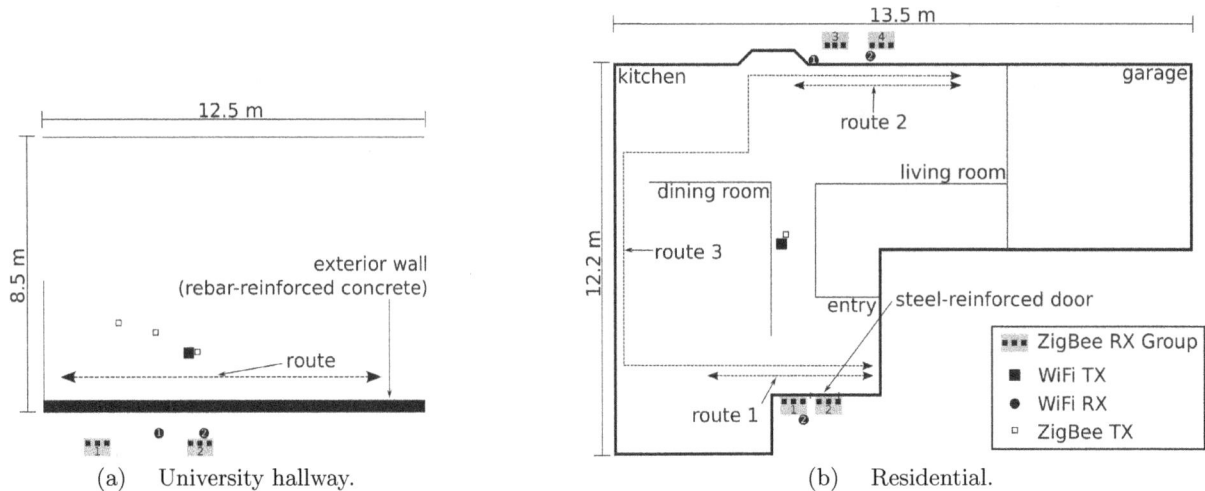

(a)　University hallway.　　　　　　(b)　Residential.

Figure 3: Network layouts. We show maps of the University Hallway and the Residential House and mark the location of the legitimate transmitter(s) and the attack receivers. We also highlight the route(s) followed by the walking person.

*TX_NORMAL:* In this case, the transmitters transmit with fixed transmit power and variations in RSS are due to person movement and noise only.

*TX_LINECROSS:* For finer control, we simulate the effect of transmit power change (for both WiFi and ZigBee) by modifying received data according to a power profile that replicates typical signal attenuation introduced by a person crossing the link line. We randomly select different time points in the measurements to introduce effect of transmit power change.

*TX_RANDOM:* Here, we experimentally implement or simulate the scenario where the transmitter may use a different power level for each transmission by randomly selecting from a predefined set of power levels supported by the hardware. For ZigBee nodes, we program the transmitter(s) to change its transmit power at each transmission by randomly selecting one among four pre-defined transmit power levels, *i.e.*, $+4.5$ dBm, $-1.5$ dBm, $-6$ dBm, and $-10$ dBm. However, we are unable to program the random power changes in WiFi nodes and hence, we simulate these power changes.

While simulating effects of transmit power change we rely on the fact that any change in the transmit power at a time instant is observed across all subcarriers for all transmitter-receiver antenna pairs in case of WiFi and across all receivers in case of ZigBee at the same instant and we change the received signal parameters accordingly. We also add a zero mean Gaussian random variable (with standard deviation 0.67) to each $H_{j,k}(n)$ measurement, in addition to the the transmit power change $t_x(n)$, to account for errors due to environmental noise.

## 4.3 Experimental Deployments

We evaluate our methodologies in two different real world settings.

### 4.3.1 University Hallway

We choose a hallway inside a university building as the area being monitored (Figure 3(a)). The hallway is adjacent to a 30 cm thick and 3.5 m tall rebar-reinforced concrete boundary wall. We note that this type of a wall causes

significant RF attenuation at WiFi frequencies and represents a worst-case scenario among typical exterior walls for our purposes [20]. We place the attack receivers outside the boundary wall parallel to the hallway approximately 1 m away from the wall, at a height of 1.2m.

For the WiFi experiment, we deploy one transmitter inside the building across the hallway, and two attack receivers separated by 3 m outside the concrete wall (Figure 3(a)). Similarly, for the ZigBee network, we deploy one transmitter across the hallway and six receivers outside the boundary wall. The attack receivers are placed in two groups of three nodes each, with the distance between the groups being 3 m (Figure 3(a)). Nodes in the same group are almost 30 cm apart. We perform both TX_NORMAL and TX_RAND experiments with the same ZigBee setup.

During the experiment, a person is walking back and forth along a predefined path (shown as route in Figure 3(a)) along the corridor between the transmitter and the attack receivers. With the help of a metronome, the person walks at a constant speed of 0.5 m/s. We collect over $12,000$ data samples for WiFi and over $20,000$ data samples for ZigBee in this experiment. In our evaluation, we use $w_s = 4$ s (short time window), and $w_l = 40$ s (long term window) (Section 3.1). Note that, $w_s$ must be chosen such that it effectively captures the effect of short term variation in signal strength due to human movement in the vicinity of the link. We observe that, for typical movements these variations last for about 2-6 seconds (Figure 5). We use the mean value for our evaluation (our results do not change significantly if we other values in the 2-6 seconds range). On the other hand, $w_l$ must be large enough to capture the long term behavior of the link, and should not get affected by short term movements. We select a moderately large value for $w_l$ that effectively captures the long term link behavior, and keeps the computation complexity under reasonable bounds so that the detection can be performed in real time.

### 4.3.2 Residential House

In this experiment, we monitor two sides of a residential house (Figure 3(b)) to detect people movement. We perform

74

two sets of experiment with the WiFi nodes. In the first experiment (House 1), we place the WiFi transmitter in a corridor centrally located inside the house and two WiFi receivers with normal antenna separation (WiFi_NORM) in the backyard of the house outside the external wall as shown in the Figure 3(b). The receivers are placed approximately 1 m away from each other, both at a height of 1.2m. For the second experiment (House 2), we use two WiFi receivers with larger antenna separation (WiFi_SEP) and place one of them in the backyard and the other outside the front entrance. The transmitter is placed in the same position as in experiment House 1.

For the ZigBee network, we place two groups of receivers, each group with three nodes, on either side of the house outside the external walls. As shown in Figure 3(b), the ZigBee groups 1 & 2 are placed outside the front entrance, and groups 3 and 4 are placed in the backyard, approximately 1 m away from the walls. Nodes in the same group are almost 30 cm apart while the inter-group distance on either side being at least 1 m. The ZigBee transmitter is placed inside the house co-located with the WiFi transmitter.

During these residential experiments, a person walks inside the house back and forth first near the front entrance of the house (route 1 in the Figure 3(b)), and then in the living room which is near the rear end of the house (shown as route 2 in the Figure 3(b)). Finally, the person makes a few rounds inside the house as shown in route 3 in the Figure 3(b). We collect over 10,000 data samples for each set of ZigBee and WiFi experiments. We video record the line crossings to test the accuracy of our detection method against ground truth. For the residential experiments, we use $w_s = 2$ s (short time window), $w_l = 20$ s (long term window) and $\Delta = 4$ s (Section 3.1). We use smaller window sizes for detection of line crossings as the person walks at a faster speed as compared to the University Hallway experiments.

In our experiments, we place the transmitter on a stand that is approximately 1.2 m high. We understand that transmitters are sometimes placed on a ceiling. However, given that transmitters are typically placed well inside boundary walls for coverage reasons, we can assume that movement behind boundary walls will still result in line of sight crossings between the transmitter and receivers that an attacker deploys at low heights. Furthermore, even if transmitter and receiver are both at ceiling height, there should be changes in CSI observed, as shown by [29]. An attacker may also use existing works on source localization [16, 17] to determine the location of the wireless transmitter, and plan the target area of detection accordingly.

We end this section by noting that while our experiments consider only one wireless transmitter, it is very likely that multiple transmitters will be present in a common home/university setting. However, WiFi transmitters actively avoid interfering with each other due to the 802.11 MAC protocol. Wireless devices, such as WiFi access points, also attempt to operate on different channels for minimizing transmission overlap. Therefore, signals from wireless transmitters can still be received at the attack receivers. Additionally, we can identify the transmitter a packet is coming from using RSS-based or other signatures. We will thoroughly investigate the impact of multiple transmitters on detection accuracy in our future work.

## 5. RESULTS

We evaluate the performance of the MRW attack in terms of false alarm and missed detection rates. False alarm (FA) rates are calculated as the number of line crossings wrongly detected by the system over the number of sample points. Missed detection (MD) rates are calculated as the number of actual line crossings not detected by the system over the total number of actual line crossings.

### 5.1 Detection of Line Crossing

In this section, we present the accuracy of detection of line crossings using the methodology as described in Section 3.1.

#### 5.1.1 University Hallway

Table 1 lists the results obtained in the University Hallway experiment using our majority vote detection. We achieve almost 100% detection rate with few false alarms and missed detections. Using a WiFi 802.11n receiver with normal antenna separation, we get zero false alarms and only 1.92% missed detections. We compare the detected crossing times with those in the recorded video footage of the experiment and find that we can detect the crossing times with an average error of 0.79 s, with minimum and maximum errors of 0.03 s and 2.73 s respectively.

We obtain zero false alarms and missed detections when using a 802.11n WiFi receiver with a large spatial separation between antennas, the mean error in this case being 1.22 s. For ZigBee, using a group of three closely located receivers, we get a 2.66% false alarm rate and a 1.67% missed detection rate in line crossing detection with an average error of 1.22 seconds. We use two groups of receivers and experiment with three different transmitter locations in case of ZigBee. We obtain the above results by averaging over all transmitter location and receiver group pairs.

Note that, while computing the errors as compared to the ground truth, we consider the line connecting the centroid of transmitter antenna locations (or the transmitter location in case of ZigBee) and the centroid of the receiver antenna locations (or the centroid of the receiver locations in the group in case of ZigBee) as the representative link line.

#### 5.1.2 Residential House

We present the detection accuracy of the Residential House experiment in Table 2. We achieve greater than 94% detection accuracy with a 0.043% false alarm rate while using WiFi receivers with normal antenna separation (WiFi_NOR-M). With larger antenna separation (WiFi_SEP) the accuracy is greater than 95% with a 0.005% false alarm rate. The mean error in detection of line crossings is $1.06s$ in case of WiFi_NORM, the same being $0.56s$ for WiFi_SEP.

For ZigBee, we achieve greater than 99% accuracy in detection with a false alarm rate of 0.004% only. The average error in time-of-crossing estimation in this case is 1.63 s. Note that during this experiment, we placed one group of ZigBee nodes (group 2) directly in front of the metal-plated entrance door. The packet reception rates for receivers in this group are much lower than the receivers in the other groups. Also, perhaps due to attenuation through the door, the RSS measurements made by this group are more noisy than those made by the other groups, leading to further degradation in performance. The missed detection rate for this group is almost 30%, about 60 times more than the

Table 1: Detection Accuracy (Hallway).

| Hallway | Accuracy | | Error (sec) | | |
|---|---|---|---|---|---|
| Experiment: | FA% | MD% | Min | Max | Mean |
| WiFi_NORM | 0 | 1.92 | 0.03 | 2.73 | 0.79 |
| WiFi_SEP | 0 | 0 | 0.27 | 2.37 | 1.22 |
| ZigBee | 0 | 1.02 | 0.27 | 2.37 | 1.22 |

Table 2: Detection Accuracy (House).

| House | Accuracy | | Error (sec) | | |
|---|---|---|---|---|---|
| Experiment: | FA% | MD% | Min | Max | Mean |
| WiFi_NORM | 0.043 | 5.70 | 0.29 | 2.78 | 1.06 |
| WiFi_SEP | 0.005 | 4.35 | 0.03 | 1.82 | 0.56 |
| ZigBee | 0.004 | 0.49 | 0.10 | 3.55 | 1.63 |

average missed detection rate of other groups (results presented in Table 2 are averaged over the other three groups). Thus, we conclude that, although an MRW attack can penetrate concrete and brick walls, metallic structures in the line of sight path of the radio signals degrades the detection accuracy significantly.

## 5.2 Determining Direction of Motion

In this section, we present the accuracy we achieve in detecting the direction of motion for each experiment.

### 5.2.1 University Hallway

In the university hallway experiment, the corridor was crossed by a moving person an equal number of times in either direction. We achieve 100% accuracy in detecting direction of movement on either side of the corridor while using two WiFi receivers or two groups of ZigBee nodes using the method described in Section 3.2.

We also achieve an accuracy as high as 90.38% in detecting direction of motion with only a single WiFi 802.11n receiver by increasing the spatial separation of the MIMO antennas. The accuracy with a single WiFi receiver with standard antenna separation is 59.62%, which is slightly better than guessing the direction of motion.

### 5.2.2 Residential House

For the experiment performed in the residential house we again achieve 100% accuracy in detection while using two WiFi receivers with standard antenna separation (experiment House 1) or two groups of ZigBee nodes on either side of the house. Individual detection accuracy of the two WiFi receivers (with standard antenna separation placed on the same side of the house as in experiment House 1) used are 100% (RX1) and 68% (RX2) respectively. Detection accuracy with spatially separated antennas for these receivers (when they are placed on opposite sides of the house as in experiment House 2) are 96% (RX1) and 52.6% (RX2) respectively. These results differ from the University Hallway experiment where we get better accuracy in detecting direction of movement while using large spatial separation between antennas as compared to using normal antenna separation. The degradation in accuracy with antenna separation in Residential House experiment may be due to the fact that during the House 2 experiment, walking speed of the person was about 20% faster as compared to the House 1 experiment with normal antenna separation, hence crossing

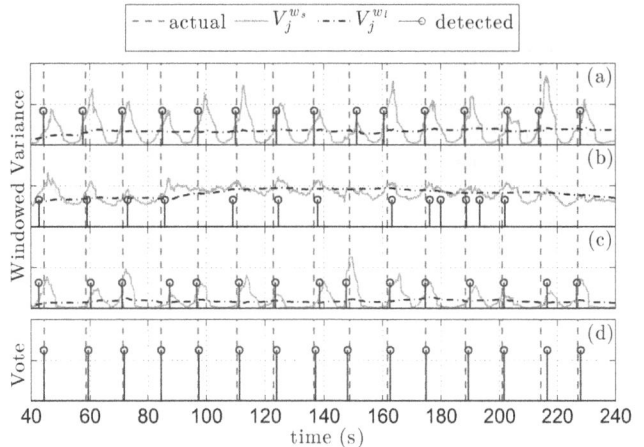

Figure 4: The majority vote over transmitter-receiver antenna pairs reduces false alarms and missed detections. (a),(b), and (c) show the results of the windowed variance based line crossing detection for three antenna pairs using Wifi. In (d), we see that the majority vote eliminates false alarms and missed detections.

times for individual antennas overlapped with each other in some cases.

To summarize, a MRW adversary should use two WiFi receivers or two groups of ZigBee nodes to detect direction of motion accurately. It is possible to achieve high accuracy even with a single WiFi receiver in some cases (e.g. RX1 in experiments House 1 and House 2), however the results depend on the environment and need further investigation.

## 5.3 Advantages of Majority Vote

In this section, we show how our majority vote approach helps overcome inherent uncertainties in wireless links. All wireless links are not equally sensitive to motion occurring in their vicinity and the sensitivity varies with link fade level along with other factors. Since it is not possible for an adversary to know beforehand whether a link is good or bad for detecting LOS crossings, he relies on correlation among multiple closely located links and infers a line crossing only when majority of these closely located links indicates a crossing. In our experiments, $3 \times 3 = 9$ links between the MIMO transmitter-receiver antenna pairs are considered for majority vote in the WiFi case, and groups of 3 single-antenna receivers in the ZigBee case. Figure 4 shows one scenario where our majority vote algorithm helps get rid of some false alarms and missed detections due to one bad WiFi link (for clarity we show three out of the nine links) from the University Hallway experiment. As can be seen the link in Figure 4(b), fails to detect a line crossing that occurs around 100 s, however the other two links (Figure 4(a) & Figure 4(c)) detect the crossing and a majority vote among these three links detects the crossing at that time (Figure 4(d)). Similarly, we see that the link in Figure 4(b) flags a false alarm at 180 s but the other two links do not indicate any crossing. Hence again the majority vote gets rid of the false alarm at time 180 s (Figure 4(d)), thereby improving the overall accuracy of the system.

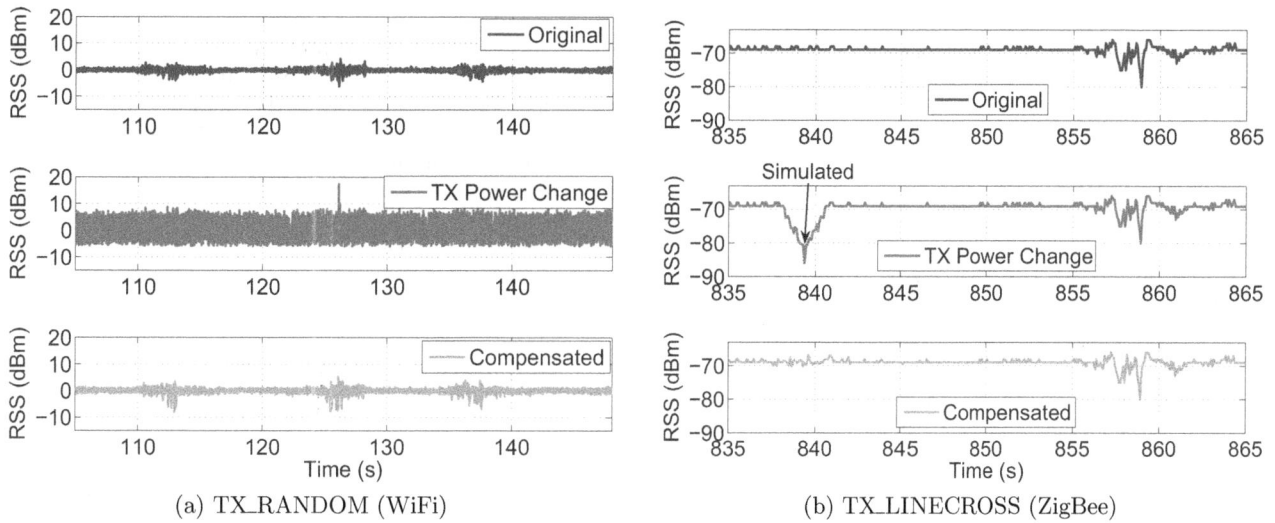

(a) TX_RANDOM (WiFi)                                (b) TX_LINECROSS (ZigBee)

Figure 5: Measured CSI and RSS (top) without and (middle) with TX power change; and (bottom) after compensation.

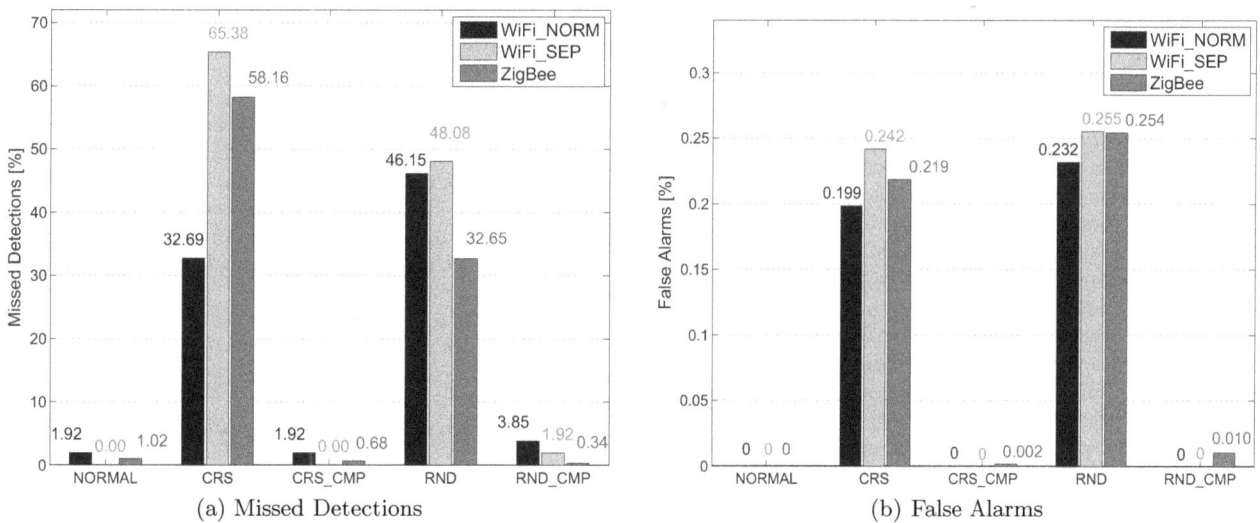

(a) Missed Detections                                (b) False Alarms

Figure 6: Compensation accuracy in the University Hallway Experiment.

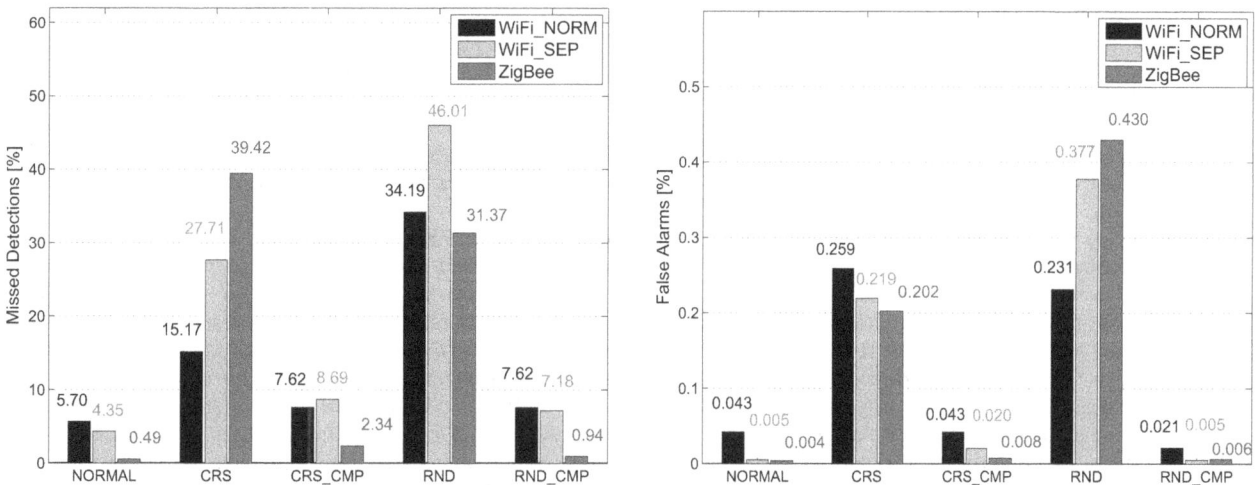

Figure 7: Compensation accuracy in the Residential House Experiment.

77

To summarize - a single wireless link suffices in some cases in detection of line crossings between a transmitter and a receiver, however the results are not always reliable due to inherent uncertainties in link sensitivity to object movements. We can improve accuracy and reliability by correlating detections across multiple co-located links using a majority vote approach.

## 5.4 Compensation for Transmit Power Change

In this section, we show how transmit power changes (random or strategic) affect line crossing detection accuracy and how our compensation method nullifies the effect of such power changes. Figure 5(a) shows the effect of random transmit power changes on line crossing detection for a WiFi link between a single transmitter-receiver antenna pair that is crossed three times by a moving person. The top figure corresponds to the case when there is no transmit power change. This figure clearly shows distinct short time periods of high variance in the CSI corresponding to the times when the person crosses the link. However, transmit power change masks these distinct short term variance regions and renders line crossing detection ineffective as can be seen in the figure in the middle. The bottom figure plots the CSI for the same link after compensating for the transmit power changes as described in Section 3.3. Clearly, our compensation method almost nullifies the masking effect of transmit power changes and the attacker can detect three line crossings (high short term variance region) from the compensated signal. Similarly, Figure 5(b) shows how strategic power changes can be used to simulate link line crossings, and how our compensation method eliminates these artificial variations. The top figure plots the RSS in dBm for a ZigBee link that is crossed during the time interval 856-860 s. The figure in the middle shows one additional line crossing (high variance region) introduced in the link by strategic transmit power changes during time interval 838-841 s. However, as seen from the bottom figure, our compensation method gets rid of the false alarm introduced by strategic power change and we can detect the original line crossing from the compensated signal.

In the Figure 6 we show false alarms and missed detections induced by transmit power changes and the accuracy of our compensation method in the University Hallway experiment. In the figure, NORMAL corresponds to the case when the transmitter transmits with fixed transmit power, CRS is when strategic power changes are introduced in the data using TX_LINECROSS simulation, CRS_CMP corresponds to the results when we apply our compensation method on TX_CRS. Similarly, RND shows results when the transmitter is changing its transmit power randomly with each transmission, while RND_CMP is the corresponding compensation results.

As an example, in the University Hallway experiment, a strategic transmit power change at the WiFi transmitter increases the missed detections rate from 1.92% to 32.69% and the false alarms rate from 0% to 0.199% when using a WiFi receiver with normal antenna separation. However, our compensation method gets rid of all the additional false alarms and missed detections. Similarly, random power changes for the ZigBee experiment increases the false alarms rate from 0% to 0.254%, but our compensation method brings it back to only 0.010%. We obtain similar results in the Residential House experiment (Figure 7). For example, for random power changes at the ZigBee transmitter, the missed de-

tections rate increases to 31.37% from 0.94% and the false alarms rate increases to 0.429% from 0.003% but our compensation method brings down the missed detection and false alarm rates to only 0.94% and 0.006%, respectively.

To summarize our findings, transmit power changes (strategic or random) increase the false alarm and missed detection rates significantly. However, using our compensation method, an attacker can accurately estimate the transmit power change amplitude and compensate for the same to get rid of the adverse effect caused by such changes and, still sense people location and motion with high accuracy.

## 5.5 Detection with Varying Transmission Rate

ZigBee applications in modern facilities use different transmission rates for communication. To understand the effect of lower transmission rates on detection accuracy, we use the data from TX_NORMAL for both the University Hallway and Residential House experiment to simulate lower transmission rates. Note that the original transmission rate is approximately 12 Hz. We simulate three additional transmission rates - 6 Hz, 4 Hz and 2 Hz respectively from the original data. Figure 8 shows the results of our simulation. We find that the overall detection rates decrease with lower transmission rates. For the transmission rate of 6 transmissions/second, accuracy of the detector is over 98% for the University Hallway experiment and over 96% for the Residential House experiment. These results are similar to what we observe for original transmission frequency of 12 Hz. The accuracy is worst for transmission frequency of 2 Hz with the detection rate being as low as 71% for the Residential House experiment. For the transmission rate of 4Hz, the detection rate degrades to 87% in the University Hallway experiment, although it remains greater than 96% for the Residential House experiment. We do not see any noticeable change in the false alarm rates with varying transmission rate.

## 6. ADDITIONAL RELATED WORK

In recent years, device-free localization (DFL), in which people who are not carrying any radio transmitters are located by a static deployed network, has been the subject of intense research. Our MRW attack is significantly different from traditional DFL work in that the MRW attack is practical for large buildings, is stealthy because no transmitters are deployed by the attacker, and is immune from jamming. DFL systems such as the ones in [4, 11–13, 15, 24, 24, 25, 30] require dozens of radio transceivers deployed throughout or on many sides of the target area. Further, through-building DFL systems such as [25, 31] assume the transmitted signal penetrates through two external walls and any internal walls in between, and as such have been tested only in buildings of small (18 - 42 m$^2$) size. In this paper, we show access to one side is sufficient for an MRW attack, and it requires a signal from inside a building to penetrate only one external wall. Other fingerprint-based DFL systems [14, 19, 23, 27] require collection of training data with a person in each possible location in the environment. In our MRW attack, we do not assume that an attacker has prior access to the inside of the building to be able to perform such data collection. Further, to perform DFL, an attacker must deploy some nodes which transmit, exposing them to being detected and located by RF source localization, while an MRW attack is stealthier in that purely passive receivers are deployed by an attacker. Finally, DFL systems' signals could be interfered

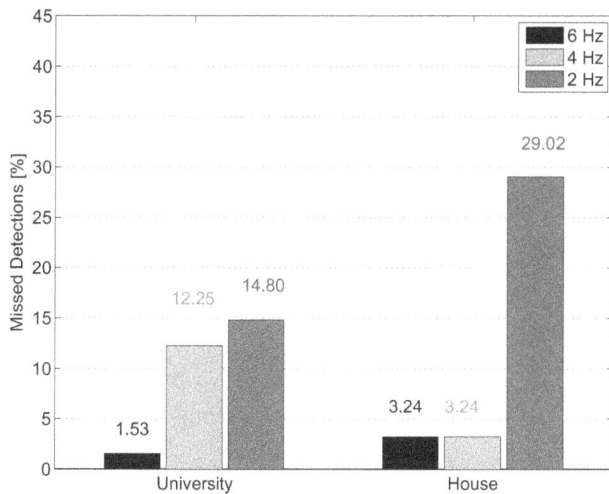

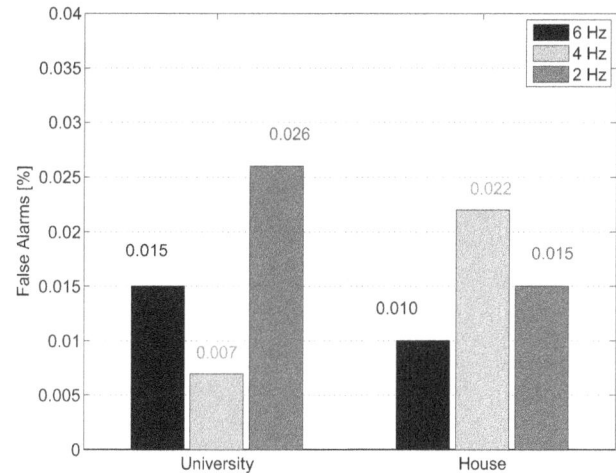

Figure 8: Detection accuracy with varying transmission rates (ZigBee).

with by a powerful jammer. In the method in this paper, any transmitter in the building, including a jammer, could be used as a source for MRW. The work in [5] presents a through-walls passive WiFi radar system. In it, a receiver is situated outside the target building and a Wi-Fi AP placed inside the building and having a narrow-beamwidth directional antenna is used as transmitter. The signal received by the passive radar detector is then used to create a range-Doppler surface and detect a moving target. Our work is complementary to [5], first, because we use different measurements. Doppler information in [5] is used to estimate relative velocity; in our work, received power or CSI is used to infer presence (even when stationary) on the link line. In theory, both could be used to improve localization accuracy. For example, while a person is crossing perpendicular to the link line, the cause no Doppler shift, but our system would detect their direction of motion. Second, we note that the receiver in [5] is a specialized radar receiver with a PC for intensive offline processing. In comparison, our system uses standard transceivers and requires little processing, and thus is suitable for real time monitoring by an adversary with only standard hardware. We demonstrate that, random or pre-defined transmit power change, used as a possible countermeasure, can not protect the privacy of the location of people inside the target area. To the best of our knowledge, no previous work on location privacy can function accurately in presence of purposeful transmit power changes.

Several existing works focusing on location privacy typically assume that the *victims* of the attack are carrying an actively communicating wireless device [3, 6–8, 10]. We focus on obtaining location information where the person being monitored does not actively participate in the detection process.

## 7. CONCLUSION

We investigated the ability of an attacker to surreptitiously use an otherwise secure wireless network to detect a moving person through walls. We designed and implemented an attack methodology, to passively obtain through wall person movement information, that reliably detects when a person crosses the link lines between the legitimate transmitters and the attack receivers by using physical layer measurements. We also developed a method to determine the direction of movement of a person from the sequence of link lines crossed during a short time interval. Additionally, we described how an attacker may estimate any artificial changes in transmit power (used as a countermeasure), compensate for these power changes using measurements from sufficient number of links, and still detect line crossings. We implemented our methodology on WiFi and ZigBee nodes and experimentally evaluated the MRW attack by monitoring people movements through walls in two real-world settings. We found that our methods achieve close to 100% accuracy in detecting line crossings and the direction of movement. The limitation of our proposed methodology is that it works for detecting movement of only a single person at a time. Future work must develop methodology for passively locating multiple people through walls in more dynamic environments.

## Acknowledgments

This material is based upon work supported by the National Science Foundation under Grant Nos. #0748206, #0855261, #1035565, and by the ARL MURI Grant #W911NF-07-0318. The many comments from our shepherd Dr. Di Ma and anonymous reviewers greatly improved the final version of the paper.

## 8. REFERENCES

[1] F. Adib, Z. Kabelac, D. Katabi, and R. C. Miller. 3d tracking via body radio reflections. In *Presented as part of the 11th USENIX Symposium on Networked Systems Design and Implementation (NSDI 14)*, Seattle, WA, 2014. USENIX.

[2] F. Adib and D. Katabi. See through walls with wifi! In *Proceedings of the ACM SIGCOMM 2013 conference on SIGCOMM*, pages 75–86. ACM, 2013.

[3] P. Bahl, V. N. Padmanabhan, and A. Balachandran. Enhancements to the radar user location and tracking system. Technical report, 2000.

[4] X. Chen, A. Edelstein, Y. Li, M. Coates, M. Rabbat, and M. Aidong. Sequential Monte Carlo for simultaneous passive device-free tracking and sensor localization using received signal strength measurements. In *ACM/IEEE Information Processing in Sensor Networks (IPSN)*, April 2011.

[5] K. Chetty, G. Smith, and K. Woodbridge. Through-the-wall sensing of personnel using passive bistatic wifi radar at standoff distances. *Geoscience and Remote Sensing, IEEE Transactions on*, 50(4):1218 –1226, april 2012.

[6] B. Danev, D. Zanetti, and S. Capkun. On physical-layer identification of wireless devices. *ACM Computer Survey*, 45(1):6:1–6:29, 2012.

[7] B. Greenstein, R. Gummadi, J. Pang, M. Y. Chen, T. Kohno, S. Seshan, and D. Wetherall. Can ferris bueller still have his day off? protecting privacy in the wireless era. In *Proceedings of the 11th USENIX workshop on Hot topics in operating systems*, HOTOS'07, pages 10:1–10:6, Berkeley, CA, USA, 2007. USENIX Association.

[8] M. Gruteser and D. Grunwald. Enhancing location privacy in wireless lan through disposable interface identifiers: a quantitative analysis. *Mob. Netw. Appl.*, 10(3):315–325, June 2005.

[9] D. Halperin, W. Hu, A. Sheth, and D. Wetherall. Tool release: gathering 802.11n traces with channel state information. *SIGCOMM Comput. Commun. Rev.*, 41(1):53–53, Jan. 2011.

[10] T. Jiang, H. J. Wang, and Y.-C. Hu. Preserving location privacy in wireless LANs. In *In Proceedings of 5th International Conference on Mobile Systems, Applications, and Services (MobiSys 2007*, pages 246–257. ACM Press, 2007.

[11] O. Kaltiokallio and M. Bocca. Real-time intrusion detection and tracking in indoor environment through distributed rssi processing. In *2011 IEEE 17th Intl. Conf. Embedded and Real-Time Computing Systems and Applications (RTCSA)*, volume 1, pages 61 –70, Aug. 2011.

[12] O. Kaltiokallio, M. Bocca, and N. Patwari. Follow @grandma: Long-term device-free localization for residential monitoring. In *Local Computer Networks Workshops (LCN Workshops), 2012 IEEE 37th Conference on*, pages 991 –998, oct. 2012.

[13] M. A. Kanso and M. G. Rabbat. Compressed RF tomography for wireless sensor networks: Centralized and decentralized approaches. In *5th IEEE Intl. Conf. on Distributed Computing in Sensor Systems (DCOSS-09)*, Marina Del Rey, CA, June 2009.

[14] A. E. Kosba, A. Saeed, and M. Youssef. Rasid: A robust WLAN device-free passive motion detection system. In *2012 IEEE International Conference on Pervasive Computing and Communications (PerCom)*, pages 180–189, 2012.

[15] R. K. Martin, C. Anderson, R. W. Thomas, and A. S. King. Modelling and analysis of radio tomography. In *CAMSAP*, pages 377–380, 2011.

[16] D. Niculescu and B. Nath. Ad hoc positioning system (aps) using aoa. In *INFOCOM*, volume 3, pages 1734–1743. IEEE, 2003.

[17] N. B. Priyantha, A. Chakraborty, and H. Balakrishnan. The cricket location-support system. In *Proceedings of the 6th annual international conference on Mobile computing and networking*, pages 32–43. ACM, 2000.

[18] Q. Pu, S. Gupta, S. Gollakota, and S. Patel. Whole-home gesture recognition using wireless signals. In *Proceedings of the 19th annual international conference on Mobile computing & networking*, pages 27–38. ACM, 2013.

[19] M. Seifeldin, A. Saeed, A. Kosba, A. El-Keyi, and M. Youssef. Nuzzer: A large-scale device-free passive localization system for wireless environments. *Mobile Computing, IEEE Transactions on*, PP(99):1, 2012.

[20] W. C. Stone. Nist construction automation program report no. 3: Electromagnetic signal attenuation in construction materials. *Building Fire Res. Lab., Nat. Inst. Standards Technol., Gaithersburg, MD, Tech. Rep. NISTIR*, 6055, 1997.

[21] C. D. Taylor, S. J. Gutierrez, S. L. Langdon, K. L. Murphy, and W. A. Walton III. Measurement of RF propagation into concrete structures over the frequency range 100 MHz to 3 GHz. In *Wireless Personal Communications*, pages 131–144. Springer, 1997.

[22] Texas Instruments. A USB-enabled system-on-chip solution for 2.4 GHz IEEE 802.15.4 and ZigBee applications.

[23] F. Viani, P. Rocca, M. Benedetti, G. Oliveri, and A. Massa. Electromagnetic passive localization and tracking of moving targets in a WSN-infrastructured environment. *Inverse Problems*, 26:1–15, March 2010.

[24] J. Wilson and N. Patwari. Radio tomographic imaging with wireless networks. *IEEE Transactions on Mobile Computing*, 9(5):621–632, May 2010.

[25] J. Wilson and N. Patwari. See Through Walls: Motion Tracking Using Variance-Based Radio Tomography Networks. *IEEE TMC*, 2010.

[26] R. Wilson. Propagation losses through common building materials 2.4 GHz vs 5 GHz. Technical Report E10589, Magis Networks, Inc., August 2002.

[27] C. Xu, B. Firner, Y. Zhang, R. Howard, J. Li, and X. Lin. Improving RF-based device-free passive localization in cluttered indoor environments through probabilistic classification methods. In *IPSN*, pages 209–220, 2012.

[28] M. Youssef, M. Mah, and A. K. Agrawala. Challenges: device-free passive localization for wireless environments. In *MOBICOM*, pages 222–229, 2007.

[29] D. Zhang, J. Ma, Q. Chen, and L. M. Ni. Dynamic clustering for tracking multiple transceiver-free objects. In *IEEE PerCom'09*.

[30] D. Zhang, J. Ma, Q. Chen, and L. M. Ni. An RF-based system for tracking transceiver-free objects. In *Fifth Annual IEEE International Conference on Pervasive Computing and Communications (PerCom-07)*, pages 135–144, 2007.

[31] Y. Zheng and A. Men. Through-wall tracking with radio tomography networks using foreground detection. In *IEEE WCNC*, pages 3278–3283, 2012.

# Short Paper: "Here I am, now pay me!": Privacy Concerns in Incentivised Location-sharing Systems

Luke Hutton
School of Computer Science
University of St Andrews
St Andrews, Fife, UK
lh49@st-andrews.ac.uk

Tristan Henderson
School of Computer Science
University of St Andrews
St Andrews, Fife, UK
tnhh@st-andrews.ac.uk

Apu Kapadia
School of Informatics and
Computing
Indiana University
Bloomington, IN, USA
kapadia@indiana.edu

## ABSTRACT

Social network sites, location-sharing services and, more recently, applications enabling the quantified self, mean that people are generating and sharing more data than ever before. It is important to understand the potential privacy impacts when such personal data are commercialised, to ensure that expectations of privacy are preserved.

This paper presents the first user study of incentivised location sharing, where people are given a direct monetary incentive to share their location with a business or their social network. We use Nissenbaum's framework of contextual integrity in a preliminary user study ($n=22$) to investigate potential privacy risks with such services. We find that monetisation changes why people share their data, but not the frequency of disclosures. Our results motivate further study and are useful for designers of location-sharing systems and researchers who wish to leverage the diverse range of personal data that are available in a privacy-sensitive manner.

## Categories and Subject Descriptors

H.1.2 [**Information Systems**]: User/Machine Systems

## Keywords

privacy; contextual integrity; location-sharing

## 1. INTRODUCTION

The rise of smartphones and mobile sensing smart devices is enabling the quantified self,[1] whereby vast amounts of personal data are collected or generated, and optionally shared with other people, services, and businesses. Such self-tracking is the logical extension of context-sharing applications such as Foursquare; as new sensors become available, new devices have exploited these and new applications have arisen to enable data collection and sharing. At the same time, operators of services using these data have aimed

---

[1] http://quantifiedself.com/

to develop sustainable business models, leading to increased commercialisation of people's data. For instance, advertisers now use location-sharing services to reach highly-targeted groups of people, who receive incentives such as cash or discounts, in exchange for promoting the business to their social networks, and releasing some personal and demographic information to the advertisers.

While previous work has identified the economics of privacy decisions in abstract scenarios [6], or suggested mechanisms for exchanging data based on people's values [2], it is also necessary to study what happens when incentives are explicitly introduced into a service's business model. It is well-known that people who use location-sharing applications are concerned about privacy [18], but how does the introduction of incentives affect these privacy concerns, or people's uses of such services? Do people's decisions change for the worse as a result of incentives, and how, or indeed should, we improve this? In this paper we look at what we term *incentivised location-sharing* (ILS) services, to determine whether they may constitute a risk to individual privacy. While the use of location-based services has been well studied, this is the first user study to examine the potential risks in embedding financial incentives in traditionally social-oriented online sharing.

To determine whether incentives may create new privacy violations, we use Nissenbaum's model of contextual integrity [16]. As the ILS context is not well-studied, we conduct a pilot user study in which 22 people use an ILS application for one week, and receive financial incentives to share their location with businesses and their social network. The user study allows us to better understand the expectations of people using such an application, their behaviour and motivations for disclosing their location for a financial incentive, and how the design of the application affects how people use it. Our early findings can help application developers to deliver incentives for disclosures in a way which preserves people's comfort and privacy, while delivering benefits to advertisers and developers. Our findings also motivate a set of research questions for further work.

## 2. BACKGROUND AND RELATED WORK

So-called "social-driven" location-sharing services, that allow people to share their location with their social network using a smart device, have existed for some time [11, 23]. More recently, systems have emerged which adopt the fundamental principles of these location-sharing services, but in addition deliver incentives to people for disclosing their location. We refer to such systems as *incentivised location-sharing* services, and these range from companies offering geo-fenced discounts to nearby users [15]; existing location-based services offering location-specific discounts for users who check in, such as Foursquare offering discounts to the "mayor" of Starbucks [22] and RadioShack [19]; to advertising-specific mobile applications such as Quidco.

To study these ILS services, we employ the contextual integrity framework. Contextual integrity has been widely used to study privacy in various services [3, 5, 9, 12, 21] but ours is the first study to use contextual integrity for location-sharing and advertising, and the first to conduct a user study to collect empirical data on these services. Privacy concerns and behaviour in location-sharing services have been extensively researched, with user studies [1, 17, 24] evincing the social norms and practices that govern the expectations of users, and their motivations for using such services.

Similarly, other work has examined online advertising [27] or location-based advertising [26]. In particular Kelley et al. study the sharing of location with advertisers [10] with a user study of 27 participants, although this is not the ILS form of advertising that we study here. Other work has also examined incentives and location-sharing, e.g., Cramer et al. identify emergent norms in the use of Foursquare, with location disclosures motivated by a desire to share interesting events as an impression management technique, and sometimes to endorse local businesses [4]. More recently, Patil et al. find increased rates of incentivised disclosures, with many people disclosing their location to receive rewards such as discounts or coupons [18].

# 3. CONTEXTUAL INTEGRITY

Nissenbaum proposes contextual integrity as a theoretical framework for describing privacy in terms of information flows, arguing that information is not inherently public or private, but privacy is violated when norms governing the appropriate flow of information are not respected [16]. These context-specific "informational norms" govern all aspects of life in which information flows between actors. Individuals, groups and sections of society have expectations about how their information is collected, processed, and transmitted to other parties, and they perceive their privacy to be violated when these expectations are not met.

For example, while many would consider medical data to be "private", they might accept that it is appropriate to disclose information about medical conditions to a doctor to receive a diagnosis and treatment. If that doctor were to then gossip about their conditions to their friends, this would be a clear violation of privacy. It is the *appropriateness* of the flows of information in different contexts that determines privacy, not the information itself.

Our specific focus is on the new privacy concerns and violations created by the introduction of incentives to location-sharing and mobile advertising applications. These violations might arise because people may be incentivised to make decisions about sharing sensitive data that they might otherwise be unwilling to do so. If so, one way to improve systems is to aid this decision-making process, and previous work [20, 25] has indeed indicated that providing feedback to users can aid in decisions about sharing data.

We apply contextual integrity to ILS by conducting a user study to capture the expectations of users before and after using a prototype ILS service, and measure their motivations for disclosing their location when financially incentivised. Assessing these factors, and the role of feedback, allows us to conduct a preliminary analysis about the potential risks of such services, identifying questions for further research.

# 4. METHOD

To apply Nissenbaum's framework of contextual integrity, we conducted a week-long pilot user study with 22 participants, to identify the prevailing norms and expectations necessary to deter-

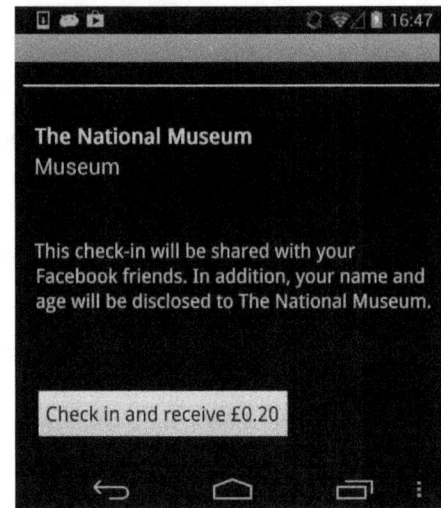

**Figure 1: Screenshot of the incentivised location sharing application created for our user study. One group of participants are shown information about the flow of PII before confirming a check-in.**

mine whether ILS constitutes a potential risk to privacy. We chose to run the study for seven days based on recommendations from the experience sampling literature [7] and from running such studies in the past.

For this user study, we developed an application for Android smartphones which closely resembled the interface and feature-set of existing commercial applications such as Quidco and Foursquare. The application consisted of a widget which used the Google Places API to periodically update and display the names of businesses close to the participant's current location. From the widget, the participant could select a nearby business and check in, thus creating a Facebook status update, in exchange for a small financial incentive. At the start of the study, participants chose six of their Facebook friends who would be able to view these stories, representing a cross-section of close friends, acquaintances, and colleagues. By choosing a small subset of people to share locations with, we mitigate potential adverse effects of the study, considering our interest in potentially inappropriate disclosures, while still making participants consider the social impact of their disclosures to a diverse audience. Participants could pause the application for a short period of time if they did not want location data to be collected.

## 4.1 Study design

Participants were randomly assigned to one of three conditions, which affected the feedback displayed to participants immediately before they checked in, and the value of the cash incentive:

- Low incentive, no feedback (**LowNo**): Participants received £0.10 for each check-in, and were not actively reminded that PII would be disclosed to the business.

- High incentive, no feedback (**HighNo**): Participants received £0.20 for each check-in, and were not actively reminded that PII would be disclosed to the business.

- High incentive, feedback (**HighYes**): Participants received £0.20 for each check-in, and were reminded that their name and age would be disclosed to the business.

Participants in the feedback condition were shown the information depicted in Fig. 1, while other participants were only informed that their check-ins would be disclosed to their Facebook friends before checking in. These incentive levels were chosen based on the distribution of incentives we find in commercial applications such as Quidco. The high incentive level was set at £0.20 because we were interested in seeing whether differences would manifest even between marginally different levels of micro-incentives, and to avoid compelling lower-income participants to check in out of financial need, which we are not investigating in this study. Participants were not aware that there were other conditions, nor how the incentives were chosen.

Before joining the study, all participants were asked to read the application's privacy policy, which specified that the business indicated would receive some PII in return for the financial incentive. Before beginning to use the application, participants completed a pre-briefing questionnaire, consisting of 15 questions drawn from the 'collection', 'control', 'awareness', and 'secondary use' dimensions of the Internet Users' Information Privacy Concerns (IUIPC) scale [13]. To these we added a question identifying expectations in the ILS context. Immediately after completing the study, participants were asked to complete the same questionnaire, allowing us to identify a relationship between different feedback conditions and a change in privacy attitudes.

In addition to recording the participant's activity during their seven days of participation, participants received an automatically-generated end-of-day questionnaire each night, based on their activity during the preceding day. This allowed us to capture qualitative data about the motivations for activity within the application, and to clean anomalous outliers (such as accidental interface taps) within hours of the activity occurring.

## 4.2 Recruitment

Participants were recruited through advertisements on Facebook and mailing lists aimed at university students and staff. Participants were not screened, with the only requirement being possession of an Android smartphone and a Facebook account. 39 participants were recruited in total, of whom 22 completed, and 17 prematurely left the study. The majority of those who did not complete the study installed the application to their mobile device but did not complete the registration and consent process. 9 participants were in the LowNo condition, 6 in the HighNo condition, and 7 in the HighYes condition. To prevent the study being affected by cultural differences in privacy expectations, we recruited all participants from the United Kingdom. Recruitment for the experiment positioned our system as a new commercial application, to closely align participant expectations with that of existing commercial applications.

## 4.3 Remuneration

Participants were told they would earn money for sharing their locations. Rather than provide the exact amount promised by the application, all participants were given an Amazon voucher of equal value at the end of the study, surpassing the value any participant accrued during normal use of the application. This strategy was employed due to ethical concerns about financially rewarding some participants more than others.

## 4.4 Ethical considerations

Data collection used our framework for privacy-sensitive handling of social network data [8]. This ensured that the proportionate set of data necessary to execute the study was collected, and

## Completed and abandoned check-in rates

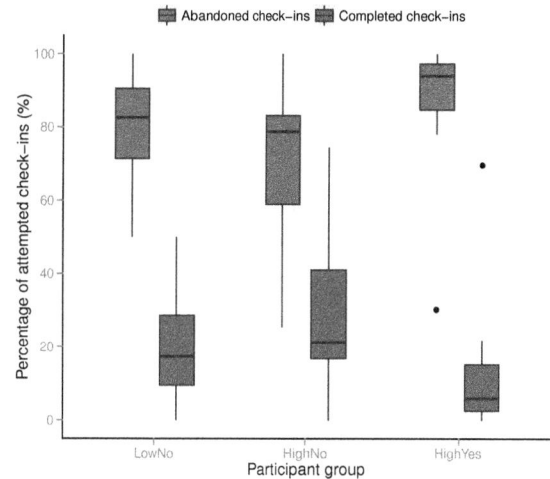

**Figure 2: Participants who receive higher incentives (the HighNo and HighYes groups) check in more often, unless more feedback about PII flows is provided.**

that personal Facebook data were sanitised and deleted at appropriate points during the lifecycle of the study.

All participants were informed of the study's deception after the experiment closed in an email providing their remuneration and explaining the motivation for the study.

The experimental design and all recruitment materials were approved by the relevant ethics committee (our institution's equivalent of an Institutional Review Board).

## 5. RESULTS

In total, our 22 participants completed 212 check-ins, and abandoned 471, and the most active user checked in 15 times in one day. We first examine the overall differences between our groups of participants to understand the effects of our feedback and incentive conditions. Our sample size is too small to make confident statistical inferences, but our findings motivate further work to investigate the specific research questions our results identify.

## 5.1 Less feedback induces greater sharing

Fig. 2 shows the proportion of completed check-ins and abandoned check-ins. We found that participants in the HighNo condition exhibited the most variable behaviour. A number of participants performed more check-ins than lower-paid participants, but this was not consistent across the group. We did, however, note a reduction in disclosure rates for participants in the HighYes condition, where most users only completed less than 10% of check-ins. Behaviour was the most consistent within this group, and the higher variance among non-feedback groups indicates that the absence of such feedback generally induced more sharing. Those who received more feedback abandoned more relative to the number of completed check-ins. We note that higher incentives without feedback leads to greater variance in check-in rates, indicating an influence on behaviour. Some participants in all conditions did not complete any check-ins throughout the study, despite continuing to interact with the application.

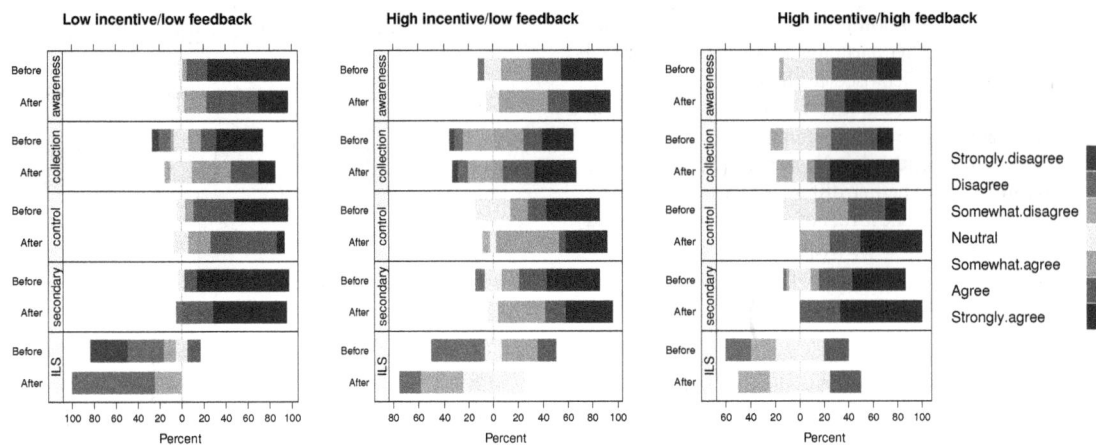

**Figure 3: Diverging stacked bar chart showing how participants responded to a questionnaire about online privacy concerns before and after participating in the study. For each dimension tested, positive answers indicate increased concern or awareness about relevant privacy practices. Participants reported high concern and awareness about online privacy issues generally, and these were reinforced when more feedback about PII flows was provided by the application. Many believed, however, that companies are "entitled" to personal information in exchange for money, and comfort with this practice increased with use of a mobile advertising check-in application, as shown by the positive tendency on the "ILS" dimension.**

## 5.2 Feedback engenders support for ILS

Fig. 3 shows the results of the IUIPC survey before and after the study. Participants exposed to more feedback about the flow of PII during the study reported greater agreement on most dimensions in our post-brief survey, particularly 'secondary use' (concern about information being used for reasons not originally sanctioned), 'control' (loss of control leads to privacy violation), and 'awareness' (of privacy practices). Participants in low feedback conditions did not significantly alter their responses in the debrief questionnaire.

We found that participants who received less feedback were less comfortable with ILS at the end of the study, although we saw increased comfort with ILS services for those in the higher feedback conditions, represented by the greater positive tendency for this question in Fig. 3.

Participants in both high incentive conditions reported greater concern about secondary use of their PII, a fundamental aspect of ILS, while lower-paid participants' concern did not change as much. This suggests neither incentives nor feedback significantly impact people's concern about the use of their information.

Our examination of attitudes before and after the study reveals that concern and awareness of privacy issues generally increases through participating in the study. Interestingly, only participants who were provided feedback about the flows of their information believed that ILS was a more legitimate practice than at the start of the study, while confidence in ILS dropped for our other participants. This mirrors our finding that high feedback participants are much more comfortable with the disclosure of their PII. We believe this can be attributed to a combination of such participants feeling more empowered by the transparent explanation of how their information is used, while other participants, without the same *in situ* assurances, may have exhibited a priming effect from the study being bookended by our IUIPC questionnaire. Participants did not frequently report such concerns in our end-of-day questionnaires, lending further support to this theory.

These results give us some insight into the expectations of people before adopting an ILS service, and their values after having experienced such a system. We observe paradoxical results, with

participants' general privacy concerns hardened, but their attitudes towards ILS more relaxed. Contextual integrity suggests if a new process perturbs the values of an existing context, there is a risk of privacy breaches. This appears to manifest in our results, as people are reporting greater concern, yet appear to be placated by the introduction of a financial incentive. Failure to reconcile these behaviours risks people feeling compelled to make disclosures they might otherwise consider inappropriate. Further work is needed to assess the significance of this effect.

## 5.3 Higher incentives change check-in motivations

Disclosures in traditional location-sharing applications are often motivated by attempts to build social capital, and this was a recurring theme in our study too. When asked in end-of-day questionnaires to explain why they checked in to certain locations, participants in all conditions frequently reported "wanting my friends to see that I was there". This motivation did not often coincide with those directly pertaining to the introduction of incentives, such as "I don't mind sharing my personal information in exchange for cash" and "wanting to promote the business", which were commonly reported independently. Interestingly, in 69.2% of cases where social capital was a motivation, it did not coincide with any other motivations, suggesting people may be motivated on two largely independent fronts — appealing to their social network, and promoting businesses for money.

Participants who were offered a higher incentive were more likely to intentionally promote local businesses to their social network. We also find that when participants cited promotion as a motivation, it coincided with no other motivation in 57.1% of cases, suggesting that participants treated these two use cases somewhat independently. Lower-paid participants did not often exhibit this motivation, suggesting they may have not considered the value of the incentive sufficient to deliberately act as an advertising agent for the business, even if the actual exposure of their check-ins was the same.

Participants who received less feedback cited social capital-building motivations most often when disclosing their location, suggesting they treated the service in the same manner as other location-sharing services. Similarly, the lowest-paid participants were unlikely to cite financial or promotional motivations, suggesting they also considered the application to be much like any other location-sharing system, despite the additional PII flows our system introduces.

# 6. IMPLICATIONS

## 6.1 People value incentives over privacy

Despite high levels of online privacy concern, our results suggest many people may be comfortable with the notion of disclosing their location and personally identifiable information for a cash incentive. When our participants were exposed to feedback about the flows of their personal information, their overall privacy concern increases, but they become even more comfortable with incentivised location sharing information flows, believing companies are "entitled" to their personal information if they are paid. This result is consistent with previous findings that people generally value money over their PII [6], and has implications for further study of ILS. We find that location disclosures were instigated by a mix of social and financial motivations which often did not coincide, which may suggest people are attempting to reconcile the context of a traditional location-sharing service with ILS. This is cause for concern as, in our system, all location disclosures reached the same audience, leading to potentially inappropriate disclosures to one's social network. Application designers can address this issue by avoiding the conflation of social and incentivised disclosures through distinct interfaces for each, and allowing people to choose different audiences for alternative types of disclosures.

## 6.2 Feedback does not discourage sharing

Participants who received more feedback about the flow of their personal information were more comfortable with the practice of ILS at the end of the study, and only made slightly fewer location disclosures than other participants. This is an important finding for application designers to note, as it contradicts any intuition that full disclosure about how people's information is used might dissuade users. Rather, our results suggest people may be empowered by understanding how their information is used. While they are more discerning about when to share their information, they are also the most confident that they are aware of the privacy implications of using such services, and that the disclosure of PII is an appropriate outcome. Furthermore, the changes in motivations among our participants should be noted by designers, who ought to design services which satisfy both the social and financial reasons for their use. Where insufficient feedback was provided, we were concerned by the conflated motivations for sharing one's location, as participants struggled to reconcile the distinct use cases. Among participants who understood how their personal information was used, however, distinct social and financial thought processes were observed. Designers should provide *in situ* disclosures of how personal information is used, as our results suggests this satisfies people's privacy concerns, without severely affecting their willingness to use such services. In addition, incentivised and non-incentivised disclosures should be represented distinctly, to ensure people's motivations for making disclosures are aligned with the exposure of their information.

## 6.3 Potential privacy risks

Based on this preliminary study, there is evidence of potential risks to users of ILS services.

Our concern is that the prominence of 'traditional' location-sharing motivations such as social capital building and impression manage-

ment, particularly among participants who received less feedback, suggests people may treat such applications in the same manner as any other social-driven location-sharing system, despite sensitive information being disclosed to advertisers, and the possibility that their social network will perceive incentivised check-ins to be of lower value [4]. When participants received clear feedback about the use of their personal information at the point of disclosure, they make slightly fewer disclosures, and while disclosures are still often socially motivated, they often constitute a deliberate effort to advertise that business to their social network. Current commercial applications often do not deliver this level of feedback, burying information about the flows of personal information within unread privacy policies [14], and we argue that if such feedback is provided, people are able to make more informed decisions about when and why their location will be disclosed. Participants who received more feedback also report slightly better awareness of online privacy issues.

We do not suggest that the introduction of new motivations for disclosure themselves constitute a breach of contextual integrity. In our user study, many participants managed the social and promotional aspects of the ILS context independent of each other. The relationship between the feedback within the application, and people's behaviour and wider attitudes towards online privacy, suggests the design of such an application can have a significant impact on people's relationship with technology. Participants who received more feedback about the flow of PII were the most comfortable with the practice of ILS.

Our results highlight interesting differences in how feedback and incentives affect behaviours and motivations in our application, but this pilot study has some limitations. Our study is limited to a small number of participants and levels of incentives, and indeed demographic information has not been studied. Future work should examine in more detail the effects of these variables over a longer period with a greater sample size. Using these results, we propose the following research questions, to be addressed in future work:

1. Do people who use location-sharing services have different expectations of privacy when their disclosures are financially motivated?

2. Do incentives perturb privacy norms in a location-sharing service to the extent that contextual integrity is violated?

3. Does greater transparency about the flow of personal information when people share their location for money affect behaviour, and reduce the risk of privacy violations?

# 7. CONCLUSION

This paper has presented the first study of what we term incentivised location-sharing — the introduction of financial incentives to traditional location-sharing and mobile advertising systems. To understand privacy violations in these systems, we employ Nissenbaum's contextual integrity framework and conduct a user study with 22 smartphone users.

Our results show that while monetisation does not change the frequency of location disclosures, people's motivations for sharing their location are altered. Also, people's concern and awareness of privacy issues increased during the study. We show that application designers can build applications to show people how their information is used in such a way to not dissuade people from using such services, while increasing their confidence in the practice. In future work we plan additional user studies to better understand the wider implications of these findings.

## 8. ACKNOWLEDGEMENTS

This material is based upon work supported by the National Science Foundation under grants CNS-1016603 and CNS-1252697, and an Engineering and Physical Sciences Research Council (EPSRC) Doctoral Training Grant.

## 9. REFERENCES

[1] D. Anthony, T. Henderson, and D. Kotz. Privacy in location-aware computing environments. *IEEE Pervasive Computing*, 6(4):64–72, Oct. 2007. doi:10.1109/mprv.2007.83.

[2] C. Aperjis and B. A. Huberman. A market for unbiased private data: Paying individuals according to their privacy attitudes. *First Monday*, 17(5-7), May 2012. doi:10.5210/fm.v17i5.4013.

[3] L. Barkhuus. The mismeasurement of privacy: using contextual integrity to reconsider privacy in HCI. In *Proc. CHI*, pages 367–376, May 2012. doi:10.1145/2207676.2207727.

[4] H. Cramer, M. Rost, and L. E. Holmquist. Performing a check-in: emerging practices, norms and 'conflicts' in location-sharing using foursquare. In *Proc. MobileHCI*, pages 57–66, Aug. 2011. doi:10.1145/2037373.2037384.

[5] F. S. Grodzinsky and H. T. Tavani. Privacy in "the cloud": applying Nissenbaum's theory of contextual integrity. *ACM SIGCAS Computers and Society*, 41(1):38–47, Oct. 2011. doi:10.1145/2095266.2095270.

[6] J. Grossklags and A. Acquisti. When 25 Cents is too much: An Experiment on Willingness-To-Sell and Willingness-To-Protect Personal Information. In *Proc. WEIS*, 2007. Online at http://weis2007.econinfosec.org/papers/66.pdf.

[7] J. M. Hektner, J. A. Schmidt, and M. Csikszentmihalyi. *Experience sampling method: measuring the quality of everyday life*. SAGE Publications, Thousand Oaks, CA, USA, 2007.

[8] L. Hutton and T. Henderson. An architecture for ethical and privacy-sensitive social network experiments. *SIGMETRICS Perform. Eval. Rev.*, 40(4):90–95, Apr. 2013. doi:10.1145/2479942.2479954.

[9] E. A. Jones and J. W. Janes. Anonymity in a world of digital books: Google Books, privacy, and the freedom to read. *Policy & Internet*, 2(4):42–74, Jan. 2010. doi:10.2202/1944-2866.1072.

[10] P. G. Kelley, M. Benisch, L. F. Cranor, and N. Sadeh. When are users comfortable sharing locations with advertisers? In *Proc. CHI*, pages 2449–2452, May 2011. doi:10.1145/1978942.1979299.

[11] J. Lindqvist, J. Cranshaw, J. Wiese, J. Hong, and J. Zimmerman. I'm the mayor of my house: examining why people use foursquare - a social-driven location sharing application. In *Proc. CHI*, pages 2409–2418, May 2011. doi:10.1145/1978942.1979295.

[12] H. R. Lipford, G. Hull, C. Latulipe, A. Besmer, and J. Watson. Visible flows: Contextual integrity and the design of privacy mechanisms on social network sites. In *Proc. CSE*, volume 4, pages 985–989, Aug. 2009. doi:10.1109/cse.2009.241.

[13] N. K. Malhotra, S. S. Kim, and J. Agarwal. Internet users' information privacy concerns (IUIPC): The construct, the scale, and a causal model. *Information Systems Research*, 15(4):336–355, Dec. 2004. doi:10.1287/isre.1040.0032.

[14] A. M. McDonald and L. F. Cranor. The cost of reading privacy policies. *I/S: A Journal of Law and Policy for the Information Society*, 4(3):540–565, 2008. Online at http://www.is-journal.org/files/2012/02/Cranor_Formatted_Final.pdf.

[15] C. C. Miller. Take a step closer for an invitation to shop. *New York Times*, page B4, Feb. 23 2010. Online at http://www.nytimes.com/2010/02/23/business/media/23adco.html.

[16] H. Nissenbaum. *Privacy in Context: Technology, Policy, and the Integrity of Social Life*. Stanford Law Books, Stanford, CA, USA, 2009.

[17] X. Page, B. P. Knijnenburg, and A. Kobsa. What a tangled web we weave: lying backfires in location-sharing social media. In *Proc. CSCW*, pages 273–284, 2013. doi:10.1145/2441776.2441808.

[18] S. Patil, G. Norcie, A. Kapadia, and A. J. Lee. Reasons, rewards, regrets: privacy considerations in location sharing as an interactive practice. In *Proc. Eighth Symposium on Usable Privacy and Security*, July 2012. doi:10.1145/2335356.2335363.

[19] M. Rost, L. Barkhuus, H. Cramer, and B. Brown. Representation and Communication: Challenges in Interpreting Large Social Media Datasets. In *Proc. CSCW*, pages 357–362, 2013. doi:10.1145/2441776.2441817.

[20] R. Schlegel, A. Kapadia, and A. J. Lee. Eyeing your exposure: quantifying and controlling information sharing for improved privacy. In *Proc. SOUPS*, 2011. doi:10.1145/2078827.2078846.

[21] P. Shi, H. Xu, and Y. Chen. Using contextual integrity to examine interpersonal information boundary on social network sites. In *Proc. CHI*, pages 35–38, 2013. doi:10.1145/2470654.2470660.

[22] E. D. Spiegler, C. Hildebrand, and F. Michahelles. Social networks in pervasive advertising and shopping. In J. Müller, F. Alt, and D. Michelis, editors, *Pervasive Advertising*, chapter 10, pages 207–225. Springer, London, UK, 2011. doi:10.1007/978-0-85729-352-7_10.

[23] K. P. Tang, J. Lin, J. I. Hong, D. P. Siewiorek, and N. Sadeh. Rethinking location sharing: exploring the implications of social-driven vs. purpose-driven location sharing. In *Proc. Ubicomp*, pages 85–94, Sept. 2010. doi:10.1145/1864349.1864363.

[24] E. Toch, J. Cranshaw, P. H. Drielsma, J. Y. Tsai, P. G. Kelley, J. Springfield, L. Cranor, J. Hong, and N. Sadeh. Empirical models of privacy in location sharing. In *Proc. 12th ACM international conference on Ubiquitous computing*, pages 129–138, Sept. 2010. doi:10.1145/1864349.1864364.

[25] J. Y. Tsai, P. Kelley, P. Drielsma, L. F. Cranor, J. Hong, and N. Sadeh. Who's viewed you?: The impact of feedback in a mobile location-sharing application. In *Proc. CHI*, pages 2003–2012, Apr. 2009. doi:10.1145/1518701.1519005.

[26] R. Unni and R. Harmon. Perceived effectiveness of push vs. pull mobile location based advertising. *Journal of Interactive Advertising*, 7(2):28–40, 2007. doi:10.1080/15252019.2007.10722129.

[27] B. Ur, P. G. Leon, L. F. Cranor, R. Shay, and Y. Wang. Smart, useful, scary, creepy: perceptions of online behavioral advertising. In *Proc. SOUPS*, July 2012. doi:10.1145/2335356.2335362.

# Practical Privacy-Preserving Location-Sharing Based Services with Aggregate Statistics

Michael Herrmann
KU Leuven ESAT/COSIC, iMinds
Leuven, Belgium
michael.herrmann@esat.kuleuven.be

Alfredo Rial
IBM Research
Rüschlikon, Switzerland
lia@zurich.ibm.com

Claudia Diaz
KU Leuven ESAT/COSIC, iMinds
Leuven, Belgium
claudia.diaz@esat.kuleuven.be

Bart Preneel
KU Leuven ESAT/COSIC, iMinds
Leuven, Belgium
bart.preneel@esat.kuleuven.be

## ABSTRACT

Location-sharing-based services (LSBSs) allow users to share their location with their friends in a sporadic manner. In currently deployed LSBSs users must disclose their location to the service provider in order to share it with their friends. This default disclosure of location data introduces privacy risks. We define the security properties that a privacy-preserving LSBS should fulfill and propose two constructions. First, a construction based on identity based broadcast encryption (IBBE) in which the service provider does not learn the user's location, but learns which other users are allowed to receive a location update. Second, a construction based on anonymous IBBE in which the service provider does not learn the latter either. As advantages with respect to previous work, in our schemes the LSBS provider does not need to perform any operations to compute the reply to a location data request, but only needs to forward IBBE ciphertexts to the receivers. We implement both constructions and present a performance analysis that shows their practicality. Furthermore, we extend our schemes such that the service provider, performing some verification work, is able to collect privacy-preserving aggregate statistics on the locations users share with each other.

## Categories and Subject Descriptors

K.4.4 [**Computers and Society**]: Electronic Commerce–Distributed commercial transactions; Security

## Keywords

Location Privacy; Broadcast Encryption; Vector Commitments

## 1. INTRODUCTION

The emergence of mobile electronic devices with positioning capabilities (e.g. through the Global Positioning System, GPS), such as smart phones and tablet computers, has fostered the appearance of a wide variety of Location Based Services (LBSs). With these services, users can find nearby places of interest, share their location with friends, and obtain information about their surroundings.

Location-sharing-based services (LSBSs) permit users to share their current location or activity with other people. The shared location data may be in the form of GPS coordinates, although in GeoSocial Networks (GSN), such as *Foursquare* and *Facebook-check-in*, it is common that users announce their location in a more socially meaningful way by providing the venue (e.g., name of the restaurant) at which they are currently present. The action is commonly referred to as *check-in*. Every day millions of users enjoy GSN and share millions of locations with each other.[1]

While LSBSs are indeed useful, the disclosure of location data raises significant privacy concerns. Service providers and other third parties with access to accurate location data can infer private user information, such as their movement patterns, home address, lifestyle and interests [25]. Further, making these inferences is even easier if users share the venue rather than just submitting coordinates, as any uncertainties introduced by possible inaccuracies in the GPS coordinates are removed. We note that, although GSNs offer configurable privacy settings [27], they are still privacy invasive, as the LSBS provider learns the users' location regardless of the privacy settings.

Location Privacy Preserving Mechanisms (LPPMs) that implement obfuscation strategies, such as adding dummy locations [35] or reducing precision [31], are unsuitable for LSBS. This is because, when transmitting an obfuscated location to the service provider, the service provider naturally is only able to forward this obfuscated location to the user's friends. This conflicts with the main functionality of LSBSs. Therefore, LPPMs have been proposed in which users share keys allowing them to encrypt and decrypt their location data [22, 45]. In those solutions, the LSBS provider stores encrypted location data and computes the reply for a user

---

[1]https://foursquare.com/about/
http://www.socialbakers.com/blog/
167-interesting-facebook-places-numbers

requesting location data of her friends. A provider offering such an LSBS is unable to learn statistics about its users' whereabouts. Consequently, this renders the common business model of offering a free service in exchange for the users' data impossible. An alternative is to offer a paid service, but this might only be feasible if the fees are sufficiently low.

In this paper we propose two schemes based on identity-based broadcast encryption [20]. The first protocol reveals the identities of the friends that should receive location information to the LSBS provider and also to the other receivers of that location information. In the second protocol, those identities are hidden towards the service provider as well as towards other users (including the receivers of the location update), thanks to the use of anonymous identity-based broadcast encryption. The advantage over existing work is that in our schemes the LSBS provider does not need to perform complex operations in order to compute a reply for a location data request, but only needs to forward data. This reduces the cost of an LSBS provider that is then able to offer its service for a lower price if pursuing a subscription-based business model. Furthermore, we extend our schemes such that the service provider is able to collect privacy-preserving statistics on the locations shared by the users. This extension does require the LSBS provider to perform additional computations. The obtained statistics could be monetized to compensate for this additional overhead or to facilitate a free service.

We have implemented both schemes on a *Samsung S III mini* smart phone and provide results on the computation time, bandwidth overhead and energy consumption. Our evaluation shows that the performance of the first scheme is independent of the number of users in the system. Furthermore, it imposes minimal computational and bandwidth overhead on both, the LSBS provider and the users' mobile devices. In the second scheme a user is able to choose a trade-off between privacy, computation and bandwidth overhead. We study this trade-off and provide recommendations to increase the level of privacy for the same amount of resources.

The remainder of this paper is structured as follows. In Section 2, we review previous work on privacy-preserving location-based services and argue that none of the existing approaches is suitable for implementing privacy-preserving LSBSs. We define privacy-preserving LSBS in Section 3. In Section 4, we introduce our two schemes. We provide a detailed performance analysis showing the feasibility of our approach in Section 5. In Section 6, we extend our schemes to allow for aggregate statistics collection. We discuss our approach and results in Section 7. Finally, in Section 8 we conclude our work.

## 2. RELATED WORK

In this section we review obfuscation-based LPPMs and argue that they are not suitable for protecting location privacy in LSBS. Subsequently, we review LPPMs that rely on cryptographic primitives. Some of them have been deliberately designed for protecting location privacy in LSBS; others have a more general purpose. Our evaluation shows that obfuscation-based LPPMs are not suitable for privacy-preserving LSBS and that our system has several advantages over existing privacy-preserving LSBS.

Other works have examined location privacy in GSNs considering a different threat model. Gambs et al. [27] and Vi-

cente et al. [48] review several GSNs and analyze their privacy issues. However, in their privacy evaluation, they do not consider it to be a privacy breach if the service provider learns the user locations. An analysis of the inferences that can be made about users based on where they check-in while using Foursquare is provided by Pontes et al. [43].

### 2.1 Obfuscation-based LPPMs

While works like [22, 45] have already noted that LPPMs based on anonymization and precision-reduction are not suitable to protect location privacy in LSBS, we provide here a more detailed evaluation. We therefore follow the categorization in [47] which distinguishes between these four obfuscation strategies: *location hiding*, *perturbation*, *adding dummy regions*, and *reducing precision*. In the following we argue that none of these obfuscation-based LPPMs are applicable to protect location privacy in LSBSs. We therefore consider the following LSBS application scenario: A user *A* is currently at one of her favorite locations and wishes to share this information with her friends. This could be either because *A* simply wants to inform her friends, or to enable them to join her at this place.

The *location hiding* strategy [4] consists of not sending the location data to the LBS and is thus impractical. In this case user *A* would not be able to share her location with her friends. Some LPPMs propose to change pseudonyms after a period of location hiding [32, 37]. However, this is also impractical, because the check-in is supposed to be received by the same set of friends and therefore identifies user *A*. LPPMs that rely on *perturbation* submit a location different from *A*'s actual location [34]. As a rather inconvenient result, the user's friends learn a wrong place and if they decide to join their friend, they would realize upon arriving that *A* is actually not present there. The *adding dummy regions* strategy [35] consists of submitting fake locations along with the user's actual location. In this case *A* would check-in at several places and her friends could not distinguish real from fake check-ins. Finally, with the *reducing precision* strategy [31] *A* would send a *cloak region* that contains her current location, but she would not reveal her precise whereabouts, making it extremely difficult for her friends to find her. We note that with all obfuscation strategies, users could rely on personal contact in order to obtain *A*'s precise location after learning the obfuscated location. However, such a system would have significant usability issues. The key limitation of these techniques is that they do not make a distinction between information revealed to friends and to the service provider. Thus, in order to protect their location information towards the service provider, users must lower the quality of location information shared with their friends.

### 2.2 Cryptographic LPPMs

Freudiger [26] proposes that users should use symmetric or asymmetric encryption and use the service provider solely as a rendez-vous point to exchange encrypted data. Longitude by Dong and Dulay [22] propose to use proxy-encryption, which guarantees that the service provider is not able to learn the location update and, furthermore, that the ciphertext can be modified by the service provider such that only intended receivers are able to successfully decrypt. Puttaswamy et al. [45] propose a scheme which combines encryption with location transformation in order to build a location-based application, such as privacy-preserving LSBS. As already mentioned in Section 1 the proposed LPPMs impose a computational overhead at the LSBS provider, which makes offering such a service more expensive. In our schemes the cost for the LSBS provider is kept at a minimum in order to make running such a service as cheap as possible. Furthermore, the service provider can decide to engage in additional computation overhead and therefore obtain statistics about its users' whereabouts. We note that this overhead is kept low since the service provider only needs to forward data and verify zero-knowledge proofs, whose cost can be reduced using batch verification. Note however that our scheme, in contrast to the works mentioned above, introduces a trusted key generation center.

Carbunar et al. [16] propose privacy preserving protocols for badge and mayor applications in GSNs. While this is closely related to our work, their scheme does not allow users to exchange their locations.

In privacy-preserving friend nearby notification, users can privately learn whether a friend is in close proximity. Such a service can be realized by homomorphic encryption [50], private equality testing [41] and private threshold set intersection [39]. These protocols are different from our solution, because in privacy-preserving location sharing protocols, location updates are sent to friends regardless of their current location, i.e. regardless of how close they are.

Bilogrevic et al. [5] propose two protocols to allow users to compute a fair rendez-vous point in a privacy preserving manner. This differs from our work in that we focus on location sharing, and not on deciding on where to meet after a group of users has deliberately decided to do so.

Popa et al. [44] propose a privacy-preserving protocol to compute aggregate statistics from users' location updates. However, in this protocol users do not share their location with other users.

Finally, some works employ Private Information Retrieval (PIR) so that the users retrieve information (e.g., points of interest) related to their surroundings [30, 42]. PIR could in principle be employed to build privacy-preserving LSBS. However, PIR operations are rather costly at the service provider side which we again argue that introduces intolerable overhead for a service provider.

## 3. DEFINITION OF PRIVACY FOR LSBS

Our LSBS involves the following parties: a key generation center, a service provider $\mathcal{P}$ and a set of users $\mathcal{U}_i$ for $i = 1$ to $n$. Figure 1 shows the parties in the system.

A privacy-invasive protocol that realizes the desired functionality works as follows. A user $\mathcal{U}_i$ sends a message to the service provider that indicates the place $loc$ that $\mathcal{U}_i$ wishes to share, and the set $S \subseteq [1, n]$ of users $\mathcal{U}_j$ ($j \in S$) that should learn that $\mathcal{U}_i$ shares $loc$. Then the service provider forwards to users $\mathcal{U}_j \in S$ the message $(\mathcal{U}_i, loc)$ to inform them that $\mathcal{U}_i$ has shared $loc$. As can be seen, this protocol is privacy-invasive. The service provider learns the location $loc$ that $\mathcal{U}_i$ shares, and the identities of the users $\mathcal{U}_j$ ($j \in S$). The privacy properties that our LSBS should fulfill are the following:

**Sender Privacy.** No coalition of users $\mathcal{U} \notin S$ and service provider $\mathcal{P}$ should learn any information on $loc$.

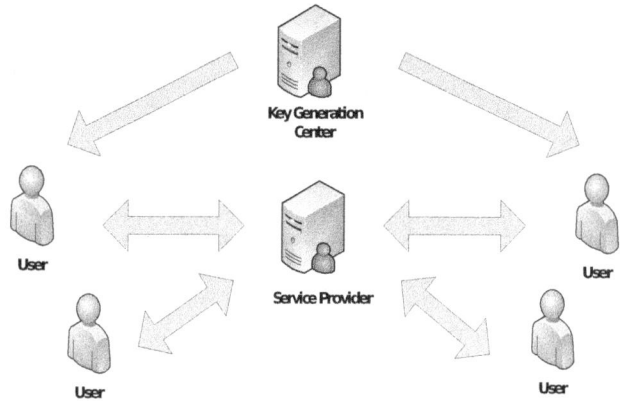

Figure 1: System Model of a privacy-preserving LSBS. The key generation center sets up the public parameters and provides users with secret keys. The service provider transfers messages between users.

**Receiver Privacy.** No coalition of users $\mathcal{U}_j$ such that $j \neq \{i, j^*\}$ and service provider $\mathcal{P}$ should learn any information on whether $j^* \in S$ or $j^* \notin S$.

Our schemes in Section 4 are secure against active adversaries, i.e., adversaries that deviate in any possible way form the protocol execution. The security of our schemes relies on the security of identity based broadcast encryption. The key generation center is trusted, which is an assumption that every identity-based cryptographic scheme makes.

## 4. CONSTRUCTIONS OF LSBS

Our schemes are based on identity-based broadcast encryption, which we describe in Section 4.1. In Section 4.2, we describe the *sender private* scheme, which fulfills the sender privacy property. In Section 4.3, we describe the *fully private* scheme, which fulfills both the sender privacy and the receiver privacy properties.

### 4.1 Identity-Based Broadcast Encryption

Broadcast encryption allows a sender to encrypt a message $m$ to a set of receivers $S \in [1, n]$, so that no coalition of receivers not in $S$ can decrypt. A broadcast encryption scheme consists of the following algorithms:

Setup($1^\lambda, n, \ell$). On input the number of users $n$, the security parameter $1^\lambda$, and the maximum size $\ell \leq n$ of a broadcast recipient group, output the public key $pk$ and the secret key $sk$.

KeyGen($i, sk$). On input an index $i$ and the secret key $sk$, output a secret key $d_i$ for user $\mathcal{U}_i$.

Enc($pk, S, m$). On input the recipient group $S \in [1, n]$, the public key $pk$ and the message $m$, output the ciphertext $c$.

Dec($pk, d_i, c$). On input the public key $pk$, the secret key $d_i$ of user $\mathcal{U}_i$ and a ciphertext $c$, output $m$ if $i \in S$ or else the failure symbol $\perp$.

In IBBE, a trusted key generation center $\mathcal{KGC}$ creates the parameters and computes the secret keys of the receivers. Note that the secret key $sk$ allows the decryption of every ciphertext. If ciphertexts $c$ do not reveal the set of receivers $S$, the broadcast encryption scheme is anonymous.

## 4.2 Sender-Private LSBS

Our sender-private LSBS (SPLS) uses an IBBE scheme that is not anonymous. In such a scheme, ciphertexts $c$ contain a description of the recipient group $S$. Our scheme works as follows:

**Setup Phase.** $\mathcal{KGC}$ executes the setup algorithm $\mathsf{Setup}(1^\lambda, n, \ell)$ on input the security parameter $1^\lambda$, the number of users $n$ and the maximum size $\ell \leq n$, publishes the public key $pk$ and stores the secret key $sk$. Users obtain $pk$.

**Registration Phase.** Each user $\mathcal{U}_i$ registers with the service provider by sending the index $i$. Additionally, $\mathcal{U}_i$ receives the key $d_i$ from $\mathcal{KGC}$, which runs $\mathsf{KeyGen}(i, sk)$.

**Main Phase.** To share a location $loc$, a user $\mathcal{U}_i$ runs $c \leftarrow \mathsf{Enc}(pk, S, i\|loc)$ and sends $c$ to the service provider $\mathcal{P}$. $\mathcal{P}$ gets $S$ from $c$ and sends $c$ to the users $\mathcal{U}_j$ $(j \in S)$. Each user $\mathcal{U}_j$ runs $\mathsf{Dec}(pk, d_j, c)$ to output the message $i\|loc$.

We note that the registration and main phases can be interleaved, i.e., users can join our SPLS dynamically.

Our scheme fulfills the sender privacy property. The IBBE scheme ensures that no coalition of service provider $\mathcal{P}$ and users $\mathcal{U} \notin S$ can decrypt a ciphertext $c$ computed on input $S$. However, this scheme does not fulfill the receiver privacy property. Since the IBBE scheme is not anonymous, the ciphertext $c$ reveals the identity of the receivers $\mathcal{U}_j$ $(j \in S)$.

### 4.2.1 Construction of IBBE

In Section 5, we instantiate our SPLS with a broadcast encryption scheme in order to implement it and evaluate its performance. Broadcast encryption was first formalized by Fiat and Naor [24]. The first fully collusion secure broadcast schemes, i.e., schemes where security holds even if all the users not in the recipient group $S$ collude, were described in [40]. The first public key broadcast encryption scheme was proposed in [21].

In the schemes mentioned above, the size of the ciphertext grows linearly with the size of the recipient group. Boneh, Gentry and Waters [8] proposed the first schemes with constant size ciphertexts. Their schemes have selective security, i.e., the adversary should decide the target recipient group to be attacked before the setup phase. Identity-based broadcast encryption was proposed in [20], which describes also selectively secure schemes.

Broadcast encryption and identity-based broadcast encryption with adaptive security was first achieved in [28]. These schemes achieve constant size ciphertexts in the random oracle model and under q-based assumptions. In [49] and [36], broadcast encryption schemes secure under static assumptions are proposed. In [36], an identity-based broadcast encryption scheme secure under static assumptions is also proposed, but it only achieves selective security.

The main property of identity-based broadcast encryption is that the scheme is efficient when the total number of users $n$ is exponential in the security parameter $1^\lambda$. Since our SPLS could have millions of users, schemes that, despite having constant size ciphertexts, have public key or user secret keys of size that grows linearly with $n$ are less suitable. Therefore, we instantiate our SPLS with the adaptively secure identity-based broadcast encryption in [28].

This scheme, which is secure in the random oracle model, in addition to constant size ciphertexts, has a public key of size independent of $n$ that grows linearly with $\ell$ and user decryption keys $d_i$ of constant size. The scheme in [28] employs bilinear maps.

*Bilinear maps.*

Let $\mathbb{G}$, $\tilde{\mathbb{G}}$ and $\mathbb{G}_t$ be groups of prime order $p$. A map $e : \mathbb{G} \times \tilde{\mathbb{G}} \to \mathbb{G}_t$ must satisfy bilinearity, i.e., $e(g^x, \tilde{g}^y) = e(g, \tilde{g})^{xy}$; non-degeneracy, i.e., for all generators $g \in \mathbb{G}$ and $\tilde{g} \in \tilde{\mathbb{G}}$, $e(g, \tilde{g})$ generates $\mathbb{G}_t$; and efficiency, i.e., there exists an efficient algorithm $\mathsf{BMGen}(1^k)$ that outputs the pairing group setup $(p, \mathbb{G}, \tilde{\mathbb{G}}, \mathbb{G}_t, e, g, \tilde{g})$ and an efficient algorithm to compute $e(a, b)$ for any $a \in \mathbb{G}$, $b \in \tilde{\mathbb{G}}$. If $\mathbb{G} = \tilde{\mathbb{G}}$ the map is symmetric and otherwise asymmetric.

Let $(\mathsf{E}, \mathsf{D})$ be a secure symmetric key encryption scheme. The scheme in [28] works as follows:

$\mathsf{Setup}(1^\lambda, n, \ell)$. On input the number of users $n$, the security parameter $1^\lambda$, and the maximum size $\ell \leq n$ of a broadcast recipient group, run $(p, \mathbb{G}, \mathbb{G}_t, e) \leftarrow \mathsf{BMGen}(1^\lambda)$. Set $g_1, g_2 \leftarrow \mathbb{G}$. Set $\alpha, \beta, \gamma \leftarrow \mathbb{Z}_p$. Set $\hat{g}_1 \leftarrow g_1^\beta$ and $\hat{g}_2 \leftarrow g_2^\beta$. Set $pk = (p, \mathbb{G}, \mathbb{G}_t, e, n, \ell, g_1, g_1^{\gamma \cdot \alpha}, \{g_1^{\alpha^j}, \hat{g}_1^{\alpha^j}, g_2^{\alpha^k}, \hat{g}_2^{\alpha^k} : j \in [0, \ell], k \in [0, \ell-2]\})$. Output $pk$ and the secret key $sk = (\alpha, \gamma)$.

$\mathsf{KeyGen}(i, sk)$. On input an index $i$ and the secret key $sk$, pick random $r_i \leftarrow \mathbb{Z}_p$ and output

$$d_i = (i, r_i, h_i = g_2^{\frac{\gamma - r_i}{\alpha - i}})$$

$\mathsf{Enc}(pk, S, m)$. On input the recipient group $S \in [1, n]$, the public key $pk$ and the message $m$, set $\tau \leftarrow \{0, 1\}^{\mathcal{O}(\lambda)}$. Set $F(x)$ as the $(\ell-1)$-degree polynomial that interpolates $F(i) = H(\tau, i)$ for $i \in S$ and $F(i) = 1$ for $i \in [n+j]$ with $j \in [k+1, \ell]$, where $H : \{0, 1\}^{\mathcal{O}(\lambda)} \times [1, n] \to \mathbb{Z}_p$ is a hash function modelled as a random oracle. Set $k = |S|$ and parse $S$ as $\{i_1, \ldots, i_k\}$. Set $i_j \leftarrow n+j$ for $j \in [k+1, \ell]$. Set $P(x) = \prod_{j=1}^\ell (x - i_j)$. Set $t \leftarrow \mathbb{Z}_p$ and set $K \leftarrow e(g_1, \hat{g}_2)^{\gamma \cdot \alpha^{\ell-1} \cdot t}$. Set $\mathrm{Hdr} \leftarrow \langle C_1, \ldots, C_4 \rangle = \langle \hat{g}_1^{P(\alpha) \cdot t}, g_1^{\gamma \cdot t}, g_1^{F(\alpha) \cdot t}, e(g_1, \hat{g}_2)^{\alpha^{\ell-1} \cdot F(\alpha) \cdot t} \rangle$. Compute $C \leftarrow \mathsf{E}(K, m)$ and output $c = (\tau, \mathrm{Hdr}, C, S)$.

$\mathsf{Dec}(pk, d_i, c)$. On input the public key $pk$, the secret key $d_i$ and a ciphertext $c$, parse $d_i$ as $\langle i, r_i, h_i \rangle$, $c$ as $(\tau, \mathrm{Hdr}, C, S)$ and $\mathrm{Hdr}$ as $\langle C_1, \ldots, C_4 \rangle$. Define $P(x)$ as above and compute $F(x)$ from $\tau$ as above. Set

$$P_i(x) = x^{\ell-1} - \frac{P(x)}{(x-i)}, \quad F_i(x) = \frac{F(x) - F(i)}{(x-i)},$$

and $e_i = -\dfrac{r_i}{F(i)}$

and

$$K \leftarrow e(C_1, h_i \cdot g_2^{e_i \cdot F_i(\alpha)}) \cdot e(C_2 \cdot C_3^{e_i}, \hat{g}_2^{P_i(\alpha)})/C_4^{e_i}.$$

Output $m \leftarrow \mathsf{D}(K, C)$.

We note that a user of LSBS usually shares her location with the same recipient group, i.e., with her friends. Therefore, broadcast encryption is used to share a symmetric key with that recipient group, and messages are encrypted using an efficient symmetric key encryption scheme. Broadcast encryption is used again only when the recipient group changes or when the symmetric key should be renewed for security reasons.

## 4.3 Fully-Private LSBS

Our fully-private LSBS (FPLS) uses an anonymous IBBE scheme. In such scheme, ciphertexts $c$ do not reveal the recipient group. The setup and registration phases of this scheme work as the ones described in Section 4.2. The main phase works as follows:

**Main Phase.** To share a location $loc$, a user $\mathcal{U}_i$ runs $c \leftarrow$ $\mathsf{Enc}(pk, S, i||loc)$ and sends $c$ to the service provider $\mathcal{P}$. $\mathcal{P}$ forwards $c$ to every user $\mathcal{U}_j$ such that $j \neq i$. Each user $\mathcal{U}_j$ runs $\mathsf{Dec}(pk, d_j, c)$ to get either the message $i||loc$ or $\bot$.

As in the construction in Section 4.2, this scheme fulfills the sender-private property. Additionally, this scheme fulfills the receiver privacy property. Since the IBBE scheme is anonymous, the ciphertext $c$ does not reveal the identity of the receivers $\mathcal{U}_j$ ($j \in S$).

This construction requires location updates to be broadcast to all users. Therefore, we propose a variant that allows to trade-off communication efficiency and location-privacy. In this variant, the map is divided into regions $reg_1, \dots, reg_r$ and users reveal to the service provider the region where they are located and the region from where they would like to receive location updates.

**Region Phase.** A user $\mathcal{U}_i$ sends to the service provider the region to which location updates she wishes to receive should be associated.

**Main Phase.** To share a location $loc \in reg$, a user $\mathcal{U}_i$ runs $c \leftarrow \mathsf{Enc}(pk, S, i||loc)$ and sends $(c, reg)$ to the service provider $\mathcal{P}$. $\mathcal{P}$ forwards $c$ to every user $\mathcal{U}_j$ such that $j \neq i$ and $reg$ equals the region sent by $\mathcal{U}_j$ in the Region Phase. Each user $\mathcal{U}_j$ runs $\mathsf{Dec}(pk, d_j, c)$ to get either the message $i||loc$ or $\bot$.

### 4.3.1 Construction of Anonymous IBBE

In Section 5, we instantiate our FPLS with an anonymous broadcast encryption scheme in order to implement it and evaluate its performance. Barth et al. [3] propose an anonymous broadcast encryption scheme secure in the random oracle model where the ciphertext size is $\mathcal{O}(S)$. The public key size is $\mathcal{O}(n)$, while user secret keys and decryption time are constant. Libert et al. [38] proposed a scheme with the same asymptotic performance but secure in the standard model.

Recently, a scheme with public key size $\mathcal{O}(n)$, secret key size $\mathcal{O}(n)$, ciphertext size $\mathcal{O}(r\log(\frac{n}{r}))$, where $r$ is the set $n - S$, and constant decryption time was proposed in [23]. Despite the fact that in this scheme ciphertexts do not grow linearly with $n$, actually $\mathcal{O}(r\log(\frac{n}{r}))$ is asymptotically larger than $\mathcal{O}(n - r)$ for large values of $r$, which are likely in our FPLS. Furthermore, the scheme in [23] does not provide anonymity with respect to users who are able to decrypt, i.e., those users can find out the identity of the other users who can decrypt.

We modify the scheme in [3] so that it employs as building block an anonymous identity-based encryption scheme instead of a key-private public key encryption scheme. This allows users to employ their identities as public keys. Such modification was suggested in Barth et al. [3] and security follows from the security of the original scheme.

An identity-based encryption (IBE) scheme consists of the algorithms ($\mathsf{IBESetup}, \mathsf{IBEExtract}, \mathsf{IBEEnc}, \mathsf{IBEDec}$). The algorithm $\mathsf{IBESetup}(1^\lambda)$ outputs parameters $params$ and master secret key $msk$. $\mathsf{IBEExtract}(params, msk, id)$ outputs the secret key $sk_{id}$ for identity $id$. $\mathsf{IBEEnc}(params, id, m)$ outputs $ct$ encrypting $m$ under $id$. $\mathsf{IBEDec}(params, sk_{id}, ct)$ outputs message $m$ encrypted in $ct$.

An IBE scheme is *anonymous* [1] if it is not possible to associate the identity used to encrypt a message $m$ with the resulting ciphertext. We employ the scheme in [7], which is anonymous [9], to implement the anonymous broadcast encryption scheme.

Another building block of the anonymous IBBE scheme is a strongly existentially unforgeable signature scheme. A signature scheme consists of algorithms ($\mathsf{Kg}, \mathsf{Sign}, \mathsf{Vf}$). $\mathsf{Kg}(1^\lambda)$ outputs a key pair $(ssk, vsk)$. $\mathsf{Sign}(ssk, m)$ outputs a signature $s$ on message $m$. $\mathsf{Vf}(vsk, s, m)$ outputs accept if $s$ is a valid signature on $m$ and reject otherwise. We employ the scheme secure in the random oracle model proposed in [6].

The remaining building block is a secure symmetric key encryption scheme ($\mathsf{E}, \mathsf{D}$). We employ the advanced encryption standard [19]. The anonymous IBBE scheme works as follows.

$\mathsf{Setup}(1^\lambda, n, \ell)$. Choose a group $\mathbb{G}$ of primer order $p$ where CDH is hard and DDH is easy and pick a generator $g \in \mathbb{G}$. Choose a hash function $H : \mathbb{G} \rightarrow \{0,1\}^\lambda$ which is modeled as a random oracle. Compute $params$ and $msk$ via $\mathsf{IBESetup}(1^\lambda)$. For $i = 1$ to $n$, pick random $a_i \leftarrow \mathbb{Z}_p$. Output Output $pk = (\mathbb{G}, g, g^{a_1}, \dots, g^{a_n}, H, params)$ and $sk = (msk, a_1, \dots, a_n)$.

$\mathsf{KeyGen}(i, sk)$. On input an index $i$ and the secret key $sk$, compute a secret key $sk_i \leftarrow \mathsf{IBEExtract}(params, msk, i)$. Output $d_i = (sk_i, a_i)$.

$\mathsf{Enc}(pk, S, m)$. On input the recipient group $S \in [1, n]$, the public key $pk$ and the message $m$, execute the following steps.

1. Compute $(ssk, vsk) \leftarrow \mathsf{Kg}(1^\lambda)$.
2. Pick a random symmetric key $K$.
3. Pick random $r \leftarrow \mathbb{Z}_p$ and set $T = g^r$.
4. For each tuple $(i, g^{a_i}) \in S$, set the ciphertext $c_i \leftarrow H(g^{a_i r})||\mathsf{IBEEnc}(params, i, vsk||g^{a_i r}||K)$.
5. $C_1$ is the concatenation of all $c_i$ ordered by the values of $H(g^{a_i r})$.
6. Compute $C_2 = \mathsf{E}_K(m)$.
7. Sign $s \leftarrow \mathsf{Sign}(ssk, T||C_1||C_2)$.
8. Return the ciphertext $C = s||T||C_1||C_2$.

$\mathsf{Dec}(pk, d_j, c)$. On input the public key $pk$, the secret key $d_j$ and a ciphertext $c$, execute the following steps.

1. Calculate $l = H(T^{a_j})$.
2. Find $c_j$ such that $c_j = l||c$ for some $c_j$ in $C_1$.
3. Calculate $p \leftarrow \mathsf{IBEDec}(params, sk_j, c_j)$.
4. If p is $\bot$, return $\bot$.
5. Parse $p$ as $vsk||x||K$.
6. If $x \neq T^{a_j}$, return $\bot$.
7. If $\mathsf{Vf}(vsk, s, T||C_1||C_2)$ outputs accept, then output $m = \mathsf{D}_K(C_2)$ else $\bot$.

We remark that, if the user is not in the recipient group and therefore she cannot decrypt, the decryption algorithm only requires the computation of a hash function.

# 5. PERFORMANCE ANALYSIS

Location-sharing-based applications are usually run on a mobile device, such as a smart phone or a tablet computer. Therefore, the available resources at the client side are limited in terms of computational power and bandwidth when on mobile connection. Furthermore, mobile devices usually have a rather low battery capacity. Thus an application must use the CPU or mobile communication interfaces, such as WiFi or 3G, as moderate as possible in order not to drain the battery too much. In order to evaluate the overhead of our schemes, we implemented them in the C programming language using the *Pairing-Based Cryptography*[2] (PBC) library. Subsequently, we imported the schemes within Android application using Android's Native Development Kit[3] (NDK) and tested the application on a Samsung S III mini (1 GHz dual-core CPU) which runs the CyanogenMod[4] operating system.

In the following we provide the *additional* overhead imposed by our schemes. This overhead is due to the computation of cryptographic operations and due to the transmission of key material and ciphertexts. Mobile applications for LSBSs, such as Foursquare, are used on a large user base and the overhead imposed by these services is accepted in practice.

For the energy consumption of our schemes, we measure the different current consumption of the phone when the CPU is idle and when the CPU load of one core is at the maximum. We found that the difference is 150 mA at 3.8 V and thus that the power consumption is 570 mW if one CPU core is at full load. Please note that we could not use PowerTutor[5] to estimate the energy consumption of our schemes, because PowerTutor was designed for a Nexus 1 mobile phone. Although PowerTutor does also run on our Samsung S III mini, the energy measurements are likely to be inaccurate, because both phones have a different CPU and we found that PowerTutor is unable to read the traffic sent and received on our phone. For the runtime estimation of our schemes, we executed our protocols 50 times and computed the average. Multiplying the runtime with the power consumption equals to the energy consumption of our schemes.

The energy consumption of data transmission via a mobile interface, such as WiFi and 3G, turns out to be significantly more difficult. This is because the actual energy consumption for sending and receiving data depends on many factors, such as amount of data, time between two consecutive data transmissions and network reception. We therefore use Balasubramanian et al. [2] work to outline ways to minimize the energy consumed by our schemes.

## 5.1 Evaluation of the Sender-Private LSBS

The complexity of the Gentry and Waters [28] scheme that we employ for our SPLS only depends on the size of the maximal broadcast group $l$. This means that for a given $l$, the computational and bandwidth overhead for computing the symmetric key stays constant, regardless of $n$ (the number of users in the system) or $k$ (actual receiver of a broadcast message). We therefore limit our evaluation to the system parameter $l$.

As we can see in Figure 2a the time for creating the symmetric key increases polynomially with $l$. For a reasonably large $l$, such as 100, our phone needs 8.66 seconds to compute the symmetric key in the encryption protocol and 7.42 in the decryption protocol. While this appears to be rather high, we must stress that a user is able to reuse a symmetric key until the broadcast group changes or the key got compromised. Therefore, a single symmetric key can be used for thousands of location shares. Furthermore, as we can see in Figure 2b, the actual energy consumed for computing a symmetric key is 4.94 Joule for the encryption protocol and 4.23 Joule for the decryption protocol, which is very low. The capacity of the standard battery of a Samsung S III mini (3.8 V and 1500 mAh) is 20520 Joule and therefore computing even dozens of symmetric keys per day would not drain the battery too much.

We show the bandwidth overhead of the FPLS in Figure 2c. For creating a new symmetric key a user needs to send 788 byte of data to the receiver of the broadcast group. Please note that even for $k > 1$ the user only needs to send 788 byte instead of $k \times 788$ byte, because the service provider forwards the traffic to the intended receivers. The public key of our scheme grows linearly in $l$. However, please note that the public key only needs to be sent very rarely. This is when a user signs up for the service, the new user receives the public key from the service provider, and if the service provider decides to increase/decrease the size of the maximal broadcast group and thus changes the parameter $l$. In those cases, all the users in the system receive the new public key.

## 5.2 Evaluation of the Fully-Private LSBS

In the following we will first show that the computational overhead that is imposed by the FPLS is feasible for current mobile devices. Subsequently we will show that the FPLS imposes a significant bandwidth overhead. This is a problem for two reasons. Firstly, data plans usually include a fixed data volume to be transmitted before either the speed of the connection gets throttled or additional costs incur. Secondly, using mobile communication interfaces, such as 3G or WiFi, is expensive in terms of energy and therefore sending and receiving higher amounts of data additionally drains the battery. However, we make several suggestions on how our protocol should be deployed to significantly reduce the energy consumption, although the transferred data volume remains the same. Furthermore, as introduced in Section 4.3, the concept of big regions greatly helps in making the FPLS feasible. We therefore consider the FPLS as a protocol which allows a very broad-ranged trade-off between location privacy and performance for users that do not wish to reveal their friendship graph. At the one extreme a very high level of location privacy is possible if the user is willing to spend the necessary resources. On the other extreme a user reveals accurate location information towards the service provider and thereby decreases the amount of data that is received.

As we can see in Figure 3a, the computation and energy overhead for encryption grows only linearly in $k$ and is there-

[2] http://crypto.stanford.edu/pbc/

[3] https://developer.android.com/tools/sdk/ndk/index.html

[4] http://www.cyanogenmod.org/

[5] http://powertutor.org/

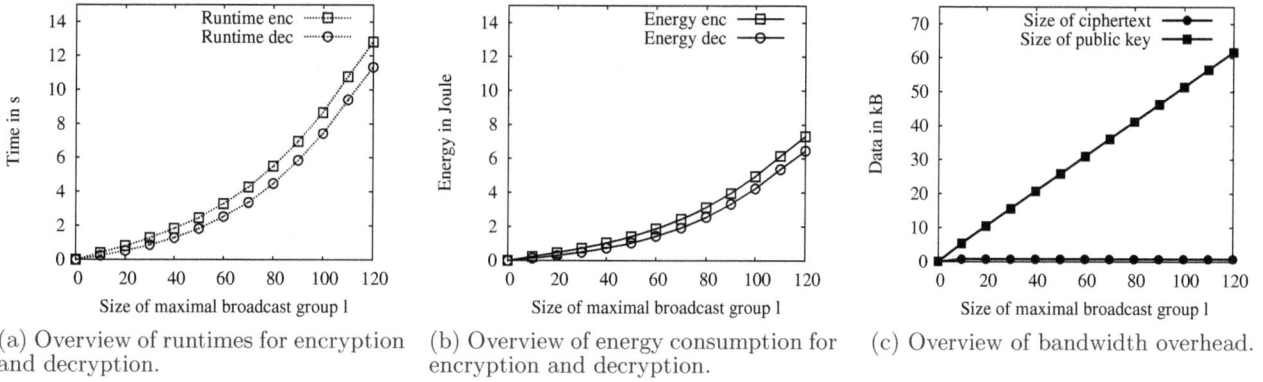

(a) Overview of runtimes for encryption and decryption.

(b) Overview of energy consumption for encryption and decryption.

(c) Overview of bandwidth overhead.

Figure 2: Runtime, energy consumption and bandwidth overhead of the SPLS for increasing $l$ and fixed $n = 1000$ and $k = 5$.

fore lower than in the SPLS. Figure 3b shows that the overhead for decryption is about two magnitudes lower than in the SPLS. Furthermore, Figure 3b shows the computation and energy overhead for fail-decryptions. These are the resources a user needs to spend in order to determine that a location update is actually not for her. Recalling the battery capacity of 20520 Joule, we can see that in terms of computational overhead the FPLS allows for sharing multiple locations per day and receiving thousands of location updates.

As already mentioned the main drawback of the FPLS is the data a user receives due to flooding. Figure 3c shows the lengths of a ciphertext as $k$ increases. In [16], the authors state that the very majority of users has less than 100 friends. Therefore, we can assume most ciphertexts to have a length of at most 60 kB. If an LSBS would have 1 million users, this would result in approximately $10^6 \times 60\text{kB} = 57.22$ GB of data every user receives per day. Clearly, this is not feasible. However, choosing a big region such that only 0.01% of all the world-wide location updates are received results in a bandwidth overhead of 5.86 MB per day.

The energy that is consumed for receiving data can be optimized with two measures. Firstly, receiving data via the WiFi interface consumes significantly less energy than receiving the same amount of data via 3G interface [2] (§ 3.6). For example receiving 500 kB of data via 3G consumes around 19 Joule and only 5 Joule via WiFi. Secondly, as noted in [2] (§ 3.6.1), the energy consumption strongly depends on the inter-transfer time between downloads. For example, receiving 50 kB transmissions with inter-transfer time 1 second consumes around 5 Joule, while it consumes 10 Joule if the inter-transfer time is 9 seconds. We therefore suggest: (i) to receive most of the traffic when a WiFi connection is available; (ii) that the service provider caches location updates for a certain period and sends them all at once in order to have few but large data transmissions to the users.

## 6. LSBS WITH AGGREGATE STATISTICS COLLECTION

In our scheme, the service provider acts as a channel between users. The service provider relays messages between the sender and the receivers, but learns nothing about the content of the messages sent. The business model of cur-

rently deployed LSBS relies on learning user check-ins. Service providers use that information in order to, e.g., give recommendations on most visited places and give discounts to users that check-in a number of times at a particular location.

We describe how our scheme can be extended to allow the service provider to collect aggregated data on how many times users visit each of the locations. In this extension, each time a user checks-in, the user increases a committed counter for that location. This committed counter is hidden from the service provider. However, after a number of check-ins, the user can choose to disclose the counter of one of the locations in order to, e.g., get a discount. The commitment ensures that the user cannot cheat and open the committed counter to a different value.

We note that, in currently deployed LSBS, users can check-in at a certain location without being present at that location. The countermeasure against that is that the wrong location disclosed to the service provider is also disclosed to the user's friends, which can cause annoyance.

Our extension provides the same countermeasure. Using zero-knowledge proofs, the user proves to the service provider that the location shared with her friends equals the location whose committed counter is increased. In order to do that, we make the following modification in our scheme. Instead of employing symmetric key encryption to encrypt the location message, we employ public key encryption. The key output when decrypting the broadcast encryption ciphertext is an ElGamal private key, while the corresponding public key is transmitted along with the broadcast encryption ciphertext.

In [16], a scheme that employs hardware devices at the physical location in order to ensure that users can check-in only if they are at the location is proposed. It is also possible to extend our scheme with hardware devices to achieve that property.

We note that the total number of locations where a user can check-in is usually large. The user should maintain a committed counter for each of the locations and, at each check-in, increment it without disclosing the location or the value of the counter, yet proving that the location equals the location shared with her friends. If we employ Pedersen commitments, this operation would have a cost linear on the total number of locations, which would make it impractical. In order to have a cost independent of the total number of

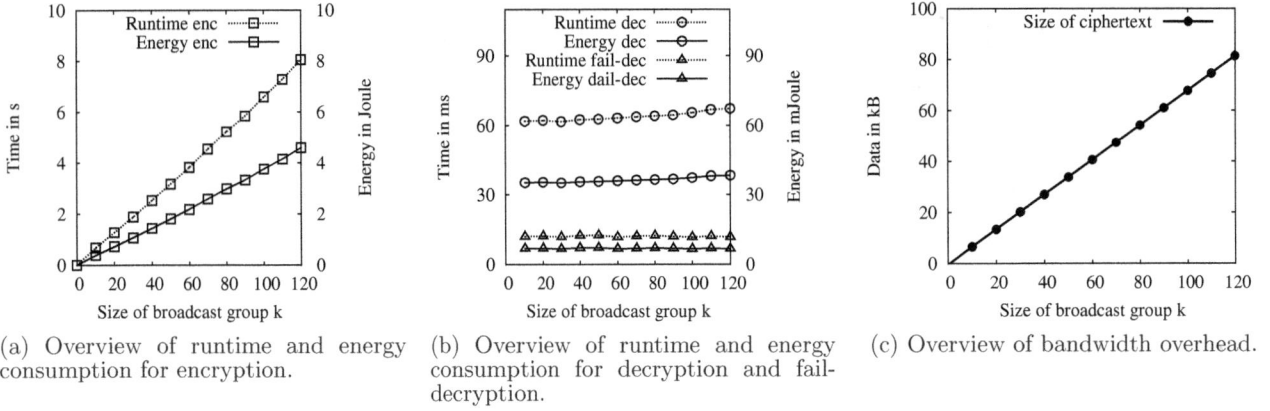

(a) Overview of runtime and energy consumption for encryption.

(b) Overview of runtime and energy consumption for decryption and fail-decryption.

(c) Overview of bandwidth overhead.

Figure 3: Runtime, energy consumption and bandwidth overhead of the FPLS for increasing $k$ and fixed $n = 1000$.

locations, we employ P-commitments [33], which are based on vector commitments.

## 6.1 Cryptographic Building Blocks

We recall the notation for zero-knowledge proofs and the definitions of P-commitments in [33].

### 6.1.1 Zero-Knowledge Proofs of Knowledge

We employ of classical results for efficient zero-knowledge proofs of knowledge (ZKPK) for discrete logarithm relations [46, 17, 15, 11, 10, 18]. In the notation of [13], a protocol proving knowledge of exponents $w_1, \ldots, w_n$ satisfying the formula $\phi(w_1, \ldots, w_n)$ is described as

$$\forall w_1, \ldots, w_n : \phi(w_1, \ldots, w_n) \tag{1}$$

Here, we use the symbol "⅄" instead of "∃" to indicate that we are proving "knowledge" of the exponents, rather than just its existence. The formula $\phi(w_1, \ldots, w_n)$ consists of conjunctions and disjunctions of "atoms". An atom expresses *group relations*, such as $\prod_{j=1}^{k} g_j^{\mathcal{F}_j} = 1$, where the $g_j$ are elements of prime order groups and the $\mathcal{F}_j$'s are polynomials in the variables $w_1, \ldots, w_n$.

There exist practical zero-knowledge proofs for the types of relations required in our protocols. We refer to Camenisch et al. [12, 14] for details.

#### Extended zero-knowledge formulas.

A proof system for (1) can be transformed into a proof system for the following more expressive statements about secret exponents $(w_i)_i = sexps$ and secret bases $(g_i)_i = sbases$:

$$\forall sexps, sbases : \phi(sexps, bases \cup sbases) \tag{2}$$

The transformation uses a blinded base $g_i' = g_i h^{\rho_i}$ for every $g_i$. It adds $h$ and all $g_i'$ to the public *bases*, $\rho_i$ to the secret *sexps*, and rewrites $g_i^{\mathcal{F}_j}$ into $g_i'^{\mathcal{F}_j} h^{-\mathcal{F}_j \rho_i}$ for all $i, j$. Finally, we observe that the proof system supports pairing product equations $\prod_{j=1}^{k} e(g_j, \tilde{g}_j)^{\mathcal{F}_j} = 1$ in groups of prime order $|\mathbb{G}|$ with a bilinear map $e : \mathbb{G} \times \tilde{\mathbb{G}} \to \mathbb{G}_t$, by treating the target group as the group of the proof system—we focus on the special case of $i = j$ for simplicity: the embedding for secret bases is unchanged, except for the case in which both bases in a pairing are secret. In the latter case, $e(g_j, \tilde{g}_j)^{\mathcal{F}_j}$ needs to be transformed into $e(g_j', \tilde{g}_j')^{\mathcal{F}_j} e(g_j', \tilde{h})^{-\mathcal{F}_j \rho_j} e(h, \tilde{g}_j')^{-\mathcal{F}_j \tilde{\rho}_j} e(h, \tilde{h})^{-\mathcal{F}_j \rho_j \tilde{\rho}_j}$.

#### Macro notation for zero-knowledge statements.

We use a macro language to specify named proof components that can be reused as sub-components of larger proofs. For example, we may define a proof macro for the long division of $a$ by $q$ as follows: $\mathbf{Div}(a, q) \mapsto (b) \equiv \forall a, q, b, r : a = b * q + r \wedge r < b \wedge 0 \leq a, b, q, r \leq \sqrt{|\mathbb{G}|} \wedge b > 1$. Semantically, the function $\mathbf{Div}$ states that the division of $a$ by $q$ gives $b$ with remainder $r$. Secret $a$ is interpreted as an initial value and secret $b$ as a new value. In terms of cryptography, it is simply syntactic sugar, but important sugar as demonstrated by the long list of side conditions to guarantee a unique positive solution modulo the order of $\mathbb{G}$. Proving these inequalities is itself non-trivial and could be further expanded using macros.

Named proof components can be used in further higher-level proofs without their details being made explicit. For example, the proof $\forall \ldots, a, q, b : \cdots \wedge b = \mathbf{Div}(a, q)$ can from now on be used in proof expressions instead of the complex restrictions above. All variables within the component declaration (e.g., variables $a, q, b$ in $\mathbf{Div}(a, q) \mapsto (b)$) can be re-used in the high level proof. Variables whose knowledge is proved, but that are not in the declaration, are considered inaccessible to the higher-level proof.

### 6.1.2 P-commitments

A vector commitment scheme allows Alice to succinctly commit to a vector $\mathbf{x} = \langle x_1, \ldots, x_n \rangle \in \mathcal{M}^n$ such that she can compute an opening $w$ to $x_i$ and can replace $x_i$ by a new value $x_i'$ by updating her commitment, such that both $w$ and the update value is of size independent of $i$ and $n$. A vector commitment scheme consists of the following algorithms.

Setup$(1^k, \ell)$. On input the security parameter $1^k$ and an upper bound $\ell$ on the size of the vector, generate the parameters of the commitment scheme $par$, which include a description of the message space $\mathcal{M}$ and a description of the randomness space $\mathcal{R}$.

Commit$(par, \mathbf{x}, r)$. On input a vector $\mathbf{x} \in \mathcal{M}^n$ ($n \leq \ell$) and $r \in \mathcal{R}$, output a commitment $com$ to $\mathbf{x}$.

Prove$(par, i, \mathbf{x}, r)$. Compute a witness $w$ for $x_i$.

Verify$(par, com, x, i, w)$. Output accept if $w$ is a valid witness for $x$ being at position $i$ and reject otherwise.

94

Update($par, com, i, x, r, x', r'$). On input a commitment $com$ with value $x$ at position $i$ and randomness $r$, output a commitment $com'$ with value $x'$ at position $i$ and randomness $r'$. The other positions remain unchanged.

A commitment scheme must be hiding and binding. The hiding property requires that any probabilistic polynomial time (p.p.t.) adversary $\mathcal{A}$ has negligible advantage in guessing which of two vectors $\mathbf{x}$ of values of its choice has been used to compute a challenge commitment. The binding property requires that any p.p.t. adversary $\mathcal{A}$ has negligible advantage in computing a vector $\mathbf{x}$ of length $n$, randomness $r$, a value $x$, a position $i \in [1..n]$ and a witness $w$ such that $\mathbf{x}[i] \neq x$ but the commitment $com \leftarrow$ Commit($par, \mathbf{x}, r$) can be opened to $x$ at position $i$ using $w$.

A P-commitment scheme is a secure vector commitment scheme that supports three ZKPKs.

**Create.** A proof of correct commitment generation that proves knowledge of $(\mathbf{x}, r)$ such that Commit($par, \mathbf{x}, r) = com$. We call the proof macro $\mathbf{Create}(\mathbf{x}) \rightarrow (com, r, (w_i)_i)$ as it proves that a P-commitment was correctly initialized to the vector $\mathbf{x}$. The prover can then use this commitment in subsequent proof steps. To simplify our macro notation, we use $M = (com, r, (w_i)_i)$ as a shorthand for the collection of $com$, $r$, and different $w_i$ values and refer to it as the memory of a P-commitment proof.

**Get.** A proof of a witness $w$ that a value $x$ was committed to in $com$ at position $i$.

$$\mathbf{Get}(M, i) \rightarrow (x) \equiv$$
$$\nexists x, i, w :$$
$$\text{Verify}(par, com, x, i, w) = \text{accept} \ \wedge i \in [1, n]$$

**Set.** A proof that a commitment $com'$ is an update of commitment $com$ at position $i$. This proof is slightly more involved because it requires the prover to prove knowledge of the old vector value for the updated position to bind the old and the new commitment together:

$$\mathbf{Set}(M, i, x') \rightarrow (M') \equiv$$
$$\nexists \mathbf{x}[i], x', i, r, r', w :$$
$$com' = \text{Update}(par, com, i, \mathbf{x}[i], r, x', r') \ \wedge$$
$$\text{Verify}(par, com, \mathbf{x}[i], i, w) = \text{accept} \wedge i \in [1, n]$$

## 6.2 Construction

As mentioned above, in this extension the location message $m$ is encrypted using an ElGamal encryption $c = (c_1, c_2) = (y^r \cdot m, g^r)$, where $y = g^x$ is the public key and $x$ is the secret key. The secret key is encrypted in the broadcast encryption ciphertext, while the public key is transmitted along with the broadcast encryption ciphertext. We employ a zero-knowledge proof of knowledge of $m$ encrypted to in $c$:

$$\nexists m, t : e(c_1, g) = e(m, g) \cdot e(t, g) \wedge e(t, g) = e(y, c_2)$$

In our scheme, the indices $(i_1, \ldots, i_n)$ of the committed vector will be the locations, and $n$ is the total number of locations. We note that the schemes proposed in [33] to implement P-commitments employ a structure preserving signature (SPS) scheme to sign together an index $i$ with the generator $g_i$ for position $i$ in the parameters of the commitment scheme. SPS sign group elements, and therefore we can

prove in zero-knowledge equality between the location message $m$ encrypted in $c$ and the index $i$ of the P-commitment. Sender and receivers employ a table or a hash function to map a location to an element of group $\mathbb{G}$.

In the registration phase, the service provider executes Setup($1^k, \ell$), where $\ell$ is the number of locations, and sends $par$ to the users. Then, each user creates a vector $\mathbf{x} = (0, \ldots, 0)$ of size $\ell$, picks $r \in \mathcal{R}$ and runs Commit($par, \mathbf{x}, r$) to get $com$. The user sends $com$ to the service provider, along with a proof

$$\nexists \mathbf{x} : \mathbf{Create}(\mathbf{x}) \rightarrow (M) \wedge \mathbf{x} = (0, \ldots, 0)$$

where $M = (com, r, (w_i)_i)$. This proof initializes the counters for each of the locations to 0 and can be done very efficiently in the P-commitment schemes in [33].

In the main phase, when a user sends a broadcast ciphertext to the service provider for location $i$ encrypted in ciphertext $(c_1, c_2)$, the user sets $\mathbf{x}[i]' = \mathbf{x}[i] + 1$, picks random $r' \in \mathcal{R}$ and runs Update($par, com, i, \mathbf{x}[i], r, \mathbf{x}[i]', r'$) to get $com'$. The user sends $com'$ to the service provider, along with a proof

$$\nexists i, t, \mathbf{x}[i], \mathbf{x}[i]' :$$
$$e(c_1, g) = e(i, g) \cdot e(t, g) \wedge e(t, g) = e(y, c_2) \wedge$$
$$\mathbf{Set}(M, i, \mathbf{x}[i]') \rightarrow (M') \wedge \mathbf{x}[i]' = \mathbf{x}[i] + 1$$

The user proves that she increments the committed counter for the same location in the message encrypted in $c$. We recall that the cost of this proof is independent of the number of locations. When the service provider receives the broadcast encryption ciphertext, the ElGamal ciphertex and public key, the commitment $com'$ and the proof, the provider verifies the proof. If it is correct, then the provider replaces the stored $com$ by $com'$ and sends the broadcast encryption ciphertext and the ElGamal ciphertext and public key to the receivers. The receivers decrypt first the broadcast encryption ciphertex to get the ElGamal secret key, which is used to decrypt the ElGamal ciphertext and get the sender's location.

When a user wishes to open the counter corresponding to one of the locations, she can use algorithm Prove($par, i, \mathbf{x}, r$) to compute a witness $w$ for location $i$ and send $(\mathbf{x}[i], i, w)$ to the provider. The service provider runs Verify($par, com, \mathbf{x}[i], i, w$) and accepts the value of the counter $\mathbf{x}[i]$ if the verification is successful. Alternatively, the user can also prove statements about the committed counter in zero-knowledge, e.g., prove that the counter has surpassed a threshold that entitles her to receive a discount. The proof $\mathbf{Get}$ is employed for this purpose.

The security of this extension relies on the security of P-commitments. The hiding property, along with the zero-knowledge property of proofs of knowledge, ensures that the service provider does not learn the values of the committed counters or the locations whose counters are increased. Additionally, the binding property of P-commitments and the extractability of proofs of knowledge ensure that the committed counters are updated correctly and that they cannot be opened to a wrong value.

## 7. DISCUSSION

The computation overhead of the SPLS is mainly due to the creation of a symmetric key. An actual location sharing operation is then encrypted using a fast encryption scheme, such as AES. While we note that the symmetric key of the SPLS can be reused for many location sharing operations, we argue that even computing several symmetric keys per day is feasible. Firstly, as our evaluation shows computing symmetric keys consumes very little energy and can thus be done several times without draining the battery. Secondly, since modern smart phones have multi-core processors embedded, one core can be occupied for creating a symmetric key while the phone is still usable for other operations, such as email checking or surfing the web. All in all we thus argue that on the user side our scheme imposes negligible overhead to the user's device.

The FPLS on the other hand imposes a significant bandwidth overhead. However, we note that it is to the best of our knowledge the only scheme that allows a user to hide her friends without relying on proxies, such as in [45]. It does so by offering a privacy/performance trade-off, which has been proposed before in schemes for privacy-preserving LSBS [45]. Note that the FPLS is not vulnerable to velocity-based attacks [29] for two reasons. Firstly location updates happen sporadically and not continuously and hence big regions are much harder to correlate. Secondly, and more importantly, the big regions are much bigger than in k-anonymity schemes, such as [31].

We note that our schemes are also suitable to implement other services, such as social recommendation applications. This is because in practice users can share arbitrary information in the ciphertext. Instead of encrypting location information, users could share their reviews, such as how they like the food in a particular restaurant. Furthermore, the low overhead of the SPLS and the strategy of reusing symmetric keys would allow to use the scheme for location tracking applications. Such applications require rather frequent location updates instead of sporadic ones, which is usually the case for check-in applications. Furthermore, we note that our schemes are more efficient than a unicast solution in which every user sends an encrypted location update to each of her friends. This is because in our schemes the user only needs to transmit the encrypted location update to the service provider that is then forwarding it to the recipients or all users of the service, respectively. This consumes significantly less bandwidth and also less energy than in the unicast solution.

Although in the setup routine of the SPLS, as well as the FPLS, the service provider initially needs to commit to a maximal number of users $n$, we note that even if there are more than $n$ users in the service, the service provider does not need to re-initialize the service. In the SPLS, $n$ is only used for checking that $l \leq n$. This condition, however, is maintained if it was true before and $n$ increases. In the FPLS, the scheme's public key can be extended, because the $g^{a^i}$ with $i > n$ can be computed when necessary and distributed among all users of the service.

Besides location-sharing, badge and mayorship protocols are another main functionality of a GSN. For the latter privacy preserving protocols have been proposed in [16]. We note that it would be possible to combine both approaches to build a privacy-preserving GSN.

## 8. CONCLUSIONS

We have defined the privacy properties that an LSBS should provide and we have proposed two LSBS based on identity-based broadcast encryption. Both constructions al-low a user to share her location with her friends without disclosing it to the service provider. The first construction discloses to the service provider the receivers of a location update, while the second does not. As advantages from previous work, in our schemes the LSBS provider does not need to perform complex operations in order to compute a reply for a location data request, but only needs to forward IBBE ciphertexts to the receivers. This allows to run a privacy-preserving LSBS at significantly lower costs. We implement both constructions and present a performance analysis that shows their practicality. Furthermore, we extend our schemes such that the service provider, performing some verification work, is able to collect privacy-preserving statistics about the places users share among each other. This could be a way to monetize the privacy-preserving LSBS.

### Acknowledgments.

We thank the anonymous reviewers for their valuable comments. We also thank Carmela Troncoso for insightful discussions and helpful feedback. This research was supported in part by the projects: IWT SBO SPION, FWO G.0360.11N, FWO G.0686.11N, GOA TENSE (GOA/11/007), iMinds SoLoMIDEM, and KU Leuven OT project Traffic Analysis Resistant Privacy Enhancing Technologies.

## 9. REFERENCES

[1] Michel Abdalla, Mihir Bellare, Dario Catalano, Eike Kiltz, Tadayoshi Kohno, Tanja Lange, John Malone-Lee, Gregory Neven, Pascal Paillier, and Haixia Shi. Searchable encryption revisited: Consistency properties, relation to anonymous ibe, and extensions. In *Advances in Cryptology–CRYPTO 2005*, pages 205–222. Springer, 2005.

[2] Niranjan Balasubramanian, Aruna Balasubramanian, and Arun Venkataramani. Energy consumption in mobile phones: a measurement study and implications for network applications. In *Proceedings of the 9th ACM SIGCOMM conference on Internet measurement*, pages 280–293. ACM, 2009.

[3] Adam Barth, Dan Boneh, and Brent Waters. Privacy in encrypted content distribution using private broadcast encryption. *Financial Cryptography and Data Security*, pages 52–64, 2006.

[4] A.R. Beresford and F. Stajano. Mix zones: User Privacy in Location-aware Services. In *Pervasive Computing and Communications Workshops, 2004. Proceedings of the Second IEEE Annual Conference on*, pages 127 – 131, march 2004.

[5] Igor Bilogrevic, Murtuza Jadliwala, Kübra Kalkan, Jean-Pierre Hubaux, and Imad Aad. Privacy in mobile computing for location-sharing-based services. In *Privacy Enhancing Technologies*, volume 6794 of *Lecture Notes in Computer Science*, pages 77–96. Springer Berlin Heidelberg, 2011.

[6] Dan Boneh and Xavier Boyen. Short signatures without random oracles. In *Advances in Cryptology-EUROCRYPT 2004*, pages 56–73. Springer, 2004.

[7] Dan Boneh and Matt Franklin. Identity-based encryption from the weil pairing. In *Advances in Cryptology-CRYPTO 2001*, pages 213–229. Springer, 2001.

[8] Dan Boneh, Craig Gentry, and Brent Waters. Collusion resistant broadcast encryption with short ciphertexts and private keys. In *Advances in Cryptology-CRYPTO 2005*, pages 258–275. Springer, 2005.

[9] Xavier Boyen and Brent Waters. Anonymous hierarchical identity-based encryption (without random oracles). In *Advances in Cryptology-CRYPTO 2006*, pages 290–307. Springer, 2006.

[10] Stefan Brands. Rapid demonstration of linear relations connected by boolean operators. In Walter Fumy, editor, *Advances in Cryptology — EUROCRYPT '97*, volume 1233 of *LNCS*, pages 318–333. Springer Verlag, 1997.

[11] Jan Camenisch. *Group Signature Schemes and Payment Systems Based on the Discrete Logarithm Problem*. PhD thesis, ETH Zürich, 1998.

[12] Jan Camenisch, Nathalie Casati, Thomas Groß, and Victor Shoup. Credential authenticated identification and key exchange. In *CRYPTO*, pages 255–276, 2010.

[13] Jan Camenisch, Stephan Krenn, and Victor Shoup. A framework for practical universally composable zero-knowledge protocols. In *ASIACRYPT*, pages 449–467, 2011.

[14] Jan Camenisch, Stephan Krenn, and Victor Shoup. A framework for practical universally composable zero-knowledge protocols. Cryptology ePrint Archive, Report 2011/228, 2011. http://eprint.iacr.org/.

[15] Jan Camenisch and Markus Michels. Proving in zero-knowledge that a number $n$ is the product of two safe primes. In Jacques Stern, editor, *Advances in Cryptology — EUROCRYPT '99*, volume 1592 of *LNCS*, pages 107–122. Springer Verlag, 1999.

[16] Bogdan Carbunar, Radu Sion, Rahul Potharaju, and Moussa Ehsan. The shy mayor: Private badges in geosocial networks. In Feng Bao, Pierangela Samarati, and Jianying Zhou, editors, *Applied Cryptography and Network Security*, volume 7341 of *Lecture Notes in Computer Science*, pages 436–454. Springer Berlin Heidelberg, 2012.

[17] D. Chaum and T. Pedersen. Wallet databases with observers. In *CRYPTO '92*, volume 740 of *LNCS*, pages 89–105, 1993.

[18] R. Cramer, I. Damgård, and B. Schoenmakers. Proofs of partial knowledge and simplified design of witness hiding protocols. In *CRYPTO*, pages 174–187, 1994.

[19] Joan Daemen and Vincent Rijmen. *The design of Rijndael: AES-the advanced encryption standard*. Springer, 2002.

[20] Cécile Delerablée. Identity-based broadcast encryption with constant size ciphertexts and private keys. *Advances in Cryptology-ASIACRYPT 2007*, pages 200–215, 2007.

[21] Yevgeniy Dodis and Nelly Fazio. Public key trace and revoke scheme secure against adaptive chosen ciphertext attack. *Public Key CryptographyâĂŤPKC 2003*, pages 100–115, 2002.

[22] Changyu Dong and Naranker Dulay. Longitude: A privacy-preserving location sharing protocol for mobile applications. In *Trust Management V*, volume 358 of *IFIP Advances in Information and Communication Technology*, pages 133–148. Springer Berlin Heidelberg, 2011.

[23] Nelly Fazio and Irippuge Perera. Outsider-anonymous broadcast encryption with sublinear ciphertexts. *Public Key Cryptography-PKC 2012*, pages 225–242, 2012.

[24] Amos Fiat and Moni Naor. Broadcast encryption. In *Advances in CryptologyâĂŤCryptoâĂŹ93*, pages 480–491. Springer, 1994.

[25] J. Freudiger, R. Shokri, and J. Hubaux. Evaluating the Privacy Risk of Location-Based Services. In *Financial Cryptography and Data Security*, volume 7035 of *LNCS*, pages 31–46. Springer Berlin, 2012.

[26] Julien Freudiger, Raoul Neu, and Jean-Pierre Hubaux. Private sharing of user location over online social networks. *3rd Hot Topics in Privacy Enhancing Technologies (HotPETs 2010)*, 2010.

[27] Sébastien Gambs, Olivier Heen, and Christophe Potin. A comparative privacy analysis of geosocial networks. In *Proceedings of the 4th ACM SIGSPATIAL International Workshop on Security and Privacy in GIS and LBS*, SPRINGL '11, pages 33–40, New York, NY, USA, 2011. ACM.

[28] Craig Gentry and Brent Waters. Adaptive security in broadcast encryption systems (with short ciphertexts). *Advances in Cryptology-EUROCRYPT 2009*, pages 171–188, 2009.

[29] Gabriel Ghinita, Maria Luisa Damiani, Claudio Silvestri, and Elisa Bertino. Preventing velocity-based linkage attacks in location-aware applications. GIS '09, pages 246–255, New York, NY, USA, 2009. ACM.

[30] Gabriel Ghinita, Panos Kalnis, Ali Khoshgozaran, Cyrus Shahabi, and Kian-Lee Tan. Private queries in location based services: anonymizers are not necessary. SIGMOD '08, pages 121–132, New York, NY, USA, 2008. ACM.

[31] M. Gruteser and D. Grunwald. Anonymous Usage of Location-Based Services Through Spatial and Temporal Cloaking. MobiSys '03, pages 31–42, New York, NY, USA, 2003. ACM.

[32] Leping Huang, Hiroshi Yamane, Kanta Matsuura, and Kaoru Sezaki. Towards modeling wireless location privacy. In George Danezis and David Martin, editors, *Privacy Enhancing Technologies*, volume 3856 of *Lecture Notes in Computer Science*, pages 59–77. Springer Berlin Heidelberg, 2006.

[33] Markulf Kohlweiss and Alfredo Rial. Optimally private access control. In *Proceedings of the 12th ACM workshop on Workshop on privacy in the electronic society*, pages 37–48. ACM, 2013.

[34] John Krumm. Inference attacks on location tracks. In Anthony LaMarca, Marc Langheinrich, and KhaiN. Truong, editors, *Pervasive Computing*, volume 4480 of *Lecture Notes in Computer Science*, pages 127–143. Springer Berlin Heidelberg, 2007.

[35] John Krumm. Realistic driving trips for location privacy. In Hideyuki Tokuda, Michael Beigl, Adrian Friday, A. Brush, and Yoshito Tobe, editors, *Pervasive Computing*, volume 5538 of *Lecture Notes in Computer Science*, pages 25–41. Springer Berlin / Heidelberg, 2009.

[36] Allison Lewko, Amit Sahai, and Brent Waters. Revocation systems with very small private keys. In *Security and Privacy (SP), 2010 IEEE Symposium on*, pages 273–285. IEEE, 2010.

[37] Mingyan Li, Krishna Sampigethaya, Leping Huang, and Radha Poovendran. Swing & swap: User-centric approaches towards maximizing location privacy. WPES '06, pages 19–28, New York, NY, USA, 2006. ACM.

[38] Benoît Libert, Kenneth Paterson, and Elizabeth Quaglia. Anonymous broadcast encryption: adaptive security and efficient constructions in the standard model. *Public Key Cryptography–PKC 2012*, pages 206–224, 2012.

[39] Zi Lin, Denis Foo Kune, and Nicholas Hopper. Efficient private proximity testing with gsm location sketches. In AngelosD. Keromytis, editor, *Financial Cryptography and Data Security*, volume 7397 of *Lecture Notes in Computer Science*, pages 73–88. Springer Berlin Heidelberg, 2012.

[40] Dalit Naor, Moni Naor, and Jeff Lotspiech. Revocation and tracing schemes for stateless receivers. In *Advances in Cryptology-CRYPTO 2001*, pages 41–62. Springer, 2001.

[41] Arvind Narayanan, Narendran Thiagarajan, Mugdha Lakhani, Michael Hamburg, and Dan Boneh. Location privacy via private proximity testing. In *NDSS*, 2011.

[42] Femi Olumofin, Piotr Tysowski, Ian Goldberg, and Urs Hengartner. Achieving efficient query privacy for location based services. In *Privacy Enhancing Technologies*, pages 93–110. Springer, 2010.

[43] Tatiana Pontes, Marisa Vasconcelos, Jussara Almeida, Ponnurangam Kumaraguru, and Virgilio Almeida. We know where you live: Privacy characterization of foursquare behavior. In *4th International Workshop on Location-Based Social Networks (LBSN 2012)*, 2012.

[44] Raluca Ada Popa, Andrew J Blumberg, Hari Balakrishnan, and Frank H Li. Privacy and accountability for location-based aggregate statistics. In *Proceedings of the 18th ACM conference on Computer and communications security*, pages 653–666. ACM, 2011.

[45] K.P.N. Puttaswamy, Shiyuan Wang, T. Steinbauer, D. Agrawal, A. El Abbadi, C. Kruegel, and B.Y. Zhao. Preserving location privacy in geosocial applications. *Mobile Computing, IEEE Transactions on*, 13(1):159–173, Jan 2014.

[46] C. Schnorr. Efficient signature generation for smart cards. *Journal of Cryptology*, 4(3):239–252, 1991.

[47] R. Shokri, G. Theodorakopoulos, J. Le Boudec, and J. Hubaux. Quantifying Location Privacy. In *Security and Privacy (SP)*, pages 247–262, May 2011.

[48] C.R. Vicente, D. Freni, C. Bettini, and Christian S. Jensen. Location-related privacy in geo-social networks. *Internet Computing, IEEE*, 15(3):20–27, 2011.

[49] Brent Waters. Dual system encryption: Realizing fully secure ibe and hibe under simple assumptions. *Advances in Cryptology-CRYPTO 2009*, pages 619–636, 2009.

[50] Ge Zhong, Ian Goldberg, and Urs Hengartner. Louis, lester and pierre: Three protocols for location privacy. In Nikita Borisov and Philippe Golle, editors, *Privacy Enhancing Technologies*, volume 4776 of *Lecture Notes in Computer Science*, pages 62–76. Springer Berlin Heidelberg, 2007.

# Short Paper: Detection of GPS Spoofing Attacks in Power Grids

Der-Yeuan Yu[†], Aanjhan Ranganathan[†], Thomas Locher[‡], Srdjan Capkun[†], David Basin[†]

[†]Department of Computer Science
ETH Zurich, Switzerland
{dyu,raanjhan,capkuns,basin}@inf.ethz.ch

[‡]ABB Corporate Research
Switzerland
thomas.locher@ch.abb.com

## ABSTRACT

Power companies are deploying a multitude of sensors to monitor the energy grid. Measurements at different locations should be aligned in time to obtain the global state of the grid, and the industry therefore uses GPS as a common clock source. However, these sensors are exposed to GPS time spoofing attacks that cause misaligned aggregated measurements, leading to inaccurate monitoring that affects power stability and line fault contingencies. In this paper, we analyze the resilience of phasor measurement sensors, which record voltages and currents, to GPS spoofing performed by an adversary external to the system. We propose a solution that leverages the characteristics of multiple sensors in the power grid to limit the feasibility of such attacks. In order to increase the robustness of wide-area power grid monitoring, we evaluate mechanisms that allow collaboration among GPS receivers to detect spoofing attacks. We apply multilateration techniques to allow a set of GPS receivers to locate a false GPS signal source. Using simulations, we show that receivers sharing a local clock can locate nearby spoofing adversaries with sufficient confidence.

## Categories and Subject Descriptors

C.2.1 [**Computer Systems Organization**]: Computer-Communication Networks—*Network Architecture and Design*

## Keywords

GPS spoofing; clock synchronization; power grids

## 1. INTRODUCTION

The power industry is deploying sensor networks in the power grid for maintenance and monitoring purposes. The state-of-the-art system, known as a wide-area monitoring system (WAMS), is an infrastructure that uses modern sensors such as phasor measurement units (PMUs) to accurately measure power lines at different locations. Obtaining

knowledge of an accurate state of the power grid requires that sensor data from PMUs is timestamped with respect to the same time reference. This implies that PMUs across the grid have synchronized clocks when timestamping their measurements. Currently, this is achieved by having PMUs synchronize to GPS time through built-in GPS modules. However, the lack of authentication in civilian GPS messages exposes the system to GPS clock spoofing attacks that could lead to inaccurate power state estimation.

In this paper, we consider the problem of GPS spoofing in power grids. We show that given their fixed deployment locations, PMUs may detect spoofing attacks by verifying their locations and checking clock offsets with other neighboring PMUs. These checks constrain the adversary's freedom of choosing where and when spoofed signals should be sent. Given sufficiently many GPS receivers, we show that the adversary cannot spoof their clocks without violating some constraints and thereby being detected by the system. Although similar mechanisms have been proposed to detect GPS spoofing [3,7,9], verification that leverages multiple receivers with different synchronization settings in the power grid has not yet been addressed. Additionally, our system enables PMUs to use multilateration to calculate the adversary's position.

Our contributions in this paper are the following. First, we define the GPS clock spoofing problem in the context of power grid infrastructures that consist of multiple spatially distributed PMUs. Second, we derive constraints imposed on the adversary to successfully execute a spoofing attack without being detected. Finally, we use existing multilateration methods to allow PMUs to locate the spoofer. In contrast to previous work, our solution considers a mixed set of receivers, which may or may not have synchronized clocks, to detect spoofing attacks by verifying the calculated location and time information. We show that, for example, spoofing can be detected with at least 5 synchronized receivers or at least 6 non-synchronized receivers.

## 2. BACKGROUND AND MOTIVATION

We introduce the power grid wide-area monitoring system and its reliance on GPS to motivate the problem.

### 2.1 Wide-Area Monitoring Systems

A WAMS [20] consists of PMUs that are installed at electrical substations to measure circuit quantities of power lines, as shown in Figure 1. An important requirement while aggregating PMU measurements from different substations is the *time alignment* of data, which implies that all the

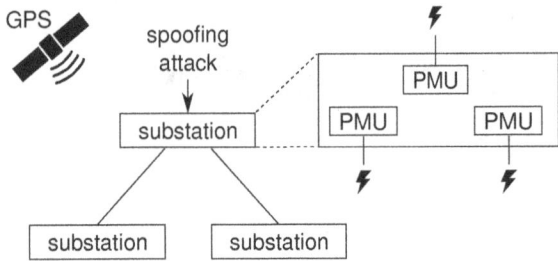

**Figure 1: Illustration of PMUs installed in substations across a power grid to measure power lines. Spoofing attacks can occur in a substation that offsets the clocks of nearby PMUs.**

PMUs should synchronize to a common time source to make synchronized measurements. The IEEE C37.118 standard governing PMU specifications defines the maximally tolerated clock synchronization error between any two measurements from different PMUs to be 31.8 or 26.5 microseconds for 50 or 60 Hertz systems, respectively [1]. As a possible solution, the precise time protocol (PTP) defined by IEEE 1588 [15] can be implemented to synchronize numerous nearby devices to a central clock with microsecond to sub-microsecond accuracy. However, for a power grid deployed on a nationwide scale, PTP is infeasible due to its dependence on specialized switches. As a more scalable alternative, modern PMUs mostly resort to GPS-based solutions [13]. The use of GPS for clock synchronization therefore exposes PMUs to intentional GPS spoofing attacks.

## 2.2 GPS Clock Synchronization and Spoofing

GPS satellites orbit the Earth and broadcast their orbit information and time. A GPS receiver receives messages from the satellites and calculates its own location and clock offset relative to the time of GPS satellites by solving a set of time-of-arrival (TOA) equations. PMUs installed across the power grid leverage clock synchronization in GPS to timestamp measurements with respect to the same time reference, referred to as GPS time.

The adversary can spoof civilian GPS messages since they are not authenticated. As a result, receivers may calculate incorrect locations or clock offsets, as shown by Shepard et al. [13]. GPS simulators are already available in the open market and allow an adversary to easily launch GPS spoofing attacks. Furthermore, these simulators are also capable of spoofing messages of other navigation systems like GLONASS.

Incorrect timestamping of phasor measurement data impacts the reliability of applications such as distance line protection and voltage stability monitoring [8]. Existing work has investigated the impact of incorrect timestamps on various power protection and monitoring mechanisms that use PMU measurements. Jiang et al. [9] demonstrate the feasibility of GPS spoofing attacks on single PMUs, and show that spoofing the GPS receiver clocks on the PMUs can cause erroneous estimates of the actual power load and trigger false warnings of power instability. Zhang et al. [18] have also investigated the impact of spoofed GPS timestamps on voltage stability monitoring. Moreover, they show that *line fault location*—an application that identifies the location of a power line failure, such as a short circuit on the transmis-

sion line—can be misled by up to 180 km if the system is subject to a GPS spoofing attack that shifts the clock by as little as 2.8 milliseconds. Motivated by the potential impact of GPS spoofing, we analyze the GPS spoofing problem and propose a solution that leverages the specific characteristics of GPS use in the power grid.

## 3. PROBLEM FORMULATION

We approach the problem of GPS spoofing on PMUs in electrical substations by first defining the system and adversarial models.

### 3.1 System Model

We assume that each PMU has its own GPS antenna, and all GPS antennas are spatially distributed along the rooftop of the substation perimeter, which is typically around 50 to 100 meters wide. The system can therefore be abstractly viewed as a set of $n_r$ GPS receivers $\mathcal{R} = \{R_1, ..., R_{n_r}\}$. Since a PMU is normally installed in a fixed position within a substation, we can assume that a GPS receiver $R_i$ knows its physical location $\ell_i$. This can be achieved by the administrator giving the location information to the GPS module, which is supported by existing GPS receivers, during initial PMU deployment. These devices communicate over an existing network to transmit measurements. We denote the set of $n_s$ GPS satellites orbiting Earth by $\mathcal{S} = \{S_1, ..., S_{n_s}\}$. At a predefined time, satellite $S_j$ broadcasts its location in space, denoted by $\ell_j^s$, and the corresponding GPS time, denoted by $t_j^s$, at which the message is sent.

### 3.2 Adversarial Model

We consider an adversary that has complete knowledge of the physical location of all the GPS receivers in $\mathcal{R}$. The adversary can place multiple antennas at arbitrary locations to send out fake GPS signals and trick PMUs into synchronizing their clocks incorrectly. When the adversary is sending spoofed signals to impersonate an authentic satellite $S_j$, we use $S_j^a$ to denote the satellite that is emulated. The entire set of emulated satellites is denoted by $\mathcal{S}^a$. For a fake GPS signal from each emulated satellite $S_j^a$, the adversary now has the following variables to assign values for a successful clock desynchronization: the claimed trajectory of the emulated satellite, and the corresponding true location of the antenna and transmit time of a fake GPS message.

We also assume that the spoofed signals are received by all GPS receivers near the targeted substation. Otherwise, if the adversary can send different signals to each GPS receiver (e.g., using directional antennas), each receiver can be independently spoofed to an arbitrary location and time without violating constraints between the receivers [14]. In addition, we focus our discussion on civilian GPS signals, which do not implement authentication, since modern PMUs produced by manufacturers without military affiliation do not have access to military GPS signals.

### 3.3 Objectives

Under the system and adversarial models, our goal is to analyze the security of clock synchronization of GPS-enabled PMUs across the power grid in the presence of spoofing attacks, and determine ways to synchronize PMU clocks such that they are accurate with respect to the error bound tolerated by standards [1]. Concretely, we aim at analyzing the

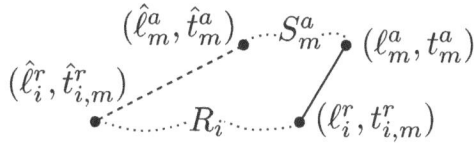

**Figure 2: The receiver perceives the TOA equation as marked by the dotted line, while the true TOA equation is marked by the solid line.**

feasibility of GPS spoofing attacks in the power grid and propose countermeasures to detect or prevent them.

# 4. DETECTION OF SPOOFING ATTACKS

We now describe the verification that can be performed by multiple GPS receivers in collaboration and the resulting constraints on undetectable spoofing attacks.

## 4.1 Formulation of GPS Spoofing

We begin by summarizing the adversary's variables for each emulated satellite $S_m^a$ and each victim receiver $R_i$ to successfully mount a spoofing attack. First, the adversary may arbitrarily announce its orbit information and thereby claim to be at location $\hat{\ell}_m^a$ at time $\hat{t}_m^a$. Second, the adversary chooses the true location $\ell_m^a$ to place the spoofing antenna and the true time $t_m^a$ when the signal is sent, where $t_m^a$ is related to $\hat{t}_m^a$ by a clock delay $\delta_m^a$: $\hat{t}_m^a = t_m^a + \delta_m^a$. Finally, for each victim receiver $R_i$ receiving the satellite signal, the adversary spoofs it to the location $\hat{\ell}_i$ and incurs a clock offset of $\hat{\delta}_{i,m}^r$. The local timestamp therefore becomes $\hat{t}_{i,m}^r = t_{i,m}^r + \hat{\delta}_{i,m}^r$. Note that the clock offset $\hat{\delta}_{i,m}^r$ is specific to each satellite-receiver pair. Table 1 summarizes the notations used throughout this paper.

The true TOA equation of the adversary's GPS satellite signal at the victim's GPS receiver can be derived as

$$c\left(t_{i,m}^r - t_m^a\right) = \left|\ell_i^r - \ell_m^a\right|, \qquad (1)$$

where $c$ is the speed of the medium. The clock synchronization of the receiver is based on the received GPS message and its perceived reception time,

$$c\left(\hat{t}_{i,m}^r - \hat{t}_m^a\right) = \left|\hat{\ell}_i^r - \hat{\ell}_m^a\right|, \qquad (2)$$

where the left-hand side is commonly referred to as the *pseudorange* between receiver $R_i$ and satellite $S_m^a$. Figure 2 illustrates the relationship between the two TOA equations.

The adversary relates its claimed/true satellite information and the desired locations and clock offsets to which a receiver would be spoofed to solve for the variables. All variables can be related by taking the difference between Equation (1) and Equation (2), resulting in

$$\left|\ell_i^r - \ell_m^a\right| + c\left(\hat{\delta}_{i,m}^r - \delta_m^a\right) = \left|\hat{\ell}_i^r - \hat{\ell}_m^a\right|, \qquad (3)$$

The adversary's goal is therefore to solve for the variable sets marked in Table 1 such that Equation (3) is satisfied for each satellite-receiver pair.

## 4.2 Verification by Receivers

Different types of verification can be implemented across the GPS receivers to place constraints on the adversary's variables and thereby limit the feasibility of spoofing attacks.

| | | Emulated satellite $S_m^a$ |
|---|---|---|
| | $\ell_m, t_m$ | Location and time of authentic satellite |
| Set 1 | $\ell_m^a, t_m^a$ | True location and time |
| Set 2 | $\hat{\ell}_m^a, \hat{t}_m^a$ | Claimed location and time |
| | | **Receiver $R_i$ when receiving messages from $S_m^a$** |
| | $\ell_i^r, t_{i,m}^r$ | True location and time upon reception |
| Set 3 | $\hat{\ell}_i^r$ | Calculated location |
| | $\hat{t}_{i,m}^r$ | Reception time recorded by local clock |
| Set 4 | $\hat{\delta}_{i,m}^r$ | Calculated clock offset |

**Table 1: Notations used in this paper and the variable sets that the adversary can influence**

We assume that the adversary sends spoofed signals of $n_a$ of satellites. Out of the given $n_r$ victim receivers, we define $n_{rc}$ as the number of receivers that share a local clock.

**Message Content Verification.** When spoofing civilian GPS messages, the adversary may freely select Variable Set 2 since there is no message authentication. However, the power company may obtain an authentic copy of the data by setting up a GPS receiver at a remote location to receive signals from authentic satellites. Receivers can therefore compare messages from the adversary with the authentic copy, imposing the following constraint on the adversary:

$$\hat{\ell}_m^a = \ell_m \text{ and } \hat{t}_m^a = t_m.$$

**Receiver Location Verification.** Given that PMUs are installed in fixed and known locations in the substation, GPS receivers can leverage this knowledge to remove the adversary's freedom on Variable Set 3. The adversary must therefore send signals that do not affect the calculated locations of the receivers:

$$\forall R_i \in \mathcal{R}_m^a, \quad \left|\hat{\ell}_i^r - \ell_i^r\right| < \varepsilon_g.$$

The choice of $\varepsilon_g$ depends the accuracy of the GPS receiver when localizing in a setting without GPS spoofing. Based on studies of localization errors of modern GPS receivers [16], $\varepsilon_g$ can be approximately 10 meters or assigned based on the specification of individual GPS receivers.

**Single Receiver Clock Offset Verification.** Given that GPS satellites themselves are tightly synchronized, the difference between a receiver's clock and that of a satellite should be similar across different satellites:

$$\forall S_m, S_n \in \mathcal{S}^a, \forall R_i \in \mathcal{R}_m^a, \quad \left|\hat{\delta}_{i,m}^r - \hat{\delta}_{i,n}^r\right| < \varepsilon_t. \qquad (4)$$

Similar to the tolerated location difference, the tolerated clock error $\varepsilon_t$ can be defined based on the specification of the GPS receiver and is typically around 100 nanoseconds [11].

**Grouped Receivers Clock Offset Verification.** Recall that in Section 2.1, clock synchronization protocols such as PTP cannot be scaled to synchronize devices throughout a wide area that is the power grid. They are still useful, however, within a local substation. As a result, a set $\mathcal{R}_{\text{sync}}$ of GPS receivers in the same substation and synchronized using PTP may compare their clock offsets with each other. This leads to another constraint:

$$\forall S_m, S_n \in \mathcal{S}^a, \forall R_i, R_j \in \mathcal{R}_m^a \bigcap \mathcal{R}_{\text{sync}}, \left|\hat{\delta}_{i,m}^r - \hat{\delta}_{j,n}^r\right| < \varepsilon_{\text{sync}}. \qquad (5)$$

Given the two variants of clock offset verification, Equation (5) implies that only 1 free variable can be assigned by the adversary as the only clock offset for the synchronized receivers. For non-synchronized receivers, the adversary is still constrained by Equation (4) for every receiver, implying that there are $n_r - n_{rc}$ clock offsets for the adversary to assign. It therefore follows that the adversary may specify $n_r - n_{rc} + 1$ separate clock offsets in Variable Set 4.

Finally, in our adversary model, the adversary can freely place the antennas and transmit signals at desired times. As a result, for Variable Set 1, the adversary can freely choose the true location (3 dimensions) and time (1 dimension) of each emulated satellite, amounting to $4n_a$ variables.

In summary, the adversary has to solve for $4n_a + n_r - n_{rc} + 1$ variables, which are subject to $n_r n_a$ instances of Equation (3), each representing the TOA relationship between an emulated satellite and a victim receiver. The variables become overdetermined if there are more equations than variables:

$$n_r n_a > 4n_a + n_r - n_{rc} + 1. \qquad (6)$$

This restricts the adversary to at most one single solution for every variable. The single solution is the trivial one, where $\hat{\ell}_m^a = \ell_m^a$ and $\hat{t}_m^a = t_m^a$, that is, the correct location and time of the satellites. If no error is tolerated in the verification process by the receivers, the adversary must transmit messages from the authentic satellite location and time as claimed in the message to prevent being detected. In this case, the adversary is essentially behaving honestly, and spoofing is not possible. As an example, if the adversary sends spoofed signals of four emulated satellites to five synchronized GPS receivers placed at different locations, then Inequality (6) is satisfied, and therefore spoofing can be detected. Based on the selection of the thresholds $\varepsilon_g$, $\varepsilon_t$, and $\varepsilon_{\text{sync}}$, however, the adversary may assign the variables to be numerically close to the theoretical solution and still affect the clock offsets of the receivers. It is therefore important to choose tight thresholds values such that spoofing attacks are infeasible due to the tightened constraints.

# 5. LOCALIZATION OF THE ADVERSARY

In this section, we evaluate the use of multiple GPS receivers to estimate the true location of the source of a received GPS message using multilateration techniques [12].

## 5.1 Multilateration

We now describe a technique that allows a set of receivers sharing a local clock to locate the source of a GPS message. Recall that PMUs are installed in fixed locations within electrical substations, and therefore such a setup is practical to realize. Combined with the knowledge of their positions, a group of GPS receivers can infer the true position of an incoming GPS signal using time-difference-of-arrival (TDOA) equations. This mechanism, referred to as multilateration, can be used to verify the location claimed in the GPS message and to locate a possible spoofing adversary.

Let $\mathcal{R}$ be a set of receivers that share a common local clock, and $S_m^a$ be the adversary's fake satellites. Each receiver $R_i \in \mathcal{R}$ may construct the following TOA relationship with the signal source using Equation (1).

$$|\ell_m^a - \ell_i^r| = c \left[ \left( \hat{t}_{i,m}^r - \hat{\delta}_{i,m}^r \right) - t_m^a \right]. \qquad (7)$$

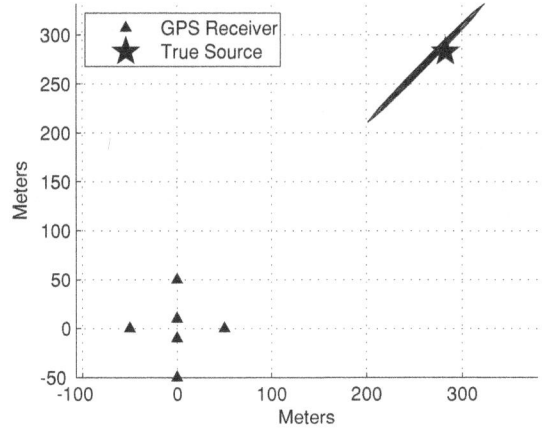

Figure 3: Locating the adversary roughly 400 meters away. The ellipse represents a 80% confidence region around the estimated location.

Taking the difference between Equation (7) for receivers $R_i$ and $R_j$, we can obtain the following TDOA relationship between the two with respect to the same GPS message:

$$|\ell_m^a - \ell_i^r| - |\ell_m^a - \ell_j^r| = c \left( \hat{t}_{i,m}^r - \hat{t}_{j,m}^r \right) = c\Delta_{ij}^m, \qquad (8)$$

where the time difference is represented as $\Delta_{ij}^m = \hat{t}_{i,m}^r - \hat{t}_{j,m}^r$.

The GPS message's source location $\ell_m^a$ computed by the receivers via Equation (8) describes a hyperboloid in 3D space. Based on multiple sets of TDOA equations between different pairs of receivers in $\mathcal{R}$, the GPS source location can be solved as the intersection of a set of hyperboloids, each corresponding to one TDOA equation between a pair of receivers. Since a minimum of 4 hyperboloids are required to generate a unique solution, this method works if there are at least 5 receivers in $\mathcal{R}$ that share a local clock.

This multilateration approach allows the receivers to verify a received GPS message's true source location, which can be compared with its claimed location in the message or used to determine the location of a spoofing GPS signal source in the event of a spoofing attack.

Obtaining the source location by solving the set of TDOA equations is non-trivial. This is due to the non-linearity of Equation (8) for every receiver pair and real-world errors such as those from multipath effects in wireless communication. Moreover, the system of equations becomes overdetermined when there are more than 5 receivers in $\mathcal{R}$, which should be taken into account when dealing with, for example, a large substation that contains many PMUs. Solutions, such as those provided by Chan and Ho [4] or Dogancay [5], already exist and can be readily adopted to obtain estimates of the source location.

## 5.2 Evaluation

In order to evaluate the localization method using an actual implementation, two types of information are needed: (1) the locations, $\ell_i^r$, of the GPS receivers; (2) the times, $\hat{t}_{i,m}^r$, when GPS messages are received. While the former is known during deployment, the latter requires that GPS receivers record the time when each individual satellite message is received. Currently, however, commercially off-the-shelf GPS receivers do not output such information. We consider the construction of specialized GPS receivers out

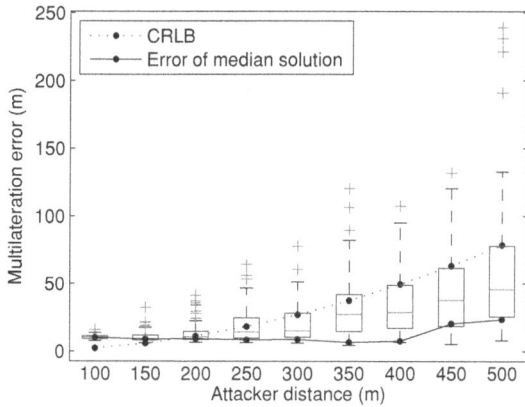

Figure 4: Box plot of multilateration errors using the solution by Chan and Ho [4], compared to the errors of the median of multiple runs (taken separately for each axis) and the theoretical CRLB for one single run.

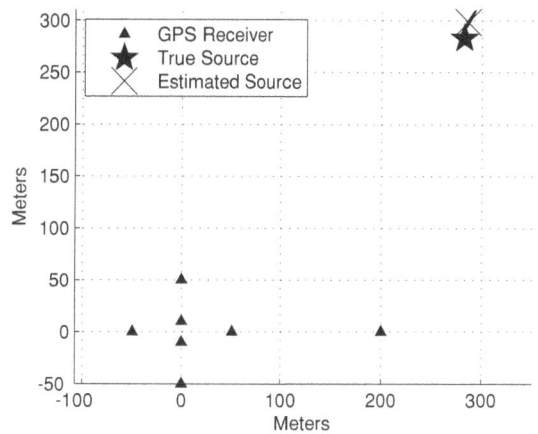

Figure 5: Signal source estimation improves when an additional GPS receiver is positioned far away from the original set.

of this paper's scope and so use simulations to generate the time differences when evaluating our approach.

We perform simulations to verify the use of signal source localization on a GPS receiver system with sufficient receivers ($> 5$) for multilateration. Our simulation consists of a set of 6 GPS receivers $\mathcal{R} = \{R_1, ..., R_6\}$, dispersed across a 100 m × 100 m × 20 m rectangular prism, which is realistic for an electrical substation. All GPS receivers synchronize their clocks to a local time source, each with an error as a random variable $\varepsilon_{\text{sync}}$. A fake GPS signal source $S^a$ is modeled as a signal source $400\,m$ away from the center of the GPS receivers. In reality, this is a plausible placement because the signal source could be, for example, a GPS simulator mounted in the adversary's vehicle that is close to the electrical substation. The distance between receiver $R_i$ and the signal source is $d_i = |\ell_i^r - \ell^a|$.

The TDOA localization method mentioned in Section 5 takes two inputs: (1) the locations of the GPS receivers, which is given based on our setup; (2) the difference of signal reception time between two receivers, which we generate in the simulation due to the lack of hardware support.

The time difference $\Delta_{ij}$ between two receivers $R_i$ and $R_j$ that receive the same signal is $\Delta_{ij} = c^{-1}|d_i - d_j| + \varepsilon_{\text{sync}}$, where $\varepsilon_{\text{sync}}$ is independently sampled for each time difference. Equation (8) for the receiver pair $R_i$ and $R_j$ becomes

$$|\ell^a - \ell_i^r| - |\ell^a - \ell_j^r| = |d_i - d_j| + c^{-1}e.$$

We simulate the time difference between receiver pairs $(R_1, R_2)$, $(R_1, R_3)$, $(R_1, R_4)$, $(R_1, R_5)$, and $(R_1, R_6)$, which results in a set of 5 TDOA equations.

The adversary's location can subsequently be solved by intersecting the hyperboloids described by the TDOA equations, and we use the maximum likelihood estimator by Chan and Ho [4]. We also model the real-world inaccuracies of clock synchronization protocols using $\varepsilon_{\text{sync}}$ in Equation (5). In our simulation, $\varepsilon_{\text{sync}}$ is assumed to be a normal random variable with a standard deviation of 1 nanosecond, which is a realistic accuracy for state-of-the-art clock synchronization protocols among devices in a local network [11].

Figure 3 illustrates our simulated environment setup and compares the estimated adversary location to the ground

truth. As observed, the location of a real-world adversary sending spoofed signals to an electrical substation from a distance of 400 meters can be estimated.

We also evaluate the errors of locating signal sources in different distances, defined as the distance between the estimated position and the true position, which is theoretically lower bounded by the Cramér-Rao lower bound (CRLB) [4]. Figure 4 is a comparison among the average errors of 100 trials, the CRLB, and the error of the median of the solutions. It shows that taking the median over multiple executions gives a superior accuracy over the CRLB of a single-iteration solution, and can be an option for GPS receivers to track the adversary over a longer period of time.

Figure 4 also shows that when the adversary is farther away from the GPS receivers, the approximation error increases. However, we observe that the direction from the receivers to the spoofed signal source can still be determined, as previously depicted by the narrow covariance ellipse in Figure 3. Furthermore, the accuracy can be further improved if other distant GPS receivers participate in solving the TDOA equations. Figure 5 illustrates the improved accuracy of multilateration by placing an additional GPS receiver farther away, around 200 m, from the original set of PMUs but still synchronized to the same local clock. In reality, if the adversary's antenna is far away from the substation, then it is reasonable to assume that GPS receivers in PMUs in other substations or in nearby transmission towers would also receive the signal and assist in multilateration.

## 6. RELATED WORK

In order to synchronize clocks across PMUs installed in a nationwide scale without requiring specialized hardware for networked time protocols, the industry often relies on GPS for clock synchronization. This has been shown by Shepard et al. [13] to be vulnerable to GPS spoofing. In our work, we propose mechanisms to increase its robustness against such malicious attacks. Jiang et al. [9] analyze how GPS spoofing can be performed on a single PMU as well as the impact on voltage stability monitoring and propose various detection techniques. Our contributions differ from theirs by analyzing the problem when multiple PMUs are deployed and how the adversary can be located.

In existing work on spoofing detection, Garofalo et al. [6] propose verifying GPS signal strengths to detect spoofing and to synchronize with other redundant clocks in a network via NTP protocols. Zhang et al. [19] propose a method of detecting clock synchronization attacks by monitoring the standard deviation of the differences in the signal-to-noise ratio from two GPS receiving antennas. Jafarnia-Jahromi et al. [7] provide an comprehensive overview of various ways single GPS receivers can use to detect spoofing. On the theory side, Tippenhauer et al. [14] investigate formulations of the GPS spoofing problem. Our work focuses on formulating the GPS problem by considering victim receivers with and without clock synchronization and their effects on reducing the feasibility of an undetectable spoofing attack.

For locating a signal source, Bhatti et al. [2] investigate possibilities of locating GPS interference signal sources in an urban setup, which assumes a 2D environment and close proximity between the source and receiver network. Strategies of placing GPS receivers to reduce the errors of multilateration has also been analyzed [17]. Various emitter localization methods based on multilateration have been proposed and compared in the past [4,10]. A closed-form and efficient estimator that is adopted in this paper is introduced by Chan and Ho [4], which employs a maximum likelihood estimator to approximate the solution for TDOA equations. We apply this to a 3D substation setup to demonstrate the feasibility of locating the adversary.

# 7. CONCLUSION

In this paper, we explored the security of GPS-based clock synchronization against spoofing attacks for phasor measurement units in power grids. The solution may also be applied to other stationary sensor networks. Receivers collaborating to verify the information from GPS navigation messages may detect spoofing attacks. Existing multilateration techniques can also be applied to locate an adversary with sufficient accuracy. We showed that deploying sufficiently many receivers increases the difficulty and risk for the adversary. For these mechanisms to work, GPS receivers should record the reception time of each individual GPS message. Future GPS receivers that make such information available for analysis would improve their robustness against spoofing attacks.

# 8. ACKNOWLEDGMENTS

We are grateful for the feedback provided by the anonymous reviewers as well as the comments from Yongdae Kim, Sebastian Obermeier, Joel Reardon, and Michael Wahler.

# 9. REFERENCES

[1] IEEE Standard for Synchrophasors for Power Systems. *IEEE Std C37.118.1-2011*, 2011.

[2] J. Bhatti, T. Humphreys, and B. Ledvina. Development and Demonstration of a TDOA-based GNSS Interference Signal Localization System. In *Position Location and Navigation Symposium, IEEE/ION*, 2012.

[3] J. V. Carroll. Vulnerability Assessment of the US Transportation Infrastructure that Relies on the Global Positioning System. *Journal of Navigation*, 2003.

[4] Y. Chan and K. Ho. A Simple and Efficient Estimator for Hyperbolic Location. *IEEE Trans. Signal Processing*, 1994.

[5] K. Dogancay. Emitter Localization Using Clustering-based Bearing Association. *IEEE Trans. Aerospace and Electronic Systems*, 2005.

[6] A. Garofalo, C. Sarno, L. Coppolino, and S. D'Antonio. A GPS Spoofing Resilient WAMS for Smart Grid. In *Dependable Computing*, Lecture Notes in Computer Science. 2013.

[7] A. Jafarnia-Jahromi, A. Broumandan, J. Nielsen, and G. Lachapelle. GPS Vulnerability to Spoofing Threats and a Review of Antispoofing Techniques. *Int'l Journal of Navigation and Observation*, 2012.

[8] J.-A. Jiang, J.-Z. Yang, Y.-H. Lin, C.-W. Liu, and J.-C. Ma. An Adaptive PMU Based Fault Detection/Location Technique for Transmission Lines. I. Theory and Algorithms. *IEEE Trans. Power Delivery*, 2000.

[9] X. Jiang, J. Zhang, B. Harding, J. Makela, and A. Dominguez-Garcia. Spoofing GPS Receiver Clock Offset of Phasor Measurement Units. *IEEE Trans. Power Systems*, 2013.

[10] G. Mao, B. Fidan, and B. D. Anderson. Wireless Sensor Network Localization Techniques. *Computer Networks*, 2007.

[11] P. Moreira, J. Serrano, T. Wlostowski, P. Loschmidt, and G. Gaderer. White Rabbit: Sub-nanosecond Timing Distribution over Ethernet. In *Int'l Symposium on Precision Clock Synchronization for Measurement, Control and Communication*, 2009.

[12] R. Schmidt. A New Approach to Geometry of Range Difference Location. *IEEE Trans. Aerospace and Electronic Systems*, 1972.

[13] D. P. Shepard, T. E. Humphreys, and A. A. Fansler. Evaluation of the Vulnerability of Phasor Measurement Units to GPS Spoofing Attacks. *Int'l Journal of Critical Infrastructure Protection*, 2012.

[14] N. O. Tippenhauer, C. Pöpper, K. B. Rasmussen, and S. Capkun. On the Requirements for Successful GPS Spoofing Attacks. In *ACM Conference on Computer and Communications Security*, 2011.

[15] A. Vallat and D. Schneuwly. Clock Synchronization in Telecommunications via PTP (IEEE 1588). In *IEEE Int'l Frequency Control Symposium*, 2007.

[16] M. G. Wing, A. Eklund, and L. D. Kellogg. Consumer-grade Global Positioning System (GPS) Accuracy and Reliability. *Journal of Forestry*, 2005.

[17] B. Yang. Different Sensor Placement Strategies for TDOA Based Localization. In *IEEE Int'l Conference on Acoustics, Speech and Signal Processing*, 2007.

[18] Z. Zhang, S. Gong, A. Dimitrovski, and H. Li. Time Synchronization Attack in Smart Grid: Impact and Analysis. *IEEE Trans. Smart Grid*, 2013.

[19] Z. Zhang, M. Trinkle, A. Dimitrovski, and H. Li. Combating Time Synchronization Attack: A Cross Layer Defense Mechanism. In *ACM/IEEE Int'l Conference on Cyber-Physical Systems*, 2013.

[20] M. Zima, M. Larsson, P. Korba, C. Rehtanz, and G. Andersson. Design Aspects for Wide-Area Monitoring and Control Systems. *Proc. IEEE*, 2005.

# Gaining Insight on Friendly Jamming in a Real-World IEEE 802.11 Network

Daniel S. Berger[*], Francesco Gringoli[†], Nicolò Facchi[†],
Ivan Martinovic[‡], and Jens Schmitt[*]
[*]DISCO Lab, University of Kaiserslautern, Germany
[†]CNIT - DII, University of Brescia, Italy
[‡]University of Oxford, United Kingdom
{berger,jschmitt}@cs.uni-kl.de,
{francesco.gringoli,nicolo.facchi}@ing.unibs.it,
ivan.martinovic@cs.ox.ac.uk

## ABSTRACT

Frequency jamming is the fiercest attack tool to disrupt wireless communication and its malicious aspects have received much attention in the literature. Yet, several recent works propose to turn the table and employ so-called friendly jamming for the benefit of a wireless network. For example, recently proposed friendly jamming applications include hiding communication channels, injection attack defense, and access control.

This work investigates the practical viability of friendly jamming by applying it in a real-world network. To that end, we implemented a reactive and frame-selective jammer on a consumer grade IEEE 802.11 access point. Equipped with this, we conducted a three weeks real-world study on the jammer's performance and side-effects on legitimate traffic (the cost of jamming) in a university office environment. Our results provide detailed insights on crucial factors governing the trade-off between the effectiveness of friendly jamming (we evaluated up to 13 jammers) and its cost. In particular, we observed – what we call the power amplification phenomenon – an effect that aggravates the known hidden station problem when the number of jammers increases. However, we also find evidence that this effect can be alleviated by collaboration between jammers, which again enables effective and minimally invasive friendly jamming.

## Categories and Subject Descriptors

C.2.1 [**Computer Communication Networks**]: Network Architecture and Design—*Wireless communication*

## Keywords

friendly jamming; jamming for good; defensive jamming; reactive jamming; IEEE 802.11; Wi-Fi; WLAN

*WiSec'14*, July 23–25, 2014, Oxford, UK.
Copyright is held by the owner/author(s). Publication rights licensed to ACM.
ACM 978-1-4503-2972-9/14/07 ...$15.00.
http://dx.doi.org/10.1145/2627393.2627403.

# 1. INTRODUCTION

Radio frequency jamming is commonly understood as a severe threat to the security and availability of wireless networks. Such intentional interference effectively disrupts communication on the physical layer making mitigation hard. In the military context, jamming is an established primitive to block an enemy's communication, and even practical handbooks on this topic are available [1–3, 25]. The same threat, however, also applies to the availability of civilian communication networks and received significant research interest (e.g., [21, 23, 24, 27, 38]). Seen from the attacker's perspective, jamming is a simple, yet effective tool. However, these are also desired properties for defense tools of a system and thus the question arises why not view jamming as a protection tool.

This question has recently motivated many researchers to envision positive use cases of jamming in wireless networks (cf. a list of proposals in Table 1). Such positive use cases, however, have different requirements on the jamming technique. In the traditional attack setting, the jammer attempts to block any communication usually only subject to stealthiness or energy constraints [23, 24]. On the other hand, realistic scenarios in which jamming is used to benefit network operations introduce an orthogonal requirement: *minimal invasiveness*. In particular, in order to coexist with other legitimate networks, only specific transmissions should be targeted, whereas the impact on other transmissions should be minimal. We henceforth denote by *friendly jamming* such use cases in which jamming is used for the good and strives to be minimally invasive.

While there are different jamming techniques (cf. a discussion in Section 2), minimal invasiveness requires reactive and frame-selective jamming. Reactive jamming has been characterized to be energy-efficient and effective [40], and is more likely to comply with legal regulations[1]. Actually applying friendly jamming in practice, however, faces many challenges. Reactive and frame-selective jamming poses strict timing constraints, and involves further engineering issues for which solutions have begun to emerge in recent years.

---

[1]For example, the maximum duty cycle (the fraction of one second a transmitter is active) is commonly limited to small values [10]. We briefly remark, however, that jamming, in general, is a sensitive topic. For example, in the US the operation, marketing, or selling of continuous jammers such as GPS jammers, or cell phone blockers is prohibited [11].

| Related Work | Technology | Problem addressed | Js | Methodology |
|---|---|---|---|---|
| Jamming for good [22] | 802.15.4 | fake messages, unauth. comm. | 3+ | implementation and evaluation |
| WiFire [36] | 802.15.4 | unauthenticated comm. | 2 | implementation and evaluation |
| IMD shield [12] | (propriet.) | unauth. comm.,eavesdropping | 1 | implementation and evaluation |
| Jamming for Throughput [7] | 802.11 | performance: hidden terminals | 1 | theoretical analysis |
| Ally Friendly Jamming [31] | 802.11 | unauthenticated comm. | 2+ | analysis, implementation, and evaluation |
| Defend your home [6] | 802.15.4 | unauth. comm., fake messages | 1 | implementation and evaluation |
| Shout to Secure [16] | 802.11 | eavesdropping | 1 | simulation |
| iJam [13] | 802.11 | key generation | 1 | implementation |
| Secure Wi-Fi Zones [17] | 802.11 | eavesdropping | 4+ | theoretical analysis and implementation |
| Wire-Tap Channel | (indep.) | eavesdropping | 1 | theoretical analysis, implementations |

**Table 1:** This study is concerned with scenarios requiring a *minimally invasive* and distributed jamming system (and an IEEE 802.11 b/g network). Similar scenarios are assumed in [6,7,12,22,31,36], whereas [13,16, 17] and also the Wire-Tap Channel scenario (umbrella term coined by Wyner [39], see also [8,20,30,33,41,42]) usually do not assume minimal invasiveness, e.g., the whole channel is often continuously blocked.

Hence, a critical issue is whether friendly jamming works as desired under *real-world* conditions, i.e., under multipath effects and attenuation, or fast channel fading in a dynamic environment. On a high level, this is thus the key question we address in this paper: *Is friendly jamming practically viable in a real-world 802.11 network?*

Answering this question by a real-world measurement study, we delve into the details of two issues, the performance of jamming and its related cost. As we will see these two have to be traded off against each other and the details of that trade-off depend on several factors that we investigate. We base our measurement study on the most widely deployed wireless communication standard, IEEE 802.11. To that end, we implemented a friendly jammer by modifying the microcode of the wireless chipset in a customer-grade access point, which has been certified to comply with legal regulations on power and spectral density requirements. Over a period of three weeks we ran a friendly jamming scenario, recorded all messages exchanged at different vantage points, and investigated the jammer's performance as well as negative side-effects on legitimate traffic. By this, we hope to provide an understanding of friendly jamming "in the wild" and thus foster further research in this promising and interesting domain[2].

Specifically, we collected the following main insights from our real-world study:

1. We found clear evidence that a large number of jammers is required to ensure high hit ratios.

2. The sequence of unjammed frames possesses a memoryless property – rendering predictions based on past observations inefficient, which makes their exploitation harder (which is good).

3. The cost of friendly jamming lies mainly in what we call the *power amplification effect*, which results in an aggravation of hidden station problems.

4. Collaboratively selecting the best jammers can boost the effectiveness of multiple jammers while minimizing the cost of jamming.

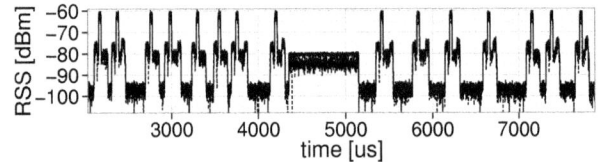

**Figure 2:** A particular challenge of friendly jamming is to enable coexistence with other legitimate networks' traffic (e.g., not to jam the beacon in the center) while accurately jamming target frames (here: all of the short frames).

5. In additional simulations based on our measurements we investigated more thorough the underlying reasons why perfect jamming is often infeasible.

The rest of this paper is structured as follows. In Section 2 we given an introduction to friendly jamming. The setup of our experiments is introduced in Section 3 and is followed by our main results in Section 4. Section 5 contains a technical analysis of jamming success. We discuss related work in Section 6 and conclude in Section 7.

## 2. FRIENDLY JAMMING: CONCEPTS AND CONSTRAINTS

There are several techniques to disrupt a wireless transmission. The most fundamental approach addresses the physical layer on which intentional interference causes errors when decoding a transmission's data. In this section we describe enabling techniques for (radio frequency) jamming; in particular, we focus on a description of reactive jamming as the technique, which lies at the foundation of friendly jamming. We conclude this section with an outlook on evaluation aspects for our real-world study.

### 2.1 Proactive vs. Reactive Jamming

There is a variety of techniques to create intentional interference. Continuously emitting a high power signal, for example, requires a lot of power and does not admit other uses of the channel. Other approaches are deceptive jamming (deceiving stations that the channel is occupied), random jamming (randomly alternating between sleeping and jamming), and reactive jamming [24,40]. In reactive jamming, the interfering signal is emitted only when another signal is detected. This can be done selectively by analyzing

---

[2]We distribute a ready-to run version of our implementation on our project page http://www.ing.unibs.it/~openfwwf/ friendlyjammer/. It also holds condensed result tables and samples of the measurement data – we ask for brief email inquiry to obtain the full source code and measurement data.

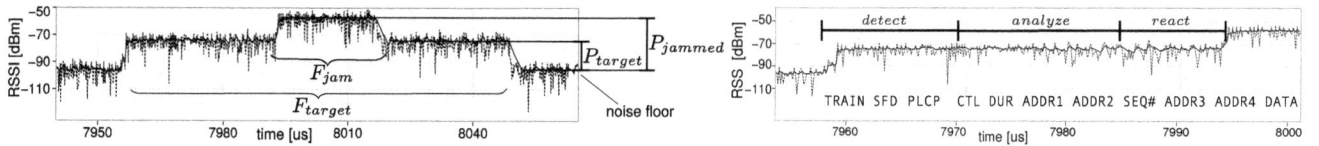

Figure 1: Left: in order for the jamming frame $F_{jam}$ to successfully interfere with the target frame $F_{target}$ (i.e., to render it irrecoverable) it is necessary that the superimposed signal's power $P_{jammed}$ is significantly higher than $P_{target}$. Right: reactive jamming involves three steps: detecting the signal by means of the training sequence, analyzing the signal to decide whether or not to jam, and, if so, emitting the jamming signal.

signals and interfering only with certain ones. Therefore, re-active jamming is the most attractive jamming technique for friendly jamming and can yield minimally invasive applications. This technique is often considered the most sophisticated jamming technique [24] and entails several challenges.

## 2.2 Reactive Jamming Challenges

Reactive jamming starts with the task of channel sensing in order to detect a target frame (a signal in IEEE 802.11 terminology). The target frame's detection and further decoding can only be achieved by jammers which are well positioned with regard to the arriving signal (to be specific: the target signal arrives with high signal-to-noise-ratio (SNR)). This position, with respect to the sender and environmental conditions, is thus an important factor for jamming success.

After having detected the signal, the jammer starts the decoding and analysis in order to take a jamming decision. In a realistic scenario, the jammer needs to distinguish between target frames and legitimate frames (Figure 2). While the jamming hit ratio (# jammed frames / # sent frames) of the former needs to be maximized, the impact of jamming on the latter shall remain small. This trade-off is further constrained by the fact that the decision has to be taken very fast. We recall these timing constraints by considering, say, a frame comprising a medium-sized 100 Bytes UDP packet. If this frame is transmitted at the fastest 802.11g Modulation and Coding Scheme (MCS), its duration is only $48\mu s$. If we further assume that the jamming decision depends on bits in the MAC header (e.g., the sender's MAC address), the remaining part of the frame is even another $24\mu s$ shorter. In the remaining time, the jammer's decision code has to be executed, the hardware needs to switch from receive to transmission mode, and the jamming signal has to be emitted.

Once the signal is emitted, successful jamming depends on the target frame's MCS and the jamming signal's power. While higher power drives high jamming success, this factor is subject to legal regulations and is a crucial factor for the detrimental impact on legitimate traffic. A final aspect concerns the systems view of jamming as concurrent jammers can improve upon both the target frame detection and the jamming signal's power level. Therefore, the number of concurrent jammer is another important success factor.

## 2.3 Evaluating Friendly Jamming

In comparison to an attacker's perspective on jamming, friendly jamming demands a broader evaluation scope. While the jammer's hit ratio (and corresponding factors) are an important performance aspect, we additionally have to consider some friendly jamming specific aspects. In particular, estimating the cost of jamming in terms of potential negative side effects on other legitimate transmissions is of great

interest. Another question poses itself for friendly jamming in a security setting: is an attacker on the network able to predict jamming misses (which could then be exploited)? This predictability constitutes the main attack vector on friendly jamming systems and, accordingly, should be kept as low as possible. Finally, we argue that an experimental friendly jamming deployment has to be considered from a worst-case perspective. Therefore, our experimental setup assumes a random placement of jammers instead of choosing preoptimized jammer positions.

## 3. EXPERIMENTAL SETUP

A practical evaluation of the factors described in the previous section requires a realistic implementation and evaluations in a complex radio communication environment. In this section we briefly introduce our realization of a friendly jammer, some micro benchmarks to ensure the system's basic operation, and the deployment used for the result in Section 4.

## 3.1 Jammer Hardware and Implementation

In order to encounter realistic hardware constraints, we implemented the reactive jammer for our experiments on cheap customer-grade hardware that has been certified to comply with regulatory rules. We start with a brief description of this jammer.

Our jammer is implemented directly on the Network Interface Card (NIC) of the popular WRT54GL platform. Access to this resource was facilitated by an open source microcode for the access point's IEEE 802.11 NIC (released by the OpenFWWF [14] project). This microcode replaces the proprietary Broadcom image and allows direct control of all medium access, decoding, and encoding operations subject to some (humble) hardware constraints due to the microcontroller's original purpose. Similarly to [5, 28] we altered the receive path in the assembly code and compiled the jammer's functionality in our own microcode that would be run directly on the NIC.

A principal advantage of the Broadcom NIC that we used is that the microcode can analyze a frame while still receiving it: this feature enables us to implement flexible filtering rules to decide whether or not to emit a jam signal. For example, the check can be based on matching an incoming frame's header to a dynamic bit mask dynamically configured from the host system. The experiments in Section 4, however, are based on a simple match of a frame's transmitter address. After the jamming decision has been positively evaluated, the jammer aborts the current reception, switches to transmission mode, and delivers the jam frame to a serializer, which further handles its emission through the RF circuitry. The jam signal has to be a standard compliant

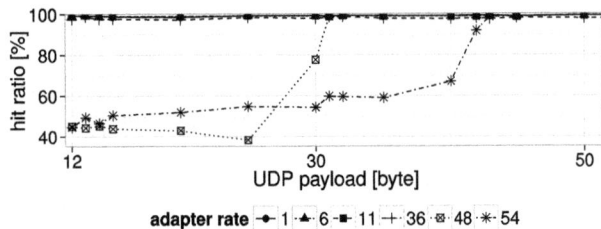

Figure 3: Impact of $F_{target}$'s duration: short frames at high rate cannot be jammed, e.g., at $54Mb/s$ frames with less than 42 bytes payload.

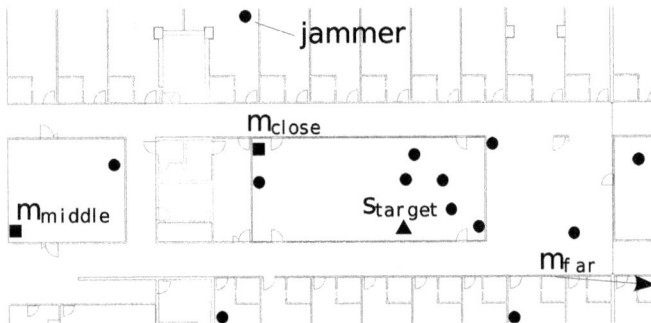

Figure 4: The target traffic source ($s_{target}$) and 13 jammers were located in a $30m \times 45m$ segment of the floor. The monitored experiment area is in total $40 \times 85m$ (extends to the right), and covered by $m_{close}$, $m_{middle}$, and $m_{far}$, which is located far to the right.

frame, but can be assembled directly on the NIC and is only constrained by the hardware's capabilities[3].

The fact that the WRT54GL is based on particularly cheap Broadcom NIC had (besides some challenges) also advantageous side-effects: due to some randomness in execution timing and significant clock skew, multiple jammers behave independently which results in a higher likelihood to cause destructive interference (cf. Section 5).

## 3.2 Micro Benchmarks and Optimal Jamming Signal

Several micro benchmarks validated the sanity of the jammer implementation. For example, traces by real-time spectrum analyzers (Figure 2) showed that target frames were jammed reliably and accurately, while legitimate traffic remained unjammed.

As a consequence of these micro benchmarks, we implemented several code optimizations to shorten the jammer's reaction time and increase jamming performance. For example, the jammer's configuration was originally stored in a part of the NIC's memory that can be accessed from the host system and the microcontroller to enable flexible reconfiguration. However, as this access is slow, we implemented a prefetching mechanism that stored the jammer's configuration in fast-access registers. Another optimization addressed the chipset's sending power management, which is based on partial information from reverse engineering the chipset. We

---

[3]To be specific the jammer can use DSSS and ERP-OFDM, but neither HT nor VHT, and only in the $2.4GHz$ band

ran comprehensive tests on corresponding hardware registers before settling on a final configuration.

We also found that the jamming frame's MCS impacts the jamming performance. We fixed it to the best configuration, which was attained by $1Mb/s$ DSSS jamming signals. For this MCS, the impact of the jamming frame's payload length was negligible and the MAC Protocol Data Unit (MPDU) was set to ten bytes (the minimal length allowed by the hardware). The jamming signal then $192\mu s$ for the transmission of the Physical Layer Convergence Protocol header, and additional $80\mu s$ for the MPDU – a total of $272\mu s$ in air time.

We also obtained the reaction time of the jammer as the time it took to react after matching a specific MAC address. By comparing original and jammed frames' content, we verify this delay to be two bytes at $1Mb/s$, i.e., $16\mu s$. Independently, the minimal frame length that can be jammed verifies this finding as Figure 3 shows that the jammer implementation can tackle frames with at least 42 bytes at 54 Mbps or 31 bytes at 48 Mbps.

## 3.3 Deployment and Device Configuration

We selected a university office floor as a representative and challenging setting since it is a particularly heterogeneous and dynamic environment. The university network's traffic is generated by a dynamic user base of faculty members and students; it comprises a variety of traffic sources such as typical back-office activities, research oriented applications, and even multimedia applications. Besides the university's main campus network, there are various smaller access points with many overlapping Basic Service Sets, so that we are able to observe different networks types in parallel.

We deployed 13 WRT54GL wireless access points as jammers, four additional WRT54GLs configured as two sources-sink pairs, and three Alix2d2 system boards as monitors on the university floor. The target traffic source was located at a fixed position, $s_{target}$ in Figure 4. It generated an iperf UDP stream at a constant rate that was sent to a corresponding sink at a short distance. We experimented with different traffic rates, inter-frame spacing (e.g., SIFS) and backoff mechanisms but finally chose a standard-compliant configuration at a low rate of $500Kb/s$ in order to allow legitimate traffic to be observed on the same (and adjacent) channels.

Our measurements are taken by additional traffic monitors, which were placed at three observation points. These locations were constrained by availability, and are shown in Figure 4: in the same room ($m_{close}$), in an adjacent room ($m_{middle}$), and in a large office room down the floor ($m_{far}$) (also see Figure 11). Another source-sink pair was placed in the same room (not shown in Figure 4) and injected additional artificial crosstraffic to measure application-level performance of regular users with ongoing jamming.

We took particular care to preserve the association of $s_{target}$ to its access point by filtering out deauthentication messages: this was necessary as the controller of the University wireless network was reacting to our experiment setup using the same channels by sending spoofed deauthentication messages. By eliminating unintended causes of lost $F_{target}$ we were able to reliably generate traffic that we transmitted using a round-robin rate selection without retransmissions, in order to obtain uniform statistics for each

| dist | 1 Jammer | 2 Jammers | 3 Jammers |
|------|----------|-----------|-----------|
| 5.4m | 98.93% ($\pm$0.19) | 100.0% ($\pm$0.00) | 99.98% ($\pm$0.02) |
| 6.7m | 98.57% ($\pm$0.85) | 99.95% ($\pm$0.04) | 100.0% ($\pm$0.01) |
| 8.1m | 77.03% ($\pm$12.30) | 98.37% ($\pm$0.29) | 99.43% ($\pm$0.14) |

Table 2: Open-space hit ratio (97.5% confidence intervals) under $1-4$ jammers and different distances.

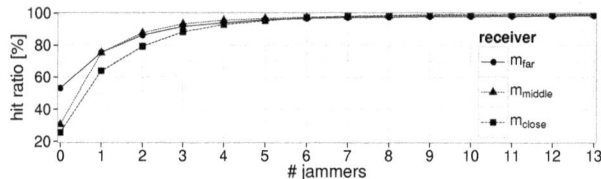

Figure 5: The hit ratio is significantly lower in-doors than in open-space due to attenuation. (0 jammers corresponds to packet loss without jamming.)

MCS. To accurately track sent, received, and valid-checksum statistics, we implemented corresponding low-level counters that were not impacted by the operation system.

In summary, our setup was carefully crafted to obtain reliable target traffic and accurate measurements.

## 3.4 Measurement Data

The experiments were conducted over a three week period In November and December 2013 to observe different conditions and utilization of the wireless channel. Time was divided into short experiments each of about 150s, where in each experiment a random number and selection of jammers were activated uniformly from all possible combinations. In total, this setup generated 13660 experiments with about 350GB of measurement data comprising almost 370 million target frames and 490 million legitimate-traffic frames.

This concludes our description of the experimental setup and we next report on the insights obtained in this setting.

## 4. RESULTS ON FRIENDLY JAMMING IN THE REAL WORLD

In this section, we investigate the trade-off between jamming performance and the cost of friendly jamming under (worst case) random selection of jammer positions; while the jamming performance increases with the number of jammers, the cost of jamming also goes up. We also find evidence that friendly jamming can overcome the constraints of this trade-off by collaboration schemes that heuristically select the most appropriate subset of jammers.

The confidence intervals throughout this section give 97.5% confidence based on the t-distribution. We start by describing performance aspects of friendly jamming under the factors discussed in Section 2.

## 4.1 The Jamming Performance

A direct metric to determine a jammer's performance is the hit ratio for which Figures 5 and 6 show a selection of significant factors.

*Number of Jammers.* We first evaluate the effect of the number of jammers being used. Both in an ideal open-space environment (Table 2) and our dynamic indoor setting (Figure 5), an increasing number of jammers increases the hit ratio due to improving the detection and emitted power of

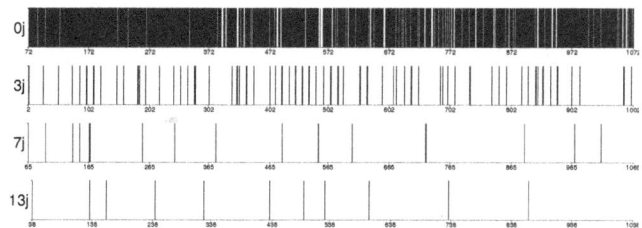

Figure 7: Sequence number diagrams visualize the requirement for several concurrent jammers. From above to below: 0, 3, 7, 13 jammers. In each, black bar: valid checksum, white bar: jammed.

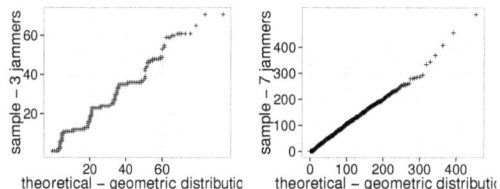

Figure 8: Quantile-quantile plots show good correspondence with a geometric distribution for seven jammers (right) but not for three jammers (left).

the jammers. Note, however, that in the open-space environment one may grossly underestimate the number of jammers necessary for the realistic environment. We observed that a single jammer significantly impacts the target packet rate. Nevertheless, some positions close to the target receiver yield low hit ratios – an observation that can be partly explained by the high and irregular attenuation of the office environment (also see the analysis in Section 5). Due to this, a single jammer's hit ratio lies between $60-90\%$ (averaged over all positions). At least three jammers are required to sustain an average hit ratio above 90%, seven jammers for 99%, and the hit ratio graph's slope only flattens out for more than eleven jammers. This appears to be robust across receivers at different proximities, which yielded distinct packets loss rates without any jammers ($19-48\%$ at $12-75m$, cf. Figure 4). These figures are probably higher than expected and must be taken as caveat for friendly jamming applications.

*Position-Dependence.* In a open-space testbed the hit ratio monotonically decreases with the jammer's distance from the receiver; in contrast to this, in-door behavior is quite erratic and there are weak positions even close to a target receiver (cf. Figure 6(left)). The impact of these weak positions is more pronounced for robust MCSs (those which are based on direct sequence spread spectrum), and lower numbers of jammers. For example, the hit ratio when averaging over random placement of three jammers decreases significantly for the robust MCS $1Mb/s$, as shown in Figure 6(center). Already for seven jammers, this issue mostly disappears as it is more likely that a good position is included in the active jammer set.

*Invariance to Seasonal Effects.* Figure 6(right) shows the average rate of legitimate traffic and the hit ratio of three and seven jammers over the measurement period. While the legitimate traffic rate shows the expected habitual variations, the hit ratio remains pretty stable for both three and seven jammers. For three jammers, we observe some exceptions to this, e.g., on November 20 the hit ratio of three

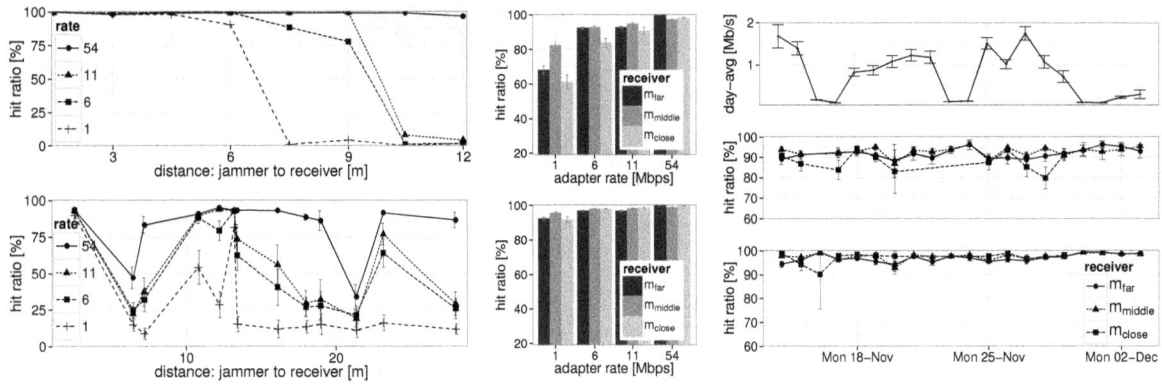

Figure 6: Left: in open space a single jammer's hit ratio decreases monotonically with the distance (top), whereas the indoor evaluation shows erratic behavior (bottom), indicating the need for careful real-world deployments. Center: robust adapter rates (MCSs) such as 1Mb/s have a tremendous impact on the hit ratio of three jammers (top), but less on seven jammers (bottom). Right: while the legitimate traffic's throughput shows weekly patterns (top), the hit ratio of three (center) and seven (bottom) jammers remain almost stable.

jammers goes down significantly due to some untraceable events about which we could only speculate. Note, however, that we observe no impact on seven jammers.

*Temporal Distribution of Misses.* Besides the hit ratio, another metric to determine a jammer's performance can be based on temporal correlations of missed frames. If jamming is used to block an attacker from sending, e.g., malicious packets, then runs of consecutively missed frames constitute a greater threat compared to the case in which the same number of frames was missed spread-out over time. Figure 7 shows a sequence number diagram of representative traces, which depicts how increasing the number of jammers yields a more uniform distribution of the missed frames over the sequence number space. We formalize this aspect by a stochastic miss model. The quantile-quantile plots in Figure 8 show that for seven jammers, the geometric distribution yields a good fit. Since the geometric distribution is memoryless, i.e., having observed any number of past misses does not yield information about a future miss, this property ensures that the prediction of future target frame misses (attack opportunities) is hard – even when an attacker is able to observe the friendly jamming system over a long time. However, our analysis shows that at least seven jammers are required to provide this property. For example, three active jammers are not enough to enforce this property (Figure 8(left)).

This section gave an overview on global jamming performance aspects. Note that the specific values of the hit ratio depend on our implementation, which we deliberately based on cheap customer-grade hardware as a feasibility study. However, we argue that some of the fundamental properties presented in this section apply to a much broader set of jammers, which adhere to FCC or EU regulations.

The next section focuses on an orthogonal aspect – how invasive is friendly jamming.

## 4.2 The Cost of Friendly Jamming

In this section, we investigate the side effects of friendly jamming on *legitimate* traffic in the network. Note that legitimate frames have not been targeted by the frame-selective jammers; instead, any adverse effect on legitimate traffic is collateral – the cost of friendly jamming.

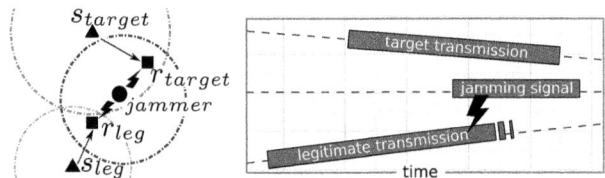

Figure 9: Assume that a target transmission and a remote legitimate transmission would be interference free without jammer. Nevertheless, a jammer located between them may interfere with both transmissions: intentionally, with the target transmission; collaterally, with the legitimate transmission. We call this effect power amplification.

In order to assess this cost, we distinguish legitimate frames from target frames (and, possibly, jamming signals) in our measurement data. This required some attention because fragments resulting from the target and jammers' frames could not easily be distinguished from actual legitimate frames due to high bit error levels. We used a two-run procedure on the measurement data: the first run discovered valid legitimate transmitter MAC addresses, and the actual analysis was carried out on a second run in which frames with small Hamming distance from the legitimate addresses were considered. This analysis was also verified selectively down to the bit level of individual frames.

*Loss of Legitimate Traffic and Power Amplification.* Increasing the number of jammers affects legitimate differently depending on their respective positions (with regard to the target sender and the jammers). We attribute this effect to what we call the power amplification effect: the jammers can significantly increase the interference radius of any target transmission. This can be seen by considering a scenario (see Figure 9 for an illustration) in which a legitimate sender is located far away from the target sender and transmissions of the two senders would be free of interference. Assume a jammer is located between the two senders and can receive and interfere with transmissions of both senders. If the legitimate sender starts a transmission, the target source could possibly start a concurrent transmission as well. Without jammers, both transmissions may proceed without prob-

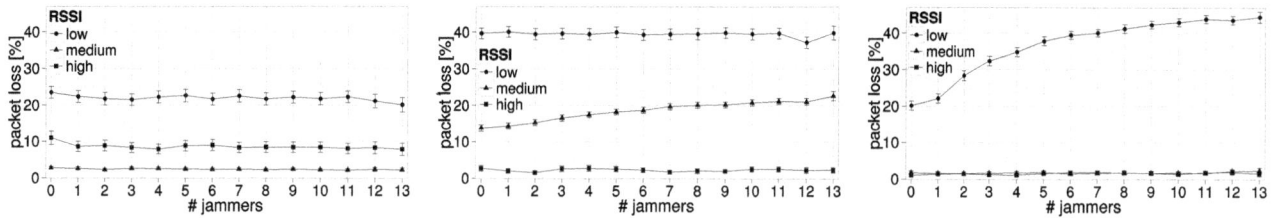

Figure 10: Packet loss of legitimate traffic characterized by respective RSSI levels. Left: the data from monitor $m_{close}$ shows stable behavior. Center: monitor $m_{medium}$ observed an increase in the packet loss for senders with medium RSSI, which we attribute to a slight power amplification effect. Right: the packet loss of traffic from low RSSI senders to $m_{far}$ doubles with an increasing jammer count.

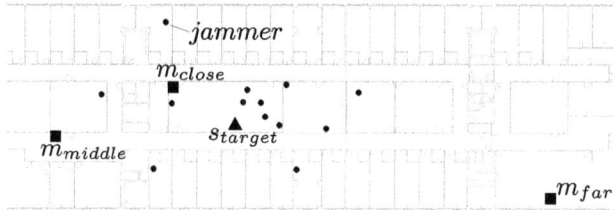

Figure 11: Monitored experimental environment.

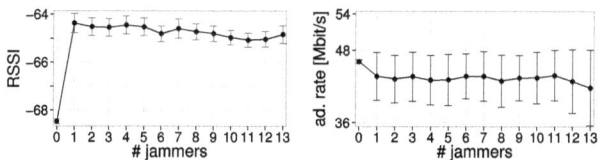

Figure 12: Left: the RSSI (at $m_{close}$) surges when enabling the first jammer, indicating an increased noise level. Right: the mean adapter rate of artificial traffic slightly decreases with the # of jammers.

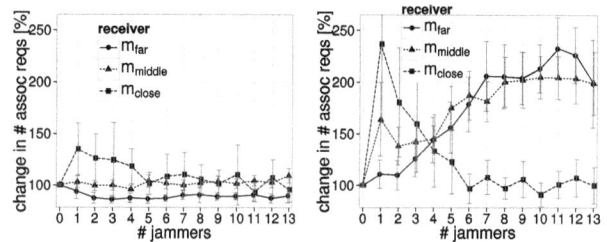

Figure 13: On average, the number of (re)association requests remains approximately stable (left). However, some particular stations are badly affected (right: most badly affected station).

lems; once the jammer selectively interferes with the target transmission, however, it also creates interference with the legitimate transmission, causing it thus to fail.

We quantify this effect by exploiting the fact that our monitors $m_{close}$, $m_{middle}$, and $m_{far}$ cover a large observation area, 85m in length (see map in Figure 11). For each of the monitors, we categorize the observed senders into three classes based on the received signal strength: low RSSI ($< -65dB$), medium RSSI ($-65dB < $ RSSI $< -55dB$), and high RSSI ($> -55dB$). The packet loss for each sender in these classes is measured with the monitor as a receiver, based on each frame's checksum. Figure 10 reveals that the packet loss increases with the number of jammers only for two classes (and is stable for the other classes). The most badly affected class is the traffic with low RSSI as observed by $m_{far}$ (Figure 10(right)): the packet loss doubles from 20.2% to 40.4%. The low-RSSI senders are located at positions to the right on the floor (Figure 11), where they do not receive the target messages but may suffer interference from the jammers in the center (i.e. the setting described in Figure 9). Accordingly, we attribute the observed increase of packet loss to the power amplification phenomenon, for which the likelihood increases with an increasing number of active jammers. The second affected class are $m_{middle}$'s medium-RSSI senders (Figure 10(center)): the packet loss increases from 13.7% to 22.6%. We also explain this obser-

vation with the jammer's power amplification; however, the effect is less pronounced than before since there are fewer candidate jammers. It is also interesting to note that the low-RSSI senders at $m_{middle}$ are not similarly affected by this phenomenon – we attribute this to erratic propagation effects of the indoor topology (cf. Figure 6(left)); for example, there is a fire door to the left of this monitor that significantly alters signal propagation paths.

Summing up, we found that friendly jamming can substantially impair the channel of legitimate transmissions due to the power amplification effect. Future studies of friendly jamming should thus seriously consider a cost perspective besides traditional metrics of performance and security.

*Interaction with Rate Adaptation.* The remaining station's packet loss is only marginally affected by higher jammer counts. Curiously, we find that the close-by traffic's loss (Figure 10(left)) slightly decreases when the first jammer is enabled. This is probably due to the close-by stations' rate adaptation algorithms. When considering the RSSI recorded at the close-by monitor, we find that it increases significantly (Figure 12(left)). From this we infer a generally increased level of channel noise, which triggers the rate adaption algorithms to select a more robust modulation. In fact, Figure 12(right) shows that the mean adapter rate shows more variance when the jammers are enabled and slightly tends towards more robust MCSs. The effect on the mean adapter rate of packets at different monitors is even smaller.

*Effect on Associations.* As a final aspect of the cost of jamming, we consider the number of (re)associations requests under different numbers of jammers. Figure 13(left) presents the change in this number with respect to the configurations without jammers. While the close-by stations seem to be affected by an increase of up to 40%, the farther-away stations exhibit approximately stable behavior. We also considered

111

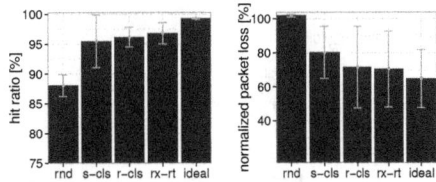

Figure 14: Left: the hit ratio of the proposed jammer-collaboration schemes. Right: the packet loss of far-away packets (affected by the power amplification phenomenon) normalized to random jammer configurations with the same hit ratio.

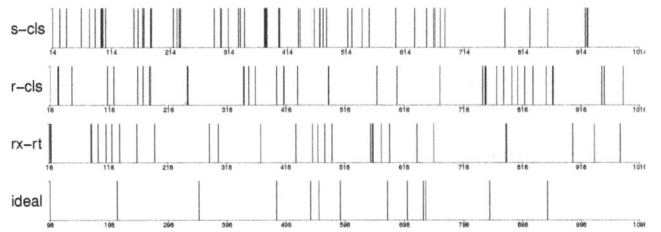

Figure 15: Sequence number diagrams shows the effectiveness of the collaboration schemes already for three jammers – compare to Figure 7.

the (re)associations of individual stations, and found that there is a small number of significantly affected stations. Figure 13(right) depicts that there exist some far-away stations that loose connectivity more likely with an increasing number of active jammers. Interestingly, we also found evidence of a close-by station, which is more badly affected when there is a small jammer count.

In summary, we again emphasize the trade-off between jamming performance and the cost of jamming: enabling a larger number of jammers is necessary to boost the hit ratio but also increases the collateral damage to legitimate traffic. While not unexpected, we obtained detailed quantitative statements on the cost of jamming in a real-world 802.11 network. These results were obtained under the assumption of random jammer placement – a limitation a jamming system might be able to overcome, and which we investigate in the following section.

## 4.3   Jammer Collaboration Schemes

In this section, we show the potential of jammer collaboration, by which we mean that jammers are selected according to some deterministic rule instead of randomly as above. This promises to improve the hit ratio while remaining marginally invasive, based on the previous section's finding that the jammer's position is critical to both the performance and cost of friendly jamming. We investigate this potential by comparing three practical collaboration schemes to the theoretic optimum observed in our experiments.

The simplest idea is to select the jammer closest to the sender (e.g., realized by trilateration) and is called s-cls. If the jamming system can observe bidirectional communication attempts between targets, the jammers may be able to infer the location of the intended receiver and the jammers closest to the receiver can be selected. One can expect the corresponding scheme, r-cls, to improve the hit ratio because respective jammers would be closer to the receiver and thus their jam signals arrive with higher energy. Our third practical scheme is based on the idea to select jammers based on their reception quality. More specifically, the scheme rx-rt selects those jammers that received the highest number of target frames. While this heuristic only considers the channel from the receiver to the jammer, one may speculate that it also corresponds to better jamming positions in general.

We evaluate these schemes' performance with three jammers. The theoretical ideal scheme, which always picks the most successful jammers based on a posteriori knowledge, and the average performance of random jammer placement are considered as ground truth. Figure 14 compares the hit ratio of the schemes and the magnitude of their respective

power amplification effects. The latter is measured as the normalized packet loss of far-away packets where normalization is done to configurations that yield the same hit ratio[4].

The simple s-cls scheme significantly increases the jamming performance and also reduces the effect of the power amplification phenomenon. We attribute this improvement to the fact that the receiver and the sender are positioned close to each other and far-away jammers are efficiently excluded. The extension, the r-cls scheme, yields a slightly better hit ratio than s-cls and can reduce the packet loss even further. However, we remark that this scheme is less practical than s-cls. The third practical scheme rx-rt can outperform s-cls slightly, but with overlapping confidence intervals. While all collaboration schemes improve significantly over random jammer selection, their hit ratios are $2.5 - 4\%$ below the ideal case – indicating some further room for improvement and more sophisticated schemes.

We also compared sequence number diagrams of the four proposed collaboration schemes. Figure 15 displays the differences of the schemes with respect to this performance metric. It again also shows the gap in performance to the ideal case. Nevertheless, while the misses of the random jammer selection do not possess the memoryless property of the geometric distribution, the misses of all collaboration schemes come closer (r-cls) or achieve it (s-cls, rx-rt).

We also studied the schemes for seven jammers. In that case, the mean hit ratio is about 98.95% for s-cls, 99.41% for r-cls, 99.62% for rx-rt, and 99.95% for the ideal case.

This completes the measurement analysis, and we next address the jamming success in more detail.

## 5.   DETAILED ANALYSIS OF JAMMING SUCCESS

In the previous section, we observed friendly jamming to hit target traffic only imperfectly as there will always be some successfully received frames under power constraints. This finding holds even under very favorable conditions: the long-term hit ratio in a static environment (at night) with large numbers of jammers with constant jamming power never reaches 100%. Under the assumption that only detection, reaction time, and power determine jamming success (for fixed MCS and other conditions), one may wonder why this is the case. This section investigates explanations for this somewhat mysterious finding. In particular, we also address the reason why jamming affects frame differently despite equal power levels.

---

[4]If scheme $x$ achieves a hit ratio of 90%, the normalized packet loss of $x$ is: (packet loss of $x$) / (packet loss of random jammer configuration, which yields a 90% hit ratio)

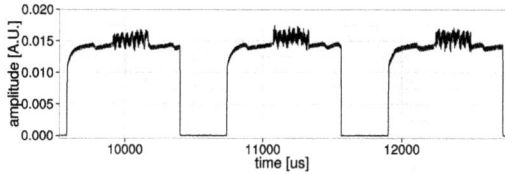

Figure 16: Three jammed frames in a Tektronix trace. The first frame is jammed and yields a wrong checksum with our software decoder, while the following two frames can be decoded correctly (despite the same relation of $P_{jammed}$ to $P_{target}$).

## 5.1 The Reception Process of DSSS

As expected and validated by our measurement results, the MCS underlying the 1 $Mb/s$ rate is particularly robust to jamming and can be considered the worst-case with respect to jamming success. Thus, we focus our study on the corresponding direct sequence spread spectrum (DSSS) scheme and first review the reception process as defined in the IEEE 802.11 standard [15].

In the encoding process, bit are first pre-processed to be balanced, i.e., to not include long runs of binary 0s or 1s, and have a self-synchronizing property ($\rightarrow$scrambling). Then, the DSSS scheme expands every bit into eleven chips that are mapped to a Barker sequence making it robust ($\rightarrow$spreading gain). The Barker chips are then modulated with (differential binary) phase-shift keying (PSK) modulation, and the resulting symbols are transmitted.

Decoding starts with the receiver detecting energy on the channel. It then starts a phase-locked loop and the PSK can be demodulated to obtain the sequence of Barker chips. With the scrambled bit's self-synchronizing property, the actual data bits can finally be obtained.

In order to reliably decode a frame, the receiver has to synchronize with the incoming transmission. For instance, the border of each eleven Barker chips corresponding to one data bit have to be found. This is accomplished at the start of a frame by the physical layer preamble, which comprises a training sequence of 128 1-bits. Because the training sequence is known, the receiver can align its decoding components with the incoming data. The end of this sequence is indicated by the start of frame delimiter (SFD) (cf. Figure 1) and the receiver goes on to decode the remainder of the frame. Therefore, the alignment of the decoder with the frame remains robust despite interference and the spreading gain (the eleven-fold redundancy) can be used to recover the original bit sequence.

## 5.2 Impact of a Jammer's Symbol Alignment

At a receiver antenna, the two streams of symbols produced by the target and the jammer will not likely align, for several reasons: first, the clocks of jammer and target are not synchronized; second, the propagation delays could be different and change at every transmission because of multipath effects; third, the microcontroller of the jammer, its execution pipeline state and the instruction that is being executed when the target frame is received, strongly influences the scheduling delay of the jam signal. All these reasons are independent, and we assume in the following that the symbols in a jam frame can have any alignment with respect to those in the target frame and that the symbol delay can be

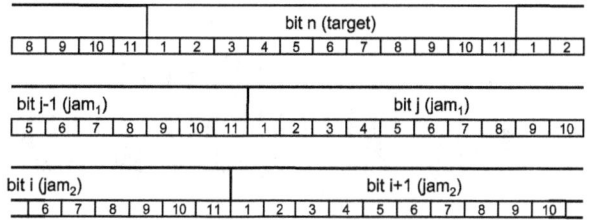

Figure 17: Alignment of two jam frames with a target frame: although none of the two jam frames is bit aligned, the top one achieves maximal, the bottom one minimal jamming success.

approximated by a uniformly distributed random variable over an interval of symbol length. On a higher order temporal scale, there is also an issue with bit alignment: however, as we will show in the following subsection, it is symbol alignment to really make a difference and, in fact, there is only one possible symbol alignment scheme that minimizes jamming performance, i.e., when each jam symbol spreads over two consecutive target symbols (which in Fig. 17 happens for the bottom jam). On the contrary, there are eleven possible bit alignments that behave in the same way, which correspond to the number of symbols (or chips for $1Mb/s$) that compose each bit.

## 5.3 Trace-based Simulation Results

We developed the software-equivalent of an IEEE 802.11 receiver in order to simulatively validate the symbol alignment explanation as a root cause for unsuccessful jamming. The following simulation results are based on an actual trace of I/Q samples recorded with a real-time spectrum analyzer (Textronix RSA3408) during the real world experiments. Our spectrum analyzer captures traces with 12 bit resolution at $51.2MS/s$ which we downsampled to $44MS/s$ leading to four samples per Barker chip.

We validated our receiver on multiple traces of frames in which acknowledgments were clearly visible. The receiver works reliably and actually outperforms the hardware receivers used in the experiments. We also reproduced the previous finding, that different frames, which were jammed but agreed on the ratio $P_{jammed}/P_{target}$ (cf. Figure 1), are sometimes successfully decoded but sometimes not. Figure 16 shows such an example in which the amplitude of three jammed frames looks similar, but only one in three can be decoded successfully.

Our first simulation of the symbol alignment addresses a valid capture of a single frame. We superpose this frame with another valid 802.11 $1Mb/s$ frame (the jam frame) at different symbol alignments and increasing amplitude (100% means same amplitude as the target). Given that we have four samples per symbol we can consider alignments in 25%-of-a-symbol steps. Figure 18(top) shows that for a fixed jam amplitude, the jamming success depends on the symbol alignment in a periodic fashion. If the jam amplitude is very low, all frames can be decoded; if it increases, jamming is successful at first in those cases in which the two frames are symbol aligned; if the amplitude is further increased, only those cases can be decoded in which the jamming frame is delayed by about 50% of a symbol. Finally, for high amplitudes, jamming is successful independently of the symbol alignment. We also evaluate for larger delays up to two

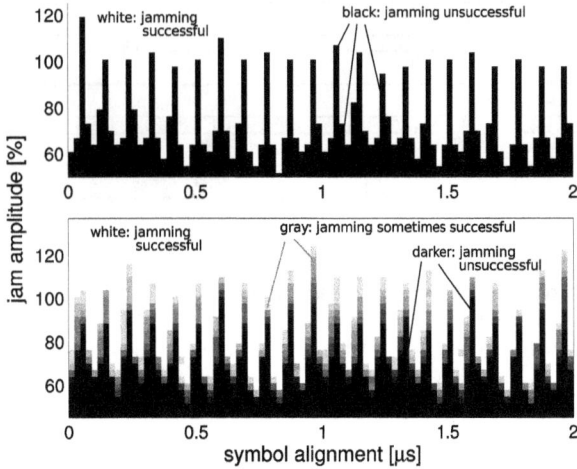

Figure 18: An explanation for the observation that jamming is only sometimes successful at the same jamming power: the jamming success depends on *both* the relative amplitude (jamming signal to target signal) *and* the symbol alignment. For each symbol, four alignments are displayed: jamming is successful for exact bit alignment (0%) and small deviation (25%, 75%). Jammed packets are often decodable for an alignment corresponding to a 50% symbol delay (the peaks). Top: single frame, bottom: entire trace with shades of gray corresponding to jamming/decoding probability.

full Barker chip sequences ($2\mu s$, 22 chips), but find that the jamming success is determined mostly by the alignment with respect to each symbol.

We next extend the same analysis to additional 27 frames. We can interpret this analysis stochastically as the probability that frames can be decoded for a specific combination of alignment and jam amplitude. Figure 18(bottom) shows that, in principle, the findings obtained for a single frame carry over to the other frames in our trace. However, note that there are subtle differences. For example, the minimal jam amplitude required increases by $3 - 5\%$ and the parameter regions indicating jamming success are less clearly defined. At the highest evaluated jamming amplitude of 120%, some frames can still be decoded for a particular configuration that corresponds to an alignment close to a full Barker sequence (close but not exactly bit alignment).

We also extended the simulations to the case of two jammers: the same method as before is used, but the jam frame is superimposed twice (independently) with all 28 frames in the capture. We explored the space of all possible symbol-alignments for both jam frames and consider the fraction of decodable packets for an equal amplitude for both jam signals. Figure 20 shows the improvement of a two-jammer configuration over a single jammer for low relative jam amplitudes of 37%, 59%, or 74% (from left to right). While most frames can be decoded for a single jammer, two jammers improve the jamming success rate significantly. Nevertheless, the actual effectiveness still depends on the respective symbol alignments: the jammers are successful if their alignment corresponds to delays close to 50%, as expected.

Finally, we connect the pieces of symbol alignment, jam amplitude, and the number of jammers: we consider the hit ratio as the average probability resulting under the assump-

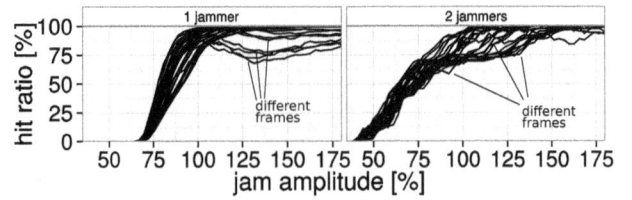

Figure 19: The simulated hit ratio for different frames (averaged over all symbol alignments) shows that two jammers significantly increase the hit ratio for low to medium jam amplitudes.

tion that any symbol alignment can occur with the same probability. Figure 19 shows that doubling the number of jammers more than doubles the hit ratio; for example, when the amplitude is 50%, a single jammer's hit ratio is maximally 20%, but with two jammers a hit ratio of $40-90\%$ can be obtained. This is due to the fact that unfavorable symbol alignments for several jammers at the same time become increasingly unlikely since the jammers behave independently (a probabilistic explanation results from the superposition of uniform distributions which result in low probability for simultaneously bad alignments).

## 6. RELATED WORK

Friendly jamming relates to a variety of research topics in the field of radio communication. In this section, we briefly review previous work on friendly jamming applications, evaluations, and studies on interference properties.

*Friendly Jamming Applications.* Recent proposals can be roughly grouped into two main categories based on their intentions: 1) jamming for blocking unauthorized communications [6, 12, 22, 31, 36], and 2) jamming for improving secrecy of communications [12, 16, 17, 33] (see also works on the Wire-Tap Channel due to Wyner [39]).The first category is the most relevant motivation our study. For example, Gollakota *et al.* [12] and Brown *et al.* [6] propose to use reactive jamming to block unauthorized commands from being transmitted to implantable medical devices (IMDs) or to devices in the smart home. Similarly, Wilhelm *et al.* [36] rely on reactive jamming to enforce rules similar to a firewall. All friendly jamming proposals of this category share the goal of jamming only particular frames in the air motivating thus the evaluation of the cost of jamming in Section 4.2.

The second category also employs jamming as a tool but addresses a different use case. Intentional interference ensures that eavesdropping is rendered infeasible since the jammed messages cannot be decoded. Authorized nodes, however, can successfully receive the messages as the interfering signal is known to them (as a shared secret): these nodes cancel out the interfering signal to recover the original message. An interesting work by Kim *et al.* [17] defines a computational model to optimize the arrangement of jammers protecting an area around an access point. Their setting differs from our setting in that the jammers continuously emit a jam signal and the corresponding negative impact on other networks can only be controlled by power settings and the use of directional antennas (and is not evaluated in their work).

*Evaluation of Friendly Jamming.* Previous works mainly implemented reactive jamming on software defined radio (SDR) platforms (e.g., [4,6,36,37]) and did not target realis-

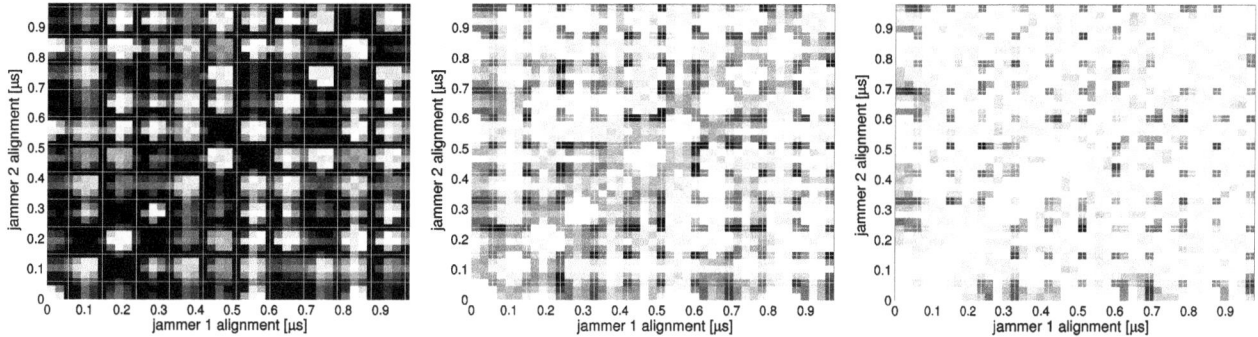

**Figure 20:** Results from simulations of two artificial jam frames indicate that the jam amplitude for successful jamming is significantly lowered, compared to a single jammer: while a relative amplitude of 37% (left) is ineffective, already 59% (center) greatly improves the jamming performance, for 74% (right) the jammers are almost always successful. These plots result from averaging over (all possible) alignments for 28 packets of a real trace (brighter shades of gray indicate higher jamming success).

tic customer-grade access points. The reaction times constitutes a particular challenge in enabling frame-selective jamming on these platforms. For example, Bayraktaroglu *et al.* [4] reports reaction times in the order of milliseconds and cannot target high-rate IEEE 802.11. Instead, the slower IEEE 802.15.4 standard has often been used to evaluate friendly jamming proposals. For example, Brown *et al.* [6] report hit ratios of $98.9 - 100\%$ in a testbed scenario and Wilhelm *et al.* [36, 37] achieve a reaction time of $39\mu s$ and a 97.6% hit ratio with one jammer (99.9 for two concurrent jammers) in an indoor office environment (however, for a short term, non-dynamic experiment).

To the best of our knowledge, we are the first to systematically evaluate the performance and cost of friendly jamming in a real-world environment. Having said that, the feasibility of friendly jamming with respect to secrecy applications, however, has recently been thoroughly evaluated by Tippenhauer *et al.* [32]. Their study focuses on a specific aspect compared to our more macroscopic view of friendly jamming: the confidentiality that can be provided by a jammer (see e.g., [8,12,20,30,31,33,41,42]). In their setting, the jammer and target source are located very close to each other $(15 - 30cm)$ and communicate using the $400MHz$ band. For an attacker that is up to $3m$ away, Tippenhauer *et al.* demonstrated that jamming does not provide strong confidentiality guarantees for all configurations.

*Interference and Collisions in 802.11.* Our simulation study of jamming success is related to the study of packet error probabilities in face of non-intentional interference in IEEE 802.11 networks. These studies are largely motivated by the capture effect. The capture effect describes the successful reception of the stronger signal under interference (even if starting a little later) [18]. Although intentional inference motivates a different perspective (such as the one in Section 5), the corresponding analysis often tries to answer the same questions. In particular, while initial models only considered the role of relative timing on the frame level and the received power [18, 19, 34], more recent capture models report observations that agrees with our analysis.

These works come to a similar conclusion to ours, i.e., that the power ratio between interfering signals is not sufficient to build a capture effect model, but other parameters, such as time and phase offset of sender and receiver, have to be incorporated into the analysis [9, 19, 26, 29, 35].

## 7. CONCLUSION

System proposals for friendly jamming applications have received substantial research interest in recent years. Yet, a reality test was lacking, which is why we investigated friendly jamming at work in a real-word 802.11 network for three weeks. The main insights we collected from these are: 1) a rather high number of jammers is required to achieve a high hit ratio across different modulations, 2) the identification and quantification of the power amplification phenomenon which represents a shadow cost of friendly jamming, and 3) the effectiveness of potential jammer collaboration schemes in achieving a good trade-off between jamming performance and cost. The actual implementation of such collaboration is left for further study as it is most likely very application-dependent which scheme is realizable protocol-wise and which performance/cost trade-off needs to achieved. Besides the rather black-box oriented measurement results on friendly jamming, we also used simulations of the reception process of superimposed signals to investigate the question why perfect jamming is not always feasible. The analysis revealed a strong dependence of the jamming success on the symbol alignment between target and jam frame(s), opening up another interesting opportunity for future research: can friendly jammers boost their hit ratios by sending jam signals that are synchronized with the target signal? Throughout the paper, we assumed jammers to have no energy restrictions, yet, in the literature there are also jammers with a limited energy budget, therefore releasing this assumption could be another future work item.

## Acknowledgments

We thank our anonymous reviewers for their insightful comments on improving various aspects of this work. In particular, we thank our shepherd, Panos Papadimitratos, for his valuable time and guidance. This research was partially supported by the EU's 7FP grant n.258301 (CREW).

## 8. REFERENCES

[1] D. Adamy. *EW 101: a first course in electronic warfare*, volume 1. Artech House, 2000.
[2] D. Adamy. *EW 102: a second course in electronic warfare*, volume 2. Artech House, 2004.
[3] D. Adamy. *EW 103: Tactical battlefield communications electronic warfare*. Artech House, 2008.

[4] E. Bayraktaroglu, C. King, X. Liu, G. Noubir, R. Rajaraman, and B. Thapa. On the Performance of IEEE 802.11 under Jamming. In *Proceedings of IEEE INFOCOM*, pages 1265–1273. IEEE, Apr. 2008.

[5] G. Bianchi, P. Gallo, D. Garlisi, F. Giuliano, F. Gringoli, and I. Tinnirello. Maclets: Active mac protocols over hard-coded devices. In *Proceedings of ACM CoNEXT*. ACM, December 2012.

[6] J. Brown, I. E. Bagci, A. King, and U. Roedig. Defend your home!: Jamming unsolicited messages in the smart home. In *Proceedings of ACM HotWiSec*, pages 1–6, New York, NY, USA, 2013. ACM.

[7] Y. Cai, K. Xu, Y. Mo, B. Wang, and M. Zhou. Improving WLAN throughput via reactive jamming in the presence of hidden terminals. In *Proceedings of IEEE WCNC*, pages 1085–1090. IEEE, Apr. 2013.

[8] L. Dong, H. Yousefi'zadeh, and H. Jafarkhani. Cooperative jamming and power allocation for wireless relay networks in presence of eavesdropper. In *Proceedings of IEEE ICC*, pages 1–5, June 2011.

[9] P. Dutta, S. Dawson-Haggerty, Y. Chen, C.-J. M. Liang, and A. Terzis. Design and evaluation of a versatile and efficient receiver-initiated link layer for low-power wireless. In *Proceedings of ACM SenSys*, pages 1–14, New York, New York, USA, 2010. ACM.

[10] ETSI. EN 300 328 V1.8.1 Electromagnetic compatibility and Radio spectrum Matters (ERM), August 2012. http://www.etsi.org/deliver/etsi_en/300300_300399/300328/01.08.01_60/en_300328v010801p.pdf.

[11] FCC. Jamming Prohibition. last accessed 2014/13/02 http://www.fcc.gov/encyclopedia/jammer-enforcement.

[12] S. Gollakota, H. Hassanieh, B. Ransford, D. Katabi, and K. Fu. They can hear your heartbeats: Non-invasive security for implantable medical devices. In *Proceedings of ACM SIGCOMM*, pages 2–13, New York, NY, USA, 2011.

[13] S. Gollakota and D. Katabi. Physical layer wireless security made fast and channel independent. *2011 Proceedings IEEE INFOCOM*, pages 1125–1133, Apr. 2011.

[14] F. Gringoli and L. Nava. Openfwwf: Open firmware for wifi networks. available at http://www.ing.unibs.it/ openfwwf/.

[15] IEEE. Standard 802.11 1999 edition (r2003) IEEE standard for information technology–telecommunications and information exchange between systems–local and metropolitan area networks–specific requirements–part 11: Wireless lan medium access control (mac) and physical layer (phy) specifications, June 2003.

[16] M. Jorgensen, B. Yanakiev, G. Kirkelund, P. Popovski, H. Yomo, and T. Larsen. Shout to secure: Physical-layer wireless security with known interference. In *Proceedings of IEEE GLOBECOM*, pages 33–38, Nov 2007.

[17] Y. S. Kim, P. Tague, H. Lee, and H. Kim. Carving secure wi-fi zones with defensive jamming. In *Proceedings of ACM ASIACCS*, pages 53–54, New York, NY, USA, 2012. ACM.

[18] A. Kochut, A. Vasan, A. Shankar, and A. Agrawala. Sniffing out the correct physical layer capture model in 802.11b. In *Proceedings of IEEE ICNP*, pages 252–261, October 2004.

[19] J. Lee, W. Kim, S.-J. Lee, D. Jo, J. Ryu, T. Kwon, and Y. Choi. An experimental study on the capture effect in 802.11a networks. In *Proceedings of ACM WinTECH*, pages 19–26, New York, NY, USA, 2007. ACM.

[20] Z. Li, W. Xu, R. Miller, and W. Trappe. Securing wireless systems via lower layer enforcements. In *Proceedings of ACM WiSe*, pages 33–42, New York, NY, USA, 2006. ACM.

[21] G. Lin and G. Noubir. On link layer denial of service in data wireless LANs. *Wireless Communications and Mobile Computing*, 5(3):273–284, May 2005.

[22] I. Martinovic, P. Pichota, and J. B. Schmitt. Jamming for good. In *Proceedings of ACM WiSec*, page 161, New York, New York, USA, Mar. 2009. ACM Press.

[23] A. Mpitziopoulos, D. Gavalas, C. Konstantopoulos, and G. Pantziou. A survey on jamming attacks and countermeasures in WSNs. *IEEE Communications Surveys & Tutorials*, 11(4):42–56, April 2009.

[24] K. Pelechrinis, M. Iliofotou, and S. V. Krishnamurthy. Denial of service attacks in wireless networks: The case of jammers. *IEEE Communications Surveys & Tutorials*, 13(2):245–257, 2011.

[25] R. Poisel. *Modern Communications Jamming: Principles and Techniques*. Artech House, 2011.

[26] C. Pöpper, N. Tippenhauer, B. Danev, and S. Capkun. Investigation of signal and message manipulations on the wireless channel. In V. Atluri and C. Diaz, editors, *Computer Security – ESORICS 2011*, volume 6879 of *Lecture Notes in Computer Science*, pages 40–59. Springer Berlin Heidelberg, 2011.

[27] D. R. Raymond and S. Midkiff. Denial-of-service in wireless sensor networks: Attacks and defenses. *IEEE Pervasive Computing*, 7(1):74–81, January 2008.

[28] P. Salvador, F. Gringoli, V. Mancuso, P. Serrano, A. Mannocci, and A. Banchs. Voipiggy: Implementation and evaluation of a mechanism to boost voice capacity in 802.11 wlans. In *Proceedings of IEEE INFOCOM*. IEEE, March 2012.

[29] N. Santhapuri, S. Nelakuditi, and R. Choudhury. On spatial reuse and capture in ad hoc networks. In *Proceedings of IEEE WCNC*, pages 1628–1633, March 2008.

[30] A. Sheikholeslami, D. Goeckel, H. Pishro-Nik, and D. Towsley. Physical layer security from inter-session interference in large wireless networks. In *Proceedings IEEE INFOCOM*, pages 1179–1187. IEEE, 2012.

[31] W. Shen, P. Ning, X. He, and H. Dai. Ally friendly jamming: How to jam your enemy and maintain your own wireless connectivity at the same time. In *Proceedings of IEEE S&P*, pages 174–188, May 2013.

[32] N. O. Tippenhauer, L. Malisa, A. Ranganathan, and S. Capkun. On Limitations of Friendly Jamming for Confidentiality. In *Proceedings of IEEE S&P*, pages 160–173, May 2013.

[33] J. Vilela, P. Pinto, and J. Barros. Position-based jamming for enhanced wireless secrecy. *IEEE Transactions on Information Forensics and Security*, 6(3):616–627, Sept. 2011.

[34] K. Whitehouse, A. Woo, F. Jiang, J. Polastre, and D. Culler. Exploiting the capture effect for collision detection and recovery. In *Proceedings of IEEE EmNetS*, pages 45–52, May 2005.

[35] M. Wilhelm, V. Lenders, and J. B. Schmitt. An Analytical Model of Packet Collisions in IEEE 802.15.4 Wireless Networks. *CoRR*, abs/1309.4, 2013.

[36] M. Wilhelm, I. Martinovic, J. Schmitt, and V. Lenders. WiFire: a firewall for wireless networks. *Proceedings of ACM SIGCOMM*, pages 456–457, 2011.

[37] M. Wilhelm, I. Martinovic, J. B. Schmitt, and V. Lenders. Short paper: reactive jamming in wireless networks: how realistic is the threat? In *Proceedings of ACM WiSec*, pages 47–52, New York, NY, USA, 2011. ACM.

[38] A. Wood and J. Stankovic. Denial of service in sensor networks. *Computer*, 35(10):54–62, 2002.

[39] A. D. Wyner. The wire-tap channel. *Bell System Technical Journal*, 54(8):1355–1387, 1975.

[40] W. Xu, W. Trappe, Y. Zhang, and T. Wood. The feasibility of launching and detecting jamming attacks in wireless networks. In *Proceedings of ACM MobiHoc*, pages 46–57, New York, NY, USA, 2005. ACM.

[41] X. Zhou and M. McKay. Physical layer security with artificial noise: Secrecy capacity and optimal power allocation. In *Proceedings of ICSPCS*, pages 1–5, Sept 2009.

[42] X. Zhou, M. Tao, and R. Kennedy. Cooperative jamming for secrecy in decentralized wireless networks. In *Proceedings of IEEE ICC*, pages 2339–2344, June 2012.

116

# Power Napping with Loud Neighbors:
# Optimal Energy-Constrained Jamming and Anti-Jamming

Bruce DeBruhl, Christian Kroer, Anupam Datta, Tuomas Sandholm, and Patrick Tague
Carnegie Mellon University
{debruhl@, ckroer@cs., danupam@, sandholm@cs., tague@}cmu.edu

## ABSTRACT

The openness of wireless communication and the recent development of software-defined radio technology, respectively, provide a low barrier and a wide range of capabilities for misbehavior, attacks, and defenses against attacks. In this work we present *finite-energy jamming games*, a game model that allows a jammer and sender to choose (1) whether to transmit or sleep, (2) a power level to transmit with, and (3) what channel to transmit on. We also allow the jammer to choose on how many channels it simultaneously attacks. A major addition in finite-energy jamming games is that the jammer and sender both have a limited amount of energy which is drained according to the actions a player takes.

We develop a model of our system as a zero-sum finite-horizon stochastic game with deterministic transitions. We leverage the zero-sum and finite-horizon properties of our model to design a simple polynomial-time algorithm to compute optimal randomized strategies for both players. The utility function of our game model can be decoupled into a recursive equation. Our algorithm exploits this fact to use dynamic programming to construct solutions in a bottom-up fashion. For each state of energy levels, a linear program is solved to find Nash equilibrium strategies for the subgame. With these techniques, our algorithm has only a linear dependence on the number of states, and quadratic dependence on the number of actions, allowing us to solve very large instances.

By computing Nash equilibria for our game models, we explore what kind of performance guarantees can be achieved both for the sender and jammer, when playing against an optimal opponent. We also use the optimal strategies to simulate finite-energy jamming games and provide insights into robust communication among reconfigurable, yet energy-limited, radio systems. To test the performance of the optimal strategies we compare their performance with a random and adaptive strategy. Matching our intuition, the aggressiveness of an attacker is related to how much of a discount is placed on data delay. This results in the defender often

choosing to sleep despite the latency implication, because the threat of jamming is high. We also present several other findings from simulations where we vary the strategies for one or both of the players.

## Categories and Subject Descriptors

[**Security and privacy**]: Mobile and wireless networks; [**Computing methodologies**]: Artificial Intelligence—*Distributed Artificial Intelligence, Multi-agent systems*

## Keywords

Jamming; Game Theory; Wireless Networks; Equilibrium Computation; Energy-Constrained Jamming

## 1. INTRODUCTION

The flexibility of wireless communication enables untethered mobility, agile deployment, and on-the-fly reorganization of connected devices. However, the openness of wireless communication and the recent development of software-defined radio (SDR) technology, respectively, provide a low barrier and a wide range of capabilities for misbehavior and attacks. One class of attacks which has benefited significantly from SDR technology is jamming, or injection of intentionally interfering signals into the wireless medium. While jamming has been a topic of research for several decades [37], partially due to the devastating potential and difficulty of defense, the SDR revolution has sparked continued innovation on jamming and anti-jamming techniques.

Much of the early work in developing jamming models and technologies focused on attackers with unlimited energy resources, postulating that a jamming attacker would use a generator or be connected to the power grid [32]. Such assumptions have led to overly wasteful or boisterous attackers that make no attempt to conserve energy or to hide their attack activity. Likewise, anti-jamming mechanisms are often designed assuming that the jamming attack is trivial to detect, so many techniques reduce to either advanced signal processing [33] or localizing the attack source to take further action [40].

Our increasingly battery-operated mobile world has recently inspired exploration of attackers with limited energy resources [29]. Constrained attackers, however, are not necessarily less effective, as they can leverage the advanced technologies of SDR, software-defined networking, agile and reconfigurable protocols, sensing, and machine learning. Such capabilities can also provide increases in attack stealth, allowing attackers to avoid detection or localization [9]. Ex-

*WiSec'14*, July 23–25, 2014, Oxford, UK.
Copyright is held by the owner/author(s). Publication rights licensed to ACM.
ACM 978-1-4503-2972-9/14/07 ...$15.00.
http://dx.doi.org/10.1145/2627393.2627406 .

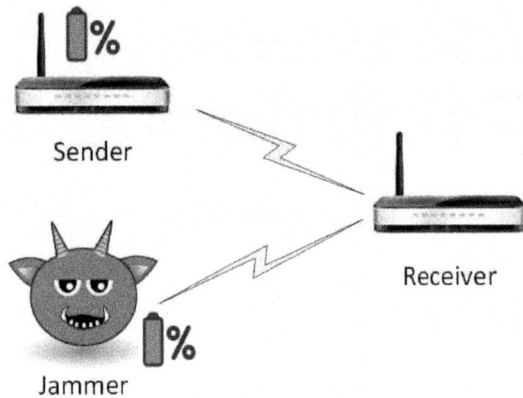

**Figure 1: The players involved in our Finite-Energy Jamming Game are the attacker and the defender, made up of the sender-receiver combination. All game decisions on the defender side are actually made by the sender in our model.**

amples of recent energy-conscious attacks include periodic jamming [10] and random jamming [40] that alternate between jamming and sleeping to save energy; control channel jamming [8] and similar attacks that leverage protocol structure for efficiency; and reactive jamming [39], adaptive jamming [9, 31], and mesh jamming [22] which respond to observed activity instead of attacking statically.

Fortunately, the same innovative technologies that enable energy-efficient and stealthy attacks can also enable more robust and agile anti-jamming techniques. The agility provided by SDRs allows defenders and attackers alike to have more fine-grained control of protocols and parameters, enabling the ability to adapt on the fly [25]. However, this mutual agility increases system complexity and presents a significant challenge to our understanding of various performance, security, and reliability metrics required for effective system design. Understanding how mutually agile opponents interact in a resource-constrained scenario remains an active research field. In this work we explore a battery-operated jammer and battery-operated sender, where the sender's goal is to successfully transmit and the jammer's goal is to prevent that.

To increase our understanding of mutually agile, resource-constrained players in the context of wireless communications, we look to game theory for tools to analyze optimal strategies for jamming and anti-jamming. We make the following contributions in this work.

- We design a new model for energy-constrained jammer-defender interaction, allowing players to transmit or sleep during any round. This provides for the exploration of a realistic scenario where opponents have similar energy levels and freedom to reconfigure.

- We model this interaction as a zero-sum finite-horizon stochastic game with deterministic transitions to find optimal player strategies. We leverage the properties of our game to design a simple polynomial-time dynamic programming algorithm that solves a series of small linear programs to compute optimal strategies (a Nash equilibrium).

- We implement a simulation of three scenarios to gain insights on the performance of energy-constrained Direct Sequence Spread Spectrum (DSSS) and Frequency Hopping Spread Spectrum (FHSS) systems.

Our first contribution is considering attacking and defending opponents that can choose (1) whether to transmit or sleep, (2) what power level to transmit with, and (3) what channel (or how many channels) to transmit on, with the understanding that each choice has a different energy usage and that the outcome also depends on the action chosen by their opponent. Due to the energy constraints and the fact that every choice has a non-zero cost (even sleeping is subject to non-trivial energy leakage), both players can only participate for a finite amount of time. Moreover, since the value of data may significantly decrease with latency, we allow the sender's utility to decay with time. Since our game incorporates aspects of power control and sleeping for throughput and latency management, we refer to our game formulation as a *finite-energy jamming game*. We are the first to mathematically model and analyze accumulative energy-constrained jammer-sender strategic interaction. In related energy-constrained work, the focus has been on average energy consumption [5] or over-heating [26].

In particular, our finite-energy jamming game formulation imposes maximum energy expenditure on both the jammer and defender, while allowing both players to adjust their transmit power levels. The sender and receiver, collectively comprising the defender in our scenario, communicate either using single-channel DSSS or multi-channel FHSS. We model DSSS and FHSS because many modern communication systems use variants of these techniques. Likewise, the attacker can jam on one or many channels depending on which technique is employed by the defender. If the sender selects a sufficiently high power level compared to the jammer's selected power level (or if the jammer chooses a different channel), then the transmission is successful. Regardless, both player's expend an amount of energy that corresponds to their chosen power level (or sleeping).

In most related work on modeling jamming games, energy constraints have not been considered, so single-shot or repeated game approaches have been adopted. In contrast to that work, the energy constraint means that our game has state, and thus needs more advanced modeling techniques. The two papers in the literature that are closest to our work are the following. First, Altman et. al. [5], consider jamming in a stochastic game setting. Whereas we assume that actions and energy levels are fully observed, their work goes the opposite direction and requires that actions are completely unobserved. The truth lies, of course, somewhere in the middle, but both our and their work can shed light on the possibilities and limitations for the general problem. Second, Mallik et. al. [26] consider a dynamic game where temporal energy constraints exist, in the form of over-heating. This means that energy usage only impacts the immediate rounds afterwards, as opposed to expending energy from a finite supply. Like us, they assume that actions are fully observed. They propose a dynamic game, almost akin to a repeated game, with slight variations in the available actions.

Our second contribution is to develop algorithms for computing optimal strategies for our system, formulating it as a zero-sum finite-horizon stochastic game with deterministic transitions. We use Nash equilibria as our framework for optimal strategies. Nash equilibria are a compelling solution concept especially for zero-sum settings such as ours, as they guarantee the highest utility against optimal opponents and sub-optimal opponents only increase our utility. As such, Nash equilibria and their associated expected utility represent the best guarantee on utility that one can hope for, when faced with potentially optimal adversaries.

We leverage the zero-sum and finite-horizon properties to design a simple polynomial-time dynamic programming algorithm that solves a series of small linear programs to compute a Nash equilibrium. The dynamic programming aspect is similar to the work of Mallik et. al. [26], who also use the finite-horizon aspect to obtain a dynamic programming description. However, they further use specific properties of their setting to derive analytical solutions, whereas our work relies on algorithms for computing strategies. Their consideration of temporal constraints could easily be incorporated into our more general framework and algorithms, along with our finite-resource energy constraints.

Our third contribution is a series of simulations of finite-energy jamming games, which provide insights into robust communication among reconfigurable yet energy-limited radio systems. To further understand the benefit of our game-theoretic models, we compare the rational player using the finite-energy jamming game model with a random player and an adaptive player, demonstrating several cases where the game-theoretic strategies provided by finite-energy jamming game provides significant gains over other strategies. The game theoretic strategies also provides interesting insights about the tradeoffs of energy-constrained jamming-defender interaction. Of particular interest and matching our intuition, we observe that the jammer's optimal strategy is extremely aggressive when the sender highly values low-latency communication, resulting in an attack strategy using high-power jamming in the beginning. This forces the sender to transmit with low probability in the beginning of the game, even when highly valuing low latency. In addition to these observations, we evaluate a number of different attack and defense scenarios, and identify a number of interesting trends and tradeoffs in the realm of finite-energy jamming games. In order to mimic a realistic scenario, we set the jammer and defender's initial energies to be within an order of magnitude of each other for our simulations.

The remainder of this work is organized as follows. In Section 2, we explore related work in jamming and game theory. We introduce our system model and assumptions in Section 3, and we present finite-energy jamming games in Section 4. In Section 5, we present our simulation and evaluation setup, and we discuss our simulation results in Section 6. Lastly, in Section 7 we briefly discuss limitations and future research directions.

## 2. RELATED WORK

Due to the potential risk of jamming, a large body of work has recently focused on how to effectively avoid and mitigate the effects of jamming attacks. Much of the work on basic and advanced jamming techniques through the last decade has been summarized in a 2010 survey [29]. Efficient jamming and anti-jamming techniques can be classified into two categories: static and adaptive. Static jamming and anti-jamming techniques rely on specification of protocols, parameters, and strategies in advance, while adaptive techniques rely on context, measurements, and observations to choose protocols, parameters, and strategies on the fly to improve performance.

Traditional jamming mitigation techniques have focused on static strategies and shared secrets to perform spread spectrum techniques such as direct sequence spread spectrum (DSSS), frequency hopping spread spectrum (FHSS), code division multiplexing (CDMA), and orthogonal frequency division multiplexing (OFDM) [28]. Efficient static strategies include random [40], periodic [10], and deceptive jamming [40]. Both random and periodic jamming alternate between attacking and sleeping in an attempt to attack in an efficient manner. Deceptive jamming on the other hand sends legitimate packets in an attempt to stealthily interfere with communications, making its effect very similar to greedy MAC misbehavior techniques [30]. More recent strategies have explored adaptation of protocols and parameters at multiple layers either randomly or in response to observations and measurements. The SPREAD system uses multi-layer adaptation as an extension of spread spectrum [25], providing a more robust communication system but still depending on the same secret-sharing fundamentals. Adaptive jamming strategies using observation-based agility [9] and offline optimization using long-term measurement data [36]. Moreover, adaptive anti-jamming techniques have included the use of advanced signal processing and filtering at the receiver [33], jamming-aware traffic management [35], and adaptive beamforming [6].

Game theory has provided a potent tool to investigate and analyze jamming and anti-jamming [1, 12, 27] as well as other security problems. In the domain of jamming, game theory has provided a framework to select parameters and strategies for both static and adaptive jamming and anti-jamming scenarios. We briefly discuss three types of related games: power management games, jammer-versus-defender games, and friendly jamming games.

Power management games study the choice of transmission power levels among nodes in a network to achieve sufficient signal quality while limiting interference with neighbors [4]. Power management games are useful in maximizing the signal-to-interference-and-noise ratio (SINR) of wireless communication in the network. The authors derive a Nash equilibrium for transmission power selection to maximize SINR over the network in both a selfish and cooperative setting.

A second class of relevant games involves explicit competition between jamming and defending players. Previous work has studied the equilibrium behavior of a rate-adaptive defender versus a power-limited jammer [13], choosing jamming power to avoid detection [23], choosing jamming and communication transmission power to balance over-heating concerns [26], choosing jamming strategies considering impact and per-round energy drain [3], and team-versus-team jamming where each team maximizes their own throughput while minimizing the opposing team's throughput [7, 17, 18].

Friendly jamming games aim to use jamming to enforce communication secrecy or privacy against eavesdroppers. In this scenario, utility is defined by the ability to relay data to an intended receiver while preventing eavesdropping by an unintended receiver [16, 19]. Variations on the game include using a coexisting network of active jamming attackers that can also prevent the intended nodes from receiving the data [41].

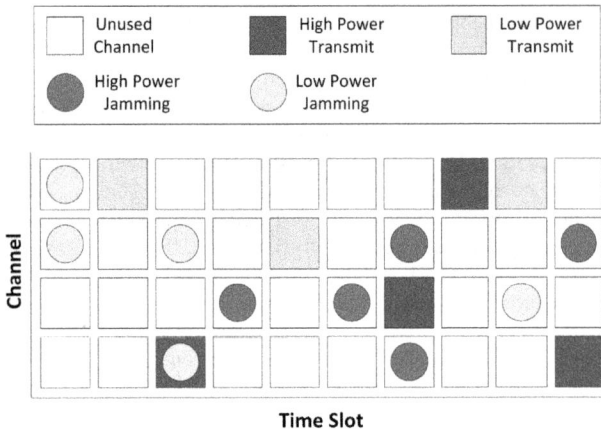

**Figure 2:** We illustrate our system and show the Finite-Energy Jamming game. The jammer and sender both are able to choose to power nap, transmit at a low power, or transmit at a high power.

Our two-player game with energy-constrained players has similarities with many of these related works, but we include the additional consideration of multi-round optimization with a fixed energy budget for the entire game. The closest of the related works in this regard is the optimal jamming and anti-jamming work of Li et al. [23], but that work differs in that the goal of the attacker is to avoid detection, while in our work the attacker aims to maximally ruin the sender's throughput.

Beyond the papers mentioned in Section 1, much work in the stochastic games literature has been focused around iterative algorithms that eventually converge to a Nash equilibrium or approximate Nash equilibrium, posing additional constraints on the game for convergence, such as existence of global optima, or saddle points [20,24,38]. For the finite-horizon case, polynomial-time algorithms have been developed, with a running time that is quadratic in the size of the state space [21]. Iterative convergence approaches have also been combined with optimal solving of stage games [14,15], but without runtime guarantees. Our context allows us to develop a significantly more efficient algorithm that only requires traversing the state space once.

## 3. SYSTEM MODEL AND ASSUMPTIONS

In this work, we explore a three-node scenario consisting of a sender, a receiver, and a jamming attacker over a time interval $\mathcal{T}$, as illustrated in Figure 1. The sender and receiver collectively comprise the defender, able to use single-channel DSSS or $N$-channel FHSS, while all of the defender's decisions in our scenario are made by the sender. We assume that both the attacker and defender are energy constrained, starting with initial energy $E_{a,0}$ and $E_{d,0}$, respectively, so they are forced to balance between maximum performance and minimum energy expenditure.

We assume that the time interval $\mathcal{T}$ is divided into distinct sub-intervals referred to as *rounds*. In each round, the defender chooses a transmission power $p_d$ from a discrete set of power levels $\mathcal{P}_d \subseteq \{0, 1, \ldots, p_{d,\max}\}$, where $p_{d,\max}$ is the defender's maximum transmission power. When the

defender transmits with power $p_d$ in a round, it incurs an energy cost $\epsilon_d(p_d)$, and we assume two fundamental properties of this cost function: monotonicity and strict positivity. Monotonicity of the cost function simply means that higher transmission power incurs higher energy cost, while strict positivity means that all actions incur an energy cost, even a play of $p_d = 0$, in which case the defender pays a leakage cost while sleeping. In the case of FHSS, the defender also chooses which of the $N$ channels it will use for communication. We assume that the underlying synchronization, configuration, and channel switching costs are negligible, and thus we treat them as free. We illustrate this system in Figure 2.

The attacker's energy model is similar. In each round, the attacker chooses a jamming power $p_a$ from a discrete set of power levels $\mathcal{P}_a \subseteq \{0, 1, \ldots, p_{a,\max}\}$, where $p_{a,\max}$ is the attacker's maximum jamming power. The energy cost of the attacker's action in the round is also dictated by a function $\epsilon_a(p_a)$, which is both monotonic and strictly positive as with the defender, but with one significant difference. In the FHSS case, the attacker is allowed to reconfigure the radio front-end to jam any $k$ out of the $N$ channels, where $1 \le k \le N$, using power $p_a$ per channel. The cost for the attacker for this round is then given by $k\epsilon_a(p_a)$ proportional to the number of channels jammed.

To measure the defender's performance in each round, we consider the throughput $T(p_d, p_a)$ achieved in the round when the defender transmits with power $p_d$ and the attacker transmits on the same channel with power $p_a$. Moreover, since the value of the sender's data to the receiver may decrease with time, we introduce a discount factor $\delta \in (0, 1]$ for every round in which the data does not reach the receiver. This discount function is representative of a system where the sender has all data at the beginning of the time interval and desires rapid transmission. To compensate for the latency induced by the jamming attack in the defender's utility function, we multiply the throughput $T(p_d, p_a)$ by $\delta$ for each round of delay, so any throughput attained during round $i$ is valued according to the *latency-adjusted throughput* $\delta^i T(p_d, p_a)$. When the attacker jams on a channel different from that used by the defender, we use the equivalent throughput $T(p_d, 0)$, since the attack has no effect.

We assume a perfect knowledge scenario starting at the beginning of the time interval, so the players know the initial energy of both players. In addition, we assume that each player can observe their opponent's actions in that round by the end of the round, so each player always has complete knowledge of their opponent's residual energy at the beginning of the next round when they have to decide what to do in that round.

## 4. FINITE-ENERGY JAMMING GAMES

We model a finite-energy jamming game in the described wireless system as a zero-sum finite-horizon stochastic game with deterministic transitions. In much of the related literature, jamming scenarios have been modeled as single-shot or repeated games [2,34]. Both of these approaches are sensible when no state is present, for example, when energy constraints do not apply, as the same strategy remains optimal throughout the game. Since our game has state in the form of residual energy, neither single-shot nor repeated game models can adequately capture our setting. Instead, we turn to stochastic games, where the game state transitions at every time step. Since residual energy is monotonically decreasing, we can model our game as a finite-horizon game. We allow all transitions between states to be deterministic, since the energy cost of different actions is assumed to be fixed and known.

In two-player zero-sum games, the solution concept of Nash equilibria is particularly compelling. In general-sum games, there can be many Nash equilibria with different expected utilities for the players, and playing a Nash equilibrium strategy says nothing about the expected utility for a player, if the opponent does not play a best response. This is not so for zero-sum games, where playing a Nash equilibrium strategy guarantees at least a certain level of utility in expectation. That guaranteed utility is called the value of the game, and it is achieved when the opponent responds optimally to the player's optimal (Nash equilibrium) strategy. The zero-sum property guarantees that the player can only benefit (and get more than the value of the game) if the opponent does not play optimally. We will formally define a Nash equilibrium in Section 4.1.

We first introduce our game framework in the context of the single-channel communication system. We then extend our study to include FHSS with the jammer transmitting on a fixed number of channels. After this, we explore a further extension using FHSS where the attacker can vary the number of jammed channels at each time step. For the FHSS settings, we are not assuming that a single channel is chosen at each time step. Rather, we assume that the frequency hopping is so effective that the best the jammer can do is jam a random subset of channels in the hopes of disrupting communication. Finally, we show how to compute Nash equilibria for these games.

## 4.1 Single-Channel Game

The first game we explore is the single-channel finite-energy jamming game. This game uses a single DSSS channel and has the attacker and defender select power levels from a discrete set. The parameters to the game are the discount factor $\delta$ and the initial energies $E_{d,0}, E_{a,0}$ for the players. Based on the defender's residual energy $E_d$ at the start of a round, the defender's action set $A_d(E_d)$ for that round is defined as $A_d(E_d) = \{p \in \mathcal{P}_d : \epsilon_d(p) \leq E_d\}$. The attacker's action set $A_a(E_a)$ is similarly defined. When the defender and attacker choose respective actions $p_d \in A_d(E_d)$ and $p_a \in A_a(E_a)$, the immediate utility to the defender is $u_d(p_d, p_a) = T(p_d, p_a)$, which is later discounted by $\delta^i$ during round $i$ to compensate for latency. The attacker's immediate utility is $u_a(p_d, p_a) = -u_d(p_d, p_a)$. The defender chooses its action based on an energy-dependent *strategy* $\sigma_d^{E_d, E_a}$ that specifies a probability distribution over actions in $A_d(E_d)$. For example, $\sigma_d^{E_d, E_a}(p)$ is the probability the defender will transmit at power level $p \in \mathcal{P}_d$. We analogously define the attacker's strategy $\sigma_a^{E_d, E_a}$. Once the players choose their actions in a round $i$, with the defender and attacker respectively transmitting at power levels $p_d$ and $p_a$, the game transitions to round $i + 1$, where the players have residual energy $E_d - \epsilon_d(p_d)$ and $E_a - \epsilon_a(p_a)$. The game continues in this way until the defender's residual energy is such that $A_d(E_d) \subseteq \{0\}$, after which $u_d = u_a = 0$.

Considering the entire game over multiple rounds, a *strategy profile* $\sigma$ is a pair of strategies $\sigma = \{\sigma_d, \sigma_a\}$ that fully specifies the game. Using the strategy profile $\sigma$, we can then compute the defender's total expected utility $u^\sigma(E_{d,0}, E_{a,0})$

using a recursive definition over diminishing energy levels as

$$u^\sigma(E_d, E_a) = \sum_{p_d \in A_d(E_d)} \sum_{p_a \in A_a(E_a)} \sigma_d^{E_d, E_a}(p_d)\sigma_a^{E_d, E_a}(p_a)$$
$$\times \Big(u_d(p_d, p_a) + \delta u^\sigma(E_d - \epsilon_d(p_d), E_a - \epsilon_a(p_a))\Big) \tag{1}$$

where $u_d(p_d, p_a) = T(p_d, p_a)$ for the single-channel game. This can be viewed as a series of normal-form games, where the payoff matrix for each game depends on the values of the subgames induced by the various choices of actions.

A Nash equilibrium is a strategy profile $\sigma^* = \{\sigma_d^*, \sigma_a^*\}$ that satisfies

$$\sigma_d^* = \arg\max_{\sigma_d} u^{\{\sigma_d, \sigma_a^*\}}(E_{d,0}, E_{a,0})$$
$$\sigma_a^* = \arg\max_{\sigma_a} u^{\{\sigma_d^*, \sigma_a\}}(E_{d,0}, E_{a,0})$$

In other words, in a Nash equilibrium, each player maximizes their own utility, given the strategy of the other player.

## 4.2 Multi-Channel Game with FHSS

We next consider a finite-energy jamming game in which the defender spreads its transmissions over $N$ orthogonal channels by choosing a different channel randomly in each round of the game. In our first FHSS-based game, the attacker chooses $k$ channels to jam every round, where $k$ is constant for the duration of the game. In each round, the attacker has a probability of $k/N$ of interfering with the defender's transmission, so the immediate utility for the defender in this case is given by

$$u_d(p_d, p_a) = \frac{k}{N}T(p_d, p_a) + \frac{N-k}{N}T(p_d, 0) \tag{2}$$

The defender's total expected utility is given by substituting (2) into (1). In this game, the energy expenditure of the attacker is increased by a factor of $k$, meaning that an attack action with power $p_a$ incurs a cost $k\epsilon_a(p_a)$.

## 4.3 Multi-Channel Game with FHSS and Selection of Number of Channels to Jam

Similar to our second game, we consider a generalization of the previous FHSS game in an $N$-channel communication system. In our second FHSS-based game, the attacker is free to choose any value of $k \in \{1, \ldots, N\}$ in each round as part of its attack strategy. Given the additional game parameter, the attacker's action set $A_a(E_a)$ in each round is extended to

$$A_a(E_a) = \{(p, k) \in \mathcal{P}_a \times \{1, \ldots, N\} : k\epsilon_a(p) \leq E_a\}$$

and the utility function $u_d(p_d, p_a)$ is extended to $u_d(p_d, p_a, k)$, using the same form as (2). In contrast to the previous game with fixed $k$, treating $k$ as a variable game parameter allows the attacker to effectively balance the tradeoff between higher utility and greater energy expenditure of jamming more channels. In addition, since the attacker's action set $A_a(E_a)$ has increased in dimensionality compared to the fixed-$k$ case, the complexity of solving the game increases linearly in $N$.

## 4.4 Computing a Nash Equilibrium

For each of the three game models described above, we can use the same basic approach for computing a Nash equilibrium. Each of those three games can be viewed as a series of normal-form games, each of which depend on the values of subgames to fill out their payoff matrix. We use this subgame property, along with the well-known fact that zero-sum normal-form games can be solved in polynomial time using linear programming, to solve our problem. Using dynamic programming, solutions are constructed bottom up through successively solving linear programs that compute Nash equilibria of subgames. The pseudocode is presented as Algorithm 1.

---

**Input**: Energy levels $E_d, E_a$, discount factor $\delta$
**Output**: Nash equilibrium strategy profile $\sigma$
$U \leftarrow [\,]$       // dynamic programming table
**for** $E'_d \in \{0, \ldots, E_d\}$ **do**
    **for** $E'_a \in \{0, \ldots, E_a\}$ **do**
        $M \leftarrow [\,]$    // payoff matrix
        **for** $p_d \in A_d(E'_d), p_a \in A_a(E'_a)$ **do**
            $M[p_d, p_a] =$
            $u(p_d, p_a) + \delta \cdot U[E'_d - \epsilon_d(p_d), E'_a - \epsilon_a(p_a)]$
        **end**
        $U[E'_d, E'_a] = \textsc{GameValue}(M)$
        $\sigma^{E'_d, E'_a} = \textsc{StrategyProfile}(M)$
    **end**
**end**

**Algorithm 1: Bottom-up dynamic program for computing Nash equilibria in finite-energy jamming games.**

---

The dynamic program iterates over all possible energy levels for the two players, starting from the smallest levels possible. For each pair of energy levels, a payoff matrix $M$ is computed. Line 1 implements the recursive equation for utility given in (1) or (2) depending on the game played. That is, it sets the payoff to the immediate payoff achieved from the actions taken plus the value of the subgame reached by the power loss, weighted by the discount factor $\delta$. Lines 1 and 1 extract the value of the game and a strategy profile that achieves a Nash equilibrium.

Our dynamic program crucially relies on the fact that every set of energies $E_d, E_a$ induces a subgame, where the path traveled to get to these energy levels does not matter. Depending on the round where the energy levels are reached, the discount factor might be different. However, in terms of computing a strategy for $E_d, E_a$, we can assume without loss of generality that we are at round 0, since for any other round $i$, every entry in $M$ will be scaled by the same discount factor $\delta^i$, and so the optimal strategies will be the same.

For the function calls GameValue and StrategyProfile in Lines 1 and 1, a solver for computing a Nash equilibrium of $M$ is needed. Since $M$ is a standard payoff matrix for a normal-form game (entries are constants, because values for the subgames have already been computed), we can adopt the standard linear programming approach for computing a Nash equilibrium strategy. We will show how to compute a Nash equilibrium strategy for the defender, with the case for the attacker being completely analogous.

The linear program is shown in Figure 3. The variable $v$ denotes the utility for the defender, which is to be maximized. The first two constraints ensure that the defender's strategy at the subgame forms a probability distribution. The last constraint ensures that no matter which action the attacker selects, the defender is guaranteed value $v$. For

any optimal solution, the value of $v$ will be the value of the game, and the computed strategy will be a Nash equilibrium strategy.

$$\max v \qquad\qquad\qquad\qquad\qquad\qquad\qquad (3)$$
$$\sum_{p_d \in A_d(E_d)} \sigma_d^{E_d, E_a}(p_d) = 1 \qquad\qquad\qquad\qquad (4)$$
$$\sigma_d^{E_d, E_a}(p_d) \geq 0 \qquad\qquad \forall p_d \in A_d(E_d) \quad (5)$$
$$\sum_{p_d \in A_d(E_d)} \sigma_d^{E_d, E_a}(p_d) \cdot M[p_d, p_a] \geq v \ \ \forall p_a \in A_a(E_a) \quad (6)$$

**Figure 3: The linear program used in computing a Nash equilibrium strategy for the defender. $A_d(E_d)$ and $A_a(E_a)$ are the sets of actions available for the defender and attacker respectively, given their current energy levels.**

The number of linear programs can be upper-bounded by the number of possible energy levels in subgames. Given initial energy levels $E_{d,0}$ and $E_{a,0}$, the number of linear programs solved is $O(\frac{E_{d,0}}{\epsilon_d(0)} \cdot \frac{E_{a,0}}{\epsilon_a(0)})$, since the power cost of sleeping divides all other power costs. Each linear program has size $O(|\mathcal{P}_d| \cdot |\mathcal{P}_a|)$.

Technically, our algorithm computes a subgame perfect equilibrium, a refinement of Nash equilibria. A subgame perfect equilibrium is a Nash equilibrium such that for any subgame, even those reached with probability zero, the players are playing Nash equilibrium strategies for the subgame. This provides an extra level of robustness over Nash equilibria, as we are not only guaranteed the value of the game, but also guaranteed to play optimally if the opponent chooses a sub-optimal action, assuming the game is played optimally onwards from there. This is not the same as optimally responding to any strategy of the opponent. Rather, it means that we optimally respond to any current game state, assuming that the opponent will play optimally from then on, even with mistakes in the past.

## 5. SIMULATION

To show the benefits of the finite-energy jamming game we simulate three different games. To use realistic parameters in the simulation we base our parameters on measurement data taken from communication nodes and a jammer implemented with GNUradio on USRP2 software-defined radio. We consider an attacker that is able to adapt their power level and also the number of channels they jam on. The defender is able to choose a channel to transmit on and also choose a power level to transmit at. For our measurements the sender and jammer are connected to the receiver via wire with equal attenuation. This mimics the location of the senders being equidistant from the receiver. In this section, we discuss the parameters we use for our simulation, the optimization results, and the game play simulation we use.

### 5.1 Game parameters

We take RF power measurements at the connection port and find that the power expended for a low-power attack as $1.16\mu w$ and for a high-power attack as $3.22\mu w$. We also

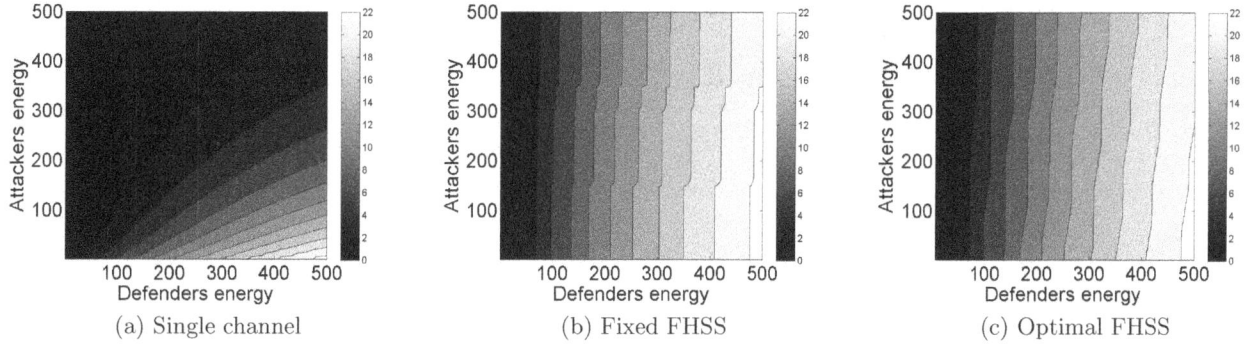

(a) Single channel      (b) Fixed FHSS      (c) Optimal FHSS

Figure 4: To demonstrate the optimization, we show the expected utility for 3 different games with varying initial energy levels. For all the games a discount factor of .975 is used and in the frequency hopping game the defender uses 50 channels. The color scale shows the utility of the game.

assume a continuous energy drain per round that we estimate as $.5\mu w$. This constant drain controls for calculation, battery leakage, and other constant sources of drainage. We normalize the cost of energy usage per round and define $\{1, 3, 7\} \in \mathcal{P}_a$ as the values for sleeping, low power, and high power attacking, respectively. The jammer is able to simultaneously jam on multiple channels during any round. We assume a linear cost increase per channel for the low- or high-power attacks. Sleeping does not use channels so we assume it has no increased costs.

Likewise for the defender we find power at the port for a low-power transmission as $6.5\mu w$ and a high-power transmission as $7.83\mu w$. We again assume a constant energy drain of $.5\mu w$. Normalizing and approximating the cost per round of each play we find costs of $\{1, 14, 16\} \in \mathcal{P}_d$ for sleeping, low power transmissions, and high power transmissions, respectively. We assume that synchronization and key-sharing is done beforehand and that there is no extra cost for the sender to use frequency hopping.

If the defender is transmitting we assume a constant rate so the normalized throughput per round is approximated by packet delivery ratio (PDR). Because of this we use packet delivery ratio in lieu of throughput when the defender is transmitting and assume zero throughput when the defender is sleeping. We measure packet delivery ratio in our single channel 802.15.4 system as

$$\mathrm{pdr}(\mathcal{P}_a, \mathcal{P}_d) = \begin{pmatrix} 0 & .96 & 1 \\ 0 & .58 & .92 \\ 0 & 0 & 0 \end{pmatrix} \quad (7)$$

where the attacker is the row player and the defender is the column player. We assume that there is no cross-channel interference so if the jammer is not attacking a particular channel there is no added interference.

In order to mimic both players using the same class of devices, we constrain the attacker and defender to have similar initial energy resources. We define similar initial energy resources as both players having an initial energy that is within one order of magnitude of the other.

## 5.2 Optimization

We use Algorithm 1 to arrive at an optimal strategy and expected utility. In Figure 4(a) we show the values for the single channel game with a .975 discount factor. In Fig-

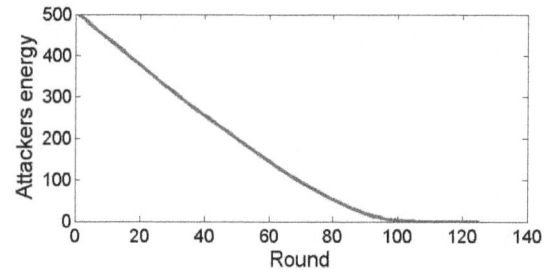

(a) Attacker's energy

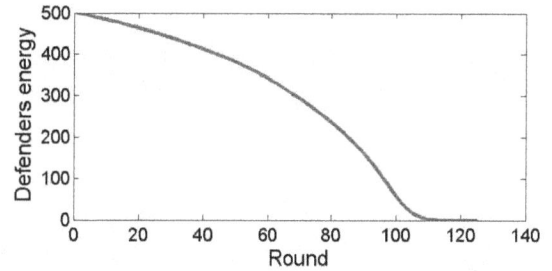

(b) Defender's energy

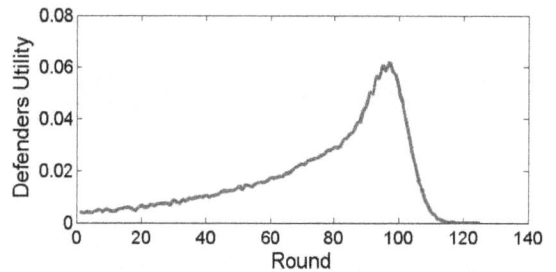

(c) Defender's utility

Figure 5: The average over 10,000 runs of a simulation of the single channel game with two rational players and a .975 discount factor.

ure 4(b) we show the expected defender utility for a defender with 50 channels and an attacker with 50 channels and .975 discount. In Figure 4(c) we show the defender's utility when the defender has 50 channels and the attacker optimizes power and number of channels. The optimization provides confirmation of what is intuitively expected. The single channel game heavily favors the attacker while either of the frequency hopping games with 50 channels favors the defender.

## 5.3 Game play

We designed a simulator to explore the performance of our computed strategies and compare them to other strategies. Other strategies we use for comparison include a constant strategy, a uniform random strategy, and a weighted average algorithm [11]. The random strategy that we consider uniformly samples from all possible strategies. The weighted average algorithm was designed for a similar power game. It works by keeping a weighted vector of the likelihood of their opponents strategy as well as a matrix of the expected utility for given combinations of plays. The player then uses these to compute their strategy.

We designed a simulator for each of the games introduced in Section 4. For the single channel, input parameters include both players' strategies as well as the initial energy of both players, and the discount factor for the players. In the frequency hopping spread spectrum case with a constant number of attacker channels the simulator also takes the number of channels used by the defender $N$ and attacker $k$. The simulator also accepts the precomputed optimal strategy for both players for the given game and the discount factor.

To demonstrate the operation of our simulator we show the average run of 10,000 trials of the single channel game with a .975 discount factor and two rational players in Figure 5. The initial energy for assigned to both player is 500 units in this experiment, and the power levels and corresponding energy usage are given in Section 5.1. Figures 5(a) and 5(b) show the average remaining energy for the attacker and defender, respectively, at the given time. Figure 5(c) on the other hand shows the average instantaneous utility for the defender.

To simulate the frequency hopping game the defender selects one channel $n \in [1, N]$ at the beginning of every round. Similarly, the attacker selects $k$ of $N$ channels to interfere with. If n is one of the $k$ channels selected then the attacker is successful and the throughput is calculated using (7). Otherwise the throughput is calculated using

$$\mathrm{pdr}(\mathcal{P}_a, \mathcal{P}_d) = \begin{pmatrix} 0 & .96 & 1 \\ 0 & .96 & 1 \\ 0 & .96 & 1 \end{pmatrix} \quad (8)$$

## 6. SIMULATION RESULTS

In this section, we discuss simulated scenarios using the setup and parameters presented in Section 5. We explore all three games from Section 4 and describe insights gained from various experiments.

## 6.1 Single-Channel Game

For the single channel game we compare the performance of the rational, random, and adaptive weighted average algorithm for both players. In Table 1 the utility averaged over

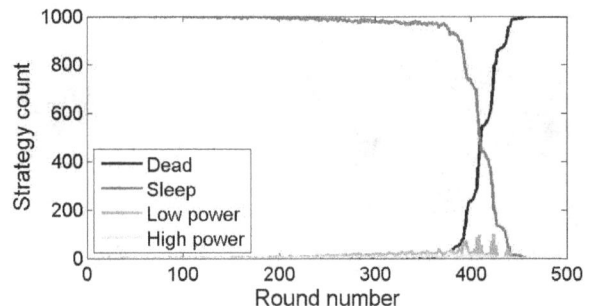

**Figure 6: Counts of how many times out of a thousand a defender chooses a strategy against a constantly sleeping attacker with a .9 discount factor. We define a dead node as a node that has expended all of its energy.**

100,000 runs for various attacker and defender strategy pairs is presented. Both players start with 200 units of energy and choose optimal strategies for the given discount factor. The results for the rational player always outperform the random and weighted average player's performance, but sometimes this is less pronounced. Although the gain from rationality is marginal with the .9 discount factor, a second factor to consider is that rationality decreases deviation of results. In Table 2 we show that either player playing rationally greatly decreases the standard deviation in utility. This decrease in variance can be a significant benefit for designing secure systems in that it is able to provide performance guarantees and less uncertainty.

The single channel game also provides an interesting insight on the effect of rationality on the defender's utility. In Table 3 we see that rational play increases the defender's overall throughput. The smaller the discount factor, the greater the gain in defender's throughput from rationality against a rational attacker.

Another interesting result is highlighted in Figure 6. In this figure the attacker always chooses to power nap while the defender is rational. This results in an attacker that has a slow but constant energy fade. The rational defender plays as if the attacker was also rational, and therefore he transmits with very low probability in the beginning of the game. This is highly counterintuitive from a throughput perspective, since the sender could transmit freely, and gain much higher utility. This is an example of how inoptimal opponents are not exploited optimally by a Nash equilibrium strategy, since the sender has to assume that the jammer might start playing optimally at each round, in order to guarantee attaining the value of the game.

We also explored the effect of a difference in energy between the two players. In Figure 7 we show the defender's utility for various advantages in the attacker's energy. The curve here, while qualitatively intuitive, can be instructive in how much extra energy a defender must have to perform well in the presence of an attacker.

## 6.2 Multi-Channel Game with FHSS

The second set of experiments we conduct considers a defender frequency hopping over a set of $N$ channels and a jammer blocking a set of $K$ channels per round. In Figure 8 we show the defender's utility for various sets of attacker

| | | Defense | | | | | | | | |
|---|---|---|---|---|---|---|---|---|---|---|
| | | .9 Discount Factor | | | .95 Discount Factor | | | .99 Discount Factor | | |
| | | Rational | Random | Weighted | Rational | Random | Weighted | Rational | Random | Weighted |
| Attack | Rational | 0.2575 | 0.2573 | 0.2564 | 1.2424 | 1.2351 | 1.2369 | 6.0236 | 6.0031 | 6.0119 |
| | Random | 0.2583 | 3.2958 | 3.1432 | 1.2452 | 4.7213 | 4.5393 | 6.08 | 7.0388 | 6.8867 |
| | Weighted | 0.2577 | 2.5974 | 2.5286 | 1.25 | 3.545 | 3.4438 | 6.425 | 5.0245 | 4.9568 |

Table 1: Mean defender's utility for the single channel game.

| | | Defense | | | | | | | | |
|---|---|---|---|---|---|---|---|---|---|---|
| | | .9 Discount Factor | | | .95 Discount Factor | | | .99 Discount Factor | | |
| | | Rational | Random | Weighted | Rational | Random | Weighted | Rational | Random | Weighted |
| Attack | Rational | 0.0956 | 0.3124 | 0.2942 | 0.3682 | 0.7693 | 0.7255 | 1.0194 | 1.3730 | 1.3590 |
| | Random | 0.2651 | 0.9328 | 0.9878 | 0.5104 | 1.1131 | 1.1843 | 1.0983 | 1.4895 | 1.5331 |
| | Weighted | 0.2554 | 1.3741 | 1.4083 | 0.5049 | 1.9931 | 2.0147 | 1.1843 | 3.1574 | 3.1580 |

Table 2: Standard deviation of the defender's utility for the single channel game.

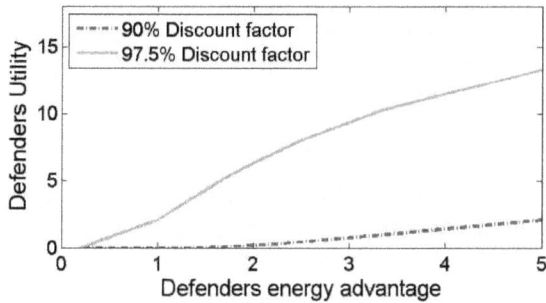

Figure 7: Advantage gained by an attacker or defender having a energy advantage with varying discount factors. The advantage shown is the multiplicative advantage such that defender's advantage $= \frac{E_d}{E_a}$.

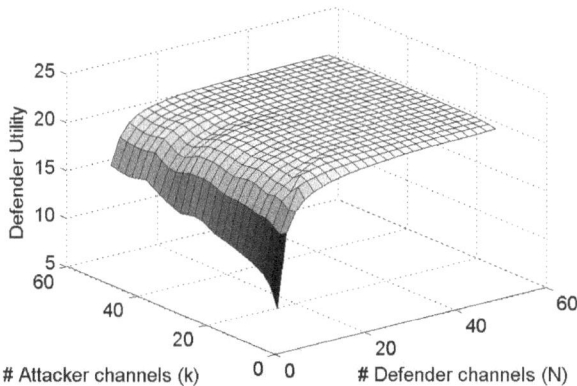

Figure 9: In this figure, we show the mean defender's utility for varying numbers of defending channels and an optimal attacker.

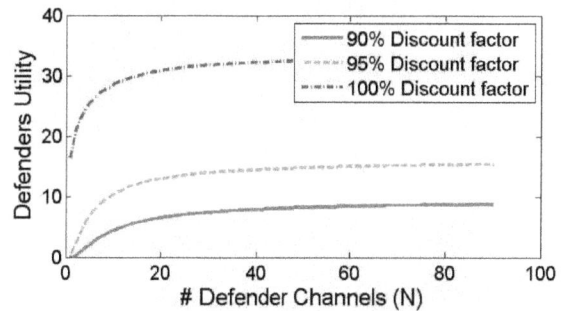

Figure 8: Defender's utility for the set number of attacker channel FHSS game. The attacker and defender both choose their power levels optimally for the number of channels they are using.

and defenders channel numbers with a .975 discount factor when both players are rational. This leads to two conclusions when the defender and attacker have similar initial energy. First, a defender with 20 or more channels effectively mitigates the jamming threat. Second, an attacker jamming fewer channels in this case can be beneficial to the attacker. One likely explanation for this would be sensitivity to power cost, since only being able to jam a large number of channels (as opposed to being able to vary this) expends a large portion of the energy.

## 6.3 Multi-Channel Game with FHSS and Selection of Number of Channels to Jam

Our third set of experiments considers the FHSS game where the attacker can choose power levels and the number of simultaneous channels to attack. In Figure 9 we show the mean defender's utility for various discount factors. This figure suggests that above a certain number of channels, even with an optimal attacker, there is a diminishing return on investment for the defender adding more channels. The attacker's strategy with the lower discount factor causes an attacker to select a very aggressive strategy, often expending all its energy as quickly as possible in hopes of causing some degradation to the transmission.

In Figure 10 we show the defender's utility for various attacker multiplicative energy advantages defined as $\frac{E_a}{E_d}$.

| | | Defense | | | | | | | | |
|---|---|---|---|---|---|---|---|---|---|---|
| | | .9 Discount Factor | | | .95 Discount Factor | | | .99 Discount Factor | | |
| | | Rational | Random | Weighted | Rational | Random | Weighted | Rational | Random | Weighted |
| Attack | Rational | 7.0159 | 0.7682 | 1.0190 | 6.4976 | 1.9530 | 2.1542 | 6.6333 | 6.1134 | 6.1242 |
| | Random | 6.8493 | 7.2073 | 7.0517 | 6.6224 | 7.2075 | 7.0662 | 6.6791 | 7.1996 | 7.0542 |
| | Weighted | 6.2695 | 5.1466 | 5.0629 | 6.4519 | 5.1496 | 5.0321 | 7.0621 | 5.1268 | 5.0613 |

Table 3: Defender's mean throughput for the single channel game.

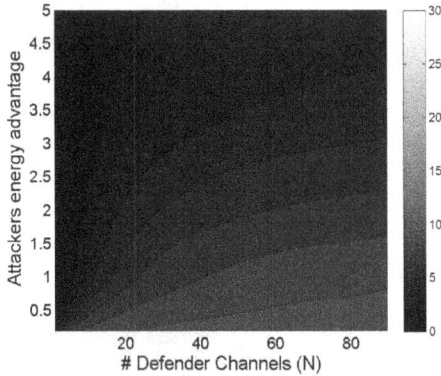

(a) .9 discount factor

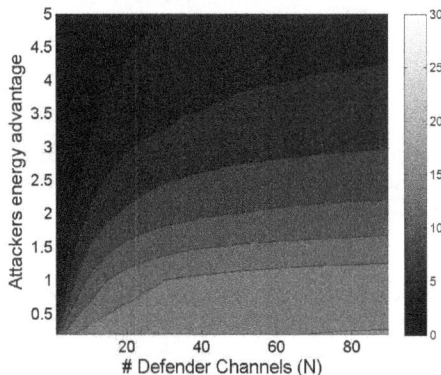

(b) .95 discount factor

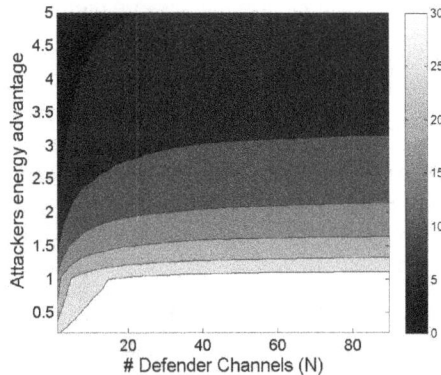

(c) .99 discount factor

Figure 10: Defender's utility for various channel numbers against an optimal attacker. We define the attacker's energy advantage as $\frac{E_a}{E_d}$.

These curves allow for a decision of how much of an energy advantage an attacker needs to overcome spread spectrum. This also illustrates that the number of channels a defender needs to be protected from a jamming attack varies on the difference in the two players energy.

## 6.4 Summary of Simulation Results

In this work, we consider three different finite-energy jamming games. The first is a single channel DSSS jamming game, the second is a FHSS game where the attacker jams a constant number of channels, and the third is a power nap game with jammer attacker the optimal number of channels.

In the first game we find that either player playing rational decreases the variance in the game, a beneficial result for designing a secure communication system. We also noted that in this game a rational defender greatly increased the overall throughput of the system. We also showed that rationality can be detrimental to the defender. When the discount factor is small and the attacker chooses a strategy of constantly sleeping the defender is intimidated into not transmitting until most of the energy is drained.

In the second game we show that the a defender that hops over at least 20 channels is effectively able to mitigate the effects of jamming. We also show, counter to intuition, in some scenarios when the attacker jams less simultaneous channels it has a greater impact.

In the third game we confirm the intuition of a diminishing return for the defender past a certain number of channels. We also show the tradeoff in the advantage in the attacker's energy level and the number of channels. These charts provide a basis for choosing the number of channels a defender needs for hopping based on how much extra energy is available for the jammer.

## 7. CONCLUSION

In this work we introduced *finite-energy jamming games*, a game-theoretic framework to understand energy-constrained jammer-defender interaction. We developed several game models within this framework, where the sender and jammer can vary their power levels and whether to send at all. In our more advanced models, we introduced frequency hopping to the game model, and investigated the effect of allowing the jammer to vary number of channels jammed on. To do this, we modeled our system as a zero-sum finite-horizon stochastic games with deterministic transitions. Leveraging the properties of our game, we designed a simple and fast polynomial-time dynamic programming algorithm for computing a Nash equilibrium. We implemented a simulator to explore the practical properties of our framework across our different game types. Using our simulator, we investigated the possible guarantees that can be achieved under various game settings. We also investigated the practical performance of Nash equilibrium strategies against simpler strategies, such as adaptive or fixed randomized strategies. An interesting result from this analysis was the decrease in variance provided from a rational player, a beneficial property for designing secure systems. Another interesting result provided by this analysis is that an inoptimal opponent that sleeps constaly still leads to a rational sender incurring large performance losses, due to the assumption that the attacker will play optimally.

There are several interesting future research directions for extending our current work. First, to make the problem more practical, it would be interesting to relax the perfect knowledge assumption and replace it with an observation based approach. This would make the game model significantly harder to solve, and so more advanced computational approached would be needed. Second, expanding this work to the setting of multiple jammers and multiple defenders would provide a better understanding of interactions of adversaries in the wild. Third, the scope of both players could be expanded to include multiple layers in the communication stack and cross-layer attacks. Finally, there are several options for expanding the action space of the players, in ways that are easily incorporated in our current model and algorithms. We currently allow the players to select a single power level per round, even when the number of channels jammed on is more than one. There could be cases where the sender and jammer would want to select different power levels for different channels. This would incur an exponential increase in the number of actions available to the players, but our algorithmic results would transfer to such a setting. Related to this, it might be possible to show that certain combinations of power levels over different channels are never optimal, in order to avoid this blowup. Likewise, in this paper we only allowed the sender to transmit on a single channel. In future work, it would be interesting to investigate whether sending on several channels at once is beneficial.

# 8. ACKNOWLEDGMENTS

DeBruhl and Tague are supported by the NSF under grant CNS-1149582, and DeBruhl is further supported by an ND-SEG fellowship. Sandholm and Kroer are supported by the NSF under grants IIS-1320620, CCF-1101668 and IIS-0964579, as well as the CMU Center for Computational Thinking funded by Microsoft Research. Datta is supported in part by the AFOSR MURI on Science of Cybersecurity. The views and conclusions contained here are those of the authors and should not be interpreted as necessarily representing the official policies or endorsements, either express or implied, of CMU, NSF, or the U.S. Government or any of its agencies.

# 9. REFERENCES

[1] T. Alpcan and T. Başar. *Network Security: A Decision and Game-Theoretic Approach*. Cambridge University Press, 2010.

[2] E. Altman, K. Avrachenkov, and A. Garnaev. Jamming in wireless networks: The case of several jammers. In *IEEE International Conference on Game Theory for Networks, 2009*, pages 585–592.

[3] E. Altman, K. Avrachenkov, and A. Garnaev. A jamming game in wireless networks with transmission cost. In *Network Control and Optimization*, pages 1–12. Springer, 2007.

[4] E. Altman, K. Avrachenkov, and A. Garnaev. Transmission power control game with SINR as objective function. In *Network Control and Optimization*, pages 112–120. Springer, 2009.

[5] E. Altman, K. Avrachenkov, R. Marquez, and G. Miller. Zero-sum constrained stochastic games with independent state processes. *Mathematical Methods of Operations Research*, 62(3):375–386, 2005.

[6] J. Becker, J. D. Lohn, and D. Linden. An in-situ optimized anti-jamming beamformer for mobile signals. In *IEEE Antennas and Propagation Society International Symposium 2012*, pages 1–2.

[7] S. Bhattacharya, A. Khanafer, and T. Başar. Switching behavior in optimal communication strategies for team jamming games under resource constraints. In *IEEE International Conference on Control Applications 2011*, pages 1232–1237.

[8] A. Chan, X. Liu, G. Noubir, and B. Thapa. Control channel jamming: Resilience and identification of traitors. In *Proc. IEEE International Symposium on Information Theory*, Nice, France, June 2007.

[9] B. DeBruhl, Y. Kim, Z. Weinberg, and P. Tague. STIR-ing the wireless ether with self-tuned, inference-based, real-time jamming. In *Proc. 9th IEEE Conference on Mobile Ad-hoc and Sensor Systems*, Las Vegas, USA, Oct. 2012. IEEE.

[10] B. DeBruhl and P. Tague. How to jam without getting caught: Analysis and empirical study of stealthy periodic jamming. In *IEEE International Conference on Sensing, Communication, and Networking, 2013*.

[11] B. DeBruhl and P. Tague. Keeping up with the jammers: Observe-and-adapt algorithms for studying mutually adaptive opponents. *Pervasive and Mobile Computing*, 2014.

[12] M. Felegyhazi and J. Hubaux. Game theory in wireless networks: A tutorial. Technical report, Technical Report LCA-REPORT-2006-002, EPFL, 2006.

[13] K. Firouzbakht, G. Noubir, and M. Salehi. On the capacity of rate-adaptive packetized wireless communication links under jamming. In *Proceedings of the fifth ACM conference on Security and Privacy in Wireless and Mobile Networks*, pages 3–14. ACM, 2012.

[14] S. Ganzfried and T. Sandholm. Computing an approximate jam/fold equilibrium for 3-player no-limit Texas Hold'em tournaments. In *International Conference on Autonomous Agents and Multi-Agent Systems (AAMAS)*, 2008.

[15] S. Ganzfried and T. Sandholm. Computing equilibria in multiplayer stochastic games of imperfect information. In *Proceedings of the 21st International Joint Conference on Artificial Intelligence (IJCAI)*, 2009.

[16] A. Garnaev and W. Trappe. An eavesdropping game with SINR as an objective function. In *Security and Privacy in Communication Networks*, pages 142–162. Springer, 2009.

[17] A. Gupta, A. Nayyar, C. Langbort, and T. Başar. A dynamic transmitter-jammer game with asymmetric information. In *51st IEEE Annual Conference on Decision and Control, 2012*, pages 6477–6482.

[18] Y. Gwon, S. Dastangoo, C. Fossa, and H. Kung. Competing mobile network game: Embracing antijamming and jamming strategies with reinforcement learning. In *IEEE Conference on Communications and Network Security*, pages 28–36. IEEE, 2013.

[19] Z. Han, N. Marina, M. Debbah, and A. Hjorungnes. Physical layer security game: How to date a girl with her boyfriend on the same table. In *IEEE International Conference on Game Theory for Networks, 2009*, pages 287–294.

[20] J. Hu and M. P. Wellman. Nash Q-learning for general-sum stochastic games. *The Journal of Machine Learning Research*, 4:1039–1069, 2003.

[21] M. Kearns, Y. Mansour, and S. Singh. Fast planning in stochastic games. In *Proceedings of the Sixteenth conference on Uncertainty in artificial intelligence*, pages 309–316. Morgan Kaufmann Publishers Inc., 2000.

[22] L. Lazos and M. Krunz. Selective jamming dropping insider attacks in wireless mesh networks. *IEEE Network*, 25(1):30–34, 2011.

[23] M. Li, I. Koutsopoulos, and R. Poovendran. Optimal jamming attacks and network defense policies in wireless sensor networks. In *IEEE 26th IEEE International Conference on Computer Communications, 2007*, pages 1307–1315.

[24] M. L. Littman. Friend-or-foe Q-learning in general-sum games. In *ICML*, volume 1, pages 322–328, 2001.

[25] X. Liu, G. Noubir, R. Sundaram, and S. Tan. SPREAD: Foiling smart jammers using multi-layer agility. In *26th IEEE International Conference on Computer Communications*, Anchorage, AK, USA, May 2007.

[26] R. K. Mallik, R. A. Scholtz, and G. P. Papavassilopoulos. Analysis of an on-off jamming situation as a dynamic game. *Communications, IEEE Transactions on*, 48(8):1360–1373, 2000.

[27] M. Manshaei, Q. Zhu, T. Alpcan, T. Başar, and J.-P. Hubaux. Game theory meets network security and privacy. *ACM transaction on Computational Logic*, 5, 2011.

[28] A. Molisch. *Wireless Communications*. John Wiley & Sons, Inc., 2005.

[29] K. Pelechrinis, M. Iliofotou, and S. Krishnamurthy. Denial of service attacks in wireless networks: the case of jammers. *IEEE Comm Surveys and Tutorials*, Apr. 2011.

[30] M. Raya, I. Aad, J.-P. Hubaux, and A. El Fawal. DOMINO: Detecting MAC layer greedy behavior in IEEE 802.11 hotspots. *IEEE Transactions on Mobile Computing*, 5(12):1691–1705, Dec. 2006.

[31] A. Richa, S. Schmid, C. Scheideler, and J. Zhang. A jamming resistant mac protocol for multi-hop wireless networks. In *Proc. of the 24th Int.Symposium on Princ. of Distributed Computing*, 2010.

[32] J. Rodgers. Pulse radar systems, 1962. US Patent 3,029,429.

[33] L. Rosenberg and D. Gray. Anti-jamming techniques for multichannel SAR imaging. *IEE Proceedings-Radar, Sonar and Navigation*, 153(3):234–242, June 2006.

[34] Y. E. Sagduyu, R. Berry, and A. Ephremides. Mac games for distributed wireless network security with incomplete information of selfish and malicious user types. In *IEEE International Conference on Game Theory for Networks, 2009*, pages 130–139.

[35] P. Tague, S. Nabar, J. A. Ritcey, and R. Poovendran. Jamming-aware traffic allocation for multiple-path routing using portfolio selection. *IEEE/ACM Transactions on Networking*.

[36] P. Tague, D. Slater, G. Noubir, and R. Poovendran. Linear programming models for jamming attacks on network traffic flows. In *Proc. 6th International Symposium on Modeling and Optimization in Mobile, Ad Hoc, and Wireless Networks*, pages 207–216, Berlin, Germany, Apr. 2008.

[37] D. J. Torrieri. *Principles of Secure Communication Systems*. Artech House, Boston, 2nd edition, 1992.

[38] X. Wang and T. Sandholm. Reinforcement learning to play an optimal Nash equilibrium in team Markov games. In *In Proceedings of the Neural Information Processing Systems: Natural and Synthetic (NIPS) conference*, 2002. Extended version at http://www.cs.cmu.edu/ sandholm/oal.ps.

[39] M. Wilhelm, I. Martinovic, J. Schmitt, and V. Lenders. Reactive jamming in wireless networks: How realistic is the threat? In *Proc. 4th ACM Conference on Wireless Network Security*, Hamburg, Germany, June 2011.

[40] W. Xu, K. Ma, W. Trappe, and Y. Zhang. Jamming sensor networks: Attack and defense strategies. *IEEE Network*, 20(3):41–47, May/June 2006.

[41] Q. Zhu, W. Saad, Z. Han, H. V. Poor, and T. Başar. Eavesdropping and jamming in next-generation wireless networks: A game-theoretic approach. In *IEEE Military Communication Conference, 2011*, pages 119–124.

# Friendly CryptoJam: A Mechanism for Securing Physical-Layer Attributes

Hanif Rahbari
rahbari@email.arizona.edu

Marwan Krunz
krunz@email.arizona.edu

Department of Electrical and Computer Engineering
University of Arizona
Tucson, AZ 85721

## ABSTRACT

The broadcast nature of wireless communications exposes various "transmission attributes," such as the packet size, the inter-packet times, and the modulation scheme. These attributes can be exploited by an adversary to launch passive or active attacks. A passive attacker threatens user's privacy and confidentiality by performing traffic analysis and classification, whereas an active attacker exploits captured attributes to launch selective jamming/dropping attacks. This so-called PHY-layer security problem is present even when the payload is encrypted. For example, by determining the modulation scheme, the attacker can estimate the data rate, and hence the payload size, and later use it to launch traffic classification or selective rate-adaptation attacks.

In this paper, we propose *Friendly CryptoJam*, a novel approach that combines analog-domain friendly jamming and modulation-level encryption. *Friendly CryptoJam* decorrelates the payload's modulation scheme from other transmission attributes by always "upgrading" it to the highest-order modulation scheme supported by the system (a concept we refer to as *modulation unification*) using a secret pseudo-random sequence. Such upgrade is a form of transmitter-based friendly jamming. At the same time, modulation symbols are encrypted to protect unencrypted PHY-layer fields (*modulation encryption*). To generate and sync the secret sequence, an efficient message embedding technique based on Barker sequences is proposed, which exploits the structure of the preamble and overlays a frame-specific seed on it. We study the implications of the scheme on PHY-layer functions through simulations and USRP-based experiments. The results confirm that *Friendly CryptoJam* is quite successful in hiding the targeted attributes, at the cost of a small increase in the transmission power.

## Categories and Subject Descriptors

C.2.1 [**Computer-Communication Networks**]: Network Architecture and Design—*Wireless Communication*

## Keywords

PHY-layer security; side-channel information; IEEE802.11; modulation encryption; friendly jamming; preamble; USRP

## 1. INTRODUCTION

As we continue to depend on the rapidly expanding wireless ecosystem, we are challenged with serious threats related to user privacy, data confidentiality, and system availability. Using commodity radio hardware, unauthorized parties can easily eavesdrop on wireless transmissions. Although advanced encryption algorithms like AES can be applied to ensure data confidentiality, parts of the frame (e.g., PHY-layer header) must be transmitted in the clear for correct protocol operation, device identification, and reduced complexity. For example, 802.11i, the primary security amendment of 802.11, provides confidentiality only for the MAC-layer payload, as well as integrity for this payload and its header [2]. Even if we hypothetically encrypt the entire frame, the transmission is not completely immune. In fact, an adversary can still perform low-level RF and traffic analysis, and estimate several transmission attributes, including packet sizes, modulation scheme, inter-packet times, and traffic directionality.

Transmission attributes can be correlated to create "fingerprints" of intercepted communications, which can be used to determine user identities, content, type, or stage of a communication. Depending on whether the frames are entirely encrypted or not, leaked attributes may consist of only side-channel information or may also contain lower-layer fields. Side-channel information refers to statistical traffic features, such as packet size distribution, inter-packet time sequence, and data rate (traffic volume). For example, by eavesdropping on an 802.11 wireless LAN traffic, an adversary (Eve) can determine the type of user activities with 80% accuracy (after only five seconds of eavesdropping) [4, 19] or the content of search query words [6]. Upper-layer traffic manipulation techniques, such as packet padding and traffic reshaping [18], aim at obfuscating side-channel information at the cost of traffic overhead [7]. Even then, they cannot completely hide all such information. For instance, the data rate and the length of a (re)transmitted frame can be estimated through RF analysis and by inspecting the PHY frames. Using an off-the-shelf device such as a vector signal analyzer (VSA), Eve can detect the payload's modulation scheme of even an entirely encrypted frame. This type of side-channel information has not been studied in the security literature. Eve would then estimate the data rate, and hence determine the packet size in bytes. Statistics of the packet size and total traffic volume [7] are key parameters in traffic analysis and classification. In fact, there is no effective and resource-efficient countermeasure to obfuscate the total traffic volume, which can be exploited independently for traffic classification [7].

Eve can also exploit unencrypted fields in the PHY and MAC headers to expose the privacy of a user [4, 19], or to identify the user and launch sophisticated active attacks. These lower-layer fields include the source and destination MAC addresses, data rate, modulation scheme, frame length (duration), the number of space-time streams of a MIMO system, and others. For example, Noubir *et al.* [14] demonstrated a reactive jammer that can significantly hamper the network throughput by intercepting the rate field of a frame and accordingly deciding whether to jam the rest of the frame. If a packet is not correctly decoded as a result of jamming, the transmitter (Alice) will mistakenly assume a poor channel and will lower the rate. Our approach belongs to the so-called PHY-layer security, which complements conventional data encryption and upper-layer traffic manipulation techniques by providing protection for the entire frame at the PHY-layer. In this paper, we focus on preventing the exposure of unencrypted header fields and the payload's modulation scheme, hence countering rate-adaptation and packet-length-based classification attacks.

Friendly jamming (e.g., [3,8,9]) is probably the most prominent method for PHY-layer anti-wiretapping. It tries to degrade Eve's channel without impacting the channel quality at the intended receiver (Bob). This is done using MIMO techniques or by having relay nodes transmit a jamming signal that is harmless (friendly) to Bob. A mixture of the information and jamming signals could also be viewed as an encrypted signal. However, three fundamental issues limit the practicality of this approach. First, if Eve is equipped with multiple antennas, she can cancel out a transmitter-based jamming signal [15,16]. For example, Schulz *et al.* [15] exploited a known part of the transmitted signal (e.g., frame preamble) to show that Eve can estimate the precoding matrix for the friendly jamming signal and nullify its effects. This matrix is supposed to be secret and unique, as it depends on the CSI for the Alice-Bob channel, i.e., it represents a signature of the Alice-Bob channel.[1] This known-plaintext attack can thwart any security scheme that relies on prefiltering (precoding) data at Alice. Furthermore, the uniqueness of the Alice-Bob CSI has been shown to be invalid in poor scattering environments [11]. Specifically, a few adversaries located just several wavelengths away from Bob (Bob's *vulnerability zone*) can cooperatively reconstruct the link signature for the Alice-Bob channel.

Second, transmitter- and receiver-based friendly jamming (such as in [9]) are still vulnerable to cross-correlation attacks on (unencrypted) semi-static header fields, where the field can take one of a few possible values. In such attacks, Eve can detect the start of a frame, even if it is combined with a jamming signal [10]. By knowing the underlying header format (i.e., where each field is supposed to start), Eve can locate the starting time of the targeted field in the header. Figure 1(a) shows an example of the measured in-phase (I) values of a complex sequence that represents the

---

[1]Once the precoding matrix is approximated, Bob multiplies the received signal by the inverse of this matrix and cancels out the friendly jamming signal.

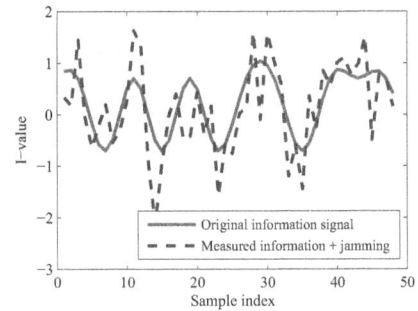

(a) I-values of a QPSK-modulated information signal when combined with a jamming signal (received JSR at Eve= 0 dB).

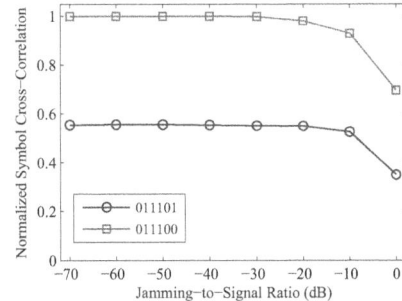

(b) Cross-correlation between received (information + jamming) signal and a possible value for the information signal vs. JSR (011100 is the correct value).

Figure 1: Cross-correlation attack on an information signal combined with a friendly jamming signal.

modulated value of a semi-static header field plus jamming signals. This field is probably not decodable at Eve because of friendly jamming. However, by correlating the modulated symbol of each possible value of this field with the received signal, Eve can guess the actual field value. In general, this cross-correlation attack can be formulated as a composite hypothesis testing. We show a simple example in Figure 1(b), which depicts the cross-correlation between two possible field values (011100 is the true value and 011101 is another possible value) and the received information + jamming signal (Figure 1(a)) as a function of the jamming-to-signal ratio (JSR). Each point is the mean of 100 simulation trials. The plots show that Eve can successfully determine the true value even when the jamming power is as high as the signal power.

Third, depending on the channel coefficients, the jamming power may need to be even higher than the information signal power to achieve non-zero secrecy capacity [8]. This motivates the need for a more robust security framework that provides protection to all lower-layer fields at a reasonably low power expenditure.

## Scheme Overview

In this paper, we propose *Friendly CryptoJam* (CJ, for short), a form of friendly jamming but with the information and jamming signals intermixed before transmission. Essentially, this intermixing makes CJ a form of robust modulation-level encryption. CJ completely encrypts a frame right after the digital modulation phase and before the frame is transmitted over the air. In contrast to classic friendly jamming techniques, a single antenna is used to transmit both the

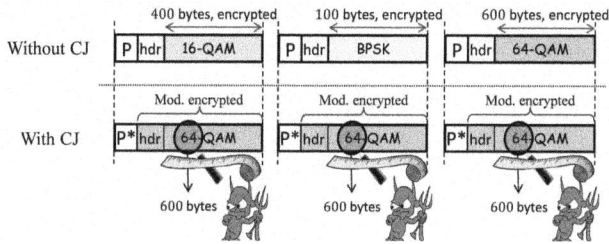

Figure 2: Example of using *Friendly CryptoJam* to hide the modulation scheme (and packet size) of three packets with the same duration. Headers and payload are modulated-encrypted and upgraded without changing the data rate. Under CJ, a seed ($\mathcal{ID}$) is overlaid on the original frame preamble ($P$), leading to a new preamble ($P^* = P + ID$).

information and jamming signals. The key idea in CJ is to first encrypt the modulated symbols. This is done by replacing each modulated symbol by another one according to a pseudo-random secret jamming sequence (i.e., the friendly jamming signal). Our specific encryption function leaves Eve with the highest entropy no matter what signal she observes, i.e., it achieves perfect secrecy. Then, while keeping an eye on the BER and without increasing the data/information rate, the encrypted modulated symbols are mapped (upgraded) to the constellation map of the highest-order modulation scheme supported by the system, using other parts of the same secret sequence that was used in the encryption phase. This secret sequence, hereafter called *bogus traffic*, is generated using a partially secret seed, which is independent of the link signature, i.e., independent of Bob's location, and is robust to known-plaintext attacks.

The combination of modulation encryption and modulation upgrade prevents any classification based on the modulation scheme (hence packet size and rate cannot be reliably determined), obfuscates the total traffic volume with little traffic overhead, and also keeps unencrypted fields and retransmissions indistinguishable (see the example in Figure 2). Our energy-efficient modulation upgrade approach, called *modulation unification*, preserves the BER with less than 2 dB increase in the transmission power. The design of CJ also takes into account issues such as interference and packet losses, retransmissions, channel estimation, and frequency offset estimation, while maintaining synchronization of the bogus traffic generation processes at Alice and Bob. In contrast to conventional (digital-domain) encryption, the encryption in CJ is modulation-aware. CJ is also transparent to upper layer.

One important challenge in designing *Friendly CryptoJam* is how to change the bogus traffic on a per-frame basis (to prevent a dictionary attack). In particular, relying on a single (long) PN sequence to generate the bogus traffic is prone to synchronization errors due to ACK packet losses, for example. To ensure consistency in the generation of per-frame bogus traffic at Alice and Bob, Alice conveys a frame-specific seed (e.g., packet number) whose modulated value is superposed onto the known frame preamble. This same seed is also concatenated to the session key and fed into an appropriately designed pseudo-random number generator (PRNG) to generate the bogus traffic. The seed is also responsible for sender identification (to pull up Alice's security credentials at Bob), since the MAC address is encrypted. However, superimposing any signal on the preamble may

degrade the preamble's crucial functions (e.g., frame detection, frequency offset estimation). To prevent that, we use cyclically rotated Barker sequences (which exhibit low cross-correlations with the preamble) to construct a seed-bearing signal. This signal will have two identical parts (similar to the preamble), so frequency offset estimation can operate as usual. Bob then extracts the embedded seed and uses it for channel estimation and bogus traffic generation. We extensively evaluate the different components of CJ by simulations. We also use a USRP-based platform to implement and experimentally verify that CJ is highly immune to PHY-layer eavesdropping.

**Paper organization–** We provide background material on 802.11 PHY-layer header and preamble functions in Section 2. In Section 3, we describe the attack model and state our assumptions. Modulation unification and encryption are presented in Section 4, followed by bogus traffic generation, shifted Barker sequences, and practical challenges of message embedding in Section 5. We present our simulations and USRP experiments in Section 6. Section 7 contains a more detailed literature review. Finally, we conclude the paper in Section 8.

## 2. PHY-LAYER ATTRIBUTES AND PREAMBLE IN 802.11 SYSTEMS

**(1) PHY-layer header fields.** 802.11 standards specify the frame length and the transmission rate in the PHY-layer header. The transmission rate is typically adjusted based on channel conditions, resulting in different frame durations (in seconds) for the same payload. In 802.11b/g, the data rate and the modulation scheme (DBPSK, DQPSK, CCK, or PBCC) are specified in the *Signal* and *Service* fields, respectively. In 802.11a, the rate field represents both the transmission rate and the modulation scheme (BPSK, QPSK, 16-QAM, or 64-QAM). The MCS field in 802.11n is similar to the rate field in 802.11a. All 802.11 standards specify a "length" field, which represents the payload size in octets (for 802.11a/n) or in milliseconds (for 802.11b).

**(2) Frame detection and frequency offset estimation.** Each PHY-layer header is preceded by a preamble, which is used to detect the start of a frame (frame detection), frequency offset (FO) estimation, and channel estimation. This preamble consists of several repetitions of a publicly known pattern. The process of FO estimation requires detecting the arrival of at least two of the repetitions. A frequency offset $\delta_f$ creates a linear phase displacement $\varphi(t)$, which accumulates over time as follows:

$$\varphi(t) = 2\pi\delta_f\, t. \tag{1}$$

To decode a frame, Bob estimates $\delta_f$ by taking one of the repetitions in the received signal as a reference and comparing it with another repetition that is $T$ seconds away. Specifically, Bob may subtract the phases of any pair of identical samples to find $\varphi(T)$. Because of noise, usually there will be a residual FO estimation error even after averaging over several of such identical pairs. In large packets, this residual error eventually shifts a data symbol to a wrong point on the constellation map, causing a demodulation error. Another reason for using a preamble is channel estimation. After compensating for FO, Bob compares the known pattern in the preamble with its received value to estimate the channel parameters (CSI).

In 802.11b systems, a scrambled version of a 128-bit preamble is modulated (spread) using an 11-chip Barker sequence (Table 1).[2] The autocorrelation of a Barker sequence at non-zero lags is very low (orthogonality property), which can be exploited for frame detection and timing. Let $\mathcal{A}(k)$ be the autocorrelation at lag $k$, $1 \leq k < N$. Then,

$$\mathcal{A}(k) = \Big| \sum_{j=1}^{N-k} a_j a_{j+k} \Big| \leq 1 \qquad (2)$$

where $\{a_j : j = 1, \ldots, N\}$ is a Barker sequence. The receiver correlates this known sequence with the received signal sequence $r$ and computes the square of the cross-correlation value, denoted by $\mathcal{R}(n)$:

$$\mathcal{R}(n) = \Big| \sum_{j=1}^{N} a_j^* r_{j+n-1} \Big|^2. \qquad (3)$$

$\mathcal{R}(n)$ is expected to peak when the n-th sample of $r$ marks the beginning of the transmitted Barker sequence.

| Input | Sequence |
|---|---|
| 0 | $+1, -1, +1, +1, -1, +1, +1, +1, -1, -1, -1$ |
| 1 | $-1, +1, -1, -1, +1, -1, -1, -1, +1, +1, +1$ |

Table 1: DSSS signal spreading based on an 11-chip Barker sequence for DBPSK modulation.

**(3) Detection of lower-layer fields.** The preamble and the PHY header are both transmitted at the lowest supported rate.[3] The MAC header is considered part of the data payload, so it may be transmitted at possibly a different rate. The security amendment 802.11i only provides integrity for the MAC header. The preamble, PHY, and MAC headers are all transmitted in the clear, allowing an adversary to intercept them. Detection of the payload's modulation is another way to obtain an estimate of the data rate, packet size, or packet type (e.g., control or data packet). A modulation scheme is usually associated with two or three data rates, with different coding rates. For example, in 802.11a, 16-QAM is used when the data rate is either 24 or 36 Mbps. Hence, by determining the modulation scheme, it is rather easy for the adversary to guess the data rate. Moreover, because control packets are often transmitted using the most robust modulation scheme (e.g., one with lowest required SINR threshold), exposure of this scheme facilitates the discovery of control transmissions.

## 3. SYSTEM MODEL

Consider a wireless link that consists of a transmitter (Alice) and a receiver (Bob). The link operates in the presence of an eavesdropper (Eve). Alice and Bob first create a shared *pairwise transient key* (PTK) through the EAPOL 4-way handshake of 802.11i [2]. PTK is used to encrypt unicast payloads, but as explained later we also use it to generate bogus traffic at the PHY layer. Every node maintains a table of the PTKs and the session IDs of other hand-

shaked neighbors in the network.[4] We assume Alice and Bob are each equipped with a single antenna. They exploit knowledge of the preamble and PHY-header format to customize *Friendly CryptoJam*, but keep the original preamble and frame content, including the header(s), intact. Any preamble modification will be in the form of superposing a signal on the original preamble rather than introducing a completely new preamble. This way, customizing the design to other systems with a known preamble structure and an arbitrary but known set of modulation schemes is straightforward. Without loss of generality, we consider a rate-adaptive system that uses the preamble and PHY format of 802.11b. For simplicity, we consider BPSK, QPSK, 16-QAM, and 64-QAM modulation schemes for the payload.

Figure 3 shows a schematic view of Alice's PHY layer and the insertion points of the proposed *Friendly CryptoJam* components, which include modulation encryption (point 1), modulation unification (point 2) and message, frame and session IDs embedding (point 3). Starting with the MAC header, once the payload arrives at Alice's PHY layer, Alice determines PHY-header fields, including the appropriate modulation scheme for this payload, based on a rate-adaptation algorithm. The preamble, PHY-header, and payload are then scrambled and modulated before being passed to the pulse filters and transmitted over the air. Bob, on the other hand, detects the preamble and extracts the frame and session IDs embedded in it to regenerate the bogus traffic and estimate the CSI. Next, he recovers and decrypts the header to extract the modulation field of the payload, which is used to recover and decrypt the rest of the frame.

Eve knows the frame structure and protocol. She can be a passive eavesdropper or a reactive jammer that jams based on her analysis of early portions of the frame. The types of attacks that can be launched by Eve include cross-correlation attacks (e.g., Figure 1(b)), rate-adaptation attack [14], known-plaintext [15] attack, and any data-rate-based traffic classification attack. We also allow Eve to be equipped with multiple antennas. She can also perform RF analysis, correlation, and modulation detection. We further assume that upper layers may employ a traffic classification mitigation technique (e.g., traffic morphing or random padding), but do not pad a packet to a set of fixed sizes (e.g., pad to MTU). For a given packet size, lower-modulation orders generate longer frame durations. So if the frames contain packets of the same size after padding, the duration of their corresponding modulation-unified signals can reveal the actual modulation order.

## 4. FRIENDLY CRYPTOJAM

In this section, we introduce the first two components of CJ, i.e., modulation unification and encryption, which are used to mask the entire frame and protect lower-layer fields. *Friendly CryptoJam* is essentially a form of friendly jamming that encrypts modulated symbols. However, it is different from conventional cryptography, friendly jamming, and scrambling in that it is applied right after digital modulation and before the up-conversion and antenna transmission. Conventional cryptography digitally encrypts (blocks

---

[2]Scrambling transforms an all-one preamble bit sequence into a sequence of zero's and one's. Methods like [20] are used to detect the zero's and change them to one's.

[3]The only exception is the short header format of 802.11b/g, which uses DQPSK.

[4]MAC address, which comes after the PHY header, is encrypted, and hence cannot be used to retrieve the corresponding PTK. Session ID will be used instead to distinguish between different transmitters.

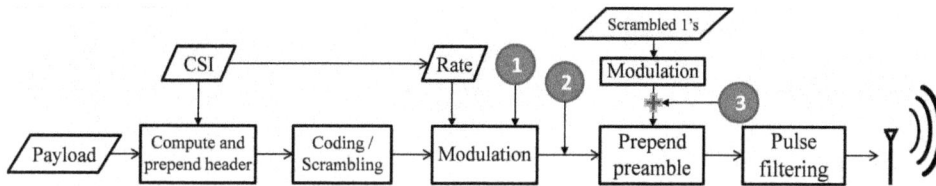

Figure 3: Transmission chain at Alice under CJ. Insertion points (1), (2), and (3) refer to modulation encryption, modulation unification, and message embedding within the preamble.

of) bits. Scrambling used in 802.11 is another digital-domain operation. Friendly jamming, on the other hand, is the concurrent transmission of analog noise from one or more antenna(s) other than the one used for the information signal.

In the following, we first explain our modulation unification and encryption scheme, assuming that the bogus traffic sequence is already available at both Alice and Bob. The problem of securely generating and synchronizing this sequence will be explained in Section 5.

## 4.1 Modulation Unification

The modulation scheme used for the frame payload should always look the same for the eavesdropper (Eve) so as to prevent any signal classification and modulation detection. To achieve that, we upgrade the payload's modulation scheme to the highest-order scheme supported by the underlying system (i.e., 64-QAM in our setup), which may result in a transmission rate that is higher than what the channel allows. In this upgrade, the original modulation symbols are embedded in the constellation map of the highest-order modulation scheme but the actual channel-dependent data rate remains unchanged.

Increasing the modulation order resembles the superposition of the constellation points of two colliding packets, i.e., as if the two packets are combined in the digital modulation space prior to transmission. One of these packets can be a digitally modulated version of conventional friendly jamming (i.e., an artificial collision). In a collision, the I and Q components of the two superimposed complex symbols are added to create a higher-order constellation map. For example, the superposition of two QPSK-modulated frames (each may contain four possible constellation points) results in a new constellation map with nine possible (I,Q) pairs (see Figure 4). Inspired by this and the fact that a collision is not recoverable if both packets are unknown, we combine Alice's frame (except the preamble) with the modulated bogus traffic but in a way that meets our uniformity and throughput requirements. The original preamble is required for performing the specific functions mentioned in Section 2. Because its content and modulation scheme are already known to Eve, such an upgrade is not beneficial for the preamble. An uncontrolled superposition of two signals (i.e., a collision) may result in a new modulation point that does not belong to any of the modulation schemes supported by the system and further may disclose the original modulation points (hence, the modulation schemes). In contrast to that, we propose a particular mapping from any of the available payload modulation schemes to the highest modulation order that is already supported by the system.

However, a higher modulation order can be more susceptible to demodulation errors. To illustrate, let the bogus traffic be $\mathcal{B}$ and let $\mathcal{F}_{\mathcal{B}}(m_i)$ be a mapping that is known for both

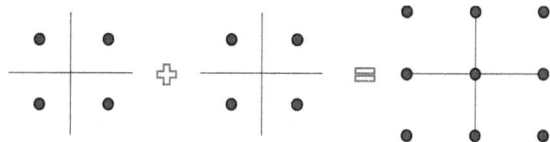

Figure 4: Combining (artificially colliding) of two QPSK-modulated signals results in a 9-symbol constellation map.

Alice and Bob and upgrades the $i$th modulation scheme $m_i$, $i = 1, \ldots, M$, to the highest-order modulation scheme $m_M$. The minimum distance between the symbols in the constellation of $m_i$, denoted by $d_{min,i}$, specifies the probability of a demodulation error at a given SNR value. This $d_{min,i}$ generally decreases with the increase in $i$. Table 2 depicts $d_{min,i}$ for the 802.11a system after taking into account modulation-dependent normalization factor $K_{MOD}$ [1]. $K_{MOD}$ is a coefficient this is multiplied by the (I,Q) values to achieve the same average power for all modulation schemes. To maintain the same $d_{min,i}$ after mapping $m_i$ to $m_M$, i.e., achieve the same BER, two neighboring points in $m_i$ should not be mapped to very close points in $m_M$, as much as possible. At the same time, all the resulting constellation points of $m_M$ as observed by Eve must be equally probable (as when a random information sequence is modulated using $m_M$). Otherwise, Eve may guess $m_i$ by performing statistical analysis. In the following, we define a mapping $\mathcal{F}_{\mathcal{B}}(m_i)$ based on $\mathcal{B}$ that achieves both of the above design requirements. Alice upgrades her modulation scheme $m_i$ only when $i < M$. In the case when $i = M$, $\mathcal{F}_{\mathcal{B}}(m_M)$ is just an affine function.

To upgrade $m_i$, our scheme defines $|m_i|$ equal-size and non-overlapping sets of constellation points in $m_M$, where $|m_i|$ is the number of constellation points in $m_i$. Each distinct constellation point (or symbol) in $m_i$, denoted as $s$, is mapped to one of these predefined target sets. The selection of a point inside a given target set depends on $\mathcal{B}$. For a given $s$, Alice needs $\log_2 |m_M| - \log_2 |m_i|$ bits of $\mathcal{B}$ to select one of the $\frac{|m_M|}{|m_i|}$ points within a target set. So Alice picks the first $\log_2 \frac{|m_M|}{|m_i|}$ bits in $\mathcal{B}$ for the first symbol to be transmitted, the next $\log_2 \frac{|m_M|}{|m_i|}$ bits for the second symbol, and so on. The same bits in $\mathcal{B}$ always point to the same constellation point within a target set, i.e., $\mathcal{F}_{\mathcal{B}}(m_i)$ is static. This ensures that the resulting constellation points are equally probable, assuming that the bits in $\mathcal{B}$ are uniformly and randomly distributed. We rely on a cryptographic hash function like SHA-2 to generate such a secret $\mathcal{B}$ (see Section 5 for details).

During the decoding process, Bob knows $\mathcal{B}$. He needs to obtain the original data symbol $s$. Let $b$ be the decimal representation of the bits in $\mathcal{B}$ that correspond to $s$. Based on $b$, Bob selects $|m_i|$ candidate points in $m_M$, denoted by $C_b$, for the unknown data symbol. Each candidate point belongs to one of the target sets. Therefore, Bob's job is

| $i$ | $m_i$ | $K_{MOD}[1]$ | $d_{min,i}$ | $d_{min}(\mathcal{F}_\mathcal{B}(m_i))$ | $b_{4,i} \overset{\text{def}}{=} \frac{d_{min,i}}{d_{min}(\mathcal{F}_\mathcal{B}(m_i))}$ |
|---|---|---|---|---|---|
| 1 | BPSK | 1 | 2 | $8/\sqrt{21}$ | $\sqrt{21}/4$ |
| 2 | QPSK | $1/\sqrt{2}$ | $2/\sqrt{2}$ | $8/\sqrt{42}$ | $\sqrt{21}/4$ |
| 3 | 16-QAM | $1/\sqrt{10}$ | $2/\sqrt{10}$ | $8/\sqrt{42}$ | $\sqrt{4.2}/4$ |
| 4 | 64-QAM | $1/\sqrt{42}$ | $2/\sqrt{42}$ | $2/\sqrt{42}$ | 1 |

Table 2: Parameters of the optimal mapping from the modulation schemes in 802.11a to 64-QAM.

| $x$ \ $y$ | 0 | 1 | 2 | 3 |
|---|---|---|---|---|
| 0 | 0 | 1 | 2 | 3 |
| 1 | 1 | 2 | 3 | 0 |
| 2 | 2 | 3 | 0 | 1 |
| 3 | 3 | 0 | 1 | 2 |

Table 3: Modulation encryption for QPSK (resulting $z$ values for various $(x, y)$ pairs).

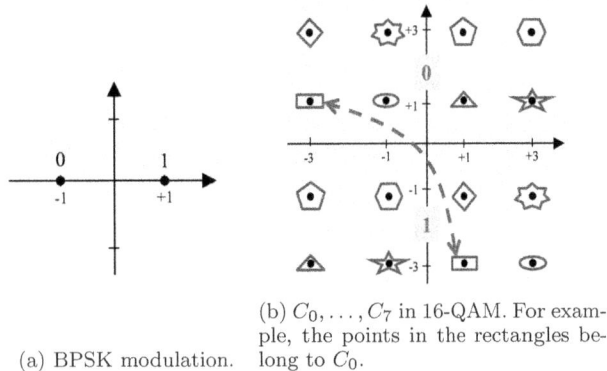

(a) BPSK modulation.

(b) $C_0, \ldots, C_7$ in 16-QAM. For example, the points in the rectangles belong to $C_0$.

Figure 5: Optimal mapping from BPSK to 16-QAM.

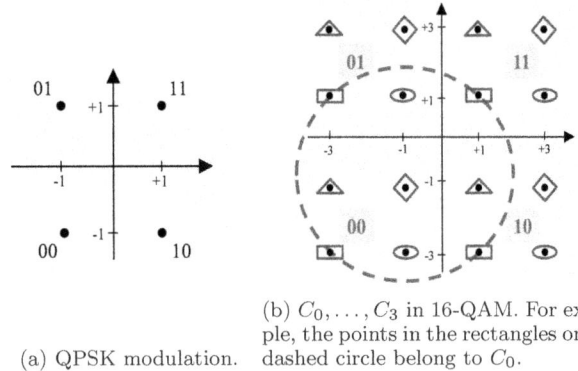

(a) QPSK modulation.

(b) $C_0, \ldots, C_3$ in 16-QAM. For example, the points in the rectangles on the dashed circle belong to $C_0$.

Figure 6: Optimal mapping from QPSK to 16-QAM.

to find the most likely symbol in $C_b$, given the observed symbol, which is a classical demodulation process. Because the modulation scheme of the PHY header portion is known a priori, Bob is able to first decode the header and obtain the original payload's modulation scheme, and then demodulate the rest of the frame.

Next, we explain an optimal strategy for selecting the target sets and mapping the original constellation points to these sets. In here, optimality is taken w.r.t. maximizing the minimum distance between symbols. Let $d_{min}(\mathcal{F}_\mathcal{B}(m_i))$ be the minimum distance between any two points in $C_b, \forall b = 0, \ldots, |m_M|/|m_i| - 1$. Bob uses a standard demodulation technique (e.g., ML) over the constellation points in $C_b$ to decode $s$. An optimal mapping for $m_i$ maximizes $d_{min}(\mathcal{F}_\mathcal{B}(m_i))$. The following formulation solves for such a mapping:

$$\max_{C_b} \quad d_{min}(\mathcal{F}_\mathcal{B}(m_i))$$
$$\text{s.t.} \quad |C_b| = |m_i|, \forall b = 0, \ldots, |m_M|/|m_i| - 1$$
$$\bigcup_{b=0}^{|m_M|/|m_i|-1} C_b = m_M \qquad (4)$$
$$\bigcap_{b=0}^{|m_M|/|m_i|-1} C_b = \emptyset.$$

Figures 5 and 6 illustrate an optimal mapping from BPSK and QPSK to 16-QAM, respectively. In part (b) of each figure, the constellation points that belong to the same set $C_b$ are enclosed in the same shape. The bits that correspond to any given constellation point in $m_M$ consist of the user payload bits (MSBs) and bogus bits $b$ (LSBs). On the constellation map of $m_M$, the MSBs specify the region (e.g., quadrant), while the LSBs specify a point inside that region. For example, in QPSK the payload data bits specify one of the quadrants in 16-QAM and $b$ specifies a point within that quadrant.

However, the optimal mapping may not fully satisfy the initial $d_{min,i}, \forall i \in 1, \ldots, M$. Let $b_{M,i}$ be the ratio between $d_{min,i}$ and $d_{min}(\mathcal{F}_\mathcal{B}(m_i))$. To guarantee $d_{min,i}$, Bob boosts the transmission power by scaling up the (I,Q) values of $m_M$ by

$$b_{M,max} = \max_i b_{M,i}. \qquad (5)$$

Although this energy boost is not required for all $m_i$'s, Alice always applies $b_{M,max}$ to eliminate any difference in the energy levels of different modulation schemes, which may leak the underlying $m_i$. For an $m_i$ with $b_{M,i} < b_{M,max}$, however, this boost will reduce the demodulation error. For the optimal mapping to 64-QAM, $d_{min,i}$ of BPSK and QPSK is not preserved, and $b_{4,max} = \sqrt{21}/4 \simeq 1.15$, which is equivalent to only $b_{4,max}^2 = 1.181$ dB increase in transmission power (see Table 2).

## 4.2 Modulation Encryption

Modulation unification introduced in the previous section hides the true modulation scheme of the frame's payload. However, because the mapping $\mathcal{F}_\mathcal{B}(.)$ is not necessarily secret (with sufficient randomness) and the modulation scheme for the PHY *header* is often fixed and publicly known, Eve may still be able to extract unencrypted fields in the PHY and (if the rate field is disclosed) MAC headers by detecting the frame preamble and obtaining the $m_M$-modulated symbols of the target header field. From the inverse function $\mathcal{F}_\mathcal{B}^{-1}$, Eve can determine the original symbols $s$ from their $m_M$-modulated counterparts, revealing the true content of that field. This is especially the case if Eve exhibits a high SNR to demodulate the received $m_M$-modulated symbols (e.g., Eve is close to Alice). To remedy this situation, we apply a modulation-level stream encryption $\mathcal{E}_\mathcal{B}(m_i)$ to the $m_i$-modulated symbols of the frame (payload + header)[5]

---

[5]We do not encrypt the preamble, since otherwise Bob cannot detect the start of the frame without knowing in advance

to randomize the location of the original symbols in constellation map of $m_i$. This way, sole knowledge of $\mathcal{F}_\mathcal{B}$ is not sufficient to disclose the symbol $s$ that corresponds to an observed $m_M$-modulated symbol. $\mathcal{E}_\mathcal{B}(.)$ is applied before $\mathcal{F}_\mathcal{B}$ and should be uniquely decodable; i.e., it is a 1-to-1 mapping. Note that if we alternatively upgrade the modulation scheme first and then apply encryption, Bob may not reliably decode an $m_M$-modulated symbol with low SNR.

The encryption function $\mathcal{E}_\mathcal{B}(m_i)$ is performed as follows. Consider $\log_2 |m_i|$ information bits, corresponding to one symbol of the modulation scheme $m_i$. Select $\log_2 |m_i|$ successive bits from $\mathcal{B}$ and modulate them using $m_i$. Let $x$ and $y$ be the decimal values of the information and bogus symbols, respectively (in the range $0, 1, \ldots, |m_i| - 1$). The value of the encrypted symbol, denoted by $z$, is given by:

$$z = (x + y) \bmod |m_i|. \tag{6}$$

Bob uses the same bogus symbol $y$ to obtain $x$:

$$x = \big(|m_i| - (z - y)\big) \bmod |m_i|. \tag{7}$$

This is a symmetric function; $x$ and $y$ are interchangeable. Table 3 depicts an example of encrypting QPSK symbols. As mentioned earlier, Eve may obtain the original $m_i$-modulated symbol of an observed $m_M$-modulated one. However, the $z$ value determined by Eve can potentially correspond to any possible $x$. In other words, the observation of $z$ does not reduce the entropy, which means mutual information is zero at Eve, and Eve cannot use $z$ to recover the original symbol $s$; i.e., we achieve perfect secrecy for the header and the payload (provided that $\mathcal{B}$ is secret).

However, the encryption operation $\mathcal{E}_\mathcal{B}(m_i)$ destroys the Gray code structure of 802.11 modulation schemes. In Gray coding, adjacent points in the constellation map differ by only one bit and a demodulation error almost always causes a single-bit error. After randomizing the points using $\mathcal{E}_\mathcal{B}$, the average BER due to demodulation errors increases by a factor that corresponds to the average hamming distance between any pair of adjacent constellation points in $\mathcal{E}_\mathcal{B}(m_i)$. This factor is about 1.33, 1.17, 2.13, and 3.04 for (D)QPSK, CCK, 16-QAM, and 64-QAM, respectively. This increase in BER is especially important when there is a considerable residual error in frequency offset estimation, which causes many demodulation errors in long frames. In Section 6 we show and argue that this loss is often small and can be compensated for with a slightly higher transmission power. For a modulation scheme $m_i$ with $b_{M,i} < b_{M,max}$, (e.g., 16-QAM and 64-QAM in Table 2), the power boost discussed in Section 4.1 can mitigate this loss.

At Bob, the modulation-encrypted header and payload are treated is the same way, except that the true modulation order for the PHY header is known a priori. So Bob knows in advance how many bits from $\mathcal{B}$ are needed to decrypt and recover the header. The modulation scheme for the payload is determined after the PHY header has been decoded and the rate field recovered. Eve, on the other hand, cannot decode the header because it is modulation-encrypted by the secret $\mathcal{B}$. As long as the rate field in the header is unknown, Eve cannot determine $m_i$ of the payload, and hence does not know how many information bits are associated with an observed symbol.

---

the sender's identity (the frame may originate from several possible sources).

Altogether, Alice applies the composite mapping $\mathcal{F}_\mathcal{B}\big(\mathcal{E}_\mathcal{B}(m_i)\big)$ to the symbols of a frame. For each $m_i$-modulated symbol, Alice (Bob) sequentially picks a block of $\log_2 |m_i| + \log_2 \frac{|m_M|}{|m_i|}$ bits from $\mathcal{B}$ to first encrypt (recover) the symbol and then upgrade (decrypt) it.

## 5. BOGUS TRAFFIC GENERATION

If Alice and Bob were to use the same secret bogus bits for different frames, a given header field that can take a few possible values (e.g., the 8-bit Signal field in 802.11b takes four possible values) would produce a fixed set of constellation points in $m_i$. After eavesdropping on several frame transmissions that may have different values for that field, Eve may estimate the part of the secret sequence used to protect that field. This can disclose the field values and facilitate a *dictionary attack* against the header content. Moreover, in the case of a retransmission, applying the same $\mathcal{B}$ results in the same sequence of modulated symbols. Eve may then correlate successive transmissions and detect retransmissions. She could then exclude these retransmissions from the statistics used to create the fingerprint of the session (e.g., packet size histogram). Furthermore, if Alice and Bob synchronously use different parts of a common $\mathcal{B}$ for different frames, the loss of an ACK would make Alice and Bob out-of-sync. For this reason, we require $\mathcal{B}$ to vary from one frame to another, in addition to being secret. In this section, we explain how a secret frame-specific $\mathcal{B}$ is generated based on the PTK.

We exploit a one-way cryptographic hash function from the SHA-2 hash family (recommended by NSA) to generate $\mathcal{B}$ based on a seed value. These functions enjoy the property that even a bit change in the seed makes the hash value ($\mathcal{B}$ in our case) completely different. Also, if the hash value is extracted, it cannot be used to recover the seed value, i.e., it is one-way. If the seed is to be completely secret, i.e., the PTK is solely the seed, the hash value $\mathcal{B}$ will always remain the same. So the idea is to concatenate an unprotected frame ID, denoted by $\mathcal{ID}$, to the PTK and compose a partially secret seed for the given frame. *Friendly CryptoJam* embeds $\mathcal{ID}$ in the frame preamble and transmits it in the clear. If there are other nodes (e.g., Charlie) that may also communicate with Bob, we assume that the session ID is part of $\mathcal{ID}$, allowing Bob to distinguish between Alice's and Charlie's transmissions in the absence of MAC addresses and accordingly apply the right PTK.

### 5.1 Embedding the $\mathcal{ID}$

To embed the non-secret $\mathcal{ID}$, we can introduce a new field between the preamble and the standard PHY header. However, to keep the standard PHY-layer frame format intact for interpretability purposes and also to avoid increasing the frame size, we take advantage of the known preamble to embed $\mathcal{ID}$ into it in the form of an analog-signal superposition. (Note that we cannot use any reserved bits in the header(s) because the entire header is supposed to be encrypted by *CryptoJam*.) The design below is specific to the 802.11b long preamble, but the basic idea can be generalized to other preamble structures.

Correct $\mathcal{ID}$ extraction from the superposition is highly critical for Bob. At the same time, Bob does not want to lose the important functions of the preamble as a result of this superposition. To satisfy both requirements, we propose

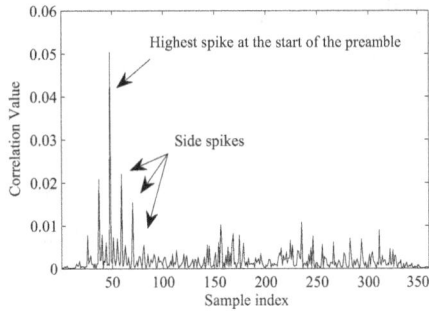

(a) The highest spike indicates the start of a frame.

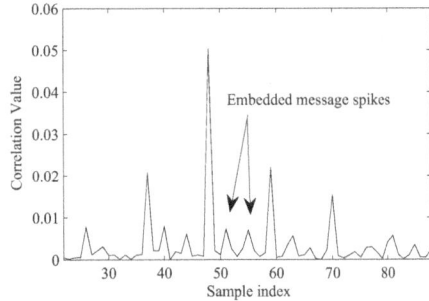

(b) Small but detectable spikes due to the embedded $\mathcal{ID}$.

Figure 7: $\mathcal{R}(n)$ computed over a frame.

using cyclically rotated Barker sequences (Section 2) to encode Alice's $\mathcal{ID}$. When a Barker sequence is aligned with the original preamble, the function $\mathcal{R}(n)$ (defined in (3)) spikes, indicating the start of a frame. To preserve this spike, we utilize cyclically shifted versions of the reference 11-chip Barker sequence. Every $k$-shifted sequence, $k = 1, \ldots, 10$, can be a message. Because of the orthogonality property of Barker sequences, this overlaid message is easily detectable with RF correlation. Moreover, the frame detection process will not be noticeably affected because the encoded message will have little contribution to the correlation with the reference sequence, when aligned properly. Figure 7(a) is an example drawn from our experiments (Section 6) that shows the value of $\mathcal{R}(n)$ when applied over a frame with two embedded rotated Barker sequences repeated in each half of the preamble. The preamble in this example consists of four Barker sequences, which create a few side spikes when the correlator is moved a multiple of 11 indices away from the beginning of the preamble. Figure 7(b) zooms into the preamble and shows the two *messages spikes* (i.e., spikes corresponding to the cyclicly rotated Barker sequences) between every two successive preamble spikes.

For each frame (including retransmissions), Alice picks a frame $\mathcal{ID}$ that has not been recently used. It is conveyed by concatenating several $k$-shifted versions of the Barker sequence, which are superimposed on the original preamble in the analog domain. Specifically, let $(k_1 k_2 \ldots k_l)_{10}$ be the decimal representation of the value of $\mathcal{ID}$, where $k_i$, $i = 1, \ldots, l$, is the i-th most-significant digit. Then, the value of $k_i$ corresponds to a cyclically shifted Barker sequence with $(k_i + 1)$ amount of shift. Concatenation of the $l$ shifted Barker sequences produces $\mathcal{ID}$. Bob is still able to detect the preamble and the $\mathcal{ID}$, as shown in Figure 7. The steps taken by Bob to extract $\mathcal{ID}$ and perform the preamble functions are summarized as follows:

1. Detect frame, estimate FO, and compensate for it.

2. Extract frame $\mathcal{ID}$.

3. Construct a new reference preamble using the original preamble and the embedded $\mathcal{ID}$.

4. Perform channel estimation using the new preamble.

5. Look up the PTK associated with the session ID and start generating $\mathcal{B}$.

## 5.2 Practical Issues

Embedding a frame $\mathcal{ID}$ in the preamble may affect some of the preamble's common functions. We discuss how an appropriately designed message embedding mechanism can maintain these functions.

**(1) Frame detection.** A typical receiver performs sliding-window correlations using different time offsets (parameter $n$ in (3)). In the case of CJ, the superposed $\mathcal{ID}$ will cause a few spikes when Bob correlates the reference preamble with the received signal at time offsets $k_1, \ldots, k_l$, from the start of the preamble. To avoid creating an alias of the actual start of the preamble, Alice makes sure that she uses different rotation values over successive preamble bits. Let the number of such successive rotations be $l < 11$ ($l \neq 6$). Excluding the noise and multipath channel effect, the message spikes cannot be larger than $\frac{(6-l)^2}{(5l)^2}$ of the highest spike. Because in every sequence of $l$ rotations, at most one of them will perfectly aligned with the correlating sequence, i.e., the original preamble. Note that the correlation value of two Barker sequences with the same (different) rotation value(s) is $|11|^2$ ($|-1|^2$).

**(2) Frequency offset estimation.** As explained in Section 2, frequency offset estimation requires two identical repetitions of an arbitrary sequence. We satisfy this requirement by repeating the $\mathcal{ID}$-bearing signal at least twice. Specifically, if Bob uses $K$ repetitions of the Barker sequence (preamble bits) for FO estimation, Alice places the $\mathcal{ID}$-bearing signal in the first $K/2$ sequences and then repeats it over the other $K/2$ sequences. (If $K > 2l$, Alice uses the last $l$ bits in each half to superimpose the $\mathcal{ID}$.) If Alice does not know $K$ a priori, she only exploits the portion of the preamble that will likely be detected by Bob. Bob then can find the start of the $\mathcal{ID}$ signal either by an energy-increase detection, or by iteratively running (on each preamble bit) a series of threshold-based correlations with nonzero rotations of the Barker sequence. Once a correlation value exceeds the threshold, this indicates the start of the $\mathcal{ID}$ signal.

**(3) Channel estimation.** A known sequence, such as the preamble, is also often used for channel estimation. Upon detection of $\mathcal{ID}$, Bob constructs a new "temporary" preamble by superposing the same message signal over the original preamble, and uses the new preamble for channel estimation.

**(4) Message capacity and error correction.** There are 10 distinct rotations of an 11-chip Barker sequence. In DBPSK, this translates into 10 different messages per preamble bit. So in every nine out of 128 bits of the preamble, 10! different $\mathcal{ID}$s of the form $(k_1 k_2 \ldots k_9)_{10}$ can be embedded. Given this large number, Alice can define a coding scheme over the set of $\mathcal{ID}$s to reduce the message detection errors (e.g., using messages with large Hamming distances).

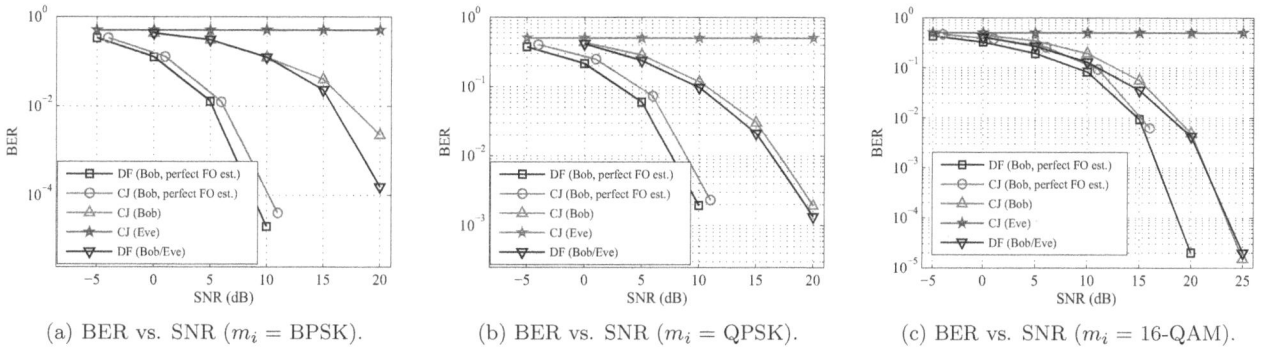

| (a) BER vs. SNR ($m_i$ = BPSK). | (b) BER vs. SNR ($m_i$ = QPSK). | (c) BER vs. SNR ($m_i$ = 16-QAM). |

Figure 8: BER performance of modulation encryption and unification (simulations).

# 6. PERFORMANCE EVALUATION

We evaluate *Friendly CryptoJam* using the LabVIEW simulation environment. We also implement it on an NI-2922 USRP testbed controlled by the LabVIEW USRP driver. Our LabVIEW PHY-layer libraries include the transmitter components in Figure 3, as well as channel and frequency offset estimations modules at the receiver. In the simulations, FO is a controllable parameter, whereas in the experiments, it is a feature of the USRP radio oscillator.

**(a) Modulation.** We use three basic modulation schemes, BPSK, QPSK, and 16-QAM. The modulation mappings follow Figures 5 and 6. When various modulation schemes are mapped to 16-QAM, $b_{M,max} = b_{3,max}^2 \simeq 1$ dB.

**(b) Physical frame.** Unless specified otherwise, each frame consists of a 44-bit Barker code DBPSK modulated preamble (four 11-chip Barker sequences) followed by a 512-bit random payload. The frame is transmitted over a 2.4 GHz frequency band at a symbol rate of 1 Msamples/s.

**(c) Bogus traffic.** For bogus traffic generation, we did not implement SHA-2. Instead, we generated a sufficiently large random sequence, shared between Alice and Bob. In [13], it was shown that the data rate of the hardware (FPGA) implementations of SHA-2 hash family exceeds one Gbps, which is quite sufficient for *Friendly CryptoJam*. To support the highest data rate in 802.11n (600 Mbit/s), a bogus traffic generator with at least this data rate is required.

**(d) Metrics.** We evaluate the BER performance and preamble-related operations, such as frame detection and FO estimation, for different SNR values and modulation schemes. The message extraction success rate is another important metric of interest.

## 6.1 Simulations

To assess the performance of individual components of CJ, in the simulations we first decouple the unification/encryption schemes from the message embedding approach. AWGN channel model is used with channel coefficient of 1. We then evaluate all the components together in the USRP experiments.

### 6.1.1 Modulation encryption and unification

Because Alice uses only 16-QAM symbols for transmission, Eve always receives 16-QAM symbols. So Eve always detects 16-QAM as the underlying modulation scheme. If Eve applies this modulation scheme to demodulate symbols that were originally modulated using BPSK or QPSK, her BER will be high. Besides the BER, we evaluate Eve's capability in wiretapping the encrypted header by assuming

that she knows *Friendly CryptoJam* and the header's original modulation scheme. BER in digital communications not only depends on SNR and $d_{min,i}$, but also on FO estimation accuracy. For this reason, we obtain the results with and without perfect FO estimation.

Figure 8 depicts the BER performance of CJ as a function of the SNR at Bob/Eve for different modulation schemes $m_i$. In the figures, the DF scheme refers to the default operation without CJ, which is used as our benchmark. When BPSK is used (Figure 8(a)), modulation encryption does not impact Gray coding, so $d_{min}(\mathcal{F}_{\mathcal{B}}(m_i))$ of modulation unification is the only important parameter. When FO estimation is perfect, CJ can achieve almost the same BER but with about 1 dB increase in the transmission power. This verifies our analysis in Section 4. However, when Bob has to estimate FO, not only the BER increases due to FO estimation errors, but also the accumulation of phase errors over time starts to impact 16-QAM-modulated symbols of CJ more than the default scheme (withe BPSK-modulated symbols). To account for the BER increase, Alice can increase her transmission power by about 2 dB. Eve, on the other hand, cannot perform better than a random guess (BER = 0.5).

For the QPSK case in Figure 8(b), 1 dB power increase may not be sufficient even with perfect FO estimation, because the structure of the Gray code is no longer preserved. However, for 16-QAM in Figure 8(c), this loss of structure is partially compensated for by the excess power boost (because $b_{3,max} > b_{3,3}$), and hence the gap between CJ and the default case narrows. Higher modulation orders are less vulnerable to FO estimation errors, because under Gray coding, a large phase offset flips a smaller fraction of bits. This explains why the perfect FO estimation case is closer to the imperfect estimation case when $m_i$ is set to 16-QAM. An interesting observation is that different modulation schemes have similar BER performance under CJ (with imperfect FO estimation). Figure 8(c) also verifies that even without modulation unification, modulation encryption is sufficient to protect unencrypted fields.

### 6.1.2 Message embedding

Next, we disable modulation encryption and unification but embed an $\mathcal{ID}$ in the preamble. We study how much the superposition of $\mathcal{ID}$ into the preamble affects frame detection (timing), FO estimation, and channel estimation. We also measure the efficiency of the embedded message extraction method. In all examined cases, the modulation scheme is QPSK and the embedded message signal has the same energy as the preamble, unless specified otherwise.

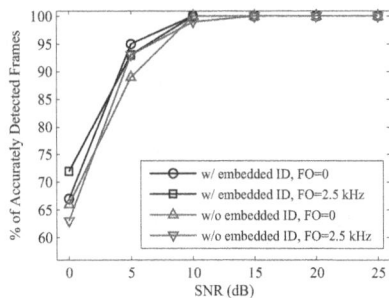

Figure 9: Frame detection accuracy vs. SNR with and without an embedded $\mathcal{ID}$ for different FO values (simulations).

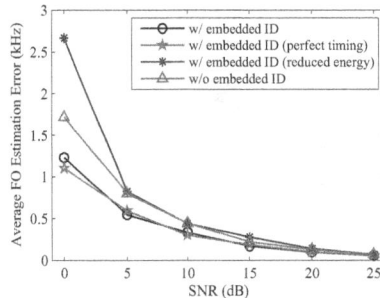

Figure 10: FO estimation error vs. SNR with and without an embedded $\mathcal{ID}$ in the preamble (simulations).

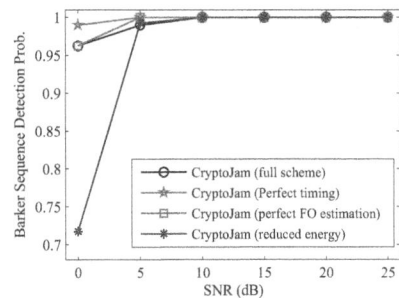

Figure 11: Performance of shifted Barker sequence ($\mathcal{ID}$) detection at Bob vs. SNR (simulations).

Accurate frame detection is the first requirement in the decoding process. It starts by a threshold-based energy detection, followed by the preamble (Barker sequence) correlation. Figure 9 shows that the embedded message does not noticeably impact frame detection even when FO is not zero. In fact, the higher received energy due to the superposition makes energy detection with message embedding slightly more accurate in presence of noise. Although four distinctly shifted Barker sequences generate additional spikes when correlated with an incorrectly aligned reference sequence, the highest of these spikes will not be more than 15% of the spike of the correctly aligned reference sequence (see Figure 7).

The receiver then moves on to the next phase; frequency offset estimation. The symmetry between two parts of the preamble-message combo together with the higher energy improves FO estimation, as illustrated in Figure 10. To specifically study the effect of $\mathcal{ID}$ embedding on FO estimation, we also simulate the scheme assuming perfect frame detection. The results show that FO estimation is not considerably impacted by the frame detection errors. The reason is that even though a frame timing error eliminates some of the samples of the combo from the FO estimation process, the symmetry property still holds for most of the samples included in the estimation process and the effect of the samples that do not belong to the combo averages out. We then add a forth curve to study the effect of the $\mathcal{ID}$ signal's energy. In particular, we multiplied its samples by $1/\sqrt{2}$ before transmission. According to this curve, Alice can reduce the $\mathcal{ID}$ signal's energy to achieve similar FO estimation performance when the noise level is not high.

The performance of CJ highly depends on correct extraction of the $\mathcal{ID}$. Figure 11 provides more details about the impacts of FO estimation and frame detection on the message detection performance by comparing the rate of correct detection of CJ with the cases when either of the aforementioned processes was perfectly done in CJ. When the SNR is high ($\geq 5$), Bob can always extract the embedded $\mathcal{ID}$. However, the error increases with the increase in the noise power and frame detection errors. Correct $\mathcal{ID}$ extraction depends more on correct frame detection than on FO estimation, as perfect FO estimation does not improve the detection rate, but perfect timing almost always extracts the message correctly. We also consider the reduced energy case of Figure 10. Inline with the effect of low SNR, the results show that a reduction in the energy is not beneficial to Alice. We also note that the preferred 3 dB energy increase during

the preamble transmission is not considerable because the duration of the preamble is much less than the duration of the payload.

Last but not least, we evaluate the BER when a message is embedded in the preamble (Figure 12). To measure the sensitivity to FO estimation errors, we also simulate the cases with perfect FO estimation. It turns out that the FO estimation has a crucial impact on the BER. This also justifies why CJ achieves a better BER when the superposition energy is higher; so FO estimation is more accurate. Likewise, when the $\mathcal{ID}$ signal's energy is reduced, the BER increases.

## 6.2 USRP Experiments

In our testbed, one of the USRPs always acts as Alice while the other one can be either Bob or Eve. Since the scheme has been extensively studied under an AWGN channel model in the simulations, we exploit our USRPs to emulate a real transmission in an indoor multipath environment. In particular, we eliminate the LOS component by placing an obstacle between Alice and Bob/Eve. The experimental scenarios, listed in Table 4, are based on the Alice-Bob/Eve distance and type of the obstacle. It is worth to mention that we also experimented with simpler scenarios without an obstacle in which the distance was the varying parameter. However, the BER under this setup is either zero (in most of the cases) or similar to the BER in the setup with an obstacle, and so we do not report them here.

| Scenario # | Alice-Bob Distance | Obstacle |
|---|---|---|
| 1 | 70 cm | Cardboard box |
| 2 | 1.2 m | Cardboard box |
| 3 | 1.2 m | PC case (metal) |

Table 4: Scenarios used in the USRP experiments.

In analyzing the measured data, we filter out cases in which transmissions were not detected by the USRP. Those cases constituted less than 0.3% of the transmitted frames. We also distinguish between cases based on whether or not the $\mathcal{ID}$ is correctly detected. Basically, any message detection error will result in a packet drop and we exclude these samples in the averaging. Nevertheless, the successful detection rate is always higher than 99.83% in our experiments.

Figure 13 depicts the BER for different payload's modulation schemes but with the same packet size. Surprisingly, QPSK shows the best performance. FO error can explain the reason. For the same frame length, BPSK results in a higher frame duration than QPSK. So due to FO

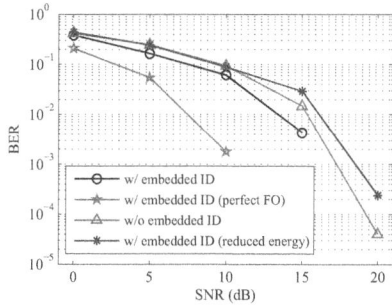

Figure 12: BER vs. SNR with and without an embedded $\mathcal{ID}$ (simulations).

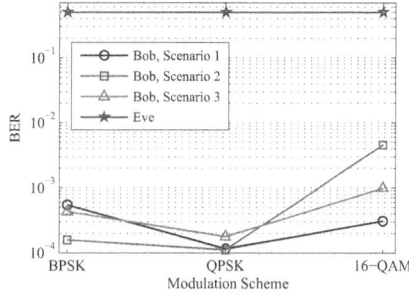

Figure 13: BER vs. modulation schemes with fixed packet size (USRP experiments).

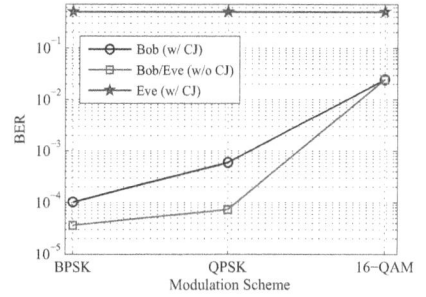

Figure 14: BER vs. modulation schemes with fixed frame duration (USRP experiments).

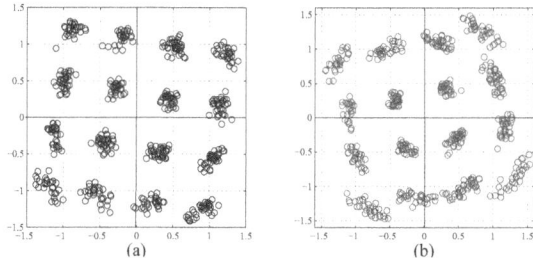

Figure 15: Examples of received 16-QAM symbols at Eve for (a) $m_i$ = BPSK, (b) $m_i$ = QPSK (USRP experiments).

estimation errors, phase error accumulation over a longer time period causes more demodulation errors when BPSK symbols are extracted from the 16-QAM constellation map. The frame durations under BPSK, QPSK, and 16-QAM in our experiments are approximately 6.78, 3.68, and 2.05 ms, respectively. On the other hand, QPSK by design has a higher $d_{min,i}$ than 16-QAM, which in this case dominates the small frame duration difference compared to the 16-QAM-modulated frame.

Next, we consider a situation in which Alice wants to confuse Eve about the actual payload size by transmitting packets of three different sizes but with the same frame duration. In particular, Alice always transmits for 3.64 ms (preamble + payload). Depending on the CSI, she may actually send 250 bits with BPSK, 500 bits with QPSK, or 1000 bits with 16-QAM. From Eve's perspective, however, these packets look the same in duration and modulation scheme. Figure 15 illustrates two example constellation maps of what Eve observes when the payload's original modulation scheme is BPSK and QPSK (assuming scenario 3). Eve will always detect 16-QAM symbols and decode them into 1000-bit packets. The corresponding BER performance was shown in Figure 14. Even when $m_i$ is 16-QAM, Eve's BER is high due to modulation encryption. As for Bob, he can identify the underlying $m_i$ and correctly decode the symbols. While Eve cannot decode a frame or estimate its size, modulation scheme, rate, etc., Bob can achieve a BER close to the default case. Disorganization of Gray code together with FO estimation errors can explain the small performance loss.

## 7. RELATED WORK

Several upper-layer techniques, such as padding, traffic morphing [17], and packet features masking at the application layer [12], have been proposed to prevent the leakage of side-channel information by changing the traffic statistics. These techniques, however, trade off higher traffic overhead for increased privacy. In fact, most of the existing techniques and in particular the padding techniques have been shown to be insufficient in thwarting classification attacks, despite their high bandwidth overhead [7]. Dyer et al. [7] demonstrated that even if packet lengths are obfuscated, training a classifier based only on the total bandwidth can result in a very high classification accuracy. They also proposed a countermeasure that obfuscates the total bandwidth, but with $100\% - 400\%$ overhead. To reduce the overhead, traffic reshaping at the MAC layer [18] is used to split the traffic among several virtual MAC interfaces; hence reshaping the statistical traffic profile of each of the interfaces. However, even if the devices support multiple virtual MAC addresses, traffic splitting requires modifying the MAC protocol. Furthermore, none of the above techniques can hide lower-layer fields such as the modulation scheme and the data rate. Friendly CryptoJam, however, obfuscates packet lengths and the total traffic volume (among others) without imposing high overhead or modifying higher-level protocols. For example, upgrading BPSK-modulated frames to 64-QAM-modulated frames can translate to 600% increase in the total traffic volume from Eve's perspective.

A number of PHY-layer protection schemes have also been proposed. Scrambling can be used to securely obfuscate the input bit sequence. However, this does not obfuscate the channel-dependent modulation scheme. Directional antennas try to shrink the vulnerability zone by steering in the direction of the legitimate receiver. Yet, the LOS from Alice to Bob is still vulnerable to wiretapping, in addition to side lobes. Also, in some circumstances, these techniques may fail to provide directionality (e.g., see [3, 5]). Other techniques such as beamforming and orthogonal blinding (e.g., [3]) are essentially based on prefiltering (precoding) a signal, which have been shown to be insufficient [15].

## 8. CONCLUSIONS

Preventing leakage of wireless transmission attributes, including unencrypted header fields and modulation scheme, is challenging. In this paper, we proposed Friendly CryptoJam, a combination of friendly jamming and low-level encryption, to effectively protect lower-layer fields using a single antenna, and prevent traffic classification and rate-adaptation attacks. The scheme employs three main techniques: First, a modulation-level encryption technique that can perfectly secure the headers and the payload. Second, an optimal and energy-efficient modulation unification technique that obfuscates the modulation scheme and partially decorrelates the modulated-frame duration from the packet size and the total traffic volume. Third, a message embedding technique that overlays an $\mathcal{ID}$ on the preamble for exchanging packet/sender identifiers instead of the (encrypted) MAC address, which is used for session-key look up in existing systems. We showed theoretically and experimentally that constructing an $\mathcal{ID}$ using a series of shifted Barker sequences and then superposing it on the 802.11b preamble is reliable, without affecting the preamble functions, such as frequency offset estimation. The simulation and experimental results also verify that with a slight increase in the transmission power, modulation unification and encryption are successful in hiding the true packet size, modulation scheme, and the content of a frame without degrading the BER.

# 9. ACKNOWLEDGEMENTS

This research was supported in part by the Army Research Office (grant # W911NF-13-1-0302) and in part by the National Science Foundation (grants # IIP-1265960 and CNS-1016943). Any opinions, findings, conclusions, or recommendations expressed in this paper are those of the author(s) and do not necessarily reflect the views of ARO or NSF.

# 10. REFERENCES

[1] Supplement to IEEE Standard for Information Technology–Telecommunications and Information Exchange Between Systems–Local and Metropolitan Area Networks–Specific Requirements: Part 11: Wireless LAN Medium Access Control (MAC) and Physical Layer (PHY) Specifications: High-Speed Physical Layer in the 5 GHz Band, IEEE Std 802.11a-1999, 1999.

[2] IEEE Standard for Information Technology–Telecommunications and Information Exchange Between Systems–Local and Metropolitan Area Networks–Specific Requirements: Part 11: Wireless LAN Medium Access Control (MAC) and Physical Layer (PHY) Specifications (Amendment 6: Medium Access Control (MAC) Security Enhancements), IEEE Std 802.11i-2004, 2004.

[3] N. Anand, S.-J. Lee, and E. Knightly. STROBE: Actively securing wireless communications using zero-forcing beamforming. In Proc. IEEE INFOCOM'12, pages 720–728, March 2012.

[4] J. Atkinson, O. Adetoye, M. Rio, J. Mitchell, and G. Matich. Your WiFi is leaking: Inferring user behaviour, encryption irrelevant. In Proc. IEEE Wireless Communications and Networking Conf. (WCNC'13), pages 1097–1102, April 2013.

[5] M. Buettner, E. Anderson, G. Yee, D. Saha, A. Sheth, D. Sicker, and D. Grunwald. A phased array antenna testbed for evaluating directionality in wireless networks. In Proc. 1st ACM Int. Workshop System Evaluation for Mobile Platforms (MobiEval'07), pages 7–12, San Juan, Puerto Rico, 2007.

[6] S. Chen, R. Wang, X. Wang, and K. Zhang. Side-channel leaks in web applications: A reality today, a challenge tomorrow. In Proc. IEEE Symp.

[7] K. Dyer, S. Coull, T. Ristenpart, and T. Shrimpton. Peek-a-boo, I still see you: Why efficient traffic analysis countermeasures fail. In Proc. IEEE Symp. Security and Privacy (SP'12), pages 332–346, May 2012.

[8] S. Goel and R. Negi. Guaranteeing secrecy using artificial noise. IEEE Trans. Wireless Communications, 7(6):2180–2189, June 2008.

[9] S. Gollakota, H. Hassanieh, B. Ransford, D. Katabi, and K. Fu. They can hear your heartbeats: Non-invasive security for implantable medical devices. In Proc. ACM SIGCOMM Conf. Data Communication (SIGCOMM'11), pages 2–13, Toronto, Ontario, Canada, August 2011.

[10] S. Gollakota and D. Katabi. ZigZag decoding: Combating hidden terminals in wireless networks. In Proc. ACM SIGCOMM Conf. Data Communication (SIGCOMM'08), pages 159–170, Seattle, WA, USA, October 2008.

[11] X. He, H. Dai, W. Shen, and P. Ning. Is link signature dependable for wireless security? In Proc. IEEE INFOCOM'13, pages 200–204, April 2013.

[12] A. Iacovazzi and A. Baiocchi. From ideality to practicability in statistical packet features masking. In Proc. 8th Wireless Commun. Mobile Computing Conf. (IWCMC'12), pages 456–462, August 2012.

[13] R. P. McEvoy, F. Crowe, C. Murphy, and W. P. Marnane. Optimisation of the SHA-2 family of hash functions on FPGAs. In Proc. IEEE symp. Emerging VLSI Technologies and Architectures, March 2006.

[14] G. Noubir, R. Rajaraman, B. Sheng, and B. Thapa. On the robustness of IEEE 802.11 rate adaptation algorithms against smart jamming. In Proc. Fourth ACM Conf. Wireless Network Security (WiSec'11), pages 97–108, Hamburg, Germany, June 2011.

[15] M. Schulz, A. Loch, and M. Hollick. Practical known-plaintext attacks against physical layer security in wireless MIMO systems. In Proc. Network and Distributed System Security Symp. (NDSS'14), February 2014.

[16] N. Tippenhauer, L. Malisa, A. Ranganathan, and S. Capkun. On limitations of friendly jamming for confidentiality. In Proc. IEEE symp. Security and Privacy (SP '13), pages 160–173, May 2013.

[17] C. V. Wright, S. E. Coull, , and F. Monrose. Traffic morphing: An efficient defense against statistical traffic analysis. In Proc. Network and Distributed System Security symp. (NDSS'09), pages 237–250, February 2009.

[18] F. Zhang, W. He, and X. Liu. Defending against traffic analysis in wireless networks through traffic reshaping. In Proc. 31st IEEE Int. Conf. Distributed Computing Systems (ICDCS'11), pages 593–602, June 2011.

[19] F. Zhang, W. He, X. Liu, and P. G. Bridges. Inferring users' online activities through traffic analysis. In Proc. Fourth ACM Conf. Wireless Network Security (WiSec'11), pages 59–70, Hamburg, Germany, 2011.

[20] Y. Zhang. Method, apparatus and system for carrier frequency offset estimation, Oct. 17 2013. US Patent App. 13/597,204.

# Duet: Library Integrity Verification for Android Applications

Wenhui Hu, Damien Octeau, and
Patrick McDaniel
Department of Computer
Science and Engineering
Pennsylvania State University
University Park, PA, USA
{whu, octeau, mcdaniel}@cse.psu.edu

Peng Liu
College of Information
Sciences and Technology
Pennsylvania State University
University Park, PA, USA
pliu@ist.psu.edu

## ABSTRACT

In recent years, the Android operating system has had an explosive growth in the number of applications containing third-party libraries for different purposes. In this paper, we identify three library-centric threats in the real-world Android application markets: (i) the library modification threat, (ii) the masquerading threat and (iii) the aggressive library threat. These three threats cannot effectively be fully addressed by existing defense mechanisms such as software analysis, anti-virus software and anti-repackaging techniques. To mitigate these threats, we propose *Duet*, a library integrity verification tool for Android applications at application stores. This is non-trivial because the Android application build process merges library code and application-specific logic into a single binary file. Our approach uses reverse-engineering to achieve integrity verification. We implemented a full working prototype of *Duet*. In a dataset with 100,000 Android applications downloaded from Google Play between February 2012 and September 2013, we verify integrity of 15 libraries. On average, 80.50% of libraries can pass the integrity verification. In-depth analysis indicates that code insertion, obfuscation, and optimization on libraries by application developers are the primary reasons for not passing integrity verification. The evaluation results not only indicate that *Duet* is an effective tool to mitigate library-centric attacks, but also provide empirical insight into the library integrity situation in the wild.

## Categories and Subject Descriptors

K.6.5 [**Management of Computing and Information Systems**]: Security and Protection—*Invasive Software*

## Keywords

Smartphone; Android; third-party library; library-centric security threat; library integrity verification

## 1. INTRODUCTION

The Android operating system holds the biggest market share in the world of smartphones [22]. For such a success, third-party applications play an important role in the whole ecosystem [14]. These application developers integrate libraries into their applications for different purposes. For example, advertising-supported free applications have become popular in the world of Android. An advertising network distributes advertising libraries. Third-party application developers collect revenue by adding these advertising libraries into their applications. Pearce et al. found that 49% of applications in their dataset are supported by advertising libraries [39].

Besides advertising libraries, Android application developers also include other libraries into their applications. For example, Zebra crossing (ZXing) [9] is a library that provides functionality of 1D/2D barcode image processing. Another example is the license verification library (LVL) [26] by Google. With LVL, applications can query Google Play to obtain their license status at runtime.

**Three Library-Centric Security Threats:** Unfortunately, third-party libraries that come with applications can be modified to be malicious. For example, *AntiLVL* [11] is a free tool available online that modifies third-party libraries in applications in order to subvert standard license protection methods such as Amazon Appstore DRM and Verizon DRM. Such attacks require reverse-engineering and a build process, which is called a repackaging process.

Besides modifying existing libraries, attackers could also create a new malicious library. To make people believe this is a good library, attackers usually would do masquerading. For example, use the same namespace that is used by good libraries. For instance, as reported in [46], *DroidKungFu*, a famous malware, uses names such as *com.google.ssearch* and *com.google.update* to pretend to be published by Google for legitimate and benign purposes.

In addition to the modification threat and the masquerading threat mentioned above, it has also been proven that some legitimate third-party libraries have aggressive behaviors such as collecting device owner's email address. Based on the report from FireEye Blog [43], one popular advertising library that has aggressive behaviors has been used in over 1.8% of the applications in their dataset and these affected applications have been downloaded more than 200 million times in total. As reported in the followup news [44], benign application developers remove problematic third-party libraries after being notified.

**Limitation of Existing Techniques:** The three library-centric security threats mentioned above cause very serious consequences in the real world. However, we find they cannot be effectively fully addressed by existing defense mechanisms. Although software analysis [30, 19], anti-virus software [5, 3] and anti-repackaging techniques [15, 45] can detect some malicious behaviors in library code, it is hard to tell whether library providers or application developers are the offenders because the application developers can modify library code during the development process.

In the case of the modification threat, the application developer could blame the library provider for malicious library behaviors, even though the application developer is the real attacker and the library provider is a victim of the attack. Regarding the masquerading threat, the application developer could also blame the library provider for malicious library behaviors, even though the real attacker is the application developer and the victim is the library provider. Regarding the aggressive library threat, the library provider could blame the application developers for aggressive library behaviors because the developer can modify the library. In this case, the real attacker is the library provider and the victim is the application developer.

However, it is important to figure out the offenders in case of library-centric security threats in order to protect the reputation of benign stakeholders. A good reputation is important to both benign application developers and benign library providers in the ecosystem. In most cases, the application developers do not know all behaviors of the library they use while library providers have no control over who will use their library. There is a need for a technique to protect the reputation of the benign party when library-centric security threats happen.

**Research Objective:** To address the limitation of existing techniques, we develop an integrity verification technique. When Android applications are submitted to Android application stores, testing the integrity of third-party libraries in applications can effectively address library-centric threats. Third-party libraries that become malicious after modifications and masquerading libraries cannot pass library integrity verification. This guarantees that the library provider is not the attacker. However, if the malicious behaviors come from aforementioned legitimate and problematic third-party libraries, benign application developers should be protected. If these problematic libraries pass library integrity verification, it proves that the malicious behaviors in these libraries are from the library providers, instead of application developers.

**Verifiers for library integrity:** How to verify the integrity of libraries relies heavily on who is going to do the verifications. It is clear that we have at least two candidates: application developers and application stores. Obviously, it is straightforward for application developers to verify the library integrity during the build process. For example, developers can verify library integrity by comparing libraries' checksums with checksums from the library providers. However, letting the developers do verification cannot effectively fully address the three library-centric security threats because developers can modify the library. As a result, the limitations of existing techniques are still not addressed.

Realizing that letting developers do verification is not enough, we look into the reason behind it: application developers and third-party library providers are different stakeholders in the ecosystem. Their code have different intentions while they do form a symbiotic relationship. Therefore, a suitable verifier for library integrity cannot be its symbiont, the application developer. We find if stores can do the verification successfully, the three library-centric security threats can be very well addressed, due to the same reasons in *Research Objective*.

**Challenges for store side verification:** There are three major challenges for the integrity verification of Android application libraries by application stores. First, in the Android application build process, library code and application-specific logic are "blended into pieces", mixed and merged into a single binary file. The application store cannot tell whether the library has been modified before compilation by reading the application binary directly. Second, in most cases, the application store cannot get the source code of Android applications to repeat the Android application compilation process for integrity verification. Finally, library files reverse-engineered from the application binary are different from original library files collected from their provider, so that the application store cannot just use reverse engineering for integrity verification.

**Our approach:** To overcome these challenges, we propose *Duet*: a library integrity verification tool for Android applications at application stores. *Duet* first collects the original library files from their providers. With the observation that reverse-engineered library files go through a build process and a reverse-engineering process, *Duet* takes a novel mirroring approach in which original files also go through a build process and a reverse-engineering process in order to create reference files. Library files reverse-engineered from applications that use unmodified libraries are exactly the same as reference files. *Duet* builds the reference database that stores all these reference files and their digests (checksums). In particular, we use *Dare* [37] as our reverse-engineering tool. The reverse-engineering is also called retargeting in this paper.

*Duet* need to use original library files to build the reference database. This assumes that third-party libraries used for Android applications are public. Considering that application developers can access libraries, it is reasonable to assume that other stakeholders in the ecosystem can also access those library files directly from the providers. With the reference database, application stores can then directly verify library integrity in applications.

**Our Main Contributions:** Our main contributions are as follows:

- To the best of our knowledge, *Duet* is the first technique/tool for application stores that can verify the integrity of libraries used in Android applications.
- We ran *Duet* on 100,000 applications to test integrity of 15 different libraries. The results indicate that *Duet* is an effective solution for library integrity verification in Android applications.
- We present in-depth analysis that illustrate the library modification by application developers in the real world.

## 2. BACKGROUND AND PROBLEM STATEMENT

### 2.1 Background

#### 2.1.1 Libraries in Android

The libraries on a smartphone can be broken down into two categories. Some libraries enable execution of the op-

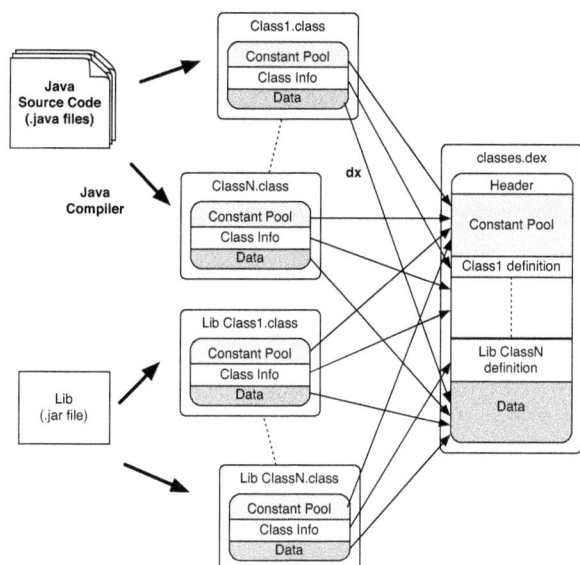

**Figure 1: Compilation process for Android applications.**

erating system. The second type of libraries are for execution of applications. Android relies on about a hundred dynamically-loaded libraries for the execution of the operating system. Some of the libraries are in fact other open source projects, such as Bionic [4]. The other libraries are generated within Android Open Source Project (AOSP) [2]. For instance, *libbinder.so* is the Binder library for Android interprocess communication. All these libraries are merged together within AOSP, and are made available by the Android software stack. Since these libraries are part of the Android framework, the operating system providers should verify the integrity of these libraries in various stages of the build process. In this paper, we do not discuss attacks on these libraries or the verification of their integrity.

This paper focuses on the second type of libraries, namely libraries for Android applications. In practice, these libraries are published by their creators in *.jar* or *.class* files. These libraries normally contain one or several packages that are collections of *.class* files, with each package defining a namespace for the *.class* files it contains. The Android application developers then use these libraries to build applications. The three library-centric security threats introduced in Section 1 target these libraries. In this paper, we propose a new integrity verification technique for these libraries, and this new technique can address these three threats.

### 2.1.2 *Android Application Compilation*

Android applications are developed in Java but compiled to Dalvik bytecode [10]. This bytecode runs in a platform-specific Dalvik Virtual Machine (DVM), which is optimized for devices with (relatively) low computing resources (e.g., smartphones and tablets). The compilation is generally a two-step process, as shown in Figure 1. In step one Java source code (*.java* files) are compiled into *.class* files. The libraries are already in the format of *.class* files coming from the library providers. Here, the developer could do some post-processing. In step two, all *.class* files are compiled into one *.dex* file. During the compilation process, the Java *.class* files composing the application are converted to a single *.dex* file. The main differences between *.class* files and the *.dex* file are as follows. The constant pools containing

the constants used by each class are merged into a single *.dex* constant pool, thereby avoiding a lot of constant replication. Other changes include: register architecture, control flow structure, ambiguous primitive types, null references, and comparison of object references [19, 37].

During the above compilation process, *.class* files are either generated based on application source code or directly from imported libraries. Then the Dalvik *dx* compiler consumes *.class* files, and recompiles them to Dalvik bytecode, which is a *.dex* file. During the compilation process, even the unused *.class* files (for both application logic and libraries) are compiled into the *.dex* file.

The *.dex* file, and other files required by the application, such as resources, assets, certificates, and manifest file, are then put into a ZIP file formatted package based on the JAR file format. This package is called Android application package (APK) file.

### 2.1.3 *Library Post-Processing*

In the real world, libraries are often not directly compiled to Dalvik bytecode. Instead, some post-processing is done before the libraries are compiled into the *.class* file. Post-processing for Java *.class* files include shrinkage, optimization, and obfuscation. Some libraries are post-processed by library providers before release. In this paper, we call this type of post-processing *Provider's Post-Processing* on the library. Some application developers perform post-processing on libraries before compilation of Android applications. In this paper, we call this type of post-processing *Developer's Post-Processing* on the library. Provider's Post-Processing helps the library providers protect source code against reversing engineering. Developer's post-processing leads to not passing the library integrity verification as discussed in Section 6.

## 2.2 Security Model

**Trust Model:** We assume application stores and security companies that use Duet are trustworthy. We also trust the library provider to provide libraries without modifications. We assume that library providers provide all versions of their libraries.

For those libraries that require the application developers to do post-processing, *Duet* cannot perform integrity verification. Google In-App Billing [24] is such a library. It is published as source code. Application developers are guided to modify the code and perform post-processing on it. This is a special category of libraries. Most libraries are published in bytecode and *Duet* can therefore be used to verify their integrity.

Reflection does not have any influence on the correctness of *Duet*. The integrity verification decision for a library is based on whether the library has been modified. Thus, cases where reflection is used as part of a library or to invoke library functions from the application do not affect the verification process. If the library code is modified by the application developer in a way that replaces API calls with reflection (e.g., for obfuscation), then the library cannot pass the integrity verification.

In this paper, we only support the official Android SDK and only support the existing compiler options. *Duet* can be extended to support customized SDK and customized compilers.

**Threat Model (Assumptions):** This work will focus on the three library-centric security threats mentioned in

Section 1, namely the library modification threat, the masquerading threat, and the aggressive library threat. We assume libraries used for Android applications are public. Other stakeholders besides application developers can also access those libraries directly from the providers. To the best of our knowledge, most libraries for Android applications are freely available online; a small portion of libraries are available online with a license fee. See Section 5.1 for demographic study.

For those libraries that are not published online, we consider them as proprietary libraries. *Duet* cannot perform integrity verification for these libraries because *Duet* cannot collect the original files for them. In such situations, application developers should take the responsibility for library-centric threats. If these application developers and library providers would like to verify the library integrity in Android applications, they can either use *Duet* themselves, or provide the libraries to third party organizations for verification.

Applications can also load libraries during runtime. *Duet* cannot be used to verify library integrity in these cases because this happens dynamically. Application stores could use other techniques such as [40] for analyzing unsafe and malicious dynamic code.

Currently, *Duet* does not support native libraries. Native code is only used in about 6.3% of Android applications [19]. In order to verify the integrity of native libraries, it is possible to simply compare the original library files with the files within the .apk file directly because the native library will not be processed by the *dx* compiler.

Note that the presence of a modified library does not necessarily imply that an attack has been performed. For example, developers sometimes perform obfuscation on library code. We argue that developers have incentives not to perform such modifications. It is usually possible to avoid modifying library code even in the case of obfuscation, since obfuscating tools can be set up not to modify certain parts of the code of an application. In cases where application developers choose to modify the library for benign purposes, they prevent integrity verification. As a result, they may be deemed responsible if a library exhibits malicious or aggressive behaviors.

## 2.3 Problem Statement

Although developers can verify the library integrity, letting developers perform integrity verification cannot effectively address the three library-centric security threats. It is clear that application store side verification is necessary and critical.

*Problem Statement:* How to enable application stores to do library integrity verification without cooperating with application developers (without knowing the source code of applications).

## 2.4 Use Cases

In the Smartphone ecosystem, different stakeholders would like to see library integrity verification results for various purposes. Library providers care about the library integrity because the library modification threat hurts the providers' benefits. Library providers also care about the masquerading threat because malware in their libraries could hurt their reputations. Because the library providers have no control of the application development process, they need store side library verification technique. In special cases, the application store is also the library provider, for instance Amazon and Google. In fact, Amazon is the victim of the library modification threat [11, 15] and Google is the victim of the masquerading threat [46]. Hence, they have motivations to perform store side library integrity verification to protect themselves.

We find that application developers also need store side library verification. Although application developers can verify the library integrity during the build process, the store still has no information about the library integrity status. In the case of the aggressive library threat [43], benign application developers need library integrity verification to prove their innocence [44]. Of course, developers can submit all source code and build configuration for repeating the build process as evidence. However, it is not only a bad idea to give source code to others, but also an extra burden for developers to keep source code and configuration for each version of applications. The store side verification can solve all these concerns.

## 3. SYSTEM OVERVIEW

### 3.1 Naive Solutions and Challenges for Store Side Verification

We find store side library integrity verification is non-trivial because the store has no control about the Android application build process. Here, we discuss several naive solutions and explain why they cannot work. One simple method to verify library integrity is to collect library files from the application package, and compare these files with the library files that are from the library provider. However, this method cannot work for Android applications. During the compilation of Android applications, the *.class* files of both libraries and application logic are merged together into one single *.dex* file. Fields and methods from each *.class* file are separated, and stored in different locations of the *.dex* file. Because each application has various *.class* files as application logic, the compilation process generates different *.dex* files for different applications even if they use the same library. To verify one must locate every piece of the library and put together each *.class* file. However, this is a very complicated thing to do. That is without reverse engineering, there seems to be no way to collect the library file.

The second method to achieve library integrity verification is to repeat the compilation process of applications. If we have the java source code or the *.class* files of one Android application, we can repeat the Android application compilation process to generate the *.dex* file. Then, we can verify the library integrity by comparing the generated *.dex* file with the *.dex* file in the application package. However, this method requires source code or *.class* files of this application. In the real world, we cannot collect these data for millions of applications. In practice, it is very difficult to convince most application developers to release source code or *.class* files. Therefore, this method can only be used in special cases when source code or *.class* files are available.

Therefore, we have to use reverse engineering technology to get the *.class* files of libraries from *.dex* files for library integrity verification. Another method is to compare the *.class* files after reverse engineering with the original library files. The reverse-engineered (retargeted) files are functionally equivalent to the original files, however they are not exactly the same. For example, original files may include debugging information, which is not necessary for their nor-

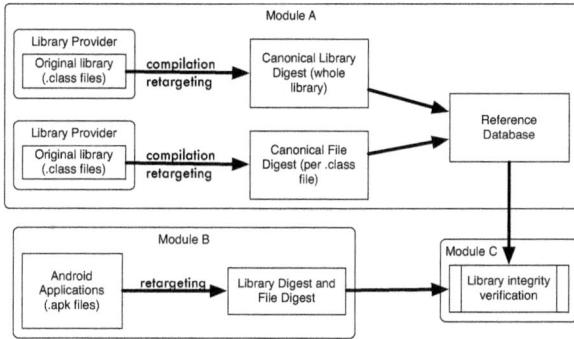

**Figure 2: Store Side Library integrity verification: system overview.**

mal execution. This debugging information is not recovered by the retargeting process. As a consequence, the retargeted files cannot directly be compared to the original library files from the library providers.

**Challenges:** To address this problem, we need to handle the following challenges:

- **C1**: The Android application compilation process mixes *.class* files of library and application logic together. The application store cannot verify the integrity of the libraries by reading the binaries of the *.dex* files.

- **C2**: The application store cannot get the source code of the application logic, and the application store has no knowledge of development configuration for each application. Therefore, repeating the compilation process of applications to achieve integrity verification of libraries is not feasible.

- **C3**: Library files from reverse engineering are different from original library files collected from their provider. Therefore, comparing *.class* files after reverse engineering and *.class* files before compilation to achieve integrity verification is not feasible.

### 3.2 Our Idea (Double Reverse-Engineering)

To overcome these challenges, we have to collect library files from the applications by using reverse-engineering. After that, we also need a correct method to compare the reverse-engineered library files with the original files from library providers. With the observation that reverse-engineered library files go through a build process and a reverse-engineering process, *Duet* takes a novel mirroring approach in which original files also go through a build process and a reverse-engineering process to create reference files. Library files reverse-engineered from applications that use unmodified libraries are exactly the same as reference files. *Duet* builds the reference database that stores all these reference files and their digests (checksums).

### 3.3 Architecture of Duet

As shown in Figure 2, *Duet* has three major modules. Module A builds the reference database; Module B processes applications; Module C compares results from Module B with the reference database for integrity verifications.

In Module A, *Duet* first downloads original libraries from the library providers. Then, *Duet* compiles original libraries to Dalvik bytecode and retargets them to get the retargeted *.class* files, which are the reference files. *Duet* merges the content of all *.class* files of a given library into a single file and calculates the hash value of this file. This value is called *canonical library digest*. *Duet* also calculates a hash value

for each *.class* file of this library. These values are called *canonical file digests*. We explain how *Duet* uses these digests when we explain Module C. The canonical library digest, canonical file digests, and reference files are all stored into the reference database.

For an Android application, Module B collects retargeted *.class* files of its libraries after retargeting. For a given library, retargeted *.class* files are used to calculate its *library digest* after being merged together. The library digest is a hash value. For every *.class* file of the library, Module B calculates its *file digest* that is also a hash value.

Then, Module C first compares the library digest with canonical library digests in the reference database. Once a match is found, the library passes the integrity verification. Otherwise, Module C compares all file digests with canonical library digests in the reference database. If every file digest can match, the library also passes the integrity verification.

Compared to file digests, calculation of library digest requires only one hash calculation. Hence, it is fast. Finding a match with canonical library digest in the reference database means that the library has not been modified. It requires that there are neither extra *.class* files nor missing *.class* files in libraries.

However, the above ideal situation does not always happen in the real world. One possible situation is that some application developers use a shrinker to remove the unused *.class* files before Android application compilation in order to reduce the size of the application. Missing some *.class* files cannot lead to meaningful security attacks. Hence, *Duet* uses file digest comparison to tolerate it.

Another situation in the real world is that several libraries from the same provider might share the same namespace. For example, *Android support* library [25] has three different libraries in the directory *"/android/support/"*. One application might contain all these three libraries. We find this is happening in the real world. *Duet* also uses file digest comparison to tolerate this situation.

## 4. DESIGN AND IMPLEMENTATION
### 4.1 Reverse-Engineering Requirements

Our double reverse-engineering idea requires the following two properties which enable our design to work very well.

**Property 1: Distinctiveness.** Different libraries compiled into Android applications should get retargeted to different code. In other words, it should be possible to distinguish the code from different libraries after the retargeting process.

**Property 2: Identity.** If the same library is compiled into different applications, retargeting these applications should yield bytecode for the library that is identical across all applications (*Identity guarantee*). In other words, the retargeting process enables us to recognize when a library has been integrated into different applications.

We select the *Dare* tool [37] as our reverse-engineering tool because we find that it provides these two guarantees. The first one is trivial. Different libraries *A* and *B* have semantically different Java bytecode, which gets compiled to semantically different Dalvik bytecode. The *Dare* retargeting process is formally defined and ensures that code semantics is preserved from Dalvik to Java bytecode. Thus, retargeting the Dalvik bytecode of *A* and *B* results in different Java bytecode.

Further, *Dare* provides identity guarantees. When a given library is compiled into different applications, it get compiled to very similar bytecode. The class names, field names, method names and the structure of the method code are identical. The only difference occurs when an instruction references a constant (e.g., integer or string constant) by using an index to a constant pool element. Since the Dalvik compilation process merges all Java constant pools together, constant indices for the library are different between applications. The retargeting process is such that, despite the differences in constant pool indices in the Dalvik bytecode, the indices in the retargeted code of the library are the same. The reason why this is true is that *Dare* uses Jasmin [36] for bytecode assembly. In order to use a constant in Jasmin code, the value of the constant has to be textually "described". For example, an integer constant is described by its value. Also, a method reference is described by the signature of the method and the name of its declaring class. This description only depends on the *value* of the constant and not on its original index in the *.dex* constant pool. Thus, the Jasmin code for a given library is the same after retargeting different applications that contain the library. This in turn results in identical Java bytecode after assembling the Jasmin code.

### 4.1.1 Potential Attach Surface

**Evading Library Integrity Verification by Duet (False Negative) :** It is fatal for an integrity verification tool if the tool/technique can be evaded by attackers. In our problem, this means that a library is detected as unmodified, even though it was in reality modified. In order for a library to be detected as unmodified, its retargeted files have to be strictly identical to the reference retargeted files. Thus, false negatives can only occur if different Dalvik code map to the same retargeted files. The only parts of the *.class* files that have an influence on runtime behavior (and are therefore potential targets of attacks) are the fields and methods. Field declarations are simply composed of a type, a name, and in some cases an initial value. Thus any modification would be detected by *Duet*. Method code is more complex, with 257 possible kinds of instructions. However, as described in [37], the mapping between Dalvik and Java bytecode is unambiguously defined. There are rare cases where different Dalvik bytecode map to the same Java bytecode. However, in these cases the different Dalvik bytecode structures are semantically equivalent. For example, there are two ways to fill an array with data in Dalvik bytecode. One is to add data to the array one element at a time. The second one consists in using a single `fill-array-data` instruction. Both cases are translated to Java bytecode using the same pattern. That is because they are semantically equivalent. In addition to this example, we have considered all other cases where different Dalvik instructions patterns map to similar Java bytecode patterns and in all cases the Dalvik semantics are the same. As a result, while it is possible that our approach may miss some code modifications, the modified code would not be semantically different. In particular, malicious modifications cannot go undetected.

## 4.2 Building the Reference Database

When building the reference database, *Duet* first downloads the original libraries from library providers. Then, *Duet* calculates the canonical library digests and canonical file digests for libraries.

### 4.2.1 Canonical Library Digest

As shown in Figure 3(a), *Duet* takes five steps to calculated the canonical library digest: compilation, retargeting, library directory information collecting, library encoding, and digest calculation.

**Compilation:** *Duet* uses the Dalvik *dx* compiler to generate the *.dex* file. Different versions of *dx* generate different *.class* files. When we build the reference database, we should consider all possibilities. We go through all versions of Android application SDK and we find that there are four different versions of *dx* so far. We also find two of them generate the same result.

**Retargeting:** We use *Dare* [37] to retarget the *.dex* to Java *.class* files. *Dare* offers a feature which consists in rewriting unverifiable (i.e., malformed) Dalvik bytecode to generate verifiable Java bytecode. This feature could potentially lead to application-specific modifications of a library. Indeed, one of the main causes of unverifiability is that sometimes Dalvik bytecode refers to missing classes [37]. If such a class is included in one application A but is excluded in application B, then *Dare* would rewrite the code in application B but not in application A (since A does not have a missing class). Therefore, we deactivate the rewriting feature in *Dare*.

**Library Directory Information Collecting:** After retargeting, the retargeted *.class* files are organized according to their package name. For example, *.class* files from *AdMob* [27] are located in directory *"/com/google/ads/"*. *Duet* needs this information in order to separate the *.class* files of the library from other parts of applications in the future.

**Library Encoding:** A single library commonly has hundreds of *.class* files. During the file encoding, we merge the content of all retargeted *.class* files of the library into one file.

**Digest calculation:** Once *Duet* gets the encoded file from the library encoding step, *Duet* calculates a cryptographic hash as the canonical library digest of the particular library.

After the above process, *Duet* stores the following information into the reference database: the library provider, version, canonical library digest, and library directory information.

### 4.2.2 Canonical File Digest

For each original library, *Duet* calculates a cryptographic hash for each retargeted *.class* file, which is a canonical file digest. These canonical file digests and the names of *.class* files are also stored into the reference database.

### 4.2.3 Issues

For the reference database, it is critical to store all legitimate canonical library digests and legitimate canonical file digests. Otherwise, *Duet* will make wrong conclusions for the integrity verification. It requires *Duet* not only supports legitimate behaviors of library providers but also supports all legitimate settings in the developers' build processes. In particular, *Duet* needs to solve the following issues: (1) Collect all history versions of original libraries from their providers; (2) Support all versions of *dx* compilers; (3) Support all possible options of *dx* compilers. We explain how *Duet* solve these three issues in Section 5.3.

## 4.3 Library Integrity Verification in Applications

As shown in Figure 3(b), the integrity verification in applications also needs five steps: decompression, retargeting,

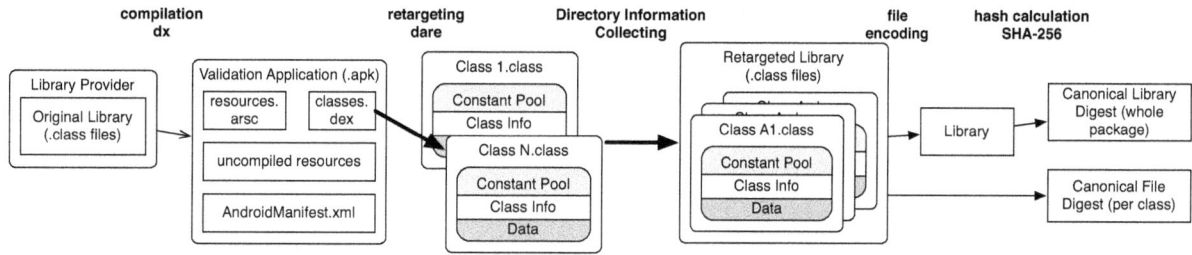

(a) Calculating the canonical library digest and canonical file digest for original libraries.

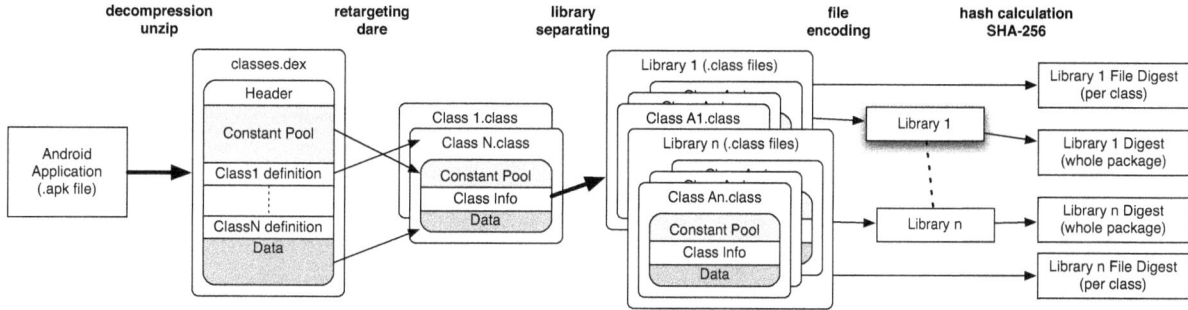

(b) Calculating library digest and file digest for libraries in Android applications.

**Figure 3: Calculation of library digest and file digest.**

library separating, library encoding, and digest calculation. Retargeting, library encoding, and digest calculation are the same as the steps when building the reference database. The other two steps, decompression and library separating, are explained as follows.

**Decompression:** In the library integrity verification, *Duet* gets the *classes.dex* from the *.apk* files of Android applications. The .apk files are in zip format. We use "unzip" to get the *classes.dex*. We also use this step to verify that the application does not be damaged during network transmissions.

**Separating library and application logic:** After retargeting, the retargeted *.class* files are organized according to their package names. With the library directory information in the reference database, we can easily separate libraries from other application logic.

## 5. EVALUATION

We have two main evaluation goals. First, we want to do library integrity verification against 100,000 Android applications in the wild to *assess the extent* to which *Duet* can help address the three library-centric security threats in the real world. Our measurements directly help the potential victims of the aggressive library threat to clear their names. The measurements also estimate an upper bound on how many library usages in the wild could suffer from the modification threat and the masquerading threat. The second goal is to validate the decisions made by *Duet*. In particular, *Duet* makes two types of decisions: (1) one library passes the integrity verification, and (2) it does not pass the integrity verification. We want to evaluate whether the decisions are trustworthy. So we will do in-depth analysis regarding whether *Duet* is making any incorrect decisions.

Our dataset has 100,000 applications downloaded from Google Play between February 2012 and September 2013. For applications that have multiple versions, only the latest

**Table 1: Categories of the top 100 detected libraries, and their source code available situation.**

|  | # of Libraries | # of Source Available | Source Available Percent (%) |
|---|---|---|---|
| App-Dev | 39 | 34 | 87.18% |
| Advertising | 34 | 0 | 0.00% |
| Service | 10 | 2 | 20.00% |
| Analytics | 9 | 0 | 0.00% |
| Game | 8 | 0 | 0.00% |
| Total | 100 | 36 | 36.00% |

version is included in the dataset. In Section 5.1, we detect the top 100 libraries used in these applications, and analyze the library usage. Then, we evaluate *Duet* by both in-lab testing and measurements on this dataset.

## 5.1 Libraries in Android Applications

For all 100,000 Android applications, we use *Dare* to do retargeting to get all *.class* files. After that, we scan Java namespaces, and count how many times each particular namespace is used. With namespace list sorted by frequency, we map namespaces to libraries with a manual online search. This process is repeated until we collect the top 100 Android application libraries. Considering that a popular library is usually reused in various applications, we get a list of most popular libraries in our dataset by this method. Figure 4(a) shows the top 20 detected libraries.

During our manual library mapping, we also identify the category of each library and its source code availability information. As shown in Table 1, there are 39 utility libraries meant to facilitate the application development process. For instance, the *Android support* library from Google can simplify the process of targeting different hardware. Many of these libraries are based on open source projects or are open source projects themselves. 87.18% of libraries in this category have source code available.

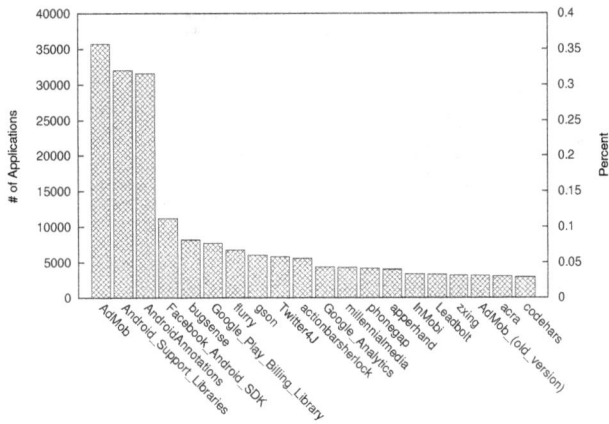

(a) Popularity of the Top 20 Libraries in Our Dataset.

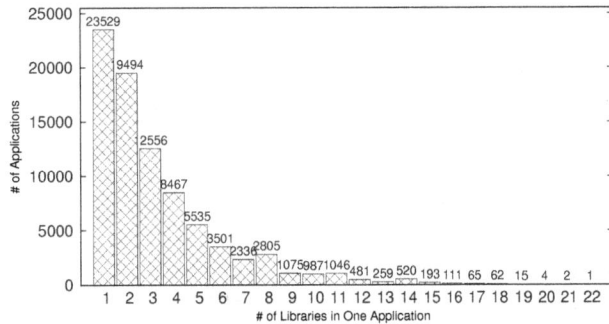

(b) Number of Libraries Contained by Each Application.

**Figure 4: Library usage information.**

The next popular popular category is advertising. We detected 34 advertising libraries. Other 10 libraries are providing important services to the Android applications. We name these libraries as the service libraries. One example is *Google Play Billing* library, which provides the service of in-application purchase. Another library category is the analytics library. An analytics library helps developers know how and when users use their applications. 9 libraries in the top 100 libraries fell into this category. The last category of libraries is the game library. There are 8 libraries in this category. The source code of most of these libraries is not available, most likely because they aim at monetizing applications.

With the top 100 library list, we then check how widely libraries are used in Android applications. As shown in Figure 4(b), one application that uses 22 libraries as the extreme case. In our dataset, 83,044 (83.04%) applications use at least one library in the top 100 list.

As shown in Table 2, we detect 276,317 library usage cases in total. 149,291 occurrences (54.04%) happen in the *App-Dev* category. These usages happened in 66,035 (66.04%) different applications. The remaining 127,026 (45.97%) usages happen in the following categories: *advertising, service, analytics,* and *game*. Correspondingly, these usages happen in 60,009 (60.01%) different applications.

Generally, the above results indicate that libraries are widely used in the Android applications. For those libraries having business behind, the modification threat could cause

**Table 2: Usage information of the top 100 detected libraries.**

| | # of Category Usage | Percent in Total Usage (%) |
|---|---|---|
| App-Dev | 149,291 | 54.03% |
| Advertising | 84,617 | 30.62% |
| Service | 16,762 | 6.07% |
| Analytics | 17,458 | 6.32% |
| Game | 8,189 | 2.96% |
| Total | 276,317 | 100.00% |

damages. 60.01% of applications in our dataset, contain these libraries. For library providers, the masquerading threat could hurt library providers' reputation. For benign application developers, the aggressive library threat could lead to being excluded from application stores. In other words, a tool that can address the three library-centric security threats is very important for building a healthy smartphone application ecosystem.

## 5.2 In-lab testing of the correctness of Duet

To ensure that we know 100% of the ground truth, instead of using a real-world library, we create a library by ourselves and denote it as the "original library". Then, we modify it manually with two different methods: (1) we modify the java source code of the library, get the modified *.class* files using a Java compiler, and compile these *.class* files to an Android application; (2) we first build an application that uses the "original library"; then, we use reverse engineering tools [1] to repackage this application and modify the library during the process. In the modifications, we make changes on different targets including APIs, fields, and *.class* files. Finally, we use *Duet* to perform integrity verification between the original library and the modified ones. As shown in the following table, *Duet* detects all these manual modifications.

| Attack Methods | Class Modification | Repackaging |
|---|---|---|
| API Removal | Not Pass | Not Pass |
| API Addition | Not Pass | Not Pass |
| API Modification | Not Pass | Not Pass |
| Field Removal | Not Pass | Not Pass |
| Field Addition | Not Pass | Not Pass |
| Field Modification | Not Pass | Not Pass |
| *.class* File Removal | Not Pass | Not Pass |
| *.class* File Addition | Not Pass | Not Pass |

## 5.3 In-the-wild Library Integrity Verification Results

After in-lab testing, we then perform in-the-wild library integrity verification. We need to build the reference database with the real-world libraries before integrity verification.

**Table 3: Information of the Reference Database.**

| | Rank | # of Version | # of Canonical Library Digest | # of Canonical File Digest |
|---|---|---|---|---|
| AdMob | 1 | 16 | 256 | 25,104 |
| Android Support | 2 | 41 | 656 | 130,080 |
| AppBrain | 40 | 89 | 1,424 | 56,316 |
| AdFonic | 57 | 9 | 144 | 5,280 |
| Others | | 63 | 252 | 35,624 |
| Total | | 218 | 2,732 | 252,404 |

**Table 4: In-the-wild Library Integrity Verification Results. (All Known Versions)**

| | Rank | # of Detection | Library Digest | File Digest | Compilation with Customized Options | # of Passings | # of not Passings |
|---|---|---|---|---|---|---|---|
| AdMob | 1 | 35,726 | 28,264(79.11%) | 40(0.11%) | 10(0.03%) | 28,314(79.25%) | 7,412(20.75%) |
| Android Support | 2 | 32,002 | 23,243(72.63%) | 37(0.12%) | 24(0.07%) | 23,304(72.82%) | 8,698(27.18%) |
| AppBrain | 40 | 1,522 | 1,050(68.99%) | 235(15.44%) | 0(0.00%) | 1,285(84.43%) | 237(15.57%) |
| AdFonic | 57 | 1,025 | 876(85.46%) | 0(0.00%) | 0(0.00%) | 876(85.46%) | 149(14.54%) |
| Average | | | (76.55%) | (3.92%) | 0(0.03%) | (80.50%) | (19.50%) |

**Building the Reference Database:** As we explained in Section 4.2.3, it is critical but non-trivial to build the reference database. The first requirement is to collect all history versions of third-party libraries. It is not difficult for application stores to request all versions from library providers by requesting them. But, it is difficult for us because we cannot afford the communication costs with a large number of library providers. Further, our demand could be ignored for various reasons. For instance, some old versions have vulnerabilities such that the provider does not want to provide them. However, we still manage to collect all known versions for 4 libraries. For example, we download all known versions of *AdMob* based on its release note [27]. Besides the above 4 libraries, we collect some versions for another 11 libraries.

For these 4 libraries with all known versions, the total number of usage cases are 70,275. These libraries cover both the most popular closed source library and the most popular open source library, as well as contain libraries from both well-known library providers and relatively small library providers. Analysis on them provides empirical insight into library integrity situation in the wild.

For the *dx* compiler, we go through all versions of the Android application SDK and find that there are four different versions of *dx* so far. We also find two of them generate the same result. In addition, *dx* compiler has two working optimization options, *Duet* supports all combinations of these options.

Overall, the reference database takes 6.28GB. As shown in Table 3, the reference database contains 218 original libraries, 2,732 canonical library digests, and 252,404 file digests. The rank in the table is the rank of the library in the top 100 list.

**Library integrity verification results:** Now, we are ready to use real-world libraries and applications to evaluate the effectiveness of *Duet*. Table 4 shows the integrity verification pass ratio of 4 libraries with all known versions. The highest passing rate is achieved with *AdFonic* with 85.46%; the lowest passing rate is 72.82%. These numbers indicate that libraries are not modified after release in 80.50% of cases on average in the wild.

The remaining 19.50% of cases do not pass the integrity verifications. These not passing, however, do not always mean malicious library modification or masquerading library. In Section 6, we will look into these not passing cases and do in-depth analysis.

We perform the integrity verification on 11 libraries with some versions in order to check whether *Duet* can be used for other Android libraries. Table 5 shows the integrity verification pass ratio of these libraries. The highest passing rate is achieved with *OldAdMob*[1] with 69.32%; the lowest

---
[1] *OldAdMob* was the library released by AdMob when it was an independent company.

**Table 5: In-the-wild Library Integrity Verification Results. (Some Versions)**

| | Rank | # of Detection | Library Digest | File Digest |
|---|---|---|---|---|
| BugSense | 5 | 8,156 | 221(2.71%) | 0(0.00%) |
| Flurry | 7 | 6,741 | 2,107(31.26%) | 0(0.00%) |
| Millennial Media | 12 | 4,296 | 1,864(43.39%) | 0(0.00%) |
| InMobi | 15 | 3,344 | 201(6.01%) | 401(11.99%) |
| OldAdMob | 18 | 3,126 | 2,167(69.32%) | 0(0.00%) |
| AdWhirl | 24 | 2,458 | 1,183(48.13%) | 2(0.08%) |
| Mobclix | 25 | 2,403 | 647(26.92%) | 0(0.00%) |
| RevMob | 31 | 1,864 | 225(12.07%) | 1(0.05%) |
| MobFox | 37 | 1,679 | 188(11.20%) | 0(0.00%) |
| ZestAdZ | 86 | 521 | 356(68.33%) | 0(0.00%) |
| Cauly | 88 | 504 | 66(13.10%) | 0(0.00%) |

passing rate is 2.71%. Every library has some samples that can pass. This indicates that *Duet* is a tool that can handle integrity verification of any Android library.

In both Table 4 and Table 5, some samples pass the integrity verification by using file digest. This fact indicates that *Duet* does tolerate two real-world issues aforementioned in Section 3.3 by introducing the file digest as the supplement of the library digest.

In Table 4, 80.47% of samples pass the integrity verification by matching the canonical digests generated with the default *dx* options. At the same time, 0.03% of samples pass the integrity verification with the canonical digests generated with customised *dx* options. This indicates that (1) *Duet* does tolerate different *dx* compiler options; (2) Very few application developers customise the *dx* compiler options.

## 5.4 Implications of Passing Rates

As we mentioned in Section 1, if we can fully trust the passing conclusions made by *Duet*, the three library-centric threats can be effectively addressed. Third-party libraries that become malicious after modifications and masquerading libraries cannot pass library integrity verification. This guarantees that library provider is not the attacker. The measurements estimate 19.50% library usages in the wild have been modified in the development process. They are the upper bound of how many library usages in the wild could suffer from these two threats. However, if the malicious behaviors come from aforementioned legitimate and problematic third-party libraries, benign application developers should be protected. If these problematic libraries pass library integrity verification, it proves that the malicious behaviors in these libraries are from the library providers, instead of application developers. Our measurements directly help 80.50% of library usages which are the potential victims of the aggressive library threat to clear developers' names.

Whether we can fully trust passing conclusions depends on whether *Duet* generate any false negatives and/or false positives. By false negative we mean that a library is detected as unmodified, even though it was in reality modified. In Section 4.1.1, we have discussed whether false negative could exist. By false positive, we mean that an unmodified library fails to pass verification. Because the false positive issue is critical, we will use dedicated one section to do in-depth analysis. In particular, we will manually check whether false positive exists in Section 6.

## 5.5 Performance

Since *Duet* is designed to be used in the real world, the performance is an important factor. Retargeting takes 5,259ms on average as the majority of the time of the library integrity verification. All other processing for the verification of one library takes 27.9ms on average that is much less than the time for retargeting. For an application, the retargeting happens just once while the other processing repeats for each detected library. In our dataset, each application has three libraries on average. Therefore, it takes less than 7 seconds on average for an application to do the library integrity verifications for all libraries that this application uses.

# 6. IN-DEPTH ANALYSIS OF APPLICATIONS THAT DO NOT PASS VERIFICATION

In our Dataset, 19.50% of libraries do not pass the integrity verification. We collect names of *.class* files in these libraries and perform manual analysis on a randomly selected set of applications in order to find the reasons of not passing integrity verification. In some situations, we also compare the decompiled code to check the not passing reasons. As shown in Table 6, we find the major reasons of not passing are code insertion, obfuscation, optimization, and missing original libraries.

**Code Insertion:** We find some libraries have code that is not from the library provider. We find these inserted *.class* files by checking if there are any *.class* files not a member of the set of *.class* files in the reference database.

We find there are several different ways to insert code into libraries: (1) Developers add their own code such as *MyViewActivity.class* into the namespace of libraries. (2) Other libraries lodge into the namespace of original libraries. For instance, *Waston* [8] lodges in the *Android Support* library. (3) The library provider may allow other libraries to use its namespace. For instance, *AdMob* allows other advertising libraries that use its mediation service to use *"/com/google/ads/mediation/"*.

For developers, it is not a good idea to use the namespace that is used by a library provider. This allows the inserted code to access the "package" methods and fields, which might cause problems. For instance, a "package" field could have the same name as another filed in another package. Inserted code by developers could use the wrong filed because of carelessness. For the library provider, allowing others' libraries to use its namespace may bring conveniences in its management. *Duet* can be extended to support this, as long as these admissive libraries are also collected.

For the four libraries, we manually checked every *.class* file. The results are as follows. 63(0.18%) applications among 35,726 applications using the *AdMob* library have code inserted. For *AppBrain* and *AdFonic* libraries, we observed similar percentages, 0.26% and 0.29%, respectively (see Table 6). However, we observed a significant high percentage of the Android Support library. 5605 applications out of 32,002 applications have code insertion. This is be-

cause Android Support library is the only open source library in these four libraries. Therefore, developers could modify its source code and add their own code as well.

Having code insertion does not really mean that the code inserted has malicious intent. A lot of code insertion is actually done by benign developers. Separating good code inserted from malicious one is out of the scope of this work.

**Obfuscation:** When we analyze names of the *.class* files to detect the code insertion, we notice that some libraries have been obfuscated by application developers from the fact that some *.class* names have been modified. For instance, *android/support/a/a/A.class* is never used in the original libraries, but is detected in the dataset. These obfuscated *.class* file names sometimes even contains special characters from Chinese or Japanese. We manually build a list of *.class* names for these obfuscated cases. As show in Table 6, on average 12.73% of libraries are detected to have been obfuscated by application developers.

Our analysis on libraries indicates one interesting thing: many libraries have been obfuscated by the library provider before release. In these cases, another obfuscation by the application developers does not benefit developers that much. We suggest the application developer should not perform obfuscation to libraries that have already been obfuscated. ProGuard [6] does have options to achieve this function.

**Optimization:** Optimization on libraries by developers is another reason for not passing integrity verification. For example, we use Soot [7] to decompile the *.class* files of one *AdMob* library to get source code and compare with decompiled source code from the original library. In this case, optimization is found as one reason for not passing verification. For instance, in *com/google/ads/AdActivity.class*, we figure out that the code inlining optimization has changed *.class* files. As another example, we find annotations in samples of *Android Support* library have been removed. There are several ways developers can remove annotations in a library. For instance, developers can use ProGuard to perform the removal. As shown in Table 6, we find 0.97% of libraries do not pass the integrity verification because of optimizations.

**Missing Original Libraries:** Another reason of not passing integrity verification is missing the original libraries. Although we manage to collect all known versions for 4 libraries, it is still possible that we missed some very old versions. For example, we download all known versions of *AdMob* based on its official release note [27]. The release note contains version information after March 15, 2011. According to our knowledge, Google also released advertising libraries that were called *GoogleAdView.jar* before that date. In the reference database, we only have two versions of *GoogleAdView.jar*.

The *GoogleAdView.jar* contains *GoogleAdView.class* that is not used in subsequent *AdMob*. With this particular *.class* name, we detect 459 samples of *GoogleAdView.jar*. However, 451 of these 459 samples do not pass the integrity verification (see Table 6). The passing ratio for *GoogleAdView.jar* is 1.74%(8 of 459) that is much less than 80.50%. Therefore, we must miss some versions of *GoogleAdView.jar* when we build the reference database.

This fact indicates that a reference database with all versions of libraries is critical for *Duet*. Library providers can provide old versions to the application store directly. They have an incentive to do so, as it protects their reputation in the event of a library-centric attack. Library providers

**Table 6: In-depth Analysis of In-the-wild Verification Not Passing Samples.**

|  | Rank | # of not Passing | Code Insertion | Obfuscation | Optimization | Missing Original Library | Remain |
|---|---|---|---|---|---|---|---|
| AdMob | 1 | 7,412(20.75%) | 63(0.18%) | 5,772(16.16%) | 509(1.42%) | 451(1.26%) | 617(1.73%) |
| Android Support | 2 | 8,698(27.18%) | 5,607(17.52%) | 2,150(6.72%) | 356(1.12%) | 0(0.00%) | 585(1.83%) |
| AppBrain | 40 | 237(15.57%) | 4(0.26%) | 213(13.99%) | 16(1.05%) | 0(0.00%) | 4(0.26%) |
| AdFonic | 57 | 149(14.54%) | 2(0.20%) | 144(14.05%) | 3(0.30%) | 0(0.00%) | 0(0.00%) |
| Average |  | (19.50%) | (4.54%) | (12.73%) | 0(0.97%) | (0.32%) | (0.96%) |

are willing to provide these information because it will protect their reputation in case of the library-centric attacks. In this process, library providers do not share extra information with application stores because libraries are publicly available.

# 7. RELATED WORK

Security and privacy in Android have become popular topics in the research community.

**Smartphone platform security:** Kirin [20] is addressing permission combinations of Android applications. Whenever third-party applications are installed, the security requirements will be checked. The limitation of this approach is that applications might collaborate to bypass the protection of Kirin. As the extension of Kirin, Saint [38] does runtime inspection on the permission state.

For application security, dynamic taint analysis is used in both Android OS [18] and iOS [17]. The results from both operating systems are similar. End users' private data might be leaked to servers on the Internet.

Static analysis is widely used in application security on Android OS. Enck et al. [19] and Chan et al. [12] obtain the application source codes by decompiler and use existing tools to do analysis. Other works [13, 19, 21, 23, 28, 29, 30, 45, 47] do the analysis on either the class bytecodes or intermediate codes. These works have detected malware and give the direction of future research to improve the security on the Android platform.

All these works treat one Android application as an unit. Libraries and application logic are treated as the same. Those techniques that use static analysis and dynamic analysis can detect malicious behaviors, even if the malicious behaviors happen in the library code. However, none of these techniques can check the integrity of library code in Android applications. Hence, they can neither help the library providers clear their names for the modification threat and the masquerading threat, nor help the application developers clear their names for the aggressive library threat.

**Android Advertising Library:** Advertising libraries have been the focus of recent works. Grace et al. [28] and Steven et al. [42] have analyzed advertising libraries in the real world. They found over one hundred types of different advertising libraries using static analysis. They found that advertising networks sometimes collect information from end users, e.g., collecting contacts in the phone. These works focus on the analysis of the behavior of advertising libraries.

Researchers proposed solutions to use different applications for application logic and for the advertising library [41, 34]. In this approach, the advertising library and the remaining application logic have their own protection domain. AdDroid [39] uses another approach to separate advertisements from application by supporting advertisements in a system service. Both of these solutions solve the problem that the application logic and the library share the same protection. However, for the modification threat and the masquerading threat, discussed in this paper, attacks still work when the library is in another protection domain. For the aggressive library threat, the problem is still the same while the victims could be the application developers or the operating system provider based on which solution is chosen.

**Library Detection:** Library detection has been well studied. IDA Pro's Fast Library Identification and Recognition Technology (FLIRT) [32] is a popular library identification technique using byte pattern matching algorithms. In another work [31], Griffin et al. detect libraries based on the heuristic that a library function cannot statically call any user-written function. Both of these techniques can be extended to detect third-party libraries for Android applications. However, none of them can verify the library integrity.

**Repackaging:** Researchers have noticed repackaged Android applications. Zhou et al. [46] found 86% of malware is repackaged. Researchers analyze either intermediate codes (smali) or java classes (from reverse engineering) of the applications to generate CFGs and program dependence graphs (PDGs) [45, 15, 16]. The CFG and PDG are then used to detect the repackaged applications. These solutions are targeting to application plagiarism. They require to remove library code for making decisions on potential repackaging. Therefore, these techniques cannot be used to address the three library-centric security threats.

**Code Clones:** Besides repackaging detection for Android applications, both the detection of similar software applications and the detection of code clones have been well studied [33] and [35]. These techniques detect similarity between applications by comparing strings, tokens, trees, or semantics. None of them can be used to verify the software integrity.

# 8. CONCLUSION

There are three security library-centric threats in the world of Android. Since there is no existing technique that can effectively fully address these threats, we propose a novel technique for library integrity verification in application stores. In the evaluation, we use a dataset with 100,000 Android applications downloaded in the wild, and perform the library integrity verification on 15 libraries. Measurement results indicate that *Duet* is a useful technique to mitigate three security library-centric threats. Measurement results also provide the first empirical insight into the library integrity situation in the wild.

# 9. ACKNOWLEDGEMENTS

We thank Matthew Dering for providing our application samples. We also thank Stephen McLaughlin, Hayawardh Vijayakumar and our shepherd David Barrera for editorial comments during the writing of this paper. This work was supported by ARO W911NF-09-1-0525 (MURI), NSF CCF-1320605, and W911NF-13-1-0421 (MURI). This material is also based upon work supported by the National Science Foundation Grants No. CNS-1228700, CNS-0905447, CNS-1064944 and CNS-0643907. Any opinions, findings, and conclusions or recommendations expressed in this material are those of the authors and do not necessarily reflect the views of the National Science Foundation.

# 10. REFERENCES

[1] android-apktool. http://code.google.com/p/android-apktool/.

[2] Android open source project. http://source.android.com.

[3] AntiVirus Security. https://play.google.com/store/apps/details?id=com.antivirus.

[4] Bionic. https://github.com/android/platform\_bionic.

[5] Kaspersky Internet Security for Android. http://www.kaspersky.com/android-security.

[6] Proguard. Available at: http://proguard.sourceforge.net.

[7] Soot: a java optimization framework. Available at: http://www.sable.mcgill.ca/soot/.

[8] Watson library. http://grepcode.com/file/repo1.maven.org/maven2/com.octo.android.robospice/robospice-motivations/1.2.0/android/support/v4/app/Watson.java.

[9] Zebra crossing (zxing). https://github.com/zxing/zxing.

[10] ANDROID OPEN SOURCE PROJECT. .dex - dalvik executable format, Nov 2007. http://source.android.com/devices/tech/dalvik/dex-format.html.

[11] ANTILVL. android cracking: Antilvl, 2013. Available at: http://androidcracking.blogspot.com/p/antilvl_01.html.

[12] CHAN, P., HUI, L., AND YIU, S. Droidchecker: analyzing android applications for capability leak. In *Proceedings of the fifth ACM conference on Security and Privacy in Wireless and Mobile Networks* (2012), ACM, pp. 125–136.

[13] CHIN, E., FELT, A., GREENWOOD, K., AND WAGNER, D. Analyzing inter-application communication in android. In *Proceedings of the 9th international conference on Mobile systems, applications, and services* (2011), ACM.

[14] CRAVENS, A. A demographic and business model analysis of today's app developer. Available at: http://appdevelopersalliance.org/.

[15] CRUSSELL, J., GIBLER, C., AND CHEN, H. Attack of the clones: Detecting cloned applications on android markets. *Computer Security–ESORICS 2012* (2012), 37–54.

[16] CRUSSELL, J., GIBLER, C., AND CHEN, H. Andarwin: Scalable detection of semantically similar android applications. In *Computer Security–ESORICS 2013*. Springer, 2013.

[17] EGELE, M., KRUEGEL, C., KIRDA, E., AND VIGNA, G. Pios: Detecting privacy leaks in ios applications. In *Proceedings of the Network and Distributed System Security Symposium* (2011).

[18] ENCK, W., GILBERT, P., CHUN, B., COX, L., JUNG, J., McDANIEL, P., AND SHETH, A. Taintdroid: an information-flow tracking system for realtime privacy monitoring on smartphones. In *Proceedings of the 9th USENIX conference on Operating systems design and implementation* (2010), pp. 1–6.

[19] ENCK, W., OCTEAU, D., McDANIEL, P., AND CHAUDHURI, S. A study of android application security. In *Proceedings of the 20th USENIX Security Symposium* (2011), vol. 2011.

[20] ENCK, W., ONGTANG, M., AND McDANIEL, P. On lightweight mobile phone application certification. In *Proceedings of the 16th ACM conference on Computer and communications security* (2009), ACM.

[21] FUCHS, A., CHAUDHURI, A., AND FOSTER, J. Scandroid: Automated security certification of android applications. *Manuscript, Univ. of Maryland* (2009).

[22] GARTNER. Android and samsung dominate the phone market in q1. Available at: http://www.engadget.com/2013/05/14/gartner-android-samsung-q1-2013/.

[23] GIBLER, C., CRUSSELL, J., ERICKSON, J., AND CHEN, H. Androidleaks: automatically detecting potential privacy leaks in android applications on a large scale. *Trust and Trustworthy Computing* (2012), 291–307.

[24] GOOGLE. Google Play In-app Billing. https://developer.android.com/google/play/billing/index.html?hl=en-Us.

[25] GOOGLE INC. Andriod Support Library. http://developer.android.com/tools/support-library/index.html.

[26] GOOGLE INC. Lvl: License verification library. http://developer.android.com/google/play/licensing/index.html.

[27] GOOGLE INC. Release Notes - Google Mobile Ads SDK. https://developers.google.com/mobile-ads-sdk/docs/rel-notes.

[28] GRACE, M., ZHOU, W., JIANG, X., AND SADEGHI, A. Unsafe exposure analysis of mobile in-app advertisements. In *Proceedings of the fifth ACM conference on Security and Privacy in Wireless and Mobile Networks* (2012), ACM.

[29] GRACE, M., ZHOU, Y., WANG, Z., AND JIANG, X. Systematic detection of capability leaks in stock android smartphones. In *Proceedings of the 19th Annual Symposium on Network and Distributed System Security* (2012).

[30] GRACE, M., ZHOU, Y., ZHANG, Q., ZOU, S., AND JIANG, X. Riskranker: scalable and accurate zero-day android malware detection. In *Proceedings of the 10th international conference on Mobile systems, applications, and services* (2012), ACM.

[31] GRIFFIN, K., SCHNEIDER, S., HU, X., AND CHIUEH, T.-C. Automatic generation of string signatures for malware detection. In *Recent Advances in Intrusion Detection (RAID)* (2009), Springer.

[32] GUILFANOV, I. Fast Library Identification and Recognition Technology (1997). https://www.hex-rays.com/products/ida/tech/flirt.shtml.

[33] JIANG, L., MISHERGHI, G., SU, Z., AND GLONDU, S. Deckard: Scalable and accurate tree-based detection of code clones. In *Proceedings of the 29th international conference on Software Engineering* (2007), IEEE Computer Society.

[34] LEONTIADIS, I., EFSTRATIOU, C., PICONE, M., AND MASCOLO, C. Don't kill my ads!: balancing privacy in an ad-supported mobile application market. In *Proceedings of the Twelfth Workshop on Mobile Computing Systems & Applications* (2012), ACM, p. 2.

[35] MCMILLAN, C., GRECHANIK, M., AND POSHYVANYK, D. Detecting similar software applications. In *Software Engineering (ICSE), 2012 34th International Conference on* (2012), IEEE.

[36] MEYER, J., REYNAUD, D., AND KHARON, I. Jasmin home page. http://jasmin.sourceforge.net/, 2004.

[37] OCTEAU, D., JHA, S., AND McDANIEL, P. Retargeting Android Applications to Java Bytecode. In *Proceedings of the 20th International Symposium on the Foundations of Software Engineering* (November 2012).

[38] ONGTANG, M., McLAUGHLIN, S., ENCK, W., AND McDANIEL, P. Semantically Rich Application-Centric Security in Android. In *2009 Annual Computer Security Applications Conference* (2009), IEEE.

[39] PEARCE, P., FELT, A., NUNEZ, G., AND WAGNER, D. Addroid: Privilege separation for applications and advertisers in android. In *Proceedings of AsiaCCS* (2012).

[40] POEPLAU, S., FRATANTONIO, Y., BIANCHI, A., KRUEGEL, C., AND VIGNA, G. Execute this! analyzing unsafe and malicious dynamic code loading in android applications. In *Proc. of the 19th Annual Network and Distributed System Security Symposium (NDSS)* (2014).

[41] SHEKHAR, S., DIETZ, M., AND WALLACH, D. Adsplit: separating smartphone advertising from applications. In *Proceedings of the 21st USENIX conference on Security symposium* (2012), USENIX Association.

[42] STEVENS, R., GIBLER, C., CRUSSELL, J., ERICKSON, J., AND CHEN, H. Investigating user privacy in android ad libraries. In *Proceedings of IEEE Mobile Security Technologies (MoST)* (2012).

[43] ZHANG, Y., XUE, H., WEI, T., AND SONG, D. Ad vulna: A vulnaggressive (vulnerable & aggressive) adware threatening millions. FireEye Blog, http://www.fireeye.com/blog/technical/2013/10/ad-vulna-a-vulnaggressive-vulnerable-aggressive-adware-threatening-millions.html, 2013.

[44] ZHANG, Y., XUE, H., WEI, T., AND SONG, D. Monitoring vulnaggressive apps on google play'. FireEye Blog, http://www.fireeye.com/blog/technical/2013/11/monitoring-vulnaggressive-apps-on-google-play.html, November 2013.

[45] ZHOU, W., ZHOU, Y., JIANG, X., AND NING, P. Detecting repackaged smartphone applications in third-party android marketplaces. In *Proceedings of the second ACM conference on Data and Application Security and Privacy* (2012), ACM.

[46] ZHOU, Y., AND JIANG, X. Dissecting android malware: Characterization and evolution. In *Security and Privacy (SP), 2012 IEEE Symposium on* (2012), IEEE, pp. 95–109.

[47] ZHOU, Y., WANG, Z., ZHOU, W., AND JIANG, X. Hey, you, get off of my market: Detecting malicious apps in official and alternative android markets. In *Proc. of the 19th Annual Network and Distributed System Security Symposium (NDSS)* (2012).

# GroupTie: Toward Hidden Collusion Group Discovery in App Stores

Zhen Xie
Dept of Computer Science and Engineering
The Pennsylvania State University
zhenxie@cse.psu.edu

Sencun Zhu
Dept of Computer Science and Engineering &
College of Information Sciences and Technology
The Pennsylvania State University
szhu@cse.psu.edu

## ABSTRACT

The current centralized application (or app) markets provide convenient ways to distribute mobile apps. Their vendors maintain rating systems, which allow customers to leave ratings and reviews. Since positive ratings and reviews can lead to more downloads/installations and hence more monetary benefit, the rating systems have become a target of manipulation by some collusion groups hired by app developers. In this paper, we thoroughly analyze the features of hidden collusion groups and propose a novel method called *Group-Tie* to narrow down the suspect list of collusive reviewers for further investigation by app stores. As members of a hidden collusion group have to work together more frequently and their ratings often deviate more from apps' quality, collusive actions will enhance their relation over time. We build a relation graph named *tie graph* and detect collusion groups by applying graph clustering. Simulation results show that the precision of GroupTie approaches to 99.70% and the recall is about 91.50%. We also apply our method to detect hidden collusion groups among the reviewers of 89 apps in Apple's China App Store. A large number of reviewers are discovered belonging to a large collusion group and several small groups.

## Categories and Subject Descriptors

K.6.5 [**Management of Computing and Information Systems**]: [Security and Protection]; D.2.8 [**Software Engineering**]: Metrics

## Keywords

App Stores; Collusion Groups; Tie Graph; Correlation Coefficient; Clusters

## 1. INTRODUCTION

To help customers find high quality apps, app stores like Apple's App Store, Google Play allow customers to write

*WiSec'14*, July 23–25, 2014, Oxford, UK.
Copyright 2014 ACM 978-1-4503-2972-9/14/07 ...$15.00.
http://dx.doi.org/10.1145/2627393.2627409.

ratings and reviews for the apps they have installed, and display average ratings and list reviews in their stores. Under this centralized environment, ratings and reviews are critical information to distinguish high quality apps from low quality ones. Positive ratings and reviews will potentially lead to more downloads/installations and more monetary benefit. Moreover, app store vendors often show various ranking charts on the front page and apps with higher ranking will attract more attentions and more downloads. Specifically, their ranking algorithms [8] take review ratings as an important factor. As such, often one would have the incentive to promote one's own app while demoting the competitors' apps. In reality, this could be achieved through hiring a group of users to give very high ratings (e.g., 5) to one's own app while giving very low ratings (e.g., 1) to the competing ones.

Recently, a number of companies have been found conducting their businesses on promoting apps (e.g., itunestop, appqibu). As advertised in their websites (www.itunestop.com[1], www.appqibu.com), these companies claim that they are able to move the ranking of an app into top 5, top 10, or top 50 in a few hours, subject to how much one is willing to pay. The way they achieve this goal is by hiring a large number of users or registering multiple accounts that collectively offer false reviews and ratings. In fact, to combat these fraud apps reviews and ratings, app stores have released an announcement on February 2012 warning the developer not to manipulate the App Store chart rankings [11]. Indeed, when we looked at the top 10 apps in Apple Store China on May 21, 2012, we found two of them clearly had their ratings manipulated. Clearly, as the key part of the smart phone ecosystem, the centralized marketplaces could be damaged by such collusive misbehavior.

In this paper, we aim to discover hidden collusion groups and systematically analyze the problems in App Stores. Specifically, we are searching for answers to the following questions: *Do hidden collusion group actually exist in current app stores? what are the characteristics of collusion groups? how to discover the hidden collusion groups efficiently and accurately?* These questions are concerned by platform vendors. Correct answers will guide the vendors to clean up app stores and catch developers who have manipulated the feedbacks. It also can help customers decide whether to trust ratings and reviews of an app. As for developers, it is useful to monitor whether their apps' feedbacks are manipulated by opponents or not.

---

[1]This website has been closed recently.

Table 1: Confusion matrix of rating behaviors

| Quality \ Rating | Positive | Negative |
|---|---|---|
| High | Honest rating | Demoted rating |
| Low | Promoted rating | Honest rating |

To discover collusion groups, the most difficult task is to identify group members. Salehi-Abari et al. [16] defined collusion as "A collaborative activity that gives to members of a colluding group benefits they would not be able to gain as individuals". The definition shows two essential characteristics of collusion groups. One is that members of a collusion group need to work together to fulfill their purposes. They have to rate together more frequently than independent reviewers because they only hold a small portion of total accounts. The other one is that their ratings consistently deviate to the same side from apps' actual quality; for example, group members usually provide high ratings to promote an app or low ratings to demote it. But for honest reviewers, their deviations are distributed more randomly.

Based on the above observations, we propose a novel method called *GroupTie* to identify group members. We first prove that correlation coefficient between the variation of average ratings in a time period (e.g., weekly) and the variation of its reviewer numbers in each period across different versions is equal to zero if all the reviewers rate independently. Then, we design a method to estimate apps' quality considering their correlation coefficient. We further calculate the pairwise tie strength between users and build a tie graph to represent reviewers' relation. By applying graph clustering on tie graph, we can classify all the nodes to several clusters which are considered to be collusion groups. Simulation results show that the precision of GroupTie approaches to 99.70% and the recall is about 91.50%.

We have further applied our method to discover collusive reviewers in Apple app store. On May 21th, 2012, we collected 200 apps from its China market, including 100 top paid apps and 100 top free apps. GroupTie identified $8,853$ reviewers among all $818,545$ reviewers as possible collusion group members, which account for 1.08%. We also find that 3,677 reviewers belong to a large group, which contains $2,652$ members, and several small groups.

## 2. PRELIMINARIES

### 2.1 Rating Behaviors

For honest reviewers, we assume their ratings are *independent*. An independent rating means its variance is independent of other ratings. As for collusion group members, their ratings are correlated and usually deviate far away from the quality. For example, most of their ratings are the same, irrespective of the app's actual quality.

All rating behaviors can be classified into three types w.r.t. apps' quality. As shown in Table 1, they are *honest rating*, *promoted rating* and *demoted rating*. Honest rating, denoted by $H$, is to leave ratings around apps' actual quality. Demoted rating, denoted by $D$, is to rate much below apps' actual quality. Promoted rating, denoted by $P$, is to rate much above than apps' actual quality.

The above rating behaviors form the basic behaviors set $\{H, D, P\}$. We define *role* as a combination of different behaviors and the possible roles are enumerated in Table 2. Every reviewer chooses a strategy on what kind of role she/he will follow each time. Similar to the player's strategy in game theory [4], there are two types of strategies. One is the pure strategy, which means that a reviewer chooses a specific behavior from the behaviors set to follow. For example, to promote an app, the reviewer chooses a behavior like $P$ and leaves a high rating. The other type of strategy is a mix strategy, which means that the reviewer chooses actions based on probabilities. For example, in the same scenario, the reviewer may choose the behavior $H$ with probability 20%, $D$ with probability 10% and $P$ with probability 70%. Clearly, the pure strategy is a special case of the mix strategy. In this paper, we adopt the pure strategy to simplify the definition of attack models.

### 2.2 Attack Model

To promote an app, members of a collusion group will collaborate and rate high no matter how bad its real quality is. Similarly, to demote an app, they work together to provide low ratings. What is more, some members could randomly act as honest reviewers to hide their purposes. These collective rating actions neglecting apps' real quality are called *collusion attacks*. According to the roles described in Section 2.1, the possible roles for collusion group members are $\{(0,0,P), (0,D,0), (0,D,P), (H,0,P), (H,D,0), (H,D,P)\}$, as shown in Table. 2.

In this paper, we classify all the collusion attacks into three types: promotion only attack, demotion only attack and orchestrated attack.

*Promotion only attack (PoA):* The collusion groups only promote apps' rating by providing higher ratings than apps' quality. The roles of group members could be $\{(0,0,P), (H,0,P)\}$.

*Demotion only attack (DoA)* The collusion groups only demote apps' rating by providing lower ratings than the real quality. The roles of group members could be $\{(0,D,0), (H,D,0)\}$.

*Orchestrated attack (OA)* The collusion groups promote the target apps and demote the opponents of the target apps at the same time. The possible roles of group members are $\{(0,0,P), (0,D,0), (0,D,P), (H,0,P), (H,D,0), (H,D,P)\}$.

For example, as shown in Fig. 1, reivewer1 and reviewer2 take roles $(H,0,P)$ and $(0,0,P)$, respectively and they together perform PoA against App2. Reviewer3 and reviewer4 take roles $(H,D,P)$ and $(0,D,0)$, respectively and they together perform DoA against App4. Reviewer5 and reviewer6 take roles $(H,D,P)$ and $(0,D,P)$, respectively and they perform both PoA and DoA. All the reviewers can form a group to single perform an OA.

In this paper, we aim to discover attackers that form collusion groups to achieve their goals like raising average scores. We do not target at detecting other types of attackers like independent attackers, one-time attackers, or random attackers. Independent attacker is the reviewer that attacks an app on his/her own. Considering the massive number of reviewers for an app, independent attack has little influence on the app's overall score. One-time attackers are those promoting or demoting an app only once. For example, a developer might ask her friends and relatives to promote her app. Theoretically, there could also be attacks launched by a collusion group that behaviors randomly. For example, they may demote an app in the first week and then promote

Table 2: Possible reviewer roles

| role | Role description |
|------|------------------|
| (0, 0, 0) | A reviewer who never provides ratings. |
| (0, 0, P) | A reviewer who always provides positive ratings. |
| (0, D, 0) | A reviewer who always provides negative ratings. |
| (0, D, P) | A reviewer who will only provide positive ratings to his partners' apps and negative ratings to his opponents' apps. |
| (H, 0, 0) | An honest reviewer. |
| (H, 0, P) | A reviewer who will provide positive ratings to his partners' apps and honest ratings to others. |
| (H, D, 0) | A reviewer who will provide negative ratings to his opponents' apps and honest ratings to others. |
| (H, D, P) | A reviewer who will provide positive ratings to his partners' apps, negative ratings to his opponents' apps and honest ratings to other apps. |

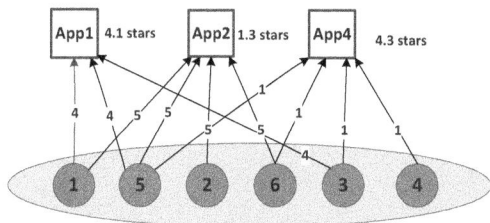

Figure 1: Collusion Attack. App1 and App4 are high quality apps and App2 is a low quality app. Several groups have been hired by the developers to promote App2 or hired by the competitors of App4 to demote App4.

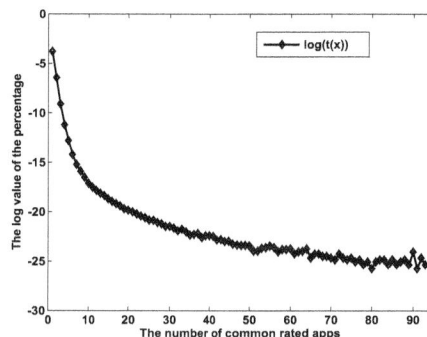

Figure 2: The probability of co-rating apps. Here the $x$-axis represents the number of commonly rated apps, and the $y$-axis represents $ln(t(x))$ where $t(x) = \frac{\#\text{pairs of reviewers co-rating } x \text{ apps}}{\text{total pairs of reviewers}}$

it in the following weeks, for whatever reasons. We will not address these types of attacks in this work.

Note that in our work we do not claim the detection results are 100% accurate due to the extreme difficulty of getting the ground truth. Rather, our algorithm output can provide a much-narrowed-down suspect list for further investigation by app stores. App stores may use additional evidences which we do not have (e.g., information about reviewer accounts) to further pinpoint the abused apps and the collusion groups.

## 3. GROUPTIE

### 3.1 Overview

User accounts in app stores (e.g., Google Play or Apple iTunes) are bound with hardware devices (e.g., smartphones or tablets), so collusion groups are only likely to account for a small portion among all user accounts. Hence, they often have to collaborate in order to impact the rating of an app significantly. More specifically, their collaboration has two essential characteristics. First, for either promotion or demotion, they provide similar ratings deliberately and collectively. Their ratings significantly deviate from the real quality in the same way, e.g., giving 5 to low quality apps of 1 or 2 stars or the other way around. But for an honest reviewer, his ratings' deviations are likely to be distributed randomly. Even though for some special apps, an individual user's ratings may have similar deviation skewness with collusion group members, such a phenomenon would not happen for most of the apps.

Second, the collaboration of collusion group members could occur many times; consequently, they have a much higher probability to rate the same set of apps than any other individual reviewers. In general, co-rating (i.e., rating the same apps) is not common. To see this, we collected 553,005 reviewers from Apple's China App Store and we found that 0.163% pairs of the reviewers had two commonly rated apps and this number decreases to 0.012% for three commonly rated apps. As illustrated in Fig. 2, co-rating probabilities decrease sharply with the increase of the number of commonly rated apps.

Because of the above characteristics, the relations of group members are increasingly strengthened when they co-rate more and more apps, and eventually their relations become very close. Detection of group members is to detect such close relations. Here we outline the three challenges to be solved for collusion group discovery.

- First, how to define and quantify users' relations and model their rating skewness?
- Second, how to discover collusion groups from pairwise relations?
- Third, how to improve detection accuracy under the influence of biased reviewers, adaptive attackers, version updating, etc.? For example, biased reviewers might be misidentified as attackers, hence decreasing the precision (See Section. 3.2). Adaptive attackers might try hard to disguise their roles and avoid being exposed. It would raise the recall (See Section. 3.2). Besides, developers usually update their apps and upload new versions for downloading. Some of the versions might include good features and thus will receive better reviews. Some of them might bear bugs acci-

dently and get low ratings. This will increase the complexity of discover collusion attacks (See Section.3.3.2).

Next, we propose a model to deal with the above three challenges. We borrow the concept of *tie* [10] to represent the relation between two reviewers and construct *tie graph* to represent the relations among all reviewers. Then, we propose a novel method to estimate apps' quality. Finally, given tie graphs, we apply a *k*-clique communities clustering algorithm to discover collusion groups.

## 3.2  Tie and Tie Graph

DEFINITION 1. *Tie is the relation between two reviewers.*

In this paper, *tie* represents the possible relation between two reviewers, where the term *relation* means the probability of two reviewers belonging to the same collusion group.

DEFINITION 2. *Deviation measures how much a rating deviates from an app's real quality.*

Formally, let the lower case letter denote a reviewer and the upper case letter denote an app. $R(i, K)$ represents the rating of reviewer $i$ to app $K$ and $Q(K)$ denotes the real quality of app $K$ (we will show how to estimate $Q(K)$ later). $Dev(i, K)$ denotes the deviation of reviewer $i$'s rating to the quality of app $K$ and it follows Eq. 1.

$$Dev(i, K) = \begin{cases} 0 & R(i, K) \text{ does not exist} \\ R(i, K) - Q(K) & \text{Otherwise} \end{cases} \quad (1)$$

DEFINITION 3. *Tie Strength measures the closeness of a relation.*

The tie strength between reviewer $i$ and reviewer $j$ is denoted by $Tie(i, j)$, which follows Eq. 2

$$Tie(i, j) = \sum_{K=0}^{N} Dev(i, K) * Dev(j, K), \quad (2)$$

where $N$ is the number of commonly rated apps by $i$ and $j$. For members of a collusion group, their tie strengths would be high positive values due to their common rating actions. Based on tie strength, we classify ties into three types: *strong ties*, *weak ties* and *absent ties* by setting a tie threshold (e.g., 16 in our experiments). A strong positive tie has tie strength larger than the threshold, which indicates attraction between two reviewers. A strong negative tie has tie strength lower than the negative threshold (e.g., -16), which indicates repulsion between two reviewers. Weak ties are neutral ties with low tie strength (e.g., between -16 and 16), which indicate the relation is uncertain between two reviewers. Absent ties means the relation information between two reviewers is missing.

DEFINITION 4. *Tie graph is a weighted undirected graph which contains all the pairwise relations among all reviewers. The vertex set is all the reviewers and the edges are the ties between them.*

For example, as shown in Fig. 3 and Fig. 4, four reviewers rate a high quality app and a low quality one, respectively. Among them, two reviewers are honest and the other two are members of a collusion group. Honest reviewers give

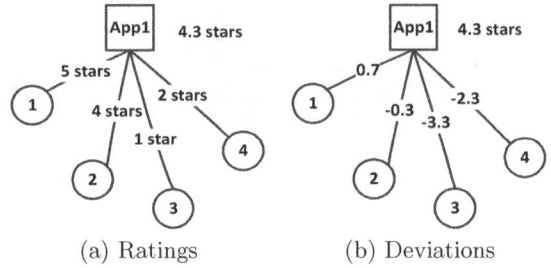

(a) Ratings                (b) Deviations

Figure 3: DoA toward an app with quality 4.3 stars.

ratings around the quality, and collusive ones perform promotion and demotion, respectively. We can calculate the tie strength for each pair of them.

By following Eq. 2, we can calculate the tie strengths in Fig. 3.

$$Tie(1, 2) = -0.21 \quad Tie(1, 3) = -2.31 \quad Tie(1, 4) = -1.61$$
$$Tie(2, 3) = -0.99 \quad Tie(2, 4) = 0.69 \quad Tie(3, 4) = 7.59$$

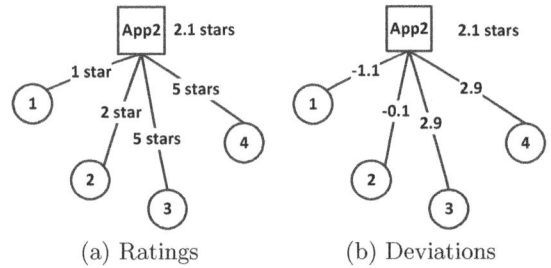

(a) Ratings                (b) Deviations

Figure 4: PoA toward an app with quality 2.1 stars.

Similarly, we can get the tie strengths in Fig. 4.

$$Tie(1, 2) = 0.11 \quad Tie(1, 3) = -3.19 \quad Tie(1, 4) = -3.19$$
$$Tie(2, 3) = -0.29 \quad Tie(2, 4) = -0.29 \quad Tie(3, 4) = 8.41$$

Finally, by combining the tie strengths generated in both figures, we can get the overall tie strengths between each pair of the four reviewers. We can further generate the tie graph shown in Fig. 5.

$$Tie(1, 2) = -0.1 \quad Tie(1, 3) = -5.5 \quad Tie(1, 4) = -4.8$$
$$Tie(2, 3) = -1.28 \quad Tie(2, 4) = 0.4 \quad Tie(3, 4) = 16$$

Obviously, the tie between two members in a collusion group is the strongest and the other ties can be considered to be weak ties compared to the strong positive ties.

In practice, biased reviewers who always rate high/low may form two different types of strong ties: one case is that when they happen to rate the same set of apps with other biased reviewers, and the other case is when they rate the same set of apps as a collusion group do. In the first case, these biased reviewers form a group. Considering the chance of co-rating illustrated in Fig. 2, the size of the group formed by chance will not be very large, and we can easily filter them out by the algorithm proposed in Section. 3.4. In reality, biased reviewers are prone to rate popular apps. However, popular apps are usually not the targets of collusion groups because popular apps have many more reviewers than a collusion group has. Thus, the attack has little influence. But theoretically, the second case could happen and

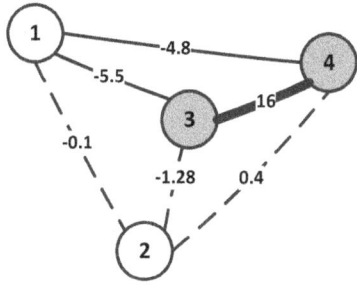

Figure 5: The tie graph including all the nodes. Thick solid line represents a strong positive tie, thin solid line represents a strong negative tie, and dashed lines represent weak ties.

these biased reviewers would be misidentified as attackers. This case will cause precision to decrease. However, if we further check other features mentioned in Section. 4.2.1, like whether they have similar review history, consecutive reviewer IDs as attackers, other type of account information, biased reviewers can also be identified and removed from suspect lists.

On the other hand, if knowing GroupTie beforehand, some attackers might choose adaptive strategies to avoid forming strong ties. For example, each attack of a collusion group will increase tie strength between any two group members. For any two of them, they have to rate another app and leave two totally different ratings (i.e., one is high and the other is low) to annihilate the past impact on tie strength. As a result, if a collusion group has $n$ members, after co-rating a single app, they have to rate $\binom{n}{2}$ different apps to reset their tie strengths caused by such a co-rating, which is very difficult to execute in reality. For example, if a collusion group has 200 members, they have to choose another 20100 apps and build negative ties to cancel out previous positive ties. This would remarkably increase the cost of their organization and what is worse, this strategy could also lead to the risk of exposing their roles.

## 3.3 App Quality Estimation

To calculate tie strength, we need to know apps' real quality. However, in reality, app's quality measurement is subjective, and its score displayed in the app store could have been severely skewed by attacks. To estimate apps' quality, our idea is to first detect the abnormality of the rating behavior for an app and then remove such abnormality. In this section, we first prove that there is no linear relation between the average rating and the number of reviewers in each period (e.g., in each week) when no attacks exist. Then, we propose a method to estimate apps' quality.

### 3.3.1 Correlation Coefficient

Correlation coefficient is a measurement of the linear relationship between two variables. If it is a positive value, the increase of one variable is likely to lead to the increase of the other one, and so is the decrease. That is, their variances are synchronous. Similarly, if the value is a negative one, their variances are opposite. Here we adopt Pearson's correlation coefficient [15] to measure the linear relationship between two variables. It is denoted by $r(Y, X)$ for variables

$Y$ and $X$, as shown in Eq. 3.

$$r(Y, X) = \frac{Cov(Y, X)}{\sigma_Y * \sigma_X} = \frac{E(Y - u_Y)(X - u_X)}{\sigma_Y * \sigma_X}, \quad (3)$$

where $Cov(Y, X)$ denotes the covariance of $X$ and $Y$. $u_X$ and $u_Y$ are the mean values of variables $X$ and $Y$, and $\sigma_X$ and $\sigma_Y$ represent the variances of $X$ and $Y$, respectively.

In this work, we divide time into periods of certain unit, e.g., weeks. Suppose an app has been updated a few times, and each version $k$ has the lifetime of $kn$ periods. Let $\bar{Y}_{ki}$ be its average rating for period $i$ w.r.t. version $k$. Its average ratings are denoted by $\bar{Y}_k = \{\bar{Y}_{k1}, \bar{Y}_{k2}, ..., \bar{Y}_{kn}\}$ with $u_{\bar{Y}_k}$ being the overall average. The number of reviewers during each period is a random variable denoted by $X_k = \{X_{k1}, X_{k2}, ..., X_{kn}\}$ with the overall average $u_{X_k}$. Then, the correlation coefficient between average rating and number of reviews in each period is $r(\bar{Y}_k, X_k)$.

### 3.3.2 Correlation Coefficient in Ideal Scenario

Intuitively, if all the reviewers of an app rate independently, then the average rating by one group of its reviewers should be about the same to that by another group if the app's quality does not change (i.e., there is no version update). In other words, the increase or decrease of reviewers' number should not change the average rating. From a different perspective, since each rating reflects the app's quality, it can be considered as a sample on app's quality. As these samples are independent and reflect the same app's quality, it is reasonable to assume they follow the same distribution and this scenario is named the *ideal scenario*.

In the ideal scenario, it can be proven that no linear correlation exists between the average rating (sample mean) and the number of reviewers (sample size). Thus, we have the following theorem.

THEOREM 1. *If the ratings of an app w.r.t. version $k$ are fully independent and have identical distribution, the correlation coefficient between average rating $\bar{Y}_k$ and number of its reviewers $X_k$ in each period is equal to zero when $X_k$ is large enough.*

PROOF. Let us first divide time into periods of certain unit, e.g., weeks, and suppose there are totally $n$ periods for an app. The average rating of each period is a random variable denoted by $\bar{Y}_k = \{\bar{Y}_{k1}, \bar{Y}_{k2}, ..., \bar{Y}_{kn}\}$. The mean value of $\bar{Y}_k$ is denoted by $u_{\bar{Y}_k}$. The number of reviewers during each period is a random variable denoted by $X_k = \{X_{k1}, X_{k2}, ..., X_{kn}\}$ with mean value $u_{X_k}$.

Let $Y_{ki} = \{Y_{ki_1}, Y_{ki_2}, ..., Y_{ki_m}\}$ denote the sequence of independent and identical distributed ratings in the $i$th period having mean $u$ and variance $\sigma^2$. $\bar{Y}_{ki}$ is the average rating in this period, which is expressed in Eq. 4. The number of reviewers in $i$th period is denoted by $Y_{ki}$.

$$\bar{Y}_{ki} = \frac{Y_{ki_1} + Y_{ki_2} + ... + Y_{ki_m}}{m} \quad (4)$$

According to the central limit theorem, $\bar{Y}_{ki}$ follows a normal distribution $N(u, \frac{\sigma}{\sqrt{m}})$ given that $m$ is large enough. That is to say, if $Z_{ki} = \bar{Y}_{ki}|X_{ki}$, $Z_{ki}$ will follow a normal distribution $N(u, \frac{\sigma}{\sqrt{m}})$ and $u = E(Z_{ki}) = E(\bar{Y}_{ki}) = E(\bar{Y}_k) = u_{\bar{Y}_k}$. The probability density of $Z_{ki}$ is denoted by $f(Z_{ki})$

157

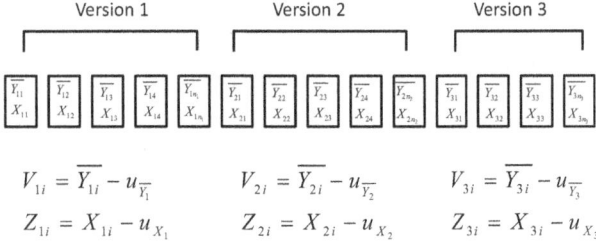

$$V_{1i} = \overline{Y_{1i}} - u_{\overline{Y_1}} \qquad V_{2i} = \overline{Y_{2i}} - u_{\overline{Y_2}} \qquad V_{3i} = \overline{Y_{3i}} - u_{\overline{Y_3}}$$

$$Z_{1i} = X_{1i} - u_{X_1} \qquad Z_{2i} = X_{2i} - u_{X_2} \qquad Z_{3i} = X_{3i} - u_{X_3}$$

Figure 6: One example of version updates.

and $f(Z_{ki}) = f(\overline{Y}_{ki}|X_{ki})$.

$$
\begin{aligned}
Cov(\overline{Y}_k, X_k) &= E[(\overline{Y}_k - u_{\overline{Y}_k})(X_k - u_{X_k})] \\
&= E(\overline{Y}_k X_k) - u_{X_k} E\overline{Y}_k - u_{\overline{Y}_k} EX_k + u_{X_k} u_{\overline{Y}_k} \\
&= E(\overline{Y}_k X_k) - u_{X_k} u_{\overline{Y}_k}
\end{aligned}
\tag{5}
$$

$$
\begin{aligned}
E(\overline{Y}_k X_k) &= E(X_k(\overline{Y}_k|X_k)) \\
&= \sum_{i=1}^{n}(X_{ki} p(X_{ki}) \sum_{j=1}^{m}((\overline{Y}_{kj}|X_{ki})p(\overline{Y}_{kj}|X_{ki}))) \\
&= \sum_{i=1}^{n}(X_{ki} p(X_{ki})(\overline{Y}_{ki}|X_{ki})p(\overline{Y}_{ki}|X_{ki})) \\
&= \sum_{i=1}^{n}(X_{ki} p(X_{ki})) \int_{Z_{ki}}(Z_{ki} f(Z_{ki})) dZ_{ki} \\
&= \sum_{i=1}^{n}(X_{ki} p(X_{ki}) E Z_{ki}) \\
&= u_{\overline{Y}_k} \sum_{i=1}^{n}(X_{ki} p(X_{ki})) \\
&= u_{\overline{Y}_k} u_{X_k}
\end{aligned}
\tag{6}
$$

Hence, $Cov(\overline{Y}_k, X_k) = E(\overline{Y}_k X_k) - u_{X_k} u_{\overline{Y}_k} = 0$.

Furthermore, according to Eq. 3, Pearson's correlation coefficient $r(\overline{Y}_k, X_k) = \frac{Cov(\overline{Y}_k, X_k)}{\sigma_{\overline{Y}_k} * \sigma_{X_k}} = 0$.

$\square$

In practice, the quality of an app might be changed due to version updates. As a result, the average rating of one group is probably different to another group who rates over another version. For example, before updating a version with good features, the developer did a lot of advertising. Now for the new version, its average rating, even without promotion attack, could be improved. Another example is mentioned at the beginning that a version of an app is updated with bugs. Honest reviewers will leave low ratings to this version even though reviewers will rate high to other versions. In this cases, the correlation coefficient between average ratings and number of reviewers across different versions is not always equal to zero. To eliminate the influence of version updates, we will need to normalize the average ratings. Specifically, we will redefine correlation coefficient as the relation between the *variation* of average ratings and the *variation* of its reviewer numbers in each period across different versions.

Fig. 6 shows how to calculate the variation of average ratings and the variation of reviewer quantities. Here, an app has been updated three times and thus it has three versions. For both version 1 and version 2, reviewers rated the app for five weeks. For version 3, only four weeks have ratings. Each rectangular in the figure represents one week. We first calculate the average ratings (e.g., $\overline{Y}_{11}$ for the first week of version 1) and the number of reviewers in each week (e.g., $X_{11}$). For version 1, we then calculate the overall average of the weekly average ratings (e.g., $u_{\overline{Y}_1} = (\overline{Y}_{11} + \overline{Y}_{12} + \overline{Y}_{13} + \overline{Y}_{14} + \overline{Y}_{15})/5$) and the overall average of weekly

Table 3: The correlation coefficient(CC) of top ten apps. Apps denoted by "NA" has lifetime less than nine weeks as of May 21, 2012 and they do not have enough data to calculate a correlation coefficient.

| Rank | App Id | App Name | CC |
|---|---|---|---|
| 1 | 483583569 | Mobilocation | 0.414 |
| 2 | 362949845 | Fruit Ninja | -0.175 |
| 3 | 449735650 | Where's My Water? | 0.023 |
| 4 | 439615801 | Plants vs. Zombies(Chinese version) | NA |
| 5 | 414664715 | Order & Chaos @Online | -0.008 |
| 6 | 491231653 | Richman 4 fun | -0.088 |
| 7 | 400973408 | Asphalt 6: A-drenaline | 0.036 |
| 8 | 508720652 | Quick Call Divert | NA |
| 9 | 435728194 | Shou Ji Ling Sheng | 0.249 |
| 10 | 449595696 | Office Assistant Pro | 0.082 |

reviewer numbers (e.g., $u_{X_1} = (X_{11} + X_{12} + X_{13} + X_{14} + X_{15})/5$). Let $V_{ki}$ be the variation of the average rating in period $i$ w.r.t. version $k$, then $V_{ki} = \overline{Y}_{ki} - u_{\overline{Y}_k}$. Similarly, we can derive $Z_{ki}$, which is the variation of the number of reviewers in period $i$ w.r.t. version $k$, as $Z_{ki} = X_{ki} - u_{X_k}$.

Formally, let $V$ represent the variation of average ratings of all the versions where $V = \{V_{11}, V_{12}, ..., V_{ki}, ...\}$ and $Z$ represents the variation of reviewer numbers of all the versions where $Z = \{Z_{11}, Z_{12}, ..., Z_{ki}, ...\}$. Based on Theorem 1, we can further derive the following lemma.

LEMMA 1. *If the ratings of an app are fully independent and have identical distribution, the correlation coefficient between the variation of average ratings $V$ and the variation of reviewer quantity $Z$ in each period is equal to zero.*

### 3.3.3 Correlation Coefficient in General Scenario

Unlike in the ideal scenario, in general scenario honest reviewers and collusion groups may coexist. For honest reviewers, they usually download apps and write comments after playing them for a while directly from mobile devices. Their experiences are independent and they usually do not refer to other reviews while leaving comments. Besides, even though human herding behavior [6] will influence their decision on buying an app, it has no explicit impact on review contents which express their own experience. For these reasons, the independency of user reviews are still held in general scenario. However, the existence of collusion groups will likely change the correlation coefficient of an app.

Since the correlation coefficient in the ideal scenario is equal to zero, its non-zero value in general scenarios could indicate the existence of collusion attacks as well as the type of collusion attacks (i.e., promotion or demotion). For example, for the top 10 paid apps in Apple App Store of China (as of May 21, 2012), we calculated their correlation coefficients (CC) by setting the time period to one week, as listed in Table. 3. We found that the app named "Mobilocation" (Rank #1) has the highest CC score of 0.414 and the app named "Shou Ji Ling Sheng" (rank #9) has the second highest CC score (0.249). We confirmed that these

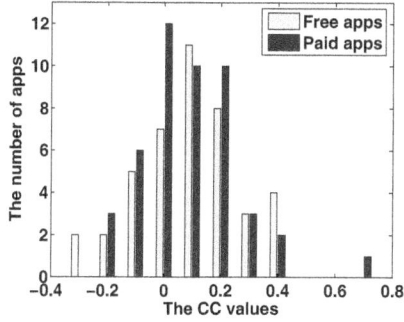

Figure 8: The distribution of CC values (rounded to nearest).

Table 4: The relation between CC value intervals and the ratio of abused apps in each interval (demoted apps indicated by *)

| CC Range | Free | Paid | Total |
|---|---|---|---|
| [0.5,1] | 0 | 1/1 | 1/1 |
| [0.4, 0.5) | 1/2 | 2/2 | 3/4 |
| [0.3, 0.4) | 4/5 | 2/2 | 6/7 |
| [0.2, 0.3) | 1/3 | 6/7 | 7/10 |
| [-0.2, 0.2) | 4/30 | 7/35 | 11/65 |
| [-1, -0.2) | 2*/2 | 0 | 2/2 |

two apps were indeed promoted because of their low quality. They were reported to abuse the rating system in some websites [17][9] and "Mobilocation"[2] has been removed from Apple App Store before May 7, 2013. We further plot the relationship between variance of weekly average rating and variance of reviewer quantities in each week for the first, second, and ninth apps, as shown in Fig. 7. From Fig. 7(a) and Fig. 7(c), it is obvious that the variation of weekly average rating of this app "Mobilocation" and "Shou Ji Ling Sheng" increase synchronously with variation of the weekly number of reviewers. However, this phenomenon does not exist in Fig. 7(b). This app did not show obvious attacks based on our checking.

We have examined the top 100 paid apps and 100 free apps (as of May 21, 2012) and filtered out those apps with lifetimes less than nine weeks (so that our result has more statistical significance). This gave us totally 89 apps and about half for each type of apps. The distributions of these apps' CC values are illustrated in Fig 8. From the shapes we can see that in both free and paid app cases, the distribution approximates to Gaussian Distribution, though skewing slightly to positive of free apps[3]. That is, while majority of the apps look normal, a good portion of them could have been attacked.

We further checked each app looking for signs of promotion or demotion (such signs are discussed in details in Section. 4.2.1). Among the 22 apps with CC larger than 0.2 and 2 apps with CC value less than -0.2, 19 apps were confirmed to be promoted and 2 apps were demoted [4]. Table 4 presents a detailed distribution of CC values for these 89 apps. We can see that large CC values indicate high possibility of attacks. Specifically, a positive CC value indicates a promotion dominating attack whereas a negative CC value indicates a demotion dominating attack.

As we discussed, CC value can reflect the abnormality of an app' rating in most of the time. However, there are

ways to manipulate it and keep it low by attackers. Some sophisticated opponents may act stealthily to avoid the fluctuation of average ratings. They have to avoid generating large amount of ratings in a short time. However, this strategy will not be able to improve average rating quickly, and it also increases their management cost. Some other attackers, for example, can demote the application in the first week of its release and then promote it in the subsequent weeks. If the strength of the promotion and defense are the same, CC of this app will be close to zero and it will not reflect the existence of attack. In these cases, attackers will not achieve their goals and have no much influence on the average ratings. Even though we cannot discover all types of collusive attackers, we can narrow down the suspicious raters as well as increase the bar of the attackers.

### 3.3.4 Apps' Quality Estimation

Normally, the square of correlation coefficient (also called *coefficient of determination*, $R^2$, or $R$ squared) is a statistical measurement of how well a regression line approximates the real data points. In our context, $R^2$ can help us determine the percentage of average rating variations that have linear relationship with rating population variations in a period. We call the average ratings of such period *abnormal ratings* because normal (honest) rating variation should have no such linear relationship with rating population variation. We aim to estimate an app' real quality by removing the impact (*not removing ratings*) from the abnormality of ratings instead of identifying which rating is abnormal. Note that in our work the goal of app quality estimation is to use estimated scores for tie strength calculation (and then collusion group discovery). We do not use estimated scores as the real scores for apps, so high estimation accuracy is not the goal (To obtain the real scores, we will need to first remove the ratings by identified collusion groups and then recalculate their scores. This is however out of the scope of our current work.) Next we introduce the detail for app quality estimation.

For an app with version $k$, the abnormal ratings cause its final rating in the app store (i.e., $R_k$) to deviate from its real quality (i.e., $Q_k$). When CC is a positive value, $R_k$ is higher than $Q_k$ and $Q_k$ is bounded between $[1, R_k]$. As shown in Fig. 9, $Q_k \in [1, R_k]$ and $R_k - 1$ is the range of $Q_k$. Here the range $R_k - Q_k$ is mainly caused by promotion attacks. The more severe the attack is, both $R^2$ and $R_k - Q_k$ will increase, and vice versa. Let $\frac{R_k - Q_k}{R_k - 1}$ be the normalized value of the range $R_k - Q_k$ indicating the severity of the attack, we can approximate it by a linear function of $R^2$; that is, $\frac{R_k - Q_k}{R_k - 1} = p * r^2(V, Z)$, where $p$ is a system parameter reflecting the linear relation between $\frac{R_k - Q_k}{R_k - 1}$ and $R^2 = r^2(V, Z)$. On the

---

[2]The app's reviews are still accessible in the iTunes through the link `http://ax.phobos.apple.com.edgesuite.net/WebObjects/MZStore.woa/wa/viewContentsUserReviews?id=xxx&pageNumber=0&sortOrdering=1&type=Purple+Software`. Make sure to change your location to China and replace xxx with an app id.

[3]One conjure is that most users are tolerant of free apps' quality. More reviewers will yield a much higher average rating and results a positive correlation coefficient.

[4]Since Apple Inc. had cleaned some of the apps and their reviews, the evidences can no longer be found online.

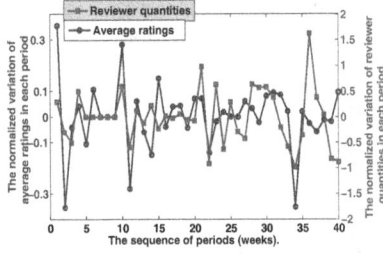

(a) App id: 483583569 (Rank #1)    (b) App id: 362949845 (Rank #2)    (c) App id: 435728194 (Rank #9)

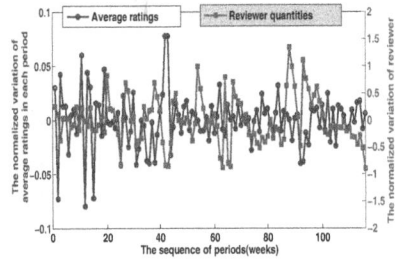

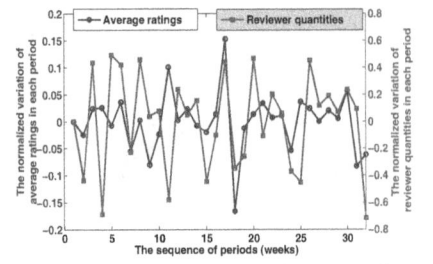

Figure 7: The variation of weekly average ratings and weekly number of reviewers. The x-axis is the index of each week ordered by date. The left y-axis represents the number of reviewers and the right y-axis represents the average rating.

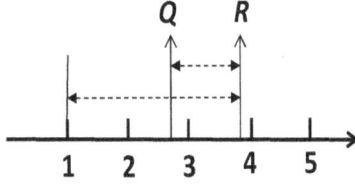

Figure 9: The positions an app's quality $Q_k$ and its final rating $R_k$ if the correlation coefficient $r(V, Z) > 0$.

Figure 10: The tie graph of two collusion groups $A=\{1, 2, 3, 4\}$ and $B=\{6, 7, 8, 9, 10\}$. In this tie graph, all the weak ties and negative ties have been removed.

other hand, when CC is a negative value, $R_k$ is below $Q_k$. Hence, $Q_k$ is bounded between $[R_k, 5]$ and $5 - R_k$ is the range of $Q_k$. Here the range $Q_k - R_k$ is mainly caused by demotion attacks. The more severe the attack is, both $R^2$ and $Q_k - R_k$ will increase, and vice versa. Similarly, we can normalize $Q_k - R_k$ as $\frac{Q_k - R_k}{5 - R_k}$ and approximate it with $R^2 = p * r^2(V, Z)$. Let $E_r$ follow Eq. 8, we can get Eq. 7.

$$p * r^2(V, Z) = \frac{R_k - Q_k}{R_k - E_r} \qquad (7)$$

$$E_r = \begin{cases} 1 & \text{if } r(V, Z) \geq 0 \\ 5 & \text{if } r(V, Z) < 0 \end{cases} \qquad (8)$$

Finally, to derive app quality $Q_k$, we can rewrite Eq. 7 as Eq. 9.

$$Q_k = R_k - p * r^2(V, Z)(R_k - E_r) \qquad (9)$$

Note that in our system, the system parameter $p$ must not be greater than $\frac{1}{r^2(V,Z)}$ to guarantee the right hand of Formula 7 will not exceed 1. In practice, once we set a threshold CC value (that is, if an app has CC value above the threshold, it will be considered as suspicious), we can set $p$ accordingly. In the simulation and experiments of this work, we set the threshold CC value as 0.25 and $p = 15$. During calculation, whenever $p*r^2(V, Z) > 1$, we will set it to 1. As a result, $Q_k = E_r$. This means, for a clearly promoted app (i.e., $|CC| > 0.25$), we will estimate its score as 1 (according to Formula 9). This may be inaccurate compared to its actual quality (again the purpose of our estimation is not to report actual score for market use). However, it has the advantage of exposing strong ties when two reviewers both gave 5 to this promoted app.

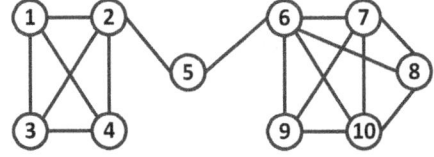

## 3.4 Collusion Groups Discovery

After estimating apps' quality following Eq. 9, we are able to calculate the pairwise tie strength following Eq. 2 and further build a tie graph to capture all the pairwise relations among reviewers. Like the scenario shown in Fig. 5, the ties between reviewers are different. Specifically, tie strength between collusion group members is accumulated through each group action and their ties will finally become strong positive ties. For honest reviewers, their rating deviations from apps' quality are randomly distributed and thus positive ties are harder to form. Therefore, to detect collusion groups, we only need to care about the strong positive ties and neglect the other types of ties.

Discovery of collusion groups finally becomes partitioning the tie graph which only contains strong positive ties. Here, we exploit two characteristics of collusion groups. First, even though collaboration enhances the relation, group members are not always connected to each other in the tie graph because they do not necessarily all participate in the same set of tasks or always behave the same. For example, as shown in Fig. 10, reviewer8 has never collaborated with reviewer9 even though they both belong to the same group $B$. It is possible that reviewer8 only promotes apps and reviewer9 only demotes apps. The other three reviewers in group $B$ perform both promotion and demotion.

Second, different collusion groups are not necessarily separated from each other. In reality, they could be connected for some reason. In Fig. 10, group $A$ and group $B$ are connected by reviewer5 because reviewer5 might by chance have rated some common apps with reviewer2 and reviewer6, respectively. As a result, even though there is a strong tie between reviewer5 and reviewer2, they do not belong to the same collusion group. The same reason holds for reviewer5 and reviewer6. Hence, one collusion group does not need to be fully separated from the other groups.

160

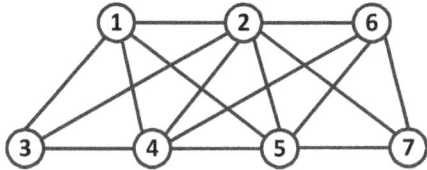

Figure 11: An example of 4-clique-community. There are four 4-cliques which are {1, 2, 3, 4}(c1), {1, 2, 4, 5}(c2), {2, 4, 5, 6}(c3) and {2, 5, 6, 7}(c4). c1 is adjacent to c2 and they share three nodes. Similarly, c2 is adjacent to c3 and c3 is adjacent to c4. Any two 4-cliques can reach each other through such adjacent neighbors.

In this section, considering the above two characteristics, we introduce an algorithm to detect collusion groups. Based on the observation that a typical member in a community is linked to many other members but not all of them, a community can be interpreted as a union of smaller complete (fully connected) subgraphs. Let $k$ refer to the number of nodes in a subgraph; then a subgraph is also called a $k$-clique. Palla et al. [14] defined a $k$-clique-community as a union of all $k$-cliques. All the $k$-cliques can be reached from each other by way of a series of adjacent $k$-cliques, where "adjacent" means sharing $k - 1$ nodes. For example, Fig. 11 shows a 4-clique-community where four 4-cliques comprise a community. This definition expresses the essential feature of community: members can be reached through well-connected subsets of nodes. The other parts cannot be reached through $k$-cliques are probably another $k$-clique community. Meanwhile, a single node can be in several communities. Thus, the whole graph consists of overlapping communities. Since these features of communities also exist in collusion groups, discovering collusion groups is equivalent to find $k$-clique-communities on the tie graph with only strong positive ties. It is called $k$-clique-groups in this work. We can adapt the algorithm introduced in [14] to discover $k$-clique-groups. The variance of $k$ influences the structure of collusion groups. If $k = 2$, a tie graph is considered to be a collusion group because all nodes are connected. For example, there is only one single collusion group in Fig. 10, which contains all the reviewers. Similarly, a 3-clique-group is given by the union of triangles that can be reached from one to another through a series of shared edges. As $k$ increases, the size of collusion groups shrinks, but on the other hand, it becomes more cohesive since their members have to be part of at least one $k$-clique. For instance, Fig. 10 is actually a 4-clique-groups which contains group $A$ and group $B$. Group $B$ contains two 4-cliques and they share a 3-clique.

Since we are looking for k-clique-groups, those groups smaller than $k$ will be discarded because they are unable to complete a successful attack with few group members. These small groups may be formed by biased reviewers who happen to rate the same apps. They can also be some random reviewers even though they rate honestly. Even though we misidentify some honest reviewers as attackers, it is easy to further filter them out with other features discussed in Section. 4.2.1. In practice, we may use GroupTie as the first round of discovery and set a small $k$ to catch as many attackers as possible during the next round of detection.

Table 5: The average value of FPR and FNR under attacks like PoA, DoA and OA.

| Attacks | precision | recall |
|---------|-----------|--------|
| PoA | 99.96% | 89.61% |
| DoA | 99.38% | 92.56% |
| OA | 99.75% | 92.34% |
| Overall | 99.70% | 91.50% |

## 4. EXPERIMENT AND RESULT ANALYSIS

We have implemented our collusion groups discovery model in JAVA based on Fedora 13 and stored all the data in MYSQL 5.1.56. Two types of experiments are conducted; one is the simulation[5] to evaluate the algorithm and the other one is to detect collusion groups in an actual app store.

### 4.1 Simulation Study

From the apps that look free of attacks (i.e., without any heuristics mentioned in Section. 4.2.1) in Apple App China Store, we randomly choose 29 apps and consider all of their original ratings honest. We set each period to be one week because it is a general period of our daily life; accordingly, the lifetime of an app is described in terms of number of weeks. We then introduce one collusion group to manipulate $N_{apps}$ apps ($N_{apps} = 4$ by default[6]) by adding positive, negative, or honest ratings. In the simulation, the collusion group controls two parameters: $P_{period}$, the percentage of weeks in an app's lifetime to introduce attacks; and $P_{raters}$, the ratio of the number of malicious raters to the population of raters in each week for an app. Once the collusion group chooses an app to attack (i.e., to promote or demote), its members may take one or more attack strategies, as described in Section 2.2: PoA, DoA and OA.

Two standard metrics of classification are used in our evaluation: *precision* and *recall*. In particular, precision measures the percentage of identified attackers which actually do belong to a collusion group and recall represents the proportion of attackers that are truly identified. Under the above attacks, we calculate the precision and recall of GroupTie, as shown in Table. 5. From the table we can see that the overall precision and recall of GroupTie is about 99.70% and 91.50%, respectively. GroupTie has higher precision but lower recall in the PoA case than in the DoA case. Its performance with OA is just between that with PoA and with DoA.

### 4.2 Discovering Collusion Groups in App Store

#### 4.2.1 Data Description and Detector Settings

We collected and analyzed the data of 200 apps from Apple's China App Store, which consist of 100 top paid apps and 100 top free apps on May 21, 2012. Among them, 111 apps have lifetime shorter than 9 weeks, so they were not included for further study. Finally, we obtained the test set of 89 apps, 818,545 reviewers and 1,042,832 reviews.

Establishing the ground truth on the suspiciousness of these apps and their reviewers is certainly a challenge here.

---

[5]For the detailed simulation result, please refer to https://www.dropbox.com/s/jhzhnlalgyeooi0/GroupTie_wisec_full.pdf

[6]We also tried 8 target apps, which showed similar results.

Manually checking all the reviews to identify possible attacks is not feasible in two aspects: scalability (the number of reviews is too huge) and accuracy (many evidences are hidden). As such, we turn to build an automatic tool that leverages several heuristics: review intensity, skewed ratings, highly similar review history, consecutive reviewer ids to expose suspicious apps and the collusion reviewer groups. Note that we cannot claim the results based on these heuristics are 100% accurate, but our algorithm output can provide a much-narrowed-down list for further investigation by app stores. App stores may use additional evidences which we do not have (e.g., information about reviewer accounts) to further pinpoint the abused apps and the collusion groups. Also note that for the objectiveness of our evaluation, these heuristics were not learned from the 89 apps under test in the next section.

***Review Intensity*** represents the distribution on the number of ratings over each unit time. Basically, if one checks all the reviews of an app and orders them by "helpfulness", one may notice that many same type of reviews are posted in a very short period. For example, among the reviews of the app with id 499814295, most five star ratings were posted on April 28, 2012 and May 22, 2012. Among all the reviews of app 499805269, there were 188 most helpful reviews and 183 of them were five star posted on June 1, 2012. This phenomenon reflects the collaborative rating behavior of collusion groups to make the attacks more effective.

***Skewed Ratings*** means that the distribution of rating scores of an app in a short time period is very skewed compared to its overall score distribution. For example, for the app with id 474429394, its overall rating summary for version 1.5.2 is $(28, 9, 25, 37, 241)$ (rating scores ordered from one star to five star). We also collected its ratings from July 1, 2012 to Aug 3, 2012 and got its rating summary $(1, 0, 0, 3, 136)$ for this time period. It is easy to observe that the ratio of five star to one star ratings increases from $241/28 = 8.61$ to $136/1 = 136.00$. Therefore, the developer might have hired a collusion group to promote its app version 1.5.0. Another example is app 499805269. Its rating summary of version 2.5.6 was $(2, 1, 0, 0, 183)$. If checking all its ratings in Jun 1, 2012, the rating summary was $(0, 0, 0, 183)$. This indicates all its five ratings appeared in one day. However, for normal apps, the ratio does not change a lot in different periods. This phenomenon is due to collaborative promotion which generates massive five star ratings in a short time window to be effective.

***Highly Similar Review History*** means group members have co-rated many common apps in the past. For example, we find a group of 171 reviewers all have rated and nearly only rated apps with ids (499814295, 525948761, 485252012, 496474967, 499805269) in the past. Only a few of them also rated 460351323.

***Consecutive Review Id*** means reviewer IDs of some groups are very close. Even though we do not know the mechanism for id (i.e., Apple ID) generation in iTunes, it is still weird that many reviewers with very close ids reviewed the same set of apps. For example, the following reviewers have commonly reviewed two apps with ids 474429394 and 525378313, respectively.

"212525736, 212525739, 212525752, 212525762, 212525765, 212525781, 212525784, 212525788, 212525795, 212525800, 212525808, 212525811, 212525825, 212525827, 212525834,

Table 6: Abuse signs of apps

| Sign | # of apps |
|---|---|
| Reviews Intensity or Skewed Ratings | 9 |
| Highly Similar Review History | 7 |
| Consecutive Ids | 3 |
| Removed Apps | 6 |

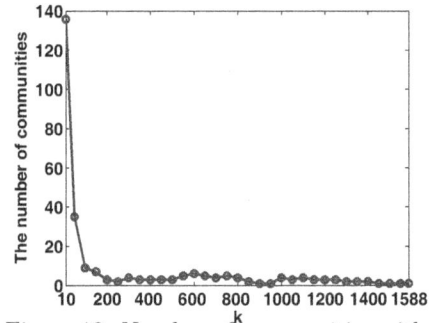

Figure 12: Number of communities with $k$.

212525847, 212525851, 212525857, 212525860, 212525864, 212525903, 212525990, 212525996"[7]

If iTunes generates user ids in an incremental way, this group probably applied these IDs in a very fast way (e.g., through bots). This sign would indicate not only the existence of a collusion group, but also the co-rated apps by these reviewers are probably abused apps.

***Removed Apps*** means some apps have been removed from app stores, due to reasons like rating manipulation as reported by the news.

### 4.2.2 Findings

Based on the above heuristics, we implemented an automated tool to check the apps for their signs of being abused. Among the 24 apps (out of the total 89 apps) whose CC values were above 0.2 or below −0.2, we identified 19 of them as suspicious (labeled as abused apps), because they bore one or more heuristics mentioned previously, as shown in Table 6. The relation between CC value intervals and the ratio of suspicious apps in each interval has been shown earlier in Table 4. Furthermore, among $818,545$ reviewers, we found that $8,853$ reviewers (i.e., 1.08%) had strong ties, and they formed $734,848$ strong positive ties. We applied the $k$-clique-communities algorithm described in Section 3.4. As illustrated in Fig. 12, when $k$ increases from 10 to 100, the number of communities decreases sharply from 136 to 9. When $k$ further increases, the number of communities continues to decrease until to the largest $k$ value (i.e., $1,588$). The reason is that when $k$ increases, more and more groups cannot satisfy the $k$-clique requirement any more and they are not considered as a group.

When $k$ equals to 100, we found $3,677$ reviewers forming 9 groups, which contained one large group with $2,652$ members and 8 smaller groups. We also checked their target apps by counting the commonly rated apps of the group members. As shown in Table 7, the 8 small groups targeted

---

[7]The review history of a reviewer can be accessed through the link https://itunes .apple.com/WebObjects/MZStore.woa/wa/viewSoftware?id=xxx. Make sure to change your location to China and replace xxx with a reviewer id.

Table 7: Collusion groups discovered by GroupTie.

| # | Group size | Target App ID |
|---|---|---|
| 1 | 104 | 363966906, 431194169 |
| 2 | 107 | 444934666, 370130751 |
| 3 | 145 | 441216572, 512500671 |
| 4 | 146 | 324101974, 444934666 |
| 5 | 151 | 324101974, 483583569 |
| 6 | 180 | 414478124, 387682726 |
| 7 | 198 | 324101974, 363966906 |
| 8 | 195 | 512500671, 387682726 |
| 9 | 2652 | 324101974, 414478124, 441216572 483583569, 512500671, 370130751 363966906, 444934666 |

at some apps to do promotion or demotion and they have some specific characteristics. For example, the target apps of group 1 actually belonged to one developer. Group 4 seemed to have two types of tasks: one was to promote 324101974 and the other was to demote 444934666. Group 9 was the largest group and it was almost 13 times larger than the other groups. Similar to group 4, its targets included both demoted (e.g., demoting the products of Tencent Inc. [19]) and promoted apps. Indeed, among all the target apps listed in Table. 7, all were labeled as abused apps previously. This indicates these 9 groups are highly likely collusion groups.

We further examined the behavior of the largest group (group # 9) and made the following observations.

- Attacks concentrated within a few days. For example, when demoting app 444934666, lots of low ratings were posted on 3/30/2012 and 3/31/2012.
- Multiple attacks to the same app were launched by the same group. For example, three separate attacks on app 324101974 were launched at around 12/1/2011, 01/19/212, and 5/14/2012.
- Group members have similar rating behaviors. When some members attacked an app, their rating scores were very close to each other. For promotion, most of them posted the highest rating (e.g., 5 star to app 324101974). For demotion, they often left the lowest rating (e.g., 1 star to app 444934666).
- Attacks often happened at the time of updating a new version. For example, the attack on app 324101974 occurred at the second day (i.e., 12/1/2011) of updating version 6.6. Similar scenarios were also found in other attacks.

Some of these observations conform with the heuristics Group-Tie applies, and the others may inspire us to define new features. For example, one may pay special attention to the ratings posted right after the publishing of an app to identify collusion groups.

## 5. DISCUSSION

Next we discuss several issues related to the limitations and future improvement of GroupTie.

*Attacks To GroupTie* GroupTie is for detecting the close relation between collusion group members. Clearly, a collusion group, once knowing that GroupTie is in place, may try its best to evade the detection, with different levels of difficulty, complexity, efficiency and cost. For example, they can try strategies like randomizing their ratings or

collaborators for different apps to make their attacks more stealthy at the cost of lower attack effectiveness. Clearly, there will be an arms race which could attract more research work in the future. We believe our current work, though as a first step, has greatly raised the bar for attackers. However, if collusion groups can hold enough accounts (e.g., millions), they might use each account only once to evade the discovery of GroupTie. The problem becomes a well-known sybil attack which has been studied a lot [20][21][22].

*Computational Complexity and Storage Overhead* We note that storage overhead is not an issue here if an app store is going to run our algorithm, because it has the rating/review information already. The computational complexity is a concern if we want to run our algorithm over the entire store, that is, for all raters and all apps. This is because we need to compute tie strength for each pair of users if they have ever co-rated an app and the number of such pairs is huge for an entire store. It will not be possible to compute tie strength for all pairs in physical memory. In practice, one optimization could be to run the algorithm only for suspicious apps and their associated reviewers. Further, we may distribute tie strength computation by leveraging the MapReduce framework to build tie graphs.

*Application to Other App Stores* GroupTie is designed based on general principles and assumptions, so it should also be applicable to Google Play or BlackBerry App World.

## 6. RELATED WORK

This section discusses a few most relevant fields.

*Clique Detection* In the context of cloud computing, collusion attack could break the integrity of the data collected from individual nodes. Du et al. [7] offered a mechanism to pinpoint the malicious service providers by detecting nodes outside maximum cliques. Stab et al. [18] presented a mechanism to detect collusion nodes by exploiting how often they work together in the majority or minority and how often they are in opposite groups. Lee et al. [12] designed an algorithm to find the cliques and furthermore, detect the malicious nodes and decrease their influence on the reputation. These methods were applied in grid computing, and after each task the result about whether a node cheats or not is easy to verify. However, reviewers' ratings to apps are subjective and not binary either. Moreover, the full graph including all the nodes is too large to detect cliques efficiently. GroupTie only builds graph for the suspects who have strong ties, which is much smaller than the full graph.

*Maximum Independent Set* Araujo et al. [3] proposed a maximum independent set approach for collusion detection in voting pools, aiming at classifying nodes as correct or incorrect. The approach first builds a vote against graph where two node in each edge voted against each other. Since each edge represents the disagreement between the nodes in two ends, they must belong to different groups, collusion group or honest group. Assuming that the largest plurality of nodes that do not vote against each other is correct, the detection of collusion groups is to find the maximum independent set from the votes against graph. Since collusion group members in an app store could rate randomly to hide their roles, the ratings to the non-target app of two members in a group could be totally different like one is "1 star" and the other one is "5 star". Thus, it is not suitable to apply maximum independent set in apps store.

*Feature Engineering* is a method to extract features of collusion groups and apply them to identify other groups. Mukherjee et al. [13] proposed algorithm which first uses a frequent itemset mining(FIM) [1] method to find candidate groups and employs an eight indicators evaluation system to detect collusion groups. Allahbakhsh et al. [2] offered a similar method employing six indicators to discriminate collusion groups with honest groups and they also built a biclique to represent the relationship between reviewers and products. Beutel et al. [5] proposed a method to catch collusive attackers which have lockstep behavior (i.e., launch attacks in a short time) when generating fraudulent "like" page in Facebook. These methods are based on features of specific collusion groups. Instead, features used in GroupTie are the essential features shared by various collusion groups.

## 7. CONCLUSIONS

In this paper, we have analyzed collusion attacks by providing falsified ratings in current apps store and proposed a novel method called GroupTie to detect collusion group members. Our simulation results showed that both the precision and recall of GroupTie is about 99.70% and 91.50%, respectively. We also applied our method to discover collusion group members among the reviewers of 200 apps in Apple's China App Store and found that 1.08% of the reviewers were likely collusive attackers belonging to one large collusion group and 8 small groups. The result calls for more attention to the collusion group problem in current app stores.

## 8. ACKNOWLEDGEMENT

This work was supported in part by NSF grant CCF-1320605 and a Google gift. We also thank the reviewers for helpful comments.

## 9. REFERENCES

[1] R. Agrawal and R. Srikant. Fast algorithms for mining association rules in large databases. In *Proceedings of the 20th International Conference on Very Large Data Bases*, VLDB '94, pages 487–499, San Francisco, CA, USA, 1994. Morgan Kaufmann Publishers Inc.

[2] M. Allahbakhsh, A. Ignjatovic, B. Benatallah, S.-M.-R. Beheshti, N. Foo, and E. Bertino. Detecting, representing and querying collusion in online rating systems. *CoRR*, abs/1211.0963, 2012.

[3] F. Araujo, J. Farinha, P. Domingues, G. C. Silaghi, and D. Kondo. A maximum independent set approach for collusion detection in voting pools. *J. Parallel Distrib. Comput.*, 71(10):1356–1366, 2011.

[4] T. Basar and G. Olsder. *Dynamic noncooperative game theory*, volume 200. SIAM, 1995.

[5] A. Beutel, W. Xu, V. Guruswami, C. Palow, and C. Faloutsos. Copycatch: stopping group attacks by spotting lockstep behavior in social networks. In *WWW*, 2013.

[6] Y.-F. Chen. Herd behavior in purchasing books online. *Comput. Hum. Behav.*, 24(5):1977–1992, Sept. 2008.

[7] J. Du, W. Wei, X. Gu, and T. Yu. Runtest: assuring integrity of dataflow processing in cloud computing infrastructures. In *AsiaCCS*. ACM, 2010.

[8] fiksu.com. http://www.fiksu.com/blog/apple-finally-adding-ratings-ranking-factors-0.

[9] Geekpark. http://www.geekpark.net/read/view/158104.

[10] M. Granovetter. The Strength of Weak Ties. *The American Journal of Sociology*, 78(6):1360–1380, 1973.

[11] A. Inc. https://developer.apple.com/news/index.php?id=02062012a.

[12] H. Lee, J. Kim, and K. Shin. Simplified clique detection for collusion-resistant reputation management scheme in p2p networks. In *Communications and Information Technologies (ISCIT), 2010 International Symposium on*, pages 273–278, Oct 2010.

[13] A. Mukherjee, B. Liu, and N. Glance. Spotting fake reviewer groups in consumer reviews. In *Proceedings of the 21st international conference on World Wide Web*, WWW '12, pages 191–200, New York, NY, USA, 2012. ACM.

[14] G. Palla, I. Derĺenyi, I. Farkas, and T. Vicsek. Uncovering the overlapping community structure of complex networks in nature and society. *Nature*, 435:814–818, June 2005.

[15] K. Pearson. *Mathematical contributions to the theory of evolution*, volume 13. Dulau and co., 1904.

[16] A. Salehi-Abari and T. White. On the impact of witness-based collusion in agent societies. In *Proceedings of the 12th International Conference on Principles of Practice in Multi-Agent Systems*, pages 80–96. Springer-Verlag, 2009.

[17] Sina. http://tech.sina.com.cn/it/2012-05-10/06197087031.shtml.

[18] E. Staab and T. Engel. Collusion detection for grid computing. In *Proceedings of the 2009 9th IEEE/ACM International Symposium on Cluster Computing and the Grid*, pages 412–419. IEEE Computer Society, May 2009.

[19] Tencent. http://www.tencent.com/en-us/index.shtml.

[20] G. Wang, M. Mohanlal, C. Wilson, X. Wang, M. J. Metzger, H. Zheng, and B. Y. Zhao. Social turing tests: Crowdsourcing sybil detection. In *NDSS*. The Internet Society, 2013.

[21] G. Wang, C. Wilson, X. Zhao, Y. Zhu, M. Mohanlal, H. Zheng, and B. Y. Zhao. Serf and turf: Crowdturfing for fun and profit. In *Proceedings of the 21st International Conference on World Wide Web*, WWW '12, pages 679–688, New York, NY, USA, 2012. ACM.

[22] Z. Yang, C. Wilson, X. Wang, T. Gao, B. Y. Zhao, and Y. Dai. Uncovering social network sybils in the wild. In *Proceedings of the 2011 ACM SIGCOMM Conference on Internet Measurement Conference*, IMC '11, pages 259–268, New York, NY, USA, 2011. ACM.

# NativeGuard: Protecting Android Applications from Third-Party Native Libraries

Mengtao Sun
Lehigh University
27 Memorial Drive West
Bethlehem, PA 18015, United States
mengtao.sun@lehigh.edu

Gang Tan
Lehigh University
27 Memorial Drive West
Bethlehem, PA 18015, United States
gtan@cse.lehigh.edu

## ABSTRACT

Android applications often include third-party libraries written in native code. However, current native components are not well managed by Android's security architecture. We present NativeGuard, a security framework that isolates native libraries from other components in Android applications. Leveraging the process-based protection in Android, NativeGuard isolates native libraries of an Android application into a second application where unnecessary privileges are eliminated. NativeGuard requires neither modifications to Android nor access to the source code of an application. It addresses multiple technical issues to support various interfaces that Android provides to the native world. Experimental results demonstrate that our framework works well with a set of real-world applications, and incurs only modest overhead on benchmark programs.

## Categories and Subject Descriptors

D.4.6 [**Software**]: Operating Systems—*Security and Protection*; D.2.12 [**Software**]: Software Engineering—*Interoperability*

## Keywords

Android; Java Native Interface; Privilege isolation

## 1. INTRODUCTION

Smartphones have been increasingly popular and widely adopted around the globe. Evolution and development of smartphones benefit from a large number of applications available in online stores such as Apple's App Store for iOS and Google's Google Play for Android. Apple adopts a confidential vetting process on all applications submitted to the App Store. On the contrary, Google has built a security framework for Android that in general keeps its ecosystem secure and at the same time open and flexible. Each Android application is assigned a unique Linux user ID and runs in a separate process. Furthermore, privileges of applications

are controlled by a dedicated permission system, where users grant permissions to applications upon installation to allow them to access certain information and resources.

Android applications are mostly written in Java. Similar to desktop Java programs, Android supports the Java Native Interface (JNI) and allows applications to incorporate native libraries. It is well known that in a conventional setting, native code defeats Java's security, as native code is not covered by Java's security model and has access to the entire address space. In Android, on the other hand, the story is different. First, previous studies (e.g., [6]) have shown low utilization of native code in Android applications. Second, process isolation, as the basis of security in Android, regulates all application components above the kernel, regardless of the programming language used in development. Therefore, it is generally believed that "native code is not pervasive", and that "native code is as secure as Java" in Android applications. Hence neither researchers in academia nor engineers in industry have paid much attention to native-code security in Android.

However, we believe Android's defense against native threats is not as strong as it appears. Our survey (detailed in Section 3) over the most popular Android applications shows that native libraries are used pervasively in popular Android applications. Nowadays, applications tend to provide diverse functionalities in order to take full advantage of cutting-edge hardware in modern Android phones. Tasks like 3D rendering and audio/video encoding have become extremely common in popular applications, where third-party native libraries are much more likely to appear. To make matters worse, these third-party native libraries enjoy all permissions the user grants to the whole application, which is often unnecessary and violates the principle of least privilege.

Given the prevalence of third-party native libraries in popular Android applications, the question is how to limit native libraries' privileges so that the damage caused by malicious or buggy third-party native libraries can be controlled. A natural idea is to design a framework in which native libraries are privilege separated from the rest of the application. Native libraries can have their own set of permissions, different from the permissions used in Java code.

For this purpose, we have designed NativeGuard, a framework that utilizes Android's process isolation to sandbox native libraries of an application. Generally speaking, NativeGuard improves Android's security in the following two aspects. First, NativeGuard separates native libraries contained within an Android application to another standalone application, where native code does not have full access to the entire application address space and the interaction between native and Java code is fulfilled via Android's interprocess communication (IPC) mechanism. Second, the native-library application is no longer granted all permissions the original application possesses; therefore, there would be much less damage if those libraries were exploited.

The main contributions of this paper are as follows:

- Our survey shows the prevalence of native libraries in popular Android applications, contrary to previous beliefs.
- To the best of our knowledge, NativeGuard is the first work on Android focusing on security threats of native libraries. We addressed multiple technical challenges in NativeGuard, involving the support of JNI function calls and the accommodation of Android's Native Development Kit (NDK) API. The framework takes advantage of the existing Android security architecture, does not need special hardware or system support, and can be easily deployed to the current Android system without much pain.
- We evaluated the prototype of NativeGuard over both the most prevalent Android applications today and industrial-strength benchmark programs, which fully demonstrated its practicality and efficiency.

We stress that, in NativeGuard's threat model, an application's Java components are trusted, while the application's native libaries are untrusted. We are mainly concerned with the scenario in which an Android developer incorporates a third-party native library into her application, treats it as a black box, and blindly assigns all permissions of the application to the library. Through NativeGuard, the developer can assign a much smaller permission set to the native libraries and as a result security is improved. Clearly, the Java components of an application could be malicious as well. But malicious applications are a well recognized threat and defenses have been proposed in many other studies. We instead focus on the security of native libraries. The threat model of NativeGuard will be detailed later in the paper.

The rest of the paper is organized as follows. We first introduce the background of Android security and the JNI interface in Section 2. In Section 3, we show the prevalence of native libraries in popular applications and explain how Android controls their security. Section 4 is an overview of NativeGuard, followed by Section 5, where we describe the isolation achieved by the framework, as well as several technical challenges and our solutions. We present in Section 6 our prototype implementation and experimental evaluation. In the end, we discuss related work, future work and conclude.

## 2. BACKGROUND: JNI AND ANDROID

In this section, we present a high-level overview of the Android architecture and its deployed security mechanisms. We also introduce the necessary background about the Java Native Interface.

### 2.1 Android Security Overview

Android is a software framework designed for mobile devices. It is built upon an adapted Linux kernel and supports Applications written in Java. Similar to desktop Java programs, they are also allowed to contain native modules. Android provides a set of security mechanisms to maintain the security of user data and system resources. Among them,

application sandboxing and the permission system are two key features.

***System-level security: application sandboxing.*** Android utilizes the Linux kernel as the basis of security and isolation. In Android, each application runs as a unique user with its own Linux user ID (UID). This design sets Android apart from the traditional Linux system, and provides natural kernel-level sandboxing among applications: each application stays within its own process boundary and does not have the privilege to interact with other applications. Thanks to the kernel-level isolation, protection covers both Java and native code.

***Application-level security: the permission model.*** As described earlier, applications on Android are sandboxed and by default do not possess permissions to access security-critical information and devices. In order to be privileged, an application has to declare its necessary capabilities and gets user approval upon installation. Most permissions are checked when sensitive APIs are invoked, which is the only way an application could access corresponding protected resources. There are also a few permissions enforced by the Linux kernel. Moreover, applications may define custom permissions to limit interactions with other applications.

It is worth mentioning that under the current Android permission model, permissions obtained by an application apply to all of its components. It is not possible to grant permissions to only part of the application.

### 2.2 The Java Native Interface

The Java Native Interface (JNI) [13] is a framework allowing Java programs to interoperate with native libraries. In Java, the `native` keyword is used to declare native methods. The following code snippet of the `PlasmaView` class is extracted from a sample of the Android NDK, which declares a native method `renderPlasma`. Once declared, native methods can be invoked in the same way as ordinary Java methods. In the example, the `onDraw` Java method invokes `renderPlasma`.

```
public class PlasmaView {
  ...
  private Bitmap mBitmap;
  protected void onDraw (Canvas canvas)
      { long time_t = ...;
        renderPlasma(mBitmap, time_t); ...;}

  private static native void renderPlasma
    (Bitmap bitmap, long time_ms);

  static {System.loadLibrary(''plasma'');}
}
```

A native method is implemented in a native language, such as C, C++, or assembly. Native code may also use JNI functions to interact with Java. Through these JNI functions, native code can inspect, modify, and create Java objects, invoke Java methods, catch and throw Java exceptions, and so on.

In Android, the NDK includes a cross-compilation toolchain, which helps generate libraries from native code. It also provides a collection of APIs and system libraries that facilitate developers to perform various tasks from traditional libc function calls to OpenGL-based 3D graphics rendering.

| Category | Apps | Apps with native libs | Percentage |
|----------|------|------------------------|------------|
| Social | 7 | 7 | 100% |
| Communication | 5 | 4 | 80% |
| Gaming | 19 | 18 | 95% |
| Entertainment | 2 | 2 | 100% |
| Other | 17 | 12 | 71% |
| Total | 50 | 43 | 86% |

Table 1: Top 50 Applications and Their Use of Native Libraries.

## 3. NATIVE CODE IN ANDROID: THE CURRENT SITUATION

In this section, we first present a small-scale study with a focus on the most popular applications on Google Play, which helps us better understand the use of native libraries in popular applications. Then we summarize how current security mechanisms in Android confine the behavior of native libraries.

### 3.1 Trends and Statistics

Native libraries are often treated as black boxes or simply trusted in past security research. In general, only a small portion of Android applications contain native libraries. A previous study showed that native libraries are found in less than 10% of the total applications inspected [6]. However, this reflects only part of the story.

More smartphone applications nowadays are about social networking, sharing, and entertainment. Social networking and gaming applications are among top categories that have been used by most users. Since native libraries are often used to perform CPU-intensive tasks such as image filtering, pixel rendering, audio/video encoding/decoding, which are common features provided by social applications, or are frequently performed in cellphone games, we expect native libraries to be much more likely to appear in popular applications.

To confirm this hypothesis, we investigated into those top applications: We downloaded the application package files (APKs) of the top 50 applications from the "Top Free in Android Apps" chart in Google Play in November 2013, which are the most popular Android applications at the time, regardless of their contents or categories. We then unpacked those APK packages and collected statistics on their usage of native libraries.

We identified 200 native libraries in total, showing an average of 4 native libraries per application. Table 1 presents the statistics. The first two columns show that according to the categorization in Google Play, applications in social, communication, gaming, or entertainment categories contribute to about two thirds of the applications in the Top 50 ranking. Among them, native libraries are pervasive: almost all applications falling in those categories carry at least one native library. Even in other categories such as music/audio or shopping, more than half of the applications inspected include native libraries. In fact, only 7 out of 50 applications surveyed are written solely in Java.

Our survey results and some previous studies (for example, [6, 31]) may seem contradictory. This can be explained by the following reasons. First, previous studies collected large numbers of applications without paying attention to their contents or popularity. As an example, Zhou *et al.* collected 204,040 applications from various online stores and reported native code deployment rate of 4.52% in total [31]. However, the majority of the applications may not be installed and used by most smartphone users: according to statistics shown in Google Play in November 2013, the No.1 application in the chart has accumulated almost a billion installs, while the application ranking 300 shows less than 500,000 installs in total, which is approximately only 0.05% of the top application. Second, the computing power in smartphones today has increased dramatically. Users are expecting more powerful applications and breathtaking games right in their palms. Hence, applications tend to be more sophisticated with more features and the possibility to incorporate native libraries increases.

### 3.2 Deployed Security Mechanisms

As introduced in Section 2.1, two core defenses are deployed in Android: the application sandbox and the permission model, which cover both Java and native code. We next take a closer look at each of them, with a focus on how the protection extends to native code.

First, the application sandbox builds upon the Linux user-based process protection, covering everthing running above the kernel, regardless of the language being used. Different from a traditional Java Virtual Machine, where native code is not covered by the Java security manager, native components in Android stay within the context of a particular application and cannot read/write other applications' data or files or perform privileged tasks, unless granted necessary permissions.

Second, the permission model ensures that only applications with necessary permissions may access resources that may harm users' privacy or lead to unexpected result if visited or used improperly. The permission model extends to native code in the following two aspects:

- Most security-sensitive system resources are accessed via Android API functions, which native code does not have direct access to. Native code may instead invoke Java methods through JNI's method-invocation functions, in which permissions are enforced.
- For those resources that are not wrapped by the API functions, they are controlled by Linux groups [7]. In these cases, the Linux kernel takes care of the permission checking when the underlying system calls are invoked.

## 4. DEFENSE OVERVIEW

In this section, we discuss the threat model of NativeGuard, as well as defenses it provides. Technical details are left to Section 5.

### 4.1 Threat Model

As shown in the survey, native libraries are prevalent in popular Android applications. Oftentimes, they are incorporated to fulfill some fixed and repeating tasks, such as file compression, 3D rendering, and audio/video stream decoding. Rather than implementing the functionalities from scratch, application developers often tend to utilize existing third-party native libraries, and connect them to their Java code via a small amount of glue code upon necessity. For instance, we have identified the same photo editing library (namely, `libaviary_native.so`) that appears in several popular social and photography applications. The downside, on the other hand, is the potential security threats brought by third-party native components: although developers can improve the quality of their work through careful examination and thorough testing, they cannnot fully trust arbitrary third-party binaries.

Despite Android's security mechanisms discussed in the previous section, native libraries still pose serious threats to the application and system security. At a high level, our threat model puts an application's Java components into the Trusted Computing Base (TCB), together with the rest of the system, while focusing on the security of native code. The threat model is justified by the following reasons:

- In the context of Android, native libraries are inherently not as safe as Java components. First, developers have no control over third-party native libraries they incorporate: in most cases these third-party components appear as black boxes with only documented interfaces. Second, native libraries are the weak link of an application because native languages are more prone to various vulnerabilities due to their lack of basic safety mechanisms, such as type checking and bounds checking.

- A large amount of research work has been performed to either strengthen Android's security mechanisms or mitigate security threats (e.g., [5, 27, 29]). Unfortunately, they do not deal with the security of native code. By concentrating on native code security, our work complements related Android security research.

In NativeGuard, we focus on the following two ways through which buggy or malicious native libraries may compromise the safety and security of the application or the Android system.

- Native libraries in an Android application reside in the same address space as the rest of the application and therefore have access to the entire address space of the application sandbox. Native code, once exploited, may potentially access/modify any data within the process boundary, leading to possible privacy violation or application malfunction.

- As per Android's permission model, once granted, permissions are applied to the entire application. Native modules possess the same privileges and may possibly abuse system resources, resulting in leak of confidential information or unexpected results.

## 4.2 Defenses Provided

In order to defend against the listed threats, native code needs to be insulated from the rest of the application, and should run without unnecessary permissions. In NativeGuard, we utilize the natural process boundary provided by the underlying Linux kernel in Android to isolate untrusted native code. Figure 1 depicts the isolation at a high level. As the basis of isolation, native libraries are relocated to a second sandbox besides the original one. The native-code sandbox runs in a separate process, so native libraries no longer have direct access to the rest of the original application. To support ordinary native method calls and JNI function calls, a stub library and a set of service trampolines are introduced, which hide implementation details of interprocess communication (IPC) from the original Java and native code. Following this design, there is no need to retrofit application code: IPC is transparent to the applica-

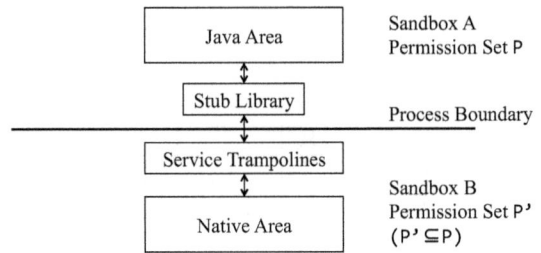

**Figure 1: Overview of the isolation.**

tion. In addition, if native libraries are separated from an application with permissions $P$, where $P$ is the set of permissions granted to the application at install time, then native libraries are jailed in another sandbox with permissions $P'$, where $P' \subseteq P$. That is, native code has only a subset of the original permission set. In fact for most applications, as is shown in Section 5 and Section 6, $P' = \emptyset$.

After separation, the process that holds native libraries can communicate with the Java process through the JNI interface, which unfortunately was not designed with security in mind. One worry is that malicious native code might misuse the JNI interface to cause integrity or confidentiality violations. For example, native code can issue JNI calls to modify fields of Java objects with values of incompatible types, which corrupts the integrity of the Java process. For another example, native code can forge a Java reference and issue a JNI call that uses the reference to read any memory in the Java process. This violates confidentiality. To prevent such violations, NativeGuard strengthens the JNI interface by performing runtime type checking when JNI functions are called. This guarantees that native code, even if malicious, can perform only type-preserving modification of the Java process and can read the Java process's memory through only the set of references passed from Java. This type safety guarantee is the same as what Robusta [21] provides to a conventional Java Virtual Machine.

One concern about process-based isolation is the performance overhead brought by context switches and interprocess communications. However, we believe it should work with most Android applications after a careful analysis of the Android NDK and usage patterns of most cellphone applications. First of all, based on the official document of the NDK [8], native code should be used only on tasks that perform CPU-intensive operations and that do not consume much memory, where context switches are not expected to occur frequently. Moreover, most applications today follow a user-driven model, where interactions with users are frequent and are the dominant factor in the application lifecycle. Hence, we consider that the idea of process isolation would not incur significant overhead most of the time. We present evaluation and performance data over benchmark programs in Section 6.

## 5. SANDBOXING NATIVE LIBRARIES

In NativeGuard, native libraries are put into another sandbox with limited permissions so that their security is controlled by Android's existing security mechanisms. We have different choices of implementing this sandbox.

(1) *Isolating native code in a second process within the same application.* By default, all components in one applica-

tion run in one process. Yet Android does allow one application to have multiple processes by supporting the `android:process` attribute in the manifest file of the application. It would be clean if native libraries run in another process but still stay in the same application as the rest of the code and resource files. However, this idea would not work with the current Android system, where permissions are enforced at the application level. Modifications to the underlying permission enforcement implementation would be inevitable, which would hinder NativeGuard from working directly with current Android smartphones.

(2) *Isolating native code in a second application.* In another approach, native libraries are moved to an entirely new *service* application running alongside the original one, the *client* application. The disadvantage is that the two applications have to be installed together, and there is no way to explicitly enforce any correlation between them. The benefit, on the other hand, is the compatibility with current Android systems. By putting native libraries into another application with less permissions, this approach sandboxes untrusted native libraries without requiring any modification to the system.

In the end, we chose the latter approach to keep NativeGuard a portable solution. Figure 2 shows the architecture of NativeGuard at a high level. An Android application is separated into two: the client application, which holds the Java side of the original application, and resource and user-interface files for interacting with users; and the service application, which takes the native libraries. The two applications interact via interfaces defined by the Android Interface Definition Language (AIDL) and the application holding native libraries acts as a service. It runs in the background and responds to requests from the client. Extra code is generated to support functionalities including native method calls, JNI function calls, NDK API invocation, and service application initialization.

We next present the detailed design of NativeGuard in four steps: (1) a brief overview of AIDL; (2) a closer look at the components and the workflow of NativeGuard; (3) how JNI function calls are handled across process boundaries; and (4) various technical issues concerning the NDK APIs.

## 5.1 AIDL Overview

AIDL is an interface definition language that defines the interface through which IPC is performed between a *client* and a *service*. AIDL follows Java's syntax. By defining the AIDL interface in an `.aidl` file and implementing necessary interface methods, Android application developers can easily utilize Android's IPC to marshall objects or perform remote method calls across processes. Specifically, the Android software development kit (SDK) takes the interface definition and generates a `stub` class in Java, which extends the `Binder` class, the core part of RPC support in Android. Developers then write code to extend the `stub` class and provide the actual implementation of interface methods. Then the interface is exposed to clients for IPC.

## 5.2 Native Code Separation

Given an Android application's APK package, NativeGuard separates native libraries in the application and the rest into two applications. In addition, it generates several AIDL interfaces and auxiliary native libraries, and slightly modifies the launcher class(es) (shown in dashed boxes in Figure 2) to achieve the separation. Next we elaborate several key components in the architecture.

***Modified launcher activities.*** Similar to the `main` method of a Java program, the launcher activity is the starting execution point of an Android application. A callback method of the activity named `onCreate` is automatically invoked by the system when the application is launched. To ensure that the service application starts together with the client and the client is *bound* to it after launched, NativeGuard locates the `onCreate` callback method in the application and adds necessary code so that when launched, the client proactively binds to the service by sending out an *intent*. In order to keep NativeGuard working with arbitrary applications, where source code is not always available, we inject crafted Dalvik bytecode sequences with the help of apktool, a widely-used reverse engineering tool for Android applications. We leave the implementation details to Section 6.

***Proxy native libraries.*** Since Java components and native libraries are put into two different applications, those Java components no longer have direct access to native libraries. NativeGuard's solution is to introduce a level of indirection through a layer of trusted proxy libraries. For each native library, there is one proxy library with the same name. Proxy libraries are put in the client application and provide implementations for exactly the same native methods as the original ones. The implementation of a native method in a proxy library invokes an appropriate AIDL interface method, which uses the IPC to invoke the corresponding native method in the service application. This level of indirection keeps changes transparent to Java code.

***The AIDL interface for native method calls.*** An AIDL interface is defined for native methods and is exposed to the client application. After the client is bound to the service, native code in proxy libraries may invoke the corresponding IPC method through the JNI interface. For each native method, there is one AIDL interface method implemented on the service side. When the method is invoked, binder IPC code generated by the SDK copies the arguments to the service process and calls the implementation in the end.

***Stub libraries.*** Calling an AIDL interface method transitions the control flow to the service application. Eventually the intended native method by Java code should be invoked. NativeGuards adds another layer of stub libraries for the purpose of maintaining a proxy table of JNI functions. The reason for this layer is the following. JNI passes object references to native methods as *opaque references*. Those references, however, no longer make sense when passed to another address space and need to be "properly translated" upon dereference. The proxy JNI function table redirects JNI calls back to the client application where opaque references could be correctly resolved. Details regarding stub libraries as well as the proxy JNI function table are presented in Section 5.3.

***The AIDL interface for JNI and NDK API calls.*** As mentioned in the previous paragraph, JNI calls in sandboxed native libraries are redirected back to the client process, which requires another AIDL interface for the necessary IPC. Similarly, the implementations of some NDK API functions cache low-level pointers to objects and manipulate them directly in native code; they also call for the IPC to

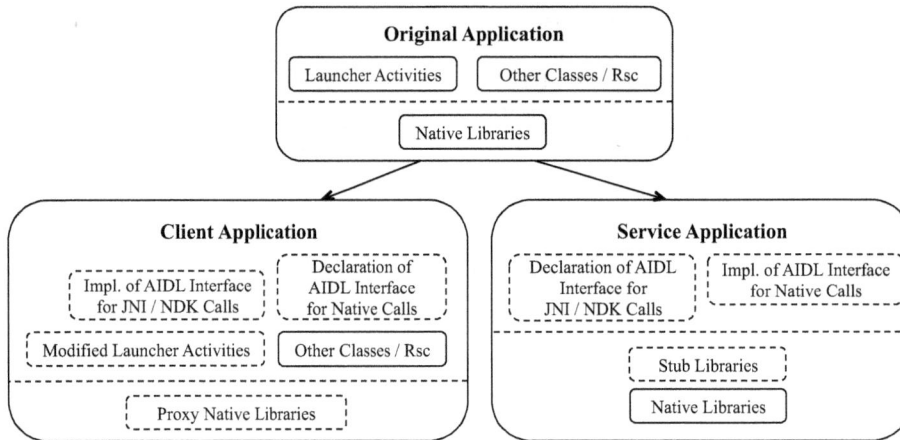

**Figure 2: Architecture of NativeGuard.**

interact with objects in the client process. Another set of AIDL interface methods are hence provided for this purpose. More details are discussed in Section 5.3 and Section 5.4, respectively.

We next walk through the basic process of native code isolation in NativeGuard using a native method example from `libjni_filtershow_filters.so`, a widely-deployed native library for photo editing. The example we present is `image-FilterVibrance_nativeApplyFilter`, a native method that applies the vibrance effect to a photo. The first step is to extract the original library and replace it with a proxy library. The proxy library contains a proxy function for each native-method implementation. The second step is to write/generate mandatory components shown in dashed boxes in Figure 2, put them in the two new applications, build and deploy them respectively. The following steps outline what happens when the user starts the instrumented application from the device.

(1) When the application is launched by the user, the client application is started first, which sends out an intent. The service application starts and responds to the intent. The client is then bound to the service.

(2) When the application loads the native library, it loads the proxy version of `libjni_filtershow_filters.so` on the client side.

(3) When the `imageFilterVibrance_nativeApplyFilter` native method is invoked, the control transfers to the proxy method. The proxy method performs a function call to the corresponding AIDL interface method.

(4) When the AIDL interface method for `imageFilterVi-brance_nativeApplyFilter` is called, the control transfers to the service application. The service application loads the stub library if it is not yet loaded and performs a native method call to the corresponding stub function.

(5) The stub function takes over the control and (a) uses `dlopen` to load the real library in the service process if it has not been loaded; (b) uses `dlsym` to find the address of `imageFilterVibrance_nativeApplyFilter` in the real library; and (c) performs a function call to the real target function.

## 5.3 Supporting JNI Calls

Native code may use JNI functions to manipulate Java objects or call Java methods. For instance, the following native method `initIDs` extracted from class `java.util.zip.Inflater`

in the Zlib library calls `GetFieldID` to obtain the JNI identifier of a field.

```
JNIEXPORT void JNICALL
Java_java_util_zip_Inflater_initIDs
  (JNIEnv *env, jclass cls){
  ...
  jfieldID strmID =
    (*env)->GetFieldID(env, cls, ``strm'', ``J'');
  ...
}
```

In the above code, `GetFieldID` returns the identifier of the field "strm" in the Inflater class, which can later be used to read from or write to the field. Note that the first two parameters of a native-method implementation are special: a JNI interface pointer, and a reference to the Inflater object or the Inflater class in the case of static native methods, similar to `this` pointer in C++ or Java. The `cls` bolded in the code above is the reference to the Inflater class.

After NativeGuard's isolation, the implementation of `ini-tIDs` is migrated to the service application. Hence when invoked, `cls` in `initIDs` becomes the reference to the service class and is no longer the one that it is expecting.

As briefly discussed in the preceding section, NativeGuard's solution is to introduce a stub library between the Java code and the real native libraries in the service application. The stub library maintains a proxy JNI interface pointer structure in the service application, but with function pointers to the AIDL interface methods for JNI functions. When the stub function calls the real target function (the last step discussed in Section 5.2), it passes the proxy JNI interface pointer to the corresponding native library. Hence, when native code in the isolated library invokes a JNI function via the proxy interface pointer, the control is transferred to an AIDL interface method, which performs IPC and jumps back to the client application and the real JNI function is called. Note that opaque references must be retained so that correct objects could be retrieved when JNI function calls are redirected back to the client application. In the example above, the value of `cls` is mandatory to find the field ID and thus cannot be lost. In NativeGuard, one more argument is added to the AIDL interface methods for native method calls. When a proxy method calls to the AIDL interface (step (2) in Section 5.2), it passes in `this` reference value. The reference is kept all the way down to the native code in the service application so that all JNI calls within this context could be properly handled back in the client application.

The benefit of this design is threefold. First, isolated native code still follows the same syntax for invoking JNI functions and thus need not be aware of the isolation. Second, only references are marshalled across processes, not Java objects. This brings down the overhead caused by IPC as object marshalling is very expensive. Also it makes the solution source-code free, as reference marshalling in AIDL does not depend on the implementation details of objects. Last, no global references are necessary in the proxy libraries on the client side, as JNI function invocations in the service application always stay within the context of a native-method call, where local references are valid during the period.

In addition, the proxy JNI interface provides a natural place for performing runtime type checking on the JNI. As we have discussed, misuse of the JNI interface by the native code can cause confidentiality and integrity violations. Therefore, NativeGuard performs checks in the proxy JNI interface to ensure type safety of JNI calls. The implementation of these checks follows previous JNI checking systems, including Arabica [22] and Jinn [12]. We omit a detailed description.

## 5.4 Supporting NDK API Function Calls

Ideally, native libraries interact only with Java code: they are not dependent upon each other albeit belonging to the same Android application. In this case, it is sufficient to support only the JNI interface in our framework as native libraries perform computation tasks and only communicate with the rest of the program via the JNI interface. The reality, however, is different when a few special NDK libraries are involved.

The NDK provides a set of API functions for native code to fulfill various tasks. Besides traditional libc support, the API also includes headers of OpenGL libraries for 3D rendering, libjnigraphics headers for bitmap pixel manipulation, and so on. As a simple example, native code may invoke `AndroidBitmap_lockPixels` implemented in `libjnigraphics` to grab the lock on a Java Bitmap object and acquire a pointer to the pixel buffer of the object, through which direct access to pixels is supported. In fact, many applications and libraries provide photo filter functionalities based on API functions in `libjnigraphics`, including `libjni_filtershow_filters.so`, the example library we introduced in Section 5.2.

It turns out that in some NDK libraries, manipulation on Java objects is directly performed via native pointers, rather than through the JNI interface. In these cases, Java objects are only "wrappers" of native data structures, which are allocated in native methods implemented in *system* native libraries. In the above example, the underlying implementation of `AndroidBitmap_lockPixels` first calls `GetIntField` to obtain the value of an integer field, specifically, `mNativeBitmap` in the Java Bitmap object, then casts the integer to a `SkBitmap` pointer, through which the Bitmap pixels can be directly modified. By further tracing down the calling sequence, we find that the Bitmap object is created by calling a native method `nativeCreate`, which (1) allocates a new `SkBitmap` object; (2) casts the pointer value to an integer; and (3) caches the integer to the `mNativeBitmap` field. `nativeCreate`, however, is implemented in `liban-`

`droid_runtime`, a system native library in Android. Since our purpose is to isolate untrusted, third-party native libraries, system libraries are considered trusted. Hence, when a native library is isolated in the service application and tries to modify a Bitmap object via the NDK API, its behavior cannot be predicted, because the pointer cached can only be interpreted in the client application and does not point to a valid object in the service application.

To support these NDK API function calls after isolation, NativeGuard intercepts an API invocation and marshalls related objects to the service application before the real API function is run. For instance, if a sandboxed native library invokes the `libjnigraphics` API, NativeGuard provides a fake `libjnigraphics` in the service application, which utilizes the dedicated AIDL interface to transport the Bitmap object from the client before calling the real API function. Correspondingly, updated Bitmap objects are marshalled back when native code finishes its work on the pixels, specifically, when it calls `AndroidBitmap_unlockPixels`, the API function that indicates the end of the native modification.

We next make a few clarifications. First, we can easily marshall Java objects like the Bitmaps as long as they support the `Parcelable` interface, which allows the system to decompose objects into primitives that can cross the process boundary. If not, then we have to implement the `Parcelable` protocol for the object on our own, which may or may not be difficult, depending on the composition of the object. Second, not all NDK libraries encounter the situation discussed in this section. Our prototype implementation provides support for `libjnigraphics`, the library we discussed earlier, and the OpenSL ES native audio library.

## 5.5 Managing Native Code Permissions

The basic idea of limiting privileges of native code in NativeGuard is to better use the Android permission mechanism. Following the principle of least privilege (POLP), native libraries are isolated in another application with only the minimum mandatory permission set granted. We next discuss how the POLP principle is enforced in NativeGuard.

Based on the guideline of the NDK and how native code is managed under current Android framework, we infer that native code *itself* seldom requires any permission. First of all, the NDK may only be beneficial when used with self-contained libraries that perform CPU-intensive operations [8], which are not likely to access system resources or devices protected by permissions. Second, native code is not allowed to interact directly with the system API and must call back to Java via the JNI interface to visit protected resources [7]. In this case, permissions are enforced on the API calls, not native libraries; JNI function calls do not require any permission either. The only circumstance under which native code does require permissions is when native code directly accesses system resources *not* protected by the system API. For instance, a native library may open and write to a file on the SD card without calling back to Java, and hence requires the `WRITE_EXTERNAL_STORAGE` permission itself.

To the best of our knowledge, there is no official document or previous research that sheds light on how native functions, library calls or NDK APIs are connected to the permission model. Intuitively, native code's access to protected resources is fulfilled by system calls and the permission check is performed in the Linux kernel. But it is hard to decide whether a system call requires an Android permission as it

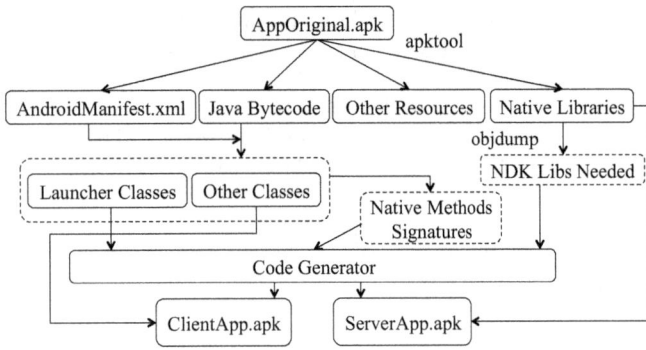

**Figure 3: Workflow of the Application Separator.**

may be dependent on its parameters. As a simple example, the system call `open` requires the `WRITE_EXTERNAL_STORAGE` permission when opening a file on the SD card with the write access, but requires no permission when opening a private file of the application or opening a file on the SD card with the read-only access. Furthermore, since NativeGuard aims to defend threats of untrusted native libraries in arbitrary Android applications from online stores, where source code of the native libraries is not available, it is even harder to find the minimum permission set efficiently solely from the binary.

Hence, we decide to follow a heuristic approach and by default grant no permission to the service application in NativeGuard. The approach is motivated by the observation that it is rare for legal native code to perform privileged operations, as it is a "bad practice" according to the NDK. In fact, as we will present in Section 6, the heuristic works with all real applications that NativeGuard has been tested on (around 30 applications). On the other hand, the drawback is that the approach does not support native code that requires privileged access to the devices. As a remedy, NativeGuard also supports a configuration file through which a developer can manually grant permissions to native libraries.

## 6. IMPLEMENTATION AND EVALUATION

In this section, we first present the prototype implementation of NativeGuard. Then we discuss its evaluation, on both benchmark programs and real-world applications.

### 6.1 Prototype Implementation

The thrust of this project, as we have discussed, is to design a framework that isolates untrusted native libraries in Android applications downloaded from online stores. Hence, we implemented NativeGuard as an "application separator", which takes as input an APK package and generates two APK files: the client and the service applications. As presented in Section 5, the client contains Java bytecode and other resources from the original application, the service isolates native libraries and by default does not require any permission. In addition, NativeGuard also supports a configuration file, where permissions can be manually granted to the service application upon separation.

Figure 3 shows the separation process in NativeGuard. At a high level, NativeGuard is composed of a code generator, and two third-party tools. First, we utilize apktool [1], an open-source tool for Android application reverse engineering, to extract native-method information and to make

slight modifications to the launcher classes. Apktool can unpack an APK file into resources and `smali` code, a human-readable format for the Dalvik bytecode, where the basic information of the program, such as method names and native method signatures, is available. It can also rebuild them into an APK file after some modifications. Second, we incorporate the `objdump` from the NDK toolchain, which can dump an Android native library built by the toolchain to reveal information regarding library dependency. The main steps of the separation process are as follows.

(1) Apktool unpacks the input APK file.
(2) The `AndroidManifest.xml` file is parsed to locate launcher class(es).
(3) All `smali` files are analyzed to record signatures of native methods.
(4) Native libraries are dumped to record the dependency to NDK libraries.
(5) Based on information collected above, the code generator generates extra AIDL interfaces and library code. It also adds mandatory `smali` code to the launcher class(es) for service binding.
(6) In the end, two applications are built as the output.

NativeGuard is implemented in Java and is comprised of about 2,000 lines of Java code and about 20 template files for fast code generation. In addition, it incorporates apktool 1.5.2 and `objdump` from the NDK Revision 8c. We choose Java as the implementation language because the package installer in Android is written in Java. Therefore, NativeGuard can be incorporated into the package installer in the future, which provides users a completely transparent solution for native code isolation.

### 6.2 Evaluation

We carried out a three-stage evaluation to fully test NativeGuard's functionality and performance. First, we created an illegal native library that abuses granted permissions to test the effectiveness of NativeGuard's defense. Afterwards, NativeGuard was tested on dozens of applications in various categories that are among the most downloaded applications in Google Play. For performance testing, it was evaluated both on a representative benchmark suite and on a hand-crafted benchmark program. Experiments were conducted on a Nexus 4 smartphone running Android 4.3. All performance numbers were averaged over 10 runs.

***Functionality testing.*** We have manually created a test native library, which *directly* accesses the location information of a phone without going through the Java side (assuming the application has been granted the location-access permission). In Android, most system resources are protected by privileged Java API methods, which are implemented in a trusted system process [7]. A typical native library has to invoke the corresponding API method through method-invocation functions in JNI in order to access the privileged resource. In contrast, our test native library directly talks to the system process and obtains the location information without going through the Java API.

The test library demonstrates that malicious native code can take advantage of permissions that are not really needed to cause security violations. NativeGuard can improve this situation. For the test native library, we used NativeGuard to isolate it into a service application with no permissions and thus its access to the location information was denied due to lack of permissions.

| Benchmark | Size of Data Set | Overhead |
|-----------|-----------------|----------|
| jpeg | 20 KB | 17.16% |
| lame | 177 KB | 1.12% |
|  | 2585 KB | 0.87% |
| tiff2bw | 6662 KB | 7.83% |
|  | 27873 KB | 2.08% |
| tiff2rgba | 6662 KB | 3.14% |
|  | 27873 KB | 0.54% |
| tiffdither | 2223 KB | 14.37% |
|  | 9303 KB | 1.40% |
| tiffmedian | 6662 KB | 5.11% |
|  | 27873 KB | 2.32% |

**Table 2: Runtime overheads on MiBench benchmarks.**

| Buffer Size | Overhead | Context Switches (per millisecond) |
|-------------|----------|-----------------------------------|
| 1KB | 183.13% | 31.89 |
| 2KB | 107.49% | 25.98 |
| 4KB | 55.02% | 18.51 |
| 8KB | 34.36% | 9.81 |
| 16KB | 26.64% | 3.96 |

**Table 3: Extreme-case runtime overheads on the Zlib benchmark application.**

*Real-world applications testing.* We collected a total of 30 applications from the official Google Play store to test NativeGuard's functionality on real applications. The applications are collected from different categories and are on the "top" charts of the store in November 2013. Note that tested applications are not strictly the overall top 30 ones, as we intended to exercise our framework on applications providing diverse functionalities and containing different native libraries. Our framework succeeds on 28 out of 30 applications. It fails on two applications because of the apktool, which fails either in the disassembling stage before separation or in the assembling stage after separation. Applications after separation are tested manually, as existing automatic testing tools that generate random inputs are not sufficient for our purpose. Since we want to make sure the native libraries are loaded and used during testing, it is much safer to just manually play with the instrumented applications and exercise various functionalities provided. For example, some applications require signing in before using any meaningful functions. In these cases, automatic testing frameworks are more likely to fail in exercising native code.

During our testing, we could perceive slightly longer response delays in some applications and use cases. For example, photo filters may take extra time to render a picture. But in general, NativeGuard introduces acceptable overhead and does not affect the functionalities delivered by the applications. Details regarding evaluated applications are presented in Appendix A.

*Performance evaluation.* For a security framework utilizing process isolation, the runtime overhead of NativeGuard depends greatly on the intensity of *context switches*, e.g. the frequency of IPC. If isolated native libraries are typical "good candidates" for the NDK and do not involve lots of context switches, the overhead caused by NativeGuard should be small.

We first evaluated NativeGuard on MiBench [9], a free and open-source benchmark suite for embedded systems. The suite provides six categories of benchmark programs for different purposes in real-world applications, and testing data sets of various sizes. MiBench is not Android-ready. We picked several benchmarks under the Consumer category (a category for consumer devices, like PDAs and smartphones) and ported them to Android. Table 2 presents the results.

In general, NativeGuard shows moderate overheads on MiBench programs. The benchmarks all utilize native libraries to perform CPU-intensive operations, such as image compression and conversion, and thus do not frequently make context switches. The result table also confirms the correlation between the overhead and the context switch intensity: programs on large data sets show less performance overheads, as they stay longer in the service application before switching back. Since native libraries in MiBench programs are representative candidates for the Android NDK, NativeGuard is promising to incur modest overhead on isolating a majority of native libraries in popular applications.

Another important factor to evaluate on mobile devices is the overhead posed on memory and storage, which are both limited resources on smartphones. Although for an application with native libraries, users with NativeGuard now have to keep two applications running simultaneously, the increase of memory utilization turns out to be moderate: NativeGuard introduces only 11.81% of memory overhead on the ported MiBench application, according to data reported by Android's `dumpsys` tool. Moreover, NativeGuard shows a tiny 130KB increase on the size of the application, being only 7.11% of the original.

But *what if the isolated library does make frequent context switches?* To further understand the performance of NativeGuard in extreme cases, we carried out another set of hand-picked benchmark programs. The programs compress a medium-sized file stored on the device using the popular Zlib library. When the user presses the start button on the user interface, the Java side of the application divides the file into data segments of smaller sizes and passes a data segment through a buffer to Zlib, which performs the compression and returns the result to the Java side. Then the Java side passes the next segment of data. Hence, when the Zlib library is sandboxed, the size of the buffer is strongly correlated to the performance overhead, as a smaller buffer results in more frequent context switches between Java and native code. We conducted experiments with different buffer sizes and the results are presented in Table 3.

As shown in the table, the runtime increase of NativeGuard on the Zlib benchmark demonstrates the similar trend: as the buffer size increases, the performance overhead decreases. The performance penalty can be as high as near two times when extremely intense context switch happens.

In summary, the experiments demonstrate that the approach of process isolation brings security to untrusted native code, and with modest overhead on most real-world applications where context switches between Java and native code are not frequent.

## 7. RELATED WORK

We next discuss related work in two categories: techniques for sandboxing untrusted components from a trusted environment, and previous studies on Android security.

***Untrusted code isolation.*** It is always desirable to isolate untrusted code to prevent uncontrolled access or malicious compromise to the trusted environment and there have been various approaches. *Language-based isolation* ensures the security of untrusted code by utilizing static types [17] or object-capability models [16, 11], but it is tied to a specific language. *Isolation based on virtual machines* regulates untrusted code by building a safety-oriented platform (e.g., [3]), which is a clean solution but incurs severe performance penalty. In comparison, NativeGuard utilizes *hardware-based process isolation*, which has long been used in various operating systems to isolate untrusted components [4, 23]. Process isolation suffers from high performance overhead with frequent interprocess communication, but can provide flexible and robust isolation if used with clever optimizations. For instance, Codejail isolates untrusted libraries into a jailed process and incurs acceptable overhead on libraries that are tightly coupled with the main program [26].

With regard to sandboxing untrusted native code in foreign function interfaces, NativeGuard is similar to several previous frameworks. Klinkoff *et al.* designed a system that sandboxes unmanaged native code in the .NET framework [10], but relies on a kernel add-on module to control system calls in untrusted code. Robusta adopts software-based fault isolation (SFI) [25] and puts native libraries in Java programs into an SFI sandbox [21]. In terms of performance, it compares favorably to other sandboxing frameworks thanks to SFI, but relies on nontrivial modification to the internal of a Java Virtual Machine. Arabica improves Robusta and achieves JVM-portability through clever use of the Java Virtual Machine Tool Interface (JVMTI) [22], which, unfortunately, is not available for the Dalvik Virtual Machine on Android. On the contrary, NativeGuard reuses Android's permission model and does not need support for special interfaces or plug-ins, hence is ready to deploy on any Android system.

***Android safety and security.*** As the most widely-adopted smartphone OS worldwide, Android has attracted much attention from academia in recent years. A couple of empirical studies provided more complete view of Android application security and its permission model. For example, Enck *et al.* designed a Dalvik decompiler `ded` and performed analysis on 1,100 Android applications [6]. Their work produced many findings, some of which might lead to ways of exploiting Android. Felt *et al.* established a mapping between the Android API and the permissions, and shed light on the pervasive overprivilege problem among Android applications [7]. PScout utilizes static analysis to further improve the completeness of the mapping and reveals the state of the art in newer versions of Android [2]. Their work is a strong motivation of NativeGuard as many applications are overprivileged with security-critical permissions, which are not needed by native libraries. Recent studies have presented various systems (e.g., TaintDroid [5] and VetDroid [29]) to detect user privacy and confidential information leaks, which increased the overall security of Android, but left native libraries unmonitored.

Much work has been performed to address various aspects of Android security, for example, advertisements (e.g., [20, 19]), application repackaging and malware detection (e.g., [30, 24]), and privilege escalation attacks (e.g., [14, 15]). Though in a different context, AdSplit and AFrame are in spirit similar to our framework, as they isolate advertising libraries into separate processes [20, 28]. To display both the advertisement and the host application on the screen after separation, AdSplit follows an emulation approach to allow two activities to share the screen, while AFrame supports embedded activities. Both of them require changes to the system. In comparison, NativeGuard isolates native libraries into a service application that does not interact with the user, avoiding unnecessary modifications to the Android framework. Moreover, a number of systems have been designed to improve the permission system's granularity and flexibility (e.g., [18, 32]). These studies increase the power of the permission model, but requires changes to the system. They also risk overprompting users to make security-related decisions. By contrast, our framework reuses the current permission model, where users still receive the same information when installing applications.

## 8. FUTURE WORK

Some parts of NativeGuard can be improved. The next step is to incorporate NativeGuard into the Android package installer. NativeGuard is currently implemented as a command line tool, which genereates APK packages according to user commands. If integrated into the Android package installer, it would bring conveniece to end users; they can download, isolate native libraries, and perform installation in a streamlined process.

We also plan to explore techniques that efficiently decide the minimum permission requirement of native binaries. Currently our framework relies on a heuristic, which worked well in our multistage evaluation, but cannot support legitimate libraries that do require permissions. Since native code may directly access certain system resources through system calls, it would be a good starting point to build a permission map to connect system calls to permission requirements.

## 9. CONCLUSIONS

Although the Android platform has a sophisticated security architecture for Java code, native libraries are uncontrolled. Given the increasing popularity of Android devices and insufficient research, native libraries pose pressing challenges to the security of the Android ecosystem. In this paper, we have proposed NativeGuard, a security framework that isolates native libraries into a non-privileged application. NativeGuard requires no change to the Android system, nor does it require access to the source code of an application. It incurs modest runtime overhead on tested real-world applications, in which interprocess communication is not intensive. We believe that our study is a good starting point for future security research on native code in Android.

## Acknowledgments

We thank anonymous referees of WiSec '14 for detailed comments on an earlier version of this paper. This research is supported by US NSF grants CCF-1217710, CCF-1149211, and a research award from Google.

# 10. REFERENCES

[1] android-apktool. https://code.google.com/p/android-apktool/.

[2] K. W. Y. Au, Y. F. Zhou, Z. Huang, and D. Lie. Pscout: Analyzing the android permission specification. pages 217–228, 2012.

[3] R. S. Cox, S. D. Gribble, H. M. Levy, and J. G. Hansen. A safety-oriented platform for web applications. In *IEEE Symposium on Security and Privacy (S&P)*, pages 350–364, 2006.

[4] J. R. Douceur, J. Elson, J. Howell, and J. R. Lorch. Leveraging legacy code to deploy desktop applications on the web. In *USENIX Symposium on Operating Systems Design and Implementation (OSDI)*, pages 339–354, 2008.

[5] W. Enck, P. Gilbert, B.-G. Chun, L. P. Cox, J. Jung, P. McDaniel, and A. N. Sheth. Taintdroid: An information-flow tracking system for realtime privacy monitoring on smartphones. In *USENIX Symposium on Operating Systems Design and Implementation (OSDI)*, 2010.

[6] W. Enck, D. Octeau, P. McDaniel, and S. Chaudhuri. A study of android application security. In *20th Usenix Security Symposium*, pages 21–21, 2011.

[7] A. P. Felt, E. Chin, S. Hanna, D. Song, and D. Wagner. Android permissions demystified. In *18th CCS*, pages 627–638, 2011.

[8] Google. Android ndk. http://developer.android.com/tools/sdk/ndk/index.html.

[9] M. Guthaus, J. Ringenberg, D. Ernst, T. Austin, T. Mudge, and R. Brown. Mibench: A free, commercially representative embedded benchmark suite. In *Workload Characterization, 2001. WWC-4. 2001 IEEE International Workshop on*, pages 3–14, 2001.

[10] P. Klinkoff, E. Kirda, C. Kruegel, and G. Vigna. Extending .NET security to unmanaged code. *Internation Journal of Information Security*, 6(6):417–428, 2007.

[11] A. Krishnamurthy, A. Mettler, and D. Wagner. Fine-grained privilege separation for web applications. In *Proceedings of the 19th International Conference on World Wide Web (WWW '10)*, pages 551–560, 2010.

[12] B. Lee, M. Hirzel, R. Grimm, B. Wiedermann, and K. S. McKinley. Jinn: Synthesizing a dynamic bug detector for foreign language interfaces. In *PLDI*, pages 36–49, 2010.

[13] S. Liang. *Java Native Interface: Programmer's Guide and Reference*. Addison-Wesley Longman Publishing Co., Inc., 1999.

[14] L. Lu, Z. Li, Z. Wu, W. Lee, and G. Jiang. Chex: Statically vetting android apps for component hijacking vulnerabilities. pages 229–240, 2012.

[15] T. Markmann, D. Gessner, and D. Westhoff. Quantdroid: Quantitative approach towards mitigating privilege escalation on android. In *IEEE International Conference on Communication*, pages 2144–2149, 2013.

[16] A. Mettler, D. Wagner, and T. Close. Joe-E: A security-oriented subset of Java. In *Network and Distributed System Security Symposium(NDSS)*, 2010.

[17] G. Morrisett, D. Walker, K. Crary, and N. Glew. From System F to typed assembly language. *ACM Transactions on Programming Languages and Systems*, 21(3):527–568, May 1999.

[18] M. Nauman, S. Khan, and X. Zhang. Apex: extending android permission model and enforcement with user-defined runtime constraints. In *5th ACM Symposium on Information, Computer and Communications Security*, 2010.

[19] P. Pearce, A. P. Felt, G. Nunez, and D. Wagner. Addroid: Privilege separation for applications and advertisers in android. In *7th ACM Symposium on Information, Computer and Communications Security*, 2012.

[20] S. Shekhar, M. Dietz, and D. S. Wallach. AdSplit: Separating smartphone advertising from applications. In *21th Usenix Security Symposium*, 2012.

[21] J. Siefers, G. Tan, and G. Morrisett. Robusta: Taming the native beast of the JVM. In *17th CCS*, pages 201–211, 2010.

[22] M. Sun and G. Tan. JVM-portable sandboxing of Java's native libraries. In *17th European Symposium on Research in Computer Security (ESORICS)*, pages 842–858, 2012.

[23] M. M. Swift, M. Annamalai, B. N. Bershad, and H. M. Levy. Recovering device drivers. In *USENIX Symposium on Operating Systems Design and Implementation (OSDI)*, pages 1–16, 2004.

[24] T. Vidas and N. Christin. Sweetening android lemon markets: Measuring and combating malware in application marketplaces. In *Proceedings of the Third ACM Conference on Data and Application Security and Privacy*, CODASPY '13, pages 197–208, 2013.

[25] R. Wahbe, S. Lucco, T. Anderson, and S. Graham. Efficient software-based fault isolation. In *ACM SIGOPS Symposium on Operating Systems Principles (SOSP)*, pages 203–216, New York, 1993. ACM Press.

[26] Y. Wu, S. Sathyanarayan, R. H. Yap, and Z. Liang. Codejail: Application-transparent isolation of libraries with tight program interactions. In *17th European Symposium on Research in Computer Security (ESORICS)*, pages 859–876, 2012.

[27] Z. Yang, M. Yang, Y. Zhang, G. Gu, P. Ning, and X. S. Wang. Appintent: Analyzing sensitive data transmission in android for privacy leakage detection. In *20th CCS*, 2013.

[28] X. Zhang, A. Ahlawat, and W. Du. AFrame: Isolating advertisements from mobile applications in Android. In *Proceedings of the 29th Annual Computer Security Applications Conference*, 2013.

[29] Y. Zhang, M. Yang, B. Xu, Z. Yang, G. Gu, P. Ning, X. S. Wang, and B. Zang. Vetting undesirable behaviors in android apps with permission use analysis. In *20th CCS*, 2013.

[30] W. Zhou, X. Zhang, and X. Jiang. Appink: Watermarking android apps for repackaging deterrence. In *8th ACM Symposium on Information, Computer and Communications Security*, pages 1–12, 2013.

[31] Y. Zhou, Z. Wang, W. Zhou, and X. Jiang. Hey, you, get off of my market: Detecting malicious apps in official and alternative android markets. In *Network and Distributed System Security Symposium(NDSS)*, 2012.

[32] Y. Zhou, X. Zhang, X. Jiang, and V. W. Freeh. Taming information-stealing smartphone applications (on android). In *Proceedings of the 4th International Conference on Trust and Trustworthy Computing*, pages 93–107, 2011.

# APPENDIX

# A. EVALUATION OF APPLICATIONS

Detailed information about applications evaluated in Section 6 is shown in Table 4. Notice that a "\*" besides the version number or the size of an application indicates that the version or the size of that application varies with different devices, and the number shown in the table is the one for our testing device and system. There is no information for native libraries in PlayKids, because apktool fails to disassemble the application. For DJ Studio 5, we include its native libraries and dependencies in the table, but apktool fails to rebuild the application after disassembling. Further experiments show that the failure is not resulted from the instrumentation of NativeGuard, as apktool fails to build the application even without any change after disassembling.

| Category | App | Version | Size | Native Libraries | Needed NDK Libraries |
|---|---|---|---|---|---|
| Photography | Snap Camera HDR | 2.1.4 | 5.3M | libjni_eglfence.so libjni_filtershow_filters.so libjni_mosaic.so | libjnigraphics.so |
| | Photo Editor by Aviary | 3.1.1 | 10M | libaviary_moalite.so libaviary_native.so libexif_extended.so | libjnigraphics.so |
| | Photo Editor | 1.3.13 | 1.9M | libIUDeskImageFilter.so libIUDeskJpegCodec.so | libjnigraphics.so libjnigraphics.so |
| Social | Snapchat | 4.0.20* | 7.5M* | libphotoeffect.so | libjnigraphics.so |
| | ooVoo | 2.0.4 | 21M | libovmedia-v7a.so | libjnigraphics.so libGLESv2.so |
| | Badoo - Meet New People | 2.27.3* | 19M | libScanPay.so | |
| Communication | WhatsApp Messenger | 2.11.109 | 11M | libframeconv.so | |
| | AntiVirus Security | 3.4.2.1* | 9.5M* | libdeng.so | |
| | Handcent SMS | 5.3 | 6.0M | libhccommon.so libmms2gif.so libspeex.so | |
| Tools | Brightest Flashlight Free | 2.4.1 | 1.2M | libndkmoment.so | |
| | GO Keyboard | 1.9.11 | 5.3M | libMFtInput.so | |
| | Android Terminal Emulator | 1.0.53 | 456k | libjackpal-androidterm4.so | |
| Shopping | eBay | 2.5.0.31* | 10M* | libredlaser.so | |
| | Walgreens | 4.1 | 18M | libaviary_moalite.so libaviary_native.so libexif_extended.so | libjnigraphics.so |
| | Out of Milk Shopping List | 4.1.6* | 8.9M* | libscanditsdk-android-3.4.0.so | |
| Games | Pou | 1.4.8 | 16M | libsonic.so | |
| | Farm Story: Thanksgiving | 1.9.6.3 | 16M | libs8.so | |
| | Cartoon Camera | 1.99 | 1.0M | libgpuimage-library.so | |
| Business | Box | 2.3.0* | 11.3M* | libleveldb.so | |
| | Call Blocker | 4.2.46.20 | 3.9M | libNqCrypto.so | |
| | Olive Office Premium (free) | 1.0.89 | 19M | libchmjni.so libpdfjni.so | libjnigraphics.so |
| Books & Reference | Cool Reader | 3.1.2-34 | 6.7M | libcr3engine-3-1-0.so | libGLESv1_CM.so |
| | Audible for Android | 1.5.3* | 9M* | libAAX_SDK.so | |
| | Ancestry | 2.2.335* | 5.7M* | libNativeTreeViewer.so | |
| Education | Mathway | 1.0.3 | 13M | libmonodroid.so | |
| | PlayKids | 1.1.1 | 17M | N/A | N/Λ |
| Music & Audio | iHeartRadio | 4.10.0* | 7.7M* | libaacarray.so | |
| | Bandsintown Concerts | 4.3.2.1 | 10M | libdeezer.so | |
| | DJ Studio 5 | 5.0.8 | 11M | libaudio-jni.so | |
| Lifestyle | AroundMe | 4.2.4 | 5.2M | libcountry-database.so | |

Table 4: Separated applications and their information.

# Short Paper
# Attacking and Defending Lightweight PHY Security Schemes for Wireless Communications

Nicholas Kolokotronis
Department of Informatics and
Telecommunications
University of Peloponnese
22100 Tripolis, Greece
nkolok@uop.gr

Alexandros Katsiotis
Department of Informatics and
Telecommunications
University of Athens
15784 Athens, Greece
akats@di.uoa.gr

Nicholas Kalouptsidis
Department of Informatics and
Telecommunications
University of Athens
15784 Athens, Greece
kalou@di.uoa.gr

## ABSTRACT

This paper investigates the security offered by PHY schemes that are well oriented towards jointly providing security and protection form channel errors. In particular, we focus on constructions that were recently proposed in the literature, whose security relies on the secrecy of parameters defining the encoding/decoding process of convolutional codes. Such schemes were shown to be quite promising in terms of error correcting capabilities, but no security analysis was provided to justify their use for wireless communications. To this end, we evaluate the strength of the PHY security scheme against chosen plaintext attacks, as well as known plaintext attacks that are built upon an extension of the known algorithm of Blum, Kalai, and Wasserman. The security analysis derives the parameters to be used for achieving a high security level against such type of attacks with low encoding and decoding complexity.

## Categories and Subject Descriptors

E.3 [**Data Encryption**]: Miscellaneous; D.4.6 [**Security and Protection**]: Cryptographic Controls

## Keywords

PHY security; code based cryptosystems; cryptanalysis; LPN

## 1. INTRODUCTION

Two important features of modern digital communication systems are security and error control coding. Traditionally, they are provided separately by schemes being employed at different layers of the protocol stack. However, a number of schemes have been proposed in literature that jointly design such functions at the physical layer (PHY) [6, 7, 12, 13]. The advantage of such constructions is that they are particularly suited for wireless devices with limited resources, since they lead to systems with reduced processing complexity, memory requirements, and power consumption. These designs, that

commonly are referred to as *secure encoders*, are based on embedding a trapdoor in the encoding/decoding process of the channel code. The trapdoor may control the way that puncturing is performed on the encoded sequence of a turbo code [12, 13], the particular mapping that is realized by the interleaver [12], the way that pruning is applied on the trellis diagram of a convolutional code [7], or generally, by keeping secret the specific code employed, from a family of codes [6]. The security of the construction proposed in [7] was conjectured to be high, since it is related to the learning subspace with noise problem [3], a generalization of *learning parity with noise* (LPN) problem [4, 8, 10]; although issues related to reliability were thoroughly discussed therein, the security analysis was left as an open problem.

In this paper, a detailed treatment of the security offered by secure encoders based on convolutional codes is provided. In particular, their strength is evaluated against chosen and known plaintext attacks, whose running time and plaintext requirements are determined for any success probability. To this end the algorithm of Blum, Kalai and Wasserman [2] which solves the LPN problem, is extended and parameters optimizing the time complexity and sample size of the new algorithm are discussed. The security analysis indicates that a high security level can be obtained for moderate values of the codes' parameters.

## 2. PRELIMINARIES

The core PHY modules of communication systems are the *channel encoder*, which encodes the information bits to allow protection from the errors induced during transmission, and the *modulator*, which maps the encoded bits to the signals (waveforms) transmitted via a communication channel [9]. The transmitted signals get corrupted due to channel noise, path loss, etc. [5]. In many cases the noise is assumed to be a Gaussian random process with zero mean and two–sided power spectral density $N_0/2$ (*additive white gaussian noise*, AWGN) [9]. One of the simplest path loss model in wireless communications is the *free space* model, where the signal's power decreases with the distance $d$ of the receiver from the transmitter. If $P_t, P_r$ are the powers of the transmitted and received signal respectively (assuming that non–directional antennas are used), then it holds

$$P_r = \left(\lambda/4\pi d\right)^2 P_t \qquad (1)$$

where $\lambda$ is the signal's wavelength [5]. At the receiver, the *demodulator* processes the received waveforms and feds its output to the *channel decoder*. If *binary phase–shift–keying* (BPSK) modulation is assumed (one bit is mapped to one

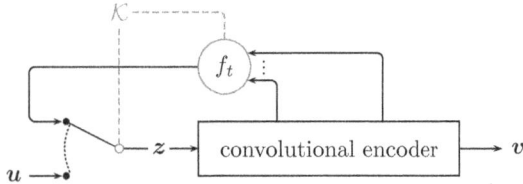

**Figure 1: Architecture of the secure encoder — the key defines the positions and values of pruning bits.**

waveform), the channel is memoryless, and the demodulator delivers hard information (i.e. bits) to the decoder, then the modulator, the channel, and the demodulator are modeled as a *binary symmetric channel* (BSC) whose probability of modifying a transmitted bit (*transition probability*) is

$$p = \frac{1}{2} - \frac{1}{2}\epsilon \qquad (2)$$

with $\epsilon \in (0,1)$ [9]. The channel decoder gives estimates of the transmitted information bits from the received ones.

*Convolutional codes* are popular channel codes for wireless communications; an $(n,k)$ convolutional encoder of memory $m$ is a linear sequential circuit with $k$ inputs and $n$ outputs [9]. Each time instant, $k$ information bits enter the encoder and $n$ encoded bits are produced (as a linear combination of the $k$ input bits and the $m$ bits being stored at the encoder's memory). Convolutional codes are represented by trellis diagrams (labeled directed graphs) that allow the use of efficient decoding algorithms, like the Viterbi algorithm [9].

Suppose that legitimate users communicate over a noisy wireless channel in the presence of eavesdroppers. They use an $(n,1)$ convolutional code $\mathcal{C}$ (called the mother code) of memory $m$ and *error correcting capability* $\omega$ [9]. The secure encoder's architecture is depicted in Fig. 1. The message $\boldsymbol{u}$ of length $k$ is multiplexed with a secret pruning sequence of length $h-k$, in order to generate the sequence $\boldsymbol{z}$ of length $h$. Then, $\boldsymbol{z}$ enters the encoder that outputs the codeword $\boldsymbol{v}$, which is transmitted through the channel. Communicating parties employ the Viterbi algorithm to decode the received sequence $\boldsymbol{r}$ on the trellis diagram of $\mathcal{C}$.

The secret key $\mathcal{K}$ controls a multiplexer that defines the positions of the pruning bits, and the possibly time–varying affine function $f_t$ that computes the values of the pruning bits by operating on the state of the secure encoder. The key space size equals $2^{h-k}\binom{h}{k}$ to account for the possible values and positions of the pruning bits. Let us define $\mathbb{F}_2 = \{0,1\}$; the embedding process of the pruning bits into the message can be described by the following (secret) affine mapping

$$\boldsymbol{z} = \boldsymbol{b} + \boldsymbol{u}\boldsymbol{A} \qquad (3)$$

where $\boldsymbol{A}$ is an $k \times h$ binary matrix of full rank, and $\boldsymbol{b}$ is an $1 \times h$ binary vector. If $\boldsymbol{G}$ is the generator matrix of the code $\mathcal{C}$, the codeword produced by the secret encoder is given by $\boldsymbol{v} = \boldsymbol{z}\boldsymbol{G}$, or equivalently by

$$\boldsymbol{v} = \boldsymbol{d} + \boldsymbol{u}\boldsymbol{C} \qquad (4)$$

where $\boldsymbol{d} = \boldsymbol{b}\boldsymbol{G}$ and $\boldsymbol{C} = \boldsymbol{A}\boldsymbol{G}$. The procedure described above guides the legitimate users in using some secret affine subspace $\boldsymbol{d} + \mathcal{C}$ of the code $\mathcal{C}$ to encode their message. The rate of $\boldsymbol{d} + \mathcal{C}$ equals $\alpha R$, where $\alpha = \frac{k}{h}$ is the information rate in sequence $\boldsymbol{z}$ and $R = \frac{h}{(h+m)n}$ is the rate of $\mathcal{C}$.

Having established a shared secret key $\mathcal{K}$, legitimate users can efficiently perform decoding on the reduced secret trellis diagram that is induced by $\boldsymbol{d} + \mathcal{C}$; due to pruning, a number

of paths in the full trellis diagram of the mother code $\mathcal{C}$ have been discarded. On the other hand, even without knowing the key, eavesdroppers can decode the received sequence by using the full trellis diagram ($\boldsymbol{v}$ is also a codeword of $\mathcal{C}$) to obtain an estimate $\boldsymbol{z}'$ of $\boldsymbol{z}$. What prevents the eavesdropper from correctly recovering $\boldsymbol{z}$ is the fact that the mother code $\mathcal{C}$ is considerably inferior (depending on the pruning rate $1-\alpha$) compared to the code $\boldsymbol{d} + \mathcal{C}$ used by the legitimate users [7]. In addition, after having obtained a noisy estimate of $\boldsymbol{z}$ after decoding, it is not easy to obtain the message $\boldsymbol{u}$.

ATTACK ASSUMPTIONS. Assume that information is transmitted over the BSC, and eavesdroppers have a set of pairs

$$\{\boldsymbol{u}_i, \boldsymbol{r}_i\} = \{\boldsymbol{u}_i, \boldsymbol{v}_i + \boldsymbol{e}_i\}, \qquad i \geq 0$$

at their disposal, where $\boldsymbol{r}_i$ is the received vector and $\boldsymbol{e}_i$ the error vector induced by the channel. Depending on the value of $p$, that is the channel conditions, and the characteristics of the mother code, adversaries may opt to mount an attack directly on the space defined by the codewords $\mathcal{C} \subset \mathbb{F}_2^{(h+m)n}$, or on the input message space $\mathbb{F}_2^h$, after having decoded the received words on the full trellis diagram. Adversaries are assumed to perform *key–recovery attacks* on secure encoders whose pruning function is not time–varying. Thus, their goal is to determine the secret quantities $\boldsymbol{b} \in \mathbb{F}_2^h$ and $\boldsymbol{A} \in \mathbb{F}_2^{k \times h}$ in (4) that completely define the secret pruning function.

## 3. CHOSEN PLAINTEXT ATTACKS

In chosen plaintext attacks, we assume the adversary can request $M$ transmissions of a chosen information message $\boldsymbol{u}$. Let $\boldsymbol{r}_1, \ldots, \boldsymbol{r}_M$ be the corresponding received words, which constitute the rows of an $M \times (h+m)n$ matrix $\boldsymbol{R}$. If $\boldsymbol{U}$ is the $M \times k$ matrix whose rows are $M$ copies of the message $\boldsymbol{u}$, then we get from (4) the following system of equations

$$\boldsymbol{R} = \boldsymbol{D} + \boldsymbol{U}\boldsymbol{C} + \boldsymbol{E} \qquad (5)$$

in the unknowns $\boldsymbol{D}, \boldsymbol{C}, \boldsymbol{E}$; the rows of $\boldsymbol{D}$ are all equal to $\boldsymbol{d}$, whereas the rows of $\boldsymbol{E}$ are the error vectors $\boldsymbol{e}_1, \ldots, \boldsymbol{e}_M$. The above structure is due to the fact that pruning parameters were assumed to be kept constant during a communications session of the legitimate users.

The first attack, which will be referred to as $\mathsf{CPA}_1$, consists of two main steps that aim at recovering the coset $\boldsymbol{d}$ first and then the matrix $\boldsymbol{C}$ in (4). Setting $\boldsymbol{U} = \boldsymbol{0}$ in (5), we get the equation $\boldsymbol{R} = \boldsymbol{D} + \boldsymbol{E}$, where the $j$th column corresponds to a rate $\frac{1}{M}$ repetition code that can be used to recover the bit $d_j$, $j = 1, \ldots, (h+m)n$, of $\boldsymbol{d}$. This is efficiently performed by using *majority logic* (MLG) decoding that is a maximum likelihood algorithm for repetition codes. Let $\boldsymbol{s}_1, \ldots, \boldsymbol{s}_k$ be the vectors in the standard basis of $\mathbb{F}_2^k$, that is

$$\boldsymbol{s}_1 = (1 \; 0 \; \cdots \; 0), \ldots, \boldsymbol{s}_k = (0 \; \cdots \; 0 \; 1).$$

Let $\boldsymbol{S}_i$ be the $M \times k$ matrix whose rows are all equal to $\boldsymbol{s}_i$; then, by setting $\boldsymbol{U} = \boldsymbol{S}_i$ in (5) we obtain $\boldsymbol{R} + \boldsymbol{D} = \boldsymbol{C}_i + \boldsymbol{E}$, $i = 1, \ldots, k$, where each row of $\boldsymbol{C}_i$ equals the $i$th row of $\boldsymbol{C}$. Likewise, we apply MLG decoding to the $j$th column to get an estimate about the bit $c_{ij}$ of $\boldsymbol{C}$ (*see* Alg. 1).

Decoding via MLG is successful as long as the number of errors $X$ in each column of $\boldsymbol{E}$ is less than $\frac{M}{2}$. As the random variable $X$ follows the binomial distribution, we have

$$\Pr\left(X < \frac{M}{2}\right) = \sum_{i=0}^{\lceil M/2 \rceil - 1} \binom{M}{i} p^i (1-p)^{M-i}$$

**Alg. 1** The CPA$_1$ attack

**input:** parameter $M$
1: request $M$ transmissions of $\mathbf{0}_k$
2: $d'_j = \mathsf{MLG}(r_{1j}, \ldots, r_{Mj})$, for $j = 1, \ldots, (h+m)n$
3: **for** $i = 1, \ldots, k$ **do**
4:    request $M$ transmissions of $\mathbf{s}_i$
5:    $c'_{ij} = \mathsf{MLG}(r_{1j}, \ldots, r_{Mj}) + d'_j$, for $j = 1, \ldots, (h+m)n$
6: **end**
**output:** estimates $\mathbf{d}'$ and $\mathbf{C}' = [c'_{ij}]$

$$= \Phi\left(\frac{M/2 - Mp}{\sqrt{Mp(1-p)}}\right) = \Phi\left(\frac{\sqrt{M}\epsilon}{\sqrt{1-\epsilon^2}}\right) \quad (6)$$

for sufficiently small $\epsilon = 1 - 2p$ where $\Phi(\cdot)$ is the cumulative distribution function, of the normal distribution. The attack is successful when $\mathbf{d}, \mathbf{C}$ are correctly recovered, that is

$$\Pr(\mathbf{d}' = \mathbf{d})\Pr(\mathbf{C}' = \mathbf{C} \mid \mathbf{d}' = \mathbf{d}) = \Phi\left(\frac{\sqrt{M}\epsilon}{\sqrt{1-\epsilon^2}}\right)^{(k+1)\frac{h}{R}} \quad (7)$$

from (6) and the fact that all errors induced by the channel are independent and identically distributed.

THEOREM 1. *The* CPA$_1$ *attack succeeds with probability at least* $1 - \delta$ *for* $N_{\mathsf{CPA}_1} = (k+1)M$ *number of pairs, where*

$$M = 2\epsilon^{-2}\ln\frac{1}{1 - (1-\delta)^{R/\ell}} \quad (8)$$

$R$ *is the rate of the mother code, and* $\ell = h(k+1)$.

PROOF. Let the success probability be equal to $1 - \delta$, for some desired probability of error $\delta$. By (6), (7) we have that the probability of MLG being unsuccessful should be

$$\Pr\left(X \geq \frac{M}{2}\right) = 1 - (1-\delta)^{\frac{R}{\ell}}.$$

Moreover, by using the fact that the expected value of $X$ is $Mp = \frac{1}{2}M(1-\epsilon)$, and taking the Chernoff bound, we get

$$\Pr\left(X \geq \frac{M}{2}\right) = \Pr\left(X \geq \mathbb{E}[X] + \tfrac{1}{2}M\epsilon\right) \leq e^{-\frac{1}{2}M\epsilon^2}.$$

Solving $e^{-M\epsilon^2/2} = 1 - (1-\delta)^{R/\ell}$ with respect to $M$ leads to (8). The fact that $M$ transmissions are needed for each of the $k+1$ distinct messages to estimate $\mathbf{d}, \mathbf{C}$ gives $N_{\mathsf{CPA}_1}$. □

The parameter $\delta$ in Theorem 1 must be chosen sufficiently close to zero to ensure the correct recovery of $\mathbf{d}$ and $\mathbf{C}$ with high probability. However, the eavesdropper could tolerate a fraction of $\delta = \frac{\omega R}{h}$ errors, as these could be corrected upon decoding the possibly noisy coset $\mathbf{d}'$ and the rows of $\mathbf{C}'$ on the (full) mother trellis. Note that this final step will not be possible if mother codes of small minimum distance are employed, forcing the adversaries to require large $M$ to get an acceptable success probability.

AN IMPROVED ATTACK. Let the adversary launch a chosen plaintext attack, referred to as CPA$_2$, after having decoded the received words in $\mathbf{R}$. Therefore, starting from (5), the following system of equations is obtained

$$\mathbf{Y} = \mathbf{B} + \mathbf{U}\mathbf{A} + \boldsymbol{\mathcal{E}} \quad (9)$$

in the unknowns $\mathbf{B}, \mathbf{A}, \boldsymbol{\mathcal{E}}$. The rows of the $M \times h$ matrix $\boldsymbol{\mathcal{E}}$ correspond to the decoding error vectors. The error rate $q$ after decoding depends on the the the mother code's *bit weight enumerating function* (bit–WEF) [9], and is given by

$$q = \tfrac{1}{2} - \tfrac{1}{2}\eta \quad (10)$$

for some $\eta \in (0, 1)$. To recover $\mathbf{b}, \mathbf{A}$ we proceed as in CPA$_1$, by forming a set of rate $\frac{1}{M}$ repetition codes from the columns of (9). The main difference with the previous attack lies in the error rate prior the application of MLG decoding, and the length of the words to be decoded. By following a similar analysis, the success probability of CPA$_2$ is found to be

$$\Pr(\mathbf{b}' = \mathbf{b})\Pr(\mathbf{A}' = \mathbf{A} \mid \mathbf{b}' = \mathbf{b}) = \Phi\left(\frac{\sqrt{M}\eta}{\sqrt{1-\eta^2}}\right)^{(k+1)h} \quad (11)$$

where $\eta = 1 - 2q$. We provide without a proof the following result that determines the number of pairs required to attain a desired success probability.

THEOREM 2. *The* CPA$_2$ *attack succeeds with probability at least* $1 - \delta$ *for* $N_{\mathsf{CPA}_2} = (k+1)M$ *number of pairs, where*

$$M = 2\eta^{-2}\ln\frac{1}{1 - (1-\delta)^{1/\ell}} \quad (12)$$

*and* $\ell = h(k+1)$.

The adversary will choose the attack which, for the same parameter $\delta$, minimizes the total number of pairs. It can be shown that CPA$_2$ outperforms CPA$_1$ for small $p$, where the (poor) error–correcting capabilities of $\mathcal{C}$ can be exploited.

## 4. THE LPN PROBLEM

The *learning parity with noise* (LPN) problem has found many applications in cryptography (amongst other areas) in the past few years [2, 4, 8, 10]. Its computational variant is an average–case version of the *computational syndrome decoding* problem, which is known to be NP–hard [1]. More precisely, let $\mathbf{x} \in \mathbb{F}_2^k$ be a secret vector and $\mathcal{O}_{k,p}(\mathbf{x})$ be an oracle providing independent uniformly distributed samples $\{\mathbf{a}, y\} = \{\mathbf{a}, \mathbf{a}\mathbf{x}^T + e\}$, where $\Pr(e = 1) = p$. An algorithm $\mathcal{A}$ is said to $(n, t, \delta)$–solve the LPN$_{k,p}$ problem if

$$\Pr\left(\mathcal{A}^{\mathcal{O}_{k,p}(\mathbf{x})}(1^k) = \mathbf{x}\right) \geq 1 - \delta, \qquad \forall \mathbf{x} \in \mathbb{F}_2^k$$

by making at most $n$ queries to $\mathcal{O}_{k,p}(\mathbf{x})$ and running in time at most $t$, where $\delta \in \left(0, \frac{1}{2}\right]$.

The algorithm proposed by Blum, Kalai, and Wasserman [2], referred to as BKW in the sequel, solves the LPN$_{k,p}$ problem with $2^{O(k/\log k)}$ sample size and running time. The BKW algorithm assumes that an example $\mathbf{a}$ is comprised by $b$ blocks of length $l$ such that $bl \geq k$, and labels each $l$-bit block with an integer in the set $\mathbb{Z}_{2^l} = \{0, 1, \ldots, 2^l - 1\}$. At each iteration BKW makes $b2^l$ queries to the oracle $\mathcal{O}_{k,p}(\mathbf{x})$, and by essentially using a block Gaussian elimination, writes the vector $\mathbf{s}_1 = (1 \, 0 \, \cdots \, 0)$ as the sum of $w = 2^{b-1}$ examples, say $\mathbf{a}_{i_1}, \ldots, \mathbf{a}_{i_{2^{b-1}}}$. This gives one equation $y = x_1 + e'$ for the first bit of $\mathbf{x}$, where $y = \sum_j y_{i_j}$ and $e' = \sum_j e_{i_j}$. These steps are repeated to get a large number $M$ of independent equations about $x_1$ and determine its correct value via MLG decoding. However, as $\Pr(e' = 1) = p'$ is given by

$$p' = \tfrac{1}{2} - \tfrac{1}{2}(1 - 2p)^w \quad (13)$$

the Chernoff bound leads to $M \geq 2(1 - 2p)^{-2w}\ln\frac{1}{\delta}$, where $\delta$ is the error tolerance. By cyclically shifting each example, we work as above to get a set of independent equations for the bits $x_2, \ldots, x_k$ of the secret vector as well.

THEOREM 3. [2] *The* LPN$_{k,p}$ *problem can be solved with sample size and total computation time* $\mathsf{poly}((1 - 2p)^{-2^b}, 2^l)$.

A more accurate complexity analysis that was performed in [4] indicates that the BKW algorithm requires $O(b^3 2^l M)$ sample size and running time. A subexponential algorithm is obtained by setting $b = \frac{1}{2}\log_2 k$ and $l = 2k/\log_2 k$, for which we get $w = \frac{1}{2}\sqrt{k}$ [2].

AN EXTENSION OF BKW. The algorithm writes a vector of the standard basis as a sum of an even number of samples; next, this is extended to an odd number of samples, as it is required by the attacks of Section 5. In particular, we write $s_1, \ldots, s_k$ as a sum of $w = 3^{b-1}$ examples, where they are likewise comprised by $b$ blocks of length $l$, with $bl \geq k$.

*Definition 1.* The binary vector $a$ of length $k$ is called an $(w, i)$–vector if $a \in \mathbb{F}_2^{(b-i)l} \times \{0\}^{il}$ for some $i = 0, \ldots, b$, and it is the sum of $w$ samples. Moreover, a set of $(w, i)$–vectors of cardinality at least $m$ is called an $(w, i, m)$–set.

Let $\theta$ be a primitive element of the finite field $\mathbb{F}_{2^l}$ [9]. In the nonzero $l$–bit blocks $(a_{i1} \cdots a_{il})$ of $a$ we associate the label $\theta^v$, $0 \leq v \leq 2^l - 2$, that is written as $\theta^v = \sum_j a_{ij}\theta^{j-1}$ in terms of the basis $\{1, \theta, \ldots, \theta^{l-1}\}$. Let us randomly draw an $(1, 0, (2b-1)2^l)$–set of samples, and let it be partitioned as $V = \{V_x : x \in \mathbb{F}_{2^l}\}$ according to the label of the last block of the examples. The list $L = \{L_x : x \in \mathbb{F}_{2^l}\}$ is constructed by choosing two elements from each class $V_x$ at random (and discarding them afterwards). In order to efficiently zero the last block —while ensuring that each nonzero label from the list is used exactly twice— we rely on the following property: given some $v \neq 0$ there exists a unique $t \neq 0, v$ (that depends on $v$) such that $1 + \theta^v = \theta^t$. Therefore, for $i = 0, \ldots, 2^l - 2$, we pick $\lambda \in L_{\theta^i}$, $\lambda' \in L_{\theta^{v+i}}$ and add $\lambda + \lambda'$ to the vectors in $V_{\theta^{t+i}}$. The exception to the rule are $\lambda, \lambda' \in L_0$ in which case $\lambda + \lambda'$ is added to $V_0$. An $(3, 1, (2b-3)2^l)$–set is thus obtained by this process which if repeated $b-1$ times (from the last block to the second) leads to an $(3^{b-1}, b-1, 2^l)$–set. At the last step, we seek for the vector $(1\ 0\ \cdots\ 0) \in V_1$ that is written as the sum of $w = 3^{b-1}$ examples; this yields one equation for $x_1$ (equations for $x_2, \ldots, x_l$ are also obtained at this step). In case one of the classes $V_{\theta^0}, \ldots, V_{\theta^{l-1}}$ is empty, which happens with probability not exceeding $1/e$, we draw a new $(1, 0, (2b-1)2^l)$–set and repeat the above process. To get equations for the rest of the bits of $x$, we cyclically shift the examples as shown in Alg. 2.

THEOREM 4. *The extended BKW algorithm can solve the* $\text{LPN}_{k,p}$ *problem with sample size and total computation time* $2^{O(k/\log k)}$.

PROOF. The sample size of the extended BKW algorithm is twice that of the original, as the number of samples drawn at the beginning of each iteration is doubled; the same holds for the number of computations, as $\lambda + \lambda'$ is computed only once and then added to the elements of a class. Hence, we get $O(b^3 2^{l+1} M)$ sample size and total running time by the analysis of [4]. Setting $b = \frac{1}{2}\log_3 2k$ and $l = 2k/\log_3 2k$, we have that $w = \frac{\sqrt{2}}{3}\sqrt{k}$. These parameters are asymptotically equivalent to the ones used in the original BKW algorithm, thus leading to the same performance. $\square$

In [2] and Alg. 2, a new set of samples is drawn at each iteration to compute a new equation for all $x_1, \ldots, x_k$ that is discarded afterwards, resulting in a waste of information [8]. At the expense of increasing the total running time to $O(kb^2 2^l M)$, we can compute the $M$ equations and estimate $x_i$ before moving on to the next one. This allows discarding

---

**Alg. 2** The extended BKW algorithm

**input:** oracle $\mathcal{O}_{k,p}(x)$, parameters $b, M$
**initialization:** set $l = k/b$ and fix a primitive $\theta \in \mathbb{F}_{2^l}$
        find $v, t$ such that $1 + \theta^v = \theta^t$
1: **for** $j = 1, \ldots, M$ **do**
2:   draw $(2b-1)2^l$ samples at random
3:   **for** $\tau = 0, \ldots, b-1$ **do**
4:     shift examples by $\tau l$ bits to get $V$
5:     **for** $\nu = b, \ldots, 2$ **do**
6:       partition $V = \{V_x : x \in \mathbb{F}_{2^l}\}$   ▷ w.r.t. $\nu$th block
7:       build $L = \{L_x : x \in \mathbb{F}_{2^l}\}$ from $V$
8:       remove $L$ from $V$
9:       **for** $i = 0, \ldots, 2^l - 2$ **do**
10:         choose $\lambda \in L_{\theta^i}$, $\lambda' \in L_{\theta^{v+i}}$
11:         add $\lambda + \lambda'$ to $V_{\theta^{t+i}}$
12:       **end**
13:       add $\lambda + \lambda'$ to $V_0$ with $\lambda, \lambda' \in L_0$
14:     **end**
15:     partition $V = \{V_x : x \in \mathbb{F}_{2^l}\}$   ▷ w.r.t. 1st block
16:     find $s_1 \in V_{\theta^0}, \ldots, s_l \in V_{\theta^{l-1}}$
17:     build $y_{ij} = x_i + e'_{ij}$ for $\tau l < i \leq (\tau+1)l$
18:   **end**
19: **end**
20: $x'_i = \mathsf{MLG}(y_{i1}, \ldots, y_{iM})$, for $i = 1, \ldots, k$
**output:** estimate $x'$ of the secret vector $x$

---

$w$ vectors at each iteration (those used in the summation), therefore reducing the sample size to $O(wM)$. The trade–off between sample size and time complexity was also explored in [10], where an algorithm (not related to ours) of reduced sample size was proposed.

## 5. KNOWN PLAINTEXT ATTACKS

Suppose that an adversary knows a set of $N$ information messages $\{u_1, \ldots, u_N\}$ encrypted by the secure encoder and the associated received words $\{r_1, \ldots, r_N\}$; the messages are drawn from $\mathbb{F}_2^k$ uniformly at random. Furthermore, let these vectors constitute the rows of the $N \times k$ and $N \times (h+m)n$ matrices $U, R$ respectively.

The first known plaintext attack, referred to as $\text{KPA}_1$, is mount prior to decoding. Due to the lack of structure within $U$, we cannot directly employ MLG decoding. However, we can recover the secret coset $d$ by constructing a low–density parity check matrix $P$ of $U$, and multiply both sides of (5) with $P$ in order to get $PR = PD + PE$. Assuming that the row weight $w$ in $P$ is constant, then by the structure of $D$ (see section 3), we have $PD = 0$ if $w$ is even, or $PD$ is a matrix whose rows are all equal to $d$ as well (and thus, we can apply MLG decoding) if $w$ is odd. This task can be performed by the extended BKW algorithm, if modified as follows: instead of seeking for the elements of the standard basis (Alg. 2, line 16), we only need to search for the all–zero vector $0_k$. This is the version utilized in the $\text{KPA}_1$ attack and is denoted by $\text{BKW}_e$ (see Alg. 3).

On the other hand, assuming that $P$ is such that its rows have constant even weight $w$ and $PU = S_i$ (all the rows are equal to $s_i$), then multiplying both sides of (5) with $P$, we obtain $PR = C_i + PE$, since $PD = 0$ and $S_iC = C_i$, for $i = 1, \ldots, k$; therefore, we can apply MLG and recover the $i$th row of the matrix $C$. This task is efficiently performed by the original BKW algorithm [2].

**Alg. 3** The KPA$_1$ attack

---
**input:** parameter $M$
1: set $b_1 = \frac{1}{2}\log_3 2k$ and $w_1 = 3^{b_1-1}$
2: set $b_2 = \frac{1}{2}\log_2 k$ and $w_2 = 2^{b_2-1}$
3: request transmission of $w_2 M$ plaintexts
4: $\boldsymbol{d}' = \mathsf{BKW}_\mathsf{e}(\{\boldsymbol{U}, \boldsymbol{R}\}, b_1, M)$
5: $\boldsymbol{C}' = \mathsf{BKW}(\{\boldsymbol{U}, \boldsymbol{R}\}, b_2, M)$
**output:** estimates $\boldsymbol{d}'$ and $\boldsymbol{C}' = [c'_{ij}]$

---

From the above description, we have that the total number of pairs required by the attack is $N_{\mathsf{KPA}_1} = \max\{w, w'\}M$, where $w$ (resp. $w'$) is the number of examples used in a sum by the original (resp. extended) BKW algorithm. Therefore

$$N_{\mathsf{KPA}_1} = wM = \frac{1}{2}\sqrt{k}\,M \tag{14}$$

for the particular parameter values suggested in Alg. 3.

Note that the known plaintext attack computes the coset $\boldsymbol{d}$ independently from the matrix $\boldsymbol{C}$. The advantage of this approach is that the probability of correctly recovering $\boldsymbol{d}, \boldsymbol{C}$ satisfies $\Pr(\boldsymbol{d}' = \boldsymbol{d}, \boldsymbol{C}' = \boldsymbol{C}) = \Pr(\boldsymbol{d}' = \boldsymbol{d})\Pr(\boldsymbol{C}' = \boldsymbol{C})$ and hence, by following an analysis similar to that of Section 3, we have the following success probability for KPA$_1$

$$\Pr(\boldsymbol{d}' = \boldsymbol{d})\Pr(\boldsymbol{C}' = \boldsymbol{C}) = \Phi\left(\frac{\sqrt{M}\epsilon^{w'}}{\sqrt{1-\epsilon^{2w'}}}\right)^{\frac{h}{R}}\Phi\left(\frac{\sqrt{M}\epsilon^{w}}{\sqrt{1-\epsilon^{2w}}}\right)^{k\frac{h}{R}}$$

$$> \Phi\left(\frac{\sqrt{M}\epsilon^{w}}{\sqrt{1-\epsilon^{2w}}}\right)^{(k+1)\frac{h}{R}} \tag{15}$$

where the lower bound is obtained using $w' < w$ and the fact that the cumulative distribution function is strictly increasing. The following result determines the number of pairs of the above described attacks, using the optimal values of the parameters $b, l, w$ in the BKW algorithm.

THEOREM 5. *The* KPA$_1$ *attack succeeds with probability at least* $1 - \delta$ *for a number of pairs*

$$N_{\mathsf{KPA}_1} = \frac{1}{2}\sqrt{k}\,\epsilon^{-\sqrt{k}+2}\,N_{\mathsf{CPA}_1} \tag{16}$$

*where* $N_{\mathsf{CPA}_1}$ *is the corresponding value of* CPA$_1$ *for the same parameters.*

PROOF. Let $1 - \delta$ be the lower bound given in (15). From (14), and working as in Theorem 1, we get that the number $M$ of equations is given by

$$M = 2\epsilon^{-2w}\ln\frac{1}{1-(1-\delta)^{R/\ell}} = \epsilon^{-2w+2}N_{\mathsf{CPA}_1}. \tag{17}$$

The claim follows from (14), and by substituting above the value of the weight $w = \frac{1}{2}\sqrt{k}$. □

DECODE–THEN–ATTACK. The attack provided above can be adapted to the case where an adversary decodes the received words on the full mother trellis diagram before the attack is performed; this attack is referred to as KPA$_2$. The starting point is (9), where the error rate $q$ characterizing $\boldsymbol{\mathcal{E}}$ is given by (10). Since the BKW algorithm operates on $\boldsymbol{U}$, any choices made regarding the optimal values of $b, l, w$ need not change with respect to the previous attack. Hence, the number of plaintexts $N_{\mathsf{KPA}_2}$ is also given by (14), but with $M$ depending on $q$ instead of $p$. The probability of correctly recovering the secret quantities $\boldsymbol{b}, \boldsymbol{A}$ in KPA$_2$ satisfies

$$\Pr(\boldsymbol{b}' = \boldsymbol{b})\Pr(\boldsymbol{A}' = \boldsymbol{A}) > \Phi\left(\frac{\sqrt{M}\eta^{w}}{\sqrt{1-\eta^{2w}}}\right)^{h(k+1)} \tag{18}$$

**Table 1: Number of times each algorithm is invoked.**

|        | CPA$_1$       | CPA$_2$        | KPA$_1$ | KPA$_2$ |
|--------|---------------|----------------|---------|---------|
| MLG    | $(k+1)(h+m)n$ | $(k+1)h$       | –       | –       |
| Viterbi| $k+1$         | $(k+1)M_2$     | $k+1$   | $wM_2$  |
| BKW    | –             | –              | $M_1$   | $M_2$   |

with $\eta = 1 - 2q$. The analogue of (16) for this type of attack can be obtained by starting from (18) to get

$$M = 2\eta^{-2w}\ln\frac{1}{1-(1-\delta)^{1/\ell}} \tag{19}$$

and then work as in the proof of Theorem 5. The number of plaintexts required by known plaintext attacks is drastically increased compared to chosen plaintext attacks.

# 6. ATTAINED SECURITY LEVEL

To determine the bit–level security attained by the secure encoders we investigate the average time complexity of the attacks —not only the number of plaintexts that should be available at the eavesdropper. This includes the complexity of the Viterbi algorithm, which is used for the decoding of convolutional codes, as well as the complexity of the MLG and BKW algorithms that are employed by the attacks.

Based on the parameters of the mother convolutional code, the Viterbi algorithm requires $O(h2^{m+1}n)$ real additions and $O(h2^m)$ real comparisons [11], therefore giving a complexity $O(h2^m(2n+1))$. Note that the adversary applies decoding on the trellis diagram of the mother code, and hence this is his decoding complexity per intercepted codeword if either attack is performed after decoding. The complexity of MLG decoding is $O(M)$. BKW and BKW$_\mathsf{e}$ compute $M$ equations for the set of vectors $\boldsymbol{0}_k, \boldsymbol{s}_1, \ldots, \boldsymbol{s}_k$, and their complexity is $O((k+1)(\log k)^2 2^{k/\log k})$ per equation from the analysis of Section 5. The base of the logarithm is 2 (resp. 3) for the original (resp. extended) BKW; both values yield asymptotically equivalent complexity expressions. The complexities of the attacks are derived below.

*a) Chosen plaintext attacks:* Let $M_1, M_2$ be given by (8), (12). The number of times MLG and Viterbi are invoked is shown in Table 1, where Viterbi is used in CPA$_1$ to decode $\boldsymbol{d}$ and the rows of $\boldsymbol{C}$ to find $\boldsymbol{b}, \boldsymbol{A}$. The total complexity of the chosen plaintext attacks is therefore given by

$$\mathcal{T}_{\mathsf{CPA}_1} = \frac{h}{R}N_{\mathsf{CPA}_1} + \ell 2^m(2n+1)$$

$$\mathcal{T}_{\mathsf{CPA}_2} = h\left(1 + 2^m(2n+1)\right)N_{\mathsf{CPA}_2}$$

*b) Known plaintext attacks:* let $M_1, M_2$ be given by (17), (19). The BKW algorithms are invoked only once; the values in Table 1 are used to highlight the number of iterations. As a result, the attacks have the following complexities, where the weight $w = \frac{1}{2}\sqrt{k}$ is used:

$$\mathcal{T}_{\mathsf{KPA}_1} = \frac{1}{w}(k+1)(\log k)^2 2^{k/\log k}N_{\mathsf{KPA}_1}$$
$$+ \ell 2^m(2n+1)$$

$$\mathcal{T}_{\mathsf{KPA}_2} = \frac{1}{w}(k+1)(\log k)^2 2^{k/\log k}N_{\mathsf{KPA}_2}$$
$$+ h2^m(2n+1)N_{\mathsf{KPA}_2}$$

In Table 2, we give the minimum values of $k$ for which a certain security level is attained, depending on the crossover probability of the BSC. A pair $(p, k)$ is such that the value of $\log_2\min\{\mathcal{T}_{\mathsf{KPA}_1}, \mathcal{T}_{\mathsf{KPA}_2}\}$ is greater than or equal to the desired

**Table 2: The pruned code's dimension $k$ needed to attain 32/64/128–bit security.**

| security | $p$ | $2^{-2}$ | $2^{-4}$ | $2^{-6}$ | $2^{-8}$ | $2^{-10}$ |
|---|---|---|---|---|---|---|
| 32–bit | CPA | $2^{11.14}$ | $2^{12.35}$ | $2^{16.03}$ | $2^{19.84}$ | $2^{23.70}$ |
|  | KPA | $2^{5.51}$ | $2^{6.82}$ | $2^{7.41}$ | $2^{7.88}$ | $2^{8.25}$ |
| 64–bit | CPA | $2^{24.97}$ | $2^{25.47}$ | $2^{25.47}$ | $2^{25.47}$ | $2^{25.47}$ |
|  | KPA | $2^{7.77}$ | $2^{8.58}$ | $2^{8.84}$ | $2^{9.07}$ | $2^{9.28}$ |
| 128–bit | CPA | $2^{25.47}$ | $2^{25.47}$ | $2^{25.47}$ | $2^{25.47}$ | $2^{25.47}$ |
|  | KPA | $2^{9.52}$ | $2^{10.05}$ | $2^{10.17}$ | $2^{10.28}$ | $2^{10.38}$ |

security level (the same holds for chosen plaintext attacks). As shown, the proposed scheme achieves 128–bit security at $p = 2^{-10}$ against KPAs for $k \geq 2^{10.38} \simeq 1332$.

EXAMPLE SCENARIO. Assume that Alice transmits encoded sequences through free space (*see* (1)). BPSK modulation is used and the signal at the receiver is corrupted by AWGN. The demodulator's output at the receiver is hard quantized and the transition probability of the respective BSC is

$$p = Q\left(\sqrt{2E_s^{(d)}/N_0}\right)$$

where $E_s^{(d)}$ is the energy of a symbol at distance $d$ from the transmitter [9]. The secret encoder employs the recursive convolutional encoder of [7, Ex. 3]. Let the distance between Alice and Bob be 200 meters, and let the SNR $E_s^{(d)}/N_0$ at Bob's receiver be $-0.5$dB; the BER experienced by Bob is $10^{-4}$. With the above parameters, Fig. 2 illustrates that a high security level is attained (for moderate $h$), even if the distance of Eve from Alice is 100 meters, i.e. Eve is closer to Alice than Bob. If the catastrophic mother encoder [9]

$$\boldsymbol{G}(D) = \left(\frac{1+D+D^2+D^4}{1+D+D^4}, \frac{1+D^2+D^3}{1+D+D^4}\right)$$

was used instead, it is shown in Fig. 2 (dashed lines) that the attained security is improved for small values of $d$, compared to the non–catastrophic encoder —this is in accordance with remarks made in [7] about possible increase in security.

## 7. CONCLUSIONS

The security of PHY schemes that provide both reliability and security —by secretly pruning a convolutional code— is studied in this paper. Known and chosen plaintext attacks have been employed, and the parameters of the system that lead to secure implementations were derived. The security offered by the proposed scheme was shown to be high, particularly in the case of known plaintext attacks. It is expected that the system's security against chosen plaintext attacks is also be increased by using time varying pruning functions. Other attack types need to be considered to fully assess the system's security (like algebraic attacks). Ongoing research seeks for optimal trade–offs between security and reliability.

## 8. ACKNOWLEDGMENTS

This work is co–financed by the European Union (European Social Fund) and Greek national funds through the operational program "Education & Lifelong Learning" of the National Strategic Reference Framework (NSRF). Research funding program THALES: investing in knowledge society through the European Social Fund.

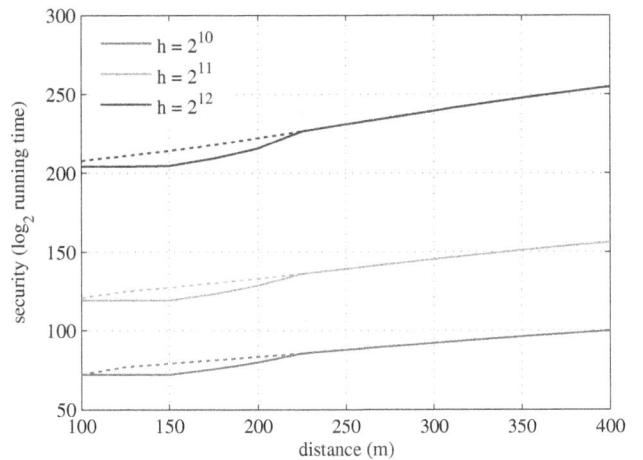

**Figure 2: Security against KPAs; dashed lines are catastrophic encoders ($\alpha = 1/2$, $\delta = 1/4$).**

## 9. REFERENCES

[1] E. Berlekamp, R. McEliece, and H. van Tilborg. On the inherent intractability of certain coding problems. *IEEE Trans. Inform. Theory*, 24(3):384–386, 1978.

[2] A. Blum, A. Kalai, and H. Wasserman. Noise–tolerant learning, the parity problem, and the statistical query model. *J. ACM*, 50(4):506–519, 2003.

[3] Y. Dodis, Y. Kalai, and S. Lovett. On cryptography with auxiliary input. In Proc. of *STOC '09*, pages 621–630. ACM, 2009.

[4] M. Fossorier, M. Mihaljevic, *et al.* An algorithm for solving the LPN problem and its application to security evaluation of the HB protocols for RFID authentication. In Proc. of *INDOCRYPT '06*, 48–62. Springer LNCS 4329, 2006.

[5] A. Goldsmith. *Wireless Communications*. Cambridge University Press, 2005.

[6] T. Hwang and T. Rao. Secret error–correcting codes (SECC). In Proc. of *CRYPTO '88*, pages 540–563. Springer LNCS 403, 1988.

[7] A. Katsiotis, N. Kolokotronis, and N. Kalouptsidis. Physical layer security via secret trellis pruning. In Proc. of *IEEE PIMRC '13*, pages 502–507, 2013.

[8] E. Levieil and P.–A. Fouque. An improved LPN algorithm. In Proc. of *SCN '06*, pages 348–359. Springer LNCS 4116, 2006.

[9] S. Lin and D. Costello. *Error Control Coding*. Prentice Hall, 2004.

[10] V. Lyubashevsky. The parity problem in the presence of noise, decoding random linear codes, and the subset sum problem. In Proc. of *APPROX. & RANDOM '05*, pages 378–389. Springer LNCS 3624, 2005.

[11] R. McEliece. On the BCJR trellis for linear block codes. *IEEE Trans. Inform. Theory*, 42(4):1072–1092, 1996.

[12] A. Nerri, D. Blasi, *et al.* Joint security and channel coding for OFDM communications. In Proc. of *EUSIPCO '08*, pages 1–5, 2008.

[13] A. Payandeh, M. Ahmadian, and M. Aref. Adaptive secure channel coding based on punctured turbo codes. *IEE Commun. Proc.*, 153(2):313–316, 2006.

# Short Paper: Gathering Tamper Evidence in Wi-Fi Networks Based on Channel State Information

Ibrahim Ethem Bagci and Utz Roedig
School of Computing and Communications
Lancaster University
Lancaster, UK
{i.bagci,u.roedig}@lancaster.ac.uk

Matthias Schulz and Matthias Hollick
Secure Mobile Networking Lab
Technische Universität Darmstadt
Darmstadt, Germany
{mschulz,mhollick}@seemoo.tu-darmstadt.de

## ABSTRACT

Wireless devices are often used in application scenarios with strict security requirements. Examples are physical intrusion detection systems commonly used to protect factories, airports or government buildings. In such scenarios, additional security features such as tamper detection are highly desirable to complement traditional cryptographic mechanisms. In this paper we use channel state information (CSI), extracted from off-the-shelf 802.11n Wi-Fi cards, to calculate a tamper-evidence value for transmitters. This value enables detection of tampering due to device movement or replacement. We describe algorithms for tamper-evidence value computation, discuss the interpretation of this value and evaluate its effectiveness.

## Categories and Subject Descriptors

C.2.3 [**Computer-Communication Networks**]: Network Operations—*Network Monitoring*

## General Terms

Security, Design, Experimentation

## Keywords

802.11; Wireless; Security; PHY; OFDM; Channel State Information; Channel Fingerprinting; Tamper Evidence

## 1. INTRODUCTION

Wireless devices are now commonplace and are often deployed in application scenarios with strict security requirements. For example, wireless devices are often part of physical intrusion detection systems used to protect critical infrastructure. Wireless surveillance cameras might be used within a physical intrusion detection system of an airport. An attacker may aim to change the camera's area of observation. Transmitted image data would still be cryptographically authenticated and tamper detection would require the

inspection of the visual data. An attacker may also obtain key material and replace a node in the deployment to inject false observation data. For these reasons, it is desirable to provide an additional layer of defence that is able to indicate node tampering. In this work, we use wireless channel characteristics to achieve this.

Communication environment changes can be observed via changes in channel characteristics and this effect can be exploited for security purposes. Previous work exploited channel characteristics to detect location changes [12] or message injection [10]. In this work, we use those characteristics to compute a tamper-evidence value for each node. In particular, and in contrast to existing work, we consider transmissions over a varying number of spatial dimensions in multi-antenna configurations of 802.11n Wi-Fi systems.

In 802.11n, the frame preamble on the physical layer is used to compute CSI for each incoming packet. We use this measurement to derive a tamper-evidence value. Moving or replacing a transmitter changes the observed channel characteristics, which results in an increasing tamper-evidence value. For example, a high tamper-evidence value may be used to dispatch security personal to check integrity of a device.

In this paper, we describe algorithms for tracking CSI values of Wi-Fi transmissions and show how to compute the tamper-evidence value. In particular, we account for 802.11n's varying number of used spatial streams. To extract CSI information from off-the-shelf hardware, we use the *Linux 802.11n CSI Tool* [6]. To compute our tamper-evidence value, no additional transmissions or protocol modifications are necessary. The contributions of this paper are:

- *Tamper Evidence:* We describe a method for device-specific tamper evidence computation based on per packet 802.11n CSI. The method handles varying numbers of used spatial streams; a feature used in 802.11n which is not yet considered by previous work.

- *Detection Analysis:* We demonstrate that device movements of just 1 cm and hardware replacements are clearly detectable. We also show that false alarms due to passing pedestrians can be suppressed.

The remaining paper is organised as follows. The next section describes related work. Thereafter, we describe in Section 3 the estimation of CSI as used in 802.11n and our algorithms for tamper evidence computation. Section 4 presents an evaluation of the proposed methods. Section 5 concludes the paper.

## 2. RELATED WORK

Existing work can be grouped into two main categories: transmitter identification and transmitter localisation. Transmitter identification aims to use received signal characteristics to identify the transmitting device (or class of device). Transmitter localisation aims to use the received signal characteristics to determine the location (or area) of the transmitter. Our work presented in this paper falls into both areas. It differs from existing work in three main ways: (i) Most existing work is not based on 802.11n Orthogonal Frequency Division Multiplexing (OFDM) and no work so far has incorporated the fact that dynamic adaptation of the number of spatial independent streams in 802.11n must be taken into account. (ii) Existing work is mostly aimed at rejecting individual messages from an attacker, while we aim to determine a tamper-evidence value based on a number of incoming transmissions. (iii) Existing work does not evaluate the relation between transmitter movement and detection capability of a detection system.

A number of recent works aim at transmitter localisation using channel characteristics. Li et al. [11] propose a method for PHY layer authentication based on measuring the *channel frequency response (CFR)*. Three USRP/GNURadio software-defined radios (SDRs) are deployed at different locations and used as transmitter, receiver and attacker. Transmitter and attacker send packets alternately to the receiver. By employing a change-point detector, transmissions can be distinguished. Patwari et al. [7] used *channel impulse response (CIR)* information to construct link signatures for location distinction. A history of $N-1$ transmission signatures is compared with the $Nth$ transmission signature using the Euclidean distance to decide whether the transmission is from a new location. The method in [7] analyses features in the time domain whereas [11] operates in the frequency domain. Additionally, [11] uses a complex-valued signature where the phase information is included, while [7] uses a real-valued signature where the phase information is excluded. Zhang et al. [12] combine the best features of [11] and [7], which are (i) the advantage of operating in the time domain and (ii) the advantage of using complex-valued signatures. Recently, Jiang et al. [10] proposed a source-authentication method to detect spoofing attacks on 802.11n management frames (MFs) by using CSI. Although this work is not aimed at location distinction, it uses the same source of information (CSI) as we do in our work. It is shown that amplitude of CSI changes for injected frames. To the best our knowledge, this work is the closest one to ours in terms of source of information, encoding methods and test devices. However, the work does not consider encoding using independent spatial streams as it is used in practical 802.11n deployments. Faria et al. [5] create *signalprints* based on Received Signal Strength (RSS) information to identify wireless devices with respect to their locations. However, our method uses a richer set of channel characteristics.

In addition to location identification, PHY-layer information is also used for device identification. Brik et al. [1] use modulation errors to identify 802.11 devices caused by modulator circuitry. The transient part of the RF signal is used to identify 802.11 [8] and 802.15.4 [2] devices. Danev et al. [3] use RF burst information to identify RFID transponders. Xiong et al. [9] identify Wi-Fi clients by looking at the angle-of-arrival information of clients' incoming signals by leveraging multi-antenna access points (APs). More detailed information about device identification based on PHY-layer information can be found in [4].

## 3. TAMPER EVIDENCE ESTIMATION

### 3.1 Channel State Information

802.11n transceivers use multiple antennas to exploit spatial diversity and spatial multiplexing. Spatial diversity is used to improve reliability by exploiting transmission of redundant data using multiple antennas. Spatial multiplexing is used to improve performance by sending independent data streams in parallel along different spatial dimensions. To correctly extract data streams at the receiver, the effects of the wireless channel and of the transmitter's filters have to be estimated and reversed at the receiver. Therefore, each 802.11n frame contains a preamble (HT-LTF) that allows an estimation of amplitude changes and phase shifts at each of the used subchannels. The estimation result is the CSI.

In this work, CSI is used at the receiver to analyse characteristics of a communication channel in order to detect tampering with the transmitter. Changes to the transmitter location or hardware are reflected in CSI changes that can be used as tamper evidence. Unfortunately, tamper-unrelated events, like changes in the environment due to moving people, also influence the CSI and have to be accounted for in order to reduce false positives. The CSI is also dependent on the number of spatial data streams used for each data transmission. As each transmission may use a different number of spatial streams, this aspect has to be accounted for in the design of a tamper detection mechanism.

### 3.2 Beamforming and Spatial Expansion

In an OFDM system, the communication on each subcarrier $sc$ can be independently represented by a linear system—describing the wireless channel as a matrix $\mathbf{H}^{sc}_{R \times T}$ projecting the signals of each transmission antenna $T^{sc}_1 \ldots T^{sc}_T$ onto the reception antennas $R^{sc}_1 \ldots R^{sc}_R$. Instead of directly transmitting data streams over each transmission antenna, transmitters can use filtering matrices $\mathbf{F}^{sc}_{T \times S}$ that perform either beamforming or spatial expansion. The former allows the transmission of multiple spatial streams $S^{sc}_1 \ldots S^{sc}_S$ in parallel, whereas the latter increases redundancy by expanding a data stream to several transmission antennas. To decide on what technique to apply, the transmitter performs a Singular Value Decomposition (SVD) on the channel matrix and analyses the singular value spread. A lower spread allows the use of more spatially independent dimensions and therefore beamforming, whereas a higher spread does not allow as many spatial streams as the transmitter has antennas—therefore spatial expansion is used. A receiver has to know the path of each data stream to each of the receiver's antennas, therefore, the preamble—used for channel estimation—also passes the transmit filter. The subcarrier-wise measured CSI matrices $\mathbf{M}^{sc}_{R \times S}$ reflect the channel characteristics related to each spatial data stream. Each matrix $M$ contains a value for each subcarrier $sc$ describing phase shift and amplitude dampening.

$$\mathbf{R}^{sc} = \mathbf{H}^{sc}_{R \times T} \mathbf{F}^{sc}_{T \times S} \mathbf{S}^{sc} = \mathbf{M}^{sc}_{R \times S} \mathbf{S}^{sc}$$

where $R$, $T$ and $S$ are number of reception antennas, transmission antennas and spatial streams respectively, and $\mathbf{R}^{sc}$, $\mathbf{T}^{sc}$ and $\mathbf{S}^{sc}$ are the corresponding signal vectors per subcarrier $sc$. The dimensions of the matrices $\mathbf{H}$, $\mathbf{F}$ and $\mathbf{M}$ are given in the subscripts.

## 3.3 Tamper Estimation Algorithm

Our proposed algorithm is split into two phases: (1) a training phase, in which we collect and store $\tau$ CSI measurements $\mathbf{M}^{sc}_{R \times S, i \in 1 \ldots \tau}$ in a tamper-free scenario; (2) a detection phase, in which we compare the CSI of new frames $\mathbf{M}^{sc}_{R \times S, i > \tau}$ to the $\tau$ measurements of the training phase by calculating the Euclidean distance. If the moving average of this distance exeeds a certain threshold, an alarm is triggered. Distance based detection algorithms are proven to work well (see previous related work [7] and [12]). Thus, we decided to use this type of algorithm in our work.

As the number of spatial streams $S$ may vary between one and the number of transmission antennas $T$, we need to perform the training phase for each possible number of spatial streams—which is equal to $T$. This leads to $T$ different models $\mathrm{Mod}_{m=1 \ldots T}$, where the CSI measurements are stored for each spatial stream. In each of those models one to $m$ spatial streams exist. In this paper, we generate separate models $\mathrm{Mod}_{m=1 \ldots T, s=1 \ldots m}$ for each spatial stream $s$.

To compute the Euclidean distance $D^i_{m,s}$ for a model $\mathrm{Mod}_{m,s}$, we calculate the Euclidean distance between a new CSI measurement $\mathbf{M}^{sc}_{R \times S, i}$ to the stored CSI measurements of the training phase. Thereby, we omit the phase information in $\mathbf{M}^{sc}_{R \times S, i}$ and concentrate on the amplitude, which we normalize to a value between zero and one by taking the 2-norm of all values in dimensions $sc$ and $r$:

$$D^i_{m,s} = \frac{1}{\tau} \sum_{j=1}^{\tau} \sqrt{\sum_{r=1}^{R} \sum_{sc=1}^{SC} \left( \frac{|M^{sc}_{r,s,i}|}{||M^{sc}_{r,s,i}||^{sc,r}_2} - \frac{|M^{sc}_{r,s,j}|}{||M^{sc}_{r,s,j}||^{sc,r}_2} \right)^2}$$

As is shown in Section 4, $D^i_{m,s}$ can have outliers that we aim to smooth out by applying a moving average filter, which we implement either sample-wise or time-wise. The sample-wise option averages over a window of $k$ samples:

$$D^i_{m,s,\mathrm{sampMA}} = \sum_{j=i-k+1}^{i} \frac{D^j_{m,s}}{k} \text{ for } i \geq k$$

For time-wise averaging, we consider the points in continuous time $t_i$—when the CSI measurement was taken—and average over a window $t_w$:

$$D^i_{m,s,\mathrm{timeMA}} = \frac{1}{\mathrm{count}(t_j)} \sum_{\substack{j \\ t_j \in (t_i - t_w, t_i)}} D^j_{m,s} \text{ for } t_i \geq t_w$$

To combine all models $\mathrm{Mod}_{m=1 \ldots T, s=1 \ldots m}$ to get the combined model $\mathrm{Mod}_c$, we take the time-wise moving average and average over all models, where $D^i_{m,s,\mathrm{timeMA}} \neq 0$:

$$D^i_c = \left[ \underset{\forall s,m}{\mathrm{count}} \left( D^i_{m,s,\mathrm{timeMA}} \neq 0 \right) \right]^{-1} \sum_{m=1}^{T} \sum_{s=1}^{m} D^i_{m,s,\mathrm{timeMA}}$$

We use the resulting value $D^i_c$ as our *tamper-evidence value*. To decide if tampering occurred, we need to set a threshold which we do by considering the metrics of maximum and mean pair-wise distance between all training CSIs $\mathbf{M}^{sc}_{R \times S, i \in 1 \ldots \tau}$:

$$D^H_{i,j} = \sqrt{\sum_{r=1}^{R} \sum_{sc=1}^{SC} \left( \frac{|M^{sc}_{r,s,i}|}{||M^{sc}_{r,s,i}||^{sc,r}_2} - \frac{|M^{sc}_{r,s,j}|}{||M^{sc}_{r,s,j}||^{sc,r}_2} \right)^2}$$

$$\mathrm{mean}(D^H) = \underset{\forall i,j}{\mathrm{mean}} \left( D^H_{i,j} \right) \quad \mathrm{max}(D^H) = \underset{\forall i,j}{\mathrm{max}} \left( D^H_{i,j} \right)$$

A further discussion about using those metrics, as well as applying the tamper estimation to channel measurements is presented in the following section on evaluation.

## 4. EVALUATION

For evaluation, we use as receiver an Intel 5300 network interface card (NIC) (3 antennas) which allows us to extract CSI measurements via the *Linux 802.11n CSI Tool* [6]. As sender, we use either an Intel 5300 NIC or an Apple Mac (3 antennas). Depending on the transmitter decision each packet is received encoded with up to three spatial independent streams. In all experiments, the transmitter is set to send a packet once a second.

In the first experiment (Experiment 1), we use an iMac as sender with an initial distance of 1.5 m between sender and receiver. After 15 min we start to move the transmitter by 1 cm; after 30 min by 2 cm; after 44 min by 3 cm; after 59 min by 5 cm; after 74 min by 10 cm and finally after 88 min by 100 cm. This experiment is to analyse the detectability of device movement. In the second experiment (Experiment 2), we analyse detectability of device replacement. An Intel 5300 NIC is used as sender; the distance is 240 cm between sender and receiver. After 10 min the sender NIC is replaced while not altering antenna positions. The third experiment (Experiment 3) is used to analyse the impact of moving pedestrians. An iMac is used as sender with distance 1.5 m between sender and receiver. After 15 min, 16 min and 17 min a person is moving slowly through the communication path (taking about 10 s each time). In the last experiment (Experiment 4), we leave an iMac sender at night transmitting over a distance of 4 m. This experiment serves as baseline without tampering or environmental changes.

Figure 1 gives a visual impression of the recorded CSI amplitude values for different experiments for a subset of the overall CSI data. For example, Figure 1d shows 30 CSI amplitude values for each incoming packet received at the first antenna $r = 1$ using spatial stream $s = 1$ and being transmitted using $S = 3$ independent spatial streams. Data for other antenna/stream combinations are not shown due to space restrictions but are later used in the tamper detection mechanism. As it can be seen in Figure 1, the different events within the 4 experimental setups are clearly visible.

### 4.1 Experiment 1: Device Movement

As described in Section 3 we use individual models for each spatial stream setting to analyse CSI data of each incoming packet. For a received packet using one spatial stream one model is used ($\mathrm{Mod}_{1,1}$). For a received packet transmitted using two spatial streams two additional models are used (one for each received spatial stream; $\mathrm{Mod}_{2,1}$, $\mathrm{Mod}_{2,2}$) and for a packet received using three spatial streams three additional models are used ($\mathrm{Mod}_{3,1}$, $\mathrm{Mod}_{3,2}$, $\mathrm{Mod}_{3,3}$). Thus, 6 spatial models can be created to analyse incoming packets; however, in practice we did not observe a useful number of packets (less than 50 packets during the entire experiment) using 3 spatial streams and, thus, only 3 models become active in this experiment ($\mathrm{Mod}_{1,1}$, $\mathrm{Mod}_{2,1}$, $\mathrm{Mod}_{2,2}$). Figure 2 shows the model output for $\mathrm{Mod}_{1,1}$, $\mathrm{Mod}_{2,1}$, $\mathrm{Mod}_{2,2}$ and of the combined Model $\mathrm{Mod}_c$ over the duration of the experiment. The output of $\mathrm{Mod}_c$ is the tamper-evidence level that

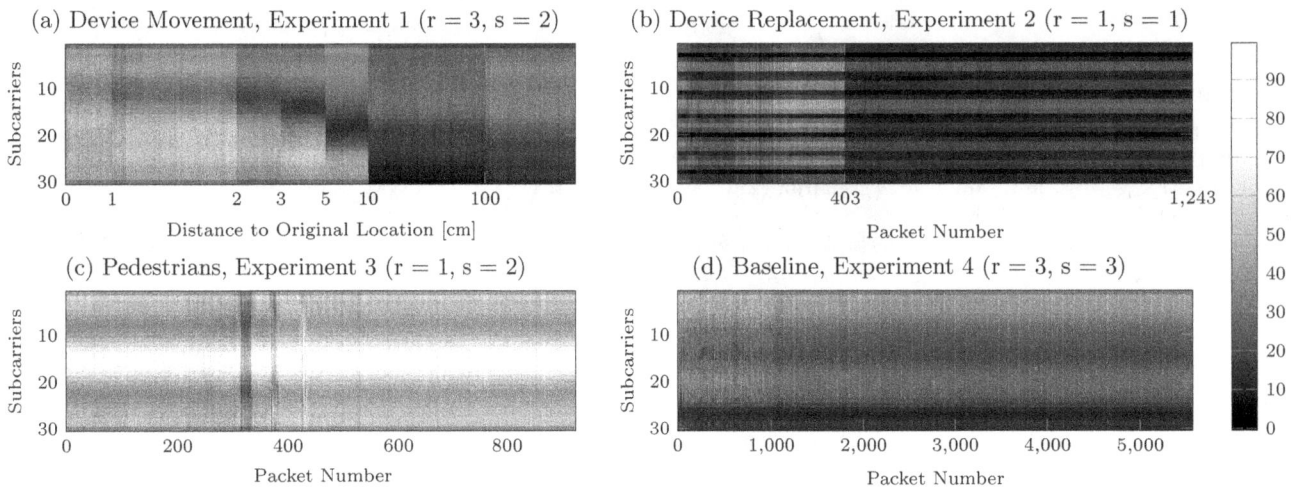

Figure 1: Amplitude CSI values for different experiments and antenna/stream combinations. Warmer colors represents higher amplitude values. Events such as device movement/replacement and environmental changes are visible.

we use to decide if a node has been tampered with. $Mod_c$ is created by combining the output of models $Mod_{1,1}$, $Mod_{2,1}$, $Mod_{2,2}$ (see Section 3.3).

Before a model becomes operational, it requires a history size of $\tau = 50$ CSI data which means that, for each model, 50 packets with the appropriate number of spatial streams must be received. A history size of 50 was chosen for the training phase as this provided stable results for our experiments. In a different scenario a shorter training phase might be possible. As the number of streams may change for each packet, a different amount of time is required for each model before it is operational. In this experiment, $Mod_{1,1}$ becomes active first after $t = 88$ s, while $Mod_{2,1}$ and $Mod_{2,2}$ become active at $t = 314$ s. The three models used for packets with three spatial streams never become active as, throughout the entire experiment, not enough packets of this type are received to fill the history. During this training phase, it must be ensured that no tamper situation is present which is the case in this experiment. (Tampering starts at $t = 15$ min.)

As can be seen in Figure 2a, model $Mod_{1,1}$ produces far fewer data points then the other two models. The reason is that the 802.11n transmitter uses for most transmissions two spatial streams, and transmissions using only one spatial transmission are rare. As a result, there are time periods (e.g. between $t = 14$ min and $t = 30$ min) where the model output is 0, which means that no recent data for this model is available and, thus, this model in these periods is not useful as a contributor to the overall model $Mod_c$. However, as long as data packets are received, there is at least one model active contributing to $Mod_c$ and, therefore, a tamper-evidence value is always provided. Only in situations where no packet is received at all would no model be active; however, in a practical setting, a lack of received data (or heart-beat messages) for a period of time may be considered as tamper situation anyway.

Tampering in the form of movement of the transmitter by 1 cm starts at $t = 15$ min. This event can clearly be seen in the tamper-evidence value provided by model $Mod_c$ (see Figure 2d). The tamper-evidence value increases from $t = 15$ min onwards with a gradient determined by the win-

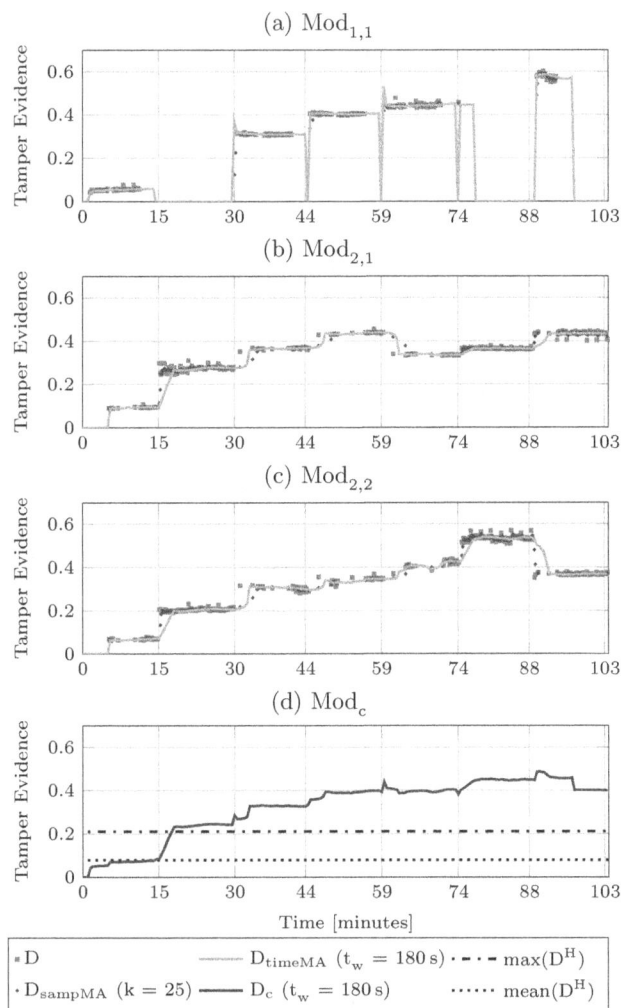

Figure 2: Experiment 1 – Tamper evidence over time with device movement. Model outputs for packets received with different spatial streams are combined into the overall model to produce a single tamper-evidence value.

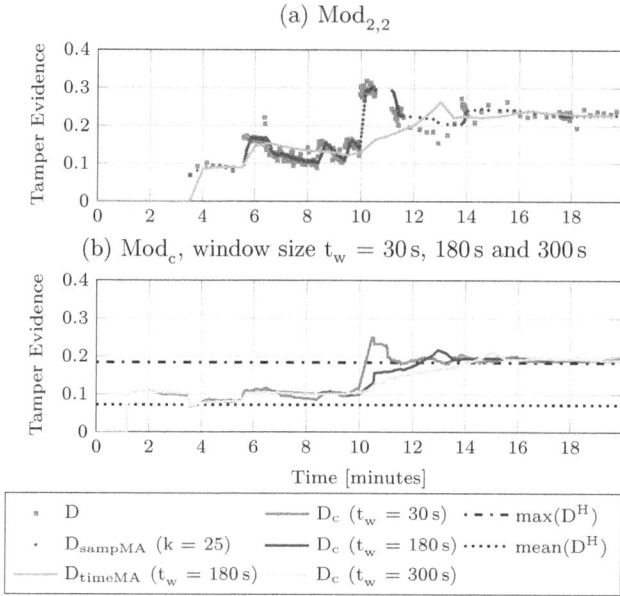

(a) Mod$_{2,2}$

(b) Mod$_c$, window size t$_w$ = 30 s, 180 s and 300 s

| | | |
|---|---|---|
| ▪ D | —— D$_c$ (t$_w$ = 30 s) | · - · - max(D$^H$) |
| · D$_{sampMA}$ (k = 25) | —— D$_c$ (t$_w$ = 180 s) | ······ mean(D$^H$) |
| —— D$_{timeMA}$ (t$_w$ = 180 s) | D$_c$ (t$_w$ = 300 s) | |

Figure 3: Experiment 2 – Tamper evidence over time in an environment with device replacement (tampering) at $t = 10\,\mathrm{min}$. Tamper-evidence levels are rising faster for smaller window sizes $t_w$.

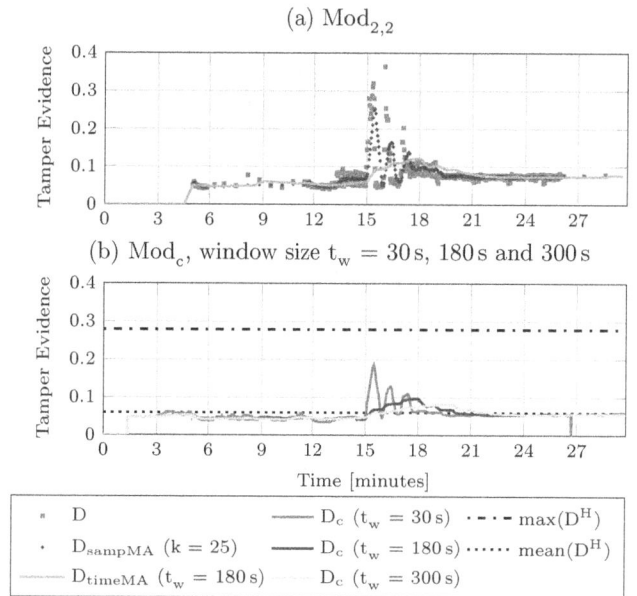

(a) Mod$_{2,2}$

(b) Mod$_c$, window size t$_w$ = 30 s, 180 s and 300 s

| | | |
|---|---|---|
| ▪ D | —— D$_c$ (t$_w$ = 30 s) | · - · - max(D$^H$) |
| · D$_{sampMA}$ (k = 25) | —— D$_c$ (t$_w$ = 180 s) | ······ mean(D$^H$) |
| —— D$_{timeMA}$ (t$_w$ = 180 s) | D$_c$ (t$_w$ = 300 s) | |

Figure 4: Experiment 3 – Tamper evidence over time in an environment with movement at $t = 15\,\mathrm{min}$, $t = 16\,\mathrm{min}$ and $t = 17\,\mathrm{min}$. Tamper-evidence levels are lower for larger window sizes $t_w$.

dow size $t_w$. A smaller window size would lead to faster increase of the tamper-evidence value. However, as we will show in Experiment 3, it is not always desirable to use a small window size, as a large window helps us to suppress high tamper-evidence levels caused by movement instead of tampering. A threshold could now be selected to decide a tamper-evidence level, beyond which the transmitter would be no longer considered to be trustworthy. The *max* and *mean* values shown in Figure 2d might help for threshold selection. For example, a threshold set to twice the value of *mean* might be a useful selection.

As shown in Figure 2d, all tested positions of the transmitter different to the original position are clearly visible as a tamper situation. It has to be noted that the tamper-evidence value, which depends on movement distance, is not a monotone increasing function. An increase in distance to the original device position may lead to a reduction of the tamper-evidence value. However, no movement in our experiment set leads to a tamper-evidence value that is close to the value associated with the un-tampered situation.

From $t = 74\,\mathrm{min}$ onwards, we see a small periodic change in the output of Mod$_{2,1}$ and Mod$_{2,2}$. This periodic change is potentially caused by an interferer (such as a heating system) active during the experiment.

## 4.2 Experiment 2: Device Replacement

The results of this experiment are shown in Figure 3. Figure 3a shows the output of the spatial model Mod$_{2,2}$; other models are not shown due to limited space. Figure 3b shows the tamper-evidence value which is the output of the combined model Mod$_c$. The output of Mod$_c$ is shown for different window sizes $t_w$. Model Mod$_{2,2}$ becomes active after $t = 213\,\mathrm{s}$ when enough packets using 2 spatial streams are received to fill the history of $\tau = 50$ values.

At $t = 10\,\mathrm{min}$ the device is tampered with and the NIC is

replaced. In this experiment, we use external antennas connected to the NIC to ensure that only the device is replaced while all antenna remain at exactly the same position.

We can clearly see in Figure 3a that the tamper-evidence value $D$ changes immediately. The output $D_{timeMA}$ is changing more slowly, as an average of values of $D$ over the past duration of $t_w = 300\,\mathrm{s}$ is used. Figure 3b shows the output of the combined model for different window sizes $t_w$ (see Section 3.3). Obviously, using a smaller window size leads to faster detection, but the algorithm would be more prone to false alarms as outliers would have a greater contribution to the tamper-evidence value.

A threshold at twice the average tamper-evidence value, *mean*, could be used as alarm threshold. In this case, the device replacement would be indicated after $t = 605\,\mathrm{s}$ when using a window size of $t_w = 30\,\mathrm{s}$. With a window size of $t_w = 300\,\mathrm{s}$, the replacement would be indicated substantially after $t = 678\,\mathrm{s}$. However, using a smaller window size is not without cost, as we will show in the next experiment.

## 4.3 Experiment 3: Pedestrians

In this experiment, a person is walking slowly 3 times through the line of sight between sender and receiver. The first walk is at $t = 15\,\mathrm{min}$, the second at $t = 16\,\mathrm{min}$, and the third at $t = 17\,\mathrm{min}$. Figure 4a is the output of the spatial model Mod$_{2,2}$. Figure 4b shows the tamper-evidence value, which is the output of the combined model Mod$_c$ (see Section 3.3). This is shown for different window sizes $t_w$.

The walks are visible in the tamper-evidence value. However, for all selected window sizes the tamper-evidence value returns after a while to the base line, indicating no tamper situation. This is different to the previous two situations of device movement and device replacement where the tamper-evidence value does not return to the original value. As can be seen in Figure 4b, the window size influences the maximum tamper-evidence value that is reached. Large windows suppress high tamper-evidence values for environmental changes such as those caused by a pedestrian. When using a threshold at twice the average tamper-evidence value, *mean*, an alarm situation can be avoided with a window size of $t_w = 300$ s, but not for a window size of $t_w = 30$ s.

Comparing the results of this experiment with the results of the previous two experiments, it becomes clear that the selection of the window size over which analysis results are averaged has an influence on i) detection time and ii) suppression of false alarms.

## 4.4 Experiment 4: Baseline

This experiment was carried out at night to avoid fluctuations of channel characteristics due to moving people and interference by electronic devices. The output of $\text{Mod}_c$ is, in this case, a flat line without significant variation; the maximum tamper-evidence value is 0.17, the minimum is 0.15 within the 1.5 h duration. This demonstrates that a continuous upgrade of the used history data (a retraining of the model) is not required. It can be expected that, in a static and tamper-free environment, the tamper-evidence value is stable.

## 4.5 Discussion and Future Work

*False Alarms:* False alarms can be triggered by changes in the environment instead of tampering. We assume that most environmental changes are of short duration (e.g. pedestrians). As shown, by selecting a large window size $t_w$, false alarms can be avoided while reducing the detection speed. If changes to the communication environment are permanent (e.g. a new structure is placed in the communication path) the models need to be trained again (history data collection). In this case, it must be ensured that training occurs in a tamper-free state. Further work is necessary to devise methods for detecting the need of retraining.

*Detection:* Our experiments have shown that device movement and device replacement can both be detected. Even small device movements of just 1 cm are clearly visible in the computed tamper-evidence value. In future work we plan to investigate how the tamper-evidence value should be used in a practical system. In particular, the methods for determination of an optimal threshold must be devised.

*Training:* The models for different spatial streams are becoming active after receiving sufficient packets transmitted with the particular number of spatial streams. Thus, different models become operational at different points in time. It must be ensured that all models are trained in a tamper-free situation. When including data in the history, it must be verified that no other already operational spatial model detects tampering.

*Experiments:* Our experiments show that the general method of using 802.11n CSI information to derive a tamper-evidence value is useful. However, our current set of experiments is limited. We plan to expand our 4 experiments into larger experiment sets investigating device movement, replacement and environmental changes in a large number of scenarios. Such experiments would also include the use of multiple receivers to improve the algorithm's performance in terms of distinction of tampering and environment changes. We also plan to apply the devised techniques in a practical setting such as a physical intrusion detection system.

*Existing work:* We explained the differences between our method and existing work in Section 2. However, performance comparisons are needed to be able to fully evaluate the effectiveness of our method over existing ones. This, we plan to investigate in future work.

## 5. CONCLUSION

We have shown that 802.11n CSI information measured at a receiver for each incoming packet can be used to create a tamper-evidence value which indicates potential tampering with the sender. In particular, our method is able to handle changing spatial stream configurations of 802.11n transmission. We have shown that tampering in the form of device movement or device replacement are clearly detectable. Furthermore, we have shown that alarms from tamper-unrelated environment changes, such as pedestrians, can be avoided.

## Acknowledgment

This work has been funded by the German Research Foundation (DFG) in the Collaborative Research Center (SFB) 1053 "MAKI – Multi-Mechanism-Adaptation for the Future Internet" and by LOEWE CASED. Many thanks go to our shepherd, Sanjay Jha.

## 6. REFERENCES

[1] V. Brik, S. Banerjee, M. Gruteser, and S. Oh. Wireless Device Identification with Radiometric Signatures. In *Proc. MobiCom'08*, 2008.

[2] B. Danev and S. Capkun. Transient-based Identification of Wireless Sensor Nodes. In *Proc. IPSN'09*, 2009.

[3] B. Danev, T. S. Heydt-Benjamin, and S. Capkun. Physical-layer Identification of RFID Devices. In *Proc. USENIX'09*, 2009.

[4] B. Danev, D. Zanetti, and S. Capkun. On Physical-layer Identification of Wireless Devices. *ACM Comput. Surv.*, 45(1):6, 2012.

[5] D. B. Faria and D. R. Cheriton. Detecting identity-based attacks in wireless networks using signalprints. In *Proc. WiSe'06*, 2006.

[6] D. Halperin, W. Hu, A. Sheth, and D. Wetherall. Tool release: Gathering 802.11n traces with channel state information. *ACM SIGCOMM CCR*, 41(1):53, 2011.

[7] N. Patwari and S. K. Kasera. Robust location distinction using temporal link signatures. In *Proc. MobiCom'07*, 2007.

[8] O. Ureten and N. Serinken. Wireless security through RF fingerprinting. *Electrical and Computer Engineering, Canadian Journal of*, 32(1):27–33, 2007.

[9] J. Xiong and K. Jamieson. SecureArray: Improving Wifi Security with Fine-grained Physical-layer Information. In *Proc. MobiCom'13*, 2013.

[10] X. L. J. H. Z. Jiang, J. Zhao and W. Xi. Rejecting the Attack: Source Authentication for Wi-Fi Management Frames using CSI Information. In *Proc. INFOCOM'13*, 2013.

[11] R. M. Z. Li, W. Xu and W. Trappe. Securing wireless systems via lower layer enforcements. In *Proc. WiSe'06*, 2006.

[12] J. Zhang, M. H. Firooz, N. Patwari, and S. K. Kasera. Advancing Wireless Link Signatures for Location Distinction. In *Proc. MobiCom'08*, 2008.

# Short Paper: Exploiting WPA2-Enterprise Vendor Implementation Weaknesses through Challenge Response Oracles

Pieter Robyns, Bram Bonné, Peter Quax, Wim Lamotte
iMinds/tUL/UHasselt
Wetenschapspark 2
3590 Diepenbeek, Belgium
{pieter.robyns, bram.bonne, peter.quax, wim.lamotte}@uhasselt.be

## ABSTRACT

Many of today's enterprise-scale wireless networks are protected by the WPA2-Enterprise Protected Extensible Authentication Protocol (PEAP). In this paper it is demonstrated how an attacker can steal a user's credentials and gain unauthorized access to such networks, by utilizing a class of vulnerable devices as MSCHAPv2 challenge response oracles. More specifically this paper explains how on these devices, Lightweight EAP (LEAP) MSCHAPv1 credentials can be captured and converted to PEAP MSCHAPv2 credentials by using a rogue Access Point. This man-in-the-middle vulnerability was found to be present in all current versions of Apple's iOS and OS X operating systems, and may impact other devices as well. A proof-of-concept implementation is available that shows how Authentication Server certificate validation and certificate pinning mechanisms may be bypassed. Mitigation strategies for the attack and protective actions which can be undertaken by end-users are also described in this paper.

## Keywords

Network security; WPA2-Enterprise; PEAP; LEAP

## Categories and Subject Descriptors

C.2.0 [**Computer-communication networks**]: Security and protection.

## General Terms

Experimentation, Security

## 1. INTRODUCTION

Since its inception, wireless networking has become increasingly popular. More and more users desire access to network resources or the internet without having to struggle with network cables. As anyone with a wireless network card can eavesdrop on data sent wirelessly, it is self-evident that data security and user privacy are crucial aspects. This is especially true for enterprises, where confidential company data may be transmitted over the air. Fortunately, this data can be encrypted using a secure communication protocol.

For the average home user, the procotol that is considered most secure for wireless communication is WPA2-PSK. Here, the user configures a single password that is used for authentication. This password is shared with all users that require access to the network. For enterprises, this approach is infeasible: different users may require different access rights on the network, access may need to be revoked to former employees or the password may unintentionally leak to unauthorized parties. Therefore, the most popular choice for enterprises is WPA2-Enterprise. When this protocol is used, each user has their own login and password.

Though WPA2-Enterprise is considered secure in general, many attacks exist that are based on the Man-In-The-Middle (MITM) principle. Here, a victim user is tricked into connecting to a rogue Access Point (AP) that has the same SSID as the enterprise network. To add to the problem, many devices on the market automatically join a wireless network in their Preferred Network List (PNL) by default. This is convenient for the user, but it also introduces the risk of joining a network under control of an attacker [15].

To solve these MITM issues, the authenticity of the APs themselves can be verified by the device. This verification happens in the background, so the user fully relies on the used network protocol for its security. In context of WPA2-Enterprise networks, the IEEE 802.1X Standard specifies that the EAP protocol should be used for this purpose. EAP is an extensible authentication protocol that implements a wide variety of authentication procedures, called EAP methods.

Though EAP methods are well-defined and thoroughly examined for flaws by security experts, a correct protocol implementation is the responsibility of the device vendor. Unsurprisingly, there are subtle differences between various vendor implementations. Some of these may contribute to significant security vulnerabilities, such as those described in this paper.

For our research we focused mainly on the PEAP method, because it is popular, widely supported and considered secure. We tested the PEAP implementation of some of the most popular operating systems used today: Windows, Mac

OS X, Android and iOS [9]. A practical attack for which Apple devices are particularly vulnerable resulted from our findings. The vulnerability has been reported to Apple prior to the release of this paper, on February 5, 2014.

## 2. ATTACK DESCRIPTION

Our attack exploits a combination of two vulnerabilities. A first vulnerability is the fact that some devices accept the older LEAP method for authentication. This EAP method is Cisco proprietary and uses the MSCHAPv1 algorithm to authenticate users. Past research has already proven that both MSCHAPv1 and MSCHAPv2 are insecure for various reasons when used without the protection of a TLS tunnel [19]. Since the LEAP method does not establish a TLS tunnel from client (or "Supplicant") to Authentication Server (AS) prior to exchanging credentials, it is vulnerable to a rogue AS MITM attack [6].

The second vulnerability is that when the user configures or joins a PEAP network, some devices reuse the supplied credentials for all supported EAP methods. Hence, LEAP credentials do not have to be entered explicitly by the user. Existing MITM attacks try to capture these LEAP credentials using a rogue AS, and then crack them with dictionary attack tools like `asleap`[1]. In our attack, we will use the credentials for a different purpose.

Before we discuss a practical implementation of our attack, let us first examine how credentials are exchanged in LEAP. The three entities participating in the authentication are the Supplicant, the Authenticator, and the AS. For simplicity, assume that Authenticator and AS reside on the same machine. The LEAP authentication procedure is performed as follows [6]:

1. The Supplicant associates with the AP and exchanges its identity with the AS. This step is identical for all EAP methods.

2. The AS sends an 8-byte challenge $C_s$, where $C_s = Random8(seed)$, to the Supplicant.

3. The Supplicant generates a 24-byte challenge response $R_p$, where $R_p = ChallengeResponse(C_s, H)$, $H = MD4(Unicode(PW))$ and $PW$ is the password of the user. $R_p$ is then sent to the AS.

4. The AS calculates $R_{check} = ChallengeResponse(C_s, H)$. The exchange is successful if $R_p$ and $R_{check}$ match.

5. In case of success, an EAP-Success message is sent from Authenticator to the Supplicant. Then, AS and Supplicant switch roles and repeat steps 2 to 4. This time we denote the challenge sent by the Supplicant as $C_p$, and the response by the AS as $R_s$.

6. The AS derives the Session Key ($SK$) as

$$SK = MD5(MD4(Unicode(H))$$
$$||C_s||R_p||C_p||R_s) \quad (1)$$

where "$||$" is the concatenation operator. The AS encrypts this value with the RADIUS secret and sends it to the Authenticator. The Supplicant also derives the

[1]This tool can be downloaded from the following URL: http://www.willhackforsushi.com/?page_id=41

$SK$, so this key can be used for WEP encrypted unicast communication. Finally, a random broadcast key is generated by the Authenticator and sent encrypted with the unicast key to the Supplicant.

Note that a LEAP exchange is practically identical to performing two MSCHAPv1 authentications (steps 2 to 4): one from AS to Supplicant ($C_s \rightarrow R_p$) and one from Supplicant to AS ($C_p \rightarrow R_s$). [25].

Next, let us examine PEAP. This authentication method is significantly more complex, and among other features supports MSCHAPv2 mutual authentication to protect against MITM attacks [16, 17]. Assuming cryptographic binding is not used (see Section 5.3), PEAP authentication is performed as follows:

1. The Supplicant associates with the AP and exchanges its identity with the AS.

2. In Phase 1, the Supplicant and AS set up a TLS tunnel similar to the procedure described in RFC 5246 [7]. From the TLS master secret, a Master Session Key (MSK) is derived via a one-way function. This key serves a comparable purpose to the Session Key from LEAP.

3. Phase 2 is performed inside the TLS tunnel and implies usage of an EAP inner authentication method. MSCHAPv2 is frequently used for this purpose. Assuming MSCHAPv2 is used, the AS starts by generating a 16-byte random server challenge $C_s = Random16(seed)$ and sends it to the Supplicant.

4. The Supplicant also generates a random 16-byte peer challenge $C_p$. Then the challenge response is calculated as $R_p = ChallengeResponse(Challenge(C_s), H)$, where $Challenge(C_s) = SHA1(C_p||C_s||U)[0:7]$, $U$ is the username of the user, $H = MD4(Unicode(PW))$, $PW$ is the password of the user and $[0:7]$ means the first eight bytes of the data. This challenge response is transmitted back to the AS, along with $C_p$ and $U$.

5. The AS calculates $R_{check}$ analogous to $R_p$ in step 4. $R_{check}$ and $R_p$ must match, or the authentication will fail.

6. The AS calculates a peer challenge response

$$R_s = PeerResponse(MD4(Unicode(H)),$$
$$M_1, R_p, Challenge(C_p), M_2) \quad (2)$$

where $M_1$ is the string "Magic server to client signing constant" and $M_2$ is the string "Pad to make it do more than one iteration". This result is SHA1-hashed and sent to the Supplicant.

7. The Supplicant authenticates the server, completing the MSCHAPv2 inner authentication.

8. An EAP-Result-TLV exchange is performed between AS and Supplicant to indicate the result of the PEAP authentication. Then an EAP-Success message is sent.

9. The MSK is used to derive the WPA2 Pairwise Master Key (PMK) and subsequent keys. Secure transmission of data can begin when the 802.11i four-way handshake [11] is completed.

When comparing the core differences between MSCHAPv1 and MSCHAPv2 credentials from RFCs 2433 and 2759, we can see that they are in fact very minor. Table 1 shows a comparison between the two methods [24, 25, 19].

Though RFC 2759 states that MSCHAPv2 is incompatible with MSCHAPv1 [24], the insignificance of the aforementioned differences led us to the conclusion that some MSCHAPv1 messages can be converted to MSCHAPv2 messages and vice versa.

We will now show that $C_s$ from MSCHAPv1 is identical to $Challenge(C_s)$ from the MSCHAPv2 AS and that $R_p$ from the MSCHAPv1 peer is identical to $R_{check}$ at the MSCHAPv2 server. This way we can be sure that all messages converted from MSCHAPv1 to MSCHAPv2 or vice versa will be accepted by the destination host. For the challenges we derive:

$$Challenge(C_s) = SHA1(C_p||C_s||U)[0:7] \qquad (3)$$
$$= SHA1(x)[0:7] \ (C_p \text{ and } C_s \text{ are random}) \qquad (4)$$
$$= Random8(seed), \quad \text{if } x = \text{random} \qquad (5)$$
$$= C_s \qquad (6)$$

Given that the $ChallengeResponse$ function is the same in MSCHAPv1 and MSCHAPv2, we derive for the challenge responses:

$$R_s = ChallengeResponse(C_s, H) \qquad (7)$$
$$= ChallengeResponse(Challenge(C_s), H) \quad (\text{Eq. } 6) \qquad (8)$$
$$= R_{check} \qquad (9)$$

With the knowledge that the challenge we get from the PEAP MSCHAPv2 AS can be converted to an MSCHAPv1 challenge (Equation 6), and that the challenge response we get from our LEAP MSCHAPv1 victim can be converted to an MSCHAPv2 challenge response that matches $R_{check}$ on the AS (Equation 9), we devised a relay attack that uses a vulnerable device as an MSCHAPv2 challenge response oracle in order to gain unauthorized access to PEAP networks. Figure 1 shows a schematic representation of our attack.

## 3. PRACTICAL LEAP RELAY ATTACK

In this section we will show how the MSCHAPv1 to MSCHAPv2 conversion can be exploited in practice. First we will discuss the preconditions for the attack. Then, a practical implementation for attacking Apple devices will be demonstrated.

### 3.1 Preconditions

A device connecting to a PEAP network is considered vulnerable to our attack when all of the following preconditions are met:

- The device supports the LEAP method.

- The device connects automatically to the PEAP network. This is the default behavior.

- The Authenticator does not require and validate client certificates. Server certificate validation and certificate pinning may be enabled on the client.

- The MSCHAPv2 or MSCHAPv1 inner authentication EAP method is supported and allowed on the AS.

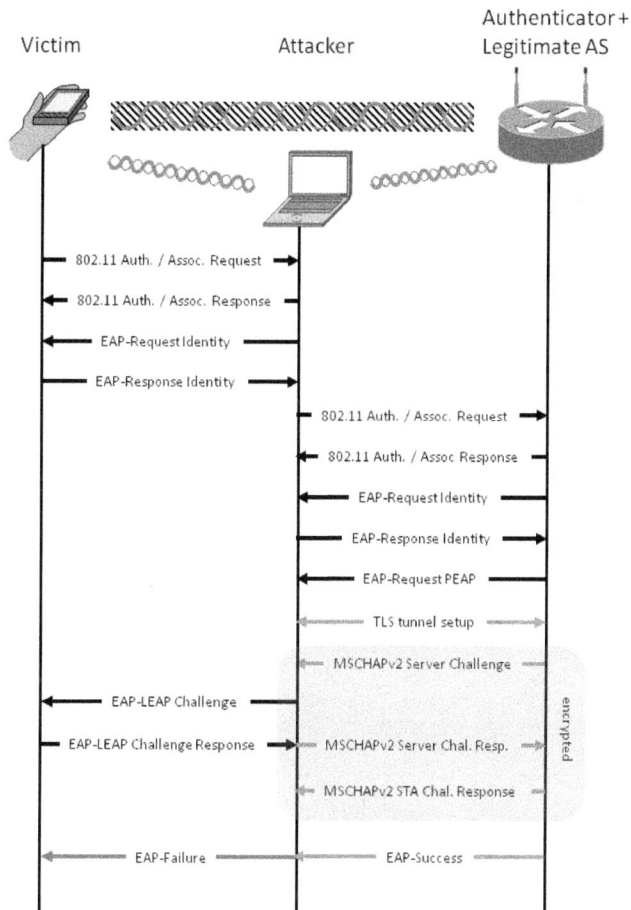

Figure 1: Schematic representation of the Apple LEAP attack

Note that most of the preconditions listed here are commonly fulfilled by default in enterprise network setups.

### 3.2 Case study: Apple devices

We will now demonstrate how the exploit can be practically applied to Apple devices (see Figure 1). Our proof-of-concept implementation uses a simple state machine to perform the attack (Figure 2). After successful execution, an attacker gains unauthorized access to the target network by impersonating a legitimate user.

#### 3.2.1 State 1: Association

Before wireless clients can begin the exchange of EAP packets to secured networks, they require association with a wireless AP. We exploit the default auto-join behavior to have clients associate to an AP under our control. In order to accomplish this, we set up a fake wireless AP with the same SSID as the target network. This fake AP broadcasts beacon packets and replies to Probe Requests from clients.

The client will associate or reassociate to our fake network AP when it is closer to the target network AP, because better signal strength is preferred [8]. Alternatively, we can force the client to connect to our fake AP by performing an attack similar to [3]. Since we do not want to receive requests from devices which are not vulnerable, our implementation uses the MAC Organizationally Unique Identifier (OUI) to

|  | MSCHAPv1 | MSCHAPv2 |
|---|---|---|
| $C_s$ | $C_s = Random8(seed)$ | $C_s = Random16(seed)$ |
| $C_p$ | $C_p = Random8(seed)$ | $C_p = Random16(seed)$ |
| $R_s$ | $R_s = ChallengeResponse(C_p, H)$ | $R_s = PeerResponse(MD4(Unicode(H)), M_1, R_p, Challenge(C_p), M_2)$ |
| $R_p$ | $R_p = ChallengeResponse(C_s, H)$ | $R_p = ChallengeResponse(Challenge(C_s), H)$ |

Table 1: Differences between MSCHAPv1 and MSCHAPv2 exchanges

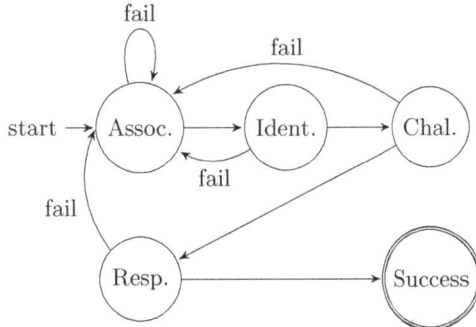

Figure 2: State machine of our attack

| Device | Vulnerable |
|---|---|
| iPod Touch (iOS 6.1.6) | Yes |
| iPhone 4 (iOS 7.1) | Yes |
| iPhone 4S (iOS 7.1) | Yes |
| Mac OS X 10.8.2 (Mountain Lion) | Yes |
| Samsung GT-S5570 (Android 2.3.4) | No |
| Google Nexus 7 (Android 4.4.2) | No |
| Samsung GT-I8750 (Windows Phone 8.0) | No |
| Windows 7 Desktop | No |

Table 2: Devices vulnerable to the LEAP relay attack

identify the device vendor. We can filter out all non-Apple devices this way.

### 3.2.2 State 2: Identification

The first step after association in WPA2-Enterprise networks is identification. The AS has to know which user wants to authenticate in order to match corresponding credentials. We can learn the identity of the vulnerable device by sending an EAP Identity Request. The device will then reply with an EAP Identity Response which contains the username of our victim.

At this point, data sent over the air is still not encrypted. Hence, some PEAP implementations use anonymous identities. In this case the real username is only disclosed when a TLS tunnel has been established between the Supplicant and the AS. Nonetheless, we can still get the real username in a later phase of our attack.

Our next goal is to get the challenge value from the target AP. We created a modified version of the `wpa_supplicant`[2] tool for this purpose. At the end of this state, the binary executable of this modified version is called from our implementation.

### 3.2.3 State 3: Challenge

In State 3, we wait for the `wpa_supplicant` tool to establish a TLS tunnel with the target AS and extract an MSCHAPv2 challenge from the inner authentication. We can now see why usage of client certificates would mitigate the attack, as the client certificate validation would not be successful in this case.

When the MSCHAPv2 challenge is retrieved, we pass it on to our tool. Upon receipt, the tool will periodically send LEAP Request messages (containing the extracted challenge) to the Apple device in order to keep the session alive.

### 3.2.4 State 4: Response

After receiving the LEAP Request, our victim will reply with a LEAP Response which contains an MSCHAPv1 challenge response to our MSCHAPv2 challenge. Should the target PEAP network enforce anonymous identities, the real or inner identity of the victim will also be revealed to the attacker through this LEAP Response. Next, our implementation will forward the received MSCHAPv1 challenge response as an MSCHAPv2 challenge response to the modified `wpa_supplicant` tool, which will in turn forward the challenge response to the legitimate PEAP network AS.

### 3.2.5 State 5: Success

When the AS receives our modified challenge response, authentication proceeds as usual, which means the AS has to authenticate to our Supplicant. However, since we are not in possession of the NT password secret, we cannot derive $H$. Hence, when receiving the peer challenge response from the AS, we are forced to accept any sent value.

After this, the MSCHAPv2 inner authentication will complete successfully and the port will be authenticated. The AS and our Supplicant will derive the $MSK$, and from this we can derive the $PMK$. We now have all components required to access resources on the internal network.

## 4. TEST RESULTS

We tested our attack on devices from multiple vendors. Table 2 shows on which devices the LEAP relay attack was successfully performed.

Assuming that the same network protocol stack is used on all Apple operating systems, we concluded from these results that all Apple devices are vulnerable. The attack was executed analogously on each device for multiple APs, using different AS implementations. These included a TP-Link WN422G using `hostapd` and the latest `freeradius` implementation on the same machine, a Linksys WRT54G AP using the latest `freeradius` implementation on a dedicated machine, and a Ubiquity UniFi AC 3.x AP using Windows RADIUS server on a dedicated machine.

---

[2]`wpa_supplicant` is an open source 802.1X Supplicant implementation by Jouni Malinen.

# 5. MITIGATION

The attack we described in this paper can be mitigated in various ways. We will discuss five methods in this section.

## 5.1 Client certificates

In State 3 of our attack, a TLS tunnel has to be established between the attacker and the target network AS. When using client certificates, each client's certificate must be provided in the "Client Hello" phase of the TLS tunnel setup. When this verification fails, the TLS setup will be aborted and hence, our attack will fail because the MSK cannot be derived from the TLS master secret.

This countermeasure is very effective and by far the most secure. However, it would require a lot of administration effort for enterprises. Especially in enterprises with a Bring Your Own Device (BYOD) policy, because a signed certificate for every device allowed on the network must be installed on the AS.

## 5.2 iPhone Configuration Utility

iPhone configuration profiles allow the network administrator to choose which EAP methods clients must use. They are the only way in which LEAP can be disabled on Apple devices. If this method is chosen to mitigate the attack, care must be taken in BYOD environments: if one user does not install the network profile, the attack can nevertheless be executed. Furthermore, network profiles can be accidentally removed by the user. For these reasons, security is put in the hands of the end user and therefore this method is not as secure as using client certificates.

## 5.3 Cryptobinding

An optional feature described in the PEAP version 2 internet draft is cryptographic binding [17]. This feature introduces the use of a new Type-Length-Value (TLV), the CryptoBinding TLV, to address MITM attacks. A two-way handshake containing a Compound MAC Key ($CMK$) proves that the two authentications terminate at the same PEAP peer and PEAP server [14].

To calculate the $CMK$, the Supplicant is required to use keying material from both Phase 1 and Phase 2 of the PEAP exchange. In practical terms this involves the calculation of the Tunnel Key ($TK$) and the Inner Session Key ($ISK$). These keys are combined in the cryptobinding algorithm to form the $CMK$.

The $TK$ is calculated similarly to the $MSK$ from the TLS master secret, and would be available to an attacker. The $ISK$ however, is calculated at the Supplicant as $ISK = InnerMPPESendKey||InnerMPPERecvKey$. The $InnerMPPESendKey$ and $InnerMPPERecvKey$ are both derived from the inner MSCHAPv2 Master Key ($MK$), which is derived as

$$MK = GetMasterKey($$
$$MD4(Unicode(H))[0:15], R_s) \quad (10)$$

Since $H$ is unknown to the attacker, the $ISK$ cannot be derived and authentication will fail.

If all consumer devices would support cryptobinding, this method would probably be the best way to mitigate our attack. However, from our experiments we concluded that Apple devices do not support cryptographic binding at this time.

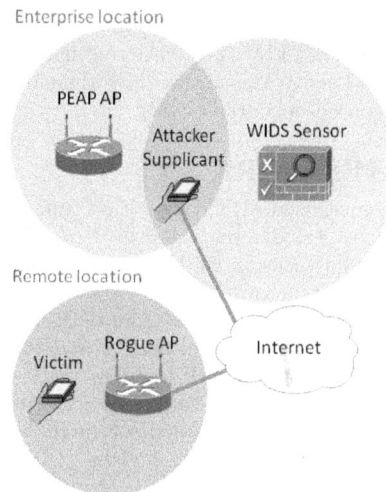

Figure 3: Remote LEAP relay attack

## 5.4 Intrusion detection

A signature based WIDS might be able to detect our attack by passively scanning for LEAP requests. Since these packets will never be sent by a legitimate AP, IDS sensor nodes have a clear indication that the network is under attack. Analytic approaches to detect our attack may include station counts, association counts, OS fingerprinting and RSSI value analysis, though these methods often lead to false positives [4, 12].

As a final note, we would like to indicate that care must be taken when relying on a WIDS for detection of an attack, as we believe that in many cases the IDS may be bypassed. For example, a victim may be in range of the rogue AP, while the latter is out of range from a WIDS sensor. In Figure 3, an example scenario is shown where the relay attack is executed over the internet.

## 5.5 Rogue AP mitigation

If one can prevent the attacker from setting up a rogue AP, the LEAP relay attack cannot be performed. Several methods have already been developed to mitigate the rogue AP attack [2, 18, 22]. However, we believe not all of these mitigation strategies will work. Context leashing will only work when creating the rogue AP in a different context, EAP-SWAT will have the same problems as PEAP, and other mitigation strategies in these works rely partly on the awareness and expertise of the user. We believe link layer protection mechanisms would be the most effective in this case.

# 6. FUTURE WORK

Future work could be done by using the same attack principles described in this paper. From our experiments we determined that other devices, for example Android devices, do not employ certificate pinning by default. If the victim user did not configure a server certificate, we believe a more generic MITM attack may be executed as described in RFC 7029 [10]. Note that in this case, the preconditions are stricter: it is required that *server* certificates are not used by the Android device, which was not the case for Apple devices.

Another option for future work would be to implement the attack for EAP-TTLS. This EAP method is similar to PEAP, and we believe the attack may therefore apply to EAP-TTLS secured networks as well.

# 7. RELATED WORK

A similar, generalized MITM attack on tunneled authentication protocols was demonstrated by N. Asokan et al. in 2002 [1]. Related attacks on PEAP vendor implementations such as the EAP dumb-down attack were introduced by Raul Siles in 2013. This attack exploits the default lack of certificate validation in mobile devices. However, for Apple devices, the dumb-down attack requires user intervention whereas our attack is automatic [20]. Furthermore, a correct configuration of authentication server certificates does not mitigate our attack for Apple devices.

Other related attacks were proposed at numerous security conferences. In 2008, Joshua Wright and Brad Antoniewicz demonstrated how EAP credentials such as MSCHAPv2 exchanges can be collected using `freeradius-wpe`, a rogue AS implementation [21]. By using the `asleap` tool, these credentials can then be cracked with a dictionary attack [5]. More recently, in 2012, Moxie Marlinspike showed how MSCHAPv2 credentials can be cracked in less than 24 hours using cloud-based FPGA nodes [13]. Finally, Josh Yavor indicated the dangers of BYOD and default certificate validation behavior of mobile devices in 2013 [23].

# 8. CONCLUSIONS

We demonstrated how MSCHAPv1 challenges and challenge responses can be converted to MSCHAPv2 challenges and challenge responses. Then, we indicated how this can be exploited in practice when a Supplicant supports the insecure LEAP method and when credentials are reused between EAP methods.

From our experiments we concluded that all Apple devices are currently vulnerable to our attack. Mitigation is possible in various ways. However, we noted why some mitigation strategies might not be feasible for enterprises. Therefore, users and network managers should take care when their devices satisfy all mentioned vulnerability preconditions.

# 9. ACKNOWLEDGEMENTS

We would like to thank Arno Barzan from the Expertise Centre for Digital Media for his support and insightful suggestions.

# 10. REFERENCES

[1] N. Asokan, V. Niemi, and K. Nyberg. Man-in-the-middle in tunnelled authentication protocols. In *Security Protocols*, pages 28–41. Springer, 2005.

[2] K. Bauer, H. Gonzales, and D. McCoy. Mitigating evil twin attacks in 802.11. In *Performance, Computing and Communications Conference, 2008. IPCCC 2008. IEEE International*, pages 513–516, Dec 2008.

[3] A. Cassola, W. Robertson, E. Kirda, and G. Noubir. A Practical, Targeted, and Stealthy Attack Against WPA Enterprise Authentication. In *Proceedings of NDSS*, volume 2013, 2013.

[4] M. Ciampa. *CWNA Guide to Wireless LANs*. Cengage Learning, 2012.

[5] Cisco. Dictionary Attack on Cisco LEAP Vulnerability, 2003. http://www.cisco.com/en/US/tech/tk722/tk809/technologies_security_notice09186a00801aa80f.html.

[6] A. DeKok and A. Sulmicki. Cisco LEAP protocol description, 2001. http://freeradius.org/rfc/leap.txt.

[7] T. Dierks and E. Rescorla. The Transport Layer Security (TLS) Protocol. RFC 5246, IETF, August 2008.

[8] M. S. Gast. *802.11 Wireless Networks: The Definitive Guide, Second Edition*. O'Reilly, 2005.

[9] A. Gupta, R. Cozza, and C. Lu. Market Share analysis: Mobile phones, worldwide, 4Q13 and 2013. *Gartner*, 2014.

[10] S. Hartman and M. Wasserman. Extensible Authentication Protocol (EAP) Mutual Cryptographic Binding. RFC 7029, IETF, October 2013.

[11] C. He and J. C. Mitchell. Analysis of the 802.11 i 4-way handshake. In *Proceedings of the 3rd ACM workshop on Wireless security*, pages 43–50. ACM, 2004.

[12] K. Hutchison. Wireless Intrusion Detection Systems. *SANS Institute InfoSec Reading Room*, October 2004.

[13] M. Marlinspike. Divide and Conquer: Cracking MS-CHAPv2, 2012. https://www.cloudcracker.com/blog/2012/07/29/cracking-ms-chap-v2/.

[14] Microsoft. Cryptobinding, 2014 (accessed). http://msdn.microsoft.com/en-us/library/cc238384.aspx.

[15] L. Nussel. The Evil Twin problem with WPA2-Enterprise. *SUSE Linux Products GmbH*, 2010.

[16] A. Palekar, D. Simon, J. Salowey, H. Zhou, G. Zorn, and S. Josefsson. Protected EAP Protocol (PEAP). Work in Progress 6, IETF, March 2003.

[17] A. Palekar, D. Simon, J. Salowey, H. Zhou, G. Zorn, and S. Josefsson. Protected EAP Protocol (PEAP) Version 2. Work in Progress 10, IETF, October 2004.

[18] V. Roth, W. Polak, E. Rieffel, and T. Turner. Simple and effective defense against evil twin access points. In *Proceedings of the First ACM Conference on Wireless Network Security*, WiSec '08, pages 220–235, New York, NY, USA, 2008. ACM.

[19] B. Schneier, Mudge, and D. Wagner. Cryptanalysis of Microsoft's PPTP Authentication Extensions. *CQRE '99*, October 1999.

[20] R. Siles. EAP dumb-down attack. In *RootedCON 2013*, pages 27–28. DinoSec, 2013.

[21] J. Wright. FreeRADIUS-WPE, 2008. http://www.willhackforsushi.com/?page_id=37.

[22] Z. Yang, A. C. Champion, B. Gu, X. Bai, and D. Xuan. Link-layer protection in 802.11i wlans with dummy authentication. In *Proceedings of the Second ACM Conference on Wireless Network Security*, WiSec '09, pages 131–138, New York, NY, USA, 2009. ACM.

[23] J. Yavor. The BYOD PEAP Show. In *DefCon 21*. iSEC Partners, 2013.

[24] G. Zorn. Microsoft PPP CHAP Extensions, Version 2. RFC 2759, IETF, January 2000.

[25] G. Zorn and S. Cobb. Microsoft PPP CHAP Extensions. RFC 2443, IETF, October 1998.

# Short Paper: Extrapolation and Prediction of User Behaviour from Wireless Home Automation Communication

Frederik Möllers*, Sebastian Seitz, Andreas Hellmann[†] and Christoph Sorge*
*Saarland University
*{frederik.moellers|christoph.sorge}@uni-saarland.de, [†] kontakt@anhellmann.de

## ABSTRACT

Wireless home automation systems are becoming increasingly popular. They can help users save energy and increase the comfort. However, this increased convenience also comes with new attack vectors. Many available systems provide little to no security. In this paper, we explore the possibilities of passive attacks against these systems. We exemplarily investigate two real-world installations of off-the-shelf home automation systems to see what amount of information can be obtained by a passive adversary.

Our results show that the systems provide no privacy. They leak information about the users' habits as well as their presence and can be abused to plan burglaries. Furthermore, we conclude that even encrypted communication does not fully protect against the attack presented here. In particular, it is still possible to predict user presence and absence even if individual actions cannot be identified.

## Categories and Subject Descriptors

K.6.5 [**Management of Computing and Information Systems**]: Security and Protection—*Unauthorized access*

## Keywords

Privacy; Home Automation; Traffic Analysis; Wireless Networks; Profile Building

## 1. INTRODUCTION

In recent years, home automation systems (HASs) have become affordable and thus very popular with private users [15]. While providing increased comfort, this also introduces new attack vectors, especially with the increasingly popular wireless systems [8]. Therefore it is necessary to consider the security regarding attacks against both the functionality of the system and the privacy of the inhabitants.

In this paper we present our security analysis of real-world HASs, using HomeMatic installations as an example. We focus on passive attacks targeting the system's communication

to create user profiles and predict user behaviour. Our passive attack consists of 3 consecutive stages. First, data is collected by sniffing the wireless communication. Semantic information is extracted from this data, such as sensor readings or actuator commands. As a second step, the attacker identifies patterns in the data, either from automation rules or from routine user behaviour. In the third step, the attacker then predicts the user's habits.

We also examine how much information can be obtained by performing *traffic analysis*, where the adversary uses timing patterns and metadata to draw conclusions about the users of the system. The information from both kinds of attacks can be used, for example, to plan a burglary when nobody is at home.

In addition to the burglary itself, insurance companies might refuse to pay the damage, given that the information was readily available from the inhabitants' own system. Thus, unsecured HASs can also be a monetary danger.

We conducted our analysis on two real-world installations of the HomeMatic HAS. To make the scenario realistic, we did not have any additional information about the two installations prior to the attack other than the fact that they were HomeMatic HASs. In the case of the second system, we were informed that it consisted of two parts that were installed in different locations and connected via a VPN.

The remainder of this paper is organized as follows. First we will provide some background information on the topic and have a look at related work in this area. Then we explain the methods we used in our analysis in Sect. 3 and present our analysis in along with its results in Sect. 4. We conclude with Sect. 5 and provide an outlook into future work.

## 2. BACKGROUND

For more than a decade now, technologies exist that enable the implementation of HASs. The type of devices in a home automation (HA) network varies from simple power switches and temperature sensors to smoke detectors and door locks. Main benefits are efficiency and comfort, but HASs can also be used or extended for security purposes. Light-controlling movement detectors can detect burglars, too, and supplementary intrusion detectors can use the existing network architecture to call the police.

### 2.1 Fundamentals of Home Automation Systems

Local communication technologies for HASs can be coarsely divided into wired (e.g. BACnet) and wireless (e.g. BidCos). There are also standards that cover both (e.g. KNX).

A major difference between wired and wireless HASs is the installation effort which disqualifies the former from installation in certain (especially rented) properties. However, traffic from a wireless system can be intercepted and possibly manipulated from anywhere nearby. Thus, protection against network attacks becomes much more important.

The topic of HA is closely related to that of building automation. Since building automation systems are usually wire-based and used in public buildings, they do not focus on privacy protection and have not been analyzed by us.

Currently, there are several HASs available on the market, e.g. HomeMatic, EnOcean and Siemens Synco Living. Our choice fell on the HomeMatic system. Due to its wide availability, the potential number of volunteers was large. In addition to this, hardware and open-source software exists that allows the capture of the communication and thus could be used for our experiments.

## 2.2 Legal Considerations

Gathering data for our analysis turned out to be problematic: only two volunteers gave us permission to analyze the traffic of their wireless HASs. A number of researchers have performed "War Driving" experiments, which essentially means getting information about a large number of WiFi networks without having asked for permission. There is, however, a legal difference to HASs—at least in Germany, where our research has been conducted. A WiFi network's beacon frames are generally broadcast messages, directed at anyone in the vicinity, to allow distinction between different networks. Data collected during War Driving might (partly) be considered as personal data, which is protected under European and national law. However, research purposes can justify the collection and processing of data under certain circumstances.

The messages exchanged by a wireless HAS, on the other hand, are only meant to be received within that system. From the perspective of legislation, the same limitations apply as in case of WiFi networks. In addition, collecting data from non-public transmissions is also a criminal offense according to section 202b of the German criminal code. We therefore decided against this option.

## 2.3 Related Work

There has been extensive research in the area of home automation in the last decade but very few have taken the aspect of secure communication into account.

Al-Muhtadi et al. proposed a very early approach [1] based on Jini and Tiny SESAME, a stripped down version of SESAME, which itself is an extension to Kerberos. Their main goals are authentication and access control and they do not consider passive attacks.

Bergstrom et al. presented an approach to secure home automation communications in 2001[2]. They assumed HA networks being controlled via the Internet using a so-called Global Home Server (GHS). The approach only focuses on securing the communication between the GHS and the individual networks, whereas the local communication is not taken into account.

Marin et al. [11] developed a middleware for home automation systems which relies on TLS for inter-node communication. They introduce different authentication procedures and encryption to secure data transmissions, but do not consider leakage of information through side channels.

Wireless sensor networks (WSNs) have similar contraints and requirements as HASs so research in this field can provide additional insight. Several surveys [9, 10, 14, 16] list known problems and solutions. De Cristofaro [5] tackles the problem of privacy protection for a user who queries a WSN. While traffic analysis and other passive attacks are a well-known threat in WSNs, the solutions rely on properties such as multi-hop routing or a local attacker. HASs differ from WSNs in exactly these aspects, so using WSN countermeasures in HASs requires extensive adaptations.

Concerns about traffic analysis in general go back as far as 1981 [3]. Numerous approaches have been developed to protect against this class of attacks [4, 6, 7, 13]. For computer networks, they have proven to even throw back the most powerful attackers [12]. However, similar to WSNs, they leverage properties that do not exist in HASs, such as routing and looser energy constraints.

## 3. ANALYSIS METHODS

For our passive attacks, we assumed a realistic attacker model: The attacker can observe the whole system at once over longer periods of time, but has no prior knowledge. This was implemented by putting a capture device inside the users' homes without receiving any information about the setup from the owners. While the position of the device is certainly different in a real attack, we assume the same coverage can be reached with multiple devices. The following sections provide an overview of the methods used in our analysis which have been implemented in a toolsuite. The modules are called *sniffer*, *cleaner* and *analyzer*.

### 3.1 Data Acquisition

A simple and way to eavesdrop on the communication is provided by the so-called CC1101 USB Lite (CUL) stick, using an open-source firmware(called `culfw`) that can decode several wireless HAS protocols. The collection of data is performed by the *sniffer* module. It reads the data and applies regular expressions which are used to preliminarily identify the type and function of each node. They are found in the FHEM (`http://fhem.de`) software. For our studies we attached the stick to a Raspberry Pi which served as a host computer and data storage.

### 3.2 Data Interpretation

The approach of applying regular expressions from the FHEM software gave us a basic idea of the device categories involved in the communication. In order to achieve maximum clarity about the packet contents, we processed the collected transmissions in 4 steps.

1. The BidCos packet structure allows the distinction of different devices based on their addresses. Counting the number of distinct addresses in the collected packets also gives the number of devices in the network.

2. To clean the collected data, we discarded all packets that were resent due to transmission errors. The remaining packets were saved in a database table whose attributes (columns) correspond to the packet fields (e.g. source address, length). The *cleaner* module performs this task.

3. The classification of devices using regular expressions is not error-free. FHEM relies on packets captured from an initial pairing procedure, which the attacker does not necessarily observe. In order to correct these

errors, we supplemented the preliminary classification with plausibility checks. These checks are explained in the next paragraph.

4. Lastly, we interpreted the messages according to their context. Messages from a temperature sensor, for example, were translated into decimal numbers. The base station, when sending messages, assumed the behaviour of a different kind of device, e.g. it would act as a remote control when sending commands to a light switch. Choosing the method of interpretation according to the destination let us correctly translate this data as well.

### Plausibility Checks

As mentioned in item 3 above, the mere layout of a certain message may not clearly indicate whether it is a temperature sensor status response or a command to a window opener. To determine which of the two was correct, we would examine the possible interpretations of the data. A temperature interpretation, for example, which results in a value outside the range from $-25°C$ to $50°C$ would be unlikely to be correct, since the systems were installed in German homes. These checks can also be automated, but have only been performed manually by us due to lower overall effort.

Another type of check is the inspection of communication links. For example, a remote control is much more likely to communicate with a window opener than with a temperature sensor. Examining the communications partners of a node thus helps to find plausible classifications. However, this would introduce dependencies and probabilities into the identification process. Thus, these checks require either manual intervention or complex logic and the gain of additional information is questionable. As a result, we have not implemented them and have used only minor manual corrections to help in the classification.

## 3.3 Profile Building

After successfully identifying the device types, an attacker can now build a profile of the inhabitants using the information he gained from the above steps. We performed this analysis in 3 different steps. All 3 steps are included in the *analyzer* module.

### 3.3.1 Visualizing the Communication

As a first step, we displayed the collected data in formats that allow a manual inspection. Two particular visualization formats have proven to be useful for our analysis. On the one hand we created a directed graph out of the collected device data. Each device corresponds to a node and an edge is created between each two devices that ever communicated with each other. The width of the edge is determined by the amount of messages on this link. On the other hand we projected the messages to and from a single device in relation to the time onto a 2-dimensional graph. This graph type helps identify temporal structures and periodic events.

### 3.3.2 Correlation Analysis

In addition to the manual identification of correlated events, we performed an automated correlation analysis using a sliding window approach. We defined an event as a 4-tuple of sender address, receiver address, message type and message content. For each event $e$, we examined other events $e^*$ that occured in a time frame after $e$. We then paired $e$ with each of these other events $e^*$ and for each pair $(e, e^*)$ calculated the number of occurences over the whole observation time. 3 parameters allow filtering out events: The minimum total number of occurences of the event $e$, the minimum chance of $e$ being followed by $e^*$ and the length of the time frame in which $e^*$ has to follow $e$ in order to be counted.

### 3.3.3 Filtering Automation Rules

With a similar approach we tried to filter out programmed automation rules. We assumed that automated events occur at a fixed time which differs only marginally. For each event we collected all occurences over the observation period. We then stripped the date so only the time of day remained. As a last step, we sorted the occurences in chronological order. The sorted list allows for an easy identification of events that often occured at similar times during a day.

## 4. RESULTS

The following sections present the analysis results.

## 4.1 Candidate 1 (C1)

The first installation is a simple single home installation. We recorded 45,679 messages over a period of 36 days. Only a few devices could not be identified with acceptable certainty. As we found out after a debriefing with the owner, this was the case for the smoke detectors that only send heartbeat messages to the central unit as well as one of the tri-state sensors that did not send any state changes during the observation period.

### 4.1.1 Communication Overview

Fig. 1 provides a graphical overview of the communication. Expectedly, the central unit $Z$ *1.1* communicates with most sensors and actuators so it could be easily identified. The graph also allows us to identify which components are directly paired with each other and do not exclusively communicate over the central unit. This information might be useful, for example for later active attacks against the system, and might also be an indicator for manual interaction.

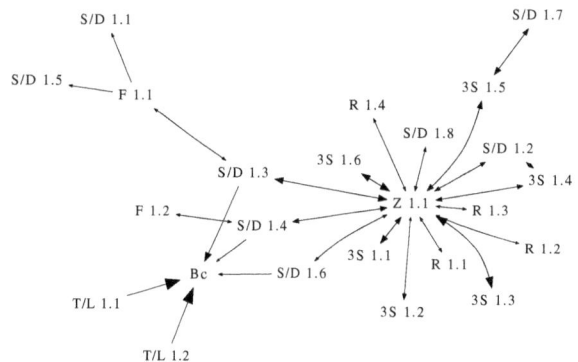

**Figure 1: Directed communication graph for candidate 1. The abbreviations used for the device types are explained in Tab. 1.**

### 4.1.2 Manual Examination of Message Graphs

Fig. 2 shows the temperature status messages of two temperature/humidity sensors $T/L$ *1.1* and $T/L$ *1.2*. What immediately leaps to the eye is the different ranges that the values lie in. We thus concluded that $T/L$ *1.1* is located outside the house whereas $T/L$ *1.2* is located on the inside.

| Abbr. | Device |
|-------|--------|
| 3S | Tri-state Sensor |
| Bc | Broadcast Address |
| F | Remote Control |
| KF | KeyMatic Remote Control |
| KS | KeyMatic Lock |
| R | Smoke Detector |
| S/D | Switch / Dimmer |
| ST | Heating Actuator / Thermostat |
| T/L | Temperature / Humidity Sensor |
| Z | Central Unit |

**Table 1: Abbreviations for the different devices.**

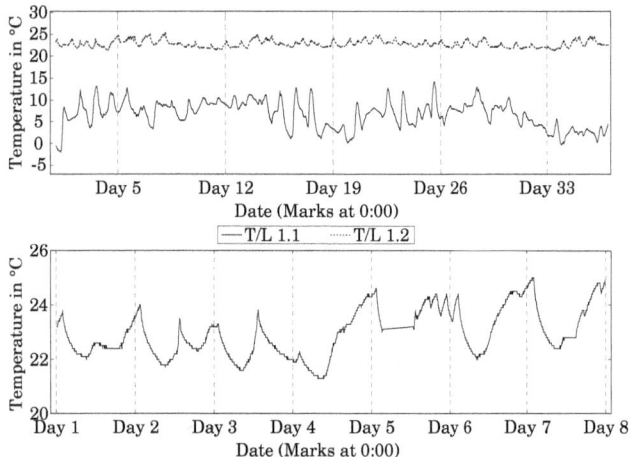

**Figure 2: Temperature values of *T/L 1.1* and *T/L 1.2* over the course of 6 weeks (upper) and values of *T/L 1.2* over the course of 7 days (lower).**

We confirmed this by comparing the recorded values with weather reports from the area.

Values of the in-house sensor *T/L 1.2* consistently lie in the range between 20°C and 25°C. The not perfectly regular rise and fall suggests that the heating is controlled manually and indicates a user habit. Furthermore we deduced from the low outside temperature and the slow temperature drop inside that the room is seldomly ventilated by widely opening the windows for at least 10 minutes.

The tri-state sensors[1] can be coarsely divided into two groups. The first group consists of only two sensors, *3S 1.2* and *3S 1.4*. Both send only very few messages with usually the same content. No conclusions could be drawn about their role. The second group consists of the remaining tri-state sensors whose traffic mainly consists of *open* and *close* state announcements.

Examining the protocol data for *3S 1.3* and *3S 1.6* reveals that they frequently switch the state. The *open* state is never held for more than 1.5 minutes and usually lies in the order of seconds, suggesting that the sensors are placed on doors rather than windows. The activity over longer time spans shows gaps during the nights and early mornings. Since tri-state sensors notify about state changes usually caused by user interaction, these gaps are good indicators for the inhabitants' sleep cycles. *3S 1.6* changes its state to *closed* some time before the gaps, which supports the assumption that it is installed on the front door. This is a major discovery for an attacker, because he can now tell

---

[1]The family of tri-state sensors includes different devices: Window sensors that distinguish between *open*, *closed* and *tilted* and door sensors which only distinguish between *open* and *closed*. Technically, they are the same kind of device.

when the first inhabitant leaves the flat/house in the morning. If there is only one inhabitant, this knowledge is already enough to plan a burglary during the owner's absence.

Similar to the tri-state sensors, the switches/dimmers can be divided into two groups. *S/D 1.2*, *S/D 1.6* and *S/D 1.8* showed very little activity over the observation period. *S/D 1.3* and *S/D 1.4* regularly alternate between *on* and *off* states. The activities of *S/D 1.4* (Fig. 3) revealed a strong regularity in the afternoon between 16:30[2] and 17:00 when the actuator is switched *on* and at 1:00 when it is switched *off* again. Each day the former action is performed 1.5 minutes earlier than the day before. This is a very strong indicator for an automation rule which compensates for the sunset times. This assumption is supported by the fact that the respective commands come directly from the base station rather than a remote control.

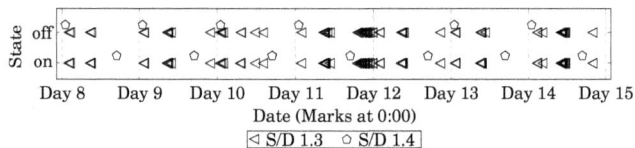

**Figure 3: Data sent to and from switches/dimmers *S/D 1.3* and *S/D 1.4*.**

Considering *S/D 1.3*, we found regular activity on weekdays between 1:00 and 2:00 as well as between 8:30 and 9:30. The slight variations support the conclusion that this indicates a user habit rather than an automation rule. The payloads of the recorded packets revealed that on weekday mornings, the base station would send timer commands to the switch between 8:00 and 9:15. These commands would turn the switch on for an hour after which it would turn itself off again. We attributed this behaviour to either a habit of the user after waking up or to an alarm function actually waking the user by e.g. turning on the lights.

Another regularity is the absence of activity of *S/D 1.3* between 13:00 and 17:30. The fact that this coincides with a lack of activity of *S/D 1.7* (12:00 to 18:30) lead us to the conclusion that the user is absent during this time of day.

### 4.1.3 Correlation Analysis

We started the correlation analysis by trying out possible parameter values. Since we had no prior knowledge about the systems, the only approach was to manually determine suitable parameters.

The results of the correlation analysis largely support the previous findings which could already be observed in the graphical analysis. Additional conclusions about the system and the user are elaborated here.

In 72.5% of all cases where sensor *3S 1.6* was turned on, it would be turned off again within 10 seconds. A similar behaviour was observed for sensor *3S 1.4*, which was closed within the 10-second interval in 58% of all cases. In accordance with our reasoning above, we concluded that the sensors are installed on doors rather than windows.

When selectively analyzing the behaviour of *3S 1.3* and *3S 1.5*, we found them to act very much alike. In most cases the state *open* did not hold for longer than 90 seconds. In the case of *3S 1.3*, this was especially interesting when considering the timer commands sent to it by the base station in the mornings. The commands would turn on the switch

---

[2]Times in this paper are expressed in the 24-hour notation.

for 300 seconds, but in 96% of these cases, the switch would be manually turned off within the first 90 seconds after reception. This supports our theory that the switch is part of an alarm function.

### 4.1.4 Filtering Automated Events

In order to filter out automated events, we initially started the analysis with very strict parameters: The minimum number of occurences of an event were set to 120, the maximum overall deviation of events possibly originating from the same automation rule was set to 60 seconds and the maximum deviation of two consecutive events from the same rule was set to 30 seconds. The only event to match at first was a command from the base station which turns off *S/D 1.4* at precisely 1:00, confirming our assumptions. We then proceeded to loosen the parameters to search for other rules. The command coming from the base station and turning on *S/D 1.4* in the afternoon between 16:25 and 17:10 came out next. Although the maximum distance between the different occurences is 38 minutes, we concluded that this event indicates the presence of an automation rule. The distance between two consecutive occurences is about 90 seconds and each event occured later than the one on the day before. Rather than a user habit, we attributed this regularity to an automation rule that incorporates sunset times.

## 4.2 Candidate 2 (C2)

The installation of C2 was somewhat special since it was split up in two parts that are interconnected via a VPN. One part was the user's private flat and the other part was his office. For this reason, we performed the data collection in two parts. We first installed the sniffer at the office, then moved it to the user's home. During this period we recorded 34,707 messages sent from 20 devices.

### 4.2.1 Communication Overview

Fig. 4 shows the communication graph for candidate 2. It can easily be seen that there is no single center of communication as opposed to the system of C1. Many devices are paired directly with each other and only 6 of 19 available sensors communicate with Z 2.1. Furthermore, neither the remote control F 2.1 nor any of the three switches paired with it communicate with Z 2.1. Thus, we can almost certainly rule out any automation rules for these devices, which gives us more insight into the habits of the inhabitants. Nevertheless, the segmentation of this installation and the VPN connection between the segments make it quite difficult to derive information about the physical presence of the inhabitants from the automated events alone. The keymatic remote controls KF 2.1 and KF 2.2 are paired with many actuators in addition to the keymatic door locks and both keymativ remote controls are paired with both door locks.

### 4.2.2 Manual Examination of Message Graphs

The temperature values given by the sensors *T/L 2.1 – 2.3* and corresponding actuators *ST 2.1 – 2.3* are strong indicators for an automated heating concept. Over the weekends, the temperatures drop gradually and then rise again sharply at the start of the week. The different temperature and humidity curves and the temperature differences of up to 10°C between the sensors lead us to the assumption that they are installed in 2-3 different rooms.

When examining the activity of the remote control F 2.1

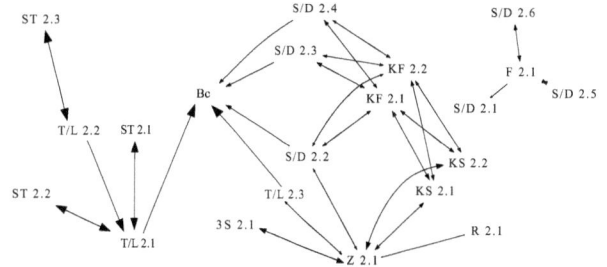

**Figure 4: Directed communication graph for C2. The abbreviations are again those from Tab. 1**

we found events only in the first part of the observation period. This means that the user only uses the remote control within the office itself and does not control any devices at home. The observed activity is thus a very reliable indicator of when the user is definitely present at the office and thus, not at home.

### Keymatic Door Lock System

The most interesting data for Candidate 2 came from the automatic door lock system. Every day at about 9:15 as well as between 20:00 and 22:00 the door locks report their status to the central unit Z 2.1. We observed that there are always two messages shortly after one another, first *3S 2.1* sends the state *open* and after a maximum of 60 seconds the state *close*. Correlating the states of *3S 2.1* and *KS 2.2*, we concluded that *3S 2.1* is installed on the same door as *KS 2.2*. Due to this combination, the presence of the inhabitants can be easily predicted. Usually there is nobody at home between 9:30 and 20:30, except for mondays, where the time of absence lies between 13:00 and 21:00.

### 4.2.3 Correlation Analysis

Our correlation analysis found strong colleations between the thermostats and the heating actuators as well as between the remote control *F 2.1* and the actuators *S/D 2.1*, *S/D 2.5* and *S/D 2.6*. The thermostats show a consecutive acknowledgement of the heating actuators new position in 98.8% of all cases. The switch and dimmmer actuators even send their status as a reaction to a previous command from the remote control in 100% of all cases.

We see similar clear results for the reactions of the Keymatic door lock systems and the switches/dimmers *S/D 2.2*, *S/D 2.3* and *S/D 2.4* to the Keymatic remote controls *KF 2.1* and *KF 2.2*, where we recorded a reaction in 90% of all cases. In addition to what we already knew, the correlation analysis revealed that the tri-state sensor *3S 2.1* seems to have a relation to *KS 2.2*, since over 60% of all status changes of *KS 2.2* result in a status change of *3S 2.1*.

### 4.2.4 Filtering Automated Events

To filter automated events we used the same approach as for the first candidate. We generally found the results to support our findings from the manual analysis.

Using the automatic filtering method we could confirm our assumption that the unlocking command sent from the base station Z 2.1 to KS 2.2 at 8:30 in the morning does belong to an automation rule. The same holds for the command that locks KS 2.2 again at 22:30.

Furthermore we found that the the heating actuators are automatically turned off at night. They regularly receive a *Pos.: 0%* command from the temperature/humidity sensors.

### 4.3 Confirmation of Results

After our experiments, we interviewed both candidates and discussed our findings with them. We were able to confirm our conclusions about the locations and purposes of the different devices. The candidates also confirmed our assumptions about automation rules and user habits.

### 4.4 Encrypted Communication

Applying encryption to all traffic in the HAS would make the aforementioned attacks harder to some degree. Both our approach to determine device types as well as our definition of an event for the correlation analysis and automation rule filtering incorporated the message payloads. They could not be applied in the same way if these payloads were encrypted.

However, encryption alone would not prevent an attacker from learning some information about the user. If the packet's source and destination address are unencrypted, an attacker can still try to identify devices by using heuristics. For example, devices that, from time to time, send two messages in short succession are usually door state sensors. Devices that only send one message each day can be assumed to be smoke detectors and devices that receive one message each morning and another one each evening can be assumed to be door locks. The devices that communicate the most are base stations, followed by temperature and humidity sensors.

Even if the complete packet, including the full header, is encrypted, some information leaks to an eavesdropping adversary. Activity in C1's HAS between 12:00 and 18:00 was 8.6% higher on weekends and holidays than it was on working days. HAS activity in C2's office was 21.3% lower during these times, strongly indicating presence and absence.

### 5. CONCLUSIONS

We have analyzed of two installations of the HomeMatic system and we have shown that this kind of system poses a significant threat to the privacy of the users. In general, systems that do not apply any kind of encryption leak a large amount of information to any observer keen enough to look for it. No prior knowledge about the installation or the victim is necessary to perform this kind of attack.

Furthermore we have gained knowledge about the traits of a HAS, such as possible communication links and how frequently a device usually sends messages. This information can be used to attack systems which apply encryption and thus at the very least identify when users are at home. As long as the systems do not provide a systematic protection against traffic analysis attacks, they should be considered vulnerable. To the best of our knowledge, no publicly available system provides this sort of protection as of now.

While we performed many tasks and checks manually during our experiments, most of them can be automated with the knowledge from our findings. Our parameters for finding automated events proved useful, as long as the automation rules did not change times themselves. Possible communication links, the usual frequencies with which the different devices send status messages and the number of messages being exchanged for each action of one device can be used to program heuristics which can then in turn identify devices in a system where packet payloads are encrypted.

### 5.1 Future Work

Considering how easy it is to attack current HASs, it is essential to protect against the attacks mentioned in this paper. While encryption schemes are available and can be readily applied, protection against traffic analysis attacks in HA networks is yet to be developed. Generating dummy traffic in an effective and efficient manner can help tackle this problem. Focus here can be put on the fact that the energy consumption of sensors and actuators has to stay as low as possible, but the base station is usually connected to a power line and can thus send dummy traffic without considerably decreasing battery lifetimes.

### 6. REFERENCES

[1] J. Al-Muhtadi, M. Anand, M.D. Mickunas, and R. Campbell, *Secure smart homes using Jini and UIUC SESAME*, ACSAC '00, ACM, pp. 77–85.

[2] P. Bergstrom, K. Driscoll, and J. Kimball, *Making home automation communications secure*, Computer **34** (2001), no. 10, 50–56.

[3] D. L. Chaum, *Untraceable Electronic Mail, Return Addresses, and Digital Pseudonyms*, CACM **24** (1981), no. 2, 84–90.

[4] G. Danezis, R. Dingledine, and N. Mathewson, *Mixminion: design of a type III anonymous remailer protocol*, Symposium on Security and Privacy, 2003. Proceedings., IEEE, pp. 2–15.

[5] E. De Cristofaro, X. Ding, and G. Tsudik, *Privacy-Preserving Querying in Sensor Networks*, ICCCN, '09, IEEE, pp. 1–6.

[6] M. J. Freedman and R. Morris, *Tarzan: A Peer-to-peer Anonymizing Network Layer*, CCS '02, ACM, pp. 193–206.

[7] D. Goldschlag, M. Reed, and P. Syverson, *Onion Routing*, CACM **42** (1999), no. 2, 39–41.

[8] M. Hatler, D. Gurganious, C. Chi, and J. Kreegar, *Smart Home Sensor Networks*, Tech. report, ON World Inc., 2011.

[9] Y.-X. Li, L. Qin, and Q. Liang, *Research on Wireless Sensor Network Security*, CIS '10, IEEE, pp. 493–496.

[10] Z. Li and G. Gong, *A Survey on Security in Wireless Sensor Networks*, (2011).

[11] A. Marin, W. Mueller, R. Schaefer, F. Almenarez, D. Diaz, and M. Ziegler, *Middleware for Secure Home Access and Control*, PerCom Workshops '07., IEEE, pp. 489–494.

[12] NSA, *Tor Stinks*, Presentation, January 2007.

[13] A. Pfitzmann, B. Pfitzmann, and M. Waidner, *ISDN-Mixes: Untraceable Communication with Very Small Bandwidth Overhead*, KiVS '91, Springer, pp. 451–463.

[14] J. Sen, *A Survey on Wireless Sensor Network Security*, IJCNIS **1** (2009), no. 2, 55–78.

[15] H. Strese, U. Seidel, T. Knape, and A. Botthof, *Smart Home in Deutschland — Untersuchung im Rahmen der wissenschaftlichen Begleitung zum Programm Next Generation Media (NGM) des Bundesministeriums für Wirtschaft und Technologie*, Tech. report, Institut für Innovation und Technik (iit) in der VDI/VDE-IT, Berlin, May 2010.

[16] Y. Wang, G. Attebury, and B. Ramamurthy, *A survey of security issues in wireless sensor networks*, Communications Surveys & Tutorials, IEEE **8** (2006), no. 2, 2–23.

# Single-stroke Language-Agnostic Keylogging using Stereo-Microphones and Domain Specific Machine Learning

Sashank Narain, Amirali Sanatinia and Guevara Noubir
College of Computer and Information Science
Northeastern University, Boston, MA
{sashank, amirali, noubir}@ccs.neu.edu

## ABSTRACT

Mobile phones are equipped with an increasingly large number of precise and sophisticated sensors. This raises the risk of direct and indirect privacy breaches. In this paper, we investigate the feasibility of keystroke inference when user taps on a soft keyboard are captured by the *stereoscopic* microphones on an Android smartphone. We developed algorithms for sensor-signals processing and domain specific machine learning to infer key taps using a combination of stereo-microphones and gyroscopes. We implemented and evaluated the performance of our system on two popular mobile phones and a tablet: Samsung S2, Samsung Tab 8 and HTC One. Based on our experiments, and to the best of our knowledge, our system (1) is the first to exceed 90% accuracy requiring a single attempt, (2) operates on the standard Android QWERTY and number keyboards, and (3) is language agnostic. We show that stereo-microphones are a much more effective side channel as compared to the gyroscope, however, their data can be combined to boost the accuracy of prediction. While previous studies focused on larger key sizes and repetitive attempts, we show that by focusing on the specifics of the keyboard and creating machine learning models and algorithms based on keyboard areas combined with adequate filtering, we can achieve an accuracy of 90% - 94% for much smaller key sizes in a single attempt. We also demonstrate how such attacks can be instrumentalized by a malicious application to log the keystrokes of other sensitive applications. Finally, we describe some techniques to mitigate these attacks.

## Categories and Subject Descriptors

K.6.5 [**Security and Protection**]: Unauthorized access; Invasive software; K.4.1 [**Public Policy Issues**]: Privacy

## Keywords

Smartphone Security; Side-Channel Attacks; Sensor Malware; Tap Detection with Motion Sensors; Keystroke Inference using Gyroscope; Keystroke Inference using Stereo-Microphones; Machine Learning; Privacy

## 1. INTRODUCTION

Mobile devices have proliferated across the globe with an estimated 1.75 billion smartphone users world-wide by the end of 2014 [9]. These smartphones are used for various day-to-day and business activities, many containing sensitive information such as Personally Identifiable Information (PII), banking and credit card numbers, passwords, health records, and location information. This means that a malicious application installed on the smartphone can siphon off sensitive information and leave millions susceptible to data theft. Operating systems on these smartphones prevent unauthorized access to application / user information by implementing security mechanisms such as sandboxing and permissions. However, side-channels such as sensors can bypass such security restrictions. Most modern smartphones contain several sensors such as microphones, cameras, gyroscopes and accelerometers that provide a better user experience but these sensors, however useful, leak information that provides an adversary opportunity to covertly infer and steal sensitive data.

In this work, we demonstrate that by recording the tap sounds and vibrations from the stereo-microphones and gyroscope of a smartphone while a target application is running, it is possible to successfully infer user typed keys with high accuracy. We also show that the audio data can be combined with the gyroscope to further boost the accuracy. Android OS is popular among users and smartphone manufacturers with more than million activations daily [15]. Owing to this popularity, we chose to perform our experiments on two popular Android smartphones and a tablet: Samsung S2, Samsung Tab 8 and HTC One. While there have been related work, to the best of our knowledge, we are the first to break the 90% accuracy barrier on the standard Android QWERTY and number keyboard. For instance, some previous work that demonstrated key inference based on Android sensors, Aviv et al. [1] reached an accuracy of 43% and 73% on PIN and pattern passwords, respectively, requiring 5 attempts, Owusu et al. [23] were able to infer 6 passwords out of 99 six-character passwords in an average of 4.5 trials on the QWERTY keyboard in landscape mode, and Miluzzo et al. [21] predicted 4x5 icon taps on iPhone and Nexus S with an accuracy of 80%. To achieve an accuracy of 90%, they relied on more than 20 repetitions. To achieve a high accuracy on the standard keyboard, we developed an algorithm and framework based on statistical methods and machine learning that can predict keystrokes without repetition or multiple attempts. Our framework is language agnostic as we do not use any lexical properties of languages, however we do assume that the adversary knows the keyboard layout. We demonstrate the algorithm using data collected at an office and in a restaurant. A malicious application and a weak permission model for Android sensors coupled with data modeling techniques make our attack feasible and consequential. We make the following contributions:

- We show that by recording the tap sounds from the stereoscopic microphone and the tap vibrations from the gyroscope on a smartphone, it is possible to infer user's typed keys with a reasonably high accuracy of above 90%. We also show that this accuracy can be boosted by combining the audio data with the gyroscope data. We design an automated system that can process this raw keystroke data, perform noise filtering, build training models and use these models to make language agnostic keystroke predictions on unknown test data.

- We develop a specialized meta-algorithm that divides the keyboard into specific areas and trains models using audio and gyroscope data for those areas. The algorithm combines character-specific and area-specific models to make more accurate predictions. We show that by combining our algorithm with meta-algorithms such as Bagging and Boosting [8], we were able to achieve higher per algorithm accuracy than an elementary use of the machine learning algorithms on unknown test data.

- We demonstrate the feasibility of a Trojan that regularly queries the Android system for the foreground application and covertly records the microphone and gyroscope when a sensitive application is used.

The rest of the paper is organized as follows. In section 2, we describe a scenario of how a stealthy attack can be launched against a sensitive Android application by a victim inadvertently downloading a malicious application. In section 3, we describe the high-level architecture of our system and discuss why the gyroscope and microphone sensors leak information about a user's typing activity. In section 4, we describe our automated keystroke inference system, data collection process and the meta-algorithm. In section 5, we present the results of our experiments. In section 6, we describe techniques that can be used to mitigate these attacks. In section 7, we describe previous related work and in section 8, we conclude and discuss future research directions.

## 2. ATTACK VECTOR

To perform a successful attack, the adversary follows the set of steps described below. The adversary develops and distributes a malicious application usually as a Trojan (step 1). They trick the victim into installing the application (step 2) through techniques such as social engineering (e.g., a malicious application disguised as a game or a note taking application or through USB connection to bogus devices [2]). Previous works have found examples of such applications with backdoors in the Android marketplace [30], [32]. After compromising the victim's smartphone, the application performs two roles. First, it presents a custom keyboard to the user to collect typing behavior for training models. Second,

after training, it listens in the background for keypresses from sensitive Android applications.

To successfully perform the first role, the malicious application starts collecting user's typing behavior by using a custom keyboard and recording the stereo microphones and gyroscope (step 3). The microphone requires explicit permissions during installation and the adversary needs to declare it in the *manifest* file. To avoid raising the victim's suspicions, the adversary justifies such permissions by providing functionality such as: note taking, supporting voice commands and voice recognition. The application must serve an actual purpose (e.g., a Todo app) so that the user actually uses the application. After monitoring the victim's behavior, the Trojan uploads the collected training data to a remote server to build models specific to the victim (step 4). The adversary can also use generic training data and prediction models as a trade-off for performance and stealth.

To accomplish the second role, the Trojan runs in the background and queries the smartphone OS for the current location and the application. To reduce battery drain, these queries run at predefined conservative intervals. On inferring that the victim is at a place of interest using the GPS or cellular and wireless networks (e.g., bank or residence garage door) or when the victim opens a sensitive application (e.g., a bank application), the Trojan starts to actively collect the microphone and gyroscope data (step 5). The current application can be found by using the `Activity-Manager` class in Android SDK if the application has the `android.permission.GET_TASKS` permission set in its manifest file. The data is filtered and keystrokes are extracted by the application and evaluated using the training models to infer the user's typed keystrokes.

## 3. APPROACH

In this section, we describe the architecture of our key inference system that performs audio and gyroscope keystroke noise filtering and extraction, data consolidation for machine learning, model training, evaluation of test instances and evaluation of accuracy.

### 3.1 Architecture

The architecture of our keystroke inference system is composed of the components shown in Figure 1. The *Application* component is the trojan application that secretly records the gyroscope and stereo microphones when a user types in our application (training data) or another security sensitive application (test data). The raw gyroscope and audio data is uploaded to a remote server that runs the remaining components of our system to process this data, create training models and perform evaluations on the test data. This raw data contains user tap vibrations and sounds mixed with pauses and noise that occur due to external factors such as unstable hands (gyroscope noise) or background music (audio noise), see Figures 6 and 7. The *Pre-processing* component removes noise from the data using adequate filtering, extracts the user taps, and performs fitting to resample the data. The techniques used for filtering and extracting gyroscope and audio data are different and require two separate pre-processing components. Once the data has been processed, it is converted to a format that is understood by Weka [16]. During conversion, the gyroscope and audio data may also be combined for inference. This means that the two need to be synchronized with each other. The

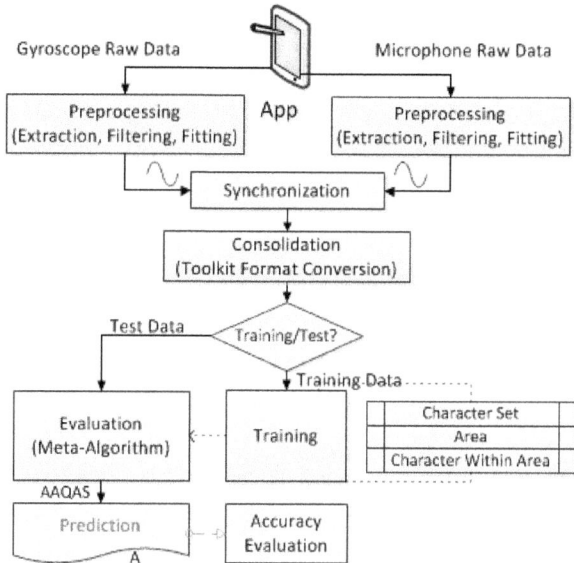

**Figure 1: Architecture of the key inference system.**

*Synchronization* component synchronizes the gyroscope and audio data and the *Consolidation* component converts the extracted and filtered inference ready data to a machine learning toolkit format. In order to classify unknown test data, the consolidated training data is used to build models. The *Training* component analyzes the data for errors, randomizes them and uses several machine learning algorithms to build different inference models for the entire character set as well as specific areas on the keyboard. These models are then used by the *Evaluation* component to perform predictions on the unknown test data. The component uses a meta-algorithm that makes a final keystroke prediction. The meta-algorithm uses a multi-step approach based on the specific layout of Android QWERTY and number keyboards to optimize the inference accuracy of test keystrokes. Once predictions have been made for all unknown test data, the *Accuracy Evaluation* component compares them with the expected keystroke to evaluate our system's performance.

## 3.2 Sensors

### 3.2.1 Gyroscope & Accelerometer

Gyroscope and Accelerometer sensors on smartphones can detect vibrations for every keystroke when a user types on a soft keyboard. Figure 2 shows the location of the gyroscope (in red), the location of keys 'I', 'Q' and 'V' on a standard QWERTY keyboard on the HTC One, and the co-ordinate system of Android sensors. The magnitude and orientation of these vibrations vary depending on the tap location with respect to the two axes which can be mapped to a standard fixed keyboard layout. In Figure 3, we see that key 'Q' shows significant vibration in the y axis and key 'V' shows significant vibration in the x axis. As the key 'I' is close to both the axes, it does not show considerable vibration in both the axes.

Gyroscope sensors are attractive targets for building smartphone keyloggers. They are easy to use in Android using the Android SDK [14] APIs defined in the **Sensor** class. They do not require special permissions and they can run in the background without prompting or notifying the user. A po-

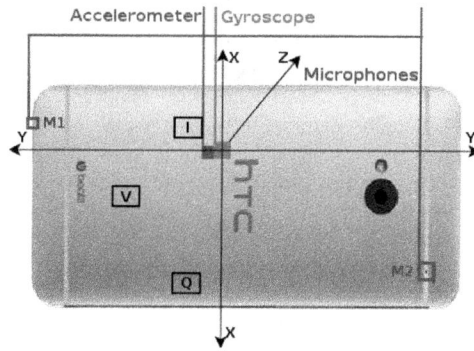

**Figure 2: Location of the Accelerometer, Gyroscope and Microphones on HTC One; Approximate location of keys 'I', 'Q' and 'V' on standard QWERTY keyboard.**

tential issue with using the SDK API is that the sampling rate is not fixed and may reduce when more processor intensive services are running, thereby reducing the inference accuracy. A solution for obtaining high and constant sampling rate on a Android smartphone even when other high priority services are running on the system is to use the Android NDK [13] APIs defined in **sensors.h**.

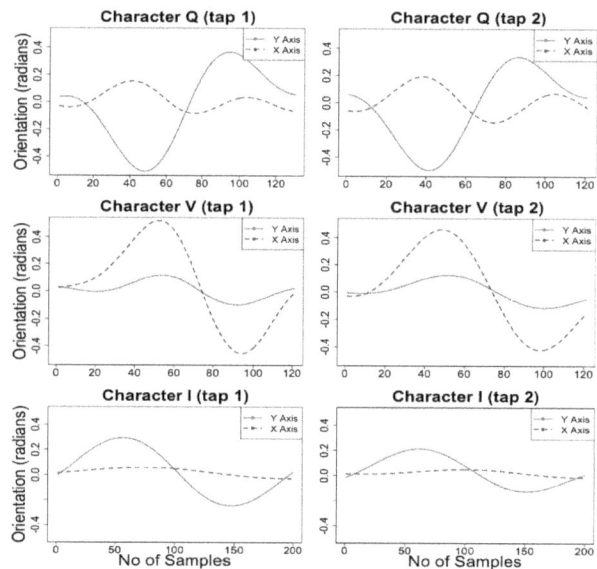

**Figure 3: (Top, middle and bottom) Similarity between two keystrokes for letters 'Q', 'V' and 'I'; Each letter pattern is visually different from other letter.**

### 3.2.2 Microphones

Microphone arrays are becoming commonplace in smartphones. Some smartphones, such as the iPhone 5s, are equipped with three microphones. Other smartphones, such as the HTC One, are equipped with dual membrane microphones that focus on capturing different sound levels (one for sensitivity and the other for distance) on a single microphone. In both these arrangements, the audio captured by the arrays are combined and processed to provide high quality and distortion free audio recording to users with the capability to detect feeble sounds. In addition, the HTC One also supports stereo recording. We observed that a soft tap on a smartphone, by a user, is audible. This tap can be covertly recorded and processed to infer a user's typing activity with relatively higher accuracy than the gyroscope. There are two techniques to infer keystrokes, one that uses the amplitude of audio signals at the two microphones and the other that uses the time delay between signals reaching the two microphones. We use a combination of both the techniques to build our inference models. Figure 2 shows the location of the microphones (in blue) on the HTC One. Since the microphones are synchronized, for a tap at location T, the delay in tap detection between the two microphones M1 and M2 can be computed using the following formula.

Number of Samples =

$$\frac{(\text{Distance}(T,M1) - \text{Distance }(T,M2)) * \text{Sampling Rate}}{\text{Speed of Sound}}$$

(1)

The distance between the two microphones on the HTC One is about 0.134 m. The current maximum supported sampling rate for Android is 48000 Hz and the speed of sound in air is about 340 m/s. Using these values with the formula, a difference of 18 samples is obtained for taps in close proximity to the microphones. This means that taps on different keys will produce varying sample differences based on their distance from the two microphones. The difference in samples will increase when smartphones start supporting higher sampling rates such as 192 KHz, currently supported by Blue-ray. Using a rate of 192 KHz with the formula, a difference of 75 samples can be obtained for taps in close proximity to the microphones. This will significantly improve the accuracy of inference and is indicative of the impact of the sampling rate on the accuracy.

To illustrate the time delay between the microphones, we recorded multiple samples for keys 'Q' and 'V' on a standard QWERTY keyboard on the HTC One at a sampling rate of 48KHz. Figure 4 shows a single tap for the two keys. We found that, for multiple taps, the two keys always have the same delay of 8 and 15, respectively, between M1 and M2. The figure also shows that the amplitudes at M1 were significantly lower than M2. This is because our application uses M2 as the primary microphone, and requests the Operating System to perform noise cancellation when supported. The lower amplitudes at M1 are a result of noise cancellation by the system.

Microphone functionality is easy to implement in Android using the Android SDK APIs defined in the `AudioRecord` class. Even though they initially require special permissions from the user, once installed, they can run in the background without prompting the user or showing a notification. This makes the microphones an attractive target for building Android keyloggers. Stereo recording is a relatively new concept in smartphones and we expect a lot of new smartphones to adopt this technology. We believe that this capability can be used maliciously and should be addressed.

## 4. SYSTEM DESIGN AND ALGORITHMS

In this section, we describe the hardware and software we developed, the data collected, the gyroscope and microphone noise filtering and extraction process, the training process and the meta-algorithm that we developed to make predictions on unknown test data.

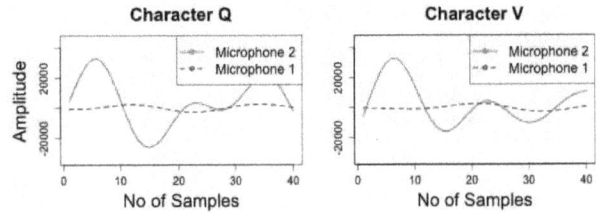

Figure 4: (Left) Sound waves received by the two microphones of HTC One for key 'Q'; (Right) Sound waves received by the two microphones for key 'V'.

### 4.1 Data Collection

#### 4.1.1 Hardware & Software

In this work, we decided to evaluate our algorithms and system on two popular Android smartphones and a tablet: Samsung S2 (Android 4.1), Samsung Tab 8 (Android 4.1) and HTC One (Android 4.4); all three using the stock Android Operating System provided by the vendor. We did not make any modifications to the operating system and its underlying mechanisms. We developed an application to collect accelerometer, gyroscope and microphones data for training the models and for generating test samples for evaluation. It runs in two separate modes for training and test data. The data collected in the training mode is used for building the inference models and the data collected in the test mode is used for making predictions using these models. In case of the test mode, the application invokes a service that runs in the background. These two modes are completely independent of each other and do not overlap. Our application implemented a custom keyboard that has the same layout and capabilities as the standard Android QWERTY and Number keyboard. The only difference is that our keyboard has the capability to detect a key press and inject a key press event in the gyroscope data. Figure 5 shows the screenshot of the custom keyboard. The user presses the 'Start Recording' button and types data on the keyboard. Whenever they are done typing their data, they press the 'Stop Recording' button that is visible after recording is started. During this typing session, the accelerometer, gyroscope and microphones are activated in the background and their data are recorded and stored on the smartphone's internal memory.

Figure 5: QWERTY and Number Keyboard with Area divisions.

#### 4.1.2 Gyroscope & Microphones

We collected accelerometer, gyroscope and audio training and test samples for both the number and QWERTY keyboard in Portrait mode on the Samsung S2, the Samsung Tab 8 and the HTC One. The data was collected by seven participants who were asked to take samples in their normal typing style. We observed their typing behavior and all of them held the device in one hand and typed using the index finger or thumb of the other. One participant (User4) held the device in their right hand and the remaining in their left hand. The main difference in typing behavior was the intensity with which the finger touched the screen and the angles at which these devices were held. These participants were asked to type anything they wanted (random characters and words) and at least 30 samples per character / number in the training mode.

The data on the HTC One was collected in two environments. Five participants typed in an office environment and two of them also typed in a restaurant. The office environment consisted of a cubicle with three computers and a server running all the time with additional noise from keyboard typing, doors opening and closing, people talking and faint noises of vehicles from on a nearby street (noise level around 49-52 dB). The restaurant was much more noisier with background music, several people talking and noise from utensils (noise level around 72-76 dB).

The data collected from the gyroscope are the smartphone's time, gyroscope accuracy, x axis orientation, y axis orientation and the z axis orientation at the maximum sampling rate for the device. We additionally collected the key press time using a custom keyboard having the same layout and capabilities as the standard Android QWERTY and Number keyboard. We chose to discard the z axis orientation as vibrations caused by keystrokes mainly affected the x and y planes.

The data collected from the microphones are the amplitudes received by the two microphones. We collected raw audio data instead of pre-processed data. A sampling rate of 48KHz was chosen because Android currently does not support higher sampling rates.

During the initial phase of the experiment, we also collected accelerometer data from the smartphone. Subsequently, we did not consider this sensor because the accuracy was significantly lower than the gyroscope. The reason was that the accelerometer combines acceleration and gravity and the gravity component varied significantly even when the phone was placed stationery on a table. Even when the gravity vibrations were removed by filtering techniques, there was not much improvement in accuracy.

### 4.1.3 Synchronization

The gyroscope and audio data are synchronized by injecting a microphone start event in the gyroscope data. The trojan application invokes two threads to start the gyroscope and microphones, however, the microphones are started only after the gyroscope has completely initialized. This is done to ensure that the gyroscope sensor starts at the highest sampling rate and does not get reduced to a lower rate due to resource consumption by the microphones. Once the microphone starts recording, the application generates a microphone start event that gets injected into the gyroscope data. The two are then recorded simultaneously.

## 4.2 Pre-processing

### 4.2.1 Gyroscope

Contrary to previous works [29], [21], [5] that extracted features from the gyroscope recordings, we use the raw gyroscope x and y axes orientations as the feature set for machine learning. The Android Sensor API returns the rate of change

of orientation in radians/second. We use this rate to construct the gyroscope recording and then use this as our raw data. The raw data is filtered, extracted, re-sampled and converted to a machine learning toolkit compatible format. Figure 6 shows the stages of pre-processing for a gyroscope sample, these stages are described below.

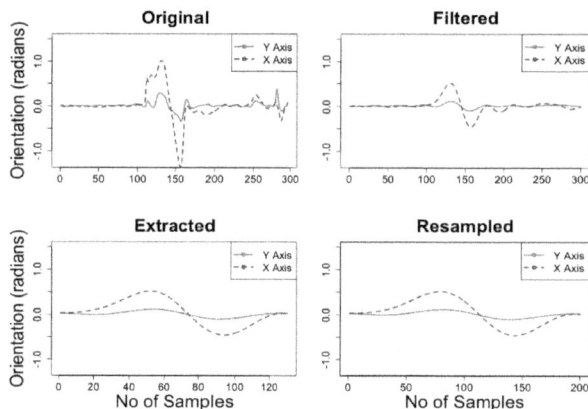

Figure 6: (Top Left) A noisy unprocessed raw gyroscope sample for letter 'V'; (Top Right) Noise removed from the sample after frequency filtering; (Bottom Left) The filtered sample after tap extraction; (Bottom Right) The sample after resampling.

*Filtering*: The gyroscope noise during a typing session occurs mainly because of the instability of the hand and this noise is typically high frequency. When the change in orientation is much higher than the noise, i.e. high signal-to-noise ratio, the noise can be removed by simple frequency filtering techniques. We use a Fast Fourier Transform filter [11] to detect frequencies corresponding to the sample values (the tap). We keep these frequencies unchanged and remove the amplitudes at the other frequencies. We then apply an Inverse Fast Fourier Transform to obtain the filtered data. The technique works quite well, however, for noisier data advanced filtering schemes such as Kalman Filtering [28] can be applied. When the signal-to-noise ratio is low, then these filters may remove significant tap specific information reducing the accuracy. One option is to use the unfiltered raw data in such cases but we observed that the accuracy with filtered data is much better than raw data. This is because the noise in the data changes the waveform and makes them dissimilar even for the same location. Another option is to observe the gyroscope vibrations and record only when the noise is under a threshold.

*Extraction*: Our trojan Android application uses a custom keyboard with the standard Android keyboard layout for tap detection. The keyboard injects an event into the gyroscope data when a key is pressed. Our system uses this as the start of the sample and uses a constant time difference to compute the end of the sample.

*Resampling*: The filtered gyroscope data are of different sizes as the Android SDK does not allow setting a fixed sampling rate for sensors. However, most machine learning toolkits are very specific about file formats and require fixed length training and test samples, therefore the data has to be resampled before consolidation. Another reason for resampling is to increase the size of the data such that minute changes in data are identified by machine learning algorithms. We use a technique known as Cubic Spline Interpolation [20] to resample the data without changing the waveform of vibrations. Our evaluation results confirm that greater number of samples increase the inference accuracy.

### 4.2.2 Microphones

Instead of extracting specific properties from the audio samples and using them as features, we use the raw audio received at the two microphones. The raw audio data is first filtered to remove noise, then extracted to obtain the tap, re-sampled and converted to a machine learning toolkit compatible format. Figure 7 shows the stages of pre-processing for an audio sample, described below.

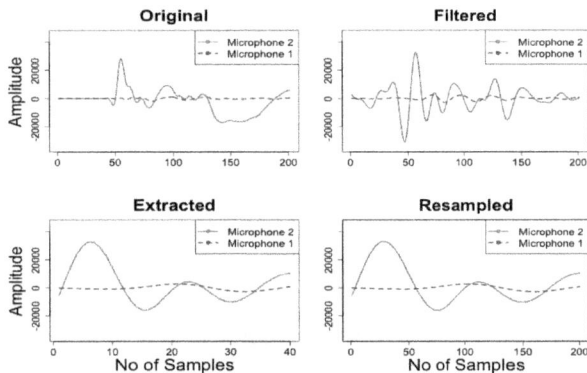

**Figure 7: (Top Left) A noisy unprocessed raw audio sample for letter 'V'; (Top Right) Noise removed from the sample after frequency filtering; (Bottom Left) The filtered sample after tap extraction; (Bottom Right) The sample after resampling.**

*Filtering*: The noise in audio signals can be present due to several factors such as background music, conversations, and moving traffic. Audio noise is typically high frequency and can be removed using frequency filtering techniques. We use a bandpass filter to pass all frequencies in the range of 1500 to 3500 Hz and stop the remaining frequencies. Bandpass filtering is an effective technique when the tap and noise frequencies don't overlap. The frequency range was obtained by analyzing recordings on the HTC One such that background noise was removed while retaining the frequencies of the tap sound. A low signal-to-noise ratio can have a significant impact on the inference accuracy and even when filters exist to remove noise, the noise removal algorithm may also change the original waveform and decrease inference. One option is to observe the microphones data and record only when the noise is under a threshold.

*Extraction & Resampling*: We use the peak amplitude at the two microphones to detect the start of the sample. The channel that has the higher amplitude becomes the base channel and about two wavelengths are extracted to ensure that the peak of the other channel is extracted as well. The audio samples are interpolated so that changes in data are detected as features by the machine learning algorithms.

## 4.3 Training Process

The system uses the specifics of Android QWERTY and number keyboard and a number of steps and algorithms to develop adequate training models.

**Table 1: Accuracies of elementary algorithms for some sample sets.**

| Keyboard | Sensor | DT | NB | NN | 10-NN |
|----------|--------|-----|-----|-----|-------|
| *HTC One* | | | | | |
| QWERTY | Mics | 86% | 85% | 90% | 80% |
| QWERTY | Comb | 85% | 81% | 89% | 84% |
| Number | Mics | 70% | 81% | 72% | 66% |
| Number | Comb | 68% | 73% | 78% | 71% |
| *Samsung S2* | | | | | |
| QWERTY | Gyro | 60% | 61% | 58% | 52% |
| Number | Gyro | 74% | 74% | 82% | 72% |

*Consolidation*: The filtered training data are consolidated into a single database file in the machine learning toolkit format. The file can contain only the gyroscope data (for non-stereo microphones), the microphone data or the microphone + gyroscope data combined (for stereo-microphones). Unlike [21], we do not use any techniques to combine the microphone + gyroscope data but simply append their contents. We reason that these sensors have different properties that may be lost if combined.

*Area Division*: The keyboards were broken down into areas such that all keys in a particular area are distinguishable from another using at least one feature. The area division for a standard QWERTY keyboard in portrait mode is shown in Figure 5. They are chosen such that the x-orientation remains constant and y-orientation varies for all keys in the area. For example, for the area 'QWE', the negative y-orientation will be higher for 'Q', lesser for 'W' and the least for 'E'. The area division for a standard number keyboard in portrait mode is shown in Figure 5 and follows the same technique except for keys '8' and '0' that will have a constant y-orientation and varying x-orientation. We tested other area divisions as well but this division worked better than the others.

*Elementary Algorithms*: The Weka toolkit offers a large variety of machine learning algorithms. The problem of predicting the keystrokes is a supervised classification problem, therefore we eliminated algorithms that do not apply in this context (e.g., K-Means). Before developing our meta-algorithm, the algorithms we tested were Decision Trees, Naive Bayes, K-Nearest Neighbor (k-NN), Hidden Markov Models, Support Vector Machines, Random Forest and Neural Networks. Of these algorithms, Decision Trees (DT), Naive Bayes (NB), 1-Nearest Neighbor (NN) and 10-Nearest Neighbor (10-NN) performed better and yielded higher accuracy rates. Neural Networks also yielded high accuracy rates but was not chosen due to heavy resource consumption. In the context of our work, instance-based methods such as k-NN yield high accuracy, since they try to find the closest match between the new prediction and the training data. Table 1 shows the performance of these elementary algorithms for three QWERTY and three number keyboard sample sets. As we can see, none of these algorithms perform well on all areas of keyboard because of overlapping instances. This observation drove us to develop a meta-algorithm which considers the areas of keyboard before making predictions.

*The Training Process*: The goal of the training process is to build inference models based on the entire character set and areas defined for the keyboard.

In step 1, training models are built for predicting areas of the keyboard using a voting [18] algorithm. The voting algorithm uses the prediction of all the algorithms and their confidence values to determine the area of the test data. The model for voting uses ensembling techniques such as Bagging and Boosting to improve the accuracy of algorithms. The Ensembling technique builds multiple models from subsets of the training data, analyzes the accuracy of the subsets to detect incorrectly classified instances, and then uses these instances again with different weights or averaging to build better predictive models.

In step 2, training models are built for the entire character set for all the algorithms. These models also use ensembling. If the training data specified is microphones + gyroscope, then training models for microphones are also built. This is because the gyroscope data for certain areas of the keyboard that are close to the actual hardware may be weaker that other areas and weak gyroscope data may reduced the overall accuracy of the model for that area.

In step 3, training models are built for all character sets within an area for each area. These models also use ensembling. If the training data specified is microphones + gyroscope, then training models for microphones are also built. Our system evaluates these models using multi-fold cross validation using varying fold values. In multi-fold cross validation, a subset of the training data is provided to the model as test data and the accuracy of the model is computed. By using multiple folds, a model can be tested multiple times with different training data and their accuracies are averaged. Our system determines which models are better for an area and uses these for predictions for that area.

In step 4, the two best algorithms for an area (determined in step 3) are combined into a single voting algorithm. This voting algorithm is used by the meta-algorithm to make a final prediction in case all previous prediction mechanisms do not conclude on a single prediction. In case the two models predict different keys, their confidence values are used to determine the final prediction.

## 4.4 The Area-Based Meta-Algorithm

Initially, we used elementary algorithms and voting schemes to make predictions on test data. Using these elementary algorithms, the accuracy achieved was not high (See Table 1), and different algorithms predicted different keys for the same test data. To address the problem, we developed a meta-algorithm that utilizes our area specific models at multiple levels to infer the key with a higher accuracy rate than traditional algorithms. The evaluation we performed shows that the meta-algorithm yields much better accuracy.

*The Inference Process*: Figure 8 shows the flow diagram of our meta-algorithm and the levels of evaluations.

In step 1, the test data is evaluated using the area voting model. The goal of this step is to identify the area where a keystroke would belong to and load the appropriate models for that area. Our system evaluates the models built for every area and maintains a list of the models that have yielded high accuracy with the training data for that area. For example, an area 'IOP' on the QWERTY keyboard may have weak gyroscope data implying that the consolidated model will be weak. The system detects this and loads the microphone model for evaluation instead of the microphones + gyroscope combined model.

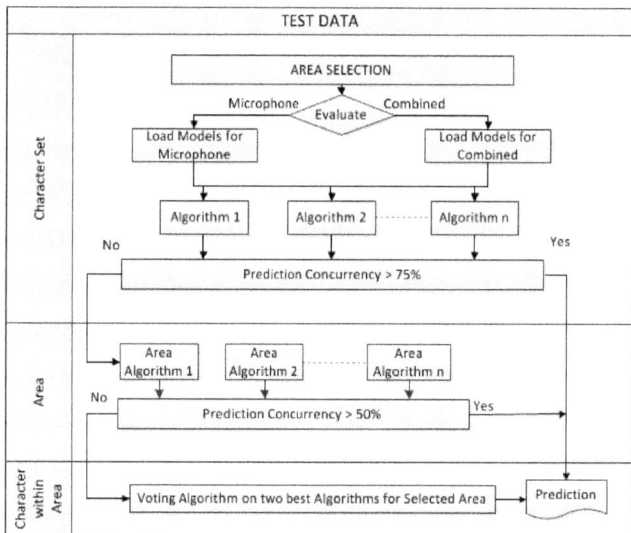

**Figure 8: Flow diagram of the Meta-algorithm.**

In step 2, the test data is evaluated using the loaded character set models. We use these models before the area-specific models to ensure that a prediction error by the voting model is detected and corrected. For example, the voting model may predict the area of a test sample on a QWERTY keyboard as 'IOP' when the key pressed was 'K'. One reason for this may be weak or noisy gyroscope data in the voting model that is similar to keys in area 'IOP'. Our system will load the microphone models when the gyroscope data is weak. These models can then evaluate the test inputs correctly based on the audio data. If more than 75% of the models predict the same key, then this key is chosen as the final prediction and no additional steps are performed.

In step 3, the test data is evaluated using the area-specific models. This step is only executed when the character models were not successful in predicting the keystroke. One reason can be the prediction of neighboring keys that belong to another area. For example, a character set based model may predict the key as 'A' when the actual key is 'Q'. These keys are neighbors on a standard Android QWERTY keyboard and may contain similar vibrations and audio characteristics. When the test data is evaluated specifically using the models for area 'QWE', then they can only predict a key from the selected area and may predict the correct key.

In step 4, the test data is evaluated using a voting model consisting of the two best algorithms for that area. The model determines the final prediction based on the prediction and confidence values of the two algorithms. This step will generally be executed when the test data is quite noisy and difficult to infer. We do not discard the data but attempt to make a final prediction based on the two best algorithms for that area.

## 5. EVALUATION

We evaluate our keystroke inference system using the following three metrics: The performance of the gyroscope, microphones and microphone + gyroscope (combined) sensors for different areas of the keyboard, the performance of our meta-algorithm applied to different machine learning algorithms in comparison to the traditional use of these algorithms, and the performance of our meta-algorithm on the sample sets that were collected.

## 5.1 The Meta-Algorithm Evaluation

Table 2 shows the area-wise accuracy of the gyroscope (Gyro), microphone (Mics) and combined (Comb) sensors for a sample set collected using the QWERTY keyboard in portrait mode on the HTC One. The evaluation is based upon the accuracy with which characters were predicted correctly in different areas of the keyboard. We can see that the gyroscope predictions are inconsistent across areas as compared to the microphone which is consistent throughout. The gyroscope results are location dependent because of its hardware location. The areas IOP, ASD and NM are close to the gyroscope and do not exhibit significant vibration on the y axis. The inference depends more on the x axis vibrations yielding lower accuracy for these areas. The areas XZ, ASD, and QWE are further from the gyroscope and exhibit significant vibrations in the y axis. The inference depends on both axes vibrations yielding higher accuracy for these areas. Microphone predictions, on the other hand are location independent as they rely on the speed of sound traveling over the surface. We also see that the accuracy of the microphones is higher than the gyroscope for most of the areas, the only exception being area XZ. Combining the data from the two sensors yields higher accuracy than the individual sensors in some cases when the gyroscope data for an area is not weak. In a situation where the gyroscope data is weak for an area, our system attempts to detect this and performs inference using microphone data for that area.

**Table 2: Area-wise accuracy of QWERTY keyboard sample set.**

| Area | Gyro | Mics | Comb |
|------|------|------|------|
| Q, W, E | 84% | 90% | 92% |
| R, T, Y, U | 86% | 86% | 92% |
| I, O, P | 79% | 90% | 99% |
| A, S, D | 84% | 94% | 97% |
| F, G, H | 70% | 89% | 92% |
| J, K, L | 71% | 84% | 89% |
| X, Z | 88% | 80% | 98% |
| C, V, B | 83% | 93% | 93% |
| N, M | 77% | 90% | 100% |

Table 3 shows the performance of our meta-algorithm when applied on individual algorithms in comparison to the traditional use of the algorithms (Table 1) for the same sample sets in Table 1. We see that our meta-algorithm can improve the accuracy of prediction for every sample set. We also see that the Decision Tree (DT) algorithm benefits the most from the meta-algorithm, with high increase in accuracies ranging from 8-13%. The Naive Bayes (NB) algorithm does not benefit much from our meta-algorithm, with lower increase in accuracies ranging from 0-4%.

Table 4 shows the final accuracy obtained by using our meta-algorithm with the sample sets that we collected in the office environment. We can see that it is possible to achieve high accuracy of predictions using the stereo-microphones on the device. We achieve an accuracy of 89.5% for the QWERTY keyboard for User3 and an accuracy of 94.5% for the Number keyboard for User2. We also see that in some cases such as the QWERTY keyboard sample for User3, combin-

**Table 3: Accuracies of meta-algorithm for some sample sets.**

| Keyboard | Sensor | DT | NB | NN | 10-NN |
|----------|--------|-----|-----|-----|-------|
| | | HTC One | | | |
| QWERTY | Mics | 94% | 86% | 93% | 85% |
| QWERTY | Comb | 95% | 80% | 93% | 91% |
| Number | Mics | 80% | 81% | 79% | 76% |
| Number | Comb | 81% | 77% | 81% | 77% |
| | | Samsung S2 | | | |
| QWERTY | Gyro | 68% | 61% | 60% | 55% |
| Number | Gyro | 82% | 76% | 84% | 79% |

ing the audio data with the gyroscope can boost the inference accuracy and it is possible to reach a higher accuracy of 94% even for the QWERTY keyboard. In some situations, using a combination of sensors may result in decrease of accuracy, such as for the number keyboard for User2. This is possible when the gyroscope data is weak. We built our system to detect such weak gyroscope samples using cross-validation of training samples but we did come across situations when the cross-validation yielded high accuracy for weak gyroscope data and used them to create models. One alternative could be to use some training samples solely for evaluating the models instead of using cross-validation with training samples that were used to create the models. There are some sample sets where the gyroscope inference accuracy is as low as 44-56%. We evaluated them carefully and found that our filtering techniques were not able to handle large gyroscope drifts. These drifts can be compensated by using Kalman or Complementary filtering on the gyroscope data.

**Table 4: Final single stroke meta-algorithm accuracy for several sample sets.**

| User | Keyboard | Count | Gyro | Mics | Comb |
|------|----------|-------|------|------|------|
| | | HTC One | | | |
| User1 | Number | 306 | 68% | 93% | 93% |
| User2 | Number | 200 | 44% | 94.5% | 93% |
| User3 | Number | 300 | 72% | 91% | 91% |
| User4 | Number | 300 | 75% | 94% | 95.5% |
| User5 | Number | 323 | 45% | 83% | 83% |
| User3 | QWERTY | 782 | 80.5% | 89.5% | 94% |
| User4 | QWERTY | 860 | 56% | 83% | 83% |
| User5 | QWERTY | 877 | 66% | 73.5% | 84% |
| | | Samsung S2 | | | |
| User1 | Number | 137 | 75.5% | - | - |
| User2 | Number | 542 | 84% | - | - |
| User3 | Number | 202 | 83% | - | - |
| User4 | Number | 200 | 81.5% | - | - |
| User5 | Number | 512 | 81% | - | - |
| User1 | QWERTY | 366 | 63.5% | - | - |
| User2 | QWERTY | 620 | 77% | - | - |
| User5 | QWERTY | 312 | 74% | - | - |

We also evaluated our keystroke inference system in environments when such an attack would not work so well. The gyroscope inference accuracy will be affected when the vibrations recorded during typing are noisy such as when typing in a running vehicle, trembling hands during typing or when the touch is too soft. The microphones inference accuracy will be affected when the background noise is too high or when the touch is too soft for the microphones to capture. In our experiments, we asked two participants to type in a noisy restaurant environment and achieved an accuracy of 42% and 56% for 212 and 226 test samples using the microphones, respectively. There were two participants who touched the screen very softly, and for them, our system achieved a low accuracy of less than 20% for both the microphones and the gyroscope. This was mainly because the keystroke could not be differentiated from the background noise. We also asked two participants to type on a tablet and achieved an accuracy of 36% and 45% for 106 and 234 test samples, respectively, using the gyroscope. These participants held the tablet in two hands and typed using their thumbs significantly reducing the vibrations caused due to typing.

## 5.2 End-to-end Attack Evaluation

To illustrate an end-to-end attack, we have also implemented a Trojan-like functionality in our Android application. The application starts a background service that queries for the foreground activity every five seconds. In Android, every UI page is known as an activity. An application may have multiple activities and every activity has a different class name. Using these class names, an adversary can determine the functionality that an application is performing. For example, for the banking application we used, the login activity is named as com.*****.mobile.*****Activity (parts of the class name hidden here for anonymity of application). The Trojan starts recording the microphones and gyroscope during the banking application login activity or when credit card input activity is in the foreground.

We collected 100 four digit random numbers and 100 sixteen digit random numbers simulating PIN numbers and credit card numbers from the Trojan service. These were recorded when users opened a particular activity of a banking application triggering the microphone and gyroscope recording. Table 5 shows the accuracy obtained by using our meta-algorithm with these PIN and credit card numbers. For four digit PIN numbers, the system correctly predicted 376 digits out of 400 digits and 8 additional keystrokes were detected by the system. Out of the 100 PIN numbers, 84 were predicted completely correctly in the first attempt. For sixteen digit credit card numbers, the system correctly predicted 1467 digits out of 1600 digits and 12 additional keystrokes were detected by the system. Out of the 100 credit card numbers numbers, 52 were predicted completely correctly in the first attempt.

**Table 5: Final meta-algorithm accuracy for 100 PIN numbers and 100 credit card numbers.**

| Total | Correct | Correct Digits | Accuracy |
|-------|---------|----------------|----------|
| PINs | | | |
| 100 | 84 | 376 | 94% |
| Credit Cards | | | |
| 100 | 52 | 1467 | 91.5% |

We, thus, show that by building area specific models combined with meta-techniques, it is possible to achieve high accuracy of predictions such as 90-94% for the QWERTY and Number keyboard.

## 6. MITIGATION

The Android platform uses a variety of security and defense mechanisms against application's misbehavior, such as sandboxing and permissions. The security and effectiveness of such techniques have been studied in previous works [26], [17], [3], [12], [22], [10]. Cai et al. [6] discussed properties of a privacy protecting sensors. Although these mechanisms have proved to be effective against a large number of attacks, they are not effective against side channel attacks that bypass them.

We broadly classify mitigation techniques against side channel attacks as blocking or limiting accuracy [24], [7].

*Blocking:* When a sensitive application starts running, it will obtain a lock on mutually exclusive sensors and hardware that are only accessible to one process (app). Some sensors, such as the microphone and camera, fall into this classification. During this period when the application is using these sensors, no other process will be able to use them. Blocking is straightforward to design and implement, e.g. in the current Android SDK, this can be done by using the system calls in `android.media.AudioRecord` and `android.media.MediaRecorder`. However, this mechanism is not practical against non-mutually exclusive sensors, such as the gyroscope and accelerometer, without significant user experience degradation.

*Limiting accuracy:* The inference accuracy for both the microphones and gyroscope is highly correlated with the sampling rate. Table 6 shows the impact of the sampling rate on these sensors. We see that by reducing the sampling rate of the gyroscope from 100 Hz to 56 Hz in sample sets collected by the same user, the inference accuracy reduced from 79% to 58%. By lowering the sampling rate to 20 Hz, most keystroke vibrations were not detected yielding a low accuracy of 18%. Similarly, by reducing the sampling rate of the microphones from 48 KHz to 22.05 KHz, the inference accuracy reduced from 91% to 31%. As mentioned in Section 3, the sampling rate of the sensors can be reduced by introducing services that use more processing power, however, an adversary can still obtain high and constant sampling rate by using the Android NDK.

**Table 6: Impact of sampling rate on inference accuracy for Number keyboard sample set.**

| Sampling Rate | Accuracy |
|---------------|----------|
| Gyroscope | |
| 100 Hz | 79% |
| 56 Hz | 58% |
| 20 Hz | 18% |
| Microphones | |
| 48000 Hz | 91% |
| 44100 Hz | 89% |
| 22050 Hz | 31% |

## 7. RELATED WORK & DISCUSSION

Cai & Chen [5] were the first to study the feasibility of number keystroke inference attacks using an Android device's orientation sensor. They developed an Android application called TouchLogger and collected three data-sets on a HTC Evo 4G phone using a Number only keypad in Landscape mode. Their experiments achieved a successful inference accuracy of about 70% on all three data-sets and showed that such an attack was indeed feasible.

Owusu et al. [23] studied the feasibility of character and area inference using an Android device's accelerometer sensor. They developed an Android application called ACCessory for collecting data-sets on a HTC ADR 6300 phone from four participants. The participants were instructed to hold the phone and enter keys in a certain manner and several data-sets were collected for screen area and characters using a QWERTY keypad in Landscape mode. The data-sets were used to build a predictive model to evaluate the accuracy of area inference as well as passwords inference. Their experiments showed that, out of 99 6-character passwords, it was possible to successfully infer 6 character passwords in 5 trials.

Xu, Bai & Zhu [29] used two motion sensors, accelerometer and orientation, to study the feasibility of inference of the lock screen password and the numbers entered during a phone call, such as credit card and PIN numbers. They developed an Android trojan application called TapLogger that stealthily logs these numbers by using the accelerometer sensor to detect the occurrence of taps and the orientation sensor to infer which number was typed by the user. They collected data-sets of several tap events from three students using two phones, HTC Aria and Google Nexus (One), and unlike other experiments, performed the training and classification on the smartphone itself. Their experiments achieved an accuracy of about 99% for one user on the Google Nexus (One) and about 70% - 85% accuracy for the other users.

Cai & Chen [4] study the impact of different settings on the accuracy of predictions. They vary different factors in their settings, such as user habits, screen size, device type, layout orientation, etc. Their results show that side channel attacks stay possible and practical regardless of the setting. Although the attacks are feasible, the accuracy of such predictions vary. They use Google Nexus S, HTC Evo 4G, Galaxy Tab 10.1, Motorola Xoom in their experiments with 21 users, and demonstrate that 4 digit PIN can be guessed correctly after 81 attempts, 65% of times.

Aviv et al. [1] examine the possibility of side channel attack on smartphones by using the accelerometer. They demonstrate the possibility of inferring PIN and pattern password on four different smartphones; Nexus One, G2, Nexus S and Droid Incredible. Their results and evaluations are based on 24 users, divided into two groups of 12. Each group performs controlled (seating) and uncontrolled (walking) experiments. In the controlled setting, they reach an accuracy of 43% and 73% on PIN and pattern passwords respectively, within 5 attempts from a set of 50 PINs and 50 patterns. In the uncontrolled setting, they can predict PINs and patterns within 5 attempts 20% and 40% of times respectively.

Miluzzo et al. [21] present a framework called TapPrints that uses the accelerometer and gyroscope to identify icon locations and infer characters typed on a keyboard. They collected a data-set on two Android devices, the Google Nexus S and Samsung Galaxy Tab 10.1, and a iPhone 4. The experiment with icon locations was performed with the device in Portrait mode while other experiments with the character keypad were performed with the device in Landscape mode. By using ensemble machine learning, the author show that on an average, locations of icons can be inferred with 79% and 65% accuracy for the iPhone and Google Nexus S respectively and characters could be inferred with 65% accuracy. They also showed that some icons or characters can be inferred with an accuracy of up to 90% and 80% respectively.

Marquardt et al. [19] demonstrated that an Android application that has access to the device's accelerometer can be used to recover text typed on a physical keyboard the device is placed in close proximity with. They showed that if a device is placed within 2 inches of a physical keyboard and the keyboard is used for typing, then by measuring the relative physical position and distance between the vibration, they could recover words with accuracy as high as 80%.

Templeman et al. [27] propose a proof-of-concept visual malware called PlaceRaider. It opportunistically uses camera and other sensory data from a smartphone to create a 3D model of the user's environment. This 3D model allows the adversary to navigate and zoom in areas of interest to examine the individual images corresponding to that region. Another example of sensory malware is Soundcomber [25] which uses microphone to steal private information such as credit card numbers from phone conversations.

Zhou et al.[31] investigate side channel attacks based on the data from different sensor. They look at ARP information, speaker status and per-app data-usage statistics. From these channels they can infer user's identity, his geo-location and his driving route. Their app is also capable of monitoring when a target app is running to stealthily collect data and report back to a remote adversary.

Our experiment is different from previous related works as we are the first in our knowledge to use the stereo recording in smartphones and to combine acoustic and sensor information to infer keystrokes. We use the entire raw data and we use keyboard specific information in our meta-algorithm. By using the combination of acoustics and sensors and a multi-tier approach based on the areas of keyboards, we achieved a higher accuracy on the standard Android keyboard. Our experiment is similar to previous works as we too have focused on predicting keystrokes on the QWERTY and number keyboard but unlike previous experiments, we focused on smaller keys. For example, [5] use a number only keypad in landscape mode, [4] use different settings but mainly in landscape mode, [23] [21] use a QWERTY keypad in landscape mode, [29] [1] use larger keypads such as the lock screen or the number keypad shown during calls. We deduce that the accuracy of these experiments may reduce when tests are performed on the default Android character keyboard in Portrait mode. We demonstrate that by using a simple attack technique, it is possible to obtain a high inference accuracy even for smaller keys. Also, we demonstrate the feasibility of number and character inference using the sounds generated by the keystrokes and recorded by a device's stereoscopic microphones.

# 8. CONCLUSION

In this paper, we investigated the feasibility of keystroke inference on a smartphone by recording the sounds of key taps by the stereo-microphone and the vibrations by the gyroscope. In the future, we plan on implementing mitigation techniques for these side-channel attacks on Android and evaluate their effectiveness on several smartphones.

# 9. ACKNOWLEDGMENTS

We would like to thank Professor Kevin Butler for his helpful comments on our paper. This material is based upon work partially supported by the National Science Foundation under Grant No. CNS 1409453.

# 10. REFERENCES

[1] A. J. Aviv, B. Sapp, M. Blaze, and J. M. Smith. Practicality of accelerometer side channels on smartphones. In *Proceedings of the Annual Computer Security Applications Conference*, ACSAC '12.

[2] A. Bates, R. Leonard, H. Pruse, D. Lowd, and K. Butler. Leveraging usb to establish host identity using commodity devices. In *The 21th Annual Network and Distributed System Security Symposium*, NDSS '14.

[3] S. Bugiel, S. Heuser, and A.-R. Sadeghi. Flexible and fine-grained mandatory access control on android for diverse security and privacy policies. In *Proceedings of the 22Nd USENIX Conference on Security*, SEC'13.

[4] L. Cai and H. Chen. On the practicality of motion based keystroke inference attack. In *Proceedings of the 5th International Conference on Trust and Trustworthy Computing*, TRUST'12.

[5] L. Cai and H. Chen. Touchlogger: Inferring keystrokes on touch screen from smartphone motion. In *Proceedings of the 6th USENIX Conference on Hot Topics in Security*, HotSec'11.

[6] L. Cai, S. Machiraju, and H. Chen. Defending against sensor-sniffing attacks on mobile phones. In *Proceedings of the 1st ACM Workshop on Networking, Systems, and Applications for Mobile Handhelds*, MobiHeld '09.

[7] S. Chakraborty, K. R. Raghavan, M. P. Johnson, and M. B. Srivastava. A framework for context-aware privacy of sensor data on mobile systems. In *Proceedings of the 14th Workshop on Mobile Computing Systems and Applications*, HotMobile '13.

[8] T. G. Dietterich. Ensemble methods in machine learning. In *Proceedings of the First International Workshop on Multiple Classifier Systems*, MCS '00.

[9] eMarketer. Smartphone users worldwide will total 1.75 billion in 2014. `http://bit.ly/LjwToI`, 01 2014. Last accessed 03/08/2014.

[10] W. Enck, P. Gilbert, B.-G. Chun, L. P. Cox, J. Jung, P. McDaniel, and A. N. Sheth. Taintdroid: An information-flow tracking system for realtime privacy monitoring on smartphones. In *Proceedings of the 9th USENIX Conference on Operating Systems Design and Implementation*, OSDI'10.

[11] M. Frigo and S. G. Johnson. FFTW: An adaptive software architecture for the FFT. In *Proc. 1998 IEEE Intl. Conf. Acoustics Speech and Signal Processing*.

[12] C. Gibler, J. Crussell, J. Erickson, and H. Chen. Androidleaks: Automatically detecting potential privacy leaks in android applications on a large scale. In *Proceedings of the 5th International Conference on Trust and Trustworthy Computing*, TRUST'12.

[13] Google Inc. Android native development kit (sdk). `https://developer.android.com/tools/sdk/ndk/index.html`, 2014. Last accessed 02/25/2014.

[14] Google Inc. Android software development kit (sdk). `http://developer.android.com/sdk/index.html`, 2014. Last accessed 02/27/2014.

[15] Google Inc. Android, the world's most popular mobile platform. `http://developer.android.com/about/index.html`, 2014. Last accessed 03/08/2014.

[16] M. Hall, E. Frank, G. Holmes, B. Pfahringer, P. Reutemann, and I. H. Witten. The weka data mining software: An update. *SIGKDD Explor. Newsl.*, 2009.

[17] H. Hao, V. Singh, and W. Du. On the effectiveness of api-level access control using bytecode rewriting in android. In *Proceedings of the 8th ACM SIGSAC Symposium on Information, Computer and Communications Security*, ASIA CCS '13.

[18] L. I. Kuncheva. *Combining Pattern Classifiers: Methods and Algorithms*. John Wiley and Sons, Inc., 2004.

[19] P. Marquardt, A. Verma, H. Carter, and P. Traynor. (sp)iphone: Decoding vibrations from nearby keyboards using mobile phone accelerometers. In *Proceedings of the 18th ACM Conference on Computer and Communications Security*, CCS '11.

[20] S. Mckinley and M. Levine. Cubic spline interpolation.

[21] E. Miluzzo, A. Varshavsky, S. Balakrishnan, and R. R. Choudhury. Tapprints: Your finger taps have fingerprints. In *Proceedings of the 10th International Conference on Mobile Systems, Applications, and Services*, MobiSys '12.

[22] M. Ongtang, S. McLaughlin, W. Enck, and P. McDaniel. Semantically rich application-centric security in android. In *Computer Security Applications Conference, 2009. ACSAC '09. Annual*, 2009.

[23] E. Owusu, J. Han, S. Das, A. Perrig, and J. Zhang. Accessory: Password inference using accelerometers on smartphones. In *Proceedings of the Twelfth Workshop on Mobile Computing Systems & Applications*, HotMobile '12.

[24] K. R. Raghavan, S. Chakraborty, M. Srivastava, and H. Teague. Override: A mobile privacy framework for context-driven perturbation and synthesis of sensor data streams. In *Proceedings of the Third International Workshop on Sensing Applications on Mobile Phones*, PhoneSense '12.

[25] R. Schlegel, K. Zhang, X. Yong Zhou, M. Intwala, A. Kapadia, and X. Wang. Soundcomber: A stealthy and context-aware sound trojan for smartphones. In *The 18th Annual Network and Distributed System Security Symposium*, NDSS '11.

[26] J. Sellwood and J. Crampton. Sleeping android: The danger of dormant permissions. In *Proceedings of the Third ACM Workshop on Security and Privacy in Smartphones & Mobile Devices*, SPSM '13.

[27] R. Templeman, Z. Rahman, D. Crandall, and A. Kapadia. PlaceRaider: Virtual theft in physical spaces with smartphones. In *The 20th Annual Network and Distributed System Security Symposium*, NDSS '13.

[28] G. Welch and G. Bishop. An introduction to the kalman filter. Technical report, 1995.

[29] Z. Xu, K. Bai, and S. Zhu. Taplogger: Inferring user inputs on smartphone touchscreens using on-board motion sensors. In *Proceedings of the Fifth ACM Conference on Security and Privacy in Wireless and Mobile Networks*, WISEC '12.

[30] W. Zhou, Y. Zhou, X. Jiang, and P. Ning. Detecting repackaged smartphone applications in third-party android marketplaces. In *Proceedings of the Second*

*ACM Conference on Data and Application Security and Privacy*, CODASPY '12.

[31] X. Zhou, S. Demetriou, D. He, M. Naveed, X. Pan, X. Wang, C. A. Gunter, and K. Nahrstedt. Identity, location, disease and more: inferring your secrets from android public resources. In *Proceedings of the 2013 ACM SIGSAC conference on Computer & communications security*, CCS '13.

[32] Y. Zhou, Z. Wang, W. Zhou, and X. Jiang. Hey, you, get off of my market: Detecting malicious apps in official and alternative android markets. In *Proceedings of the 19th Annual Network and Distributed System Security Symposium*.

# Short Paper: CHIPS: Content-based Heuristics for Improving Photo Privacy for Smartphones

Jiaqi Tan
Carnegie Mellon University
Pittsburgh, PA, USA
tanjiaqi@cmu.edu

Utsav Drolia
Carnegie Mellon University
Pittsburgh, PA, USA
utsav@cmu.edu

Rolando Martins
Carnegie Mellon University
Pittsburgh, PA, USA
rolandomartins@cmu.edu

Rajeev Gandhi
Carnegie Mellon University
Pittsburgh, PA, USA
rgandhi@ece.cmu.edu

Priya Narasimhan
Carnegie Mellon University
Pittsburgh, PA, USA
priya@cs.cmu.edu

## ABSTRACT

The Android permissions system provides all-or-nothing access to users' photos stored on smartphones, and the permissions which control access to stored photos can be confusing to the average user. Our analysis found that 73% of the top 250 free apps on the Google Play store have permissions that may not reflect their ability to access stored photos. We propose CHIPS, a unique content-based fine-grained run-time access control system for stored photos for Android which requires minimal user assistance, runs entirely locally, and provides low-level enforcement. CHIPS can recognize faces with minimal user training to deny apps access to photos with known faces. CHIPS's privacy identification has low overheads as privacy checks are cached, and is accurate, with false-positive and false-negative rates of less than 8%.

## Categories and Subject Descriptors

D.4.6 [**Operating Systems**]: Security and Protection—*Access control*

## Keywords

Android; Photo Privacy; Access Control

## 1. INTRODUCTION

Smartphones are becoming increasingly ubiquitous, and they are carried and used everywhere. Users are likely to capture and store photos of the people and events in their daily lives on their smartphones, creating collections of potentially privacy-sensitive photos. At the same time, smartphone platforms such as iOS and Android allow users to install third-party applications (apps), which can interact with other apps and data on the smartphone, including retrieve photos stored on the smartphone, and connect to the

Internet to exfiltrate data. This creates a privacy concern where photos which a user considers private can be inadvertently extracted by an app and exfiltrated without the user's knowledge. In this paper, we show concrete, real-world evidence that there are privacy issues with how the Android platform controls access to stored photos. Then, we hypothesize that photos containing faces of persons known to the user, e.g. family or close friends, are privacy-sensitive, as the user would not want these photos to be inadvertently leaked. Using this hypothesis as a heuristic, we develop a *unique content-based approach, CHIPS, to provide finer-grained access control for stored photos for the Android platform.*

**Contributions.** Our contributions in this work are: (i) we review the privacy risks to stored photos due to Android's architecture, (ii) we analyzed the top 250 free apps on the Google Play store to evaluate how current apps may pose unintended privacy risks to stored photos, (iii) we design and implement a novel content-based access control system for photos: we present CHIPS, a practical face recognition-based, fine-grained, run-time access control system for stored photos which denies unauthorized apps access to photos containing faces of user-specified persons, (iv) we show in this initial prototype that using an off-the-shelf face recognition algorithm, we can attain good accuracy with low training requirements (optimal accuracy with 4 training images per face) on frontal faces in reasonable lighting conditions, and (v) we focus on our novel system architecture for privacy enforcement for photos, which provides strong enforcement with acceptable runtime overhead. *To the best of our knowledge, CHIPS is the first technique to apply face recognition to photos locally on smartphones to automatically determine if they are privacy-sensitive (based on prior user input), and to implement access control at run-time to deny untrusted apps access to sensitive photos.*

## 2. BACKGROUND

### 2.1 Motivation

**Android's Photo Permissions.** To understand how Android controls access to stored photos, we have to understand how photos are stored, how apps access photos, and the permissions system of the Android framework.

Photos captured by the camera of an Android device are stored in the external storage directory, or "SD card", which

*WiSec'14*, July 23–25, 2014, Oxford, United Kingdom.
Copyright 2014 ACM 978-1-4503-2972-9/14/07 ...$15.00.
http://dx.doi.org/10.1145/2627393.2627394.

is either a physical removable memory card, or a logical area in the device's memory. Android is based on Linux, and it uses Linux file owners and permissions to control access to files. Android provides per-app isolation for data files belonging to different apps. However, this per-app file isolation does not apply to stored photo files, as photos are stored in the external storage location, /sdcard. All files in the external storage location of an Android device are owned by the system user and sdcard_rw group, and they are group-readable and group-writable by default.

An Android app can access stored photos in a number of ways. (i) An app can list the files in the system-wide photo directory and open the file storing the photo. (ii) An app can use the Android MediaStore API to retrieve a list of available photos and their metadata (e.g. full path, thumbnails). Then, the app can open the file for the photo at its given path. (iii) An app can delegate photo selection to the system by using the Android framework's "Image Picker" interface (in the com.android.gallery3d package), and the framework returns an internal URI (Uniform Resource Identifier). Then, the app can use the framework's ContentResolver object to obtain an Java InputStream to read the photo, and the framework opens the file containing the requested photo on behalf of the app. Hence, in each of the ways that an Android app can access stored photos, filesystem permissions control access to each photo.

There are two problems with Android's access control for stored photos. First, permissions controlling access to photos stored in a smartphone are currently coarse-grained. Android allows users to choose whether to allow an app to access photos stored on the SD card; however, users can only choose to allow the app access to all stored photos, and cannot selectively deny access to individual photos, because access to the SD card location is controlled by the READ_EXTERNAL_STORAGE system permission. While an app might present users with an "Image Picker" interface, an Android app can access any photo, and not just the user-selected ones. Hence the app will be able to read all stored photos. Second, while READ_EXTERNAL_STORAGE controls access to stored photos on Android, this may be unintuitive to the average user. The CAMERA permission is described as allowing the app to "take pictures and videos", while the READ_ and WRITE_EXTERNAL_STORAGE permissions are described as allowing the app to "modify or delete the contents of your SD card". Hence, it may appear to the average user that the permission which controls access to photos is the CAMERA permission, as it is the only permission whose description mentions photos. Unfortunately, this is not the case, and only the READ_EXTERNAL_STORAGE, but not the CAMERA, permission is required to access stored photos, which we verified empirically.

**Evidence of Unintended Photo Access.** Next, we identify apps which appear to not access stored photos based on their requested permissions, but which in fact have access to stored photos. We analyzed the top 250 free apps from the Google Play store (e.g. Facebook, Pinterest, etc.) to identify apps which requested the READ_EXTERNAL_STORAGE permission, but which did not request the CAMERA permission. We believe that a novice user, when shown this combination of permissions, would not believe that these apps are accessing any stored photos from the device, when it can in fact do so. In this group of apps, we also further distinguish between apps which requested the INTERNET per-

mission, which would be able to exfiltrate stored photos, as compared to those which did not. We used the Androguard analysis tool [1], which allowed us to extract the permissions requested by each app from its Manifest. We found that 183 out of 250 apps (2 apps excluded due to bytecode analysis difficulties) requested READ_EXTERNAL_ STORAGE but not CAMERA permissions, and 181 of these apps also requested the INTERNET permission. Based on their requested permissions, *73% of the top 250 free apps on the Google Play store have unexpected and complete access to the photos stored on a user's smartphone, and can even exfiltrate these photos* (further analysis is needed to determine if these apps actually exfiltrate photos without the user's knowledge). Next, we analyzed the bytecode of these 181 apps using Androguard, and found that 120 of these apps launched the Android-supplied Image Picker, in which case users would know that the app was accessing stored photos, even though the app's permissions may not reflect so. Nonetheless, these apps can still access all stored photos, regardless of which photos users picked. Thus, there is a need for stronger, finer-grained access control for stored photos.

## 2.2 Problem Statement and Limitations

**Goals.** Our goals for the design and implementation of CHIPS are: (i) not require any changes to the way third-party apps access photos, or to the way the Android platform stores photos, (ii) minimize the false-negative and false-positive rates of our face recognition for privacy identification, (iii) run all face detection and recognition locally on the smartphone to preserve privacy, (iv) minimize the user assistance required during the training for privacy identification, (v) have the training process for privacy identification complete in a reasonable amount of time (e.g. $< 1$ hour for 500 images on an average smartphone), (vi) have the dynamic privacy enforcement decision be reached in a reasonable amount of time ($< 1$ second on an average smartphone), (vii) third-party apps should not be able to circumvent CHIPS's decision to deny access to a stored photo.

**Assumptions.** We make a number of assumptions about users' apps and smartphones, although most of these assumptions are artifacts of our current implementation rather than necessitated by our design, and we intend to address some of these assumptions in our future work. First, we assume that file extensions accurately describe file contents, and we only perform our privacy checks on files with image extensions (e.g. .jpg). This technique is not robust to user apps renaming files to non-image extensions before accessing them, and we plan to implement file content checking in future versions. Second, we assume that the Android core libraries, framework, and operating system are isolated from user apps, and that user apps are unable to modify the core libraries, framework, or operating system. This assumption is necessary as our privacy enforcement relies on the Linux kernel (with our added modifications) to report file accesses to the CHIPS system service, and our CHIPS system service is implemented as part of the Android framework.

**Threat Model.** Our goal is to guard against unauthorized retrieval of potentially private photos on users' smartphones by untrusted apps. We assume that the smartphone OS and framework are trusted, and are not circumvented by malicious attackers. Hence, all access to a smartphone's stored photos must be via the authorized means described in §2.1. We also assume that the CHIPS user app is not exploited by malicious users, and that the data of the CHIPS user app cannot be modified by other apps.

**Limitations.** We do not develop novel face detection or recognition algorithms. We use the implementation of the well-known Eigenfaces [14] algorithm in the OpenCV library [4] as an initial proof-of-concept to show that a standard face recognition algorithm can be run entirely locally on average smartphones today while achieving good performance, while focusing on the system architecture (i.e. mediation mechanisms) necessary for enforcing photo privacy. Hence, we do not address face recognition challenges, such as occluded faces, poor lighting, and side poses. As such, our initial evaluation of the face recognition accuracy of CHIPS uses a dataset (§4) of frontal faces without difficult lighting conditions, side poses, nor occluded faces. We also currently require changes to the Linux kernel so that our privacy enforcement cannot be circumvented by low-level means e.g. using the Java Native Interface (JNI) to access photos.

# 3. DESIGN AND IMPLEMENTATION

## 3.1 Design

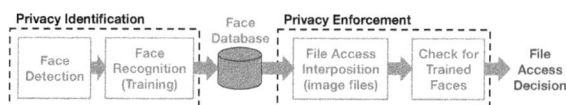

**Figure 1: Overall approach of CHIPS**

In place of Android's current all-or-nothing permissions for photo access by apps, CHIPS consists of a 2-step process (shown in Figure 1) which empowers users to indicate their privacy preferences for stored photos at a finer granularity.

### 3.1.1 Privacy Identification

CHIPS's privacy identification consists of an offline training phase, and a background classification phase. The offline training phase is carried out before privacy-sensitive photos are accessed: users assist CHIPS in training a face database. This database contains sample faces of persons whom the user considers privacy-sensitive (e.g. family, close friends). The background classification phase involves extracting faces from stored photos, and checking if these faces match any faces in the trained database.

Both the offline training and background classification phases begin with face detection to extract rectangular regions in a photo containing faces. This ensures that our face recognition works only on faces, and does not need to work with other unrelated parts of each photo. We used the Local Binary Patterns (LBP) [9] classifier to detect faces. Next, we use the well-known algorithm, Eigenfaces [14], for face recognition. The training step builds a database of sample faces for each person, so that during the classification step, the algorithm can tell if a given face belongs to a person whose face was in the training database, and which person the face belongs to. As Eigenfaces is a supervised algorithm, we require that for each person that the user would like CHIPS to later recognize, the user assists CHIPS by selecting faces of that person as training data.

### 3.1.2 Privacy Enforcement

Next, we describe the design of CHIPS's privacy identification and enforcement mechanisms for photo privacy. We

need to interpose on all file accesses to identify when image files are being accessed. Then, when an image file is accessed, we need to check if there is privacy-sensitive content (i.e. faces of persons in the training database from §3.1.1), before deciding whether to block access to the file.

**Kernel Interposition.** As photos are accessed as regular files in Android rather than through a specialized interface (§2.1), we must interpose on all file accesses to identify accesses to image files for which our privacy checks must be applied. We need to interpose on file accesses in the kernel, rather than in the Android framework (e.g. `java.io` classes), because apps can access files using the Java Native Interface (JNI) to make C library calls, or directly invoke system calls, which would bypass any framework or library interposition. CHIPS's kernel interposition also checks if the accessed file has an image format extension, e.g. `.jpg`, before deciding whether to perform further security checks. If the accessed file is not an image, CHIPS's kernel interposition allows the kernel's regular file permission checks to proceed. CHIPS needs to decide in the kernel whether the accessed file is an image which requires additional access control (i.e. detect and recognize faces) so that access to non-image files can proceed with minimal latency.

**System Service for Access Decisions.** Next, CHIPS runs a system service as part of the Android framework (runs in user-space, but as the special Android framework user) to receive notifications of file accesses from the kernel and provide access decisions for photos. This system service performs initial checks against an app whitelist, moving the burden of maintaining app whitelists out of the kernel, so that we can minimize kernel modifications. Deciding whether an app is whitelisted to access all images is a security-sensitive operation, hence we place this functionality in the Android framework so that the CHIPS system service is at the same level of protection as the Android framework [12]. The CHIPS system service communicates with the CHIPS user app to request face recognition in accessed photos.

**User-level Privacy Checks.** Finally, we place the privacy checks (§3.1.1) in a user app, so that the most complex part of the privacy checks (face detection and recognition) are outside the protected Android framework's process to prevent privilege escalation attacks in the event of crashes. Image files accessed by apps not in CHIPS's whitelist are forwarded to the CHIPS user app which performs the face detection and recognition. CHIPS checks the image to determine if there are any trained faces. If there is no match, the file access is allowed; if there is a match, then access to the image file is blocked, and the offending access is logged to allow the user to make a decision later. The CHIPS user app also maintains a cache of face recognition results for photos stored in the smartphone. This is to reduce the latency that would result from having to perform face detection and recognition on-demand on a photo when it is being accessed.

**Whitelists.** CHIPS also allows users to specify which apps are to be given access to all stored photos without privacy checks, and to allow users to specify which stored photos are not privacy-sensitive, so that all apps can access them.

## 3.2 Implementation

We implement CHIPS for Android 4.2, and our implementation has three components (Figure 2). The first component is the kernel-level file access interposition. We added 1.2 KLOC (thousands of lines of code) to the Linux kernel used

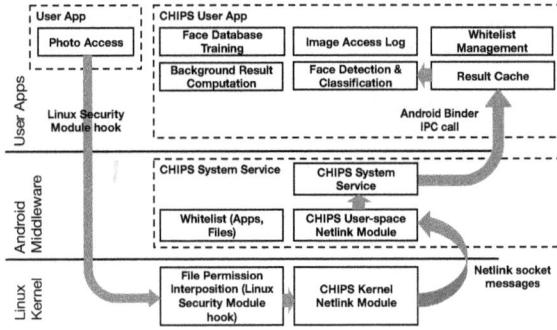

**Figure 2: Architecture of CHIPS**

in Android. The second component is the CHIPS System Service, which manages file access decisions, and is implemented as an Android System Service, and runs as part of the Android Framework. The system service consisted of 2.4 KLOC. The third component is the CHIPS user app, which is an Android app which allows users to train the face database, and which performs face recognition on accessed files, and also allows users to view a log of photos accessed by other apps, and to whitelist photos or apps. The CHIPS user app consisted of 8.5 KLOC.

### 3.2.1 Face Detection and Recognition

CHIPS's privacy identification component uses implementations of well-known face detection and recognition algorithms from the OpenCV [4] library. We used pre-trained LBP classifiers [9] included with the OpenCV library for face detection. To improve runtime, we scaled images down to a size of $600 \times 600$ pixels before face detection. To improve detection accuracy, we first used the frontal-face classifier to extract faces, and then used LBP classifiers for eyes, noses, and mouths on the extracted faces as a sanity check. We ensured that only one nose, two eyes, and one mouth are detected, and that their relative positions in the face are correct. Next, we used the OpenCV [4] implementation of the Eigenfaces [14] algorithm on faces from the face detection step for training and classification. To improve the runtime of Eigenfaces, we first scaled down detected faces to $100 \times 100$ pixels, and we found no degradation in accuracy.

### 3.2.2 Privacy Enforcement: Access Control

To demonstrate the privacy enforcement of CHIPS, we modified the Android framework. We used the CyanogenMod [3] distribution of the Android Open-source Project (AOSP), which includes device-specific code e.g. device drivers. We used CyanogenMod 10.1 (based on Android 4.2).

**Kernel File Access Interposition.** We interposed on all file accesses in the Linux kernel used in Android by implementing a Linux Security Module (LSM) [15]. To interpose on file accesses, we implemented our own `file_ permission` security hook, which is called on every file read and write. We also implemented a kernel module for communicating with the CHIPS system service using Netlink sockets.

**CHIPS System Service.** The CHIPS system service acts as an intermediary between the CHIPS kernel-level file interposition, and the CHIPS user app which runs face recognition on accessed photos. The CHIPS system service is implemented as part of the Android framework. The CHIPS system service receives kernel notifications when files with im-

age extensions are accessed, and it checks against its whitelist of filenames and the user IDs of accessing apps to determine if access should be allowed, or if the image needs to be checked. In the latter case, the system service requests for a privacy check on the image filename accessed.

**CHIPS User App.** The CHIPS user app provides the privacy checking functionality for privacy enforcement. The user app is started when the smartphone boots up. It also provides an interface to manage the whitelists of apps (allowed access to all photos) and photos (allowed access by all apps) in the CHIPS system service. When the CHIPS user app receives a file access notification, it checks its cache (described next) for a face recognition result for the accessed photo, and if there is no result present, the user app proceeds to carry out face recognition. If any faces in the trained database are present in the photo, the user app instructs the system service to deny the app access to the photo.

**Result Caching and Background Scanning.** To improve the performance of CHIPS's privacy enforcement, the CHIPS user app runs a background service to run face recognition on all stored photos and cache the results. This is to eliminate the need to run face recognition when the user is accessing photos. The cache is invalidated when the user retrains or updates the face recognition model, or when a stored photo is modified. This background face recognition runs only when the smartphone is connected to an external power source to prevent battery drainage.

## 4. EVALUATION

To evaluate CHIPS, we used the Caltech Faces 1999 dataset [2], which contains 450 color photos of frontal faces of 27 individuals with different lighting conditions, expressions, and realistic backgrounds. We believe this dataset bears some similarity to photos that average users would capture of people on their smartphones. Our experiments used a Google Nexus S (1 GHz Cortex-A8 processor, 16 GB storage, 512 MB RAM) smartphone, with our modified version of Android 4.2.

### 4.1 Case Studies of Enforcement

We demonstrate CHIPS's photo privacy enforcement on the Android app for Facebook. We trained a database containing the faces of 19 (out of 27) of the persons from the Faces 1999 dataset, and loaded a number of photos from the dataset onto our test phone. These photos contained both persons whose faces were in and not in the trained database. Figure 3 shows CHIPS's photo privacy enforcement blocking the Facebook app's access to stored photos containing trained faces. We tried to share a photo in the Facebook app. Figure 3(a) shows the Facebook app's internal image picker. There are 9 stored photos, and 5 of the photos have no displayed thumbnails. This is because CHIPS has detected faces from the trained database in these photos, and denied access to them, while the other 4 photos have faces not in the trained database. Figure 3(b) shows the error message that occurs when a user selects one of these blocked photos due to CHIPS's kernel interposition denying access to the accessed photo. CHIPS also alerts the user that access to the photo has been denied (Figure 3(c)).

### 4.2 Face Recognition Performance

**Face Detection.** We evaluated CHIPS's face detection on the Caltech Faces 1999 dataset. A false-positive occurs

216

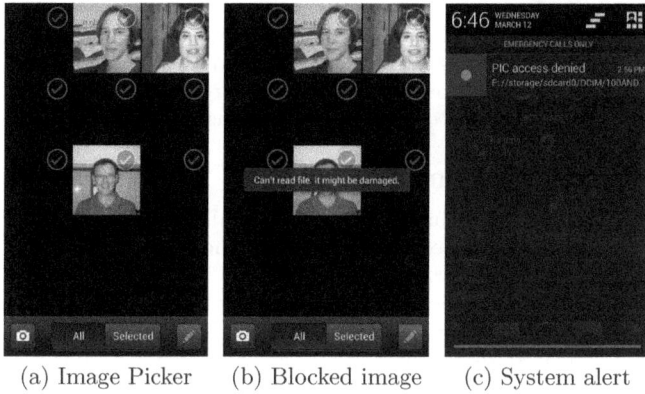

(a) Image Picker    (b) Blocked image    (c) System alert

**Figure 3: CHIPS enforcement on the Facebook app.**
(Stored photos © California Institute of Technology [2])

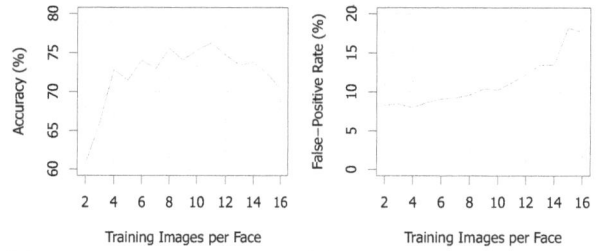

(a) Face recognition accuracy.    (b) False-positive rate (privacy identification).

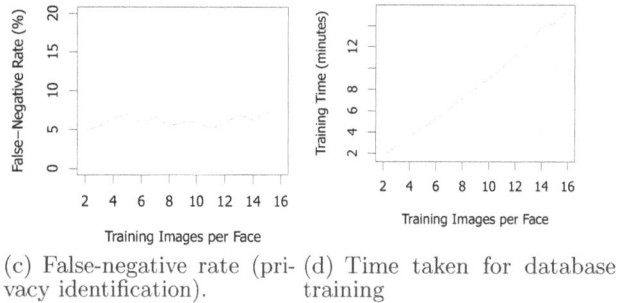

(c) False-negative rate (privacy identification).    (d) Time taken for database training

**Figure 4: Performance for face recognition and privacy identification, and time taken for training.**

when our algorithm reports a face in a region of the photo which is not a face, and a false-negative occurs when our algorithm reports that there are no faces in a photo that contains a face. We found that our face detection algorithm had no false-positives, and a false-negative rate of 2.0%.

**Face Recognition Accuracy.** The accuracy of CHIPS's face recognition is the percentage of faces in the test set for which the face recognition algorithm returns the correct label for a given face in the training database, and of faces not in the training database for which CHIPS returns "unknown". We varied the number of training images per face from 2 to 16. In addition, the test set included a number of faces for which we provided no training images. We report the average accuracy over 5 iterations of the experiment. From Figure 4(a), we can see that the face recognition accuracy improves significantly as we increase the number of training images per face from 2 to 4. Any additional training images per face only improves the face recognition accuracy slightly. The optimal face recognition accuracy is obtained with 11 training images per face, although the accuracy varies between 72% and 76% when there are between 4 and 15 training images per face. Hence, we can see that: (i) CHIPS's face recognition algorithm performs adequately, achieving more than 70% accuracy, and (ii) CHIPS's face recognition does not require significant amounts of training data, and CHIPS can achieve near-optimal (within 4%) face recognition with just 4 training images per face.

**Privacy Identification.** The goal of CHIPS's privacy enforcement is to identify whether a given face is in its database rather than to correctly label every face. Hence, it is sufficient for CHIPS to identify if a face is in the database, even if the algorithm misidentifies the face as belonging to a different person in the database. Thus, a false-positive for CHIPS's privacy identification occurs when a photo does not contain any faces in the trained database, but CHIPS labels it as one of the faces in the trained database, while a false-negative occurs when a photo contains a face in the trained database, but CHIPS labels it as not belonging to the database. We report the false-positive and false-negative rates for CHIPS's privacy identification over 5 iterations for each number of training images per face. The false-positive rate increases with more training images per face, and the optimal false-positive rate occurs at 4 training images per face, with a 8% false-positive rate (Figure 4(b)). This is

likely due to overfitting when there are too many training images. On the other hand, the false-negative rate stays below 8% (Figure 4(c)) regardless of the number of training images per face. Thus, CHIPS's privacy identification performs well, with low false-positive and false-negative rates. CHIPS can block access to privacy-sensitive photos about 92% of the time, and it wrongly blocks access to non-sensitive photos not more than 8% of the time when there are at most 4 training images per face.

## 4.3 Performance

**Training Time.** Figure 4(d) shows the time taken to train CHIPS's face recognition for a 19-person database, averaged over 5 runs. All timing experiments ran on the Google Nexus S smartphone. The time taken for CHIPS's model training increases linearly with more training images per face. For optimal privacy identification, CHIPS should use 4 training images per face (§4.2), and CHIPS takes slightly under 4 minutes to train a database using 4 training images per face. Also, CHIPS can complete training in under 10 minutes when there are 10 or less training images per face for a 19-person database. Hence, CHIPS's face recognition training can be completed in a reasonable amount of time.

|   | Photo Access Scenario | Time |
|---|---|---|
| 1 | No kernel interposition (Baseline) | 95.8 ms |
| 2 | App/photo not whitelisted, results not cached | 3677 ms |
| 3 | App/photo not whitelisted, results cached | 190.0 ms |
| 4 | App whitelisted | 117.0 ms |

**Table 1: Average access times to stored photos**

**Enforcement and Classification Time.** Next, we measure the time taken by CHIPS to enforce photo access control decisions, and to classify photos to determine access control decisions. We measure the time taken by an Android app to access stored photos in various scenarios. Table 1 shows the times taken to access each photo, averaged over 50 random photos from the Caltech Faces 1999 dataset. Scenario 1 establishes the baseline time taken to access each stored photo without CHIPS. While it takes 3.6 seconds to perform a privacy check for a photo without result caching (Scenario 2), we believe that the majority of photo access decisions will have been precomputed and cached by CHIPS's background service. Hence, for the majority of image file accesses for which photo access decisions have been cached, CHIPS would add 94.2 ms (98% overhead) to the critical execution path of accessing the photo (Scenario 3). Finally, Scenario 4 shows that for whitelisted apps, CHIPS adds only 21.2 ms (22% overhead) to the critical path of photo access.

## 5. RELATED WORK

**Android Permissions.** Apex [10] and Jeon et al. [7] propose finer-grained permissions for Android, but do not specifically target stored photos, unlike CHIPS. AppFence [5] modified the Android framework to preserve privacy by covertly substituting shadow data for sensitive data. AppFence protects only the camera, and does not protect stored photos, unlike CHIPS. Aurasium [16] mediates third-party apps using intercepts at the C and Java library level, whereas CHIPS uses mediation in the kernel to prevent apps from directly invoking system calls to bypass mediation.

**Photo Privacy.** P3 [11] protects the privacy of photos stored on third-party Photo-sharing Service Providers (e.g. social networks, photo-sharing sites). Darkly [6] is a privacy-preserving computer-vision library based on the OpenCV library [4], and it protects users from privacy loss due to continuously-sensing perceptual applications. PlaceAvoider [13] proposed new image analysis techniques for recognizing sensitive places in video streams from first-person cameras. PlaceAvoider focuses on image analysis, whereas CHIPS focuses on the systems architecture needed for enforcing stored photo privacy. Klemperer et al. [8] designed a series of user-studies which evaluated the effectiveness of using user-assigned tags to build access control rules for photos.

## 6. CONCLUSION AND FUTURE WORK

We have presented CHIPS, a fine-grained, face-recognition-based run-time access control system for stored photos on Android smartphones, which overcomes Android's current all-or-nothing access model for stored photos. We have demonstrated that CHIPS's privacy enforcement prevents unauthorized access to privacy-sensitive photos in unmodified real-world Android apps (Facebook), and that this enforcement imposes acceptable overheads of just 94.2 ms (98% overhead) per accessed photo when results are cached. We have also demonstrated that existing face detection and face recognition algorithms are sufficiently accurate, so that we can identify if a given face belongs to a trained database with a false-negative rate of 8%, and with a false-positive rate of 8%, and that they require minimal training, attaining optimal performance with just 4 training images per person.

In future, we intend to expand the CHIPS framework to support other types of media such as audio/video, along with other algorithms. For instance, we can extend CHIPS to run optical character recognition (OCR) algorithms on accessed photos to search for sensitive information, such as credit-card numbers and addresses, to proactively block access to photos containing such information. We also intend to explore the use of content-type checks to robustly identify files requiring privacy checks without relying on file extensions.

## Acknowledgements

This research is funded in part by CMU-SYSU Collaborative Innovation Research Center and the SYSU-CMU International Joint Research Institute. We would like to thank the anonymous reviewers and our shepherd, Apu Kapadia, for their comments and constructive feedback. We would also like to thank Anupam Datta for his feedback on earlier versions of this work.

## 7. REFERENCES

[1] Androguard. https://code.google.com/p/androguard/.

[2] Computational Vision at CalTech. http://www.vision.caltech.edu/archive.html.

[3] CyanogenMod. http://www.cyanogenmod.org.

[4] OpenCV. http://opencv.org/.

[5] P. Hornyack, S. Han, J. Jung, S. Schechter, and D. Wetherall. These Aren't the Droids You're Looking For: Retrofitting Android to Protect Data from Imperious Applications. In *ACM CCS*, 2010.

[6] S. Jana, A. Narayanan, and V. Shmatikov. A Scanner Darkly: Protecting User Privacy From Perceptual Applications. In *IEEE Security and Privacy*, 2013.

[7] J. Jeon, K. Micinski, J. Vaughan, A. Fogel, N. Reddy, J. Foster, and T. Millstein. Dr. Android and Mr. Hide: Fine-grained Permissions in Android Applications. In *IEEE SPSM*, 2012.

[8] P. Klemperer, Y. Liang, M. Mazurek, M. Sleeper, B. Ur, L. Bauer, L. Cranor, N. Gupta, and M. Reiter. Tag, You Can See It! Using Tags for Access Control in Photo Sharing. In *ACM SIGCHI*, May 2012.

[9] S. Liao, X. Zhu, Z. Lei, L. Zhang, and S. Li. Learning Multi-scale Block Local Binary Patterns for Face Recognition. In *International Conference on Biometrics (ICB)*, 2007.

[10] M. Nauman, S. Khan, and X. Zhang. Apex: Extending Android Permission Model and Enforcement with User-defined Runtime Constraints. In *ASIACCS*, 2010.

[11] M. Ra, R. Govindan, and A. Ortega. P3: Toward Privacy-Preserving Photo Sharing. In *NSDI*, 2013.

[12] A. Shabtai, Y. Fledel, U. Kanonov, Y. Elovici, S. Dolev, and C. Glezer. Google android: A comprehensive security assessment. *IEEE Security and Privacy*, March 2010.

[13] R. Templeman, M. Korayem, D. Crandall, and A. Kapadia. PlaceAvoider: Steering First-Person Cameras away from Sensitive Spaces. In *NDSS*, 2014.

[14] M. Turk and A. Pentland. Eigenfaces for Recognition. *Journal of Cognitive Neuroscience*, 3(1), 1991.

[15] C. Write, C. Cowan, S. Smalley, J. Morris, and G. Kroah-Hartman. Linux Security Modules: General Security Support for the Linux Kernel. In *USENIX Security Symposium*, Aug 2002.

[16] R. Xu, H. Saidi, and R. Anderson. Aurasium: Practical Policy Enforcement for Android Applications. In *USENIX Security Symposium*, 2012.

# Enabling BYOD through Secure Meta-Market*

Alessandro Armando
Security and Trust
Fondazione Bruno Kessler
Via Sommarive, 18
Trento, Italy
armando@fbk.eu

Gabriele Costa
DIBRIS - University of Genoa
Via all'Opera Pia, 13
16145, Genova (Italy)
gabriele.costa@unige.it

Alessio Merlo
E-Campus University
Via Isimbardi, 10
22060, Novedrate (Italy)
alessio.merlo@uniecampus.it

Luca Verderame
DIBRIS - University of Genoa
Via all'Opera Pia, 13
16145, Genova (Italy)
luca.verderame@unige.it

## ABSTRACT

Mobile security is a hot research topic. Yet most of available techniques focus on securing individual applications and therefore cannot possibly tackle security weaknesses stemming from the combined use of one or more applications (e.g. confused deputy attacks). Preventing these types of attacks is crucial in many important application scenarios. For instance, their prevention is a prerequisite for the widespread adoption of the BYOD paradigm in the corporate setting.

To this aim, in this paper we propose a secure meta-market which supports the specification and enforcement of security policies spanning multiple applications. Moreover, the meta-market keeps track of the security state of devices and—through a functional combination of static analysis and code instrumentation techniques—supervises the installation of new applications thereby ensuring the enforcement of the security policies. Also, we developed a prototype implementation of the secure meta-market and we used it for validating a wide range of popular Android applications against a security policy drawn from the US Government BYOD Security Guidelines. Experimental results obtained by running the prototype confirm the effectiveness of the approach.

## Categories and Subject Descriptors

D.4.6 [**Operating Systems**]: Security and Protection—*Information flow controls*; D.2.4 [**Operating Systems**]: Software/Program Verification

## Keywords

Application Meta-Market; Android Security; Formal Verification; Code Instrumentation;

## 1. INTRODUCTION

The world-wide spread of smartphones and tablets as well as the emerging "Bring Your Own Device" (BYOD) paradigm are pushing mobile devices towards a professional use. Many device manufacturers are thus considering the development of architectural solutions supporting the use of personal devices in corporate environments, e.g., Apple[1], Samsung[2], Blackberry[3], Huawei[4]. Yet, the level of protection offered by current mobile operating systems does not allow to cope with the complexity and the stringent security requirements arising in corporate environments. As a matter of fact, business activities carried out on mobile devices can handle valuable resources on platforms where users, which cannot be expected to understand all the security implications, are likely to install harmful applications.

The current trend for mobile code distribution is based on application markets. Markets allow users to browse and install myriads of applications. A centralized application repository offers some advantages for the security assessment as the market can implement procedures for the analysis and testing of the mobile code. However, the most popular markets offer very limited security guarantees (see for instance [31, 41, 39]).

In this paper we propose a security-enabled application marketplace, namely *meta-market*, which enforces BYOD security policies through analysis and monitoring of mobile applications. The meta-market masks the actual application markets by mediating all the application installation requests. A fruitful combination of static and dynamic techniques is used to check whether the applications comply with the organizational security policy. More in detail, the meta-market supports: *(i)* the definition of fine-grained security

*This work has been partially funded by the Italian PRIN project *Security Horizons* (no. 2010XSEMLC).

[1] http://www.apple.com/ipad/business/it/byod.html
[2] http://www.samsung.com/global/business/mobile/solution/security/samsung-knox
[3] http://it.blackberry.com/business/software/bes-10.html
[4] http://enterprise.huawei.com/en/solutions/byod/byod-mobility/index.htm

policies, *(ii)* the static verification of applications against the security policy and *(iii)* the runtime monitoring of applications failing the verification step.

We present an implementation of the meta-market[5] which deals with Android-based devices and supports the security assessment of the Google Play application market against corporate BYOD policies. To assess the effectiveness of our approach, we applied our meta-market to check the compliance of 860 Android applications taken from the Google Play store. Applications are validated against a real world BYOD security policy (extracted from the US Government BYOD Security Guidelines [17]) expressed in ConSpec [2], a well-known security specification formalism. The experimental results confirm the effectiveness of the proposed approach.

*Structure of the paper.* In Section 2 we discuss the state-of-the-art of the security assessment of mobile applications and some related work. Section 3 introduces the formal application and security framework adopted in this paper. In Section 4 we present the techniques and logical workflow of the proposed meta-market solution. Then, in Section 5 we describe our prototype implementation and in Section 6 we report and discuss the experimental results. We conclude in Section 7 with some final remarks and future research directions.

## 2. RELATED WORK

Recent researches on the security of mobile devices outline that malware are appearing more and more frequently in official application markets. In [41] the authors systematically evaluate the malware affecting Android OS which have been discovered in the last years. Also, they check the presence of malware in application markets and they consider whether most used anti-virus applications succeed in detecting them. They find that all the application markets they inspected contain several malware instances and, even worse, anti-viruses very often fail in discovering them.

The weakness of application markets security checks is also reported by Wang et al. [39]. Briefly, they developed a method for injecting malicious control flows in the application code. Applying their technique, they could modify and submit an iOS application to the Apple Store. After passing the review process of the market, the application carrying illegal instructions was successfully published. These works indicate that security mechanisms adopted by application markets are far from being sufficient to guarantee that the applications they deploy are safe for the user's device.

Furthermore, the basic security mechanisms offered by mobile OSes seem to be inadequate for providing actual security guarantees, e.g., see [21]. Moreover, OSes implementations are not immune to vulnerabilities. Indeed, some of them have been already identified and fixes have been proposed, e.g., see [8]. Clearly, unsafe applications acquired from markets can exploit these weaknesses to perform disruptive attacks. Several proposals advocate extensions to the native Android security mechanisms (e.g., permissions system and application sandboxing). For instance, in [29] the authors present an enhancement of the basic Android permission system, while in [42] the authors suggest new privacy-related security policies for protecting users' personal data. Similarly, [11]

presents a mixed static and dynamic approach for both detecting suspicious patterns in an installing application and, possibly, running it in a sandboxed environment.

A few approaches where security activities are carried out by the application market have been proposed. Among them, Google Bouncer[6] is a malware detector running on the Google Play store. However, it has been recently shown how it can be easily circumvented [31].

All the proposals listed above, although indirectly dealing with security policies, do not support user-defined security policies. In this respect, [19] presents Kirin, a local service certifying that an application under installation complies with user-defined security rules. Similarly, Saint [32] assigns privileges to applications at install time and monitors them at run time. Although both systems use security rules which can be arbitrarily complex, they still refer to the existing, insufficient set of permissions[7]. Since these are coarse-grained and informally defined, building security mechanisms on top of them is rather controversial.

A different approach is the *Security-by-Contract* [16] (SxC). SxC is an integrated framework exploiting several techniques for granting that a mobile application respects the policy of the device running it. Roughly, application developers attach a contract to their code through *proof-carrying code* [30]. After downloading the application, the mobile platform automatically verifies the correctness of the contract, i.e., whether it effectively models the application. If the check succeeds, the application is validated by comparing its contract against the platform policy, e.g., via *model checking* [12]. If one of these two steps fails, i.e., whenever the contract is incorrect or the policy is not fulfilled, the application is rejected, otherwise it is installed. Software installed in this way is proved to never violate the policy.

Although the Security-by-Contract prevents the execution of dangerous mobile code, it hardly copes with the current market-based distribution paradigm. In fact, the SxC tasks executed on the mobile device, i.e., contract validation and model checking, are non trivial. In particular, model checking requires heavy computation which may take long time and rapidly exhaust the device resources. Moreover, proof-carrying code significantly increase the size of the mobile code (as it injects proof annotations). Larger software packages would require extra storage space, which is usually non-free, on actual application markets.

Our proposal aims at effectively enforcing fine-grained BYOD security policies. Unlike the approaches listed above, our solution is designed to apply to the current market-based application distribution paradigm without executing cumbersome tasks on resource-constrained mobile devices.

## 3. SECURITY FRAMEWORK

Our approach relies on formal descriptions of the application behavior and the policy specification. In particular, two aspects are crucial under our assumptions, i.e., modeling the interactions among applications and the specification of fine-grained BYOD policies. A convenient abstraction of the behavior of a program is provided by its *execution trace* [1], representing the sequence of security-relevant operations it performs. In this respect, security policies

---

[5]Further information can be found at
`http://www.ai-lab.it/byodroid/`

[6]`http://googlemobile.blogspot.it/2012/02/android-and-security.html`

[7]`http://source.android.com/tech/security/`

are defined as temporal properties over an execution trace. Below we present our history-based application and policy modeling frameworks.

### 3.1 Mobile Application Framework

Mobile code is typically distributed in the form of application packages. For instance, a package may contain application code and resources (e.g., audio files and pictures). A common way to represent the behavior of a piece of code is by building its *control flow graph* (CFG). Briefly, a CFG is a data structure representing all the possible execution flows of a program. It basically consists of states and transitions. States denote linear, i.e., jumps-free, fragments of code. In contrast, transitions represent (un)conditional jump instructions that correspond to computational branches. CFGs can be extracted from assembly code [13] as well as intermediate languages like the Java bytecode [3].

In [10] a proof system allowing to prove that a CFG complies with a security specification is discussed. A similar approach is not viable under our assumptions. Here, we are interested in considering BYOD policies regulating the behavior of the mobile device as a whole. In principle, illegal executions may involve more than one application. This is typical of well-known privilege escalation attacks, e.g., based on the application collusion and confused deputy problems [23].

Hence, we follow a different approach. In particular, we translate the CFG into a corresponding *history expression*, i.e., a process algebraic representation of a set of execution traces. The procedure resembles the one in [9] with some crucial differences. First of all, we adopt an extended version of history expressions which has been specifically designed for Android applications (see [6] for a detailed presentation). These history expressions can represent the *inter-process communication* (IPC) which is a common mechanism of interaction among applications running on mobile devices. In this way we capture the possible flows of information among applications.

### 3.2 Policy Specification

Several policy specification languages have been presented for defining temporal properties over the execution traces. Among them, temporal logics, e.g., LTL [33], are a major proposal. Briefly, they extend first-order logic with temporal modalities, e.g., saying that a certain property will hold on a certain trace segment.

Automata-based formalisms have similar features and are also widely adopted. For instance, each LTL formula can be efficiently translated into a corresponding *Büchi automaton* [22] which accepts a trace if and only if it satisfies the original formula. *Security automata* [35] behave similarly. Intuitively, a security automaton defines an abstract controller which reads the elements of an execution trace. As far as the next symbol is accepted by the automaton, it respects the policy. Security automata have been also used for defining the formal semantics of some policy specification languages like PSLang [20] and ConSpec [2]. In particular, ConSpec has been specifically designed for high level languages, e.g., Java, which makes it suitable for the Android environment.

For the sake of presentation, we do not provide a full description of the ConSpec syntax and semantics. Here, we simply provide the basic intuition about the language and its features. A ConSpec policy consists of a *security state*

and a list of *security rules*. The state contains a set of variables representing the configuration of the policy. Variables have a scope defining how they behave on multiple targets, e.g., *session* means that the variable is reinitialized at every execution of an application (see [2] for further details). Moreover, rules define how the state changes when a certain security-relevant operation is evaluated. In order to give a basic intuition, we propose the following ConSpec policy.

```
1  SECURITY STATE
2    SESSION Str[11] agency_host = "agency.gov/";
3    SESSION Obj agency_url = null;
4    SESSION Bool connected = false;
5
6  /*(R1) No download of business data on device
       */
7  AFTER Obj url = java.net.URL.<init>(Str[64]
       spec)
8    PERFORM
9    (spec.contains(agency_host)) -> { agency_url
         := url; }
10   ELSE -> { skip; }
11
12 AFTER Obj url = java.net.URL.<init>(Str[0]
       protocol, Str[64] host, Nat[0] port,
       Str[0] file)
13   PERFORM
14   (host.contains(agency_host)) -> { agency_url
         := url; }
15   ELSE -> { skip; }
16
17 BEFORE java.net.URL.openConnection()
18   PERFORM
19   (this.equals(agency_url)) -> { connected :=
         true; }
20   ELSE -> { skip; }
21
22 BEFORE java.io.FileOutputStream.write(int i)
23   PERFORM
24   (!connected) -> { skip; }
25
26 /* (R2) "When in Doubt, Delete it Out"
       */
27 AFTER Obj file = java.io.File.createTempFile()
28   PERFORM
29   (true) -> { file.deleteOnExit(); }
30
31 /* (R3) No transfer of sensitive data
32          to non-agency devices
              */
33 BEFORE android.bluetooth.BluetoothSocket.
       getOutputStream()
34   PERFORM
35   (!connected) -> { skip; }
```

The policy encodes three clauses[8] informally stated in the US Government BYOD security guidelines [17].

Intuitively, the first group of rules (R1) says that users cannot store sensitive data on their device. We encoded this behavior by means of four rules. The first two (lines 7 and 12) say that after an application creates a URL object, the policy checks whether it points at some sensitive data sources (here we identify it with the "agency.gov/" path). If this is the case (lines 9 and 14), the policy stores the URL reference in the variable agency_url, otherwise (lines 10 and 15) the operation is simply allowed (skip command). The third rule (line 17) is triggered before a URL is used to create a data connection. If the URL is the same stored in agency_url (line 19), the policy state changes by setting the connected

---

[8] For brevity, here we omit few irrelevant elements.

flag to true, which means that the application has accessed to sensitive data. Finally, according to the fourth rule (line 22), the target can write on local files only if `connected` is false (following a *default-deny* approach, the policy blocks an operation whenever none of its rules apply to it). In addition, rule (R2, line 27) states that temporary data, which could include sensitive information, must be deleted at the end of each application session. To do that, right after the creation of every temporary file, the policy requires the invocation of `deleteOnExit()` (line 29). Eventually, rule (R3, line 33) exploits the same flag `connected` used in (R1) to decide whether to disable the Bluetooth output streaming for an application which might have accessed a sensitive `URL`. Again, when evaluating the Bluetooth operation, if the rule does not apply, i.e., if `connected` is true, the action is blocked.

## 4. META-MARKET PARADIGM

In this section we present the architectural aspects of the *meta-market* software distribution model. In particular, we explain how it provides formal security guarantees. Then we give a detailed description of the meta-market components and their behavior.

### 4.1 Formal Security Assessment Workflow

Intuitively, our proposal consists in moving most of the security assessment steps and logic on a meta-market. The meta-market holds the security policies of one or more organizations, e.g. private companies or public agencies, and its customers are the organizations' members, e.g. the employees of a company. For simplicity, in the rest of the paper we assume the meta-market to handle a single policy of a single organization. Figure 1 shows the code deployment workflow in the meta-market paradigm.

Code producers compile their applications and publish them through a standard application market. An application market simply implements a database of applications that registered devices can browse. Then, the meta-market interacts with an application market by passing the customers requests, e.g. to obtain the list of applications. In this way, the meta-market is totally transparent to the application market, which handles standard user sessions. Also, it only requires minor extensions of the user's device, which only needs to mount a dedicated installer (as most of the application markets do).

Our model works as follows. Code producers compile (P.0) and generate mobile applications[9] (P.1). Then, they publish their applications (P.2) on a standard application market which stores (M.0) the software packages in a database (ADB).

When a code consumer requires an application from the meta-market, the corresponding code package is retrieved. Then, a model extraction procedure is applied to the code (B.0) to generate an application model (B.1). Since the model is extracted from the mobile code, no further validation is required (as needed, for instance, by the Security-by-Contract approach [16]). Hence, the model can be directly passed (B.2) to a verification process which checks its compliance against the security policy (B.3). Security policies are retrieved (B.4) from a policy database (PDB) handling

policy instances customized over the devices' configuration. More details about this aspect are discussed in Section 4.2. If the verification succeeds (B.5 → YES) the policy database is updated and the application is delivered to the user's device with no further action (B.6). Otherwise (B.5 → NO), the meta-market attaches monitoring information to the application (B.7). Mainly, monitoring information consists of a digital signature which will be used by the code consumer to obtain a correct instrumentation of the application as detailed in Section 4.2. When the consumer receives a mobile application package, she checks whether it was marked for monitoring (C.0). If this is the case, before installation the mobile device instruments the application package with security checks by using information attached by the meta-market (C.1). Otherwise, it is directly installed.

### 4.2 Meta-Market Components and Activities

The workflow of the secure meta-market is obtained by a fruitful combination of techniques we describe in the following.

#### Model validity.

Model-based verification systems rely on the validity of models. Indeed, fake or incorrect models can compromise the whole verification process. To be valid, a model must denote (at least) every security-relevant behavior of the application it refers to. For instance, since in [16] the application model is created by an untrusted producer, it must be validated at consumer-side.

Model validation is a non-trivial task. To reduce the consumer's overhead, a possible solution is *model-carrying code* [37] (MCC). MCC is a variant of *proof-carrying code* [30] in which a piece of code, i.e. the mobile application, is instrumented with the steps of a proof of compliance against its own model. Although the proof instrumentation allows for a faster validation, it significantly increases the size of the software package [30]. Such a growth depends on the proof size and poorly fits with large scale distribution paradigms. Moreover, as model extraction is performed without knowing the consumers' policies, applying this method requires to generate inclusive, large models. Clearly, larger models exacerbate the problem of instrumenting and storing the model-carrying packages.

In our approach, the verification process takes place on the meta-market. Thus, application models can be generated locally with some clear advantages. Mainly, to obtain correct models the system just needs to rely on a sound model extraction procedure and validity proofs must be neither generated nor verified[10]. Moreover, being aware of the policy, the meta-market can extract models that only refer to the policy-relevant operations. In this way, models do not contain irrelevant information and their size is substantially reduced.

#### Policy compliance verification.

Policy compliance is the central activity of the secure application deployment process. Model checking [12] can be suitably applied to verify whether a given model satisfies a formal specification, i.e., a security policy. Models and specifications are often given as (labeled) transition systems (see,

---

[9]For the sake of brevity, we do not distinguish here between applications and their code.

[10]The model extraction program can be verified and tested before adopting it.

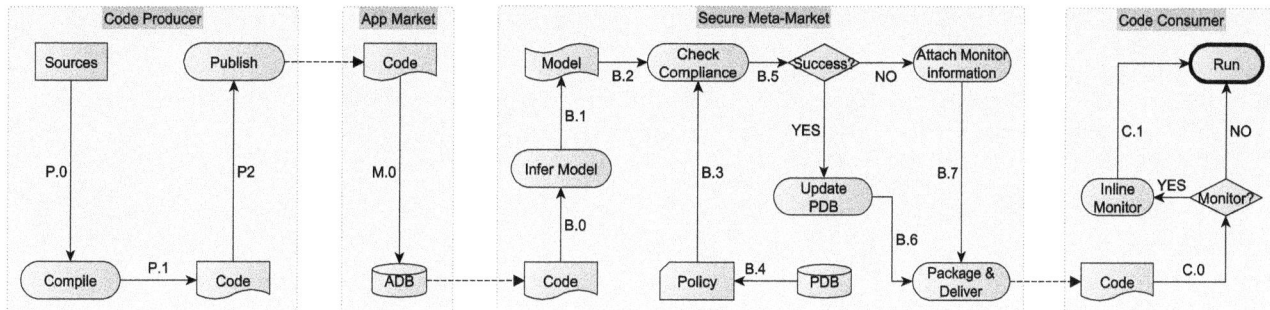

Figure 1: The meta-market software distribution workflow.

e.g. [26]) and temporal logic formulae, e.g., linear-time temporal logic [33], respectively. Several model checkers have been proposed in the last decades and many of them have been successfully applied to verification the correctness of real systems, e.g., see for instance [40, 27, 28].

Nevertheless, in some cases solving the model checking problem can be extremely hard and model checkers poorly scale over the size of their search space (see [36] for a survey). More specifically, it is well known that model checkers suffer from the state explosion problem [38], that is the exponential growth of the search space due to the representation of concurrent agents. Since they can run in parallel, mitigating this issue is crucial for applying model checking to the verification of mobile applications.

A first step consists in using previous analysis results in order to avoid repeated instances of the same model checking problem. This approach can be effectively supported by centralizing the use of the model checking process in the proposed meta-market architecture. In particular, the meta-market disposes of both the security policy and the application models. Hence, the system can store verification results and check whether a given instance was already considered in the past without running the model checker again. Although this approach can avoid repetitions of cumbersome computations, it does not reduce the complexity of the model checking.

A further optimization derives from including platform-specific aspects in the model generation process as it is has been proposed in [6] for the Android inter-process communication (IPC) framework.

Briefly, IPC defines application-level primitives for data and control flow composition. Each IPC function abstracts low-level operations which actually implement the communication. Hence, IPC-based communications can be modeled as simple messages over reserved channels. Since the IPC mechanisms also rules the application life-cycle, we can avoid concurrency in many models. For more details on the Android IPC and its formalization we refer the reader to [6]. A similar reasoning can be applied to other mobile platforms, e.g., see [5].

Moreover, we upper-bound the model checking phase, i.e., we force the model checker to terminate after a finite number of steps (visited states or amount of time). Setting a threshold guarantees the model checker to terminate within a fixed time but introduces a third analysis outcome, i.e., the timeout. A similar approach is also adopted in [18]. In

this way, the meta-market prevents indefinitely long executions which would be unacceptable in the workflow outlined above. The meta-market treats a timeout as a verification failure and marks the application for security instrumentation and monitoring. Clearly, this may cause false positives, i.e., harmless applications being monitored. Hence, the time threshold is a parameter that need to be carefully considered to obtain a reasonable trade-off. In Section 6 we describe how we deal with timeouts in our implementation. We will discuss in detail the advantages of adopting runtime monitoring below, at the end of this section.

*Partial policy evaluation and storage.*

As we outlined in the previous paragraph, models and policies play a central role for the feasibility of model checking-based validation. In particular, the security state of each mobile device is evaluated against the models of the installed applications. This implies that the meta-market must keep track of all the set of installed applications for each device. Also, these records must be updated whenever a device installs or removes an application. Hence, we use a *direct acyclic graph* (DAG) to represent device configurations and their dependencies [7]. For instance, consider the DAG depicted in Figure 2. Node $R$ is the root configuration denoting the original policy. The installation of applications $A_1$, $A_2$ and $A_3$ leads to a new configuration $N$ (solid path). Also, installing the three applications in a different order can generate a different path from $R$ to $N$ (dashed path). Eventually, installing application $A_4$ on a device being associated to $N$ can cause the migration to a different configuration (node $M$). This happens only if $A_4$ does not violate the policy holding in $N$, i.e., $\phi$. Summing up, each device is associated to a node, e.g., $N$. The node corresponds to a record containing the current policy of the device, e.g., $\phi$, the set of installed applications, e.g., $\{A_1, A_2, A_3\}$, a list of applications known to be safely installed (pointing to the corresponding node), e.g., $A_4 \to M$, and a set of applications that are known to violate the policy of the node, e.g., $\{A_5\}$. The implementation and the management of the DAG is done through a relational database as described in Section 5.3.

Beside implementation, the way device configurations are encoded must be carefully considered. Observe that a mere list of application models can be very inefficient. Indeed, consider a device which already installed applications $A_1, \ldots, A_k$, wanting to install a new application $A$. If the meta-market uses the models of the installed applications, i.e., $C_1, \ldots, C_k$, to represent the configuration of the device, the model checking problem to be solved for validating $A$ through its model $C$ is $C_1 \mid \ldots \mid C_k \mid C \models \phi$. Where $\phi$ is the security policy and $\mid$ the parallel model composition operator. As we discussed above, the complexity of this problem rapidly grows when $k$ increases.

**Figure 2: Policy data structure.**

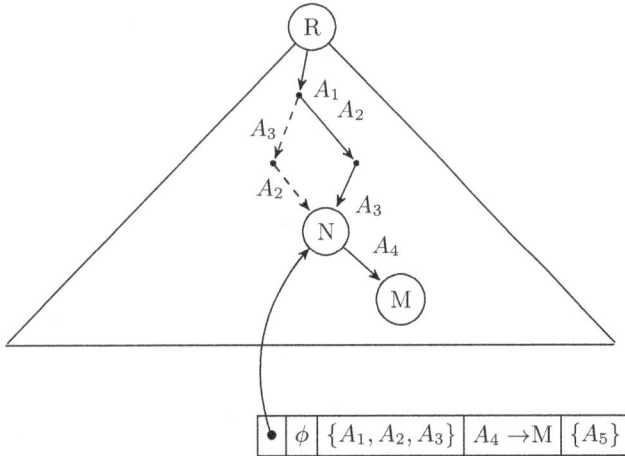

In [4] Andersen presents partial model checking (PMC). Roughly, PMC consists in partially evaluating a specification against a model. In a nutshell, given one or more models $C_1 \mid \ldots \mid C_k$ and a formula $\phi$, PMC returns a new formula $\phi'$ such that for every $C$

$$(C_1 \mid \ldots \mid C_k) \mid C \models \phi \text{ if and only if } C \models \phi'$$

Moreover, in [4] the author reports experimental results showing that PMC outperforms model checking when dealing with a model resulting from the parallel composition of smaller models. This is mainly due to a number of simplification techniques which can be applied for simplifying a formula. Hence, relying on PMC we just need to associate each device to its customized policy, i.e., the policy which has been partially evaluated against the device's configuration. When a new application is evaluated for installation, its model can be directly model-checked against the customized policy. If the verification is successful the model is included in the configuration via PMC, i.e., a new policy is obtained by partially evaluating the old one against the model.

For these reasons, we exploit PMC in the policy customization and device configuration management processes of the meta-market workflow. Further details about the PMC framework adopted in the meta-market are provided in Section 5.3.

*Application instrumentation and monitoring.*

Mobile application monitoring is a consolidated technique for enforcing policy compliance at runtime. Several implementations appeared in the literature, also running on mobile, resource-constrained devices [15, 14]. Typically, a monitoring environment consists of a *policy decision point* (PDP) and many *policy enforcement points* (PEPs). The

**Listing 1: A fragment of instrumented code.**

```
URL url;
PDP.checkBefore("java.net.URL.<init>",addr);
try {
  url = new URL(addr);
} catch(Exception e) {
  PDP.checkException
  ↪("java.net.URL.<init>",e,addr);
  throw e;
}
PDP.checkAfter("java.net.URL.<init>",url,addr);
```

PDP holds the security policy and the current security state, the PEPs control invocations to critical operations. When an application attempts to perform a security-relevant access, a corresponding PEP is activated. The PEP triggers the PDP which checks the security state and policy and grants or rejects the permission. Finally, the PEP enforces the PDP's response by allowing or blocking the requested access.

Monitoring environments may differ for the PEPs deployment strategy. Traditionally, two strategies exist, i.e., customizing the execution environment and instrumenting the application code. In both cases, the PDP is installed as a background service. For our purposes, PEP instrumentation is the best option. As a matter of fact, platform customization requires heavy modification of the mobile devices in order to replace/rewrite system components. For instance, for virtual machine-based systems, e.g., Java/Android, the customization consists in replacing the standard VM with a new one including the PEPs. On the contrary, under the same assumptions, the application instrumentation is much less invasive. Indeed, it only requires to slightly modify the intermediate code, i.e., the VM instructions, of the application. For a more detailed discussion about the PEP inlining for mobile applications see [14].

We implement instrumentation directly on the mobile device. As described in Section 4.1, mobile devices may receive applications to be instrumented. In this case, the instrumentation procedure injects instructions implementing the PEPs. These instructions wrap security-relevant invocations. In Listing 1 we show a code fragment obtained by instrumenting the instruction `Url url = new URL(addr)`. Methods `checkBefore`, `checkException` and `checkAfter` implement the PEP logic by requesting authorizations to the PDP. Briefly, they interrupt the code execution and alert the PDP about the ongoing operation and its parameters. The PDP evaluates the action according to the current security state. The evaluation changes the security state and produces a return value for the PEP, i.e., *allow* or *deny*. If the PEP receives an *allow* signal, the execution is resumed, otherwise it throws a security exception. We refer the interested reader to [34] for further details.

Clearly, application instrumentation invalidates the original software signature and, since most mobile OSes, e.g., Android and iOS, do not allow for the installation of unsigned contents, a new, valid one must be computed. For this reason, the application package to be instrumented contains the original code together with an *instrumentation signature*. The signature is computed by the meta-market and only applies if the application is modified in the right way. After the instrumentation, the signature is attached and the application installed. Moreover, the signature prevents from illegal instrumentation which could modify the code in arbitrary ways.

## 5. META-MARKET IMPLEMENTATION

In this section we present a prototype implementation of the meta-market. The current implementation of the meta-market is meant to interact with the Android software development and distribution framework and adopts all techniques previously discussed. In the following we assume the code receiver to be an Android device and the application market to be Google Play.

### 5.1 Model Extraction

Models are extracted directly from the application bytecode. The (Dalvik) bytecode is the intermediate language interpreted by the standard Android virtual machine, namely the Dalvik Virtual Machine (DVM). The application code is typically written in Java and then compiled in Dalvik bytecode. Actually, application packages consist of compressed Dalvik bytecode and resources, like audio files and pictures. Occasionally, application packages may also carry native code, i.e., libraries of machine-executable procedures. Although we do not present it below, the same approach can be applied for that kind of code (e.g., see [13]).

Basically, the model extraction process consists in building a CFG representing the behavior of the application. The CFG generation is a widely adopted technique [3] and several tools support the CFG extraction for bytecode. To this aim, we adopt Androguard[11], a state-of-the-art Android package analyzer and CFG extractor. Unfortunately, Androguard extracts large and non optimized CFGs and we had to customize the tool for our specific purpose. Briefly, we implemented ad-hoc procedures for optimizing the CFG construction in terms of generated nodes and transitions. Part of this activity consists in pruning those parts of a CFG which do not refer to any security-relevant method.

### 5.2 Model Checking

Application validation is carried out through model checking. Although several model checkers exist, we opted for Spin [24] since it offers some practical advantages. Spin has been applied to the verification of a plethora of practical case studies in several different contexts (see [27] for a survey). In terms of reliability, Spin has been included in industrial verification activities as reported, for instance, in [28]. Moreover, Spin includes features for optimizing the use of CPU and memory. For instance, since version 5 Spin supports multicore computation [25]. Pragmatically, this allows Spin to perform better when running on powerful hardware, as we assume for a server hosting the meta-market.

The specification language for Spin is Promela. Hence, we implemented a translator to convert the CFGs extracted from application packages into corresponding Promela specifications. The definition of Promela specifications from transition systems or state machines is a quite consolidated technique, see [27]. However, in our context two aspects require more attention, i.e., IPC facilities and policy encoding. Roughly, each component of an application results in a subgraph of the overall CFG. Since components pass each other

[11]https://code.google.com/p/androguard/

the control state through internal IPC messages, their subgraphs should not be considered as concurrent agents. In fact, we model special IPC channels in the Promela specification for simulating these interactions. Briefly, this approach prevents many states, representing impossible configurations, from being considered by the model checker. Moreover, since IPC can also occur among different applications, we apply a similar reasoning to interface components, i.e., those that can be invoked by other applications. Such components are known through the application interface definition contained in its manifest file.

Usually, Promela specifications contain both the system and the property for the model checker. For instance, a LTL formula defined over the agents' states can be (automatically) translated into an invariant, i.e., a *never* claim, and applied to the Promela agents. However, the properties we want to verify here are related to the messages sent from applications to the platform, i.e., the system calls. Hence, we are interested in evaluating sequences of messages, rather than the states of the Promela agents. For this reason, we directly encode the policy as an extra Promela agent. Clearly, this step relies on the formal definition of the transitional semantics of the ConSpec policy language.

The Promela agent obtained from the policy represents an abstract controller reading the abstract traces generated by the model. If the application model carries some policy-violating behavior, the policy controller reaches a faulty state causing Spin to report an error. In that case, the output contains the trace of transitions which can be mapped back to the application code in order to locate the illegal flow.

### 5.3 Policy Management and Partial Evaluation

In Section 4.2 we highlighted the advantages of applying partial model checking to the partial evaluation of security policies. Also, we described the importance of an efficient organization of mobile devices configurations. Below, we provide technical details about these two aspects.

*Partial policy evaluation.*

We implemented a partial model checking tool from scratch. Indeed, at the best of our knowledge, no implementations of the algorithm presented in [4] are publicly available. Beside the mere implementation details, two aspects must be considered: transition system and policy representations. As a matter of fact, the procedure defined in [4] uses finite transition systems as modeling formalism. Our approach directly generates transition systems from CFGs. In fact, CFGs correspond to transition systems having a fixed, maximum branching degree, i.e., two.

Policy conversion is slightly more complex. Indeed, partial model checking deals with equational $\mu$-calculus specifications. However, since the $\mu$-calculus is extremely expressive, it is possible to express ConSpec policies in that formalism. These aspects required us to develop proper compatibility components, but they lay out of the scope of this work.

The partial model checking mainly applies to the policy management process. This part is not included in our current experimental activity. As a matter of fact, it heavily depends on the specific application scenario and it can only be evaluated against a real BYOD environment or via its application usage statistics. Future developments include setting up this kind of environment.

*Database design and management.*

The secure meta-market uses a database for storing data on the security configuration of the registered devices. Mainly, installation and removal of applications are the two activities impacting the security state of a device. In general, we expect the meta-market to handle an arbitrary amount of devices, each of them running a set of applications. The number of devices may vary according to several factors, e.g., the size and purpose of the organization adopting the meta-market. In addition, the number and the kind of mobile applications changes from device to device. According to recent statistics, it seems reasonable to assume that devices install dozens of applications[12].

Considering the situation depicted in Figure 2, we have that node $N$ is represented by a corresponding row in a table called *policy_instance*. The entry for $N$ refers to a *green_list* table which includes $A_4$. Similarly, $A_2$ and $A_3$ belong to the *green_list* tables associated to other two entries of *policy_instance*. These two represent nodes in which the installation of $A_2$ ($A_3$, respectively) is legal and leads to the configuration of node $N$.

The dimension of the configurations DAG and database can rapidly increase with the number of devices and applications. This might negatively impact the scalability of the meta-market. For coping with this issue, we introduces simplification techniques based on heuristics. For the time being, we included two of them in our prototype, i.e., equivalence-based and frequency-based node elimination. The former consists of an asynchronous process which visits the DAG looking for pairs of nodes referring to equivalent policies, i.e., such that they are satisfied (violated, resp.) by exactly the same traces. If such a pair exists, the process starts a procedure for collapsing them in a single record. Furthermore, the frequency-based elimination looks for nodes which are rarely used, e.g., because some of the applications they refer to no longer exist. Again, when one of these nodes is discovered, the process decides whether to remove it and, eventually, reorganize part of the DAG accordingly. Other heuristics can be also considered and included (notice that some could also be context-dependent).

## 5.4 Client-side components

Below we discuss the components and technologies hosted by the mobile devices registered to the meta-market.

*Meta-market client application.*

The meta-market client application provides access to the application installation/removal operations through a user interface which mostly resembles those of standard market client applications. Figure 3 depicts the client GUI in two different activities: applications browsing and application description. Briefly, the client is responsible for providing the user with details about the security of the available applications, e.g., green, VERIFIED labels identify secure applications. Also, it mediates the operations usually carried out by the application market clients, e.g., contents purchasing and refunding procedures[13].

---

[12]http://www.phonearena.com/news/The-average-global-smartphone-user-has-downloaded-26-apps_id47160

[13]Clearly, some of these tasks could need to be slightly reconsidered before integration in the meta-market. For the time being, our prototype does not support purchase refunding.

When the user selects an application for installation, the meta-market client triggers the request and, consequently, the meta-market workflow. Eventually, the meta-market returns a software package which, depending on the verification outcome, can require security instrumentation and monitoring. We describe these two activities of the client application in the next paragraph.

**Figure 3: Meta-market client interface.**

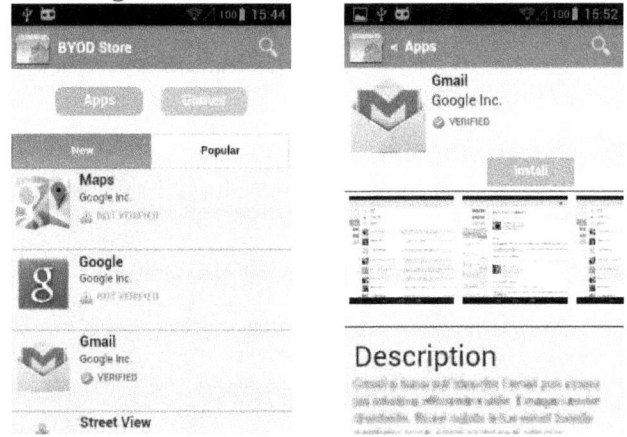

*Application instrumentation and monitoring.*

As discussed in Section 4.2, PEP inlining is a well known approach for enabling the security monitoring of mobile applications. Hence, some directions for implementing the instrumentation of Android application bytecode are viable. The current implementation of the meta-market relies on a modified version of *Redexer* [34] for instrumentation. Redexer is an OCaML implemented suite including several features for the assessment of some specific aspects of the Android application security, e.g., privilege exploitation analysis. Also, Redexer includes Dalvik bytecode parsing and rewriting facilities which we isolated and imported in our prototype. Although not designed for running on Android platforms, it can be ported by means of the Java native interface[14]. Briefly, the instrumentation is carried out by defining a *visitor* which inspects the bytecode and injects PEP instructions as described in Section 4.2. Eventually, the instrumented application is repackaged for installation. The PDP component is implemented as a background Android service running a policy interpreter. The service receives messages from the PEP instrumented in running applications. These messages are converted into events feeding the policy interpreter. Then, the interpreter simulates a corresponding step in the policy and returns a value representing the policy state, i.e., either *allow* or *deny*, as discussed in Section 4. An implementation of a ConSpec policy interpreter for mobile devices can be found in [14].

## 6. EXPERIMENTAL RESULTS

We applied the implementation of the meta-market to test the compliance of a large number of real-world applications against an instance policy, extracted from the US Government BYOD security guidelines presented in [17].

---

[14]See https://sites.google.com/site/keigoattic/ocaml-on-android for a technical explanation.

Roughly, experiments consist in performing multiple installation requests from the client application running on an emulated device. The meta-market reacts by running its workflow for achieving a policy-compliant installation. We evaluate the performance of each component taking part in the meta-market activity.

In the remaining of this section we discuss the experimental setup and test cases (Section 6.1), we provide results (Section 6.2) and, eventually, we critically discuss them (Section 6.3).

## 6.1 Experimental setup

The meta-market has been deployed on an Intel Quad-Core i7-2770 @ 3.40 GHz architecture, with 16 GB RAM and 1TB of hard drive, running Ubuntu Server 12.04 64bit. The server is also equipped with Java JDK 1.7.0_40 and Androguard 1.3 we customized for the model extraction. The meta-market client runs on an emulated Nexus 4 device mounting an ARM v7 CPU @ 1.5 GHz and 2 GB RAM.

We used the meta-market to analyze a group of 860 Android applications taken from the *"top selling free"* chart of the Google Play store. They include the most downloaded applications belonging to heterogeneous categories, e.g., business, entertainment and games.

In our experiments we considered the BYOD security policy given in Section 3 Also, we applied a time threshold of 300 seconds to the execution of each instance of the model checker. .

## 6.2 Results

We measure the time needed for each operation carried out by the meta-market server and client. Table 1 shows an excerpt of the experimental results[15]. A detailed explanation of each experimental phase is provided below.

### Model extraction.

At first, the meta-market extracts the model of each application, using our customization of the Androguard tool. The CFG is generated parametrically w.r.t. the system action expressed in the security policy and all inter-application communications. Then, the server performs an optimization step consisting in simplifying the CFG by pruning unreachable nodes. Column $T_{ext}$ reports the time needed (in seconds) for the generation of the final CFG while the size of the model is given in terms of number of nodes (column N) and edges (column E).

### Promela encoding and model checking.

As explained in Section 5.2, the use of the Spin model checker passes through two consecutive phases, i.e., Promela encoding and verification. The duration of the encoding phase for each application is listed under $T_{enc}$ in Table 1. The duration of the model checking verification step is reported in column $T_{mc}$. Moreover, we provide in column *Valid* the outcome of the model checker. We write YES to denote that the application successfully passed the verification, NO for the applications failing the verification, and Time Out (T.O.) for analysis that reached the time threshold.

---

[15]The complete results can be accessed online at `http://www.ai-lab.it/byodroid/experiments.html`.

### Application instrumentation.

Application instrumentation is performed when the model checking fails in validating the application. The instrumentation execution times are reported under $T_{ins}$ in Table 1. Moreover, since instrumentation may enlarge the original dimension of the software packages, we also report the package size change (column G), in percentage.

## 6.3 Discussion

The global values in Table 1 summarizes the overall statistics of our experiments. Although preliminary, the experimental results are promising. As a matter of fact, the meta-market validates more than 89% (column Y/N/TO) of applications within an average time of about 3 minutes $(\mu T_{ext} + \mu T_{enc} + \mu T_{mc})$. The remaining 11% (i.e. 94 applications), being rejected or leading to a time out, was successfully instrumented. The instrumentation process took an average time of 72 seconds (column $\mu T_{ins}$) and slightly enlarges the application packages by less than 0,1% on average (column $\mu G$).

It is worth noticing that our experiments have been carried out on a prototype implementation which can be further optimized. For instance, the definition of an optimized model extraction tool (different from Androguard) may reduce the extraction time; moreover, memory caching or task concurrency can improve the global performance.

Furthermore, consider that the meta-market validation is immediate when an application has been already checked in the current configuration. Hence, if devices share significant set of applications, we expect to observe a drastic increment of the skipped analysis phases.

## 7. CONCLUSION

We have presented a mobile application distribution system based on the notion of meta-market. The meta-market lays between standard, public application markets and the mobile devices. In practice, the meta-market guarantees that applications deployed on mobile devices do not violate a given security policy. This result is obtained by implementing a security workflow including model extraction and formal verification steps. When the verification rejects the application, the deployment process leads to the instrumentation of the potentially dangerous code. Instrumented code is then monitored for avoiding illegal behavior.

The whole system has been designed to be transparent to the users, the application developers, and the application markets. We have experimentally assessed the feasibility of the approach by testing the performance of an implementation of the meta-market on a large number of popular Android applications for both leisure and work. For the experimentation, a real world BYOD security policy taken from the US Government guidelines has been modeled. Eventually, we showed that the meta-market succeeds in detecting applications which can violate the security policy and in sanitizing them. All the activities carried out by the meta-market have been measured in terms of time and resources in order to witness the feasibility of our approach under realistic assumptions.

*Future directions* of this research include the extension of the experimental activity. Indeed, a crucial aspect of the meta-market is its capability to scale over a large number of devices and applications. In particular, we need to define new tests for showing the effectiveness of the PMC compo-

Table 1: Computation times and outcomes.

| Application | Size(Mb) | $T_{ext}$(s) | N | E | $T_{enc}$(s) | $T_{mc}$(s) | Valid | $T_{ins}$(s) | G(%) |
|---|---|---|---|---|---|---|---|---|---|
| Adobe Connect Mobile | 11,71 | 1,5 | 11 | 63 | 0,1 | 2,1 | YES | - | - |
| Adobe Reader | 6,63 | 11,5 | 36 | 157 | 0,6 | 2,1 | YES | - | - |
| AndrOpen office | 49,59 | 20,2 | 39 | 164 | 0,4 | 2,3 | YES | - | - |
| Angry Birds | 33,9 | 106,7 | 93 | 367 | 1,7 | 300 | T.O. | 38,7 | 0.14 |
| Angry Birds Rio | 32,61 | 106,6 | 93 | 367 | 1,7 | 300 | T.O. | 38,2 | 0.14 |
| Angry Birds Seasons | 42,27 | 112,3 | 94 | 373 | 1,7 | 300 | T.O. | 43,2 | 0.11 |
| Candy Crush Saga | 38,45 | 8,3 | 41 | 169 | 21 | 3,1 | YES | - | - |
| Dropbox | 5,59 | 32 | 33 | 168 | 11,1 | 4,9 | YES | - | - |
| Extreme racing | 8,02 | 62,5 | 112 | 403 | 2,1 | 2,4 | YES | - | - |
| Facebook | 15 | 30,2 | 25 | 112 | 0,2 | 2,3 | YES | - | - |
| FB Messenger | 12 | 314,3 | 41 | 180 | 12 | 4,3 | YES | - | - |
| Fruit Ninja free | 18,34 | 33,8 | 78 | 287 | 1,1 | 300 | T.O. | 29 | <0,01 |
| Gems Journey | 11,19 | 53,6 | 51 | 201 | 0,8 | 300 | T.O. | 33 | 0,23 |
| Gmail | 3,57 | 23 | 36 | 157 | 0,4 | 2,1 | YES | - | - |
| Google Chrome | 24,6 | 36,3 | 54 | 230 | 10,1 | 2,3 | YES | - | - |
| Google Play Music | 7,53 | 68,1 | 64 | 276 | 1 | 2,1 | YES | - | - |
| Google Street View | 0,25 | 1,8 | 13 | 57 | 0,1 | 2,1 | YES | - | - |
| Instagram | 14,87 | 93,1 | 60 | 244 | 4 | 3,8 | YES | - | - |
| LinkedIn | 6,56 | 65,1 | 69 | 292 | 4,2 | 2,1 | YES | - | - |
| Microsoft Lync 2010 | 3,61 | 3,5 | 8 | 41 | 0,1 | 2,1 | YES | - | - |
| Microsoft Remote D. | 4,50 | 16,622 | 15 | 64 | 0,1 | 2,1 | YES | - | - |
| Mozilla Firefox | 23,13 | 36,7 | 60 | 226 | 1,1 | 2,2 | YES | - | - |
| OpenDocument Reader | 1,61 | 45,8 | 44 | 188 | 0,6 | 3,0 | YES | - | - |
| PocketCloud Remote | 11,25 | 73,2 | 198 | 660 | 4,8 | 2,4 | YES | - | - |
| Tiny Flashlight | 1,28 | 16,4 | 61 | 223 | 0,8 | 3,2 | YES | - | - |
| T.N.T. Italy | 5,54 | 77,7 | 54 | 209 | 0,7 | 2,9 | YES | - | - |
| TripAdvisor | 6,31 | 24,1 | 74 | 269 | 1,1 | 2,1 | YES | - | - |
| TuneIn Radio | 6,58 | 154,4 | 174 | 649 | 8,3 | 13,3 | NO | 66 | 0,71 |
| Twitter | 5,18 | 42,7 | 62 | 256 | 10,7 | 2,3 | YES | - | - |
| SMS backup & restore | 1,33 | 35,5 | 74 | 298 | 1,3 | 2,9 | YES | - | - |
| Skype | 14,73 | 56 | 34 | 147 | 2,8 | 5,5 | YES | - | - |
| Splashtop 2 Remote D. | 17,78 | 58,46 | 90 | 357 | 1,7 | 2,2 | YES | - | - |
| Spotify | 3,65 | 8,1 | 18 | 79 | 2,3 | 2,1 | YES | - | - |
| WhatsApp | 9,75 | 369,4 | 223 | 715 | 8,8 | 2,1 | YES | - | - |
| **Global values** | | | | | | | | | |
| # Applications | $\mu$Size | $\mu T_{ext}$ | $\mu$N | $\mu$E | $\mu T_{enc}$ | $\mu T_{mc}$ | Y/N/TO | $\mu T_{ins}(94)$ | $\mu G(94)$ |
| 860 | 11,53 | 69 | 71 | 271 | 4,8 | 114,9 | 89/0,2/10,8 | 72,6 | 0,08 |

nent in improving the verification and management of large, i.e., involving several applications, device configurations. Moreover, we want to apply the meta-market to real BYOD scenarios. As a matter of fact, the behavior and performances of some meta-market components, e.g., the partial model checker, can depend on the specific environment it has to deal with. For instance, the average number of applications per device and their occurrences may affect the database management. Moreover, we plan to investigate different instances of BYOD policies involving various aspects of the security of mobile devices. Among them, contextual policies, e.g., those referring to the geographical location of the device, need further investigation. Indeed, they may be useful for some kind of organizations.

Furthermore, we plan to research on the possibility of including novel optimization heuristics for the policy database management. We already investigated double implication and low frequency. Other approaches might include policy inclusion/implication, i.e., using a more restrictive policy which, for some reason, is more convenient or easier to handle. We believe that this represents a problem of general interest and it could be interesting to consider "garbage collection" techniques for this kind of policy management systems.

## 8. REFERENCES

[1] M. Abadi and C. Fournet. Access Control based on Execution History. In *Proceedings of the 10th Annual Network and Distributed System Security Symposium*, pages 107–121, 2003.

[2] I. Aktug and K. Naliuka. ConSpec – A formal language for policy specification. *Science of Computer Programming*, 74(1-2):2–12, Dec. 2008.

[3] A. Amighi, P. de Carvalho Gomes, and M. Huisman. Provably Correct Control-Flow Graphs from Java Programs with Exceptions. In *Formal Verification of Object-Oriented Software*, volume 26 of *Karlsruhe Reports in Informatics*, pages 31–48, Karlsruhe,

Germany, October 2011. Karlsruhe Institute of Technology.

[4] H. R. Andersen. Partial Model Checking (Extended Abstract). In *In Proceedings, Tenth Annual IEEE Symposium on Logic in Computer Science*, pages 398–407. IEEE Computer Society Press, 1995.

[5] Apple Inc. Secure Coding Guide, 2012. `https://developer.apple.com/library/ios/documentation/Security/Conceptual/SecureCodingGuide/SecureCodingGuide.pdf`, accessed on 4-Dec-2013.

[6] A. Armando, G. Costa, and A. Merlo. Formal modeling and reasoning about the android security framework. In C. Palamidessi and M. Ryan, editors, *Trustworthy Global Computing*, volume 8191 of *Lecture Notes in Computer Science*, pages 64–81. Springer Berlin Heidelberg, 2013.

[7] A. Armando, G. Costa, A. Merlo, and L. Verderame. Bring your own device, securely. In *Proceedings of the 28th Annual ACM Symposium on Applied Computing*, SAC '13, pages 1852–1858, New York, NY, USA, 2013. ACM.

[8] A. Armando, A. Merlo, M. Migliardi, and L. Verderame. Breaking and fixing the android launching flow. *Computers & Security*, 39, Part A(0):104 – 115, 2013. 27th IFIP International Information Security Conference.

[9] M. Bartoletti, G. Costa, P. Degano, F. Martinelli, and R. Zunino. Securing Java with Local Policies. *Journal of Object Technology*, 8(4):5–32, June 2009.

[10] F. Besson, T. Jensen, D. Le Métayer, and T. Thorn. Model checking security properties of control flow graphs. *J. Comput. Secur.*, 9(3):217–250, Jan. 2001.

[11] T. Blasing, L. Batyuk, A.-D. Schmidt, S. Camtepe, and S. Albayrak. An Android Application Sandbox system for suspicious software detection. In *Malicious and Unwanted Software (MALWARE), 2010 5th International Conference on*, pages 55–62, 2010.

[12] E. M. Clarke, Jr., O. Grumberg, and D. A. Peled. *Model checking*. MIT Press, Cambridge, MA, USA, 1999.

[13] K. D. Cooper, T. J. Harvey, and T. Waterman. Building a control-flow graph from scheduled assembly code. Technical report, Department of Computer Science, Rice University, 2002.

[14] G. Costa, F. Martinelli, P. Mori, C. Schaefer, and T. Walter. Runtime monitoring for next generation Java ME platform. *Computers & Security*, 29(1):74–87, 2010.

[15] L. Desmet, W. Joosen, F. Massacci, K. Naliuka, P. Philippaerts, F. Piessens, and D. Vanoverberghe. The S3MS .NET Run Time Monitor. *Electronic Notes in Theoretical Computer Science*, 253(5):153–159, Dec. 2009.

[16] L. Desmet, W. Joosen, F. Massacci, P. Philippaerts, F. Piessens, I. Siahaan, and D. Vanoverberghe. Security-by-contract on the .NET platform. *Information Security Technical Report*, 13(1):25–32, Jan. 2008.

[17] Digital Services Advisory Group and Federal Chief Information Officers Council. Bring Your Own Device – A Toolkit to Support Federal Agencies Implementing Bring Your Own Device (BYOD) Programs. Technical report, White House, August 2013. Available at `http://www.whitehouse.gov/digitalgov/bring-your-own-device`.

[18] N. Dragoni, F. Massacci, T. Walter, and C. Schaefer. What the heck is this application doing? - A security-by-contract architecture for pervasive services. *Computers & Security*, 28(7):566 – 577, 2009.

[19] W. Enck, M. Ongtang, and P. McDaniel. On lightweight mobile phone application certification. In *Proceedings of the 16th ACM conference on Computer and communications security*, CCS '09, pages 235–245, New York, NY, USA, 2009. ACM.

[20] U. Erlingsson. *The Inlined Reference Monitor Approach to Security Policy Enforcement*. PhD thesis, Ithaca, NY, USA, 2004.

[21] A. P. Felt, E. Chin, S. Hanna, D. Song, and D. Wagner. Android permissions demystified. In *Proceedings of the 18th ACM conference on Computer and communications security*, CCS '11, pages 627–638, New York, NY, USA, 2011. ACM.

[22] P. Gastin and D. Oddoux. Fast LTL to Büchi Automata Translation. In *Proceedings of the 13th International Conference on Computer Aided Verification*, CAV '01, pages 53–65, London, UK, UK, 2001. Springer-Verlag.

[23] N. Hardy. The Confused Deputy: (or Why Capabilities Might Have Been Invented). *SIGOPS Oper. Syst. Rev.*, 22(4):36–38, Oct. 1988.

[24] G. Holzmann. *The Spin model checker*. Addison-Wesley Professional, first edition, 2003.

[25] G. Holzmann and D. Bosnacki. The design of a multicore extension of the spin model checker. *IEEE Transactions on Software Engineering*, 33(10):659–674, 2007.

[26] R. M. Keller. Formal verification of parallel programs. *Communications of the ACM*, 19(7):371–384, July 1976.

[27] R. V. Koskinen and J. Plosila. Applications for the SPIN Model Checker – A Survey. Technical Report 782, Turku Centre for Computer Science, Lemminkäisenkatu 14 A, 20520 Turku, Finland, September 2006.

[28] B. Long, J. Dingel, and T. N. Graham. Experience Applying the SPIN Model Checker to an Industrial Telecommunications System. In *Proceedings of the 30th International Conference on Software Engineering*, ICSE '08, pages 693–702, New York, NY, USA, 2008. ACM.

[29] M. Nauman, S. Khan, and X. Zhang. Apex: extending android permission model and enforcement with user-defined runtime constraints. In *Proceedings of the 5th ACM Symposium on Information, Computer and Communications Security*, ASIACCS '10, pages 328–332, New York, NY, USA, 2010. ACM.

[30] G. C. Necula. Proof-carrying code. In *Proceedings of the 24th ACM SIGPLAN-SIGACT symposium on Principles of programming languages*, POPL '97, pages 106–119, New York, NY, USA, 1997. ACM.

[31] J. Oberheide and C. Miller. Dissecting the Android Bouncer. In *SummerCon*, June 2012. `http://jon.oberheide.org/research/`.

[32] M. Ongtang, S. McLaughlin, W. Enck, and P. McDaniel. Semantically Rich Application-Centric Security in Android. In *Proceedings of the 2009 Annual Computer Security Applications Conference,* ACSAC '09, pages 340–349, Washington, DC, USA, 2009. IEEE Computer Society.

[33] A. Pnueli. The temporal logic of programs. In *Proceedings of the 18th Annual Symposium on Foundations of Computer Science,* SFCS '77, pages 46–57, Washington, DC, USA, 1977. IEEE Computer Society.

[34] N. Reddy, J. Jeon, J. A. Vaughan, T. Millstein, and J. S. Foster. Application-centric security policies on unmodified Android. Technical Report UCLA TR 110017, University of California, Los Angeles, Computer Science Department, July 2011.

[35] F. B. Schneider. Enforceable security policies. *ACM Trans. Inf. Syst. Secur.,* 3(1):30–50, Feb. 2000.

[36] Ph. Schnoebelen. The Complexity of Temporal Logic Model Checking. In Ph. Balbiani, N.-Y. Suzuki, F. Wolter, and M. Zakharyaschev, editors, *Proceedings of the 4th Workshop on Advances in Modal Logic (AIML'02),* pages 481–517. King's College Publications, 2003.

[37] R. Sekar, V. Venkatakrishnan, S. Basu, S. Bhatkar, and D. C. DuVarney. Model-carrying code: a practical approach for safe execution of untrusted applications.

[38] A. Valmari. The state explosion problem. In *Lectures on Petri Nets I: Basic Models, Advances in Petri Nets. The volumes are based on the Advanced Course on Petri Nets, held in Dagstuhl, September 1996,* pages 429–528, London, UK, UK, 1998. Springer-Verlag.

[39] T. Wang, K. Lu, L. Lu, S. Chung, and W. Lee. Jekyll on iOS: When Benign Apps Become Evil. In *Proceedings of the 22nd USENIX Security Symposium,* pages 559–572, 2013.

[40] J. Yang, P. Twohey, D. Engler, and M. Musuvathi. Using model checking to find serious file system errors. *ACM Transactions on Computer Systems,* 24(4):393–423, Nov. 2006.

[41] Y. Zhou and X. Jiang. Dissecting Android Malware: Characterization and Evolution. In *Proceedings of the 2012 IEEE Symposium on Security and Privacy,* SP '12, pages 95–109, Washington, DC, USA, 2012. IEEE Computer Society.

[42] Y. Zhou, X. Zhang, X. Jiang, and V. W. Freeh. Taming information-stealing smartphone applications (on Android). In *Proceedings of the 4th international conference on Trust and trustworthy computing,* TRUST'11, pages 93–107, 2011.

*SIGOPS Operating Systems Review,* 37(5):15–28, Oct. 2003.

# Short Paper:
# WifiLeaks: Underestimated Privacy Implications of the ACCESS_WIFI_STATE Android Permission[*]

Jagdish Prasad Achara[†]
Mathieu Cunche[‡†] and Vincent Roca[†]
[†]Inria, Grenoble, France
[‡]University of Lyon, France
firstname.lastname@inria.fr

Aurélien Francillon
EURECOM, Sophia-Antipolis, France
aurelien.francillon@eurecom.fr

## ABSTRACT

On Android, installing an application implies accepting the permissions it requests, and these permissions are then enforced at runtime. In this work, we focus on the privacy implications of the ACCESS_WIFI_STATE permission. For this purpose, we analyzed permissions of the 2700 most popular applications on Google Play and found that the ACCESS_WIFI_STATE permission is used by 41% of them. We then performed a static analysis of 998 applications requesting this permission and based on the results, chose 88 applications for dynamic analysis. Our analyses reveal that this permission is already used by some companies to collect user Personally Identifiable Information (PII). We also conducted an online survey to study users' perception of the privacy risks associated with this permission. This survey shows that users largely underestimate the privacy implications of this permission. As this permission is very common, most users are therefore potentially at risk.

## Categories and Subject Descriptors

K.4.1 [**Public Policy Issues**]: Privacy

## Keywords

Android Permissions; Wi-Fi; Personally Identifiable Information (PII) leakage; Static/Dynamic Analysis; User survey

## 1. INTRODUCTION

Mobile devices have become ubiquitous and are a crucial part of our lives today. These devices handle a lot of private data such as our email, communications, location, etc. As useful as they are, they also became a serious threat to user's privacy. Indeed, very accurate profiles can be created using the vast amount of data available on them. Advertising

and Analytics (A&A) companies have therefore shifted their focus from traditional desktop computers and browsers to applications running on mobile devices.

Today a large fraction of mobile devices are running Android, where access to user data is controlled by the permission system. However, users have a poor understanding of the permissions and do not pay enough attention to these messages; they therefore often do not realize the kind of information accessible to an application once installed [7]. In order to help users perceive the potential risks, Android classifies the permissions based on their expected risk[1]. ACCESS_WIFI_STATE, on which we focus in this work, allows an application to access various information related to the the Wi-Fi interface. As such it is categorized as normal as compared to, e.g., ACCESS_FINE_LOCATION which is classified as dangerous. In this work we show that the ACCESS_WIFI_STATE permission is actually dangerous as a user's PII can be (and is already) derived from the use of this permission. Also, as the use of this permission by ad libraries has increased over time [3], the problem is severe.

More specifically the contributions of this work are threefold: First, we consolidate what PII can be derived from the data related to Wi-Fi interface (Section 3), namely unique identifiers (useful for tracking purposes), device geolocation, travel history and social links between users. Second, we analyze the current situation on Google Play employing both static and dynamic analysis of Android applications (Section 4), revealing that a large number of applications have actually started to exploit this permission to obtain user PII. Finally, we analyze the user perception of this permission using an online survey to which 156 Android users answered (Section 5). The results clearly demonstrate that users do not understand the privacy implications of this permission.

## 2. BACKGROUND AND RELATED WORK

### 2.1 Android Permission System

As Android gives no privilege to applications by default, applications must ask the user for privileges by statically declaring the list of permissions it requires. There are a total of 145 different permissions available (as of Android version 4.4) for an application to ask for. Many of these permissions are required by applications to access user sensitive information (e.g. ACCESS_FINE_LOCATION and READ_CONTACTS are

---

[*]A full version of this paper is available at [1].

[1]http://developer.android.com/guide/topics/manifest/permission-element.html

**Table 1: WifiManager's method restricted by the ACCESS_WIFI_STATE permission.**

| Method name | Description | Retrievable Information |
|---|---|---|
| **isWifiEnabled()** | Returns whether Wi-Fi is enabled or disabled. | Returns true if Wi-Fi is enabled. |
| **getWifiState()** | Gets the Wi-Fi enabled state. | (Currently being) enabled/disabled or unknown |
| **getConfiguredNetworks()** | Returns a list of all configured networks. | **For each configured network/AP**: SSID, allowed protocols and security schemes |
| **getConnectionInfo()** | Returns dynamic information about the current Wi-Fi connection, if any is active. | **About AP**: BSSID, SSID, RSSI **About Device:** Wi-Fi MAC address, IP address |
| **getScanResults()** | Returns the results of the last AP scan. | **For each AP**: BSSID, SSID, signal strength, channel, capabilities |
| **getDhcpInfo()** | Returns the DHCP-assigned addresses from the last successful DHCP request, if any. | IP address, DNS server address, gateway and netmask |

the permissions required to respectively geolocalize the device and read user's contact data).

**The ACCESS_WIFI_STATE permission.** It makes some of the methods of the WifiManager class[2] available to be accessed by applications (Table 1) and falls in the 'Network communications' group of permissions. It is worth mentioning that these methods only allow to read the data associated with the Wi-Fi interface, but not to modify it: a different permission, CHANGE_WIFI_STATE, is required to change the state of the Wi-Fi interface.

## 2.2 Related Work

Zhou et. al. [13] show how PII (e.g., geolocation, identity) can be inferred from *publicly* available information in the Android system. We note that getting device geolocation is common in both ours and [13]. However, in [13], device geolocation is only obtained when the device is connected to a Wi-Fi network, whereas in our study, we show that it can be obtained as long as the Wi-Fi interface is enabled.

Book et al. [3] investigates changes over time in the behavior of Android ad libraries. The study reveals that number of libraries able to use different permissions, ACCESS_WIFI_STATE permission is one among them, drastically increased over time. Also, Nguyen et al. [10] show that Wi-Fi information could be used to breach location privacy. However, [3] and [10] did not analyze the current situation on Google Play. As opposed to these studies, our study employs in-depth analysis of applications requesting ACCESS_WIFI_STATE permission and shows that a number of user PII can be and are already derived from the data accessible using this seemingly network-related permission.

The user comprehension of Android permissions have been studied in [7]. The study considered a total of 11 permissions but left out ACCESS_WIFI_STATE and the ACCESS_FINE_LOCATION permissions. Likewise our specific study of ACCESS_WIFI_STATE permission, the results of this study also indicate that users have a poor understanding of the Android permission system.

## 3. USER PII INFERRED FROM WI-FI DATA

As we have seen, the ACCESS_WIFI_STATE permission enables an application to read data related to the Wi-Fi configuration of the device. This raw data may look innocuous, but it is actually possible to either directly access or infer several user PII. In this section, we describe such user PII.

**A unique device identifier.** Using the getConnectionInfo() method, an application can obtain the MAC address

of the Wi-Fi interface. In fact, there are other hardware-tied identifiers available to be accessed by applications, e.g., IMEI and MEID with READ_PHONE_STATE permission. As these unique identifiers could be used by advertisers to track user activities across all applications, they pose serious threat to user privacy. In particular, Wi-Fi MAC is also used to track users in the physical world [12, 6] and therefore, allows trackers to link both online and physical profiles of the user.

**Geolocation.** The list of surrounding Wi-Fi APs can be obtained thanks to the ACCESS_WIFI_STATE permission through the getScanResults() method of WifiManager class. This method does not trigger the scanning of Wi-Fi APs, but return the list of last scanned Wi-Fi APs. Wi-Fi scan is performed automatically by the system every 15 seconds and can also be triggered by other applications, therefore this list of surrounding Wi-Fi APs is often up-to-date. By submitting the raw result of a Wi-Fi scan to a remote geolocation service[3], the device gets geolocation information (coordinates and accuracy metric) in return. Wi-Fi based geolocation is accurate to 20 meters in urban areas [9]. The Wi-Fi, GSM and GPS-based geolocation systems are employed by the Android system, but access to this information is restricted by the ACCESS_FINE/COARSE_LOCATION permissions. On the opposite, the raw Wi-Fi scan information is not protected by any of these two geolocation permissions. By using a third party Wi-Fi based geolocation service, it is therefore possible for an application to obtain geolocation information without having to explicitly ask for geolocation permissions as long as the application has both the ACCESS_WIFI_STATE and INTERNET permissions. And in Section 4, we show that this is often the case.

Therefore in practice the list of surrounding Wi-Fi APs is often up-to-date and an application does not really need to start the scanning by itself.

**Travel history.** The list of Wi-Fi networks to which the device has been connected to in the past is stored in the *Configured Networks List* that can be accessed through the getConfiguredNetworks() method of WifiManager class. For each of these configured networks, the SSID is available along with other information such as the supported security protocols and authentication algorithms used. It has been shown in [8] that the data stored in the *Configured Networks List* can be combined with external resources[4] to obtain information such as the previously visited locations.

**Social links.** It is possible to predict the existence of a social or professional link between the owners of devices by

---

[2]http://developer.android.com/reference/android/net/wifi/WifiManager.html

[3]https://developers.google.com/maps/documentation/business/geolocation/
[4]http://wigle.net/

**Table 2: Most commonly used methods of WifiManager class, in 998 applications.**

| Method call | # of Apps |
|---|---|
| getConnectionInfo() | 753 (75.45%) |
| isWiFiEnabled() | 344 (33.47%) |
| getScanResults() | 156 (15.63%) |
| getConfiguredNetworks() | 59 (5.91%) |
| getWifiState() | 76 (7.62%) |
| getDhcpInfo() | 63 (6.31%) |

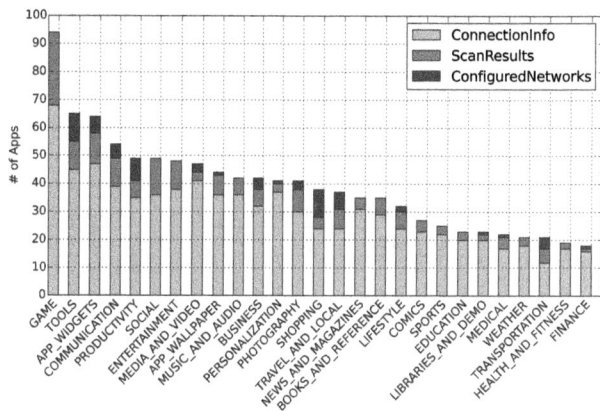

**Figure 1: Per category popularity of 3 privacy-sensitive methods (100 applications/category).**

comparing the list of SSIDs known by any two devices [5]. By collecting this data on a large population, an application could gather information that would make it possible for them to build a social network between their users. The *Configured Networks List* returned by the `getConfiguredNetworks()` method can be used for the same purpose. In fact, it also contains some other information about the configured Wi-Fi AP (e.g., allowed protocols, authentication algorithms, key management). This information can be leveraged to improve the quality of the social link establishment as [5] relies only on the SSID.

**Other PII derived from SSIDs.** SSIDs are often made to be meaningful to users and potentially contain information about the network owner or its users (e.g., name of institutions, individuals or locations [11]). Extraction of this information can be done manually or could be automated using techniques like Named Entity Recognition [4] and could then be used, for example, by advertisers to enrich the profile of the user to serve targeted ads.

## 4. ANDROID APPLICATIONS ANALYSIS

We have analyzed the 100 most popular free applications in each of the 27 categories present on Google Play, i.e., 2700 applications in total. We focused only on those that require both the `ACCESS_WIFI_STATE` and the `INTERNET` permissions (only 5 applications ask for the first permission but not the second one). To that purpose, we crawled Google Play[5] and collected the list of required permissions. Then we statically analyzed 998 applications requesting these permissions and based on the results, we chose 88 applications for an in depth, dynamic analysis. This section details our findings.

### 4.1 Static analysis

We used custom scripts (based on Androguard[6]) to statically analyze the 998 APK files corresponding to applications requiring both the `ACCESS_WIFI_STATE` and the `INTERNET` permissions.

#### 4.1.1 Use of the WifiManager class' methods

We note that 17% (165) of the applications request `ACCESS_WIFI_STATE` permission but do not access any of its methods. Those over privileged applications present a privacy risk as later revisions of those applications will be able to use the protected methods by this permission.

Table 2 presents the number of applications calling the `WifiManager` class' methods. In fact, ∼76% (762) applications are accessing at least one of these three privacy-sensitive methods whereas ∼1% (11) of them are accessing

all 3 privacy sensitive methods. Among the 6 methods protected by this permission, we chose to focus on the ones that pose serious privacy risks to the user, namely: `getScanResults()`, `getConfiguredNetworks()` and `getConnectionInfo()`. Note that the access to `WifiManager` class' methods might be legitimate, for example, in case of a Wi-Fi manager application in the `Tools` or `App Widget` categories, but probably not for a cooking or wallpaper application. From now on, our analysis only focuses on these three methods.

Figure 1 presents a per category distribution of the applications accessing these privacy-sensitive methods. Overall, applications in the `Game` category are the ones that use these 3 privacy-sensitive methods the most. There are also several other categories of applications that show a high usage of those methods without an obvious reason, like `Lifestyle`, `Comics` and `App Wallpaper`.

#### 4.1.2 Analysis of third-party code inside applications

It is interesting to identify if the method calls are made by code written by the application developer ("first-party") or by the libraries (e.g., advertisement, analytics, performance monitors, crash reporters) included by the application developer ("third-party"). For this purpose we use a heuristic: classes belonging to a package whose name is the same as the application package name is considered coming from the application developer, otherwise it is considered as third-party code. Based on this, we find that 18% (136) of the applications accessing at least one of these methods are doing so only from third-party code. This confirms that third-party code is often responsible for the usage of the `ACCESS_WIFI_STATE` permission. Access to an API call by third-party code is sometimes legitimate, but there are cases where it is clearly not (e.g., Wi-Fi scanning is performed by `inmobi.com` and `skyhookwireless.com` in 13 applications out of 156 that scan for Wi-Fi APs).

Figure 2 presents, for each of the three privacy-sensitive methods, whether a first-party, third-party, or both access these methods. It reveals that there are some applications in which only the third-party code accesses these privacy-sensitive methods. This means that if the code written by the application developer does not require the `ACCESS_WIFI_STATE` permission, the third-party library does need it. The motivation for a third party library can be to secretly collect user information, or to provide a functionality

---

[5]Using https://github.com/egirault/googleplay-api
[6]https://code.google.com/p/androguard/

**Table 3: Top 5 third-parties in each category and their corresponding number of applications.**

| ConnectionInfo | | ScanResults | | ConfiguredNetworks | |
|---|---|---|---|---|---|
| Third-party | # Apps | Third-party | # Apps | Third-party | # Apps |
| inmobi.com | 74 | inmobi.com | 9 | google.com | 10 |
| chartboost.com | 55 | domob.cn | 9 | mobiletag.com | 4 |
| tapjoy.com | 49 | mologiq.com | 6 | lechucksoftware.com | 2 |
| vungle.com | 47 | tencent.com | 5 | android.com | 2 |
| jirbo.com | 43 | skyhookwireless.com | 4 | Unibail.com | 1 |

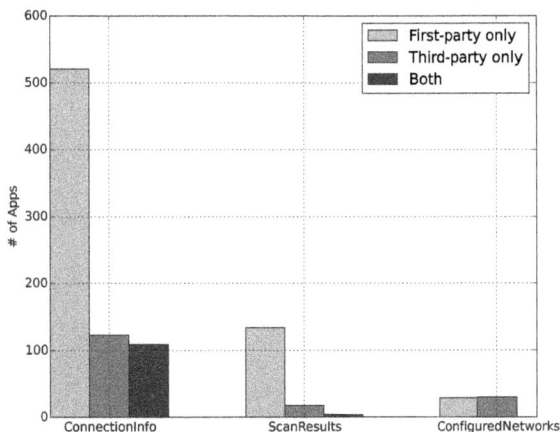

**Figure 2: Distribution based on the party accessing privacy-sensitive methods, in 762 applications.**

to the application. For example, an application developer or a third-party can use the code from `skyhookwireless.com` to retrieve device geolocation without needing explicit dedicated geolocation permissions. It is worth mentioning that `skyhookwireless.com` retrieves the list of surrounding Wi-Fi APs in 4 applications (Table 3). In any case deriving device geolocation without any explicit user permission is not legitimate and should be prevented by Android.

Table 3 presents the top 5 third-parties in each category and the number of applications in which they are present. Looking at the web pages of these third-parties, one may understand the purpose of these third-parties in various applications. It seems like most of them (`inmobi.com`, `jirbo.com`, `vungle.com`, `chartboost.com`) belong to A&A business, whereas others are different kinds of service providers, e.g., `skyhookwireless.com`. Here it is worth noting that `skyhookwireless.com` provides geolocation service among other kinds of services. With this service, an application can get the location of the phone with the use of `ACCESS_WIFI_STATE` and `INTERNET` permissions and without explicitly requesting a geolocation related permission.

## 4.2 Dynamic analysis

In Section 3 we speculated that applications can infer PII using the methods made available with the `ACCESS_WIFI_STATE` permission. We now analyze their network communications to check if these applications (or third-party libraries they embed) actually send private information to remote servers. We performed this dynamic analysis on 88 applications that access, at least, two privacy sensitive methods. For this purpose, we modified the Android OS to log in-

---

[7]The Wi-Fi MAC address is hashed (SHA-1) before being sent over the network in clear-text.

teresting method calls in a local SQLite database. We modified several methods in `WifiManager` and `WifiInfo` classes along with network (both in clear and with SSL) and data modification (encryption and hash) related methods. The rest of the OS remains unmodified. This SQLite database is later analyzed to know if a particular application is accessing some information and leaks it over the network.

Table 4 presents the list of servers to which PII obtained with the `ACCESS_WIFI_STATE` permission was sent. A number of third-parties present inside these applications are collecting the Wi-Fi MAC address and send it to their servers (sometimes in clear). Accessing Wi-Fi MAC address is really serious as it is a hardware-tied unique identifier that remains the same all along the lifespan of the device and can be used to tie both on-line and physical profile of a user (see Section 3). Looking at this list of servers in the Table 4 where Wi-Fi MAC address is sent, most of them belong to A&A companies. This clearly suggests that those actors use the MAC Address as a unique identifier to track users.

Also, both first (`Badoo.com`) and third-parties (`inmobi.com`) collect the SSID and BSSID of the AP to which the device is connected. Such a database of users and their Wi-Fi APs can easily reveal various relationships between users: a lot of information can be derived on the social relationships between users based on type of Wi-Fi APs to which users are connect to. For example, a protected Wi-Fi at home/work or the time/location at which two users connect to reveal close connections between them.

We found that Badoo and Foursquare applications send the list of surrounding Wi-Fi APs (SSIDs, BSSIDs, signal strength, etc.) to their respective servers. However, both applications have `ACCESS_FINE_LOCATION` permission and can get precise device geolocation from the regular Android APIs.

We even found some third-parties (e.g., `inmobi.com` and `fastly.net`) sending the list of surrounding Wi-Fi APs to their servers, and they are present inside various applications. Focusing on the communication inside various applications to `inmobi.com` server, we find that `inmobi.com` library works in two modes: if it is included in an application having `ACCESS_FINE_LOCATION`, it accesses the fine-grained geolocation retrieved by the system along with nearby Wi-Fi APs (possibly to enrich their own database); otherwise, if the application doesn't have this permission, it derives device geolocation by querying their geolocation server with the list of surrounding Wi-Fi APs. As an example, code from `inmobi.com` inside SimSimi (com.ismaker.android.simsimi) application sends the list of surrounding Wi-Fi APs to its server to derive device geolocation, because this application has neither the `ACCESS_FINE_LOCATION` nor `ACCESS_COARSE_LOCATION` permissions.

Finally, we didn't encounter any application sending Wi-Fi configuration information over the network (which is good

**Table 4: Servers where Wi-Fi related information is sent by 88 dynamically analyzed applications.**

| Info | Third-parties | First-parties | # Apps affected |
|---|---|---|---|
| MAC Address | appsflyer.com (SSL), revmob.com (SSL), adsmogo.mobi (plain-text), adsmogo.org (plain-text), vungle.com (plain-text), supersonicads.com (plain-text), trademob.net (SSL), sponsorpay.com (SSL), beintoo.com (SSL), adsmogo.com (plain-text), 115.182.31.2/3/4 (plain-text)[7], tapjoyads.com (SSL) | Not found | 13 |
| (B)SSID of connected AP | inmobi.com (SSL), 93.184.219.82 (plain-text) | Not found | 2 |
| Wi-Fi Scan Info | inmobi.com (SSL), fastly.net (SSL) | badoo.com (SSL), foursquare.com(SSL) | 5 |

for privacy) but this might be the case in near future. Also it might be possible that our dynamic analysis technique could not detect PII leakage in case applications employ custom data modification methods.

## 5. USER PERCEPTION

Sections 3 and 4 have respectively demonstrated the potential privacy threats and the actual situation today on Google Play. In this section we study how users perceive the ACCESS_WIFI_STATE permission. More precisely we conducted an on-line survey involving 156 Android users and we studied their perception of the privacy risks associated with this permission. We show that Android permissions are often misunderstood by users who do not necessarily understand their privacy implications [7].

### 5.1 Survey description

Our survey has been performed with Google Docs and diffused through social media and multiple mailing-lists. It was composed of 12 questions divided into 3 parts:

- the first part focuses on demographic information such as age, gender and professional category;

- the second part is about user attitude towards privacy and user's experience in using the Android system;

- the third part evaluates user's perception of the relative privacy risks associated with several permissions, and in particular how users understand the implications of the ACCESS_WIFI_STATE permission.[8]

The third part of the survey starts with a series of questions where the respondent must evaluate the privacy risks associated with 5 selected Android permissions on a scale of 1 to 10. Along with ACCESS_WIFI_STATE permission, we selected CHANGE_WIFI_STATE and ACCESS_NETWORK_STATE permissions in the 'Network Communications' group to understand how the user differentiates permissions belonging to the same group but giving access to different type of network-related data. We also selected ACCESS_FINE_LOCATION that is the permission explicitly required by applications to get device geolocation. As a device can also be geolocated indirectly by applications having the ACCESS_WIFI_STATE permission, the ACCESS_FINE_LOCATION permission is selected in order to compare how users evaluate the privacy risks of both permissions. Finally, the READ_CONTACTS permission

---

[8]The permission were presented using a screenshot of the permission's description (as showed to the user by the Android system).

is selected as a reference since the name clearly indicates the associated privacy risks.

One might argue that the geolocation information obtained using Wi-Fi APs might not be as accurate as the geolocalization obtained through GPS with the ACCESS_FINE_LOCATION permission. However Wi-Fi based geolocation can be as accurate as GPS in urban scenarios [9, 2]. In addition, contrary to GPS, the Wi-Fi based geolocation can be used both indoors and when a user turns the GPS off to save battery.

### 5.2 Results of the survey

In total, 190 users completed the survey from February 22 to 27, 2014. We discarded responses from 34 users who never used an Android device. So the results and analysis presented below are based on the responses of 156 users who have some experience with Android.

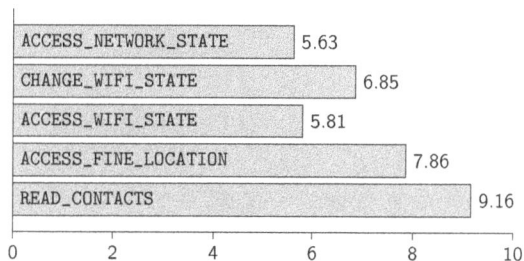

**Figure 3: Average privacy risk rating for the considered permissions on a scale of 10.**

The responses to the questions for each permission allowed us to have a comparative view of the perceived privacy risks. The average privacy risk ratings on a scale of 10 is presented in Figure 3. Overall, ACCESS_FINE_LOCATION and READ_CONTACTS are rated the highest for privacy risks whereas ACCESS_NETWORK_STATE and ACCESS_WIFI_STATE are rated the lowest. In particular, users rate ACCESS_WIFI_STATE as less risky than ACCESS_FINE_LOCATION. This is typically an error: not only geolocalization but also many other PII can be obtained through it (see Section 3). Therefore the privacy risks of this permission should have been rated higher than that of ACCESS_FINE_LOCATION.

The results for the question about the fine understanding of ACCESS_WIFI_STATE permission are presented in table 5. The correctness of the answers greatly varies across the questions. Thus we organized them into three groups, based on the fraction of correct answers they received.

The first group includes questions correctly answered by the majority of respondents (more than 75% of correct answers). We find questions about the basic functionalities

**Table 5: User understanding of the `ACCESS_WIFI_STATE` permission. Correct answers are shown in green cells.**

| *With `ACCESS_WIFI_STATE` permission and an Internet access, an application can ...* | Responses | | |
|---|---|---|---|
| Options | True | False | Don't know |
| ✓ Check if the device is connected to the Internet through Wi-Fi | 89.74% | 5.77% | 4.49% |
| ✗ Turn the Wi-Fi on or off | 6.41% | 85.26% | 8.33% |
| ✗ Get the list of your contacts | 6.41% | 86.54% | 7.05% |
| ✓ Get the list of surrounding Wi-Fi networks | 75.00% | 12.18% | 12.82% |
| ✓ Get the list of configured Wi-Fi networks | 65.38% | 16.67% | 17.95% |
| ✗ Connect the device to a Wi-Fi network | 21.79% | 67.31% | 10.90% |
| ✓ Get the device location | 48.08% | 41.67% | 10.26% |
| ✓ Get one of the device unique identifiers | 46.79% | 17.31% | 35.90% |
| ✓ Get some of the previously visited locations (even before the App is installed) | 35.90% | 42.95% | 21.15% |

of the `ACCESS_WIFI_STATE` permission (e.g., checking Internet connectivity through Wi-Fi and getting the list of surrounding Wi-Fi networks) as well as privileges that are not granted by the permission (e.g., turning the Wi-Fi on or off and getting the list of contacts).

The second group includes questions having received a majority of correct answers, but fewer than for the first group (in practice more than 60%). We find questions about the ability of the application to access the list of configured networks and to connect the device to a Wi-Fi network.

Finally, the third group includes questions having received the lowest rate of correct answers (below 50%). Those questions concerns the ability of getting current or past geolocation information as well as a device unique identifier. We remark that these poorly understood capabilities are also the most privacy invasive. Even though a majority of the respondents failed to correctly answer the last set of questions, there is still a significant proportion of respondents who answered correctly (more than 35% correct answers).

## 6. CONCLUSION AND POTENTIAL SOLUTIONS

The paper, first, presented what PII could be directly obtained or indirectly derived from data accessible to applications thanks to the `ACCESS_WIFI_STATE` permission. We showed that a large number of applications request this permission and then, with the help of an online survey, we found that users often fail to perceive privacy implications associated with this permission. Our analysis of a representative set of most popular applications in each category on Google Play revealed that a number of both first and third-parties have already started to exploit this permission to access or derive user PII.

The results of this study call for changes in the Android permission system. First of all, the access to Wi-Fi scan results should be protected with location permissions as is currently the case to access neighboring cell towers information. Secondly, the `ACCESS_WIFI_STATE` permission description should explicitly state the various PII that can be directly obtained (e.g., MAC address that can be used for tracking) or inferred from it (e.g., travel history). Finally, the `ACCESS_WIFI_STATE` permission should be placed in the list of dangerous permissions as it is more privacy-sensitive than some of the permissions already in the list.

## 7. REFERENCES

[1] J. P. Achara, M. Cunche, V. Roca, and A. Francillon. WifiLeaks: Underestimated Privacy Implications of the ACCESS_WIFI_STATE Android Permission. INRIA Research Report N°8539, http://hal.inria.fr/hal-00994926/en, May 2014.

[2] J. R. Blum, D. G. Greencorn, and J. R. Cooperstock. Smartphone sensor reliability for augmented reality applications. In *Mobile and Ubiquitous Systems: Computing, Networking, and Services*. Springer, 2013.

[3] T. Book, A. Pridgen, and D. S. Wallach. Longitudinal analysis of android ad library permissions. *arXiv preprint arXiv:1303.0857*, 2013.

[4] J. Cowie and W. Lehnert. Information extraction. *Communications of the ACM*, 39(1), 1996.

[5] M. Cunche, M.-A. Kaafar, and R. Boreli. Linking wireless devices using information contained in wi-fi probe requests. *Pervasive and Mobile Computing*, 2013.

[6] C. Daniel and W. Glenn. Snoopy: Distributed tracking and profiling framework. In *44Con 2012*, 2012.

[7] A. P. Felt, E. Ha, S. Egelman, A. Haney, E. Chin, and D. Wagner. Android permissions: User attention, comprehension, and behavior. SOUPS '12, New York, NY, USA, 2012. ACM.

[8] B. Greenstein, R. Gummadi, J. Pang, M. Y. Chen, T. Kohno, S. Seshan, and D. Wetherall. Can Ferris Bueller still have his day off? protecting privacy in the wireless era. In *USENIX HotOS workshop*, 2007.

[9] A. LaMarca, Y. Chawathe, S. Consolvo, J. Hightower, I. Smith, J. Scott, T. Sohn, J. Howard, J. Hughes, F. Potter, et al. Place lab: Device positioning using radio beacons in the wild. In *Pervasive computing*. Springer, 2005.

[10] Y. T. Le Nguyen, S. Cho, W. Kwak, S. Parab, Y. Kim, P. Tague, and J. Zhang. Unlocin: Unauthorized location inference on smartphones without being caught.

[11] J. Lindqvist, T. Aura, G. Danezis, T. Koponen, A. Myllyniemi, J. Mäki, and M. Roe. Privacy-preserving 802.11 access-point discovery. In *ACM WiSec*, 2009.

[12] A. B. M. Musa and J. Eriksson. Tracking unmodified smartphones using Wi-Fi monitors. In *ACM SenSys'12*, 2012.

[13] X. Zhou, S. Demetriou, D. He, M. Naveed, X. Pan, X. Wang, C. A. Gunter, and K. Nahrstedt. Identity, location, disease and more: Inferring your secrets from android public resources. In *ACM CCS 2013*.

# Author Index